Man, State, and Society in the Soviet Union

ER

MAN, STATE, AND SOCIETY

Man, State, and Society in the Soviet Union

EDITED BY

Joseph L. Nogee

PRAEGER PUBLISHERS
New York · Washington · London

For Leah and Jyle and their mother

PRAEGER PUBLISHERS
111 Fourth Avenue, New York, N.Y. 10003, U.S.A.
5, Cromwell Place, London SW7 2JL, England

Published in the United States of America in 1972
by Praeger Publishers, Inc.

© 1972 by Praeger Publishers, Inc.

Library of Congress Catalog Card Number: 69–12712

Printed in the United States of America

CONTENTS

v

ACKNOWLEDGMENTS

With the exception of Chapter I, all of the articles reproduced in this volume have previously been published. Appropriate acknowledgments are made throughout the text. I wish to thank the authors and publishers for their permission to reprint. I want also to express my gratitude to the University of Houston, where most of the manuscript was prepared, and to Vanderbilt University, where the text was completed. The library services of both institutions were extremely helpful, and the departments of political science at both provided generous secretarial assistance. Finally, I thank my wife, Jo, who frequently and with good cheer adjusted the family schedule to accommodate my working on the manuscript.

Man, State, and Society in the Soviet Union

I

Introduction

The Bolsheviks came to power in Russia in 1917 committed to building a new and higher form of social organization, a society without injustice or class distinction. Their scheme, perhaps inevitably, was modified by the social structure over which it sought to impose itself. Russian culture and tradition and what Alex Inkeles calls "the modal personality patterns of the population" [1] forced accommodation and adjustment in the institutions of communist rule. Other factors have qualified the impact of doctrine on Soviet life: Stalin's paranoid personality, for one; the scientific, technical, and administrative demands of a complex modernizing economic system, for another. It is a matter of some contention among scholars as to what the major determinants of the contemporary Soviet system are, though most would agree that communist rule has effected fundamental and irreversible changes in Russian society. Now that the Soviet Union has moved well into its sixth decade, a sharper focus on some of the changes is possible.

[1] Alex Inkeles, *Social Change in Soviet Russia* (Cambridge, Mass.: Harvard University Press, 1960), p. 15.

We might note at the outset that Soviet Communism works. That might seem a superfluous observation for a system that has celebrated its fiftieth anniversary, but there has been no lack of prophets who have predicted either the total collapse of the Soviet system or a sharp break with the Bolshevik heritage. Neither has occurred. The Soviet Union has survived civil war, famine, violent purges, economic upheaval, and devastating military reversals to become a ranking world power. But more significant than mere survival and growth are the qualitative changes that have come with modernization. Soviet Russia has developed the science and technology, the literate and skilled populace, and the extensive educational system necessary for an advanced industrial society. Large urban complexes—not Communist doctrine—have produced a new Soviet man endowed with attitudes and motivations appropriate to modern life. Soviet Communism now offers itself to the world as a model for development, and many nations are impressed with the example.

In spite of many changes, the present Soviet system maintains a striking continuity with the past. Political power remains today, as it has been for half a century, in the hands of a small elite committed to the ideology of Marxism-Leninism. The operational significance of the ideology has changed, as have the size and *modus operandi* of the ruling oligarchy, but the Communist Party remains the locus of political sovereignty in the Soviet Union. It is as true now as in the past that he who controls the Party controls the country.

The revolution introduced by Lenin affected primarily the structure of formal power and authority. Communist rule during the 1920's drastically altered property relationships and destroyed the old class structure, but among the masses it did not fundamentally change patterns of social behavior or work habits. It remained for Stalin, through his programs of collectivization and industrialization, to produce a thoroughgoing social and economic revolution. Most of the institutions and patterns of social organization of present-day Soviet life have their origins in the period of Stalinist rule. Under Stalin there was a steady erosion of old Russia's cultural values. The values of the peasant family, rooted in the rural community and the church, suffered severe attrition. In their place came the culture of the cities and the values of a rapidly changing industrial order.

Some features of the old social structure remained stubbornly durable, and for the sake of social stability the Communist rulers made vital concessions at the expense of doctrine. For example, early policies designed to undermine the institution of the family (easy divorce, free abortion, state rearing of children) were abandoned. Today the family is treated as one of the pillars of Soviet society. Children are taught respect for parents, and parents are encouraged to rear children who will be motivated by a work-loving, loyal, and disciplined ethic. Compromises have been made in the collectivization of agriculture to permit the cultivation of private plots and the operation of peasant markets. Educational policies again stress a traditional curriculum. Stalin even went so far as to permit the restoration of the Patriarchate of the Russian Orthodox Church as part of his program to mobilize patriotic sentiment behind the war effort. The point is that the regime has proved adaptable in the interests of stability and efficiency. Since the end of World War II, the Soviets have produced a relatively stable social order that combines elements of the old and the new.

The Soviet political system modifies—and is in turn modified by—the society it controls. Indeed, societal inputs have produced several radical changes in the political system since the Revolution. None of the changes, however, has disturbed the essentially oligarchic character of Soviet politics. To show the continuity from the Bolshevik Revolution to the present, as well as to mark the changes, descriptive labels have been attached to different periods of rule: "revolutionary oligarchy" for the system developed under Lenin, "totalitarian oligarchy" for that under Stalin, and "bureaucratic oligarchy" [2] for the present system.

Sovereignty in the Soviet Union is vested in the Communist Party. Virtually all important questions of public policy are raised, developed, and decided within its structure. Lenin conceived the Party as an instrument for the revolutionary transformation of society, and that is how it functioned in the past. But it no longer does so. Since World War II, Soviet society has stabilized to the point where the Party can no longer transform its basic structure without an unacceptable level of violence. Russia's industrial society has developed its own dynamic, powered largely by the impetus for economic growth and development, which circumscribes the Party's freedom of maneuver. This, it should be noted, in no way lessens the dictatorial character of Party rule. Within the framework of a modernized society there is an enormous range of options for public policy decisions, particularly in the area of foreign policy. It remains the prerogative of those in control of the Party to select the options to be taken, and it is within the power of the Party to ensure their implementation. So the mainsprings of change no longer reside within the Party, but their operation depends heavily on Party approval.

Though superimposed on society, the Party is not (nor could it be) completely divorced from its social underpinings. Its membership includes representatives from every important social grouping—industrial workers, administrators, peasants, intellectuals, scientists, the military, and other professional groups. Interests are articulated both outside and within the Party. Many Party members wear two hats: as Communists and as representatives of special interests. It is the function of the Party leadership to aggregate these interests—that is, resolve conflicting demands—and for-

[2] For amplification of this concept, see Richard Lowenthal, "The Soviet Union in the Post-Revolutionary Era: An Overview," in Alexander Dallin and Thomas B. Larson, eds., *Soviet Politics Since Khrushchev* (Englewood Cliffs, N.J.: Prentice-Hall, 1968), pp. 1–11, and Henry W. Morton, "The Structure of Decision-Making in the U.S.S.R.: A Comparative Introduction," in Peter H. Juviler and Henry W. Morton, eds., *Soviet Policy-Making: Studies of Communism in Transition* (New York: Praeger Publishers, 1967), pp. 3–27.

mulate broad public policies. In its calculations the Party elite must reconcile institutional needs not only with each other but also with the maintenance of the supremacy of Party rule. In this sense, the Party is not only a reconciler of interests but also a special interest itself.

Special qualities of leadership are called for in such a system. The political elite must have an understanding of the relationships among the various institutional groups in Soviet society and of the needs of an expanding industrial order. Given the complete domination by the Party and state over all economic life, this is no small requisite. One characteristic of a developed society is a proliferation of diverse interests and opinions to which some independence of expression must be given by those in power. Scientists must be guided by the findings in the laboratory—not by a Party catechism—if they are to be productive. Economic administrators, when judged by performance, will prefer a course of rational management to doctrinal conformity. The challenge confronting the oligarchy is to determine the point where freedom of expression must be curbed to prevent an undermining of its political authority.

Within the Communist Party of the Soviet Union, power is concentrated in the two dozen or so individuals who make up the Central Committee's Politburo and Secretariat. (The Twenty-fourth Congress in April, 1971, approved a Politburo of fifteen full members and six candidate members and a Secretariat of ten members. Six men were members of both, so the combined membership of both organs totaled twenty-five.) As of 1971, Party membership totaled 14,455,321, of which it is estimated that 250,000 are full-time paid Party functionaries (members of the apparatus, or "apparatchiki"). Although the rank-and-file member belongs to the reservoir from which the ruling elite comes, his Party card by itself gives him little political power. The apparatchiki are in a special position to influence the leadership, but the authority to speak decisively for the Party rests with the leadership concentrated in the highest Party organs. Power has at times been shared with individuals in the Central Committee and the higher organs of government, though only the oligarchy itself determines how broadly power will be shared, if at all. Decision taken by the leadership are binding upon all lower Party organs and are authoritative for every sector of Soviet society to which they apply. This hierarchical system is today by no means as monolithic in operation as it was under Stalin. Numerous interest groupings make known their needs and wants, which can be ignored only at the risk of creating serious problems of morale, inefficiency, and even latent opposition.

Membership in the ruling group is determined by the oligarchy itself— that is, according to the principle of co-optation. Only the Politburo can determine who will be demoted and who elevated. Under the Party Statutes, the Central Committee elects the membership of the Politburo (and the Secretariat), and the Central Committee itself is chosen by the Party Congress (theoretically the highest organ of Party authority). But since the ascendency of Stalin those elections have amounted to unanimous ratification of candidates selected by the Politburo. Indeed, the

Party Congress met only irregularly during the 1930's and not at all between 1939 and 1952. Although the post-Stalin leadership has restored to practice many of the previously unobserved rules of Party life—such as regular convocations of the Congress—there is no indication that the restoration of meaningful electoral contests for high Party position is in prospect. Those who are in a position to make such a restoration are the ones who can only lose by it—if not their high status, at least the highly valued appearance of Party unanimity.

In theory the leadership of the Party is "collective." It has not always been so in fact. Lenin was unqualifiedly recognized as the Party's leader because of his intellect, the force of his personality, and the special role he played in building the Party and leading it to power. Stalin acquired supreme power by clever political manipulation of his colleagues and control over the Party bureaucracy; he kept it through violence and terror. Khrushchev's power was less absolute. Through techniques not dissimilar to Stalin's, Khrushchev advanced to the top political position in the system, but never was his control as firm as his predecessor's.[3] Even as the "first among equals," [4] Khrushchev could not act without the ac-quicscence of his colleagues at the apex of the hierarchy. Between the periods of one-man rule or qualified one-man rule—1923–28, 1954–57, and 1964 to the present—decision-making power has in fact been collec-tive or oligarchic, that is, rule by committee, lacking an individual arbiter.

Since Khrshchev's overthrow in 1964, Leonid Brezhnev has held what is called the "number one" position within the Party leadership. As Gen-eral Secretary (head of thc Secretariat), he is the administrative head of the Party. He shares executive power with his colleagues in the Politburo. Perhaps it is because both Stalin and Khrushchev used the post of head of the Secretariat as a lever for supreme political power that Brezhnev has so far been unable to do so. At any rate, Brezhnev has not succeeded in acquiring the primacy that even Khrushchev had (nor has anyone else). His power, though considerable, is circumscribed by his colleagues. Wcre they to agree to dismiss him they could probably make it stick.[5] Brezhnev cannot on his own authority change the composition of either the Party command or the government. Heading the government (for-mally, Chairman of the Council of Ministers) is Aleksei Kosygin. He is also a member of the Politburo and one of the more powerful figures of the current leadership. But Kosygin too must negotiate with his col-leagues for any important policy or personnel change. Khrushchev and (for a time) Stalin both held the position as head of government and Party simultaneously. It seems likely that the decision to fill these posi-

[3] For a detailed analysis of the constraints on Khrushchev, see Michel Tatu, *Power in the Kremlin from Khrushchev to Kosygin* (New York: The Viking Press, 1969).

[4] This apt phrase is applied by Morton, "Structure of Decision-Making," p. 7.

[5] A coalition led by Georgi Malenkov, Vyacheslav Molotov, and Lazar Kaganovich tried to unseat Khrushchev in 1957 and failed, in part because it did not coordinate its plans with strategic elites in the Central Committee of the Party or with the army. See Roger Pethybridge, *A Key to Soviet Politics* (New York: Praeger Publishers, 1962). The coalition that ousted Khrushchev in 1964 learned the lesson well.

tions with two individuals is part of a strategy to prevent a return to
one-man rule.

Since the Soviet oligarchy is essentially a nonresponsible body, any
change in its composition must come from within. Outside pressures from
important elites in the Party or state bureaucracies, the military, the
secret police, or possibly the scientific and intellectual community can
influence actions taken by the leadership, though the prospects of forcing
a change against its will are rather slim. The evidence of the post-Stalin
period seems to lead to the conclusion that outside influence is greatest
when the leadership is divided and least when the leadership is united
and certain of its position.[6] Some division within the oligarchy is almost
inevitable, inasmuch as those in the elite represent diverse constituencies
and interests and are engaged in unceasing jockeying for power. Very little
concrete information is available about the "rules of the game" in this
power struggle. Apparently those in power seek to promote and protect
their protégés and to advance those interests they represent or upon
whose support they count. It is a contest in which personalities and issues
play an important part. Frequently the conflict centers upon factions
or groups. Individuals may attempt to enlarge their bases of support
by forming alliances with influential leaders in sectors of society outside of the ruling oligarchy. Only the counter-actions of the leadership
can keep an ambitious politician from appropriating the position of
supreme ruler. Stalin's immediate successors most probably agreed that
none of them would attempt to fill his boots. Even though Khrushchev
eventually outmaneuvered his colleagues, he was kept from exercising
anything like Stalin's power. The present leadership has proved vigilant
and cohesive enough to prevent anyone from achieving even the status of
a Khrushchev. Thus, until a single leader does emerge—and there is no
compelling reason why one must—there is a constant struggle for succession. As we shall note below, the lack of an established procedure for
political succession is a serious weakness of the Soviet political system.

One of the few distinguishing characteristics of a Communist regime is
the adherence of the rulers to Marxist-Leninist ideology. The question is:
What impact, if any, does the ideology have on the political system and
society? There are so many obvious contradictions between Soviet life
and the doctrinal prescriptions of Marx and Lenin that one might be
tempted to dismiss the tributes of the oligarchy to the ideas of Communism as nothing more than rationalization. It should be noted that
neither Marx nor Lenin had much to say about how a Communist
society and its institutions would be organized. Marx was primarily concerned with an analysis of capitalism and its contradictions, while Lenin

[6] An interesting example of outside pressure contributing to a decision that some
elements of the leadership opposed is the repeal in August, 1964, of Khrushchev's pet
education reform for production education. See the article by Joel J. Schwartz and
William R. Keech, selection 15 below, and Philip D. Stewart, "Soviet Interest Groups
and the Policy Process: The Repeal of Production Education," *World Politics* 22,
No. 1 (October, 1969): 29–50.

focused on the role of the Party as an instrument of revolution. Still, there are enough prescriptions in Marxism-Leninism to provide some measure of doctrinal purity in the Soviet system. Among the contemporary Soviet institutions that are incompatible with the vision of Marx and Engels would be the state, family, educational, and legal systems. Communist equalitarianism is certainly not reflected in the income differential among social groupings, ranging from the very affluent government and Party administrators and the scientific and intellectual elites to the unskilled workers and peasants on the bottom of the economic scale. As much an affront to Communist norms as the low economic position of the proletariat is the labor discipline imposing a work regimen on the worker. There is also the contradiction between the democratic norms of Marxism and the chronic absence of civil liberties in the Soviet Union. Quite obviously, Communist ideology has not provided a clear-cut guide to the ordering of social relations in the Soviet Union—or in any other socialist society for that matter.

Yet it would be erroneous to dismiss references to doctrine as mere cant or hypocrisy. To do so would be to underestimate the extent to which Marxism-Leninism has become a part of the Soviet political culture. Almost three generations of citizens have now undergone intensive indoctrination in the symbols and ideas of the ideology. A citizen could not avoid exposure even if he so desired. It is made part of the educational curriculum; repeated in virtually every newspaper, magazine, and reference work; and constantly cited in important statements of public policy. The ideals of Communism have been firmly implanted in the minds of millions of Soviet citizens, and they provide a transcendental meaning that makes routine activities and labor significant. Public morale and social unity is enhanced by the ideology. Social cohesion is strengthened when the masses are conditioned to respond affirmatively and automatically to ideological symbols such as the red flag, the hammer and sickle, and portraits of Lenin and Marx.

Some features of Soviet society, of course, are highly compatible with the basic premises of Marxism-Leninism. The elimination of private ownership of industry and the transfer of the means of production to the community are a case in point. So is collectivization of agriculture. Indeed, the authoritarian character of the regime has clear roots in Leninist doctrine. Lenin's theory of the Party was highly elitist and is well reflected in the structure that prevails in the Soviet Union. Lenin viewed the proletariat as politically inert, lacking a revolutionary consciousness, and therefore requiring direction from without. Sometimes the nondemocratic elements of the Soviet system are erroneously assumed to be deviations from "pure" Communist doctrine.

Probably the most vital function of ideology in the Soviet system is to legitimize the rule of the Communist Party. In the words of the 1961 Party Program:

> The Party is the brain, the honor and the conscience of our epoch, of the Soviet people, the people effecting great revolutionary transformations. It

looks keenly into the future and shows the people scientifically-motivated roads along which to advance, arouses titanic energy in the masses and leads them to the accomplishment of great tasks.[7]

Communist ideology identifies the Soviet Union as the highest form of social organization ever established on earth and credits its achievement to the guidance of the Party. Authority in the Soviet Union is premised on the syllogism: Marxist-Leninist doctrine explains the laws of history and social development; only the Communist Party interprets the ideology and correctly applies it to particular events and circumstances; therefore, the decisions of the Party must prevail. There is no other source of legitimacy in a Communist system. Within the Party individual politicians justify their authority with the argument that they, rather than their rivals, correctly apply the doctrine. Thus did Stalin denounce Trotsky's brand of Bolshevism and Khrushchev condemn his opponents in 1957 as constituting an "anti-Party" faction. The claim of ideological rectitude has been a part of every Soviet politician's baggage. Only at his peril can a Soviet leader ignore identifying his program with Communist doctrine.

Without the ideology to legitimize the regime the cost of ruling would be higher than it is. Resistance to the demands of the leadership would unquestionably be greater were the demands not linked to a scheme for improving man and society. Even Stalin, who came close to ruling by naked terror, attempted to justify his harshness on the ideological grounds that as the construction of socialism proceeded the class struggle intensified—a tenet that his successor repudiated along with Stalin's terror.

Another function ideology serves is communication. The categories of social analysis established in Marxism-Leninism offer a common framework not only in the Soviet Union but throughout the Communist world. Terms such as "bourgeois," "revisionist," and "counterrevolutionary," for example, may have different empirical referents depending upon time and circumstances, but wherever used they clearly define the relationship of social forces, separate the good from the bad, and identify friend and foe.

Ideology serves a psychological function also. For the believing Communist Marxism-Leninism helps to establish a purpose in life. It identifies one's position in history and offers a guide toward a purposeful, creative, and idealistic life. It satisfies intellectual and emotional desires to understand the past and to have some insight into the future.

As already noted, ideology does not provide a clear-cut guide for policy decisions. At the same time it is only reasonable to assume that the constant reiteration of doctrinal themes and the continuous references to Marxist-Leninist categories of social analysis do influence the substance of Communist decision-making. The Communist view of politics as a constant struggle between intensely antagonistic forces in the domestic and international arenas has made efforts at cooperation with non-Communist forces difficult and tenuous. The success of Soviet propaganda in

[7] *The Road to Communism, Documents of the 22nd Congress of the Communist Party of the Soviet Union, October 17–31, 1961* (Moscow: Foreign Languages Publishing House, n.d.), p. 583.

making "imperialist" synonymous with the United States or "revenge-seeking" with Germany is bound to influence relations with the West above and beyond the nonideological conflicts of interest. Domestically, ideology offers a framework through which the leadership is likely to organize its vision of social, political, and economic change. Long- and short-range goals and the methods to be utilized in their attainment are shaped by doctrine. An argument can be made that the net impact of ideology on public policy is both innovative and conservative. By stressing the inevitability and desirability of historical change, the ideology creates a built-in compulsion for social engineering. Until the final stage of Communism is reached, society must always move forward. At the same time, however, doctrine acts as a brake, limiting the options the oligarchy might take. There is a built-in bias against individual initiative, decentralization of control, and the autonomous interplay of forces in Soviet society. A case in point is agriculture, which would unquestionably benefit from a radical overhaul of the collectivized system. An expansion of the highly productive private sector would encounter sharp resistance on ideological grounds.

Today the role of ideology has diminished more than at any time in the Soviet past, though the doctrinal utterances continue unabated. Ideology is no longer seen as the blueprint for the transformation of society. It does not inspire the faith that moved millions to make sacrifices and perform heroic feats for a better future. In its place has developed the motivation appropriate to a bureaucratically organized, highly industrial society: material incentives, patriotism, a sense of professionalism. Communism has come to be identified with the creation of an affluent society, the raising of the standard of living through increased production and the organization of a welfare state. The road to affluence is mapped by science and education.

As a consequence, doctrinal assertions made by the Brezhnev-Kosygin administration have increasingly assumed a hollow, routine character. Never before have Soviet scientists been so free of ideological controls in the pursuit of their endeavors. Even some of the social scientists are beginning to develop studies that draw their conclusions from empirical data rather than doctrine. There are limits, of course, as there always will be in any oligarchy whose primary claim to authority is derived from dogma. Certainly no group will be permitted to question the authority of the Party or its leadership, whether on scientific or political grounds. Ideological control today is not so much concerned about doctrinal purity as it is with maintaining a basic respect for authority. The sin of so many of the writers in the late 1960's and early 1970's is not so much that they describe some of the ugliness of Soviet life as that in doing so they are challenging their elders and undermining respect for authority. Agitprop, the Party's organization for ideological education, is first and foremost an instrument for cracking down on dissent.

As noted earlier, the Soviet Union has demonstrated that Communism is workable. More than that, the rulers of Soviet Russia have organized one of the most powerful and stable regimes of modern times. Of all the nations that have played an important part in world politics since the Bolshevik Revolution, only the United States and Great Britain share with the Soviet Union the distinction of having avoided drastic changes in their political systems. Yet despite its great strength and considerable achievement the Soviet system is plagued with a number of persistent problems and chronic dilemmas, some of which are not at all unique to the Soviet Union. Social disorders such as crime, delinquency, alcoholism, drug addiction, divorce, and mental illness have arisen in all the countries of the world that have experienced industrialization and urbanization. For a long time Soviet leaders denied that social disorganization was possible under socialism and attributed such disorders as did exist to remnants from the capitalist past. Statistical data on social disorders in the Soviet Union are still scarce, though the Soviet press is increasingly paying attention to some of the problems.

There are a number of problems unique to the Soviet Union that threaten its growth and stability. In one way or another they are related to the tensions generated between the demands of dynamic elements in Soviet society for change and the resistance to them of a highly authoritarian political structure. No single problem among them is likely to undermine the maintenance of the present system, but collectively they do pose a serious threat; they suggest that the Soviet Union is a nation in trouble. These problems can be divided into political, economic, and social categories.

Politically a major weakness of the Soviet system is the lack of a recognized and established method of selecting its leadership. Every change in leadership has involved a struggle for power, with each contender devising his own strategy to conform to his strengths and purposes. There have been so clearly agreed-upon rules of the game. The provisions in the Party Statutes governing executive leadership have generally gone unobserved in practice. Theoretically the Party Congress elects the Central Committee, which in turn elects the Politburo and Secretariat; in reality the latter two organs determine their own composition as well as that of the more numerous organs. Executive power in the Soviet Union has ranged from autocracy to collegiality. Each individual who has acquired power has done so through an *ad hoc* strategy as required by the political circumstances of the time. Unlike the British, who operate without the benefit of a written constitution, the Soviets have not yet developed a set of traditional rules. Thus there is no precise way of knowing which offices are stepping stones to power, how long the leadership will remain in power, or the manner in which a change will be made. Nor are the Soviet people any better informed than observers on the outside. Khrushchev's removal was as much as a surprise to the Soviet people as it was to the non-Soviet world.

A corollary to the problem of executive selection is the issue of tenure of office. There are no limits to the length of time an individual may hold office as General Secretary of the Party, Chairman of the Council of

Ministers, or Politburo member. Khrushchev attempted to deal with the issue by revising the Party Statutes to provide for a limited rotation in office. Under rules adopted at the Twenty-second Party Congress in 1961, not less than one-quarter of the membership of the Central Committee and Politburo (then named the Presidium) would have to be changed at all regular elections, and Politburo members would as a rule be limited to three successive terms. This reform, however, was qualified by the provision that in exceptional cases individuals could serve in the Politburo for a longer period. Even those limited measures of democratic constitutionalism were revoked by the leadership under Brezhnev at the Twenty-third Congress in 1966.

The lack of set procedures makes for structural fluidity, with potentially serious implications. Every new administration must go through a trial period in which its legitimacy has to be established. Were a political transition to take place in a severe military, economic, or social crisis, a struggle for power might intensify the crisis and seriously weaken the system. The existing arrangements are an invitation to civil disorder and violence under conditions of extreme disharmony in the ruling oligarchy. It is not at all inconceivable that a struggle for power among several contenders may so divide the civilian elements that the military would attempt to seize power. It is widely believed that Khrushchev successfully overcame the attempt to displace him in 1957 in large part because he had the support of General Zhukov and the army. Violence among civilian elements is also possible, should factions within the Party reach out for the support of specific social groups in a bid for power. This may not be likely, but it is possible.

Some analysts have questioned the stability of an oligarchic leadership without a single leader. Collective decision-making poses the problem of a protracted deadlock. Who is there to arbitrate at the highest level and resolve irreconcilable policy differences? There seems to be a greater danger of stalemate and paralysis in a system of collective leadership than in one providing for a single chief executive. Certainly there are few historical instances where powerful nations (or empires) have successfully operated over a long period of time without a single leader. On the other hand, the Soviet experience in 1923–28, in 1953–57, and since 1964 shows that collective decision-making is workable.

According to the Leninist principle of "democratic centralism," decisions once made by the Party leadership must be accepted by all elements in the Party. Factionalism is not tolerated. In practice this has resulted in the stifling of debate within all but the highest echelons of the Party. Sessions of the Party congresses and plenums of the Central Committee have been little more than rubber-stamp operations to approve decisions made elsewhere. Lower Party organs and rank-and-file members have even less influence over political decisions. Divisions and differences of opinion do exist within the Party, but they cannot be openly and honestly debated, unless the oligarchy wishes to permit such debate. It seems reasonable to assume that the Party itself would benefit from an open confrontation of views and arguments; then not only would the quality of decisions be improved but the atmosphere of intrigue and conformity that permeates the Communist Party would diminish. Indeed, the introduction of open discussion could go a long way toward revitalizing morale among the Party membership.

Related to the problem of autocratic rule within the Party is that of the dictatorship of the Party over Soviet society. While many see the concentration of political power in the hands of a small oligarchy as a source of strength in the Soviet Union, it is also a source of weakness. So long as the Soviet masses are not brought into the decision-making processes of Soviet politics, there will exist a large reservoir of discontent with the system. There will be constant tension between the Party and those highly developed interests in society pressing for a voice in the decisions that govern them. Consent in the Soviet Union must now be engineered or coerced. And that invariably entails a cost. Administration at the middle and lower levels of society is undermined by the remoteness of authority. Initiative is weakened and fresh ideas stifled. Public morale is sapped. One of the outstanding characteristics of the attitudes of the Soviet people toward their government is a sense of alienation. A strong dichotomy exists in the popular mind between the people and their rulers. This has produced an endemic mood of apathy toward the regime.

Many, inside the Soviet world and outside, are willing to sacrifice freedom for security. To some, the hallmark of civic success is not the extent and health of democratic processes but the standard of living. Unfortunately the Soviet achievement here, substantial as it is, falls far short of meeting the extravagant claims of its leaders or matching that of its foremost capitalist competitors. In the economic sector too, the system is plagued by chronic difficulties. The underlying problem for Soviet planners is how to organize the production and allocation of the country's economic resources. Within the framework of a highly centralized system of planning and control Soviet leaders have experimented with a wide variety of reforms, none of which has proved completely satisfactory. The difficulties of centralized planning without the benefit of market forces are well known: A giant bureaucracy is created, which must coordinate the activities of thousands of enterprises. In 1966 Soviet industry had 300 branches and 47,000 enterprises working on independent budgets. In addition there were 12,800 construction enterprises, 12,200 state farms, and 37,100 collective farms, making approximately 110,000 productive enterprises working under one series of coordinate plans. It is virtually impossible for the system to digest and coordinate the vast amount of data fed into it. An enormous amount of paper work is generated. Decisions are made at the center that fail to take into consideration conditions at the local level. Initiative at the local level is discouraged. Waste develops because of the inability of enterprises under different government ministries to coordinate their activities and avoid duplicating productive and distributive facilities. Factories that cannot be guaranteed a smooth flow of supplies find it necessary to overstock and hoard reserves. Factory managers, guided by a system of quotas, find it advantageous to conceal their resources and production potential from authorities and to falsify statistics regarding output. The final victim is always the consumer, who is offered shoddy goods at relatively high prices.

Periodic efforts to overcome the flaws of centralization by decentralizing reforms inevitably have seen one set of problems abate somewhat only to be supplanted by a new set. Decentralization has often produced its own inefficiencies, as regional and local agencies have attempted to create self-contained empires at the expense of other regions and the nation.

The reforms introduced in 1965—sometimes referred to as Libermanism after the Soviet economist who promoted them—attempted to combine the advantage of centralized planning and management with those of a market economy. Managers are now given a freer hand, are rewarded for profitable operations, and are encouraged to raise labor productivity through labor incentive funds. By the beginning of 1969, more than 26,000 Soviet industrial enterprises were working under the new reforms. They produced 75 per cent of the total output of Soviet industry. After more than seven years of experimentation the 1965 reforms failed to produce the benefits anticipated. The year 1969 witnessed a general economic decline, with industrial output increasing at a slower rate than at any time since the overthrow of Khrushchev. While some efficiency has undoubtedly been introduced by calculating profit consideration in cost accounting, the 1965 reforms basically retain the old system of centralized planning with most of its impediments to local autonomy and initiative.

As perplexing as are the problems of industry, those of agriculture are worse. Agriculture remains the Achilles' heel of the Soviet economy. No longer do Soviet leaders echo the promises of the 1961 Program to overtake the United States in agricultural production in the 1970's. With more than 30 per cent of the Soviet working population employed in agriculture, the system is unable consistently to meet the basic food and fiber needs of the nation. It is a source of unremitting chagrin to Soviet planners that without the foodstuffs produced on private plots, which occupy less than 4 per cent of the cultivated area of the country, the shortage of some foods would reach crisis proportions.

Finally, the regime faces difficulties in creating a new "civic culture" of Communism. Soviet successes to date have been much closer to the minimum objective of securing popular acceptance of Party rule than to the maximum goal of molding social values and benefits to create a "new soviet man." Indeed, all indications are that the idea of creating a unique Soviet personality has for practical purposes been abandoned. Even now, after more than half a century in power, the Party has been unable to liquidate large pockets of opposition to Soviet authority and values. The leadership betrays its awareness of popular resistance in periodic press, radio, and television campaigns against "bourgeois ideology." The populace is periodically exhorted to be vigilant against the influence of reactionary capitalist ideas. In the spring of 1968, a campaign against Western influences was launched. The country was made to appear to be practically in a state of seige. The issue is not one of overt opposition; there is little of that and not much doubt that the masses are loyal to the system. But there are many signs of latent opposition, rejection of Soviet values, and, perhaps most widespread of all, alienation and withdrawal from matters of civic concern.

One might have expected the passage of time to remove all doubts and doubters. The generation of the 1970's is the third to be reared in relative isolation from the outside world and, like its predecessors, has been socialized by institutions under Party control. Three generations would seem to be enough to eliminate bourgeois influence. Ironically, some of the dilemmas of Soviet indoctrination increase with the passage of time. Today it is more difficult than in the past to isolate a nation from outside influences. Modernization has brought with it new developments in communication, which make it possible for Soviet citizens to receive information from the non-Soviet world. No longer can the Party maintain the monopoly of information for its citizens and be certain that its voice will be unchallenged. The leadership today suffers from a "credibility gap" that is unprecedented in the Soviet experience.

Furthermore, as the distance between the Revolution and the present increases, the excuses and rationalizations for failure to achieve the goals of the Revolution wear thin. Sacrifices of untold magnitude were borne in the 1930's because society was building the economic basis for socialism. During the 1940's the war and postwar reconstruction justified deferring the satisfaction of popular aspirations for a better life. In the 1950's and 1960's, Khrushchev promised material abundance within a decade as the Soviet Union moved into the final stage of full Communism. Increasingly, payment is demanded, or at least expected, on checks written long ago. The failure of the regime to fulfill the promises of the Revolution has led to widespread disillusionment and cynicism. The profound gap between the realities of Soviet life—its authoritarian politics, its material austerity for the majority, its gross inequalities, and its cultural sterility and conformity—and the claims of Soviet propaganda has created a widespread mood of political apathy. Many have withdrawn into their own private, personal world. A few have openly expressed their opposition.

The extent of alienation and dissatisfaction with Soviet rule varies considerably among different groups. Soviet society is striking in the unevenness of its development, in the gap between its most progressive and modern sectors and its least advanced, if not backward, sectors. Those who are among the greatest beneficiaries of Soviet rule include the Party and state administrators and bureaucrats, scientists, artists and writers, technicians, highly skilled workers, the urban dweller in general, and the European and Slavic peoples. At the lower end of the scale are groups that have fared less well and that, while they may not oppose the entire structure of Soviet rule, are by no means reconciled to many of the Party's specific policies. Certainly the peasants and unskilled workers are the largest number in that category. Their standard of living is low, their economic incentives are weak, and their opportunities are few. In 1964 the peasant, even with his private plot, earned a cash income only one-third that of the city worker.[8] From his labor comes the surplus product that has built Soviet industry and the cities. He remains society's most exploited class. National aspirations are frustrated among a number of non-Russian minorities, particularly in the Baltic and Caucasian regions. Ukrainian intellectuals are protesting to the Russification of their culture. The Tartars seek a return of their people to the Crimean homeland from which they were deported by Stalin. Religious groups want an opportunity to practice their faiths without the discrimination that is public policy against believers. Jews not only are the victims of latent anti-Semitism, a traditional characteristic of the Slavic cultures, but also must overcome official obstacles in the pursuit of their traditional cultural and religious practices.

For intellectuals a special problem exists. They do not fare badly economically. Many, however, particularly writers, resent the restrictions of Soviet censorship. Most have no quarrel with the over-all system, but they object to the hypocrisy and dishonesty of some features of Soviet life, particularly the cant and fatuity of the Party line in literature. They want simply to express themselves openly and honestly. The oligarchy has yet to find a workable boundary between free and restricted expression in literature.

The existence of these dissatisfied elements serves to highlight the heterogeneity of Soviet society. The political system, however autocratic, cannot be monolithic because the social structure over which it rules is not homogeneous. However firmly established its control, the Party cannot ignore the pressures of these and other groups.

At the same time, the system is not pluralistic. The subsocieties and interest groups that make up the social structure are amorphous and compartmentalized. They do not constitute autonomous and independent forces with the right to organize, communicate with each other, and appeal to the public at large for support. Thus, while the pressures for change in the Soviet system are powerful, the prospects for democracy remain rather remote.

[8] Inkeles, *Social Change*, p. 50.

Part One

SOCIAL THEORY

II

The Ideological Heritage

Communist ideology fails to describe what a Communist or socialist society (Marx used the terms interchangeably) would be like. Pre-Marxian socialists who attempted to describe future social organization in some detail were derided by Marx and Engels as "utopian," because they failed to explain in any scientific way how such societies would come into existence. Marx wrote more about capitalism than about socialism. The core of his theories is the attempt to explain why capitalism must eventually give way to socialism. Neither of the founders of Marxist ideology nor any of the leaders of the Communist movement has attempted a detailed description of how social life in a Communist society would be organized, what institutions would exist, or what kinds of activities would occupy its members. Actually, any attempt to do so would be "un-Marxist," because Marx maintained that social and economic institutions were determined by the conditions of production, which no one could foresee. Indeed, Marx is reported to have said that "the man who draws up a programme for the future is a reactionary." [1]

[1] Quoted in E. H. Carr, *The Bolshevik Revolution* 1917–1923 (London: Macmillan, 1952), 2:5.

Although the blueprint is lacking, a general vision of the classless society exists. It will be a collective society based upon common ownership of the means of production. Freed from the fetters of profit and the market, production will expand as necessary to meet the needs of every member of society. Human poverty will be eliminated. Gone also will be ignorance, injustice, and exploitation, the fruits of private property and class conflict. The state will disappear, as will all coercive institutions. Many of the functions of the state, such as economic planning, organization, and administration, will still be necessary, but they will not be exercised through state or political organs. Communist ideological sources are vague as to who will perform them. Marx refers only to "society," meaning the producers themselves. Lenin mentions public agencies similar to labor unions as agents of organization in the future society. Most theorists seem certain that these tasks need no specialists and will be undertaken by ordinary workers.

A major feature of socialism will be the transformation of man's nature. The predatory and competitive characteristics developed under capitalism will give way to man's true nature as a peaceful and cooperative creature. Man will work not because he is compelled to but out of enjoyment, for the satisfaction of inner creative drives. A new morality will prevail in which each person will understand the necessity of his own labor as part of the harmonious cooperation of society's productive forces. Socialism will see not only the end of exploitation but also the elimination of the class character of work as expressed in the division of labor, the antithesis between mental and manual work, and the distinction between town and country. Machines will perform the routine and tedious tasks. No one will specialize all his life in the same profession or activity. People will be trained and educated to perform many social functions and will change jobs periodically as they desire.

As everyone will be a producer, so will each be a consumer. No need will go unattended, though Marx never distinguished between want and need. Presumably public institutions such as laundries and public housing will satisfy most consumption needs. Some contemporary theorists see all of society organized around communes in which will exist common facilities for lodging, eating, recreation, education, and the like. Everyone will be educated to the utmost of his mental and physical abilities, though with less emphasis on formal instruction and more on integrating education with work and play. Life itself will replace many of the formal features of institutionalized schooling. The function of education will be to develop the natural talents of the child toward a socially useful life. Culture will lose its class character and become the common property of all. Artistic expression will be a natural way of life for all.

Finally, the character of the family will change. The monogamous family unit will remain under Communism, but only on the basis of mutual love and need between the two partners. Absolute equality of the sexes will prevail. No longer will the wife be bound to household drudgery. Women will participate in public life as much as men. The family will cease to be an economic unit and the home will lose its private character as a refuge from public life. Many of the functions of the bourgeois family, such as child care and education, will be assumed by society. A child will continue to have two parents, but every child will be responsible to, and the concern of, all of society. The distinction between legitimate and illegitimate children will disappear.

This capsule summary raises more questions about life under Communism than it answers. So will the excerpts that follow. Communist doctrine abounds in ambiguities and contradictions. It nevertheless has inspired millions of Soviet citizens with the belief that they are building a new and better society.

These particular selections will not strike many as inspirational. They are useful primarily because they contain important statements made by Marx, Engels, and Lenin on the socialist society of the future. The first three excerpts reflect the polemical origin of much of Communist ideology. Marx's critique is a passionate diatribe against Ferdinand Lasselle and the program of the German Social Democratic Party presented at its Gotha congress in 1875. Engel's essay, published in 1878, is part of a violent criticism of the German philosopher and economist Karl Eugen Dühring, who sought to reform the abuses of capitalism with a strong labor movement. Lenin's pamphlet, written in 1917, is largely directed against the ideas of Karl Kautsky, German socialist and leader of the Second International. The selections from the *Fundamentals of Marxism-Leninism* are taken from a one-volume summary of doctrine prepared for popular consumption by a group of Soviet writers and scholars under the direction of the veteran Marxist Otto V. Kuusinen. The 1961 Party Program, adopted by the Twenty-second Party Congress, was intended to be Khrushchev's blueprint for the attainment of Communism by 1980. His successors for the most part have ignored it as a policy guide. It stands, however, as the most contemporary formal statement of where the Soviet Communist Party stands in the global struggle for Communism.

1

CRITIQUE OF THE GOTHA PROGRAM

KARL MARX

The emancipation of labor demands the promotion of the instruments of labor to the common property of society and the cooperative regulation of the total labor with a fair distribution of the proceeds of labor.

"Promotion of the instruments of labor to the common property" ought obviously to read their "conversion into the common property"; but this only in passing.

What are "proceeds of labor"? The product of labor or its value? And in the latter case, is it the total value of the product or only that part of the value which labor has newly added to the value of the means of production consumed?

"Proceeds of labor" is a loose notion which Lassalle has put in the place of definite economic conceptions.

Reprinted from Karl Marx and Friedrich Engels, *Selected Works* (Moscow: Foreign Languages Publishing House, 1951), 2:19–23.

What is "a fair distribution"?

Do not the bourgeois assert that the present-day distribution is "fair"? And is it not, in fact, the only "fair" distribution on the basis of the present-day mode of production? Are economic relations regulated by legal conceptions or do not, on the contrary, legal relations arise from economic ones? Have not also the socialist sectarians the most varied notions about "fair" distribution?

To understand what is implied in this connection by the phrase "fair distribution," we must take the first paragraph and this one together. The latter presupposes a society wherein "the instruments of labor are common property and the total labor is cooperatively regulated," and from the first paragraph we learn that "the proceeds of labor belong undiminished with equal right to all members of society."

"To all members of society?" To those who do not work as well? What remains then of the "undiminished proceeds of labor"? Only to those members of society who work? What remains then of the "equal right" of all members of society?

But "all members of society" and "equal right" are obviously mere phrases. The kernel consists in this, that in this communist society every worker must receive the "undiminished" Lassallean "proceeds of labor."

Let us take first of all the words "proceeds of labor" in the sense of the product of labor; then the cooperative proceeds of labor are the *total social product*.

From this must now be deducted:

First, cover for replacement of the means of production used up.

Secondly, additional portion for expansion of production.

Thirdly, reserve or insurance funds to provide against accidents, dislocations caused by natural calamities, etc.

These deductions from the "undiminished proceeds of labor" are an economic necessity and their magnitude is to be determined according to available means and forces, and partly by computation of probabilities, but they are in no way calculable by equity.

There remains the other part of the total product, intended to serve as means of consumption.

Before this is divided among the individuals, there has to be deducted again, from it:

First, the general costs of administration not belonging to production. This part will, from the outset, be very considerably restricted in comparison with present-day society and it diminishes in proportion as the new society develops.

Secondly, that which is intended for the common satisfaction of needs such as schools, health services, etc.

From the outset this part grows considerably in comparison with present-day society and it grows in proportion as the new society develops.

Thirdly, funds for those unable to work, etc., in short, for what is included under so-called official poor relief today.

Only now do we come to the "distribution" which the program, under Lassallean influence, alone has in view in its narrow fashion, namely, to that part of the means of consumption which is divided among the individual producers of the cooperative society.

The "undiminished proceeds of labor" have already unnoticeably become converted into the "diminished" proceeds, although what the producer is deprived of in his capacity as a private individual benefits him directly or indirectly in his capacity as a member of society.

Just as the phrase of the "undiminished proceeds of labor" has disappeared, so now does the phrase of the "proceeds of labor" disappear altogether.

Within the cooperative society based on common ownership of the means of production, the producers do not exchange their products; just as little does the labor employed on the products appear here *as the value* of these products, as a material quality possessed by them, since now, in contrast to capitalist society, individual labor no longer exists in an indirect fashion but directly as a component part of the total labor. The phrase "proceeds of labor," objectionable also today on account of its ambiguity, thus loses all meaning.

What we have to deal with here is a communist society, not as it has *developed* on its own foundations, but, on the contrary, just as it *emerges* from capitalist society; which is thus in every respect, economically, morally and intellectually, still stamped with the birthmarks of the old society from whose womb it emerges. Accordingly, the individual producer receives back from society—after the deductions have been made—exactly what he gives to it. What he has given to it is his individual quantum of labor. For example, the social working day consists of the sum of the individual hours of work; the individual labor time of the individual producer is the part of the social working day contributed by him, his share in it. He receives a certificate from society that he has furnished such and such an amount of labor (after deducting his labor for the common funds), and with this certificate he draws from the social stock of means of consumption as much as costs the same amount of labor. The same amount of labor which he has given to society in one form he receives back in another.

Here obviously the same principle prevails as that which regulates the exchange of commodities, as far as this is exchange of equal values. Content and form are changed, because under the altered circumstances no one can give anything except his labor, and because, on the other hand, nothing can pass to the ownership of individuals except individual means of consumption. But, as far as the distribution of the latter among the individual producers is concerned, the same principle prevails as in the exchange of commodity-equivalents: a given amount of labor in one form is exchanged for an equal amount of labor in another form.

Hence, *equal right* here is still in principle— *bourgeois right*, although principle and practice are no longer at loggerheads, while the exchange of equivalents in commodity exchange only exists *on the average* and not in the individual case.

In spite of this advance, this *equal right* is still constantly stigmatized by a bourgeois limitation. The right of the producers is *proportional* to the labor they supply; the equality consists in the fact that measurement is made with an *equal standard*, labor.

But one man is superior to another physically or mentally and so supplies more labor in the same time, or can labor for a longer time; and labor, to serve as a measure, must be defined by its duration or intensity, otherwise it ceases to be a standard of measurement. This *equal* right is an unequal right for unequal labor. It recognizes no class differences, because everyone is only a worker like everyone else; but it tacitly recognizes unequal individual endowment and thus productive capacity as natural privileges. *It is, therefore, a right of inequality, in its content, like every right.* Right by its very nature can consist only in the application of an equal standard; but unequal individuals (and they would not be different individuals if they were not unequal) are measurable only by an equal standard in so far as they are brought under an equal point of view, are taken from one *definite* side only, for instance, in the present case, are regarded *only as workers*, and nothing more is seen in them, everything else being ignored. Further, one worker is married, another not; one has more children than another, and so on and so forth. Thus, with an equal performance of labor, and hence an equal share in the social consumption fund, one will in fact receive more than another, one will be richer than another, and so on. To avoid all these defects, right instead of being equal would have to be unequal.

But these defects are inevitable in the first phase of communist society as it is when it has just emerged after prolonged birth pangs from capitalist society. Right can never be higher than the economic structure of society and its cultural development conditioned thereby.

In a higher phase of communist society, after the enslaving subordination of the individual to the division of labor, and therewith also the antithesis between mental and physical labor, has vanished; after labor has become not only a means of life but life's prime want; after the productive forces have also increased with the all-round development of the individual, and all the springs of cooperative wealth flow more abundantly—only then can the narrow horizon of bourgeois right be crossed in its entirety and society inscribe on its banners: From each according to his ability, to each according to his needs!

*　　*　　*

2

THEORETICAL SOCIALISM

FRIEDRICH ENGELS

The materialist conception of history starts from the proposition that the production [of the means to support human life] and, next to production, the exchange of things produced, is the basis of all social structure; that in every society that has appeared in history, the manner in which wealth is distributed and society divided into classes or orders is dependent upon what is produced, how it is produced, and how the products are exchanged. From this point of view the final causes of all social changes and political revolutions are to be sought, not in men's brains, not in man's better insight into eternal truth and justice, but in changes in the modes of production and exchange. They are to be sought, not in the *philosophy*, but in the *economics* of each particular epoch. The growing perception that existing social institutions are unreasonable and unjust, that reason has become unreason, and right wrong, is only proof that in the modes of production and exchange changes have silently taken place with which the social order, adapted to earlier economic conditions, is no longer in keeping. From this it also follows that the means of getting rid of the incongruities that have been brought to light must also be present, in a more or less developed condition, within the changed modes of production themselves. These means are not to be *invented*, spun out of the head, but *discovered* with the aid of the head in the existing material facts of production.

What is, then, the position of modern socialism in this connection?

The present structure of society—this is now pretty generally conceded—is the creation of the ruling class of today, of the bourgeoisie. The mode of production peculiar to the bourgeoisie, known, since Marx, as the capitalist

Reprinted from Friedrich Engels, *Anti-Dühring*, 2d ed. (Moscow: Foreign Languages Publishing House, 1959), pp. 367–91. The footnotes have been omitted. Brackets were added by the Soviet translator.

mode of production, was incompatible with the local privileges and the privileges of estate as well as with the reciprocal personal ties of the feudal system. The bourgeoisie broke up the feudal system and built upon its ruins the capitalist order of society, the kingdom of free competition, of personal liberty, of the equality, before the law, of all commodity owners, of all the rest of the capitalist blessings. Thenceforward the capitalist mode of production could develop in freedom. Since steam, machinery, and the making of machines by machinery transformed the older manufacture into modern industry, the productive forces evolved under the guidance of the bourgeoisie developed with a rapidity and in a degree unheard of before. But just as the older manufacture, in its time, and handicraft, becoming more developed under its influence, had come into collision with the feudal trammels of the guilds, so now modern industry, in its more complete development, comes into collision with the bounds within which the capitalistic mode of production holds it confined. The new productive forces have already outgrown the capitalistic mode of using them. And this conflict between productive forces and modes of production is not a conflict engendered in the mind of man, like that between original sin and divine justice. It exists, in fact, objectively, outside us, independently of the will and actions even of the men that have brought it on. Modern socialism is nothing but the reflex, in thought, of this conflict in fact; its ideal reflection in the minds, first, of the class directly suffering under it, the working class.

Now, in what does this conflict consist?

Before capitalistic production, i.e., in the Middle Ages, the system of petty industry obtained generally, based upon the private property of the laborers in their means of production; [in the country,] the agriculture of the small peasant, freeman, or serf; in the towns, the handicrafts [organized in guilds]. The instruments of labor—land, agricultural implements, the workshop, the tool—were the instruments of labor of single individuals, adapted for the use of one worker, and, therefore, of necessity, small, dwarfish, circumscribed. But for this very reason they belonged, as a rule, to the producer himself. To concentrate these scattered, limited means of production, to enlarge them, to turn them into the powerful levers of production of the present day—this was precisely the historic role of capitalist production and of its upholder, the bourgeoisie. In the fourth section of *Capital* Marx has explained in detail how, since the fifteenth century, this has been historically worked out through the three phases of simple cooperation, manufacture, and modern industry. But the bourgeoisie, as is also shown there, could not transform these puny means of production into mighty productive forces without transforming them, at the same time, from means of production of the individual into *social* means of production only workable by *a collectivity of men*. The spinning wheel, the hand loom, the blacksmith's hammer were replaced by the spinning machine, the power loom, the steam hammer; the individual workshop by the factory implying the cooperation of hundreds and thousands of workmen. In like manner, production itself changed from a series of individual into a series of social acts, and the products from individual to social products. The yarn, the cloth, the metal articles that now came out of the factory were the joint product of many workers, through whose hands they had successively to pass before they were ready. No one person could say of them: "I made that; this is *my* product."

But where, in a given society, the fundamental form of production is that spontaneous division of labor [which creeps in gradually and not upon any preconceived plan], there the products take on the form of commodities, whose mutual exchange, buying and selling, enable the individual producers to satisfy their manifold wants. And this was the case in the Middle Ages. The peasant, e.g., sold to the artisan agricultural products and bought from him the products of handicraft. Into this society of individual producers, of commodity producers, the new mode of production thrust itself. In the midst of the old division of labor, grown up spontaneously and upon *no definite plan*, which had governed the whole of society, now arose division of labor upon *a definite plan*, as organized in the factory; side by side with *individual production* appeared *social* production. The products of both were sold in the same market, and, therefore, at prices at least approximately equal. But organization upon a definite plan was stronger than spontaneous division of labor. The factories working with the combined social forces of a collectivity of individuals produced their commodities far more cheaply than the individual small producers. Individual production succumbed in one department after another. Socialized production revolutionized all the old methods of production. But its revolutionary character was, at the same time, so little recognized that it was, on the contrary, introduced as a means of increasing and developing the production of commodities. When it arose, it found readymade, and made liberal use of, certain machinery for the production and exchange of commodities: merchants' capital, handicraft, wage labor. Socialized production thus introducing itself as a new form of the production of commodities, it was a matter of course that under it the old forms of appropriation remained in full swing and were applied to its products as well.

In the medieval stage of evolution of the production of commodities, the question as to the owner of the product of labor could not arise. The individual producer, as a rule, had, from raw material belonging to himself, and generally his own handiwork, produced it with his own tools, by the labor of his own hands or of his family. There was no need for him to appropriate the new product. It belonged wholly to him, as a matter of course. His property in the product was, therefore, based *upon his own labor*. Even where external help was used, this was, as a rule, of little importance, and in many cases received other compensation in addition to wages. The apprentices and journeymen of the guilds worked less for board and wages than for education, in order that they might become master craftsmen themselves.

Then came the concentration of the means of production [and of the producers] in large workshops and manufactories, their transformation into actual socialized means of production [and socialized producers]. But the [socialized producers and] means of production and their products were still treated, after this change, just as they had been before, i.e., as the means of production and the products of individuals. Hitherto, the owner of the instruments of labor had himself appropriated the product, because, as a rule, it was his own product, and the assistance of others was the exception. Now the owner of the instruments of labor always appropriated to himself the product, although it was no longer *his* product but exclusively the product of the *labor of others*. Thus, the products now produced socially were not appropriated by those who had actually set in motion the means of production and actually produced the commodities, but by the *capitalists*. The means of production, and production itself, had become in essence socialized. But they were subjected to a form of appropriation which presupposes the private production of individuals, under which, therefore, every one owns his own product and brings it to market. The mode of production is subject to this form of appropriation, although it abolishes the conditions upon which the latter rests.

This contradiction, which gives to the new mode of production its capitalistic character, *contains the germ of the whole of the social antagonisms of today*. The greater the mastery obtained by the new mode of production over all decisive fields of production and in all economically decisive countries, the more it reduced individual production to an insignificant residuum, *the more clearly was brought out the incompatibility of socialized production with capitalistic appropriation*.

The first capitalists found, as we have said [alongside other forms of labor], wage labor ready-made for them [on the market]. But it was exceptional, complementary, accessory, transitory wage labor. The agricultural laborer, though, upon occasion, he hired himself out by the day, had a few acres of his own land on which he could at all events live at a pinch. The guilds were so organized that the journeyman of today became the master of tomorrow. But all this changed as soon as the means of production became socialized and concentrated in the hands of capitalists. The means of production, as well as the product, of the individual producer became more and more worthless; there was nothing left for him but to turn wage worker under the capitalist. Wage labor, aforetime the exception and accessory, now became the rule and basis of all production; aforetime complementary, it now became the sole remaining function of the worker. The wage worker for a time became a wage worker for life. The number of these permanent wage workers was further enormously increased by the breaking up of the feudal system that occurred at the same time, by the disbanding of the retainers of the feudal lords, the eviction of the peasants from their homesteads, etc. The separation was made complete between the means of production concentrated in the hands of the capitalists, on the one side, and the producers, possessing nothing but their labor power, on the other. *The contradiction between socialized production and capitalistic appropriation manifested itself as the antagonism of proletariat and bourgeoisie.*

We have seen that the capitalistic mode of production thrust its way into a society of commodity-producers, of individual producers, whose social bond was the exchange of their products. But every society based upon the production of commodities has this peculiarity: that the producers have lost control over their own social interrelations. Each man produces for himself with such means of production as he may happen to have, and for such exchange as he may require to satisfy his remaining wants. No one knows how much of his particular article is coming on the market, nor how much of it will be wanted. No one knows whether his individual product will meet an actual demand, whether he will be able to make good his costs of production or even to sell his commodity at all. Anarchy reigns in socialized production.

But the production of commodities, like every other form of production, has its peculiar, inherent laws inseparable from it; and these laws work, despite anarchy, in and through anarchy. They reveal themselves in the only persistent form of social interrelations, i.e., in exchange, and here they affect the individual producers as compulsory laws of competition. They are, at first, unknown to these producers themselves and have to be discovered by them gradually and as the result of experience. They work themselves out, therefore, independently of the producers, and in antagonism to them, as inexorable natural laws of their particular form of production. The product governs the producers.

In medieval society, especially in the earlier centuries, production was essentially directed towards satisfying the wants of the individual. It satisfied, in the main, only the wants of the producer and his family. Where relations of personal dependence existed, as in the country, it also helped to satisfy the wants of the feudal lord. In all this there was, therefore, no exchange; the products, consequently, did not assume the character of commodities. The family of the peasant produced almost everything they wanted: clothes and furniture, as well as means of subsistence. Only when it began to produce more than was sufficient to supply its own wants and the payments in kind to the feudal lord, only then did it also produce commodities. This surplus, thrown into socialized exchange and offered for sale, became commodities.

The artisans of the towns, it is true, had from the first to produce for exchange. But they, also, themselves supplied the greatest part of their own individual wants. They had gardens and plots of land. They turned their cattle out into the communal forest, which, also, yielded them timber and firing. The women spun flax, wool, and so forth. Production for the purpose of exchange, production of commodities, was only in its infancy. Hence, exchange was restricted, the market narrow, the methods of production stable; there was local exclusiveness without, local unity within; the mark in the country; in the town, the guild.

But with the extension of the production of commodities, and especially with the introduction of the capitalist mode of production, the laws of commodity production, hitherto latent, came into action more openly and with greater force. The old bonds were loosened, the old exclusive limits broken through, the producers were more and more turned into independent, isolated producers of commodities. The anarchy of social production became apparent and grew to greater and greater height. But the chief means of aid of which the capitalist mode of production intensified this anarchy of socialized production was the exact opposite of anarchy. It was the increasing organization of production, upon a social basis, in every individual productive establishment. By this, the old, peaceful, stable condition of things was ended. Wherever this organization of production was introduced into a branch of industry, it brooked no other method of production by its side. [Where it laid hold of a handicraft, that old handicraft was wiped out.] The field of labor became a battleground. The great geographical discoveries, and the colonization following upon them, multiplied markets and quickened the transformation of handicraft into manufacture. The war did not simply break out between the individual producers of particular localities. The local struggles begat in their turn national conflicts, the commercial wars of the seventeenth and the eighteenth centuries.

Finally, modern industry and the opening of the world market made the struggle universal, and at the same time gave it an unheard-of virulence. Advantages in natural or artificial conditions of production now decide the existence or nonexistence of individual capitalists, as well as of whole industries and countries. He that falls is remorselessly cast aside. It is the Darwinian struggle of the individual for existence transferred from nature to society with intensified violence. The conditions of existence natural to the animal appear as the final term of human development. The contradiction between socialized production and capitalistic appropriation now presents itself as *an antagonism between the organization of production in the individual workshop and the anarchy of production in society generally.*

The capitalistic mode of production moves in these two forms of the antagonism immanent to it from its very origin. It is never able to get out of that "vicious circle" which Fourier had already discovered. What Fourier could not, indeed, see in his time is that this circle is gradually narrowing; that the movement becomes more and more a spiral, and must come to an end, like the movement of the planets, by collision with the center. It is the compelling force of anarchy in the production of society at large that more and more completely turns the great majority of men into proletarians; and it is the masses of the proletariat again who will finally put an end to anarchy in production. It is the compelling force of anarchy in social production that turns the limitless perfectibility of machinery under modern industry into a compulsory law by which every individual industrial capitalist must perfect his machinery more and more, under penalty of ruin.

But the perfecting of machinery is making human labor superfluous. If the introduction and increase of machinery means the displacement of millions of manual by a few machine workers, improvement in machinery means the displacement of more and more of the machine workers themselves. It means, in the last instance, the production of a number of available wage workers in excess of the average needs of capital, the formation of a complete industrial reserve army, as I called it in 1845, available at the times when industry is working at high pressure, to be cast out upon the street when the inevitable crash comes, a constant dead weight upon the limbs of the working class in its struggle for existence with capital, a regulator for the keeping of wages down to the low level that suits the interests of capital. Thus it comes about, to quote Marx, that machinery becomes the most powerful weapon in the war of capital against the working class; that the instruments of labor constantly tear the means of subsistence out of the hands of the laborer; that the very product of the worker is turned into an instrument for his subjugation. Thus it comes about that the economizing of the instruments of labor becomes at the same time, from the outset, the most reckless waste of labor power and robbery committed upon the normal conditions under which labor functions; that machinery, the most powerful instrument for shortening labor time, becomes the most unfailing means for placing every moment of the laborer's time and that of his family at the disposal of the capitalist for the purpose of expanding the value of his capital. Thus it comes about that the overwork of some becomes the preliminary condition for the idleness of others, and that modern industry, which hunts after new consumers over the whole world, forces the consumption of the masses at home down to a starvation minimum, and in doing thus destroys its own home market. "The law that always equilibrates the relative surplus population, or industrial reserve army, to the extent and energy of accumulation, this law rivets the laborer to capital more firmly than the wedges of Vulcan did Prometheus to the rock. It establishes an accumulation of misery, corresponding with accumulation of capital. Accumulation of wealth at one pole is, therefore, at the same time accumulation of misery, agony of toil, slavery, ignorance, brutality, mental degradation, at the opposite pole, i.e., on the side of the class that produces *its own product in the form of capital*" (Marx). And to expect any other division of the products from the capitalistic mode of production is the same as expecting the electrodes of a battery not to decompose acidulated water, not to liberate oxygen at the positive, hydrogen at the negative pole, so long as they are connected with the battery.

We have seen that the ever increasing perfectibility of modern machinery is, by the anarchy of social production, turned into a compulsory law that forces the individual industrial capitalist always to improve his machinery, always to increase its productive force. The bare possibility of extending the field of production is transformed for him into a similar compulsory law. The enormous expansive force of modern industry, compared with which that of gases is mere child's play, appears to us now as a *necessity* for expansion, both qualitative and quantitative, that laughs at all resistance. Such resistance is offered by consumption, by sales, by the markets for the products of modern industry. But the capacity for extension, extensive and intensive, of the markets is primarily governed by quite different laws that work much less energetically. The extension of the markets cannot keep pace with the extension of production. The collision becomes inevitable, and as this cannot produce any real solution so long as it does not break in pieces the capitalist mode of production, the collisions become periodic. Capitalist production has begotten another "vicious circle." . . .

The fact that the socialized organization of production within the factory has developed so far that it has become incompatible with the anarchy of production in society, which exists side by side with and dominates it, is brought home to the capitalists themselves by the violent concentration of capital that occurs during crises, through the ruin of many large, and a still greater number of small, capitalists. The whole mechanism of the capitalist mode of production breaks down under the pressure of the productive forces, its own creations. It is no longer able to turn all this mass of means of production into capital. They lie fallow, and for that very reason the industrial reserve army must also lie fallow. Means of production, means of subsistence, available laborers, all the elements of production and of general wealth, are present in abundance. But "abundance becomes the source of distress and want" (Fourier), because it is the very thing that prevents the transformation of the means of production and subsistence into capital. For in capitalistic society the means of production can only function when they have undergone a preliminary transformation into capital, into the means of exploiting human labor power. The necessity of this transformation into capital of the means of production and subsistence stands like a ghost between these and the workers. It alone prevents the coming together of the material and personal levers of production; it alone forbids the means of production to function, the workers to work and live. On the one hand, therefore, the capitalistic mode of production stands convicted of its own incapacity to further direct these productive forces. On the other, these productive forces themselves, with increasing energy, press forward to the removal of the existing contradiction, to the abolition of their quality as capital, to the *practical recognition of their character as social productive forces.* . . .

State ownership of the productive forces is not the solution of the conflict, but concealed within it are the technical conditions that form the elements of that solution.

This solution can only consist in the practical recognition of the social nature of the modern forces of production, and therefore in the harmonizing of the modes of production, appropriation, and exchange with the socialized character of the means of production. And this can only come about by society openly and directly taking possession of the productive forces, which have outgrown all control except that of society as a whole. The social character of the means of production and of the products today reacts against the producers, periodically disrupts all production and exchange, acts only like a law of nature working blindly, forcibly, destructively. But with the taking over by society of the productive forces, the social character of the means of production and of the products will be utilized by the producers with a perfect understanding of its nature and, instead of being a source of disturbance and periodical collapse, will become the most powerful lever of production itself.

Active social forces work exactly like natural forces: blindly, forcibly, destructively, so long as we do not understand, and reckon with, them. But when once we understand them, when once we grasp their action, their direction, their effects, it depends only upon ourselves to subject them more and more to our own will, and by means of them to reach our own ends. And this holds quite especially for the mighty productive forces of today. As long as we obstinately refuse to understand the nature and the character of these productive forces—and this understanding goes against the grain of the capitalist mode of production and its defenders—so long these forces are at work in spite of us, in opposition to us, so long they master us, as we have shown above in detail.

But when once their nature is understood, they can, in the hands of the producers working together, be transformed from master demons into willing servants. The difference is as that between the destructive force of electricity in the lightning of the storm and electricity under command in the telegraph and the voltaic arc; the difference between a conflagration and fire working in the service of man. With this recognition, at last, of the real nature of the productive forces of today, the social anarchy of production gives place to a social regulation of production upon a definite plan, according to the needs of the community and of each individual. Then the capitalist mode of appropriation, in which the product enslaves first the producer and then the appropriator, is replaced by the mode of appropriation of the products that is based upon the nature of the modern means of production; upon the one hand, direct social appropriation, as means to the maintenance and extension of production—on the other, direct individual appropriation, as means of subsistence and of enjoyment.

Whilst the capitalist mode of production more and more completely transforms the great majority of the population into proletarians, it creates the power which, under penalty of its own destruction, is forced to accomplish this revolution. Whilst it forces on more and more the transformation of the vast means of production, already socialized, into state property, it shows itself the way to accomplishing this revolution. *The proletariat seizes political power and turns the means of production in the first instance into state property.*

But, in doing this, it abolishes itself as proletariat, abolishes all class distinctions and class antagonisms, abolishes also the state as state. Society thus far, based upon class antagonisms, had need of the state, that is, of an organization of the particular class, which was *pro tempore* the exploiting class, for the maintenance of its external conditions of production, and, therefore, especially, for the purpose of forcibly keeping the exploited classes in the condition of oppression corresponding with the given mode of production (slavery, serfdom, wage labor). The state was the official representative of society as a whole; the gathering of it together into a visible embodiment. But it was this only in so far as it was the state of that class which itself represented, for the time being, society as a whole: in ancient times, the state of slave-owning citizens; in the Middle Ages, the feudal lords; in our own time, the bourgeoisie. When at last it becomes the real representative of the whole of society, it renders itself unnecessary. As soon as there is no longer any social class to be held in subjection; as soon as class rule, and the individual struggle for existence based upon our present anarchy in production, with the collisions and excesses arising from these, are removed, nothing more remains to be repressed, and a special repressive force, a state, is no longer necessary. The first act by virtue of which the state really constitutes itself the representative of the whole of society—the taking possession of the means of production in the name of society—this is, at the same time, its last independent act as a state. State interference in social relations becomes, in one domain after another, superfluous, and then withers away of itself; the government of persons is replaced by the administration of things, and by the conduct of processes of production. The state is not "abolished." *It withers away.* This gives the measure of the value of the phrase "a free people's state," both as to its justifiable use at times by agitators, and as to its ultimate scientific insufficiency; and also of the demands of the so-called anarchists for the abolition of the state out of hand.

Since the historical appearance of the capitalist mode of production, the appropriation by society of all the means of production has often been dreamed of, more or less vaguely, by individuals, as well as by sects, as the ideal of the future. But it could become possible, could become a historical necessity, only when the actual conditions for its realization were there. Like every other social advance, it becomes practicable not by men understanding that the existence of classes is in contradiction to justice, equality, etc., not by the mere willingness to abolish these classes, but by virtue of certain new economic conditions. The separation of society into an exploiting and an exploited class, a ruling and an oppressed class, was the necessary consequence of the deficient and restricted development of production in former times. So long as the total social labor only yields a produce which but slightly exceeds that barely necessary for the existence of all; so long, therefore, as labor engages all or almost all the time of the great majority of the members of society—so long, of necessity, this society is divided into classes. Side by side with the great majority, exclusively bond slaves to labor, arises a class freed from directly productive labor, which looks after the general affairs of society: the direction of labor, state business, law, science, art, etc. It is, therefore, the law of division of labor that lies at the basis of the division into classes. But this does not prevent this division into classes from being carried out by means of violence and robbery, trickery and fraud. It does not prevent the ruling class, once having the upper hand, from consolidating its power at the expense of the working class, from turning its social leadership into an [intensified] exploitation of the masses.

But if, upon this showing, division into classes has a certain historical justification, it has this only for a given period, only under given social conditions. It was based upon the insufficiency of production. It will be swept away by the complete development of modern productive forces. And, in fact, the abolition of classes in society presupposes a degree of historical evolution at which the existence, not simply of this or that particular ruling class, but of any ruling class at all, and, therefore, the existence of class distinction itself, has become an obsolete anachronism. It presupposes, therefore, the development of production carried out to a degree at which appropriation of the means of production and of the products and, with this, of political domination, of the monopoly of culture, and of intellectual leadership by a particular class of society, has become not only superfluous but economically, politically, intellectually a hindrance to development.

This point is now reached. Their political and intellectual bankruptcy is scarcely any longer a secret to the bourgeoisie themselves. Their economic bankruptcy recurs regularly every ten years. In every crisis, society is suffocated beneath the weight of its own productive forces and products, which it cannot use, and stands helpless, face to face with the absurd contradiction that the producers have nothing to consume, because consumers are wanting. The expansive force of the means of production bursts the bonds that the capitalist mode of production had imposed upon them. Their deliverance from these bonds is the one precondition for an unbroken, constantly accelerated development of the productive forces, and therewith for a practically unlimited increase of production itself. Nor is this all. The socialized appropriation of the means of production does away not only with the present artificial restrictions upon production but also with the positive waste and devastation of productive forces and products that are at the present time the inevitable concomitants of production, and that reach their height in the crises. Further, it sets free for the community at large a mass of means of production and of products, by doing away with the senseless extravagance of the ruling classes of today and their political representatives. The possibility of securing for every member of society, by means of socialized production, an existence not only fully sufficient materially, and becoming day by day more full, but an existence guaranteeing to all the free development and exercise of their physical and mental faculties—this possibility is now for the first time here, but *it is here.*

With the seizing of the means of production by society, production of commodities is done away with, and, simultaneously, the mastery of the product over the producer. Anarchy in social production is replaced by plan-conforming, conscious organization. The struggle for individual existence disappears. Then for the first time man, in a certain sense, is finally marked off from the rest of the animal kingdom, and emerges from mere animal conditions of existence into really human ones. The whole sphere of the conditions of life which environ man, and which have hitherto ruled man, now comes under the dominion and control of man, who for the first time becomes the real, conscious lord of nature, because he has now become master of his own social organization. The laws of his own social action, hitherto standing face to face with man as laws of nature foreign to, and dominating him, will then be used with full understanding, and so mastered by him. Man's own social organization, hitherto confronting him as a necessity imposed by nature and history, now becomes the result of his own free action. The extraneous objective forces that have hitherto governed history pass under the control of man himself. Only from that time will man himself, with full consciousness, make his own history—only from that time will the social causes set in movement by him have, in the main and in a constantly growing measure, the results intended by him. It is the ascent of man from the kingdom of necessity to the kingdom of freedom.

* * *

3

STATE AND REVOLUTION

V. I. LENIN

With What Is the Smashed State Machine to Be Replaced?

In 1847, in the *Communist Manifesto*, Marx's answer to this question was as yet a purely abstract one, or, to speak more correctly, it was an answer that indicated the tasks, but not the ways of accomplishing them. The answer given in the *Communist Manifesto* was that this machine was to be replaced by "the proletariat organized as the ruling class," by the "winning of the battle of democracy."

Marx did not indulge in utopias; he expected the *experience* of the mass movement to provide the reply to the question as to what specific

Reprinted from V. I. Lenin, *Selected Works* 2, Part 1 (Moscow: Foreign Languages Publishing House, 1952): 240–44, 249–51.

forms this organization of the proletariat as the ruling class will assume and as to the exact manner in which this organization will be combined with the most complete, most consistent "winning of the battle of democracy."

Marx subjected the experience of the Commune, meager as it was, to the most careful analysis in *The Civil War in France*. Let us quote the most important passages of this work.

> Originating from the Middle Ages, there developed in the nineteenth century "the centralized State power, with its ubiquitous organs of standing army, police, bureaucracy, clergy, and judicature." With the development of class antagonisms between capital and labor, "the State power assumed more and more the character of the national power of capital over labor, of a public force organized for social enslavement, of an engine of class despotism. After every revolution marking a progressive phase in the class struggle, the purely repressive character of the State power stands out in bolder and bolder relief." After the Revolution of 1848–49, the State power became "the national war engine of capital against labor." The Second Empire consolidated this.
>
> "The direct antithesis to the Empire was the Commune." It was the "positive form" of "a republic that was not only to supersede the monarchical form of class-rule, but class-rule itself."

What was this "positive" form of the proletarian, the socialist republic? What was the state it began to create?

> "The first decree of the Commune . . . was the suppression of the standing army, and the substitution for it of the armed people."

This demand now figures in the program of every party claiming the name of Socialist. But the real worth of their programs is best shown by the behavior of our Socialist-Revolutionaries and Mensheviks, who, right after the revolution of February 27, actually refused to carry out this demand!

> The Commune was formed of the municipal councillors, chosen by universal suffrage in the various wards of the town, responsible and revocable at short terms. The majority of its members were naturally working men, or acknowledged representatives of the working class. . . .
>
> Instead of continuing to be the agent of the Central Government, the police was at once stripped of its political attributes, and turned into the responsible and at all times revocable agent of the Commune. So were the officials of all other branches of the Administration. From the members of the Commune downwards, the public service had to be done at *workmen's wages*. The vested interests and the representation allowances of the high dignitaries of State disappeared along with the high dignitaries themselves. . . . Having once got rid of the standing army and the police, the physical force elements of the old Government, the Commune was anxious to break the spiritual force of repression, the "parson-power." . . . The judicial functionaries were to be divested of that sham independence . . . they were to be elective, responsible and revocable.

Thus the Commune appears to have replaced the smashed state machine "only" by fuller democracy: abolition of the standing army; all officials to be elected and subject to recall. But as a matter of fact this "only" signifies a gigantic replacement of certain institutions by other institutions of a fundamentally different order. This is exactly a case of "quantity becoming transformed into quality": democracy, introduced as fully and consistently as is at all conceivable, is transformed from bourgeois democracy into proletarian democracy; from the state (a special force for the suppression of a particular class) into something which is no longer really the state.

It is still necessary to suppress the bourgeoisie and crush its resistance. This was particularly necessary for the Commune; and one of the reasons for its defeat was that it did not do this with sufficient determination. But the organ of suppression is now the majority of the population, and not a minority, as was always the case under slavery, serfdom, and wage slavery. And since the majority of the people *itself* suppresses its oppressors, a "special force" for suppression is *no longer necessary!* In this sense the state *begins to wither away.* Instead of the special institutions of a privileged minority (privileged officialdom, the chiefs of the standing army), the majority itself can directly fulfill all these functions, and the more the functions of state power devolve upon the people as a whole the less need is there for the existence of this power.

In this connection the following measures of the Commune emphasized by Marx are particularly noteworthy: the abolition of all representation allowances, and of all monetary privileges in the case of officials, the reduction of the remuneration of *all* servants of the state to the level of *"workmen's wages."* This shows more clearly than anything else the *turn* from bourgeois democracy to proletarian democracy, from the democracy of the oppressors to the democracy of the oppressed classes, from the state as a *"special force"* for the suppression of a particular class to the suppression of the oppressors by the *general force* of the majority of the people—the workers and the peasants. And it is precisely on this particularly striking point, perhaps the most important as far as the problem of the state is concerned, that the teachings of Marx have been most completely forgotten! In popular commentaries, the number of which is legion, this is not mentioned. It is "good form" to keep silent about it as if it were a piece of old-fashioned "naïveté," just as the Christians, after their religion had been given the status of a state religion, "forgot" the "naïveté" of primitive Christianity with its democratic revolutionary spirit.

The reduction of the remuneration of the highest state officials seems to be "simply" a demand of naïve, primitive democracy. One of the "founders" of modern opportunism, the ex-Social Democrat Eduard Bernstein, has more than once indulged in repeating the vulgar bourgeois jeers at "primitive" democracy. Like all opportunists, and like the present Kautskyites, he utterly failed to understand that, first of all, the transition from capitalism to Socialism is *impossible* without a certain "reversion" to "primitive" democracy (for how else can the majority, and then the whole population without exception, proceed to discharge state functions?); and, secondly, that "primitive democracy" based on capitalism and capitalist culture is not the same as primitive democracy in prehistoric or precapitalist times. Capitalist culture has *created* large-scale production, factories, railways, the postal service, telephones, etc., and *on this basis* the great majority of the functions of the old "state power" have become so simplified and can be reduced to such exceedingly simple operations of registration, filing, and checking that they can be easily performed by every literate person, can quite easily be performed for ordinary "workmen's wages," and that these functions can (and must) be stripped of every shadow of privilege, of every semblance of "official grandeur."

All officials, without exception, elected and subject to recall *at any time*, their salaries reduced to the level of ordinary "workmen's wages"— these simple and "self-evident" democratic measures, while completely uniting the interests of the workers and the majority of the peasants, at the same time serve as a bridge leading from capitalism to Socialism. These measures concern the reconstruction of the state, the purely political reconstruction of society; but, of course, they acquire their full meaning and significance only in connection with the "expropriation of the expropriators" either being accomplished or in preparation, i.e., with the transformation of capitalist private ownership of the means of production into social ownership.

"The Commune," Marx wrote, "made that catchword of bourgeois revolutions, cheap government, a reality, by destroying the two greatest sources of expenditure—the standing army and State functionarism."

From the peasantry, as from other sections of the petty bourgeoisie, only an insignificant few "rise to the top," "get on in the world" in the bourgeois sense, i.e., become either well-to-do people, bourgeois, or officials in secure and privileged positions. In every capitalist country where there is a peasantry (as there is in most capitalist countries), the vast majority of the peasants are oppressed by the government and long for its overthrow, long for "cheap" government. This can be achieved *only* by the proletariat; and by achieving it, the proletariat at the same time takes a step towards the socialist reconstruction of the state.

.   .   .   .

There can be no thought of abolishing the bureaucracy at once, everywhere and completely. That is utopia. But to *smash* the old bureaucratic machine at once and to begin immediately to construct a new one that will permit to abolish gradually all bureaucracy—this is *not* utopia, this is the experience of the Commune, this is the direct and immediate task of the revolutionary proletariat.

Capitalism simplifies the functions of "state" administration; it makes it possible to cast "bossing" aside and to confine the whole matter to the organization of the proletarians (as the ruling class), which will hire "workers, foremen, and bookkeepers" in the name of the whole of society.

We are not utopians, we do not indulge in "dreams" of dispensing *at once* with all administration, with all subordination; these anarchist dreams, based upon a lack of understanding of the tasks of the proletarian dictatorship, are totally alien to Marxism, and, as a matter of fact, serve only to postpone the socialist revolution until people are different. No, we want the socialist revolution with people as they are now, with people who cannot dispense with subordination, control, and "foremen and bookkeepers."

But the subordination must be to the armed vanguard of all the exploited and toiling people, i.e., to the proletariat. A beginning can and must be made at once, overnight, of replacing the specific "bossing" of state officials by the simple functions of "foremen and bookkeepers," functions which are already fully within the capacity of the average city dweller and can well be performed for "workmen's wages."

We ourselves, the workers, will organize large-scale production on the basis of what capitalism has already created, relying on our own experience as workers, establishing strict, iron discipline supported by the state power of the armed workers; we will reduce the role of the state officials to that of simply carrying out our instructions as responsible, revocable, modestly paid "foremen and bookkeepers" (of course, with the aid of technicians of all sorts, types and degrees). This is *our* proletarian task, this is what we can and must *start* with in accomplishing the proletarian revolution. Such a beginning, on the basis of large-scale production, will of itself lead to the gradual "withering away" of all bureaucracy, to the gradual creation of an order, an order without quotation marks, an order bearing no similarity to wage slavery, an order in which the functions of control and accounting—becoming more and more simple—will be performed by each in turn, will then become a habit and will finally die out as the *special* functions of a special section of the population.

A witty German Social Democrat of the seventies of the last century called the *postal service* an example of the socialist economic system. This is very true. At present the postal service is a business organized on the lines of a state-*capitalist* monopoly. Imperialism is gradually transforming all trusts into organizations of a similar type, in which, standing over the "common" toilers, who are overworked and starved, is the same bourgeois bureaucracy. But the mechanism of social management is here already to hand. We have but to overthrow the capitalists, to crush the resistance of these exploiters with the iron hand of the armed workers, to smash the bureaucratic machine of the modern state—and we shall have a splendidly equipped mechanism, freed from the "parasite," a mechanism which can very well be set going by the united workers themselves, who will hire technicians, foremen, and bookkeepers, and pay them *all*, as, indeed, *all* "state" officials in general, a workman's wage. Here is a concrete, practical task, immediately possible of fulfillment in relation to all trusts, a task that will rid the toilers of exploitation and take account of what the Commune had already begun to practice (particularly in building up the state).

To organize the *whole* national economy on the lines of the postal service, so that the technicians, foremen, bookkeepers, as well as *all* officials, shall receive salaries no higher than "a workman's wage," all under the control and leadership of the armed proletariat—this is our immediate aim. It is such a state, standing on such an economic foundation, that we need. This is what will bring about the abolition of parliamentarism and the preservation of representative institutions. This is what will rid the laboring classes of the prostitution of these institutions by the bourgeoisie.

* * *

4

FUNDAMENTALS OF MARXISM-LENINISM

Origin and Essence of the State

History shows that the existence of the state is linked with the existence of classes. In the early stages of human development, under the classless primitive-communal system, there was no state. The functions of managing the affairs of society were carried out by society itself.

But when private ownership had come into being, and along with it economic inequality, when society had split up into hostile classes, the system of managing public affairs underwent a radical change. These affairs could no longer be settled on the basis of the agreed will of the whole or the majority of society. The dominating position was seized by the exploiting classes. Since they composed only an insignificant minority of society, these classes had to rely on direct coercion as well as on their economic power to maintain the system that suited them. For this a special apparatus was required—detachments of armed men (army and police), courts, prisons, etc. Control of this apparatus of coercion was placed in the hands of men devoted to the interests not of the whole of

Reprinted from O. V. Kuusinen, ed., *Fundamentals of Marxism-Leninism* (Moscow: Foreign Languages Publishing House, 1961), pp. 192–93, 636–39, 728–43, 755–59.

society but of the exploiting minority. In this way the state was built up as a machine for maintaining the domination of one class over another. With the help of this machine the economically dominant class consolidates the social system that is to its advantage and forcibly keeps its class opponents within the framework of the given mode of production. For this reason, in an exploiting society the state, in essence, always represents the dictatorship of the class or classes of exploiters.

In relation to society as a whole, the state acts as an instrument of direction and government on behalf of the ruling class; in relation to the opponents of this class (in an exploiting society this means the majority of the population), it acts as an instrument of suppression and coercion.

Thus, the state is the result of the irreconcilability of class contradictions. It "arises when, where, and to the extent that class antagonisms objectively *cannot* be reconciled." The political power of the economically dominant class—such is the essence of the state, the nature of its relations with society. But in addition to this it has other characteristics.

One can speak of the state as such only when the political power of this or that class extends over a certain *territory* and over the *population* living on that territory—its citizens or subjects.

Size of territory, as well as the number and composition of the population may, of course, influence the power of the state and, in a number of cases, its structural form. But the essence of the state is not determined by these features but by its class character.

.   .   .   .

DEMOCRACY FOR THE WORKING PEOPLE

In its time, bourgeois democracy was a major step forward. But with the advent of the era of socialist revolutions it is being replaced by a new political system. In Lenin's words, this system provides "the maximum of democracy for the workers and peasants; at the same time it marks a break with *bourgeois* democracy and the rise of a *new* type of democracy of world-historic importance, viz., proletarian democracy, or the dictatorship of the proletariat."

Influenced by bourgeois propaganda and Social Democratic pronouncements, some people in the capitalist countries think that dictatorship and democracy are mutually exclusive. Either there is democracy, they reason, which applies equally to all, and then there is no dictatorship, or there is the dictatorship of one class and then there is no democracy.

Such arguments can only be advanced by those who are under the delusion that there is such a thing as "above-class," "universal," or, as it is sometimes called, "integral" democracy. In actual fact, in every society with opposing classes political power, however democratic it may look, is always of a class nature and serves the ruling class. In bourgeois-democratic countries power is often disguised by a democratic appearance: There are regular general elections, the government is responsible to parliament, etc. But the real face of this power is revealed as soon as the working masses become conscious of their class interests and begin to present demands to the capitalists. Then even the most "democratic" power sides with the employers and does not shrink from sending troops and police against the workers, opening fire on peaceful demonstrations, arresting workers' leaders, etc. And when the struggle of the working people attains such dimensions that it begins to threaten the rule of big capital, the ruling power completely discards its democratic mask and resorts to openly terroristic methods. It means that democracy in the imperialist countries is a screen for the very real dictatorship of the big capitalist monopolies, directed against the working class, against the working people.

Such revelation of the class essence of the state occurred in all the eras when the exploiting classes were in power. "Everyone knows," Lenin wrote, "that rebellions, or even strong unrest, among the slaves in ancient times at once revealed the fact that the ancient state was essentially a *dictatorship of the slave-owners.* Did this dictatorship abolish democracy *among,* and *for,* the slave-owners? Everybody knows that it did not."

In other words, history confirms that dictatorship and democracy could very well go together. *Being a dictatorship in relation to certain classes, the state can at the same time be a democracy in relation to others.*

The whole question is what sort of dictatorship it is and what sort of democracy it is. Speaking of the state in the period of transition, Lenin said it should be "a state that is democratic *in a new way* (for the proletariat and the propertyless in general) and dictatorial *in a new way* (against the bourgeoisie)." The very nature of the dictatorship of the working class makes it a profoundly democratic power because it means the rule of the *majority* over the minority, while the dictatorship of the big bourgeoisie is the rule of the *minority* over the majority.

Therefore, there is no contradiction in saying that the dictatorship of the proletariat is at the same time a new type of democracy. One and the same power (the power of the working class) is a dictatorship as regards the enemies of socialism, and employs "dictatorial measures" (Lenin), and genuine democracy as regards the working people, and employs democratic methods. The dictatorship of the proletariat and proletarian democracy are thus the two sides of one medal. Lenin regarded the concepts "proletarian democracy" and "dictatorship of the proletariat" as synonymous.

It is very important for the proletarian state to observe the correct relationship of dictatorial and democratic methods in its policy, applying the former to the counterrevolutionary bourgeoisie and the latter to the working people. Giving freedom of action to the reactionary forces and narrowing down democracy for the toilers are both equally inadmissible. The 1956 events in Hungary give an idea of the consequences that may result from a violation of this principle. Reactionary onslaughts there were not suppressed resolutely enough, while at the same time the democratic rights of the working people were seriously infringed.

Not infrequently, bourgeois scientists and publicists put forward the following argument. Democracy, they declare, definitely presupposes the struggle of parties, a parliamentary opposition, etc. Having enumerated these formal signs of bourgeois democracy and failed to find one or the other of them in the socialist states, they triumphantly proclaim that the system of the proletarian dictatorship is an undemocratic system.

The Marxists judge the democratic character of a political system in a different way. The criterion that must be applied is: whose interests does the state power defend, whom does it serve, what policy does it pursue? From this—the only scientific—angle, it is impossible to find any genuine democracy in the bourgeois states. There are rival parties in the United States and opposition in Congress, yet the whole policy of the government serves the interests of an insignificant handful of multimillionaires. As a matter of fact, the power there is the dictatorship of the capitalist monopolies.

Proletarian democracy is the sole genuine democracy because it serves the interests of the working people, that is, the majority of society. The policy of the proletarian state aims at eliminating exploitation, raising the living standards and cultural level of the masses, defending universal peace, and strengthening international friendship. That accords with the most vital aspirations of the popular masses, of all progressive people.

At the same time it would be wrong to think that the proletarian state regards the question of the methods and forms of government as one of secondary importance. The strength of the dictatorship of the proletariat fundamentally lies in its connection with the masses, with the people. And these connections are strong only when government is democratic both in essence and in form. That is why the republic of a socialist type is a form of the dictatorship of the proletariat.

Enhancing democracy for the working people on an unprecedented scale, proletarian democracy, however, cannot be extended to include the overthrown reactionary forces of the bourgeoisie and all the other elements fighting for the restoration of capitalism. That is where proletarian democracy draws the line. The socialist revolution would suffer very great harm if the proletariat granted political freedoms to the organizations of the big capitalists. Is it not obvious that the dissolution of the parties and unions of the counterrevolutionary bourgeoisie and the prohibition of fascist and other antipopular propaganda not only do not restrict freedom and democracy for the working people but, on the contrary, are dictated by their interests?

.   .   .   .

SOCIALIST DEMOCRACY

Thoroughgoing democracy is the cardinal political characteristic of socialist society. Democracy permeates the diverse aspects of society's life, giving rise to new relations, habits, norms of behavior, and traditions.

Socialist democracy is a new, higher historical type of sovereignty of the people, which grew out of the proletarian democracy of the period of transition from capitalism to socialism. In comparison with preceding formations, socialism has extended the very concept of democracy to include not only the political but also the social rights of the working people. It has vested democracy with a new meaning and, by extending it to all of society, has made it true democracy of the entire people. Lastly, socialism has made the central question of democracy not the formal proclamation of rights, as is the case in bourgeois society, but the provision of the possibilities for exercising these rights.

We shall examine now the most important aspects of socialist democracy associated with the specific features of the class structure of society, the state, and the social and political rights of the citizens. . . .

A *Society of Friendly Working Classes.* A new class structure of society is formed as a result of the economic and social changes of the transition period.

The exploiting classes—capitalists, landlords, and kulaks—have been completely abolished. Society has become a community of working people: workers, peasants, and the intelligentsia. Their position has been radically changed.

This applies first and foremost to the *working class*. From a class deprived of the means of production it has become, together with all the people, their owner; from an exploited class it has become the leading force of society. The leading position of the working class in socialist society is determined by the fact that this class, which played the decisive part in the revolution, is connected with the most advanced form of socialist economy owned by the entire people. This class is also the main bearer of the communist ideas. In the midst of the workers there are incomparably fewer survivals of the psychology of the private owner, still inherent in part of the peasantry, and of the individualism preserved among some of the intellectuals. It is among the workers that the traditions of socialist mutual assistance and comradely solidarity are most deeply rooted.

The professional skill and culture of the workers rises immeasurably under socialism.

Another class of socialist society, *the peasantry*, has also undergone profound changes. Under capitalism it was a class of small producers little connected among themselves, who were doomed to eke out a miserable livelihood from their tiny plots. Village life gave rise to cultural backwardness, which bordered on savagery. Collectivization of agriculture and the cultural revolution have radically altered the aspect of the peasantry.

The overwhelming majority of peasants in socialist society are collective farmers. In the Soviet Union, for example, peasants farming on their own account constituted less than 0.5 per cent of the total in 1957. The socialist peasantry is a class freed from the exploitation of landlords and kulaks, a class which is working collectively and makes extensive use of machinery.

The culture of the peasants rises swiftly owing to the advantages of the collective farm system. True, for a long time after the victory of socialism the cultural level of the peasantry still lags behind that of the working class, and the rural mode of life is inferior to the urban. But this distinction is gradually being eliminated. A stratum of skilled farm machine-operators, associated with advanced technology and culture, is growing in the countryside. As it develops, the entire peasantry is coming up to the level of this stratum.

The collective-farm system broadens the outlook of the peasant, draws him into public activities, makes him interested in the success of his own collective (team or collective farm) and of the entire country. This is how the selfishness and seclusion of the small owner, proclaimed by bourgeois literature to be a "natural trait of the peasant," are being overcome.

In contrast to the working class, the proportion of the peasantry in the total population does not increase but declines. For countries which prior to the socialist revolution had been backward agrarian lands, this is a progressive and natural phenomenon. Mechanization of agriculture makes it possible to reduce considerably the number of people engaged in it, who are needed for the development of other branches of the economy, industry in the first place.

The *intelligentsia*, the brain workers, comprises an important section of the working people in socialist society. It cannot be grouped either with the working class or with the peasantry. Nor does it form a special class, because it does not hold an independent position in social production, although it plays a big part in the life of socialist society. The engineering and technical intelligentsia holds an important place in material production. Writers, painters, actors, and scientists contribute to the treasury of intellectual creation and enrich culture. The large bodies of teachers and physicians educate the people and safeguard their health. Lastly, many persons who have a specialized education (lawyers, economists, financial experts) do necessary work in the management of the economy, in the state administration, etc. . . .

The socialist intelligentsia is not an isolated social stratum, but a truly people's intelligentsia, bone of the bone and flesh of the flesh of the workers and peasants. To serve the people is its cherished aim. Service to the people not only advances the culture of society but also spiritually enriches the intelligentsia itself and lends purpose to its work.

The new class structure formed in socialist society radically changes the entire picture of class relations.

By abolishing exploitation of man by man completely and finally, social-ism does away forever with the class hierarchy, the system of subjugation of some classes by others, which existed for thousands of years.

All classes and strata become equal in their relation to the means of production, the state, and political power, in their rights and duties. No one can any longer appropriate the means of production and use them for exploiting other people. All social and political privileges and restrictions are abolished, including also those which were introduced in a number of countries during the period of transition from capitalism to socialism to protect the gains of the working people (preferential rates of representation for workers and poor peasants, disfranchisement of some social groups, etc.). Solid foundations are laid for social equality and justice in all spheres of life.

This is not in the least affected by the preservation of the leading role of the working class under socialism. This role is based not on some kind of exclusive rights, acquired and maintained at the expense of other classes and strata, but on the high moral and political prestige of the working class.

It follows from the above that although social distinctions do not vanish under socialism, their nature is radically altered. They are already no longer connected with relations of domination and subordination, but represent distinctions between separate groups of the working people which have equal rights, distinctions resulting from the different forms of one and the same socialist property (state property and cooperative–collective–farm property). This is a distinction between people engaged in different branches of one socialist national economy, engaged in different forms of labor.

Thus, the distinctions between classes still existing under socialism are of a different nature in principle than under capitalism; they are of a non-antagonistic character and, as society develops, steadily decrease, a process that is actively promoted by the policy of the Party and the state. Under capitalism, on the contrary, social barriers are not demolished but are raised higher; social injustice, far from declining, becomes more flagrant.

Lastly, under socialism class distinctions no longer affect the lives of people as they do under capitalism. In any bourgeois country it is enough for a person to be born into the family of a banker or manufacturer to be ensured comforts and a high income, opportunities for an education and an enviable social position, with very little merit or effort on his own part. On the other hand, the son of a worker, despite the legend spread by the bourgeoisie that any bootblack can become a millionaire, finds it almost impossible to escape from the grip of poverty and "make good." In socialist society differences in the position of people depend on their personal qualities, capabilities, knowledge, and industry, and not on social origin or position. . . .

The obliteration of class distinctions is also facilitated by the fluidity and relative nature of the very boundaries between classes in socialist society, the ease of passing from one class or section into another. This is true not only of the boundary between the working class and the peasantry but also of that separating these classes (manual workers) from the intelligentsia (brain workers). The new, socialist intelligentsia in its overwhelming majority is of working-class or peasant origin. But that is not the only thing that matters. No less important is the fact that the ranks of the workers and peasants are increasingly swelled by educated people, whose daily work in production is distinguished by many features of creative, mental labor.

It goes without saying that to master certain trades one must study a great deal, must have an education. But under socialism a higher education entirely loses the nature of a social privilege. Society carefully sees to it that even the advantages preserved so far, which consist of a more cultured environment at home, greater leisure, better material conditions for study, etc., should not turn into such a privilege. For this purpose priority in enrollment in universities and institutes is given to those who have a record of work in production; stipends are paid to students who are less secure materially; the system of evening and correspondence studies is extensively developed, etc.

Full equality, the gradual effacement of distinctions between classes, and social justice are characteristic features of class relations under socialism, which help consolidate the unity of society. . . .

Change in the Functions of the State. The victory of socialism leads to a further important change of the state, a change directly associated with the abolition of the exploiting classes and the development of the moral and political unity of society.

With the disappearance of classes hostile to the working people, the state, if we speak of its internal functions, *loses the character of an instrument of class suppression.* The cardinal aspect of activity of a state, the one which comprised its essence throughout its history, ceases to exist.

It is already on the approaches to socialism, as the economic, political, and ideological positions of the exploiting classes are undermined, that, as a rule, the intensity of the class struggle is moderated. This reduces the sphere of class suppression. No room at all remains for it when socialism triumphs.

That is why the Communist Party of the Soviet Union has so roundly criticized as deeply erroneous the theory which claims that the class struggle grows sharper with the progress of socialist construction. This theory was particularly dangerous because it justified gross violations of the principles of socialist democracy and legality.

But the withering away of the function of class suppression does not mean that under socialism the state must vanish. Socialist society cannot get along without it. Why?

Firstly, because after the victory of socialism statehood remains for a long time the most suitable and rational form of public leadership of the economy, social relations, and cultural development. The expediency of this form is determined by the level of economic, social, and spiritual development of society.

Secondly, because under socialism a certain inequality in the satisfaction of the requirements of the people still remains; there remain manifestations of the psychology of the private owner and other survivals of capitalism in the minds of some members of society. In these conditions society cannot get along without a special machinery which controls the measure of labor and consumption, protects public and personal property, and cuts short antisocial actions dangerous to the socialist system.

Thirdly, the state is preserved for external reasons. So long as socialism has not triumphed on a worldwide scale, the danger of attack by the imperialist states remains and, therefore, there also remains the need to have armed forces and other state bodies called upon to ensure the country's defense power and also to combat spies, saboteurs, and other subversive elements sent in by the imperialists.

Thus, under socialism the state is still needed by the working people. The need for some measures of state compulsion also remains. But it is the other functions and tasks that come to the fore in the activities of the state.

In the first place, the *economic role of the state* is substantially enhanced. Whereas in the transition period, at the time when several types of economic structure existed, the state was unable to control, plan, and direct all sectors and branches of the national economy, under socialism the state actually concentrates in its hands all the threads of the country's economic development. The organization of social production—direction of the economy—becomes its cardinal function.

The *cultural and educational function* of the state becomes widely expanded in socialist society: it includes the development of socialist culture—science, the arts, and literature—the cultural advancement of the people, and their communist education.

The function of *safeguarding socialist property*, the cornerstone of the new system, plays a big part in the activities of the state.

Wide scope in socialist society is attained by activities of the state in connection with the *protection of the rights and interests of the citizens, of their personal property, and of public order.*

Thus, following the victory of socialism the state acts primarily as the organizer of economic and cultural development, directing the creative activities of the working masses.

Together with this, inasmuch as the capitalist system exists and the danger of armed attack has not been removed, the function of *defending the country from outside attack* is fully preserved. The socialist state is compelled to strengthen its armed forces, army and navy, counterintelligence and intelligence agencies in order to defend successfully the gains of socialism. Its activities in the international arena, however, are not limited to military defense. They include economic, cultural, and political relations with foreign states, and their purpose is to ensure peaceful coexistence of countries with different social and political systems, to strengthen peace among the nations. The formation of the world socialist system has given rise to another task of the socialist state's foreign policy, namely, the consolidation of the unbreakable friendship, cooperation, and mutual assistance between the fraternal socialist countries.

The change in the functions and tasks of the state under socialism, as compared with the transition period from capitalism to socialism, cannot but affect the methods of its activities as well. First of all, the sphere of application of administrative compulsory measures is sharply curtailed and these measures are increasingly replaced by methods of persuasion of people, the organization of their collective endeavors.

Improvement of the methods of leadership by the state is an important problem that arises following the victory of socialism. On its successful solution largely depend both the rate of economic growth and progress in the social, cultural, and other spheres. Elaboration of proper methods and forms of state activities, conforming to the new class structure and the new type of the economy, is not an easy task. Here socialist society is not immune from mistakes. That is why the Communist Party is devoting unflagging attention to problems of developing the state.

Improvement of the socialist state demands determined eradication of bureaucracy. In conditions of victorious socialism its manifestations are even more intolerable than in the transition period. For the state now handles an incomparably greater volume of affairs. In particular, the socialist state guides all industries and trade (except cooperative trade). It directs the activities of most institutions which serve the daily needs of the citizens (health services, social maintenance, education, etc.). The state also is the main contractor of the collective farms. In these conditions bureaucracy can inflict great harm on society, both economically and politically. Taking this into account, the Party wages a consistent struggle against bureaucracy, for the consolidation of the bonds between the machinery of state and the masses, it develops and strengthens socialist democracy.

Extension of the Political and Social Rights of the Working People. Socialism for the first time creates the economic, social, and political requisites for achieving real nationwide democracy. Only socialism creates such unity of interests of all sections of society that under it all political problems can be settled without any class coercion, in a democratic way.

Genuine political equality of the citizens is achieved only under socialism. It is ensured by the fact that the people are actually equal in relation to the means of production and hence have an equal right to participate, as real masters, in taking decisions which affect all of society.

Under socialism the members of society receive not only formal rights and freedoms but also the actual opportunity to enjoy them. Nor is it accidental that socialist constitutions, proclaiming the basic freedoms—freedom of speech, press, assembly, street processions, etc.—lay special emphasis on the guarantees which ensure the actual opportunity to enjoy these freedoms and stipulate that all stocks of paper, printing presses, meeting halls, etc., be placed at the disposal of the working people.

It goes without saying that even in conditions of socialism unlimited freedom of the individual is out of the question. Unlimited freedom of the individual would be not freedom but arbitrariness, since it would infringe the interests of other people, of society as a whole. Granting man the broadest freedoms, the socialist state at the same time prohibits any activity which is harmful to other people. For example, it metes out punishment for spreading racialist and fascist views or for advocating war. In contrast to the bourgeois state, the socialist state does not allow the circulation of books, magazines, and films which corrupt youth and extol immorality, brutality, and violence. Such restriction is undoubtedly in the interest of the people and therefore does not undermine but, on the contrary, reinforces the democratic nature of the new system.

Hence socialist democracy differs essentially from the unlimited, directionless "freedom," of which anarchists love to chatter. Such "freedom," incidentally, exists only in their heated imagination, but not in society. As for socialist democracy, it is not directionless democracy, but *directed democracy*, i.e., democracy directed by the Party and the state in the interest of the further development of socialism and the building of communism. This is stated by the Communists straightforwardly and openly.

This fact infuriates the revisionists. They keep on asserting that democracy is incompatible with any restriction or direction, and on these grounds call for socialist democracy to be replaced by "unrestricted" democracy, or, putting the same thing more hazily, by "integral" democracy. The bombastic words of the advocates of such views conceal a very definite political aim—to push socialism back to bourgeois democracy, which means not to any sort of unlimited democracy but to democracy directed by the bourgeoisie, with the introduction of various limitations conforming to the interests of capitalism.

Another object of the revisionists is to undermine the leadership of society by the Party, which would in fact result in the curtailment, and not the development, of democracy. For the Party embodies in its activities the will of the masses, millions strong, and represents the most democratic organization of socialist society. Its leadership most fully personifies the principles of genuine democracy.

While sweeping aside the theories of the revisionists, and particularly their recipes for "democratization," Marxist-Leninist parties at the same time regard the consistent development and extension of socialist democracy as a prime task. But, in contrast to the revisionists, they see the way to attain this not in copying the institutions and principles of bourgeois democracy but in perfecting socialist democracy, i.e., in consolidating the links of the state and the Party with the mass of the working people, in boldly stimulating their constructive activities and initiative in all spheres of society's life.

Here the Party is confronted with great tasks, because such genuinely socialist democracy does not arise of itself in an unchanging form but develops as socialism gains in strength. This is a process which claims constant attention and effort on the part of society, the state, and the Party, and demands struggle against wrong views, against administrative-bureaucratic tendencies, and against disbelief in the intelligence and power of the people.

Why does the Party attach such great importance to the development of socialist democracy?

Because under socialism the broadest democracy of the highest type in history becomes not only possible but also necessary. In socialist conditions democracy is not a concession the ruling classes are forced to make, as it is under capitalism, but a law of life which ensures the normal and rapid development of society. Lenin wrote that "victorious socialism must necessarily give effect to complete democracy." Socialism and democracy are inseparable. . . .

The constitutions of the socialist countries embody legislatively the principle of electivity, removability, and accountability of all persons holding office, the principle of electivity and accountability of all state bodies. The voters have a right to recall any deputy who has not justified their trust before the expiration of his term of office. Public organizations of the working people exercise ever wider control over the activities of executive bodies and themselves take part in these activities.

State bodies of a socialist country enjoy the assistance of activists, a vast number of public-spirited citizens who work in factories and collective farms, in cultural and educational establishments. In the U.S.S.R., from 14 to 15 million people take part in canvassing and organizational work during election campaigns. Millions of people work in standing and *ad hoc* committees of local Soviets; as public instructors or inspectors, as members of various public assistance committees elected in factories, offices or neighborhoods; as members of control groups set up by public organizations. This vast army of people is taking part in the activities of the state and going through a big political schooling, improving its political consciousness, knowledge, and culture. The masses also exert their influence on the machinery of state through the press, which serves as a medium for the exchange of experience, control, and criticism.

The growing role of public organizations—the Party, trade unions, Komsomol [Young Communist League], and others—is an important feature of socialist democracy. Millions of people take part in the work of these organizations and in this way influence various aspects of society's life. Suffice it to note that in 1958 there were over 8 million people in the ranks of the Party, 18 million in the Komsomol, and over 50 million in the trade unions in the Soviet Union.

One of the cardinal distinctive features of the Marxist understanding of democracy is that, while attaching great importance to political rights and freedoms, it does not limit democracy to them alone. Marxists regard as a prime integral part of democracy the social and economic rights of the working people: the right to work, to rest and leisure, to education, to material maintenance in old age or in case of illness, etc. For these rights are the basis of man's genuine freedom and happiness.

The historic advantages of the socialist system are revealed with especial clarity in the way the social rights of the working people are ensured.

Can capitalist society with its chronic unemployment ensure each citizen the opportunity to work, let alone to choose the work he likes? Clearly, it cannot. But the socialist system makes the right to work a constitutional right of a citizen, delivering him from the oppressive anxiety and uncertainty over the morrow. Free labor becomes not only a means of subsistence but also the chief measure of the social value of man, a matter of honor and valor for him.

Can capitalist society guarantee its citizens the right to rest and leisure? Again the answer is no. What does the capitalist care for the health of his workers or the provision of holiday and recreation facilities for them? He sees in them merely a source of profit. Graphic proof of this is furnished by the high cost of medical service in most bourgeois countries, which makes it ruinous for the working people. Under capitalism limitation of the working day by law, paid vacations, and other social rights of the working class are won only through prolonged struggle by the laboring people, who have to exert great efforts to preserve and extend these gains.

On the contrary, in socialist society where both the means of production and political power belong to the working people themselves, concern for the health and welfare of the people are in the focus of attention of public and state organizations.

Can capitalist society guarantee its citizens the right to education? No, and not only because it takes no interest in the cultural requirements of the working people, at any rate in the requirements that go beyond the level necessary for work at a factory. The bourgeoisie, as all exploiting classes, regards the monopoly of education and culture as one of the principal instruments for the preservation of its monopoly of political power. It is much easier to keep the working people in check so long as they are illiterate, uneducated and are held in the grip of all kinds of prejudices and superstitions.

Socialist society, on the contrary, is vitally interested in making all its members educated and cultured. In a society where power belongs to the working people themselves the advance of their culture and political consciousness, the widening of their outlook, is a source of strength for the state, a way to multiply the public wealth, to accelerate progress.

Socialist society devotes special attention to the political and cultural advancement of that part of the population which in the past was the most downtrodden socially and suffered the greatest oppression. This applies especially to women.

In some capitalist countries even to this day women are deprived of many political and civil rights, get less pay for equal work with men and are kept in a subordinate position even in the family.

Marxim-Leninism holds that the emancipation of women presupposes, firstly, full equalization in rights with men both in the family and in political life; secondly, the enlistment of women in public activities and productive work; and, thirdly, abolition of the system of domestic drudgery under which housekeeping absorbs all the time and energies of women.

The socialist system is successfully solving this intricate problem. It not only gives women equal rights with men, but it also accords the mother honor and respect. The state grants working mothers long paid maternity leaves, gives monthly allowances to mothers of large families and unmarried mothers, and decorates mothers of large families with orders or medals. The rights of mother and child in the family are protected by law. . . .

We must not forget that socialism is only the first, lower phase of the new social formation. Naturally, at this stage it is impossible as yet to solve completely all the numerous difficult and involved problems which socialism has inherited from the rule of the exploiters over thousands of years. But now it is already clearly seen that socialism, as no other system, ensures the working people real democratic rights and extends the sphere of democracy to an unprecedented degree. It could not be otherwise in a society which assumes care for all its members, their happiness, welfare, and personal destinies.

As socialist society develops, more social benefits are enjoyed by the citizens and they have greater opportunities for active participation in political life. This makes all the working people deeply interested in the prosperity and progress of society.

.   .   .   .

Socialism and the Individual

Bourgeois critics of the socialist system try to prove that it is incompatible with the freedom of the individual. Revolutionary Marxism, they allege, does not regard human personality as having any value. Hundreds of books and thousands of articles have been written about the "totalitarianism" of the socialist system, "the submerging of the individual in the collective," and the "levelling" of people. Nothing could be falser than this conception.

Emancipation of the Individual Through the Emancipation of the Working Masses. The spiritual aspect of man, his relations with the people around him, and his personal consciousness depend on the nature of the society in which he lives.

Bourgeois propaganda depicts the capitalist system as a realm of freedom of the individual and presents the formal legal equality of people as the only possible form of equality. But actually the rule of capital is the greatest mockery of the freedom of the individual.

Capital bases relations between people on selfish calculation. Money replaces all personal traits of man. In capitalist society, Marx wrote,

> what I *am* and *am capable of* is by no means determined by my individuality. I am ugly, but I can buy for myself the most *beautiful* of women. Therefore I am not *ugly*, for the effect of *ugliness*—its deterrent power— is nullified by money. I, in my character as an individual, am *lame*, but money furnishes me with twenty-four feet. Therefore I am not lame. I am bad, dishonest, unscrupulous, stupid; but money is honored, and therefore so is its possessor. Money is the supreme good, therefore its possessor is good.

At one pole, man is worn out and benumbed by exhausting toil and the all-absorbing concern for daily bread. At the other pole, a surfeit of the good things of life and the absence of fruitful social activity lead man to confine himself to the intimate emotions of his ego. Such individualism leads to an impoverishment of man's inner world, produces a feeling of moral emptiness, melancholy and divided personality. In the decay of bourgeois society this individualism easily turns into brutal selfishness, the ideology of the "superman," so clearly expressed in the philosophy of Nietzsche, which became one of the cornerstones of the fascist world outlook. All this represents the real "destruction of the personality."

Only the socialist revolution provides a way out. "If man is shaped by his surroundings," Marx wrote, "his surroundings must be made human." There can be no freedom of man from society, freedom is possible only in society. To free the individual it is necessary to free the entire mass of people, by changing the social relations which enslave them. Emancipation of the individual through the emancipation of the working masses—this is the substance of the Communists' position, the cornerstone of their collectivist ideology.

When bourgeois propaganda accuses Marxists of "destruction of the personality," it tacitly proceeds from the assumption that private property is the basis of the personality. But the abolition of private property is horrifying only to those whose entire social position, beginning with their comforts and ending with their prestige among the people around them, is based not on personal abilities and personal merits but on the privileges of wealth. To such men the abolition of private ownership of the means of production used for the exploitation and degradation of other persons really seems to be the destruction of their own personality, all the more so since this deprives them of the opportunity of leading a life of idleness, and for the bourgeois parasite work is the most horrible misfortune.

To men of labor and talent, on the other hand, socialism opens up broad opportunities for the development and application of their personal gifts. Only the socialist system allows for "actually drawing the majority of toilers into an arena of such labor in which they can display their abilities, develop their capacities, reveal their talents, of which there is an untapped spring among the people, and which capitalism crushed, suppressed, and strangled in thousands and millions" (Lenin).

Socialism for the first time recognizes the right to development and independent creative endeavor of ordinary working people, whom bourgeois ideologists have always scornfully regarded as "a colorless mass." It at the same time guarantees this right, placing in the hands of society all the material means which make it possible to develop the talents and abilities of people. As the socialist system grows stronger, as the material and spiritual good things of life are produced in greater abundance and social relations are improved, all members of society have ever greater opportunities for development and creative effort, for the all-round development of their personality.

Combination of Personal and Social Interests. The antithesis of personal and social interests arose together with private property, under the domination of which man, regarding society as a hostile, oppressing force, seeks to give society as little as possible and grab for himself as much as possible.

The socialist system is concerned first of all for the common interests. For on them depends the welfare not only of the entire society, but also of each of its members. That is why socialist morality condemns the signs of individualism and small-proprietor selfishness, rightly considering them survivals of the capitalist past in the minds of men. But, on the other hand, Engels already pointed out that "society cannot free itself unless every individual is freed." Care for man, a thoughtful, attentive attitude to him, is one of the cardinal demands of socialist morality.

Socialism opens before every member of society a way to improve his position, the way of more productive and skilled labor. Naturally, the desire of people to raise their living standard in this way conforms to the interests of society and is supported by it to the utmost. This is the objective basis on which the organic unity of personal and social interests arises in socialist society. This distinctive feature of the socialist system is reflected in the minds of the people. As the socialist consciousness of the masses grows, moral stimuli begin to play an ever greater part in the activities of the people and concern for public affairs becomes a personal affair of everyone. A man reared in the spirit of socialist morality cannot look on with indifference at shortcomings, at anything that runs counter to the interests of society, even though it does not concern him directly. The feeling of being master and the sense of responsibility for the common cause inseparably associated with it constitute a major feature of the spiritual makeup of the new man. Members of socialist society have not only great rights, but great duties as well. But these are the duties of masters, of real citizens of their country, and not the obligations of downtrodden subjects.

It is understandable that in the course of a few decades it is impossible fully to eradicate all the conceptions and habits which struck deep root during the domination of private property for thousands of years. Various traits of the old morality and way of life still survive in the minds of some members of socialist society: a dishonest attitude to work, money-grabbing, selfishness, nationalistic prejudices, a wrong attitude to women, drunkenness, and antisocial views which at times lead to hooliganism and crime. We speak of all such phenomena as being survivals of capitalism. Thereby we also stress that these phenomena are alien to socialism and that in themselves social relations in socialist society, far from producing such ugly phenomena, on the contrary, gradually oust them.

The survivals of capitalism persist tenaciously in the minds of some members of society. We must not forget that there are large spheres of human relations in which antisocial habits, views, and customs exert a particularly great influence, for example, family relations and the general way of life. Such relations, undoubtedly, can be affected not only by advanced socialist morality and ideology, which is gaining a dominating position in society, but also by backward views and customs preserved among some of society's members. If such views and customs are not opposed properly, they can have a harmful influence on the minds of other people, especially the younger generation.

That is why even after the victory of socialism there remains the need for patient and constant educational work. Socialism is inconceivable without social discipline which obliges the citizen to abide by the demands of society and to observe the norms of behavior of the socialist community. This also conforms to the interests of each person, if these interests are understood correctly and their dependence on the prosperity of society as a whole is appreciated.

The developing unity of personal and social interests is a very important moral advantage of the socialist system which removes the old tragedy of the "divided human mind," and brings up harmonious, cheerful, and courageous people who are not daunted by difficulties. The victory of socialism is a tremendous moral revolution.

*　　*　　*

5

THE TASKS OF THE COMMUNIST PARTY OF THE SOVIET UNION IN BUILDING A COMMUNIST SOCIETY

COMMUNISM—THE BRIGHT FUTURE OF ALL MANKIND

The building of a communist society has become an immediate practical task for the Soviet people. The gradual development of socialism into communism is an objective law; it has been prepared by the development of Soviet socialist society throughout the preceding period.

What is communism?

Communism is a classless social system with one form of public ownership of the means of production and full social equality of all members of society; under it, the all-round development of people will be accompanied by the growth of the productive forces through continuous progress in science and technology; all the springs of cooperative wealth will flow more abundantly, and the great principle "From each according to his ability, to each according to his needs" will be implemented. Communism is a highly organized society of free, socially conscious working people in which public self-government will be established, a society in which labor

Reprinted from *The Road to Communism: Documents of the 22nd Congress of the Communist Party of the Soviet Union,* October 17–31, 1961 (Moscow: Foreign Languages Publishing House; n.d.), pp. 509–13, 553–56, 582–89.

for the good of society will become the prime vital requirement of every-one, a necessity recognized by one and all, and the ability of each person will be employed to the greatest benefit of the people.

A high degree of communist consciousness, industry, discipline, and devotion to the public interest are qualities typifying the man of communist society.

Communism ensures the continuous development of social production and rising labor productivity through rapid scientific and technological progress; it equips man with the best and most powerful machines, greatly increases his power over nature, and enables him to control its elemental forces to an ever greater extent. The social economy reaches the highest stage of planned organization, and the most effective and rational use is made of the material wealth and labor reserves to meet the growing requirements of the members of society.

Under communism there will be no classes, and the socio-economic and cultural distinctions, and differences in living conditions, between town and countryside will disappear; the countryside will rise to the level of the town in the development of the productive forces and the nature of work, the forms of production relations, living conditions, and the well-being of the population. With the victory of communism mental and physical labor will merge organically in the production activity of people. The intelligentsia will no longer be a distinct social stratum. Workers by hand will have risen in cultural and technological standards to the level of workers by brain.

Thus, communism will put an end to the division of society into classes and social strata, whereas the whole history of mankind, with the exception of its primitive period, was one of class society. Division into opposing classes led to the exploitation of man by man, class struggle, and antagonisms between nations and states.

Under communism all people will have equal status in society, will stand in the same relation to the means of production, will enjoy equal conditions of work and distribution, and will actively participate in the management of public affairs. Harmonious relations will be established between the individual and society on the basis of the unity of public and personal interests. For all their diversity, the requirements of people will express the sound, reasonable requirements of the fully developed person.

The purpose of communist production is to ensure uninterrupted progress of society and to provide all its members with material and cultural benefits according to their growing needs, their individual requirements and tastes. People's requirements will be satisfied from public sources. Articles of personal use will be in the full ownership of each member of society and will be at his disposal.

Communist society, which is based on highly organized production and advanced technology, alters the character of work, but it does not release the members of society from work. It will by no means be a society of anarchy, idleness, and inactivity. Every able-bodied person will participate in social labor and thereby ensure the steady growth of the material and spiritual wealth of society. Thanks to the changed character of labor, its better technical equipment, and the high degree of consciousness of all members of society, the latter will work willingly for the public benefit according to their own inclinations.

Communist production demands high standards of organization, precision, and discipline, which are ensured not by compulsion but through an understanding of public duty, and are determined by the whole pattern of life in communist society. Labor and discipline will not be a burden to people; labor will no longer be a mere source of livelihood—it will be a genuinely creative process and a source of joy.

Communism represents the highest form of organization of public life. All production units and self-governing associations will be harmoniously united in a common planned economy and a uniform rhythm of social labor.

Under communism the nations will draw closer and closer together in all spheres on the basis of a complete identity of economic, political, and spiritual interests, of fraternal friendship and cooperation.

Communism is the system under which the abilities and talents of free man, his best moral qualities, blossom forth and reveal themselves in full. Family relations will be freed once and for all from material considerations and will be based solely on mutual love and friendship.

In defining the basic tasks to be accomplished in building a communist society, the Party is guided by Lenin's great formula: *"Communism is Soviet power plus the electrification of the whole country."*

The CPSU [Communist Party of the Soviet Union], being a party of scientific communism, proposes and fulfills the tasks of communist construction in step with the preparation and maturing of the material and spiritual prerequisites, considering that it would be wrong to jump over necessary stages of development, and that it would be equally wrong to halt at an achieved level and thus check progress. The building of communism must be carried out by successive stages.

In the current decade (1961–70) the Soviet Union, in creating the material and technical basis of communism, will surpass the strongest and richest capitalist country, the U.S.A., in production per head of population; the people's standard of living and their cultural and technical standards will improve substantially; everyone will live in easy circumstances; all collective and state farms will become highly productive and profitable enterprises; the demand of Soviet people for well-appointed housing will, in the main, be satisfied; hard physical work will disappear; the U.S.S.R. will have the shortest working day.

The material and technical basis of communism will be built up by the *end of the second decade* (1971–80), ensuring an abundance of material and cultural values for the whole population; Soviet society will come close to a stage where it can introduce the principle of distribution according to needs, and there will be a gradual transition to one form of ownership— public ownership. Thus, *a communist society will in the main be built in the* U.S.S.R. The construction of communist society will be fully completed in the subsequent period.

The majestic edifice of communism is being erected by the perserving effort of the Soviet people—the working class, the peasantry, and the intelligentsia. The more successful their work, the closer the great goal—communist society.

.   .   .   .

The Further Heightening of the Role of Social Organizations, the State, and Communism

The role of social organizations increases in the period of the full-scale construction of communism. The *trade unions* acquire particular importance as schools of administration and economic management, as schools of communism. The Party will help the trade unions to take a growing share in economic management and to make the standing production conferences increasingly effective in improving the work of enterprises and exercising control over production. The trade unions shall:

work constantly to increase the communist consciousness of the masses; organize an emulation movement for communist labor and help the working people in learning to manage state and social affairs; take an active part in controlling the measure of labor and the measure of consumption;

encourage the activity of factory and office workers, enlisting their aid in the work for continuous technical progress, for higher productivity of labor, for the fulfillment and overfulfillment of state plans and assignments;

work steadfastly for the improvement of the skill of factory and office workers and their working and living conditions; protect the material interests and rights of the working people;

ensure that housing and cultural development plans are fulfilled and that public-catering, trade, social insurance, and health resort services are improved;

ensure control over the spending of public consumption funds and over the work of all enterprises and institutions serving the people;

improve cultural services and recreation facilities for the working people; encourage physical training and sports.

The *Young Communist League* [YCL], an independently acting public organization of the youth which helps the Party to educate young people in a communist spirit, enlist them in the practical job of building the new society, and train a generation of harmoniously developed people who will live, work, and manage public affairs under communism, will play a greater role. The Party regards the youth as a great creative force in the Soviet people's struggle for communism.

The YCL must display still greater initiative in all spheres of life, must encourage the activity and labor heroism of the youth. YCL organizations must concentrate on educating the youth in a spirit of utmost devotion to their country, the people, the Communist Party and the communist cause, constant preparedness for labor for the good of society and for overcoming all difficulties and improving the general education and technical knowledge of all young men and women. It is the sacred duty of the YCL to prepare young people for the defense of their socialist country, to educate them as selfless patriots capable of firmly repelling any enemy. The YCL educates the youth in a spirit of strict adherence to communist moral principles and standards. Its activities in the schools and Young Pioneer organizations must contribute to the molding of a buoyant, industrious, and physically and morally sound generation.

A greater role will be played by *cooperatives*—kolkhozes [collective farms], consumers', housing, and other cooperative organizations—as a form of drawing the masses into communist construction, as media of communist education and schools of public self-government.

Other social associations of the working people—scientific, scientific-technical, and popular-science societies; rationalizers' and inventors' organizations; associations of writers, art workers, and journalists; cultural-education organizations; and sports societies—will likewise be developed.

The Party regards it as a major task of the social organizations to promote labor emulation in every possible way and to encourage communist forms of labor, to stimulate the activity of working people in building a communist society, to work for the improvement of the living conditions of the people and the satisfaction of their growing spiritual requirements. Mass organizations should be given a greater part in managing cultural, health, and social insurance institutions; within the next few years they should be entrusted with the management of theaters and concert halls, clubs, libraries, and other state-controlled cultural-education establishments; they should be encouraged to play a greater part in promoting law and order, particularly through the people's volunteer squads and comradely courts.

To extend the independent activities of mass organizations, the Party considers it necessary further to reduce their salaried staffs from top to bottom, to renew each elective body by roughly as many as one-half of its membership at the regular election. It is advisable for the leading functionaries of social organizations not to be elected, as a general rule, for more than two consecutive terms.

As socialist statehood develops, it will gradually become *communist self-government* of the people, which will embrace the Soviets, trade unions, cooperatives, and other mass organizations of the people. This process will represent a still greater development of democracy, ensuring the active participation of all members of society in the management of public affairs. Public functions similar to those performed by the state today in the sphere of economic and cultural management will be preserved under communism and will be modified and perfected as society develops. But the character of the functions and the ways in which they are carried out will be different from those under socialism. The bodies in charge of planning, accounting, economic management, and cultural advancement, now government bodies, will lose their political character and will become organs of public self-government. Communist society will be a highly organized community of working men. Universally recognized rules of the communist way of life will be established, whose observance will become an organic need and habit with everyone.

Historical development inevitably leads to the withering away of the state. To ensure that the state withers away completely, it is necessary to provide both internal conditions—the building of a developed communist society—and external conditions—the victory and consolidation of socialism in the world arena.

. . . .

The Party in the Period of Full-Scale Communist Construction

As a result of the victory of socialism in the U.S.S.R. and the consolidation of the unity of Soviet society, the Communist Party of the working class has become the vanguard of the Soviet people, a Party of the entire people, and extended its guiding influence to all spheres of social life. The Party is the brain, the honor, and the conscience of our epoch, of the Soviet people, the people effecting great revolutionary transformations. It looks keenly into the future and shows the people scientifically motivated roads along which to advance, arouses titanic energy in the masses, and leads them to the accomplishment of great tasks.

The period of full-scale communist construction is characterized by a further *enhancement of the role and importance of the Communist Party* as the leading and guiding force of Soviet society.

Unlike all the preceding socio-economic formations, communist society does not develop spontaneously but as a result of the conscious and purposeful efforts of the masses led by the Marxist-Leninist Party. The Communist Party, which unites the foremost representatives of the working class, of all working people, and is closely connected with the masses, which enjoys unbounded prestige among the people and understands the laws of social development, provides proper leadership in communist construction as a whole, giving it an organized, planned, and scientifically based character.

The enhancement of the role of the Party in the life of Soviet society in the new stage of its development derives from:

the growing scope and complexity of the tasks of communist construction, which call for a higher level of political and organizational leadership;

the growth of the creative activity of the masses and the participation of fresh millions of working people in the administration of state affairs and of production;

the further development of socialist democracy, the enhancement of
the role of social organizations, the extension of the rights of the
Union republics and local organizations;

the growing importance of the theory of scientific communism, of its
creative development and propaganda, the necessity of improving the
communist education of the working people and struggling to overcome the survivals of the past in the minds of people.

There must be a new, higher stage in the development of the Party
itself and of its political, ideological, and organizational work that is in
conformity with the full-scale building of communism. The Party will
continuously improve the forms and methods of its work, so that its
leadership of the masses, of the building of the material and technical
basis of communism, of the development of society's spiritual life will
keep pace with the growing requirements of the epoch of communist
construction.

Being the vanguard of the people building a communist society, the
Party must also be in the van in the organization of internal Party life
and serve as an example and model in developing the most advanced
forms of public communist self-government.

Undeviating observance of the Leninist standards of Party life and the
principle of collective leadership, enhancement of the responsibility of
Party organs and their personnel to the Party rank and file, promotion of
the activity and initiative of all Communists and of their participation
in elaborating and realizing the policy of the Party, and the development
of criticism and self-criticism, are a law of Party life. This is an imperative
condition of the ideological and organizational strength of the Party itself,
of the unity and solidarity of Pary ranks, of an all-round development of
inner-Party democracy and an activation on this basis of all Party forces,
and of the strengthening of ties with the masses.

The cult of the individual, and the violations of collectivism in leadership, of inner-Party democracy and socialist legality arising out of it, are
incompatible with the Leninist principles of Party life. The cult of the
individual belittles the role of the Party and the masses and hampers
the development of the ideological life of the Party and the creative
activity of the working people.

In the period of full-scale communist construction the role and responsibility of every Party member will steadily increase. It is the duty
of a Communist, in production, in social and personal life, to be a model
in the struggle for the development and consolidation of communist
relations, and to observe the principles and norms of communist morality.
The CPSU will reinforce its ranks with the most politically conscious and
active working people, and keep pure and hold high the name of Communist.

The development of inner-Party democracy must ensure greater activity
among Communists and enhance their responsibility for the realization

of the noble ideals of communism. It will promote the cultivation in them of an inner, organic need to act always and in all matters in full accordance with the principles of the Party and its lofty aims.

The Party will continue to strengthen the unity and solidarity of its ranks, and to maintain the purity of Marxism-Leninism. The Party preserves such organizational guarantees as are provided by the Rules of the CPSU against all manifestations of factionalism and group activity incompatible with Marxist-Leninist Party principles. *The unshakable ideological and organizational unity of the Party is the most important source of its invincibility, a guarantee for the successful solution of the great tasks of communist construction.*

The people are the decisive force in the building of communism. *The Party exists for the people, and it is in serving the people that it sees the purpose of its activity.* To further extend and deepen the ties between the Party and the people is an imperative condition of success in the struggle for communism. The Party considers it its duty always to consult the working people on the major questions of home and foreign policy, to make these questions an object of nationwide discussion, and to attract more nonmembers to participating in all its work. The more socialist democracy develops, the broader and more versatile the work of the Party among the working people must be, and the stronger will be its influence among the masses.

The Party will in every way promote the extension and improvement of the work of the Soviets, the trade unions, the YCL, and other mass organizations of working people, and the development of the creative energy and initiative of the masses, and will strengthen the unity and friendship of all the peoples of the U.S.S.R.

The CPSU is an integral part of the international Communist and working-class movement. The tried and tested Marxist-Leninist principles of proletarian internationalism will continue to be inviolable principles which the Party will follow undeviatingly.

The Communist Party of the Soviet Union will continue to strengthen the unity of the international Communist movement, to develop fraternal ties with all the Communist and Workers' parties and to coordinate its actions with the efforts of all the contingents of the world Communist movement in the joint struggle against the danger of a new world war, for the interests of the working people, for peace, democracy, and socialism.

Such is the program of work for communist construction which the Communist Party of the Soviet Union has mapped out.

The achievement of communism in the U.S.S.R. will be the greatest victory mankind has ever won throughout its long history. Every new step made towards the bright peaks of communism inspires the working masses in all countries, renders immense moral support to the struggle for the liberation of all peoples from social and national oppression, and brings closer the triumph of Marxism-Leninism on a world-wide scale.

When the Soviet people will enjoy the blessings of communism, new hundreds of millions of people on earth will say: "We are for communism!" It is not through war with other countries, but by the example of a more perfect organization of society, by rapid progress in devcloping the productive forces, the creation of all conditions for the happiness and well-being of man, that the ideas of communism win the minds and hearts of the masses.

The forces of social progress will inevitably grow in all countries, and this will assist the builders of communism in the Soviet Union.

The Party proceeds from the Marxist-Leninist proposition: history is made by the people, and communism is a creation of the people, of its energy and intelligence. The victory of communism depends on people, and communism is built for people. Every Soviet man brings the triumph of communism nearer by his labor. The successes of communist construction spell abundance and a happy life to all, and enhance the might, prestige and glory of the Soviet Union.

The Party is confident that the Soviet people will accept the new Program of the CPSU as their own vital cause, as the greatest purpose of their life, and as a banner of nationwide struggle for the building of communism. The Party calls on all Communists, on the entire Soviet people—all working men and women, collective farmers and workers by brain—to apply their energies to the successful fulfillment of the historic tasks set forth in this Program.

UNDER THE TRIED AND TESTED LEADERSHIP OF THE COMMUNIST PARTY, UNDER THE BANNER OF MARXISM-LENINISM, THE SOVIET PEOPLE HAVE BUILT SOCIALISM.

UNDER THE LEADERSHIP OF THE PARTY, UNDER THE BANNER OF MARXISM-LENINISM, THE SOVIET PEOPLE WILL BUILD COMMUNIST SOCIETY.

THE PARTY SOLEMNLY PROCLAIMS: THE PRESENT GENERATION OF SOVIET PEOPLE SHALL LIVE IN COMMUNISM!

*   *   *

Part Two

SOCIAL INSTITUTIONS

III

The Communist Party

Soviet society is today effectively dominated by the Communist Party of the Soviet Union. The Party fashioned by Lenin to overthrow the Tsarist regime has been converted into an instrumentality of government. It is a role for which the Party theoretically was never intended. The present status of the Party is a result of a complex of historical circumstances. Lenin substituted the authority of the Party for that of the government. Stalin used the Party machinery in his rise to power but, once firmly in control, subjected it to his whim, as he did every other Soviet institution. Stalin's successors have differed in their uses of the Party, though both Khrushchev and Brezhnev worked to consolidate the Party's dominance in Soviet society.

In theory there is a clear distinction between the machinery and functions of the Party and those of the government. In fact the distinctions are blurred. Formal descriptions of the Party and government fail to describe adequately the changing character and functions of the Party in Soviet society. Today the major functions of the Party can be summed up as follows: (1) The Party legitimizes the nation's highest political leadership. Whomever the Central Committee and its Politburo (formerly the Presidium) designate or approve as the nation's political leadership is accepted by the Soviet citizen as legitimate. Indeed, the average citizen looks to the Party to choose the rulers—whatever the title of the positions involved. (2) The Party maintains an extensive system of control to ensure the observance of Party and state rules and regulations throughout Soviet society. This control is maintained by means of the strategic location of Party personnel in positions of importance at every level of Soviet society. (3) Finally, the Party mobilizes public opinion and generates mass support for communist mores and policies. It is able to accomplish this through its manipulation of the press, radio, and television and also through personal contact between millions of Party members and nonmembers. Political legitimization, control, and propaganda are by no means the only functions of the Party, but they are among the most important.

Paralleling these functions are three categories of Party personnel into which all members may be divided. At the top are the full-time, paid professional functionaries—often referred to as the apparatchiki (men of the apparatus). They include the secretaries and other Party executives from the national to the local level. It is from these ranks that the highest leadership emerges. A second category of Party members includes those individuals who occupy key positions in governmental, economic, cultural, or professional organizations that are distinct from the Party structure. These members create the interlocking links between the Party and all other important institutions in Soviet society. Their first loyalty is supposed to be to the Party, though many develop occupational and professional interests that from time to time clash with Party norms. Finally, at the base are the rank-and-file Party members. They hold no high Party, state, or public office, though they constitute the reserves from which positions of authority are filled. They are the link between the Party and the masses. To the public they explain current Party policies, encourage support for them, and set an example of superior work performance; to the Party leadership they communicate information useful for the formulation of public policy.

The Party Statutes contain the main outlines of the Party structure. At the national level the main organs are the Party Congress, theoretically the highest organ of Party power; the Central Committee, elected by the Congress to act for the Party between congresses; the Politburo, the *de facto* source of high policy decisions; the Secretariat, which handles organizational and administrative functions. Theoretically the Congress elects the Central Committee, which in turn elects the Politburo and Secretariat. In fact the Party leadership in the Politburo and Secretariat co-opt, or select from below, personnel for higher office. A system of comparable Party organs exists at the republic level (except for the Russian Federation) and the intermediate and local administrative subdivisions into which the country is divided. The lowest Party organ is the primary party organization (the cell).

Leonid Brezhnev holds the position of General Secretary, in charge of the Secretariat, and as such is the titular head of the Party. His leadership was reaffirmed by the Twenty-third and Twenty-fourth Party congresses and is reflected in the revised Party Statutes. In 1962 Khrushchev revised the statutes thoroughly, giving them a distinct anti-Stalinist tone. Khrushchev's revised rules broadened inner-Party democracy and made mandatory a periodic turnover of top Party leaders. The 1966 revisions not only repealed those innovations but reintroduced the names "Politburo" and "General Secretary," with their Stalinist connotations, in place of "Presidium" and "First Secretary."

Though Brezhnev is a leading member of the ruling oligarchy, his power is circumscribed by his colleagues in the Politburo, who, with the support of the Central Committee, could remove him at any time. The primacy of the Party leader that prevailed under Khrushchev has given way to a genuine collective leadership. Also, there has been a shift in the relative importance between the Secretariat and the Politburo, with the latter now recognized as the predominant center of political power.

Michael P. Gehlen is Professor of Political Science at the University of New Mexico. He is the author of *The Politics of Coexistence: Soviet Methods and Motives* and *The Communist Party of the Soviet Union*. Michael McBride is Assistant Professor of Political Science at Whittier College. Robert Conquest, a former member of the British Diplomatic Service, has written extensively on Soviet politics. His books include *The Great Terror, Russia After Khrushchev,* and *Power and Policy in the U.S.S.R.* Jerry F. Hough is Professor of Political Science at Toronto University and the author of *The Soviet Prefects: The Local Party Organs in Industrial Decision Making.* Leonard Schapiro is Professor of Russian Government and Politics at the London School of Economics and Political Science. Among his many books are *The Government and Politics of the Soviet Union* and *The Communist Party of the Soviet Union.*

6

REPORT OF THE CPSU CENTRAL COMMITTEE TO THE TWENTY-THIRD CONGRESS OF THE COMMUNIST PARTY OF THE SOVIET UNION

LEONID I. BREZHNEV

1. Strengthening the Party and Raising the Level of Its Organizational and Political Role

Comrades! The period under review has been characterized by a further growth of the Party's role in the life of Soviet society, a strengthening of its ranks, improvement of the forms and methods of its work, and the consolidation and development of the Party's ties with the masses. Our Leninist Communist Party is the guiding and directing force of Soviet society. It unites in its ranks the most advanced representatives of the working class and of all working people and is guided by the mili-

Pravda, March 30, 1966. Translation copyright 1966 by *The Current Digest of the Soviet Press,* published weekly at The Ohio State University by the American Association for the Advancement of Slavic Studies; reprinted by permission of *The Digest.* Translation appeared in Vol. XVIII, No. 13 (1966), pp. 3–10, of *The Digest.*

tant revolutionary ideology of the working class of the entire world—Marxism-Leninism; it is confidently leading the Soviet people forward along the path of the construction of communism, is channeling and organizing the life of socialist society, and is successfully fulfilling the role of teacher, organizer and political leader of the entire Soviet people. (*Applause.*) The Party's political and organizational work among the masses and the selfless labor of the Soviet people have ensured the further growth of the country's economy and a rise in the well-being of the Soviet people, have made it possible to strengthen our socialist state still more and to increase the international prestige of the Soviet Union. . . .

Comrades! The Communist Party of the Soviet Union now numbers 12,471,000 members and candidate members of the Party. In the period under review its ranks grew by 2,755,000 people. The growth of the ranks of the CPSU reflects the high prestige of the Party and the Soviet people's boundless trust in it.

We are proud of the millions of our Communist comrades, who bear the ideas of the Party to the masses in all sectors of communist construction and march in the front ranks of the Soviet country's working people. The millions-strong army of Communists devotes all its forces, knowledge, and organizational ability to strengthening the homeland's might, to our great revolutionary cause.

Permit me to inform you of the qualitative composition of the CPSU. As of January 1, 1966, it stood as follows:

(a) *by social status:* workers, 37.8 per cent; peasants (collective farmers), 16.2 per cent; office and professional personnel and others, 46.0 per cent;

(b) *by Party tenure:* less than ten years, 47.1 per cent; ten to thirty years, 47.3 per cent; more than thirty years, 5.6 per cent;

(c) *by age:* under twenty-five, 6.2 per cent; twenty-six to forty, 46.8 per cent; forty-one to fifty, 24.9 per cent; over fifty, 22.1 per cent;

(d) *by education:* higher or incomplete higher, 18.2 per cent; secondary, 30.9 per cent; incomplete secondary, 27.5 per cent; primary, 23.4 per cent.

As is evident from the data cited, workers and collective farmers constitute a majority in our party. In recent years, the percentage of workers accepted as candidate members of the Party has risen. Whereas between the Twentieth and Twenty-second congresses 40.6 per cent of those accepted as candidate members of the Party were workers, in the period under review this figure was 47.6 per cent. The working class must in the future as well occupy a leading position in the social composition of the Party.

Of the office and professional personnel entering the Party, more than two-thirds are members of the engineering-technical intelligentsia, specialists in various branches of the national economy. One out of every two Communists has a secondary, incomplete higher, or higher education.

The composition of the CPSU in terms of length of membership in its ranks is noteworthy. Here we see veterans of the Party who have gone through three revolutions, Communists tempered in the struggle for the industrialization of the country and the collectivization of agriculture, for the great socialist transformations of the homeland; we see here also those who linked their lives with the Party in the arduous years of the Great Patriotic War and who after the war raised the Soviet homeland up from ruins and ashes. All of them, in a single army of political fighters, are now actively building a communist society. (*Applause.*)

The qualitative composition of the Party excellently reflects the combination of old and young Communists. Today more than half of the members and candidate members of the CPSU are under forty. Vladimir Ilyich Lenin was always proud of the fact that young people entered our party; he saw this as an expression of the close tie between generations, of the continuity of the Party's revolutionary spirit, its militant traditions.

The historical role of the CPSU in the great victories of socialism and its high prestige naturally evoke in many Soviet people a desire to link their lives with the Party ideologically and organizationally and to consecrate themselves to the revolutionary struggle for the transformation of society, for the victory of communism. The high demands made on everyone who enters the Party are dictated by the enormous responsibility the Party bears to the Soviet people.

The Central Committee recently checked into the work of a number of Party organizations and established that some of them have lowered the demands made on those entering the CPSU. Individual Party committees have been prompting Party organizations to speed up the acceptance of members, as a result of which unprepared and immature people have in some cases made their way into the Party. This situation is now being rectified.

Concern for the purity of the Party's ranks, concern that each Communist bear worthily and justify the lofty title of a member of Lenin's party, must be a law of life for the Party and for all its organizations. V. I. Lenin said it is better for ten men who work not to call themselves Party members than for one chatterbox to have the right and opportunity to be a Party member.

The task of further strengthening the Party insistently demands a rise in the combat efficiency of the primary Party organizations, which constitute its basis. The primary Party organizations, with their broad network of shop organizations and Party groups, play a decisive role in implementing the Party's policy and in rearing Communists; they bind the Party to the masses, operating where the direct process of construction and creation is under way. There are now more than 320,000 primary Party organizations in the Party; they exist at almost every enterprise and institution. . . .

It is the obligation of all Party organs to display tireless concern for the primary Party organizations. It is necessary that Party committees be in constant contact with the primary Party organizations, that the leading officials of district, city, and province Party committees and the

Central Committee of the Union-republic Communist Parties regularly visit the Party organizations, converse and hold counsel with Communists, and appear before them with reports.

The activities of the primary Party organizations must be directed toward rearing Communists and non-Party people in a spirit of lofty ideology, a conscientious attitude toward their obligations, and a profound understanding of the policy of the CPSU. The Party organizations are obliged to raise still higher the level of political and organizational work among the masses, to develop the creative activeness of the working people in the struggle for the successful fulfillment of the new five-year plan, and to display constant concern for improving the conditions of labor and everyday life for workers, collective farmers, and office and professional personnel.

Everyone is well aware of how great a role is played by the territory, province, city, and district Party committees in the practical implementation of the Party's policy and measures in the localities. We are pleased to be able to remind the Congress that the November, 1964, plenary session of the CPSU reunited the province industrial and rural Party organizations into single entities, thereby restoring the Leninist principle of Party structure and eliminating the serious errors that had been committed in this matter. (*Applause.*) Also reinstated were the rural district Party committees, which in a short time have firmly reasserted their status as militant and authoritative propagators of Party policy in the countryside. (*Applause.*)

Comrades! Strict observance and consistent development of inner-Party democracy must be the object of constant attention for the Party and all its guiding bodies. Recently the CPSU Central Committee has taken a number of important steps in this direction. The development of the principle of democratic centralism has found expression in the further strengthening of the principle of collective leadership at the center and in the localities, in the enhancement of the role of plenary sessions of the CPSU Central Committee and also of plenary sessions of local Party organs, in the manifestation of complete trust in cadres, and in the improvement of inner-Party channels of information.

It is necessary that the members and candidate members of the Presidium of the Central Committee, Secretaries of the Central Committee and members of the CPSU Central Committee, members of the government, Ministers, and other leading officials regularly address the Party *aktiv*, Communists, and working people on urgent problems of economic and cultural construction, of domestic and international life. (*Applause.*)

It is necessary to give more attention and respect to the opinions and proposals of Communists, to create conditions for broad criticism and self-criticism, so that the Party organizations can promptly correct any Communist who is guilty of diverging from the requirements of the Party Statutes and can prevent the spread of shortcomings in work. Suppressors of criticism must be brought to the strictest account.

The development of inner-Party democracy simultaneously presupposes an all-round strengthening of discipline within the Party. These two aspects are inextricably bound together. Complete democracy and freedom of opinion in the discussion of all questions, and iron discipline once a decision has been adopted by the will of the majority—such is the immutable law of the Party. And we must demand its steadfast observance by all Communists, no matter where they work or what post they occupy. (*Applause.*) . . .

Comrades! Today the scale of economic and cultural construction has grown and the tasks of domestic policy have become complicated as never before. In these conditions, the correct promotion and training of the leading cadres of the Party and the state assume decisive importance.

The Party has reared and advanced into leadership a millions-strong army of ideologically tempered, well-trained, energetic officials who with the sweep and efficiency inherent in our system are carrying out the Party's line. In recent years the qualitative composition of leadership cadres has improved substantially. The overwhelming majority of the Party cadres are experienced officials who have passed through the fine school of political and organizational activity. This is an accomplishment of the Communist Party, and it is rightfully proud of its cadres.

However, the frequent restructuring and reorganizations of Party, Soviet, and economic bodies that were carried out in recent years had a negative effect on the selection, promotion, and training of cadres. As a rule, they were attended by an unwarranted shuffling and replacement of cadres, which engendered a lack of self-assurance in officials, prevented them from demonstrating their abilities to the full, and created the soil in which irresponsibility could sprout.

At present we have truly inexhaustible opportunities for ensuring that Party and state bodies and economic and public organizations are headed by skillful organizers who know their business thoroughly and enjoy prestige among Communists and non-Party people. The interests of the cause require that young, energetic officials be promoted more boldly. In so doing, it is necessary always to keep in mind the need for the correct combination of old and young cadres. Comrades who have gone through the great school of practical activity in the localities should be more vigorously promoted to leadership posts.

The matter of the selection and education of cadres must be elevated to a Partywide, statewide level. We must focus the attention of all Party organizations, from top to bottom, on the main thing—the selection, promotion, and education of cadres, verification of the fulfillment of Party directives, improvement of the work of Party organizations and the state apparatus.

There must be serious improvement in the training and retraining of Party, Soviet, and economic cadres. A wide network of permanent courses for raising qualifications and for the ideological-theoretical preparation of leading officials should be developed both at the center and in the localities, and the system of Party educational institutions should be perfected.

Life also demands that Party and state bodies improve the placement and utilization of specialists in the national economy. . . .

The socialist democracy of the Soviet state system is best embodied in the *Soviets* of Working People's Deputies, which are both organs of state authority and the public organizations embracing the broadest masses of our people. The local Soviets are called upon to improve public education, public health, social insurance, trade and public catering, and cultural-everyday services for the Soviet people and to engage more vigorously in the improvement of cities, villages, and settlements and in housing and highway construction.

Improvement of the activity of the Soviets must be effected on the basis of their further democratization. It is necessary to raise still higher the importance of sessions of the Soviets of Working People's Deputies, to grant the local Soviets greater independence in deciding economic, financial, and land questions and in guiding enterprises of local industry and everyday and social-cultural services for the population, and also to step up the work of the standing committees and to ensure regular reports to the voters by the Deputies. It must become the practice for the U.S.S.R. Council of Ministers to report to the sessions of the U.S.S.R. Supreme Soviet, and for the Union-republic Councils of Ministers and territory, province, city, and district executive committees to report to the sessions of their respective Soviets of Working People's Deputies. The most important draft laws and other legislative acts should be presented for general public discussion.

The U.S.S.R. Supreme Soviet and the Union-republic Supreme Soviets are called upon to intensify work on developing Soviet legislation and on verification of the execution of laws and to submit for the consideration of their sessions a broader range of questions of economic, social-cultural, and state construction. The work of Deputies to the U.S.S.R. Supreme Soviet and the Union-republic Supreme Soviets must become more active. The formation of new standing committees of the chambers of the U.S.S.R. Supreme Soviet might possibly contribute to this.

Party agencies must outgrow once and for all the practice of petty tutelage and usurpation of the functions of Soviet agencies, for this engenders irresponsibility and inertia among officials. It is the duty of Party organizations to develop the activeness of the Soviets in every way, to support their initiative, to be constantly concerned about the selection and promotion of cadres for work in the Soviets, about the observance and further development of the principles of socialist democracy. . . .

In developing democratic principles of state construction, the Party proceeds from the premise that the entire activity of Soviet agencies and the broad creative participation of citizens in managing the country's affairs must be based on the strictest observance of socialist legality. Soviet laws, embodying norms of socialist law and order that have been tested by life, are the expression of the will of all the working people. They are permeated with concern for the people and reliably safeguard our social order and the interests and rights of Soviet citizens. The agencies of the militia, prosecutors' offices, and the courts are doing much in the struggle for the further consolidation of socialist legality. The agencies of state security and our glorious border guards are vigilantly on duty exposing and preventing the intrigues of imperialist intelligence services and their agents.

Comrades! Constant concern for strengthening the country's defenses and the power of our glorious armed forces is a highly important task of the Soviet state. The Soviet Army showed, both in the years of the Civil War and in the years of the arduous trials of the Great Patriotic War of the Soviet people, that it is a worthy offspring of the working class, peasantry, and intelligentsia of our country. Soviet fighting men heroically defended the homeland's freedom and independence. (*Stormy applause.*)

Successes in the development of the economy, science, and technology have enabled us to equip the army and navy with the most modern nuclear-rocket weapons and with other armaments of the latest types. The arms of Soviet troops are equal to present-day requirements, and their growing striking power and firepower are fully adequate to smash any aggressor. (*Applause.*)

We must never forget the possibility of future tests that might again fall to the lot of the Soviet people. In the present complex and tense international situation, it is our duty to display unflagging vigilance. The Party deems it necessary to ensure the further development of the defense industry, the perfection of nuclear-rocket weaponry and all other types of equipment. The security of our homeland demands this.

It is necessary to perfect civil defense, to improve military-patriotic work among the working people, especially the young, to strengthen the sponsorship ties of collectives of enterprises, educational institutions, and collective state farms with military units and elements, and to show more concern for the soldiers and officers of the Soviet Army and their families. This matter demands the constant attention of the entire Party and all of Soviet society.

The Communist Party, the Soviet government, and all our people have a high regard for the honorable and exacting labor of soldiers, sailors, noncommissioned officers, petty officers, officers, generals, and admirals, have a warm affection for their armed forces, and are proud of their combat glory. The Party will continue to strengthen in every way the defense capability of the Soviet Union, to augment the power of the U.S.S.R. Armed Forces and to maintain a level of military preparedness of troops that will reliably ensure the peaceful labor of the Soviet people. (*Stormy, prolonged applause.*)

Comrades! A big role in solving the tasks of communist construction belongs to the *trade unions*, which number about 80,000,000 people in their ranks. In present-day conditions, the trade unions are charged with new content as schools of communism. . . .

Questions of the political upbringing of the working people, of improving the organization of labor and pay and of raising the skills of workers, and concern for sanitary and hygienic conditions and the protection of labor in production must always be at the center of attention of the trade unions. The trade unions must inquire daily into the matter of everyday services and the fulfillment of plans for the construction of housing and children's institutions. . . .

The *Leninist Young Communist League,* which unites about 23,000,000 young men and women, and the glorious Soviet youth led by it constitute a vigorous creative force in Soviet society. The Party is rightfully proud that it has reared whole generations of people in a spirit of selfless dedication to the great ideals of communism. It sees the YCL as the militant vanguard of Soviet youth and as its own dependable reserve. At all times, at all stages of the life and development of our society, the YCL has sacredly preserved and carried on the tradition of following the Communist Party in all things, of being its loyal and reliable assistant. (*Applause.*)

Young Communists, young Soviet men and women regard the destinies of the people and the state with lofty responsibility and awareness. The continuity of the generations and the powerful force of revolutionary traditions are brilliantly manifest in the practical deeds of young people and in their lofty ideological aspirations. The labor feats of young people —the builders of giant power plants and railroad lines, of new cities, the conquerors of the virgin lands, the pioneers in the conquest of space— have written wonderful pages in the history of the Soviet homeland. . . .

The Party and the entire people believe in the creative strength of youth. We want the lives of young people to be filled every day with concrete deeds that are useful to our homeland. Young Soviet men and women respond with great enthusiasm to all the appeals of the Party and the government.

At the same time, life makes high demands on the content of YCL activity and of all work done with youth. There are more than a few organizations and institutions in the country that are called upon to engage in the upbringing of the younger generation. But their activities are often uncoordinated. Yet it should not be disregarded that our country is young, so to speak, that half its population consists of people under twenty-six. It is therefore extremely important to intensify the attention paid by the Party, the YCL, and all other organizations to the rearing of young people. Raising the level and enriching the content and forms of ideological-upbringing work among the young is one of the most important tasks of the activity of Party and YCL organizations. It is very fine that Young Communists and other young people are working with such enthusiasm on construction projects and are taking part in the solution of other economic tasks. But at the same time we cannot forget that the main thing in the work of the YCL is the upbringing of youth.

It must be admitted that there are shortcomings in ideological-upbringing work with youth. Some Party and YCL organizations at times fail to consider the fact that the present generation of boys and girls has not passed through the harsh school of revolutionary struggle and tempering that fell to the lot of the older generation. Individual young people wish to stand aloof from seething life, are inclined toward dependency, and demand much from the state while forgetting their obligations to society, to the people. Our foes the bourgeois ideologists are taking note of precisely such unseasoned people, receptive to any ideological infections, and are attempting to use them in their own interests. Fortunately, however, we have only a handful of them. . . .

The Party nucleus in the YCL organizations should be strengthened. It cannot be acknowledged as proper that of the 2,500,000 Communists under the age of thirty, only about 270,000 work in the YCL. The young Communists must be more actively drawn into work in the YCL organizations, and this must be regarded as a highly important Party assignment for them. We must also make higher demands on the content of the activity of the YCL organizations themselves. It is necessary to bolster organization and discipline in the YCL and to perfect the forms and methods of upbringing work. The YCL must intensify work among children and take measures to improve the activity of the Young Pioneer organization. . . .

As a mother carefully nurtures her children, so must the Party raise the young generation, the hope and future of our great homeland, spiritually strong, steadfast and selfless fighters for our great cause. (*Prolonged applause.*)

2. On Certain Changes in the CPSU Statutes

Comrades! The CPSU Statutes adopted at the Twenty-second Congress conform to the norms of Party life, the demands of the times, and the tasks of communist construction. At the same time, the experience of the past few years has shown that it is necessary to make certain amendments and additions to the Statutes. A number of proposals were made in this connection at the report-and-election Party meetings and conferences and the congresses of the Communist Parties of the Union republics, as well as in letters to the CPSU Central Committee. In the main, they all call for raising still higher the title of Party member, for expanding inner-Party democracy, ensuring the further development of the initiative and activeness of Party organizations, and increasing the responsibility of Communists for the activity of their organizations and of the Party as a whole.

The Central Committee, having summed up the practical experience in the period between Congresses and also the proposals made by local Party agencies and Communists, considers it necessary to submit for the consideration of the Congress the following amendments and additions to the CPSU Statutes. Permit me, comrades, to report them to the Congress.

With a view to heightening the demands on persons joining the CPSU, it is proposed that young people under the age of twenty-three be admitted to the Party only through the Young Communist League. This will enhance the YCL's role as a reserve for the Party and will help select for the Party the most active section of young people who have gone through a school of upbringing in the ranks of the YCL. (*Applause.*)

In our view, those organizations and comrades are correct who believe that the right to give recommendations for Party membership should be granted to Communists who have been in the Party for at least five years, rather than three years, as the Statutes now stipulate. (*Shouts of approval. Applause.*)

It is suggested that the introductory section of the Statutes stipulate that the Party rid itself of persons who violate the CPSU Program and Statutes and who by their behavior compromise the lofty title of Communist. (*Applause.*)

It is proposed that a procedure be established under which a decision of a primary Party organization regarding expulson from the Party becomes valid once it has been approved by the district or city Party committee. (*Applause.*) It will be considered final, just as their decision on admission to the Party is final. (*Applause.*) This will increase the responsibility of district and city Party committees in the examination of individual cases of Communists. The rights of Communists will not be infringed thereby, inasmuch as they will, as formerly, be able to appeal to any superior Party body up to and including the CPSU Central Committee. It goes without saying that the province and territory Party committees and the Central Committees of the Communist Parties of the Union republics will be obliged, as they are at present, to supervise the examination of individual cases in district and city Party organizations.

It would appear to serve no purpose to continue resorting to such a measure of Party influence as transferring a Party member to the status of candidate member. This has not justified itself in practice. (*Applause.*) Party organizations have a sufficient number of other educational measures at their disposal. If a comrade is not worthy of the lofty title of Party member, then the Party organization must take up the question of whether he should remain in the ranks of the CPSU. (*Applause.*)

Certain amendments and additions concern the section of the Statutes dealing with higher Party bodies.

In conditions of the constantly growing tasks and the increasing role of the Party in communist construction, it may become necessary during the period between Congresses to discuss the most important political problems at Party forums that are more widely representative than plenary sessions of the CPSU Central Committee. In V. I. Lenin's lifetime and continuing right up to 1941, general Party conferences were held in such cases. It should be stipulated in the Statutes that the Central Committee may when necessary convoke all-Union Party conferences, while the Central Committees of the Communist Parties of the Union republics may convoke republic Party conferences. (*Applause.*)

It is suggested that the proposals of the Central Committees of the Communist Parties of the Union republics that uniform dates be set for the holding of congresses of the Communist Parties of the Union republics be adopted, that it be stipulated that they are to be convoked at least once every four years. (*Applause.*)

The proposal has been made in many letters from Communists that the Presidium be renamed the Politburo of the CPSU Central Committee. (*Shouts of approval. Stormy applause.*) Communists give as their motivation for this proposal the fact that for a long time, during V. I. Lenin's lifetime and subsequently, there was a Politburo of the Central Committee. The name Politburo more fully expresses the nature of the activities of our party's highest political body, which guides the Party's work between plenary sessions of the CPSU Central Committee. We support this proposal. (*Applause.*)

The opinion has been expressed that there is no need at the present time to retain the CPSU Central Committee's Bureau for the Russian Republic. Practice has shown that, even with the existence of the Central Committee's Bureau for the Russian Republic, all the most important matters pertaining to the work of the territory and province Party organizations in the Russian Federation are handled by the Presidium and the Secretariat of the CPSU Central Committee. Therefore there is no purpose in having another, parallel body of the CPSU Central Committee for the Russian Federation. The CPSU Central Committee agrees with this opinion. (*Applause.*)

Because the CPSU Central Committee and the Twenty-third Party Congress have received many proposals concerning the provisions for the renewal and turnover of the membership of Party bodies and their leading cadres, we must discuss whether those provisions should be retained in the Statutes. The principle of systematic renewal and continuity in itself has been operating in our party for a long time. And it is a correct principle. The Party has always shown concern for advancing new matured cadres to leading Party and state work.

As for the norms regulating that process now in operation, life has shown that they have not justified themselves. (*Applause.*) Here and there during elections of Communists to leading bodies, the principles of the selection of cadres for their business and political qualities have been replaced by formal attitudes. As a result, excellent workers who might still continue to work actively in Party committees are often compelled to step down from work in elective bodies.

The compulsory restriction of a Communist's term as secretary of a primary Party organization to two years has caused a heavy turnover. Whereas formerly 30 to 35 per cent of the secretaries of primary organizations were changed annually, in recent years this number has risen to 60 per cent. Moreover, two-thirds of the secretaries have been released only because the statutory term has expired. This has begun to have a negative effect on the work of primary Party organizations.

The statutory requirement that at least half the membership of the region, city, and district Party committees and the Party committees and bureaus of primary Party organizations be replaced at each regular election has also brought about the unjustified restriction of the circle of mature and experienced workers who may be elected to Party committees.

In view of this, the aforementioned provisions of the CPSU Statutes should be taken up at the Congress. Apparently it would be expedient to retain in the Statutes only the fundamental programatic provision that in elections to Party bodies, from primary organizations to the Central Committee, the principle of the systematic renewal of their membership and continuity of leadership be observed, while norms regulating that process should be excluded from the Statutes. (*Applause.*) It is more correct and more democratic for Communists to decide for themselves whether a given Party member has the political and business qualities to make him worthy to serve in a leading Party body.

It is also suggested that the established practice of granting the Party committees of large Party organizations the rights of district Party committees be fixed in the Statutes, with a provision that such Party committees are elected for a term of two years.

The Party Central Committee is convinced that the adoption of the proposed amendments and additions to the CPSU Statutes will further raise the level of Party organizational work and improve the Party's activity. (*Applause.*)

3. THE IDEOLOGICAL-UPBRINGING WORK OF THE PARTY

Comrades! Theoretical work, the ideological-political upbringing of Communists and of all working people, is a most important component part of the activity of the Communist Party. Our party has always held high the all-conquering banner of the revolutionary theory of Marxism-Leninism. Fidelity to this revolutionary teaching and irreconcilability in the struggle against its enemies is an immutable principle in all its multi-faceted activities.

V. I. Lenin always called on Party members to work tirelessly to master the revolutionary theory of Marxism and to develop it creatively. He is a great example for us of a creative approach to theory; he provided unsurpassed models of the theoretical and practical solution of many basic questions of the development of the socialist revolution and the building of a new society. His ideas, outlines, and instructions still exert an invaluable influence today on all our daily public, political, and economic life.

All of socialism's great victories in our country have been achieved on the basis of the Marxist-Leninist teaching. In vain do our enemies nurture hopes for the ideological degeneration of the Communist Party and the Soviet people. This will never happen! There is no force in the world capable of undermining or weakening our unshakable dedication to Marxism-Leninism. (*Stormy, prolonged applause.*) . . .

The social sciences, in which the Party has always placed and continues to place great hopes and great responsibility, are called upon to play an important role in this matter. To elaborate important problems of economics, politics, philosophy, sociology, history, law, and other social sciences in close tie with the practice of communist construction is a most important task of Soviet scientists. They are called upon to conduct all-round research on such problems as the direction and nature of the process the formation of communist social relations, perfection of the state system, and the development of socialist democracy, the forms and methods of economic management, the scientific organization of labor, the content and methods of communist upbringing work, and other urgent themes.

It is necessary to put an end to the idea, prevalent among a portion of our cadres, that the social sciences have propaganda value only, that they are called upon merely to explain and comment upon practice. The development of the social sciences and the implementation of their recommendations are of no less importance than the utilization of the achievements of the natural sciences in the sphere of material production and development of the people's spiritual life.

The struggle against bourgeois ideology, revisionism, dogmatism, and reformism is of great importance. We must always remember that our class enemy is imperialism. It conducts subversive activities against the socialist system, its principles, ideology, and morals. Imperialism's gigantic propaganda apparatus corrupts the individual and tries to divert the masses from politics. The struggle against bourgeois ideology must under all circumstances be uncompromising, for this is a class struggle, a struggle for man, for his dignity and freedom, for a consolidation of the positions of socialism and communism; it is a struggle in the interests of the international working class. (*Prolonged applause.*) . . .

The rearing of the new Soviet man is one of the greatest results of the Party's many years of efforts in the field of ideological work. Continuing the revolutionary traditions of the generation of fighters who established the world's first workers' and peasants' state, Soviet man has built socialism, withstood and in mortal combat won victory over fascism, defended the great gains of our revolution, and is now building communism for the first time in history. The working class, the collective farm peasantry, and the Soviet intelligentsia display an example of lofty socialist consciousness and heroic labor. The victory of socialism has wrought a most profound change in the consciousness of Soviet people.

The main thing now is to raise the level of all links of the Party's ideological work still higher. We must remember Lenin's instruction to the effect that without conscious labor and public activity there is not and cannot be any communist upbringing. All ideological work must be closely linked with life, with the practice of communist instruction; otherwise, as V. I. Lenin stressed many a time, it turns into political gibberish. The mobilization of the working people for the successful achievement of the tasks of creating the material and technical base of communism, the formation of a scientific world outlook and communist morals among all members of society, and the rearing of a comprehensively developed individual—such are the aims of the Party's ideological work.

The Soviet people are carrying out the greatest social task in the history of mankind—the building of communism. Tens of millions of people are taking part in the active creative process of construction. We must teach first the majority and then all working people to work as our glorious shock workers and masters of labor are working today. This task is perfectly feasible. Today's shock workers and innovators of production are ordinary people. But they stand out because they have fully mastered technology, because they serve society consciously, display high moral and ethical qualities, a spirit of collectivism, and are carrying out their duties to the people self-sacrificingly and to the fullest of their abilities. These are people of the future, as it were. They work as all people will work under communism. This is of tremendous significance for the success of ideological work. Here is an example, a model that should be followed and from which it is possible to learn. Party organizations are called upon to do all in their power so that every Soviet person may see in the assignments of the new five-year plan a program for his own personal labor and may make a worthy contribution to its fulfillment.

Our party has always attached primary significance to instilling conscious discipline in all members of society. The strengthening of labor discipline and the demand for the unconditional observance of all the laws and rules of socialist society not only do not contradict the democratic principles of the Soviet system but, on the contrary, constitute a condition for the development and expansion of Soviet socialist democratism. The socialist organization of the whole of society for the sake of each individual and the socialist discipline of each individual for the sake of the whole society—such is the substance of socialist democracy. It is the task of the Party constantly to strengthen the high discipline and organization of all links of the Party and the state.

The inculcation of a sense of thrift in Soviet people, of concern on the part of each individual for the preservation and augmentation of the public wealth, must play an important part in the work of Party organizations. Soviet society already possesses gigantic riches belonging to all the people. But the homeland's wealth must be tirelessly multiplied and must be used carefully and economically. Unfortunately, we still have cases of extravagance and of a prodigal attitude to material values. How much richer and stronger our state would be if we all learned to treat every kilogram of metal, coal, cement, and oil, every ruble of the people's money carefully and economically. The instilling of a sense of thrift should play as important a part in the Party's ideological work as labor upbringing.

Comrades! Our homeland, the great Soviet Union, is based on the fraternity, friendship, and cooperation of all the peoples of the country, on a common socio-economic system, a common political system, a single socialist ideology. The economic and cultural ties of the peoples of the

U.S.S.R. are becoming steadily closer and more varied. A great process of the rapprochement of peoples, of the strengthening of the unbreakable ties of their friendship and fraternity, unity and solidarity, is under way.

For almost half a century the Party has indefatigably strengthened, forged, and perfected this alliance until it has turned into the inviolable and powerful force of our state that the friendship and fraternity of the peoples of the Soviet Union is today. (*Applause.*) Our enemies have repeatedly tried to undermine and to shake the strength of this friendship both by force of arms and by the poison of their bourgeois ideology. But all their hopes have been scattered like ashes, while the friendship of the Soviet peoples is confidently gathering force, flourishing, gaining strength, and developing. (*Applause.*)

The Communist Party of the Soviet Union serves as the living embodiment of the ideas of proletarian internationalism, friendship, and fraternity of the peoples. The finest sons and daughters of the 131 nations and peoples of our country are in its ranks. We are proud that all the national detachments of our party merge, as the waters of rivers merge in a mighty ocean, in the Communist Party of the Soviet Union—a union of like-minded Leninists, with one will, one aim, one ideology. (*Prolonged applause.*)

Our Congress is a remarkable example and proof of this. Look around the hall, comrades: Present here are representatives of many peoples and nationalities of our country. Each of them is the son of his own socialist nation, but at the same time he is a son of the Party, a soldier of it; he is an internationalist Communist for whom the interests of any of the other peoples of the Soviet Union are as dear, close, and understandable as his own. Herein lies the strength of our party; herein is the strength of our multinational Soviet state, of our Soviet people. (*Prolonged applause.*)

The Party and all Communists, irrespective of their nationality, are called upon to continue to work indefatigably to bring about the further comprehensive rapprochement of the peoples of the Soviet Union and the strengthening of their friendship and fraternity, to make their economic, cultural, and spiritual ties closer and more varied. In solving any problem, whether it be of the political, the economic, or the cultural development of our country, the Party will continue to show solicitude for the interests and the national characteristics of each people, to instill in all Soviet people a spirit of the ideas of proletarian internationalism, a spirit of inviolable loyalty to the fraternity and friendship of the peoples of the U.S.S.R. This is the only correct national policy. The entire experience of the development of the U.S.S.R. confirms its viability and correctness. (*Applause.*) . . .

Comrades! Great tasks in the sphere of improving ideological and political work in the countryside confront us. In the course of the struggle for the socialist transformation of agriculture the psychology of the rural toiler has changed radically; his education and culture have grown; the alliance of the working class and the peasantry has become even stronger.

At the same time, it is necessary to point out the existence of serious shortcomings in the field of cultural-enlightenment work in the country-side. For a long time too little attention was given to expanding the network of clubs, libraries, movie theaters, and sports facilities in rural areas.

Party, Soviet, trade union, and YCL organizations and all ideological institutions must direct their attention to the elimination of these short-comings. There must be a radical improvement in the political and cultural upbringing of rural toilers, a stepping up of assistance to the country-side on the part of urban cultural-enlightenment institutions, theaters, and artistic unions and organizations. This work must be carried out along a broad front. Raising the cultural standard and improving ameni-ties in the countryside will unquestionably foster the more successful development of the productive forces of the collective and state farms.

Comrades! The scope of ideological-upbringing work among the masses is closely linked with raising the theoretical and political level of Com-munists. We must also take into account that our party has become numerically larger. Almost one-quarter of its membership consists of Com-munists who have been in the Party less than three years and of candidate members. . . .

The tasks of ideological work are great and complex. They require a decisive improvement in Party leadership in this most important field. The Soviet man today is an active participant in the struggle for the Party line, the true master of his country. His range of interests is broad, his cultural requirements are many. All this must be taken into account in ideological work.

We have considerable material possibilities for further developing up-bringing work among the masses. There are 7,700 newspapers and almost 4,000 magazines published in the country. In the period under review their combined circulation has risen by 74,000,000, or 60 per cent. More than 1,250,000,000 copies of books and pamphlets appear every year. There are more than 70,000,000 radio receivers and plug-in sets and 120 television centers in the country. According to the directives for the new five-year plan there will be 40,000,0000 television sets in the Soviet Union in 1970.

The Party has splendid cadres of propagandists, agitators, journalists, and workers in television, the cinema, radio, and the theater. These are indeed a golden fund of the Party that must be cherished, solicitously nurtured, and correctly utilized.

The erroneous idea that ideological work is the affair solely of spe-cialists in this sphere of Party activity must be resolutely rejected. Such a view is contrary to the Party's traditions and narrows the front of its ideological influence. Ideological work is a cause of our entire party, of all Communists. We must always remember that the ideological effect on the masses, the high effectiveness of all agitation and propaganda work, depends directly on the force of the personal example of Party members and leaders. Unity of word and deed—this most important Leninist requirement—must continue to be a law of the activity of our party, of each Communist, of each leading official. (*Applause.*) . . .

Comrade delegates! The Twenty-third Congress of the Communist Party of the Soviet Union is meeting on the eve of two great dates. Next year, 1967, will mark the fiftieth anniversary of the victory of the Great October Socialist Revolution and the founding of the world's first socialist state—the Soviet Union. And 1970—that is, the last year of the new five-year plan—will be the centenary of the birth of the greatest of geniuses, the founder and leader of our party and state, Vladimir Ilyich Lenin. And there need be no doubt but that the working people, all Soviet people, will mark these dates with outstanding new successes in communist construction. (*Applause.*) . . .

While devoting all their energies to the building of the future, our party and all Soviet people at the same time look back with pride over the incredibly difficult but glorious path they have traversed in the past half-century.

We have something to be proud of, comrades. No other people in the entire history of mankind has ever in so short a period and under such incredibly difficult conditions performed such feats of inimitable grandeur in building a new society, in developing the economy, science, and culture as our Soviet people. (*Applause.*) All that has already been accomplished by the labor of the Communist Party and the Soviet people, our new achievements and exploits will all be a worthy crown for the heroic fifty-year history of the world's first socialist society.

Today the difference between what our socialist state was at its inception and what it has become is evident with particular clarity.

Permit me to recall an episode from history. Early in March, 1918, when the Soviet government was moving from Petrograd to Moscow, Vladimir Ilyich Lenin wrote his famous article "The Main Task of Our Day" in a train at night by the dim light of a small lamp.

The socialist fatherland, as we know, was living through very, very difficult days then. German imperialism had frenziedly attacked the young Soviet state. A mood of despair and hopelessness had come over many people in the Party at that time. But Lenin was not the kind of person to become panic-striken or confused even for an instant. Addressing the Party and the people in this article, he called upon them to display an inflexible determination to advance along the path of socialism, to build stone by stone a strong foundation for a socialist society, to work indefatigably to create an up-to-date machine industry, to establish discipline, to strengthen order, efficiency, and the cooperation of the forces of the entire people. He ended his article with a brilliant prophecy. Listen to these words, comrades: "It is precisely this that the Russian Soviet Socialist Republic needs in order to cease being wretched and impotent, in order to become irreversibly mighty and abundant."

This prophecy has come true. Yes, this irreversibly mighty and abundant socialist state exists on this earth! (*Applause.*) It is our Soviet homeland—

the Union of Soviet Socialist Republics. (*Applause.*) Its might is indeed irreversible, economically, militarily, and in every other respect. And this is solely because year after year the Party and the people advanced unswervingly along the path charted by V. I. Lenin.

Our multinational socialist state will observe its fiftieth anniversary at the height of its strength, glory, and power. In the past half-century it was attacked more than once by brutalized imperialist enemies, but each time our people routed the enemies in fierce and bloody battles and continued their triumphant journey forward. The Soviet people achieved the majestic gains of which they are rightly proud under the leadership of the Communist Party of the Soviet Union. . . .

Permit me on behalf of the Congress, which is an embodiment of our entire Communist Party, to thank the Soviet people warmly for their great trust and support, for their great work, for their wisdom, courage, persistence and valor in the struggle for the cause of Lenin, the cause of the Party! (*Stormy, prolonged applause.*)

The Soviet people regard the Party as their leader and guide, the organizer of all their victories. They have been convinced and are convinced every day by deeds that the policy of the Party, both foreign and domestic, is the only correct policy, that the road along which the Party is leading the Soviet people is the only true Leninist road. (*Applause.*)

Permit me on behalf of the Congress, which represents all detachments of our multimillion-strong Communist Party, to assure the working class, all the working people, all the peoples of our multinational country that the Communist Party will continue in the future to devote all its energies to the cause of the struggle for the happiness of the people and the prosperity of our homeland, for communism, and that by its practical deeds it will justify the Soviet people's great trust. (*Prolonged applause.*)

Long live the Communist Party of the Soviet Union—the party of Lenin! (*Prolonged applause.*)

Long live the glorious, industrious, and heroic Soviet people! (*Applause.*)

Long live and prosper our great, multinational homeland—the Union of Soviet Socialist Republics! (*Prolonged applause.*)

Long live the mighty commonwealth of the countries of socialism! (*Prolonged applause.*)

May the international Communist and workers' movement develop and grow stronger! (*Prolonged applause.*)

Long live Marxism-Leninism through the ages! (*Prolonged applause.*)

Long live communism! (*Stormy, prolonged applause, turning into an ovation. All rise.*)

*   *   *

7

THE STATUTES OF THE COMMUNIST PARTY OF THE SOVIET UNION

The Communist Party of the Soviet Union is the militant, tested vanguard of the Soviet people, uniting on a voluntary basis the advanced, most socially conscious part of the working class, collective farm peasantry, and intelligentsia of the U.S.S.R.

Founded by V. I. Lenin, the Communist Party, the vanguard of the working class, has traversed a glorious path of struggle and has led the working class and working peasants to the victory of the Great October Socialist Revolution, to the establishment of the dictatorship of the proletariat in the U.S.S.R. Under Communist Party leadership the exploiting classes were eliminated in the Soviet Union and the moral and political unity of Soviet society has taken shape and grown in strength. Socialism has triumphed completely and finally. The Communist Party, the party of the working class, has now become the party of the entire Soviet people.

The Party exists for the people and serves the people. It is the highest form of sociopolitical organization, the leading and guiding force of Soviet society. The Party directs the great creative activity of the Soviet people and imparts an organized, planned, and scientific character to their struggle to achieve the ultimate goal, the victory of communism.

The CPSU organizes its work on the basis of unswerving observance of the Leninist norms of Party life—the principle of collectivity of leadership, the comprehensive development of inner-Party democracy, the activeness and initiative of Communists, and criticism and self-criticism.

Ideological and organizational unity, monolithic solidarity of its ranks, and conscious discipline on the part of all Communists are the inviolable law of the life of the CPSU. Any manifestation of factionalism or clique

Pravda, November 3, 1961. Translation copyright 1961 by *The Current Digest of the Soviet Press*, published weekly at The Ohio State University by the American Association for the Advancement of Slavic Studies; reprinted by permission of *The Digest*. Translation appeared in Vol. XIII, No. 47 (1961), pp. 3–8, of *The Digest*.

activity is incompatible with Marxist-Leninist Party principles and with Party membership.

In all its activity the CPSU is guided by the Marxist-Leninist teaching and the Program based on it, which defines the Party's fundamental tasks for the period of the construction of communist society.

The CPSU, creatively developing Marxism-Leninism, resolutely combats any manifestations of revisionism and dogmatism, which are profoundly alien to revolutionary theory.

The Communist Party of the Soviet Union is an inseparable part of the international Communist and workers' movement. It firmly adheres to the tested Marxist-Leninist principles of proletarian internationalism, actively promotes strengthening of the unity of the entire international Communist and workers' movement and fraternal ties with the great army of Communists of all countries.

I. Party Members, Their Duties and Rights

1. Any citizen of the Soviet Union who accepts the Party Program and Statutes, takes an active part in communist construction, works in one of the Party organizations, carries out Party decisions, and pays membership dues may be a member of the CPSU.

2. It is the duty of a Party member:

(a) to fight for the creation of the material and technical base of communism, to set an example of the communist attitude toward labor, to raise labor productivity, to take the initiative in all that is new and progressive, to support and propagate advanced experience, to master technology, to improve his qualifications, to safeguard and increase public, socialist property—the foundation of the might and prosperity of ·the Soviet homeland;

(b) to carry out Party decisions firmly and undeviatingly, to explain the policy of the Party to the masses, to help strengthen and broaden the Party's ties with the people, to be considerate and attentive toward people, to respond promptly to the wants and needs of the working people;

(c) to take an active part in the political life of the country, in the management of state affairs, and in economic and cultural construction; to set an example in the fulfillment of public duty; to help develop and strengthen communist social relations;

(d) to master Marxist-Leninist theory, to raise his ideological level, and to contribute to the molding and rearing of the man of communist society; to combat resolutely any manifestations of bourgeois ideology, remnants of a private-property psychology, religious prejudices, and other survivals of the past; to observe the principles of communist morality, and to place public interests above personal ones;

(e) to be an active proponent of the ideas of socialist internationalism and Soviet patriotism among the masses of the working people, to combat survivals of nationalism and chauvinism, to contribute by work and deed to strengthening the friendship of peoples of the U.S.S.R. and the fraternal ties of the Soviet people with the peoples of the socialist countries and the proletarians and working people of all countries;

(f) to strengthen the ideological and organizational unity of the Party in every way, to safeguard the Party against the infiltration of persons unworthy of the lofty title of Communist, to be truthful and honest with the Party and people, to display vigilance, to preserve Party and state secrets;

(g) to develop criticism and self-criticism; to boldly disclose shortcomings and strive for their removal; to combat ostentation, conceit, complacency and localism; to rebuff firmly any attempts to suppress criticism; to resist any actions detrimental to the Party and the state and to report them to Party bodies, up to and including the Central Committee of the CPSU;

(h) to carry out unswervingly the Party line in the selection of cadres according to their political and work qualifications, to be uncompromising in all cases of violation of the Leninist principles of the selection and training of cadres;

(i) to observe Party and state discipline, which is equally binding on all Party members; the Party has a single discipline, one law for all Communists, regardless of their services or the positions they hold;

(j) to help in every way to strengthen the defense might of the U.S.S.R., to wage a tireless struggle for peace and friendship among peoples.

3. A Party member has the right:

(a) to elect and be elected to Party bodies;

(b) to discuss freely questions of the Party's policies and practical activities at Party meetings, conferences and Congresses, at the meetings of Party committees, and in the Party press; to introduce motions; openly to express and uphold his opinion until the organization has adopted a decision;

(c) to criticize any Communist, regardless of the position he holds, at Party meetings, conferences, and Congresses and at plenary meetings of Party committees; persons guilty of suppressing criticism or persecuting anyone for criticism must be held to strict Party responsibility, up to and including expulsion from the ranks of the CPSU;

(d) to participate in person at Party meetings and bureau and committee meetings at which his activity or conduct is discussed;

(e) to address questions, statements, or proposals to Party bodies at any level, up to and including the Central Committee of the CPSU and to demand an answer on the substance of his address.

4. Admission to membership in the Party is exclusively on an individual basis. Membership in the Party is open to socially conscious and active workers, peasants, and representatives of the intelligentsia, devoted to the cause of communism. New members are admitted from among the candidate members who have completed their period as candidates.

Persons may join the Party on attaining the age of eighteen. Young persons up to twenty years of age, inclusive, may join the Party only via the Young Communist League.

The procedure for the admission of candidate members to full Party membership is as follows:

(a) Applicants for Party membership shall submit recommendations from three Party members who have a Party standing of not less than three years and who know the applicant from having worked with him on the job and in volunteer work for not less than one year;

Note 1. In admitting members of the YCL to membership in the Party, the recommendation of the YCL district or city committee is equal to the recommendation of one Party member.

Note 2. Members and candidate members of the Central Committee of the CPSU shall refrain from giving recommendations.

(b) The question of admission to the Party is discussed and decided by a general meeting of the primary Party organization; the decision comes into force upon ratification by the district Party committee or, in cities where there is no district subdivision, upon ratification by the city Party committee.

The presence of the persons recommending admission is not essential at the discussion of the application;

(c) Citizens of the U.S.S.R. who formerly belonged to the Communist or Workers' Party of another country are admitted to membership in the Communist Party of the Soviet Union on the basis of rules established by the Central Committee of the CPSU.

Persons who had formerly belonged to other parties are admitted to membership in the CPSU in conformity with the regular procedure, but only if their admission is approved by a province or territory Party committee or the Central Committee of a Union-republic Communist Party.

5. Those who recommend applicants are responsible to the Party organizations for the objectivity of their description of the applicant's political, work, and moral qualifications.

6. Tenure of membership dates from the adoption, by a general meeting of the primary Party organization, of a resolution to admit the candidate to Party membership.

7. The procedure for registering members and candidate members in the Party organization and for transferring them to another Party organization is determined in accordance with instructions of the Central Committee of the CPSU.

8. If a Party member or candidate member has without valid reason failed to pay membership dues for three months, the matter shall be discussed in the primary Party organization. Should it turn out that the Party member or candidate member has in effect lost contact with the Party organization, he shall be considered to have dropped out of the Party; the primary Party organization shall adopt a decision to this effect and shall submit it to the district or city Party committee for ratification.

9. A Party member or candidate member who fails to perform the

duties set forth in the Statutes or commits other offenses shall be called to responsibility and may be punished by admonition, by reprimand (or severe reprimand), or by reprimand (or severe reprimand) with entry in his registration card. The highest Party penalty is expulsion from the Party.

When it is necessary as a Party penalty, a Party organization may transfer a member of the Party to the status of candidate member for a period of up to one year. The decision of a primary Party organization to return a Party member to candidate status is ratified by the district or city Party committee. On expiration of the established period the person who has been returned to candidate status is admitted to Party membership on the regular basis and retains his former tenure of Party membership.

For minor offenses measures of Party education and influence, in the form of comradely criticism, Party censure, warnings, or reproof, should be taken.

When deciding the question of expulsion from the Party, the maximum thoughtfulness must be exercised and a thorough examination must be made of whether the accusation against the Party member is justified.

10. The question of expelling a Communist from the Party is decided by a general meeting of the primary Party organization. The decision of the primary Party organization on expulsion from the Party is considered adopted if no less than two-thirds of the Party members present at the meeting vote for it, and it is ratified by the district or city Party committee. The decision of a district or city Party committee on expulsion from the Party comes into force after it is ratified by a province or territory Party committee or the Central Committee of a Union-republic Communist Party.

Until the province or territory Party committee or Union-republic Communist Party Central Committee ratifies the resolution expelling the Communist from the Party, his Party card or candidate's card remains in his hands, and he has the right to attend closed Party meetings.

A person expelled from the Party retains the right to submit an appeal within two months to superior Party bodies, up to and including the Central Committee of the CPSU.

11. Questions of Party penalty for a member or candidate member of the Central Committee of a Union-republic Communist Party or of a territory, province, region, city, or district Party committee, and also of a member of an inspection commission, shall be discussed in the primary Party organizations.

Decisions of Party organizations on penalties for members and candidate members of these Party committees and members of inspection commissions shall be adopted by the regular procedure.

The proposals of the Party organizations regarding expulsion from the Party shall be reported to the Party committee of which the given Communist is a member. A decision to expel a member or candidate member of the Central Committee of a Union-republic Communist Party or of a territory, province, region, city, or district Party Committee or a member of an inspection commission shall be adopted at a plenary session of the respective committee by a two-thirds majority vote of its members.

The question of expelling from the Party a member or candidate member of the Central Committee of the CPSU or a member of the Central Inspection Commission shall be decided by a Party congress or, in the interval between Party congresses, at a plenary session of the Central Committee members.

12. If a Party member has committed an offense punishable under criminal procedure, he is expelled from the Party and held liable under the law.

13. Appeals by those expelled from the Party or subjected to penalties, as well as decisions of Party organizations to expel members from the Party, shall be reviewed by the Party bodies concerned within a period of not more than one month from the day of their receipt.

II. Candidates for Party Membership

14. Those entering the Party pass through a candidate stage, which is essential in order that the candidate may acquaint himself with the Party Program and Statutes and prepare for admission to the Party. The Party organization must help the candidate to prepare for admission to the Party and must verify his personal qualifications.

The period of candidacy is set at one year.

15. The procedure for admitting candidates (individual admission, presentation of recommendations, the resolution of the primary Party organization on admission, and its ratification) is identical with that for admission to Party membership.

16. Upon expiration of the candidature, the primary Party organization takes up and decides the question of admitting the candidate to membership in the Party. If during his candidature the candidate has not proved himself and because of his personal qualifications cannot be admitted to Party membership, the Party organization adopts a resolution to refuse him admission to Party membership, and, after ratification of this resolution by the district or city Party committee, he is considered dropped from candidature for Party membership.

17. Candidates for Party membership take part in the entire activity of the Party organization and enjoy the right to a consultative vote at Party meetings. Candidates for Party membership may not be elected to executive Party bodies or as delegates to Party conferences and congresses.

18. Candidates for Party membership pay the same Party dues as Party members.

III. Organizational Structure of the Party: Inner-Party Democracy

19. The guiding principle of the organizational structure of the Party is democratic centralism, meaning:

(a) election of all Party executive bodies from bottom to top;

(b) periodic accountability of Party bodies to their Party organizations and to higher bodies;

(c) strict Party discipline and subordination of the minority to the majority;

(d) the unconditionally binding nature of the decisions of higher bodies upon lower ones.

20. The Party rests on a territorial-production basis: The primary organizations are created at the Communists' places of work and are territorially united in district organizations, city organizations, etc. The organization serving a given area is superior to all Party organizations serving parts of this area.

21. All Party organizations are autonomous in deciding local questions, provided that the decisions are not contrary to the Party's policy.

22. The highest executive body of a Party organization is the general meeting (for primary organizations), the conference (for district, city, region, province, and territory organizations), and the congress (for the Communist Parties of Union republics and the Communist Party of the Soviet Union).

23. The general meeting, conference, or congress elects a bureau or committee, which is the executive body and directs the entire current work of the Party organization.

24. Elections of Party bodies are held by closed (secret) ballot. In elections all Party members have the unrestricted right to challenge candidates and to criticize them. Voting must be on individual candidates. Candidates who receive more than one-half of the votes of the participants in the meeting, conference, or congress are considered elected.

25. The principle of systematic turnover of the membership of Party bodies and of continuity of leadership is observed in elections of Party bodies.

At all regular elections of the Central Committee of the CPSU and its Presidium, not less than one-fourth of the membership shall be newly elected. Presidium members shall as a rule be elected for not more than three successive terms. Particular Party workers may, by virtue of their recognized authority and high political, organizational, or other abilities, be successively elected to executive bodies for a longer period. In such cases, election requires a majority of at least three-fourths of the votes cast by closed (secret) ballot.

At least one-third of the members of the Central Committees of the Union-republic Communist Parties and of territory and province committees chosen at each regular election, and one-half of the members of region, city, and district Party committees and the committees and bureaus of primary Party organizations shall be new members. Furthermore, members of these executive Party bodies may be elected for not more than three successive terms. The secretaries of primary Party organizations may be elected for not more than two successive terms.

A meeting, conference, or congress may, in consideration of political and work qualities of an individual, elect him to an executive body for a longer period. In such cases election requires that not less than three-fourths of the Communists participating in the voting cast their ballots for him.

Party members who are not re-elected to an executive Party body on the expiration of their terms may be re-elected in subsequent elections.

26. A member or candidate member of the Central Committee of the CPSU must by his entire activity justify the high trust placed in him by the Party. If a member or candidate member of the Central Committee of the CPSU has sullied his honor and dignity, he cannot remain a member of the Central Committee. The question of removing a member or a candidate member of the Central Committee of the CPSU from membership in the Central Committee is decided at a plenary session of the Central Committee by closed (secret) ballot. The decision is regarded as adopted if at least two-thirds of all the members of the Central Committee of the CPSU vote for it.

The question of removing a member or candidate member of the Central Committee of a Union-republic Communist Party committee from the given Party body is decided at a plenary session of the given committee. A decision is considered adopted if at least two-thirds of all the members of the committee vote for it by closed (secret) ballot.

If a member of the Central Inspection Commission does not justify the high trust placed in him by the Party, he must be removed from the Commission. This question is decided at a meeting of the Central Inspection Commission. A decision is considered adopted if at least two-thirds of all the members of the Central Inspection Commission vote for removal of a given member of the Central Inspection Commission from that body by closed (secret) ballot.

The question of removing members of inspection commissions of republic, territory, province, region, city, and district Party organizations from these commissions is decided at meetings of the given commissions under the procedure established for members and candidate members of the Party committees.

27. The free and businesslike discussion of questions of Party policy in individual Party organizations or in the Party as a whole is an inalienable right of the Party member and an important principle of inner-Party democracy. Only on the basis of inner-Party democracy can criticism and self-criticism be developed and Party discipline, which must be conscious and not mechanical, be strengthened.

Discussions on disputed or insufficiently clear questions are possible within the framework of individual organizations or of the Party as a whole.

General Party discussion is necessary:

(a) if this need is recognized by several Party organizations at the province or republic level;

(b) if within the Central Committee there does not exist a sufficiently firm majority on major questions of Party policy;

(c) if the Central Committee of the CPSU considers it essential to consult with the entire Party on given questions of policy.

Broad discussion, especially discussion on an all-Union scale, of questions of Party policy must be carried out in such a way as to ensure the free expression of the views of Party members and to prevent the possibility of attempts to form factional groupings destructive to Party unity or attempts to split the Party.

28. The highest principle of Party leadership is collectivity of leadership—the indispensable condition of the normal functioning of Party organizations, the correct rearing of cadres, and the development of the activeness and initiative of Communists. The cult of the individual and the violations of inner-Party democracy connected with it cannot be tolerated in the Party; they are incompatible with the Leninist principles of Party life.

Collective leadership does not absolve officials of individual responsibility for matters entrusted to them.

29. In the period between congresses and conferences the Central Committees of the Union-republic Communist Parties and the territory, province, region, city, and district Party committees shall keep Party organizations periodically informed about their work.

30. Meetings of the *aktiv* of district, city, region, province, and territory Party organizations and of the Union-republic Communist Parties are called to discuss major Party decisions and to work out measures for implementing them, and also to consider questions of local life.

IV. The Supreme Bodies of the Party

31. The highest body of the Communist Party of the Soviet Union is the Party congress. Regular congresses are convened by the Central Committee not less often than once every four years. Convocation of a Party congress and the agenda are announced at least one and one-half months before the congress. Extraordinary congresses are convened by the Party Central Committee on its own initiative or on the demand of not less than one-third of the total Party membership represented at the preceding Party congress. Extraordinary congresses are convened on two months' notice. A congress is considered valid if no less than one-half of the total Party membership is represented at it.

The norms of representation at the Party congress are fixed by the Central Committee.

32. If no extraordinary congress is convened by the Party Central Committee within the term indicated in Art. 31, the organizations demanding the convocation of an extraordinary congress have the right to form an organizational committee possessing the rights of the Party Central Committee to convene an extraordinary congress.

33. The congress:

(a) hears and approves reports of the Central Committee, the Central Inspection Commission, and other central organizations;

(b) reviews, amends, and approves the Program and Statutes of the Party;

(c) determines the line of the Party on questions of domestic and foreign policy and considers and decides major questions of communist construction;

(d) elects the Central Committee and the Central Inspection Commission.

34. The number of members of the Central Committee and the Central Inspection Commission is determined and their members are elected by the congress. In the event of vacancies in the membership of the Central Committee, they are filled from among the candidate members of the Central Committee of the CPSU elected by the Congress.

35. In the intervals between congresses, the Central Committee of the Communist Party of the Soviet Union directs the entire work of the Party and local Party bodies; selects and places executive cadres; directs the work of central state organizations and public organizations of the working people through the Party groups within them; creates various agencies, institutions, and enterprises of the Party and directs their work; appoints the editorial boards of central newspapers and magazines that function under its control; and distributes the funds of the Party budget and supervises its implementation.

The Central Committee represents the CPSU in its relations with other parties.

36. The Central Committee of the CPSU keeps Party organizations regularly informed about its work.

37. The Central Inspection Commission checks on the promptness of the conduct of affairs in central bodies of the Party and audits the treasury and undertakings of the Central Committee of the CPSU.

38. The Central Committee of the CPSU holds not less than one plenary session every six months. Candidate members of the Central Committee attend plenary sessions of the Central Committee with the right to a consultative vote.

39. The Central Committee of the Communist Party of the Soviet Union elects a Presidium to direct the work of the Central Committee between plenary sessions and a Secretariat to direct current work, chiefly in the selection of cadres and organization of checkup on fulfillment; it creates a Bureau of the CPSU Central Committee for the Russian Republic.

40. The Central Committee of the Communist Party of the Soviet Union organizes a Party Control Committee under the Central Committee.

The Party Control Committee under the Party Central Committee:

(a) verifies the observance of Party discipline by members and candidate members of the CPSU; calls to account Communists guilty of violating the Party Program and Statutes or Party and state discipline, as well as violators of Party ethics;

(b) examines appeals against decisions of the Central Committees of the Union-republic Communist Parties and of territory and province Party committees concerning expulsion from the Party and Party penalties.

V. The Republic, Territory, Province, Region, City, and District Organizations of the Party

41. The republic, territory, province, region, city, and district Party organizations and their committees are guided in their work by the Program and Statutes of the CPSU; carry out within the limits of the republic, territory, province, region, city, or district the entire work of implementing Party policy; and organize execution of the directives of the Central Committee of the CPSU.

42. The chief duties of republic, territory, province, region, city, and district Party organizations and their executive bodies are:

(a) political and organizational work among the masses and their mobilization for accomplishment of the tasks of communist construction, for all-round development of industrial and agricultural production, and for the fulfillment and overfulfillment of state plans; concern for a steady rise in the living standard and cultural level of the working people;

(b) organization of ideological work; propaganda of Marxism-Leninism; increasing the communist awareness of the working people; guidance of the local press, radio, and television; supervision of the work of cultural-enlightenment institutions;

(c) guidance of the Soviets, trade unions, the Young Communist League, cooperative enterprises, and other public organizations through the Party groups within them; and ever broader enlistment of the working people in the work of these organizations; development of the initiative and activeness of the masses as a necessary condition for the gradual transition from a socialist state system to communist public self-government.

Party organizations do not supplant Soviet, trade union, cooperative, and other public organizations of the working people and must not permit a merging of the functions of Party and other agencies or unnecessary parallelism in work;

(d) selection and placement of executive cadres and the rearing of them in a spirit of communist ideology, honesty, and truthfulness and a high sense of responsibility to the Party and the people for the work entrusted to them;

(e) broad enlistment of Communists in the conduct of Party work as unsalaried workers, as a form of public activity;

(f) organization of various institutions and enterprises of the Party within the bounds of their republic, territory, province, region, city, or district and guidance of their work; distribution of Party funds within their organizations; systematic reporting to the higher Party body and accountability to it for their work.

The Executive Bodies of Republic, Territory, and Province Party Organizations. 43. The highest body of the province, territory, or republic

Party organization is the province or territory Party conference or the congress of the Union-republic Communist Party, and in the intervals between them the province committee, the territory committee, or the Central Committee of the Union-republic Communist Party.

44. A regular province or territory conference or regular congress of a Union-republic Communist Party is convened by the province or territory committee or the Central Committee of the Union-republic Communist Party once every two years, and extraordinary sessions by decision of the province or territory committee or the Central Committee of the Union-republic Communist Party or upon the demand of one-third of the total number of members of the organizations belonging to the province, territory, or republic Party organization. Congresses of the Communist Parties of the Union republics having province divisions (the Ukraine, Belorussia, Kazakhstan, and Uzbekistan) may be held once in four years.

The norms of representation at the province or territory conference or congress of a Union-republic Communist Party are fixed by the given Party committee.

The province or territory conference or congress of a Union-republic Communist Party are fixed by the given Party committee.

The province or territory conference or congress of a Union-republic Communist Party hears the reports of the province or territory committee or the Central Committee of the Union-republic Communist Party and of the inspection commission; discusses at its own discretion other questions of Party, economic, and cultural work; and elects the province or territory committee or Central Committee of the Union-republic Communist Party, the inspection commission, and delegates to the congress of the CPSU.

45. Each province and territory committee and Central Committee of a Union-republic Communist Party elects a bureau, which includes the secretaries of the committee. Party membership of not less than five years is compulsory for secretaries. The plenary sessions of the committees also approve the chairmen of Party commissions, the heads of the departments of these committees, and the editors of Party newspapers and magazines.

Secretariats may be set up in the province and territory committees and Central Committees of the Union-republic Communist Parties to handle current questions and check on fulfillment.

46. The plenary session of the province committee, territory committee, or Central Committee of the Union-republic Communist Party is convened not less than once in four months.

47. The province committees, territory committees, and Central Committees of the Union-republic Communist Parties direct the region, city, and district Party organizations, check on their work, and periodically hear the reports of the region, city, and district Party committees.

The Party organizations of the autonomous republics, as well as of autonomous and other provinces within territories and Union republics, work under the direction of the territory committees or the Central Committees of the Union-republic Communist Parties.

The Executive Bodies of the Region, City, and District (Rural and Urban) Party Organizations. 48. The highest body of the region, city, or district Party organization is the region, city, or district Party conference or the general meeting of Communists convened by the region, city, or district committee not less than once in two years, and the extraordinary conference convened by decision of the committee or on demand of one-third of the total number of members of the Party in the given Party organization.

The region, city, or district conference (meeting) hears the reports of the committee and the inspection commission; discusses at its own discretion other questions of Party, economic, and cultural work; and elects the region, city, or district committee, the inspection commission, and the delegates to the province or territory conference or congress of the Union-republic Communist Party.

The norms of representation at the region, city, or district conference are fixed by the given Party committee.

49. Each region, city, or district committee elects a bureau, which includes the secretaries of the committee, and also approves the heads of the departments of the committee and the editors of newspapers. Party membership of at least three years is compulsory for secretaries of a region, city, or district committee. The secretaries of the committees are approved by the province committee, territory committee, or Central Committee of the Union-republic Communist Party.

50. The region, city, and district committees organize and approve the primary Party organizations, direct their work, periodically hear reports on the work of the Party organizations, and keep the records of the Communists.

51. The plenary session of the region, city, or district committee is convened not less than once in three months.

52. The region, city, or district committee has unsalaried instructors, sets up permanent or temporary commissions for various questions of Party work, and employs other forms of enlisting Communists in the work of the Party committee as a public duty.

VI. Primary Organizations of the Party

53. The primary organizations are the foundations of the Party.

The primary Party organizations are set up at the places of work of Party members—at plants, factories, state farms, and other enterprises; collective farms; units of the Soviet Army; offices; educational institutions, etc., wherever there are no fewer than three Party members. Primary Party organizations may also be set up on a territorial basis at the places of residence of Communists in villages or in apartment house administrations.

54. At enterprises, collective farms, and offices where there are more than fifty Party members and candidate members, Party organizations may be set up within the over-all primary Party organization in shops, sectors,

livestock sections, brigades, departments, etc, with the authorization of the district, city, or region Party committee.

Party groups by brigades and other production units may be set up within shop organizations, sector organizations, etc., and also within primary Party organizations with fewer than fifty members and candidate members.

55. The highest body of the primary Party organization is the Party meeting, which is held not less than once a month.

In large Party organizations with more than 300 Communists, the general Party meeting is convened when necessary at times fixed by the Party committee or on the demand of several shop Party organizations.

56. The primary or shop Party organization elects a bureau for a term of one year to conduct current work; the number of its members is fixed by the Party meeting. Primary and shop Party organizations with fewer than fifteen Party members elect a secretary and an assistant secretary of the Party organization instead of a bureau.

At least one year's membership in the Party is compulsory for secretaries of primary and shop Party organizations.

Full-time paid Party posts are as a rule not set up in primary Party organizations embracing fewer than 150 Party members.

57. In large enterprises and institutions with more than 300 Party members and candidate members, and also in organizations with more than 100 Communists in cases where special production conditions or geographical dispersion makes it necessary, Party committees may be set up, with the authorization of the province or territory Party committee or the Central Committee of the Union-republic Communist Party; the shop Party organizations of these enterprises and institutions are granted the rights of primary Party organizations.

The Party organizations of collective farms that have fifty Communists may set up Party committees.

The Party committee is elected for a term of one year, and the number of its members is fixed by the general Party meeting or conference.

58. The primary Party organization is guided in its work by the Program and Statutes of the CPSU. It conducts work directly among the working people, rallies them around the Communist Party of the Soviet Union, and organizes the masses for carrying out the Party's policy and for the struggle to build communism.

The primary Party organization:

(a) admits new members to the CPSU;

(b) rears Communists in a spirit of devotion to the cause of the Party, ideological conviction, and communist ethics;

(c) organizes the study by Communists of Marxist-Leninist theory in close connection with the practice of communist construction, and opposes any attempts at revisionist distortions of Marxism-Leninism and at its dogmatic interpretation;

(d) concerns itself with enhancing the vanguard role of Communists in labor and in the sociopolitical and economic life of the enterprise, collective farm, office, educational institution, etc.;

(e) acts as the organizer of the working people in carrying out routine tasks of communist construction; heads socialist competition for the fulfillment of state plans and pledges of the working people; mobilizes the masses for disclosing and making better use of the internal reserves of enterprises and collective farms and for widely introducing in production the achievements of science, technology, and the experience of leading workers; works for the strengthening of labor discipline and for a steady rise in labor productivity and an improvement of quality of output; shows concern for protecting and increasing public wealth at enterprises and state and collective farms;

(f) conducts mass agitation and propaganda work; rears the masses in the spirit of communism; helps the working people to develop skills in administering state and public affairs;

(g) on the basis of broad development of criticism and self-criticism, combats manifestations of bureaucracy, localism, and violations of state discipline; thwarts attempts to deceive the state; takes measures against laxity, mismanagement, and waste at enterprises, collective farms, and institutions;

(h) assists the region, city, and district Party committees in all their activity and accounts to them for its work.

The Party organization must see to it that every Communist observes in his own life and inculcates in the working people the moral principles set forth in the Program of the CPSU, in the moral code of the builder of communism:

devotion to the cause of communism, love of the socialist homeland, of the socialist countries;

conscientious labor for the good of society: He who does not work, neither shall he eat;

concern on the part of everyone for the preservation and growth of public wealth;

a high sense of public duty, intolerance of violations of the public interest;

collectivism and comradely mutual assistance: One for all and all for one;

humane relations and mutual respect among people: Man is to man a friend, comrade, and brother;

honesty and truthfulness, moral purity, guilelessness, and modesty in public and private life.

mutual respect in the family and concern for the upbringing of children;

an uncompromising attitude to injustice, parasitism, dishonesty, careerism, and money-grubbing;

friendship and brotherhood of all peoples of the U.S.S.R., intolerance of national and racial animosity;

an uncompromising attitude to the enemies of communism, peace, and the freedom of peoples;

fraternal solidarity with the working people of all countries and with all peoples.

59. Primary Party organizations of production and trade enterprises, state and collective farms, and planning organizations, design bureaus, and research institutions directly connected with production have the right to supervise the work of the administration.

The Party organizations of ministries, state committees, economic councils, and other central and local Soviet and economic institutions and agencies, which do not have the function of supervising the work of the administration, must actively promote improvement of the work of the apparatus, foster among the personnel a high sense of responsibility for the work entrusted to them, take measures to strengthen state discipline and improve services to the public, vigorously combat bureaucracy and red tape, and inform the proper Party bodies in good time about shortcomings in the work of the institutions as well as of individuals, regardless of the posts they occupy.

VII. The Party and the Young Communist League

60. The All-Union Leninist Young Communist League is an independent public organization of young people, an active assistant and reserve of the Party. The Young Communist League helps the Party to rear young people in the spirit of communism, to enlist them in the practical work of building a new society, and to train a generation of harmoniously developed people who will live, work, and direct public affairs under communism.

61. Young Communist League organizations enjoy the right of broad initiative in discussing and submitting to the appropriate Party organizations questions of the work of an enterprise, collective farm, or institution. They must be really active champions of Party directives in all spheres of communist construction, especially where there are no primary Party organizations.

62. The YCL works under the guidance of the Communist Party of the Soviet Union. The work of local YCL organizations is directed and supervised by the appropriate republic, territory, province, region, city, and district Party organizations.

In their work in the communist education of young people, local Party bodies and primary Party organizations rely on Young Communist League organizations and support and disseminate their useful undertakings,

63. YCL member who are admitted to the Party leave the Young Communist League from the moment they join the Party, unless they occupy executive posts in Young Communist League organizations.

VIII. Party Organizations in the Soviet Army

64. Party organizations in the Soviet Army are guided in their activity by the Program and Statutes of the CPSU and function on the basis of instructions approved by the Central Committee.

The Party organizations of the Soviet Army ensure the implementation of Party policy in the armed forces; rally their personnel around the Communist Party; educate servicemen in the spirit of the ideas of Marxism-Leninism and selfless devotion to the socialist homeland; actively help to strengthen the unity of the army and the people; show concern for strengthening military discipline; and mobilize personnel for fulfilling the tasks of combat and political training, mastering new equipment and weapons, and irreproachably carrying out their military duty and the orders and instructions of the command.

65. The guidance of Party work in the armed forces is exercised by the Central Committee of the CPSU through the Chief Political Administration of the Soviet Army and Navy, which functions with the powers of a department of the Central Committee of the CPSU.

Party membership of five years is compulsory for the heads of the political administrations of military districts and fleets and the heads of the political departments of armies, and Party membership of three years for the heads of the political departments of military units.

66. The Party organizations and political bodies of the Soviet Army support close contact with local Party committees and keep them periodically informed about political work in the military units. The secretaries of military Party organizations and the heads of political bodies participate in the work of the local Party committees.

IX. Party Groups in Non-Party Organizations

67. Party groups are organized at congresses, conferences, and meetings convened by Soviet, trade union, cooperative, and other mass organizations of the working people as well as in the elective bodies of these organizations where there are at least three Party members. The task of these groups is to strengthen the influence of the Party in every way and to carry out its policy among non-Party people, to strengthen Party and state discipline, to combat bureaucracy, and to check on the fulfillment of Party and Soviet directives.

68. Party groups are subordinate to the appropriate Party bodies: the Central Committee of the Communist Party of the Soviet Union, the Central Committee of the Union-republic Communist Party, or the territory, province, region, city, or district Party committee.

In all matters the Party groups must be guided strictly and undeviatingly by the decisions of the executive Party bodies.

X. Party Funds

69. The financial resources of the Party and its organizations consist of membership dues, revenue from Party undertakings, and other revenue.

70. The monthly membership dues for Party members and candidate members are established as follows.

Monthly earnings	Dues
up to 50 rubles	10 kopeks
from 51 to 100 rubles	0.5 per cent of monthly earnings
from 101 to 150 rubles	1.0 per cent of monthly earnings
from 151 to 200 rubles	1.5 per cent of monthly earnings
from 201 to 250 rubles	2.0 per cent of monthly earnings
from 251 to 300 rubles	2.5 per cent of monthly earnings
over 300 rubles	3.0 per cent of monthly earnings

71. An initiation fee in the amount of 2 per cent of monthly earnings is assessed upon admission as a candidate member of the Party.

CHANGES IN THE STATUTES

RESOLUTION OF THE TWENTY-THIRD CONGRESS OF THE COMMUNIST PARTY OF THE SOVIET UNION ON PARTIAL CHANGES IN THE CPSU STATUTES *

The Twenty-third Congress of the Communist Party of the Soviet Union resolves to make the following changes in the CPSU Statutes:

1. For the purpose of further improving the qualitative composition of those admitted to the CPSU and raising the responsibility of Party organizations for the admission into the Party of new members, to establish that:

(a) young persons up to twenty-three years of age inclusive may join the Party only via the Young Communist League. YCL members entering the CPSU shall submit a recommendation from a district or city YCL committee, which is equal to the recommendation of one Party member.

(b) Persons recommending applicants for admission to the Party must have a Party standing of not less than five years;

(c) a decision of a primary Party organization on admission to the Party shall be considered adopted if not fewer than two-thirds of the Party members present at the meeting vote for it.

2. Proceeding from the tasks of further strengthening Party discipline and raising the responsibility of Communists for the fulfillment of statutory obligations:

(a) to supplement the introductory section of the Statutes with a provision that the Party rids itself of persons who violate the CPSU Program and Statutes and who by their behavior compromise the lofty title of Communist;

(b) to establish that a decision of a primary Party organization on the expulsion of a Communist from the Party becomes valid once it has been approved by a district or city Party committee;

* *Pravda*, April 9, 1966. Translation copyright 1966 by *The Current Digest of the Soviet Press*, published weekly at The Ohio State University by the American Association for the Advancement of Slavic Studies; reprinted by permission of *The Digest*. Translation appeared in Vol. XVIII, No. 15 (1966), pp. 9 and 43, of *The Digest*.

(c) to abolish the transfer of a Party member to the status of a candidate member as a Party penalty.

3. In view of the proposals of many Party bodies and Communists, and taking into consideration that in Party elections the membership of Party committees is regularly renewed, depending on specific local conditions and also upon the work and political qualities of the officials, and that the regulations on these questions have not justified themselves in practice, it is considered inexpedient to retain in the CPSU Statutes the provisions determining the norms of renewal and turnover of the composition of Party bodies and the secretaries of Party organizations. In this connection, paragraph 25 of the Statutes is canceled. Paragraph 24 is supplemented with the provision that in elections to all Party bodies, from the primary organizations to the CPSU Central Committee, the principle of systematic renewal of their composition and of the continuity of leadership is observed.

4. The section of the Statutes on the Primary Party organizations is supplemented with a new paragraph stipulating that the Party committees of primary Party organizations numbering more than 1,000 Communists may, with the permission of the Central Committee of the Communist Party of the Union republic, be granted the rights of a district Party committee on questions concerning admission to the CPSU, registration of Party members and candidate members, and review of the personal affairs of Communists. Within these organizations, in the necessary cases, Party committees may be created in the shops, while the Party organizations of production sectors may be granted the rights of a primary organization. Party committees that are granted the rights of a district Party committee are elected for a period of two years.

5. Paragraph 57 of the Statutes is supplemented with a provision that Party committees may be set up on state farms if there are fifty Communists.

6. Taking into consideration the proposals of Party organizations that the CPSU Statutes should provide for greater differentiation in the holding of meetings in the primary organizations, depending on the conditions of their work, structure, and size, it is established that in primary Party organizations that number up to 300 Communists and have shop organizations, a general party meeting is to be held at least once every two months.

7. It is stipulated in the Statutes that congresses of the Communist Parties of all the Union republics are to be held at least once every four years.

8. It is provided in the Statutes that in the period between Party congresses the Central Committee may as necessary convene an All-Union Party Conference to discuss urgent questions of Party policy, and the Central Committees of the Communist Parties of the Union republics may call republic Party conferences.

The procedure for holding an All-Union Party Conference is determined by the CPSU Central Committee and for holding republic Party conferences by the Central Committees of the Communist Parties of the Union republics.

9. It is stipulated in the Statutes that the Central Committee of the Communist Party of the Soviet Union elects a Politburo to guide the work of the Party between plenary sessions of the Central Committee; and a Secretariat to guide current work, chiefly the selection of cadres and organization of checkups on fulfillment. The Central Committee elects a General Secretary of the CPSU Central Committee.

The provision in paragraph 39 of the Statutes that the Central Committee creates a Bureau of CPSU Central Committee for the Russian Republic is deleted.

10. The reference to economic councils in paragraph 59 of the Statutes is deleted.

RESOLUTION OF THE TWENTY-FOURTH CONGRESS OF THE COMMUNIST PARTY OF THE SOVIET UNION ON PARTIAL CHANGES IN THE CPSU STATUTES*

The Twenty-fourth Congress of the Communist Party of the Soviet Union resolves:

1. To establish that:

(a) regular congresses of the Communist Party of the Soviet Union are to be convened by the Central Committee at least once every five years;

(b) regular congresses of the Union-republic Communist Parties are to be convened by the Communist Party Central Committees at least once every five years;

(c) regular territory, province, regional, city, and district Party conferences are to be convened by the respective Party committees twice during the five-year period between CPSU congresses, i.e., every two or three years;

(d) report-and-election meetings (conferences) in primary Party organizations having Party committees are to be held once every two or three years, in accordance with the time periods of the convocation of district and city Party conferences. In other primary Party organizations and in shop Party organizations, report-and-election meetings are to be held every year.

2. For the purpose of further increasing the responsibility and activeness of the primary Party organizations in the implementation of the Party's policy and intensifying their organizational and upbringing work in the collectives of working people:

(a) to extend the clause of the CPSU Statutes on the right of control over the activity of administration to the primary Party organizations of all design organizations, design bureaus, research institutes, educational

* *Pravda*, April 10, 1971. Translation copyright 1971 by *The Current Digest of the Soviet Press*, published weekly at The Ohio State University by the American Association for the Advancement of Slavic Studies; reprinted by permission of *The Digest*. Translation appeared in Vol. XXIII, No. 17 (1971), p. 129, of *The Digest*.

establishments, and cultural-enlightenment, medical, and other institutions and organizations the functions of whose administration do not extend beyond their collectives.

With respect to the Party organizations of ministries, state committees, and other central and local Soviet and economic institutions and departments, it is determined that they exercise control over the work of the apparatus in fulfilling the directives of the Party and the government in the observance of Soviet laws;

(b) to establish that when necessary and with the permission of the province or territory Party committee or the Union-republic Communist Party Central Committee, primary Party organizations can be created within the framework of several enterprises that form a production association and are located, as a rule, on the territory of one borough of a single city;

(c) to permit province and territory Party committees and Union-republic Communist Party Central Committees to form, in individual cases in Party organizations with more than 500 Communists, Party committees in large shops, and to grant the rights of primary Party organizations to the Party organizations of production sectors.

3. To make partial changes in the text of the present Party Statutes in accordance with this resolution.

* * *

8

THE SOVIET CENTRAL COMMITTEE: AN ELITE ANALYSIS

MICHAEL P. GEHLEN AND MICHAEL McBRIDE

This paper is a study of the backgrounds of the members of the Central Committee of the Communist Party of the Soviet Union. The purpose of its first part is to present and interpret certain quantitative material concerning the background characteristics of the members of the Central Committee. The conclusion elaborates premises regarding the function of co-optation in the higher Party organs and suggests possible relationships of this function to the education and career experiences of the Central Committee membership as discussed in the first part. To pursue an ideal study of this type, we recognize that extensive interviews and depth exploration of the sociological histories of the members would be desirable. In the case of the Soviet political elite such a course is obviously not possible at the present time. Nevertheless, sufficient data exist to make a modest beginning toward what we hope will help to lay a foundation for more extensive analysis of elites in the Soviet system in the future.

Two basic assumptions underlie our interest in the backgrounds of the Soviet political elite. First, and more important for this paper, is the premise that persons are co-opted into the Central Committee primarily, though not exclusively, as a result of the group associations they have made during the courses of their careers. These associations are largely career associations, and most of the members become part of the elite of important functional groups before they become members of the Party elite. Educational backgrounds, age, Party status, role associations, occupation, and other factors all converge to influence the development of the careers of the members. Our concern is with the general patterns of these and related variables among the total membership of the Central Committee.

Reprinted, by permission of the publisher and authors, from *The American Political Science Review* 62, No. 4 (December, 1968): 1232–41.

A second and corollary premise is that the attitudes and value orientations of individual members are shaped in significant part by these background factors, especially by education, occupation, and role associations. This assumption, of course, opens the Pandora's box of how to determine ideological influence. More to the point here, however, the premise is intended to underscore the belief that many members are co-opted precisely because of their different backgrounds and career associations in order to bring people of varying experience, perceptions, and abilities toward the center of the decisional processes. This premise is predicated on the view that the Central Committee of the CPSU has become a composite of the representatives of key functional groups and is the principal medium, either through individual members or as a collective, through which the members of the Politburo regularly exchange information with the elites of the major interests in the system. Co-optation is viewed here as a rational process of attaining group representation in order to facilitate the communications flow between the principal decision-makers and the functional groups of Soviet society and to integrate group elites into the Party-dominated system. Co-optation, therefore, is interpreted as having both representative and regulatory functions. In short, we see the membership selection and function of the Central Committee as an institutionalization of a high-level communications network.

I. Findings on Biographical Characteristics

The empirical portion of this study consists of the examination of background factors of members of the Central Committee selected at the Twenty-third Congress of the Communist Party of the Soviet Union, held in 1966. The data were collected from written sources, primarily from *Who's Who in the USSR*, other information made available by the Institute for the Study of the U.S.S.R. in Munich, and official Soviet sources.[1] Of the 195 full members, sufficient information was obtained on 184. Of the 165 candidate members, similar information was available on 125. The basic total population of the sample therefore is 309, although in some categories information was available on a larger number of candidates.

The data collected on the 309 members were classified into twenty-eight variables. Among the more important were date of birth, level of education, source of education, the learned occupation, the practiced occupation, date of admission to the CPSU, date of admission to the Central Committee, record of Party work, occupational status before and after

[1] The most accessible source of biographical data is *Who's Who in the USSR*, 1965–1966, compiled by the Institute for the Study of the U.S.S.R., Munich, Germany, and published by the Scarecrow Press, Inc., 1966. Additional information is available in the files of the Institute. Short but current biographical sketches are published in the *Ezhegodnik* (Yearbook) of the *Great Soviet Encyclopedia*. More extensive biographies, though sometimes less up to date, are found in the biographical dictionaries produced at different times by different professional groups (scientists, engineers, and so forth) in the U.S.S.R.

1953, and region of residency. Insufficient data made some variables impossible to use. These were population of place of birth, region of birth, social class of parents, and recent technological education or retooling. Others, which will be considered later, proved of only limited value. After the data were assembled, frequency distributions were made of all variables and their subdivisions. Then a correlation matrix was employed in order to ascertain patterns of interrelatonships between pairs of variables.

Age and Sex. Examination of age and sex of the members of the Central Committee (CC) reveals what one might expect. The full members were slightly older than the candidates, but the average age of both groups fell into the fifty-four–to–sixty age category. Thirty-eight and six-tenths per cent of the full members and 22.6 per cent of the candidates were born in the decade 1900–1909, while 45.7 per cent of the former and 52.4 per cent of the latter were born between 1910 and 1919. Only one person in each group was born after 1930, and only eleven of the full members and seven of the candidates were born before 1900. In 1967, the average age of the full members was fifty-seven and that of the candidate was slightly under fifty-five. These figures indicate that the newly elected members kept the average age at about the same level as it had been for the CC elected in 1961.[2] (At that time 58.5 per cent of the total membership had been born in the decade 1900–1909.) The overwhelming number of both types of members were male. Only five full members and five candidates were women (two of the candidates for whom biographical data were unavailable were also women).

Education. The level of education of the CC membership continued to show a gradual increase, as did the tendency to co-opt persons who had basically a specialized higher educaton. Table 8–1 indicates the level of education attained by the members. These figures may be compared with those representing the source of the highest degree attained by the member (Table 8–2). These two tables indicate a slight decline in the number of persons educated at universities and military academies from the CC elected in 1961. There was a simultaneous increase in the number that had Party schools as their only source of higher education. In regard to the technically trained, there was an increase in both number and percentage in the ranks of the full members—from 58 to 61 per cent. However, there was a substantial decrease in technical education among the candidates. This number dropped from eighty-three to sixty-four, while the size of the candidate ranks was being increased. The percentage of those so classified declined from 53.4 per cent to 38.8 per cent. The reasons for this shift among the candidate membership toward more exclusive education in Party schools and less technical education was probably to provide compensation to the so-called reds, or more ideolog-

[2] References to the background characteristics of the Central Committee membership between 1961 and 1966 are based on Michael P. Gehlen, "The Educational Backgrounds and Career Orientations of the Members of the Central Committee of the CPSU," *The American Behavioral Scientist* 9 (April, 1966): 11–14.

ically oriented members, while the "experts" were being rewarded with full membership.

Occupation. An important aspect of education is the learned occupation. The frequency of this variable was also tabulated with the related

Table 8–1. Level and Types of Education

	Full Members		Candidate Members	
	No.	%	No.	%
University	17	9.3	11	8.8
Party school anly	8	4.4	15	12.0
Military academy	15	8.1	10	8.0
Technical *	120	65.2	64	51.2
Secondary	4	2.2	2	1.6
Other	1	.5	0	0.0
No data/none reported	19	10.3	23	18.4
Totals	184	100	125	100

* Technical includes institutes, polytechnical schools, and specialized academies other than military.

Table 8–2. Source of Highest Degree

	Full Members		Candidate Members	
	No.	%	No.	%
University	14	7.6	9	7.2
Party schools	32	17.4	28	22.4
Military academy	16	8.7	10	8.0
Technical	100	54.4	49	39.2
Secondary	4	2.2	2	1.6
No data/none reported	18	9.7	27	21.6
Totals	184	100	125	100

Table 8–3. Learned Occupation
(percentage of number known)

	Full Members	Candi- dates	Total
Engineering	42.1	30.3	37.5
Science & mathematics	5.6	3.0	4.7
Agronomy	18.5	16.2	17.5
Military	8.3	14.1	10.6
Arts & letters	12.7	16.2	14.0
Other (mostly Party training)	12.8	20.2	15.7
Totals	100	100	100

factor of the occupation practiced by the CC members during the early parts of their careers. Table 8–3 lists the percentages of the membership in the principal categories of learned occupations. The information in this table corresponds fairly closely with the occupations practiced by the members of the CC in the early parts of their careers. Table 8–4 provides the later information, indicating the slightly higher percentage of people drawn immediately into Party work than were specifically educated for that purpose. This practice was quite probably the result of the need to fill Party posts that were associated with some productive function (e.g., factory or kolkhoz management) that demanded technical competence.

It is suggestive from the principal occupational lines followed during the bulk of their careers that the "learned" occupations of the CC members were only selectively significant. Scientists had obviously been trained as scientists, for example, but Party workers came from a variety of educational backgrounds. In order to ascertain the career orientations pursued by individuals over a longer-term period than was indicated in Table 8–4, occupational status was examined in two parts: first, the career orientation of each member before 1953 and, second, the career orientation after 1953. The 1953 was chosen as the dividing line between Stalinist and post-Stalinist Russia, so that any significant variation in career patterns and in means of mobility might be more accurately assessed. Career orientation was determined by the number of years a CC member had spent in a particular type of occupation. Table 8–5 presents the data collected on the occupational status of full members, and Table 8–6 presents the data for candidate members.

The most striking difference between the occupational associations of the full members before and after 1953 is the sharp increase in apparatus assignments from 40 per cent to 54.9 per cent. This very strongly suggests the importance of ties with the apparatus for upward mobility in the higher levels of the Party. Since most of those moving into apparatus posts had devoted most of their careers to economic or cultural activities, the increase also underscores the emphasis placed on experience in a relatively broad range of economic and cultural areas as one condition for the co-optation of nonprofessional aparatchiki into important apparatus positions. The data indicate that about one-third of the members of the Party apparatus in the 1966 Central Committee had built their earlier careers in the economic or cultural bureaucracy or some related unit of Soviet society. In addition, many of those who had been professional aparatchiki from near the outset of their careers had been intensively trained in economic and technological matters in Party schools. As a consequence of these factors, a substantial proportion of the apparatchiki themselves had acquired some measure of expertise or specialization in one or more areas outside of Party administration. The co-optation of such experienced persons into the apparatus suggests an effort on the part of the apparatchiki to enrich their own numbers with highly competent individuals who have succeeded in careers outside the apparatus and to help assure the loyalty of such experienced persons to the role of the apparatus in the system.

The priority given to the continuation of the influence of the Party apparatus and to the development of heavy industry is attested to by the paucity of formal representation accorded persons in light industry

Table 8–4. PRACTICED OCCUPATION
(percentage of number known)

	Full Members	Candi-dates	Total
Engineering	38.0	26.7	33.6
Science & mathematics	4.9	2.8	4.2
Agronomy	16.6	19.4	17.5
Military	9.2	13.2	10.8
Arts & letters	15.3	16.1	15.6
Other (mostly Party work)	16.0	21.8	18.3
Totals	100	100	100

Table 8–5. OCCUPATIONAL STATUS OF FULL MEMBERS

Occupational Status	Before 1953		After 1953	
	No.	%	No.	%
Party apparatchiki	74	40.0	101	54.9
High-level bureaucrats:				
heavy industry	25	13.6	23	12.5
light industry	1	.5	1	.5
agriculture	5	2.7	10	5.4
Low-level bureaucrats:				
heavy industry	15	8.2	0	0.0
light industry	1	.5	0	0.0
agriculture	11	6.0	0	0.0
Other bureaucrats *	5	2.7	12	6.5
Indeterminate †	3	1.6	5	2.7
Military officers	15	8.2	14	7.6
Scientists	4	2.2	4	2.2
Writers	3	1.6	3	1.6
Journalists	1	.5	1	.5
Trade union officers	4	2.2	6	3.3
Workers	3	1.6	2	1.1
Others	2	1.1	2	1.1
No data	12	6.5	—	—
Totals	184	100.0	184	100.0

* Other bureaucrats include those in the cultural, welfare, planning, and security ministries of the government.

† Indeterminate includes those who spent such equal portions of their careers in both Party and state work as to make it impossible to place them in either category.

Table 8–6. Occupational Status of Candidate Members

Occupational Status	Before 1953		After 1953	
	No.	%	No.	%
Party apparatchiki	50	40.0	63	50.4
High-level bureaucrats:				
heavy industry	9	7.2	14	11.2
light industry	4	3.2	5	4.0
agriculture	4	3.2	5	4.0
Low-level bureaucrats:				
heavy industry	4	3.2	0	0.0
light industry	0	0.0	0	0.0
agriculture	4	3.2	1	.8
Other bureaucrats *	3	2.4	7	5.6
Indeterminate †	3	2.4	4	3.2
Military officers	11	7.2	11	8.8
Scientists	3	2.4	3	2.4
Writers	4	3.2	4	3.3
Journalists	3	2.4	2	1.6
Trade union officers	1	.8	4	3.2
Workers	2	1.6	2	1.6
Others	0	0.0	0	0.0
No data	20	16.0	—	—
Totals	125	100	125	100

* Other bureaucrats include those in the cultural, welfare, planning, and security ministries of the government.
† Indeterminate includes those who spent such equal portions of their careers in both Party and state work as to make it impossible to place them in either category.

and in intermediate and lower level bureaucratic positions. The fact that only one full member was associated with light industry both before and after 1953 indicates that careers in that sector of the economy have afforded little opportunity for upward mobility. On the other hand, it should be noted that a small number of the apparatchiki and of those now in the Council of Ministers have developed special competence in the light industry sector.

The same general pattern exists for the candidate membership as for the full members.

Prior Positions. A related point of particular importance is the relationship between the position occupied by an individual and his co-optation into the Central Committee. Examination of the compositions of the Central Committees elected in 1952, 1956, 1961, and 1966 reveals that at least eighty and possibly one hundred of the full members are chosen as a result of their holding particular positions.[3] The figure cannot be

[3] Compilations of the members and their positions at the time of election to the Central Committee are available in *Current Soviet Policies*, Volumes I–IV, published by Columbia University Press and by Praeger Publishers.

more precise, for the size of the Central Committee has tended to increase with each election, thereby making it difficult to ascertain whether the holders of some posts will continue to serve in the CC regardless of their personal identities. In addition to the members of the CPSU Politburo and Secretariat, who are always members of the Central Committee, there are sixty-five or more posts that carry CC membership with them. These include all the first secretaries of the Union-republic Parties, thirty-five or more first secretaries of important provincial Party organizations (Moscow, Leningrad, Kiev, Stalingrad-Volgograd, etc.), and the first secretaries of the Moscow and Leningrad city Party organizations. From the government, the Chairman of the All-Union Council of Ministers—also a member of the Politburo—and at least two First Deputy Chairmen of the Council are members, along with the Ministers and First Deputy Ministers of Defense and Foreign Affairs. Besides these, the chairmen of the republic Councils of Ministers of the Russian Federation, the Ukraine, Belorussia, and probably Georgia and Uzbekistan are Central Committee members. From the mass organization, the First Secretary of the Komsomol and the Chairman of the Trade Union Council are members. Although supporting data come from a rather limited time span, it can be stated that the editor of *Pravda*, the President of the Academy of Sciences, and at least one Deputy Chairman of the Trade Union Council have probably become positions bringing automatic membership in the Central Committee. There have also regularly been other members of the Council of Ministers represented on the Central Committee, but they have not been associated with any particular ministry.

As yet, candidate membership appears to have no such strong association with particular positions, although there are some indications of change in this regard. Perhaps as many as twenty-five provincial Party first secretarial posts have reached the point where they carry with them candidate membership. Some particular types of specialists may consistently be given candidate status, but thus far there is no indication that they are chosen as a result of positions already held. In general, the Party leaders may be expected to have more flexibility in the selection of candidates.

The remaining members and candidate members of the Central Committee are not commonly associated with any special position, although the great majority of them also seem to be selected as a result of a combination of their reputations and positions. The co-optation of certain military officers, scientists, literary figures, journalists, economic planners, and managers of *sovnarkhozy* [economic councils] and industrial and agricultural enterprises round out the representative significance of the institution. Some of these may achieve permanent membership. This is a distinct possibility for marshals in command of crucially stationed troops or the admirals of key fleets. It is certainly less likely for less highly institutionalized professional groups, such as writers and scientists.

The association of some positions with CC membership is undoubtedly a major reason for the relative stability of membership in recent years. Whereas there were at least two fairly sharp turnovers on the CC during the 1950's, the membership has been relatively stable since the election of the CC of 1961. In 1966, 79.4 per cent of the 175 full members from the preceding Central Committee were re-elected, although the size was increased to 195 to allow for the co-optation of additional persons. Only twenty-six living members of the previous Central Committee were not returned. Seventy per cent of the full members had never served as candidates, having been drawn directly into voting status. Twenty-two (12 per cent) had served as candidates in the preceding committee. Seventy-eight per cent were elected in 1956 or later, over one-half of these in 1961.

The candidate membership experienced greater changes in 1966 than the full membership. Here it should be remembered that data were not available on forty of the 165 candidates. The vast majority of these were new admissions. However, the data referred to in this paragraph consist of references only to 129 candidates for whom information could be collected on those variables dealing with candidate status. Of these, fifty-one were elected in 1966, fifty-four in 1961, and six in 1956. In short, over 84 per cent of the 129 reached the Central Committee at or after the Twentieth Party Congress of 1956.

A related matter worthy of attention is that the proportion of apparatchiki and bureaucrats among the full members of the CC of 1966 did not differ significantly from that found in the CC selected in the Twenty-second Party Congress of 1961. On the other hand, the number of bureaucrats in the candidate membership decreased from 29 per cent to 25.6 per cent, while the proportion of apparatchiki increased over 3 per cent. Both the apparatchiki and bureaucrats who were full members immediately prior to the Twenty-third Party Congress were sufficiently entrenched to discourage a serious turnover. The pressure from the conservatives, who apparently were still anxious to prevent a resurgence of Khrushchev-type reformism, was felt more keenly in the candidate membership, where the percentage of bureaucrats and technocrats declined due to an increase in apparatchiki.

Occupational Changes. Of particular interest is the question of who changed occupational classifications after 1953. A total of fifty-four full members, forty-one with technical education, changed job classifications in the post-Stalin years. These figures include twelve for whom there were no data for the years before 1953. Of these twelve, nine had assumed career associations with the Party apparatus after 1953. Sixteen of the others moved from positions in the lower and intermediary levels of the agricultural and industrial bureaucracies into the ranks of the apparatchiki. All but one of these had records of technical education. Six achieved upward mobility in their initial career areas, moving from low-level to high-level bureaucratic positions. No pattern existed among the remaining twenty full members who changed from one job classification to another.

Of the candidate members, twenty changed kinds of positions and another twenty moved from the unclassified (no data) category before 1953 to identifiable posts after that date. Twelve of those unclassified occupied positions in the apparatchiki after 1953. Nine others moved from the low- or middle-level bureaucracy into the Party apparatus, eight of these having had technical education. Eleven others changed kinds of positions without a pattern. Of the forty candidates, there was no information on the educational backgrounds of nineteen, while nineteen others had technical training and two had nontechnical higher education.

Of those occupational associations changed after 1953, there was a primary movement from specialized bureaucratic positions to the Party apparatus and a secondary movement from low-level to high-level positions in the same general occupational category. The primary movement indicates a tendency of the Party to recruit and promote at least partly on the basis of specialized education and experience. The secondary movement of promotion within the ranks of a particular organization is probably typical of non-Party institutional processes. The primary movement is undoubtedly more important as a means of providing the apparatus with the intelligence necessary to exert effective control over non-Party institutions by giving the apparatus groups of experts with previous or continuing association with those institutions.

Place of Residence. Although the place-of-residence factor did not have a significant correlation with the other variables considered, it does indicate the shifting living habits of the Soviet elite. Seventy-eight per cent of the full members and 63 per cent of the candidates listed their current residences in cities of 500,000 or more. Of the total membership, 91 per cent lived in cities of 100,000 or more. Moscow was by far the most widely claimed residence, despite the fact that many who lived there were formally associated with republic Party organizations. Of the full membership, 46 per cent had residences in Moscow, while 44 per cent of the candidates had the same. Also, 65 per cent of the full members and 62 per cent of the candidates resided in the Russian Federation, with the Ukraine and the Central Asian republics following as the next most widely claimed places of residence.

Party Status. The status of each member in the CPSU is another major area of consideration. Factors examined here are date of admission to the CPSU, the tenure of each member in the Central Committee, and the record of service in the central, republic, and regional Party organs. Then attention will be focused on the backgrounds of the members who were newly elected at the Twenty-third Party Congress.

The record of the dates of admission to Party membership is found in Table 8–7. The large percentage of candidates for whom there is no information suggests that those individuals were admitted fairly recently (at least, postwar) and that they are probably younger than the members for whom there is information. Assuming this is to be the case, well over one-half the candidates were admitted after the great purges of the 1930's. In contrast, about 45 per cent of the full members attained membership prior to or during the great purges. Nevertheless, the old Bolsheviks have almost entirely vanished; only five members of the CC joined the Party prior to the Revolution.

Another aspect of Party status concerns the records of those who had worked as apparatchiki in the Party before being co-opted into the Central Committee. Tables 8–8 and 8–9 indicate the Party status of the CC members before and after 1953. Party status here refers to the level

Table 8–7. DATE OF ADMISSION TO THE CPSU

	Full Members		Candidates	
	No.	%	No.	%
Pre–1917	5	3.7	0	0.0
1918–37	76	41.3	34	27.2
1938–45	88	47.8	62	49.6
1946–52	4	2.2	6	4.8
1953 or after	4	2.2	1	.8
No data	7	3.8	22	17.6
Totals	184	100	125	100

Table 8–8. PARTY OFFICES HELD BY FULL MEMBERS

Office	Before 1953		After 1953	
	No.	%	No.	%
Central apparatus	6	3.4	8	4.4
Central & republic apparatus	1	.5	17	9.2
Republic apparatus	13	7.1	16	8.7
Republic & regional apparatus	17	9.2	31	16.8
Regional apparatus	42	22.8	43	23.4
All three levels	3	1.6	13	7.1
None	102	55.4	56	30.4
Totals	184	100	184	100

Table 8–9. PARTY OFFICES HELD BY CANDIDATE MEMBERS

Office	Before 1953		After 1953	
	No.	%	No.	%
Central apparatus	5	4.0	11	8.8
Central & republic apparatus	0	0.0	6	4.8
Republic apparatus	4	3.2	21	16.8
Republic & regional apparatus	6	4.8	17	13.6
Regional apparatus	34	27.2	36	28.8
All three levels	0	0.0	3	2.4
None	76	60.8	31	24.8
Totals	125	100	125	100

Table 8–10. EDUCATIONAL BACKGROUNDS OF NEW MEMBERS

	Full Members	Candidate Members
Engineering	10	9
Agronomy	7	4
Science	3	2
Military	2	4
Arts & letters	2	7
Party schools only	3	4
No data	11	21
Totals	38	51

Table 8–11. OCCUPATIONS OF NEW MEMBERS

	Full Members		Candidate Members	
	Before 1953	After 1953	Before 1953	After 1953
Apparatchiki	17	23	16	27
High-level bureaucrats	6	8	2	10
Low-level bureaucrats	5	0	1	1
Military officers	2	2	3	5
Writers	0	0	1	1
Journalists	0	0	2	1
Scientists	3	3	2	2
Trade union officers	0	0	1	4
Indeterminate	0	1	0	0
No data	4	0	23	0
Totals	37	37	51	51

of official positions held in the organs of the CPSU. Well over one-half of both the full members and candidates had no record of regular service in Party organs before 1953. In the post-Stalin period this situation was reversed with the reversal being most sharp among the candidates. This information suggests two important possibilties that tend to enforce the findings on occupational backgrounds presented in Tables 8–5 and 8–6. First, many members made themselves accessible to co-optation into the apparatchiki as a means of increasing their upward mobility after having already established themselves in other occupational endeavors. This means that a significant portion of the CC who would now be classified as apparatchiki would not have been so classified during most of their careers. For the most part, they appear to be specialists who demonstrated their abilities as engineers or administrators and were only later drawn into full-time Party work. Second, the turnover in candidate membership in 1966 suggests that some individuals who had been members primarily as a result of their specialization and who had not become apparatchiki were removed from candidacy in favor of those who had given more regular administrative service to Party organs in the past.

New Members. Examination of the backgrounds of the newly elected members can be expected to shed further light on patterns of continuity or change in the membership of the Central Committee. Consequently, the educational backgrounds and careers of the thirty-eight new full members and the fifty-one new candidates are highlighted in Tables 8–10 and 8–11. Of the eighty-nine new members and candidates considered, fifty (56 per cent) had been regularly associated with the Party apparatus after 1953. All but eighteen (20 per cent) had had at least periodic occupational association with the apparatus. This suggests a possible effort on the part of the ruling coalition of the Party to check the influence of the technocrats and to stabilize, if not accelerate, the influence of the apparatchiki in the hierarchy of the CPSU. At the same time it should be emphasized that this effort had more effect on the candidate membership than on the full membership.

II. Correlations

Age. Although there were only about three years separating the average ages of the full and candidate members of the Central Committee, age proved to have statistical importance as a factor influencing other variables and demarking differences between the two classes of membership. Date of birth was related both to the level and to the source of education. Despite the small difference in age, the candidates had had greater access to higher forms of education. The higher correlations for the candidates lead one to assume that a larger number of them were co-opted into the Central Committee on the basis of their specialized training than was the case with the full members, who were often selected on the basis of their positions. In related areas, date of birth had an expectedly high correlation with date of admission to the CPSU. . . . The lower correlation for the candidates indicates a wide distribution of age of admission, thereby reducing, to a modest extent, the importance of age as a significant determinant to admission.

Sex. Sex is an obvious influence on the selection of members when one considers that only five of the 184 full members and five of the 125 candidates for whom informaton was available were women. Elite status in the CPSU is clearly reserved largely for males. What, then, are the factors that help to create the exceptions? For the full members no definite pattern was observed. However, two factors stood out in regard to the women candidates. All five of the latter had records as active members of the Komsomol, working in the apparatus of that organization. and four of the five had careers as apparatchiki. Two of the full members had the same backgrounds. The single exception among the candidates was the Minister of Social Security, who was associated with the state bureaucracy. Only one of the five was newly elected to the Central

Committee. The foregoing factors indicate that those women who were able to overcome the political obstacle created by their sex did so largely through their records as political activists in youth organizations and their willingness to seek careers in the Party apparatus rather than through specialization in technical areas. Moreover, it should be noted that the women tended to be younger than the male members, for the eldest was fifty-six, and two of the ten were in their thirties.

Education. Level and source of education proved to be of greater significance for candidates than for full members, although it was important for both. . . . [The] patterns suggest rather strongly that the candidates were co-opted more for their degree of specialization than the full members. If such is the case, it can be hypothesized that candidate members in the Central Committee elected at the Twenty-third Party Congress were selected because they were thought to provide a communications input into the higher decison-making centers of the CPSU. It appears that the full members, as distinct from the candidates, became less directly associated with the occupational specialty for which they were educated as they moved to higher positions in the political structure.

Regional Factors. . . . Candidacy is used more to give recognition to the geographic divisions and ethnic groups of the U.S.S.R. than full membership. . . . Related to this is the relationship of experience in a large city Party organization to the levels of the Party apparatus in which members of the CC who had such experience worked. These levels were identified by the Party offices that were held in the central, republic, and regional Party organizations. The correlations suggest that work in a city Party organization was more important for the full members than for the candidates in terms of their movement upward in the Party apparatus. It also suggests that the younger full members and most of the candidates had found other means of attaining upward mobility in the system. The days of intense rivalry between the Moscow and Leningrad Party organizations are probably about over, and the importance of association with one or the other has apparently declined despite the increasing tendency to move to the larger cities. This indicator, especially when considered in combination with the background of the members in the Party apparatus, bears out the basic contention that factors other than professional association with the apparatus are of considerable significance in determining the co-optation of persons into the Central Committee, even during a period of conservative reaction to the reformism of the Khrushchev years and even though many of them may be assigned positions in the apparatus after becoming CC members or candidates.

Foreign Travel. Among the other relationships examined, only two merit attention, and these may be only of passing interest. There was no apparent difference between the number of awards and decorations bestowed upon the two classes of CC members. What difference existed can probably be accounted for by the slight age difference. On the other hand, one curious differential may be construed as indicating the greater status of the full members in comparison with the candidates. This factor is foreign travel. There is a positive correlation . . . between full membership and foreign travel and a slight inverse correlation between candidate membership and foreign travel. This may be interpreted as a distinction in status, although it should be pointed out that the number of full members who had had diplomatic experience may have accounted for part of the difference in correlation.

III. Summary and Conclusions

The evidence presented indicates the importance of education to members of the Soviet political elite in terms both of influencing how they launched their careers and of influencing their status in the CPSU. Most of this educational preparation was specialized rather than general, with the four largest categories being engineering, agronomy, Party, and military in that order. Of our sample, 65 per cent (120) of the full members and 51 per cent (64) of the candidates had a technical education (excluding military officers and scientists). The career patterns of the members included 55 per cent (101) of the full members and 50 per cent (63) of the candidates who had primary associations in the Party apparatus after 1953. In addition, 25 per cent (46) of the full members and 26 per cent (32) of the candidates had primary associations with the state bureaucracy (excluding the military). Of those in the bureaucratic category members attached to the heavy industry segment of the state machinery were clearly predominant, with modest representation being given to agricultural administrators and specialists and only token recognition to those associated with light industry.

Despite the fact of considerable experience in the Party apparatus after 1953, a clear majority of both full and candidate members held no Party posts on the central, republic, or regional levels of the apparatus prior to 1953. This was true of 55 per cent (102) of the full members and 60 per cent (64) of the candidates. It was only after 1953—that is, the period during which increasing emphasis was given to co-opting persons into Party leadership positions who had specialized training and experience in some functional service (economics, agronomy, military technology, etc.)—that many of the members were assigned positions, temporarily or otherwise, in various levels of the Party apparatus. During this period all but 30 per cent (56) of the full members and 24 per cent (30) of the candidates held official posts in Party organs.

The correlation study demonstrated a modest though meaningful relationship between degree earned and Party office and between the Party office held by candidates and their occupational status after 1953. These correlations, especially when considered in the light of the data concerning backgrounds in Party posts, and a general survey of the 1956 and 1961 Central Committees support the contention that co-optation is developing largely into a rational process and not merely into a device with which to play games of musical chairs. In short, at least a large percentage, though undoubtedly not all, are drawn into the Central Committee as a result of their knowledge, demonstrated abilities, and occupational role associations. Their presence helps to assure an inflow of information from others with whom the members have occupational associations. It is in the sense of accessibility that the members of the Central Committee may be considered representatives, though certainly at this stage of development they are not equal voting deputies.

The role functions of the persons in the Central Committee, especially their representative role, are closely associated with *who* they are and *why* they were co-opted. The question of who they are is partially answered by the foregoing empirical study. They are persons with key occupational assignments, most of whom had acquired reputations as successes in their respective career specializations. Most are also associated with an important functional group in the Soviet system. To be sure, the evidence presented here does not deal with the difficult and important question of the degree of group solidarity and the extent to which the persons in the same group share or contest particular values. The situation of the apparatchiki, who constitute such a significant pecentage of the membership, is a case in point. The very fact that some of them have joined the apparatus rather late in their careers, that some are in Party posts that require technical training and special skills as well as administrative ability, and that still others have spent their adult lives in Party administration or in propaganda and security organs indicates the range of experiences and attitudes that they may carry into the Central Committee. The point here is simply that most have been associated with particular functional groups that have particular interests. From these associations and interests they can be expected to have acquired specialized knowledge and abilities that influence their perceptions of systemic goals as well as of their own roles in the system.

The question of why they were co-opted relates to the practice of co-optation and the kind of representation they are able to perform. Philip Selznick has argued that organizations adopt two principal mechanisms of defense as means of enhancing the security of the organization in its relation to the social forces around it.[4] These mechanisms are ideology and co-optation. The use of ideology as a device of political socialization in the Soviet system is widely recognized by Western observers. The

---

[4] See Philip Selznick, *TVA and the Grassroots*, University of California Publications in Culture and Society 3:259–61. For other works involving either elite or group analysis, see Bernard M. Bass, *Leadership, Psychology, and Organizational Behavior* (New York: Harper, 1960); Dorwin Cartwright and Alvin Zander, *Group Dynamics: Research and Theory* (Evanston, Ill.: Row, Peterson, 1960); Lewis J. Edinger, *Political Leadership of Industrial Societies* (New York: John Wiley & Sons, 1967); Thomas Gordon, *Group-Centered Leadership* (Boston: Houghton Mifflin, 1955); Morris Janowitz, *The Professional Soldier* (New York: The Free Press of Glencoe, 1960); Harold D. Lasswell, *Power and Personality* (New York: Viking Press, 1948); Dwaine Marvick, *Political Decision-Makers* (New York: The Free Press of Glencoe, 1961); Robert Tannenbaum, *Leadership and Organization: A Behavioral Science Approach* (New York: McGraw-Hill, 1961). For one of the few in-depth analyses of an important segment of the Soviet elite, see John A. Armstrong, *The Soviet Bureaucratic Elite* (New York: Praeger Publishers, 1959).

rational use of co-optation in the system has been noted but not deeply explored. Selznick suggests that there are two types of co-optation: formal and informal. Informal co-optation involves the actual sharing of power by the old elite with the co-opted persons. While this has occurred in the case of the Central Committee in leadership disputes (e.g., the anti-Party crisis of 1957), the actual sharing of power is undoubtedly the exception rather than the rule. On the other hand, the concept of formal co-optation appears to have more meaningful application in analyzing why persons are co-opted into the Central Committee. This mechanism is used to maintain or increase general acceptance of the legitimacy of the Party elite as the highest decision-making authority in the system by establishing definite means of accessibility to key individuals and especially to key groups. This is accomplished by the selection of persons who are part of group elites. Such use of co-optation also consists of selecting persons who are dependable sources of information. The in-flow of knowledge that they bring helps the elite to make more effective operational decisions than they otherwise might make. By co-opting persons on the basis of these two factors—accessibility and communications—the ruling elite may have the advantage of increased stability and information without a complementary loss of power.

The sharing of the symbols of authority, however, opens the door to pressure for a transfer of real power to the co-opted parties. The prevention of this development requires some form of control (Selznick contends informal control) over the co-opted elements. These forces—the sharing of symbols of authority and the placement of controls over those with whom authority is seemingly shared—create tension between representation and participation on the one hand and integration and regulation on the other. Such tension is suggested by the addition of apparatus-associated persons to the Central Committee in 1966 (especially among the candidates) and the corresponding decrease in the more diffuse technocratic contingent. The relative stability of the full membership, however, indicates that certain groups and individuals had acquired representation by right and that only a major conflict would overturn the general balance of forces. Candidacy may be a means of giving ostensible authority and recognition to those less firmly entrenched but ambitious to secure recognition to themselves and those with whom they are professionally associated.

These interpretations must, for the present, be tentative, although they are definitely suggested by the history of the Central Committee since 1956 and by the examination of the backgrounds of the members. The paucity of reliable information on informal channels of communications makes the problem of a more comprehensive empirical study virtually insurmountable for the time being. However, it is our hope that the methods used and the hypotheses set forth in this study will be suggestive to others of related and more comprehensive projects that might be developed in the future.

*   *   *

9

STALIN'S SUCCESSORS

ROBERT CONQUEST

It is common ground that something roughly describable as "re-Staliniza-tion" has been taking place in the Soviet Union over the past five years. More precisely, the present leaders are re-Stalinizing in the sense that they are consolidating the Stalinist institutions (a little shaken by Khrushchev's various reorganizations); preserving the rule of Stalin's cho-sen personnel; restoring the rigor of his doctrines; putting a stop to the exposure of any more indecent facts of Soviet history; and tightening up the ideological and political disciplines required by his system. They are not reinstituting (and are occasionally and mildly deploring) those ele-ments of Stalin's technique which were directing indiscriminate repression against the population. Stalin, to atomize society and build his new system on its ruins, relied on creating total insecurity among friend and foe alike. The present rulers have neither the need nor the will to do this: Only their critics have anything to fear from them. Stalin revolutionized a so-ciety; the present-day "Stalinists" wish to consolidate the new one. The aim is different; but above all the mood is different—a timid (though sometimes panicky) mediocrity has replaced a raging will.

In a world of rapid communication an impression is given of greater cultural unity than anyone would have suggested 100 or 500 years ago. Where every political leader wears trousers, it seems to be felt that basic cultural differences cannot exist as they would have been understood to do between a turban-clad Sultan and a periwigged Hanoverian King. It is always tempting for us to take the unconscious assumptions of our own society as natural and universal. The polity created by Stalin and inherited by the present leaders does not have the norms of our own (though in many respects it *claims* to have them, thus further confusing the outside observer).

The Soviet leaders speak, in however debased a form, one of the political dialects of the West. In it they constantly imply that the main
difference between the United States and the U.S.S.R. is one of social
organization. In reality this has little bearing on the matter—as can perhaps be deduced from the Soviet use of almost identical propaganda
criteria in differentiating between the U.S.S.R. and Yugoslavia and between the U.S.S.R. and the United States. The differences, in reality, are
at basic levels of civic culture and cannot be understood in terms of
"capitalism" and "socialism." (And if socialism has anything to do with
the idea of society exerting some control over the economy, the United
States is more socialist than Russia as well as more capitalistic.)

Understanding the different attitudes of this alien culture is difficult,
but the effort must be made. It depends partly on imagination. It is
always difficult, for example, for us really to grasp in ancient times the
powerful element of inhumanity, of minds entirely closed to the idea that
a slave could have the same feelings as other men. History itself, in the
ordinary sense, cannot give us this feeling: We have to read *Salammbô*.
In the Soviet case, fiction is unnecessary, but we still have to avoid lifeless
general concepts divorced from historical or current reality. . . .

On the sanguine view, the U.S.S.R. is in principle much like any other
country, and if its political principles are at the present time to some
degree aberrant, this is a minor phenomenon, rapidly being overcome by
the forces of convergence, common sense, and the natural law. Close and
concerned observers, on the other hand, see a different picture. Reports
from the Czechoslovak Communist leaders who were taken to Moscow
under arrest after the 1968 invasion all emphasize that, while they had
expected the Soviet leaders to be narrow dogmatists, they were surprised
at their coarseness and thuggishness. Observers in the U.S.S.R. have similar opinions of the low standards and the narrow horizons prevailing.
American readers will, or should, have read Anatole Shub's striking series
in *The Washington Post* last year.[1] The British left-wing *New Statesman's*
even more left-wing East European correspondent, K. S. Karol, writes:

> Stalin's heirs have shown themselves completely incapable of carrying on
> either his mission or his methods. They have forgotten all he previously
> taught them on the art of dividing the opposition, or of dressing up every
> action in plausible doctrinal robes. In a word, they are completely ignorant
> of politics, which they have replaced with plain brute force incapable of
> deceiving even the citizens of their own country.[2]

Karol quotes a Russian who remarked that the Soviet Government had
contrived to antagonize nearly all the nations in the world, and adds that
propaganda attacking, for example, complicity between Mao Tse-tung
and West Germany and between Mao Tse-tung and the "imperialists of
Israel" inspires genuine fear in Russia for its lack of any sense of propor-

[1] Now in book form: Anatole Shub, *The New Russian Tragedy* (New York: Norton,
1969).
[2] *New Statesman*, April 25, 1969.

tion: "Instead of stimulating, it demoralizes an already traumatized and apolitical country."

Roger Garaudy, the noted French Communist recently deposed from the Politburo of the French Communist Party, points out that "the present Soviet leaders" had by 1966 "completely interred the criticism of Stalinism," and gives the reasons:

> The leaders who form the essential framework of the Party and the State were formed by Stalinism and put in position in Stalin's time on the basis of the criteria of the epoch: the acceptance of official dogmas; the fulfillment without discussion, at every level, of directives coming from above; and centralized, bureaucratic and authoritarian functioning.[3]

Andrei Amalrik, in a profound analysis, similarly notes that not merely is the present degree of freedom in the U.S.S.R. minimal compared with what is required of a developed society, and is moreover shrinking, but that the whole concept of "liberalization" is misleading, since it implies some sort of deliberate plan to adapt the Soviet system to modern conditions: "As we know, there was, and there is, no such plan." At the same time he feels that it is equally false to think of the regime making piecemeal concessions to the pressures of society. On the contrary, "the regime regards itself as the acme of perfection and so deliberately does not want to change its ways either of its free will, or, still less, by making concessions to anyone or anything." In so far as relaxation takes place, it is merely a sign of "growing decrepitude," of a decline, in this as in every other field, of the vigor and energy of the ruling caste.[4]

Michel Tatu—long, as the Moscow correspondent of *Le Monde*, the most respected of all direct observers of the Soviet scene—takes a similar view, and sees no way out except through either a disintegration of the system or a reversion to one-man rule, as the result of some form of coup.[5] Garaudy, from his different political position, also sees no hope for the present leadership, and equally no hope of "change of political orientation" except by "the way of an explosion, or of a 'palace revolution.'" And failing any democratic development, he envisions the "bureaucratic-military" leadership perhaps developing into "a reactionary neo-Bonapartism and a dictatorship of the army."

But how does the contrary conception arise? Professor Hugh Seton-Watson, head of London University's School of Slavonic Studies, remarks sardonically that, evidently, "What 200,000 Communist Party officials, from Brezhnev down to the secretaries of party branches in factories or collective farms, tell their subjects is all camouflage. The *real* views of the Soviet leaders are what some nice guy from the Soviet delegation at the U.N. said over a drink or what an itinerant Midwestern scientist heard from some friendly academician in Novosibirsk."[6]

[3] *Le Grand Tournant du Socialisme* (Paris: Gallimard,1969), p. 135.
[4] *Survey*, London, No. 73, pp. 47–79.
[5] *Power in the Kremlin* (London: Collins, 1969), pp. 538–39.
[6] *The Washington Post*, September 14, 1969.

Dr. Ronald Hingley of Oxford University remarks upon a certain type of Westerner who "has seen the bastions of Soviet reaction fall again and again," and "remains permanently poised for the great moment when, somehow, all will change and the dawn of enlightenment, reasonableness, ease and prosperity will suddenly break. . . . In an instant of time (and with luck as the result of a 'summit conference') a new era of sweetness and light will be ushered in on the international and Soviet domestic arena." Hingley comments that basic misapprehensions about the U.S.S.R., almost unknown among specialists in Soviet affairs, are also rare among the ordinary people, being confined to men of fair intelligence. "For it is surely true, if not generally recognized, that real prowess in wrong-headedness, as in most other fields of human endeavor, presupposes considerable education, character, sophistication, knowledge, and will to succeed." [7]

These more or less frivolous, or unconscious, misapprehensions are compounded by certain writers with something resembling a general theory of the "convergence" of the Western and Soviet systems. Both are largely industrial (this view has it), so economic pressures will impel them, and in fact are already impelling them, into an essential similarity.

Of course it is true that economic pressures, like all other living forces in the U.S.S.R., tend constantly against the present system. But there is no evidence, as opposed to sanguine generalities, to show that the present regime is likely to bend to them more than minimally. Their release, when it comes, can hardly be other than as part of a general disintegration of the system. The collective farm system, for example, is quite alien to genuine productive principles and constitutes a vast investment in inefficiency and inadequacy. Yet there is no sign whatever of its abandonment; here, as everywhere, political dogma and political discipline are decisive for the present ruling group.

Rather than examining general probabilities, we must examine the available evidence as to the actual cultural-political content of Soviet society. The political machine Stalin created was designed, among other things, to enable him to impose his will against the natural economic trends. For perhaps the first time in history, a political organization was created that was powerful enough to take on the social forces and break them.

The present leaders started for the most part in humble posts in the newly Stalinized Party of the early 1930's, whose main activity (particularly in the Ukraine) was an almost unbelievably brutal crushing of the peasantry. Most of them made their careers in the great purge of 1936–38, a period when the qualifications required for promotion were denunciation of one's comrades and servility to the Stalin machine.

At the February–March, 1937, plenum of the Central Committee, which marked the final establishment of Stalin's personal autocracy, he told those present that all Party officials should "select, within a certain period, two people in each case, two Party workers capable of being their real substitutes." As it turned out, his estimate was conservative. Through-

[7] *Survey*, London, No. 51, pp. 102–10.

out the country, it was very common for only the third or fourth of a series of Party secretaries—or of army commanders or factory directors—to be holding their positions by the end of the purge. Academician Andrei Sakharov, the atomic scientist, has lately told us that one-half of the Party membership (over 1,200,000) was actually arrested in 1936–39—and that of these only 50,000 ever came out of jail again.[8] Moreover, this casualty rate was highest among those who held any sort of responsible position.

Nor was it possible to rise without full complicity in the terror. A typical instruction put out in April, 1938, made a special call to those conducting the purge not to forget to bring the "silent, politically spineless ones" to account.[9] That is to say, no one could remain in good odor at all without denouncing and exposing "enemies." And we can be quite certain that anyone who rose rapidly must have given particularly acceptable service in this field.

In fact the Brezhnev-Kosygin generation is the actual product of the Stalin terror. The rulers who preceded the present group—Molotov and Malenkov, Khrushchev and Beria—had a record of ruthless brutality. But they had reached positions of influence before the terror. They were its creators rather than its products, Frankensteins rather than Monsters. (Indeed, it was only from them, with their residual independence of mind, that the various attempts at de-Stalinization could come.) This is not an ethical differentiation; the most noticeable change seems to be, rather, that the later generation is far more constricted in imagination, in the ability to look at the world and the ability to conceive new policies. As a victim, and close observer, of the purge pointed out of those who then came up, "They had not even the normal advantages of youth in their favor, for the choosing had been a very negative one. They were men who had denounced others on innumerable occasions. They had bowed the knee whenever they had come up against higher authority. They were morally and intellectually crippled."[10]

To see how these processes took place, how the present leadership was formed, it is worth examining the facts of their political origins in some detail. Leonid Brezhnev became a member of the Communist Party in the Ukraine in 1931, at a time when its main activity was the crushing of the peasantry. The Party membership was mobilized to extract from the peasantry a certain amount of food for export, regardless of whether that left the peasants anything to eat. As one Soviet novelist, Ivan Stadnyuk, has put it, "First the children died, then the men and finally the women." Alexander Solzhenitsyn, in his *The First Circle*, has a peasant describing how earlier in that year someone would drive round the village shouting at each house "Anyone dead?" but later on this was changed to

[8] Andrei D. Sakharov, *Progress, Coexistence and Intellectual Freedom* (New York: W. W. Norton, 1968), pp. 55–56.

[9] Yu. P. Petrov, *Partiinoye Stroitelstvo v Sovietskoy Armii i Floty* (Moscow, 1964), p. 301.

[10] Alexander Weissberg, *Conspiracy of Silence* (London: Hamilton, 1952), p. 364.

"Anyone alive?" Five and a half million is the most probable figure for deaths simply by famine. In all, 10 million peasants were starved, killed, or deported. Party members, and particularly the students among them, were formed into squads to carry out these actions. Brezhnev was at this time a student at the Dneprodzerzhinsk Metallurgical Institute, with previous agricultural experience, and he did his duty.

From 1935 he held a post in a local factory. The Great Purge was just about to begin. From 1936–39 the Ukraine suffered more heavily than almost any other part of the country under Stalin's new super-terror. Of the 1937 Ukrainian Central Committee of 102 members, only three reappeared the following year. The whole Politburo went. All the secretaries of the provincial committees and all their successors disappeared. The entire Ukrainian government was replaced, and then its successors were replaced in their turn. The Party and state virtually ceased to exist except as appendages of the NKVD. The Prime Minister, Lyubchenko, committed suicide with his wife. The First Secretary, Kossior, was shot with his wife and two brothers. Lyubchenko's successor, Bondarenko, and *his* successor, Marchak, were shot. Every profession and every industry were ruthlessly purged. The general commanding the Kiev military district, Yakir, was shot, and so was his successor, Fedko. The head of the opera, Yanovsky, was shot, and the purge raged through the cultural institutes. Of the thirteen secretaries of the Kiev Academy of Sciences who succeeded each other between 1931–38, none was spared. Of the seven principals of Kiev University, one died a natural death and the others were all arrested.

In the factories the same atmosphere prevailed. Dr. Weissberg, who worked with the foundry industry, recalls that usually it was the third or fourth director who kept his place. To please the Party a factory executive of the time required certain qualities. Brezhnev had them. In 1937 he was promoted—to be deputy chairman of the local executive committee (i.e., deputy mayor). In 1938 he became a full-time Party organizer, which at this time bore its own meaning. Starting as head of a department in the Dneprodzerhinsk Province Party Committee, by 1939 he had become its Secretary. By 1950 he was First Secretary in Moldavia, a "republic" formed from territories annexed from Rumania, and noted for a particularly harsh style of Party rule. Stalin appointed him one of the Secretaries of the Central Committee in Moscow in 1952 at the height of the gathering new wave of terror centered on the Doctors' Plot. He was only demoted, for the time being, after Stalin's death.

The present leadership contains a number of other veterans of the Stalin machine in the Ukraine. Andrei Kirilenko's career is very similar. He, too, was a Party member in the Ukraine from 1931 and by 1938 had become Party secretary of a district committee and by 1939 Secretary of the Zaporozhye Province Committee. President Podgorny joined the Communist Party in 1930 and he too worked in the Ukraine from 1931–37, and by 1939, after various promotions, was a Deputy Minister. In 1944 he held for a time the post of plenipotentiary of the Ukrainian Republic in Poland, to supervise the deportation of Soviet citizens.

Outside the Ukraine, the worst-hit area was Leningrad, where (apart from two honorary non-Leningrad figures) *none* of the city's 152 delegates to the 1934 Party congress was there for that of 1939. In 1935 Aleksei Kosygin graduated from the Leningrad Textile Institute, then became a foreman in a textile mill. He advanced his career as a result of the purge, and "played an active role" in Leningrad's Party life as a member of the city's Vyborg District Committee, when the main "activity" was the denunciation and purge of previous secretaries and bureaus. In 1937 he filled a gap left by the purge when he became director of the October Textile Works. In 1938 he moved up to head the Transport-Industry Department of the Leningrad Province Party organization, and then to be Mayor of Leningrad (replacing the executed I. F. Kodatsky), and in January, 1939, was already a People's Commissar in the central government.

Mikhail Suslov worked from 1931 with the disciplinary bodies of the Party and took part in the official Party purges from 1933–34 in the Urals and elsewhere. At Rostov-on-Don, the notorious former NKVD man Yevdokimov was in charge. Even he is said to have protested against the extent of the purges, and he and his colleagues were shot. Suslov became a secretary of the Rostov Province Committee in their wake. He was promoted again and by 1939 was first secretary on another much-purged provincial committee, Stavropol. In this area he covered the Karachai, a Turkic people of the Caucasus. Their deportation *en bloc*, as part of Stalin's genocide policy, came in 1944. It was, of course, a police action, but Suslov seems to have had the immediate political responsibility. We do not know the casualties of the Karachai, but Academician Sakharov has recently told us that in the parallel case of the Crimean Tatars, 46 per cent died, mainly children and old people. Perhaps as a result, Suslov was transferred later in 1944 as one of the three plenipotentiaries reimposing Soviet power in the Baltic states. Suslov got Lithuania, the most difficult of the three, and there supervised the ruthless crushing of the local partisan movement—which, however, continued to fight on after his departure in 1946. In 1947 Stalin made him a Secretary of the Central Committee of the Party, the position he has held ever since.

Kiril Mazurov, a younger man, went into the political administration of the railways in Belorussia in 1938. The railways were among the most purged section of Soviet life. At this time vast nests of "Trotskyite-Japanese spies" had been uncovered on every track in Russia. Railwaymen were held by the thousand in prison trucks in sidings where special courts presided over their execution. By 1940 Mazurov had become First Secretary of the Province Komsomol Committee at Brest in the territories newly seized from Poland, where the main Party activity was mass terror, and organizing the deportation of the Poles and Western Ukrainians by the hundred-thousand.

Aleksandr Shelepin was too young to be involved in the early purges but became important in the Moscow Committee of the Young Communist League from 1940, and from 1943–50 was a secretary of Stalin's Young Communist Central Committee. Stalin promoted him to head this body in October, 1952, the worst period. Stalin's idea of a Komsomol, since officially stated in a speech of S. Pavlov at the November, 1962, plenum of the Soviet Party's Central Committee, was that "the very first task of all Komsomol education work was the necessity to seek out and recognize the enemy, who then were to be removed purely forcibly, by methods of economic pressure, organizational-political isolation, and methods of physical destruction." Shelepin held this post till 1958 and then became head of the KGB, which organized such actions as the assassination of the Ukrainian leader Bendera and other anti-Communist leaders in exile, by means of the notorious gas-gun pistols.

Similar things, at various levels within the Stalin machine, could be said of the remaining members of the Politburo and Secretariat. No less than thirty-six members of Stalin's 1952 Central Committee are members of the current one elected in 1966. They are even more strongly represented in the leadership. Brezhnev, Kosygin, Shelepin, Suslov, Voronov, Grishin, Ustinov, Kapitonov were all full members, and Ponomarev was a candidate member. In general, the mere continuity of the present regime with Stalin's is remarkable. Khrushchev's attack on Stalin rid the Central Committee, in all, over a period of eight years, of eight "Stalinists," of whom one, Voroshilov, was restored to his position by Khrushchev's successors. In fact, there is now an increasing tendency to rely on old trusties of Stalin. Aleksandr Yepishev, Stalin's nominee as Deputy Minister of State Security during the horrible Doctors' Plot period, now plays a most important role. General Shtemenko, Stalin's Chief of Staff in the postwar years, who was much despised in professional circles and degraded two ranks at Stalin's death, is now back in high position and played an important part in organizing the invasion of Czechoslovakia.

It was of the political origins of such men as these that Aleksandr Solzhenitsyn suggests, in *The First Circle*, that "while Stalin would not tolerate failure, he also hated it if people were too efficient. . . . So Stalin's touch turned everything into mediocrity." Other accounts of the period, for example that of Professor Tokaty (Tokayev), who had direct experience of the top leadership, also give the impression that, while a handful of the younger members in the postwar Politburo, such as Malenkov and Voznesensky, were men of decisive intelligence, immediately below them one found nothing but bureaucratic windbags, whose main concern and only skill was in shifting the blame.

The anti-Semitism of the *apparat* is another sign of intellectual degeneration. Anti-Semitism cannot be traced in the regime until about 1943–44. By 1948, junior *apparatchiki*, of the type now at the top, were boasting to the Yugoslavs of how "Comrade Zhdanov purged all the Jews from the apparatus of the Central Committee and how the Assistant Chief of the General Staff General Antonov, was exposed "as being of Jewish origin." [11]

Later came the arrest of the Jewish Anti-Fascist Committee and the horrors of the Crimean Affair and the Doctors' Plot. There is little reason

[11] Milovan Djilas, *Conversations with Stalin* (New York: Harcourt, 1962), p. 170.

to believe that Stalin himself was seriously anti-Semitic except for what he took to be political advantage. But the attitudes which were now absorbed by the apparatus in general did not have this cynical limitation. It was *after* Stalin's death that the crudest anti-Semitic attitudes prevailed. Konstantin Paustovsky, the writer, noted the "pogromist" jokes of senior officials in 1956, and we later saw such things as the by no means isolated case of the notorious book *Judaism Without Embellishment,* by Z. T. Kitchko (1963). That these feelings thoroughly permeated the present leadership became obvious at the meetings between the Soviet and Czech Communist leaders—still in slightly toned-down form—at Cierna-nad-Tiszu, and in their full crudity when the Czechoslovak leadership was kidnapped after the invasion and taken to Moscow, where Kriegel was openly referred to in front of his colleagues as "that damned Galician Jew."

Any serious estimate of the Soviet leaders must deal, too, with the built-in tendency to irrationality which has pervaded the Soviet Communist Party from early days. The irrational element may be seen in scandalous form in spheres usually regarded as nonpolitical, for example in the medical area, always a favorite stamping ground for the irrational layman. Lenin, in a well-known letter to Gorky in November, 1913, advised him to avoid Bolshevik doctors: "But really, in 99 cases out of 100, doctor-comrades are asses. . . . To try on yourself the discoveries of a Bolshevik—that's terrifying!" He realized, in fact, that the intellectual likely to be attracted to Bolshevik political theory was only too likely to be "advanced" in crackpot fashion in other fields.

During the great "show trial" of 1938, it came out in evidence that a number of high Party officials had been receiving treatment from one of the accused, Kazakov, who was admittedly a complete quack. After the war the regime sponsored the notorious "longevity" quack, Lepeshinskaya, and others—as well as the terrorist charlatan, Lysenko, in biology. Lysenko was discredited with his protector, Khrushchev.

None of this is, of course, to deny a rational component in Soviet political decisions. It is, however, to assert the existence and the importance of the irrational. Observers who do not make allowances for this sort of thing, who do not correct their own natural tendency to impute rational (even if mistaken) motives to policy decisions, will surely fall into misinterpretation.

It is also true and important that the present leaders have no natural ascendancy over the other members of the Central Committee, including men (themselves comparative third-raters like Patolichev, Mikhailov, and Pegov) who were in positions just below the most senior long before Podgorny or Kirilenko was ever heard of. It seems clear that a good number of *apparatchiki* of the second rank must regard the present Politburo as a more or less accidental concatenation of nonentities who could in principle be replaced. That any replacements now visible would also, in general, equally lack credibility is one of the cruxes. It implies that the decadence of the present leaders is not an accident of personalities but inherent in the whole political situation.

As Rosa Luxemburg long ago predicted, the absence of political liberty has resulted in the dying out of true political life and intelligence. The sequence Lenin-Stalin-Malenkov-Khrushchev-Brezhnev is a rapidly plunging graph. The present Politburo is the first to show no superiority in ability or prestige over the main body of the Party *apparat*. One is reminded, on its different scale, of the "heat-death of the universe." In this closed system entropy has done its work. There is now hardly a sign of anything rising above the mediocre norm.

Moreover, the current Politburo has not, as I write, produced any one figure capable of providing genuine direction. It operates, rather, as what the science fictioneers have hypothesized for us as a "hive-mind." But the linking of eleven third-rate members has not produced the single will required. Vacillation, the attempt to combine contradictory drives, has been the pattern. The predominant motive seems to be a desire to avoid all change and reform in the hope that no crisis will spring up and that the contradictions within their society and economy will go away. There is an absence of motivation, except for the apologetics—and the defense—of power.

One of the strongest impressions given by the 1968 invasion of Czechoslovakia is of the extraordinary political incompetence of the Soviet action. Even Hitler's comparable invasion of March, 1939, crude and brutal though it was, showed a far higher degree of political finesse. First, a more or less spurious, but at least detectable, Slovak appeal against Prague was set in motion. Then, President Hacha was actually induced (by the most bullying methods, it is true) to sign the appeal to Hitler. The German troops met almost no overt opposition, and marched through and out of the cities. The Czechoslovak ministers formally handed their powers over to the Protector in the Hradcany. None of this in any way implies that the Czechs were not as wholeheartedly opposed in principle to the Nazis as they are to the Russians. It was simply and solely a matter of the superior exercise of political technique. It was thought clumsy at the time; and Ribbentrop became notorious as the most oafish of top diplomats. Since then, standards of duplicity, of competence in villainy, have sunk.

They have sunk even since 1956, when Khrushchev could at least produce some sort of puppet government among the Hungarians. And this diplomatic degeneration, as one might put it, can be seen not only in such major crises, but also in the day-to-day conduct of Soviet foreign policy. The ambassador in Prague, Chervonenko, was, indeed, an all-purpose square peg, responsible in his last post for the immediate conduct of the split with Peking, and therefore evidently regarded as suitable to exacerbate the next intra-Communist crisis.

In fact, what we are seeing is not simply a more or less chance taking of power by a Stalinist faction. It is not the equivalent of a return to political control of Molotov or Kaganovich. On the contrary, it is a much deeper phenomenon (and one less easy to reverse). It represents, in effect, the taking of power by representatives—one might almost say extrusions—of the lower-level, narrow, heavily indoctrinated products of the Stalinist political tradition.

Neither in foreign relations nor toward their own people do they nourish the active, aggressive malice of the founder of Stalinism. Nor do they reach his level of intellect. Nor, too, do they possess his single, and enormous, will power. It is as though the death of a sultan were to be followed by the rule of a committee of his eunuchs.

They, or their carbon copies, will, at least for the present period in which we now have to formulate a foreign policy, be the dominant factor on the "other side of the hill." No good can come of imagining that anonymous economic or other forces can be relied upon to change their political psychology.

As Orwell shrewdly remarked, "The early Bolsheviks may have been angels or demons, according as one chooses to regard them, but at any rate they were not sensible men." Over half a century, the angelic, or demonic, drive has departed. Yet it is still not as sensible men that the rulers in Moscow should be regarded, but rather, perhaps, if we are to keep within Orwell's metaphor, as trolls.

I would share the view of M. Tatu and others that revolutionary changes are possible in Russia, and perhaps in the fairly near future. But the mere strength of the Party and state machinery in being at present should not be underestimated. So long as it does not (and it certainly might) commit suicide in the course of an ungovernable faction fight at the top, or is not overwhelmed by some vast objective crisis (as is again possible), it is fully capable of blocking and containing all the economic, intellectual, and other forces which run continually against it. Changes, if they come, will not come with its collaboration or permission. Whatever our hopes for the long run, the political regime whose characteristics we have been considering is the one which will participate in and cope with the crises of the period immediately upon us.

The most urgent, and most immediately dangerous, of these is clearly the confrontation with China. In principle, of course, the Brezhnev doctrine has established the right of the Soviet Union to intervene in any other communist country by armed force in order to install a government and leadership of which it approves. (And its specific right to do so in China has been implied in a recent Prague broadcast.) To be empowered to do something in principle is not the same as to feel capable of doing it in practice. But the Chinese problem is a refractory one at every level. China is not merely aberrant from "true" communist doctrine, but also shows every sign of being actively and dangerously hostile to the U.S.S.R. The motives for a Soviet pre-emptive attack before the development of adequate Chinese rocketry are thus both ideologically and militarily compelling. The arguments against it are merely practical: that the installation of an anti-Maoist regime by Soviet arms does not look an easy proposition;

and that the Chinese air force may already be in a position to carry out suicidal nuclear bombardments of Soviet cities. What decision will be taken cannot, of course, be predicted, and we may hope that the dangers and complexities may be enough to prevent the outbreak of a possibly uncontrollable war in Asia. All the same, it is clear that the narrow ideological pretensions of the Soviet leaders make such a war more rather than less probable.

As to Soviet-American relations, one can say that in principle, for a communist leadership which regards even non-Soviet-style communist regimes as necessarily illegitimate, no "capitalist" societies have a right to exist at all (though, indeed, in practice heresy is and has always been hated more than unbelief). This regime will never abate its total theoretical hostility to the United States. On the other hand, it has long accepted as a principle that it should reach temporary accommodations where these are beneficial. Unlike China, the Soviet Union for the past fifteen years has usually shown a healthy revulsion from the idea of nuclear war with the United States. At present, with enemies on both flanks, it is showing some desire for a measure of détente, if only temporary, with the West, though here one remarks (in the Helsinki negotiations, for example) an absence of any clear-cut willingness to see the full logic of the position and cut through the old line as Stalin did in 1939. And as we refer to the Nazi-Soviet pact, it is worth recalling that, of all the treaties signed by the Soviet Government during the Stalin period, this is the only one which it did not break—because Hitler was too strong. The present neo-Stalinists, clearly enough, will seek to avoid serious trouble with a United States which remains strong. Unfortunately, this is no guarantee that they will not blunder into unforeseen confrontations by pursuing a policy of petty advances, local pinpricks, and a general, continuous, low-pitched hostility to the West throughout the oceans and continents of the world.

Informed and intelligent opinion in the U.S.S.R. has few delusions about the competence and vision of the present leadership (fewer, indeed, than are found in the West). They see rulers who have contrived to antagonize almost the entire world (and have even produced that totally unprecedented phenomenon—a Yugoslav-Albanian détente); who have got the economy, once again, into an impasse; who show no signs of being able to handle the nationalities problem—for example, the Crimean Tatars—either by Stalin's simple methods of oppression, or by the alternative of concession. This sort of disillusionment is at present politically negligible, but it forms an important part of the pressures which, if ever given a chance, could destroy the regime.

It may well be true, as Engels commented of an earlier time in his *The Foreign Policy of Russian Czardom*, that "as soon as Russia has an internal development, and with that, internal party struggles, the attainment of a constitutional form under which these party struggles may be fought without violent convulsions . . . the traditional Russian policy of conquest is a thing of the past!" That, however, is not yet. In the meantime, various evolutions are possible. But for the immediate future Russia is stuck with a group of rulers who, though faced by a society tending in every respect away from their concepts, are in possession of an immensely powerful instrument for blocking social and political change—and immensely powerful military resources.

Hostile, suspicious, shortsighted, timid—and with the timid man's tendency to lash out at what he fears—the Soviet ruling group is not the one we might wish to see in power. Meanwhile, there it is, and any tendency in the West to pretend otherwise, to see it in a delusive light, may be comforting for the moment, but may also be lethal in the long run. About Russia we need, as ever, not stronger feelings, but stronger understandings.

* * *

10

THE SOVIET CONCEPT OF THE RELATIONSHIP BETWEEN THE LOWER PARTY ORGANS AND THE STATE ADMINISTRATION

JERRY F. HOUGH

To Westerners one of the most confusing aspects of the Soviet administrative system has been the role played by lower officials of the Communist Party. It has long been clear that the top policy decisions are made within the central Party organs, but the relationship between the lower Party officials and the governmental administrators has been obscured by a number of seeming ambiguities and inconsistencies in Soviet administrative theory. The Party apparatus has been assigned the duty of supervising and controlling the state administration, but the mandates and powers of the two hierarchies appear ill-defined and overlapping.

On the one hand, Soviet legal and textbook discussions of the administrative system seem to indicate the necessity for a strict line of com-

From Richard Cornell, ed., *The Soviet Political System: A Book of Readings* (Englewood Cliffs, N.J.: Prentice-Hall, 1970), pp. 250–71. © 1970. Reprinted by permission of Prentice-Hall, Inc., Englewood Cliffs, N.J.

mand (particularly in such realms as industry) with single and undivided responsibility in the hands of the governmental administrator at each level. Organs such as the *sovnarkhozy* (regional economic councils) are said to "bear full responsibility for the fulfillment of the production plan [and to have been] granted all the powers necessary for carrying out their economic and financial activity." Lower managers perform their duties in accordance with the principle of *yedinonachaliye* (one-man management and control), a principle which "demands the complete subordination of all the employees in the production process to the will of one person—the leader—and his personal responsibility for the assigned work." These managers, according to one authority, enjoy "the right of decision" for all questions within the jurisdiction of their organization.

Yet Soviet administrative theory contains equally emphatic statements that "the leading and directing role of the Communist Party is the foundation of Soviet state administration." Indeed, the standard Soviet textbook on administrative law declares that "not one important question is decided without supervisory instruction of the Party organs." There are many indications that these quotations are not merely formal generalities. For example, we may find in the Soviet press a matter-of-fact report that a Party *obkom* [province committee] "obligated the *sovnarkhoz* to prepare 300 bulldozer attachments for the DT-54 tractor" or that the bureau of another *obkom* "removed M. R. Kulik from his duties as regional prosecutor (*prokuror*) because of his unsatisfactory supervision of the procuracy."

The first purpose of this article is to explore these apparently conflicting concepts of the Party-state relationship and to attempt to clarify the ambiguities involved. In doing this we hope to illuminate the operational principles implicit in the formal administrative theory and to explain them in terms familiar in Western administrative theory.

The second purpose is to suggest the reasons why the Party organs have been assigned control responsibilities and to speculate on the effect of lower Party participation in decision-making upon the nature of the decisions being made. To use the categories suggested by Barrington Moore, we shall ask the questions: To what extent have the responsibilities of the Party apparatus reflected the desire of the leadership to solidify its political power? To what extent have these responsibilities resulted in decisions which deviate from a "rational-technical" norm?

The Limited Meaning of *Yedinonachaliye*

For a Westerner the most unfortunate aspect of Soviet administrative theory is its failure to use familiar concepts in discussing familiar administrative problems and situations. To a large extent the problem is one of language. For instance, the word "policy" and the phrase "policy implication" are covered by the Russian word *politichesky*, a word usually translated into English as "political"; or, the phrase "delegation of authority" has no easy Russian equivalent. Consequently, in grappling with the problems of "delegation of authority" and "the policy implications of administrative decisions," Soviet administrative theorists have often used language that has often been understood by Westerners to mean a chain of command far clearer and an allocation of power far broader than the Soviet leaders ever intended. In particular, the concept of *yedinonachaliye* has a much more limited meaning than the usual English translation would indicate.

Although all lower officials work within the framework of higher policy, Soviet administrative theory implicitly recognizes that the decisions delegated to each level often may entail policy considerations, and it attempts to distinguish between these decisions and those that are truly routine. The sweeping statements in the legal documents and textbooks about the authority of the state official pertain almost exclusively to the location of the power to take "nonpolicy" decisions and the power to issue the formal decrees by which all decisions must be implemented; these statements do not imply that the "policy" decisions at a given level are within the sole jurisdiction of the one-man manager.

If our understanding of *yedinonachaliye* is correct, then it is—and always has been—a very limited concept that denotes only three things: (1) Hour-to-hour, day-to-day decisions of a fairly routine nature are to be made by a single man, the duly constituted administrator. He need not clear each of these routine decisions with the Party or trade union organization. (2) Although important decisions can and must be influenced by groups other than the state officials (notably the Party organs), every decision must be formally implemented by a governmental organ, specifically by the man or institution which has the legal, formal authority to do so. This aspect of Soviet administrative theory is epitomized in the well-known regulation that Party organizations desiring some action must work "through" the state organs, not "apart from them." Even when Party organizations have been granted the power to take a particular kind of decision, they cannot issue the necessary formal decree themselves but must compel the appropriate governmental official or agency to do it. (3) An employee is obligated to obey any order or instruction emanating from his formal administrative superior. He has no right to appeal to any Party or trade union organization to have any specific order countermanded, or at least he has no such right of appeal if the order requires immediate execution.

The meaning of *yedinonachaliye* is illustrated in a practice that is sometimes mentioned in the Soviet press. This is the willingness of many managers to use even design engineers for such tasks as unloading vital supplies from a truck if the rush for plan fulfillment at the end of the month demands it. Even though this practice has been severely criticized by the Party leadership, an engineer receiving such an order from his superior is bound to carry it out. This is the essence of *yedinonachaliye*. The engineer does, however, have the right, and even the duty, to protest later through the Party organization and to demand that the manager be punished and prohibited from repeating the practice. Of course, the effectiveness of such a protest will depend upon the attitude of the higher authorities, particularly the Party organs.

Any reader familiar with the long Western discussion about "policy" and "administration" knows how difficult it is to distinguish between a routine administrative question and one that has policy implications, and Soviet theorists frankly admit they have not solved the problem. Lower Party officials themselves have inquired as to what kind of questions should be decided by soviet organs and what kind by Party organs, and have been answered by the foremost of Soviet theorists that it is impossible to give a recipe or some sort of catalog. This official, the head of the "Party Life" department of *Pravda*, cautioned that in certain cases there might be questions which seemed minor at first glance "but which in reality should be raised to the level of important political significance."

The inability of Soviet administrative theory to distinguish precisely between a policy and a nonpolicy question inevitably means a certain ambiguity in the Soviet administrative system, but it is an ambiguity that in one form or another is inherent in large-scale organization everywhere. Once it is conceded that lower-level decisions may have policy implications—and all Western administrative theorists would concede that point— then the Soviet distinction makes at least some sense. For the sake of convenience here, a lower-level policy question may be defined as one on which two technically qualified persons, both working within the framework of central directives and rules, might still arrive at different decisions. Thus, a policy question arises when a Party secretary differs with the decision made by the state administrator or feels it necessary to advance a suggestion himself. The "political maturity" of the Party secretary becomes defined in terms of "his ability to pick out the most significant matters from the mass of current business."

Admittedly, our hypothesis about the reconcilability of *yedinonachaliye* and official statements about the Party's role is not the usual one. It is difficult to prove its correctness conclusively because a question of interpretation and translation is involved. The hypothesis does, however, "work" in the sense that it explains a considerable body of data which must otherwise be dismissed as inexplicable or deliberately confusing.

First, the interpretation fits the history of the concept of *yedinonachaliye*. *Yedinonachaliye* was not invented by Stalin as he moved to reduce the independence of the Party apparatus that had placed him in power; rather it was vigorously advocated by Lenin in the first months after the Revolution—a period when he surely had no desire to limit the authority of lower Party officials.

When quoted in the abstract or in a contemporary Soviet source, there seems to be a categorical quality to an assertion by Lenin that "*incontrovertible subordination* to a single will is unconditionally indispensable for the success of work [in] large-scale industry." Yet, in the context of early 1918, such statements surely were not an appeal for a plant manager who would be an independent decision-maker subject only to higher administrative authorities. They are much better understood as an attempt to combat the utopian interpretations of workers' control and trade union control prevailing in this period (and encouraged by Lenin's own prerevolutionary slogans).

From this perspective the advocacy of *yedinonachaliye* and "incontrovertible subordination to a single will" represented little more than Lenin's conviction that the complicated processes of industry would require planning, coordination, and labor discipline under socialism as well as under capitalism. Although the worker would have to accept orders from a directing figure, Lenin had no intention of suggesting that the orders of the "single will" would be based on the manager's independent decisions. It is for this reason that the early debate about *yedinonachaliye* hardly touched on the question of the role of the Party.

In the second place, the hypothesis is in accord with the examples which Soviet spokesmen use to illustrate the importance of *yedinonachaliye*. When Party organs are criticized for interfering in the business of management, the examples almost always involve very minute details rather than questions of any significance. Thus, one Party handbook argued against excessive Party involvement in the following terms: "What would happen if the district (*raion*) Party committee told a collective farm chairman where to send a particular tractor or instructed the shop heads of an enterprise as to which worker should be placed on a particular operation?" Similarly, after Khrushchev's removal the *Pravda* criticisms of local Party organs which usurped the functions of the administrative organs featured such examples as Party determination of traffic rules, the location of a street sign, the method of street-cleaning, or the schedule for digging the foundation of a building. It is particularly instructive that "such a style of work" is criticized on the grounds that "it does not permit the political leader to concern himself with his real job—the resolution of the important problems which are within his competence."

Finally, the interpretation offered here makes sense of one of the most puzzling paradoxes in Soviet administrative theory, namely, the repeated instruction to Party organs to strive "to strengthen *yedinonachaliye*" and the assertion that "the Party committee of the plant, in using its right of verification (*pravo kontrolya*), is strengthening *yedinonachaliye*." If *yedinonachaliye* implies autonomy for the manager in decision-making, this type of statement obviously contradicts other statements about the role of the Party, and in some formulations it becomes ridiculous; but if *yedinonachaliye* has the more limited meaning suggested here, then the strengthening of *yedinonachaliye* can mean little more than the strengthening of labor discipline—a much more understandable demand.

THE RELATIONSHIP OF PARTY ORGANS AND GOVERNMENTAL ADMINISTRATION

To state that *yedinonachaliye* is compatible with an active Party role in decision-making is not to indicate the nature of that role. This will be the subject of the remainder of the article.

It is actually misleading to speak of "a" role for the lower Party organs in Soviet decision-making, for, in reality, there is more than one Party-state relationship. The role of the primary Party organization (summarized in the term *pravo kontrolya,* that is, the right of verification) is different from that of the local Party committees (summarized in the terms *rukovodstvo* and *napravleniye,* that is, executive leadership and direction, respectively). An understanding of the distinctions made in Soviet administrative theory between these two roles is vital for a comprehension of the complex role of the lower Party apparatus in Soviet decision-making.

The relationship of the primary Party organization and of its secretary to the chief administrator of an enterprise or institution can be quite varied. If the organization is located within a governmental administrative office (for example, a ministry, *sovnarkhoz,* or department of a soviet), it has no right to interfere in policy decisions but should simply ensure that decisions are made smoothly and that a "bureaucratic" atmosphere with red tape, toadyism, and excessive self-satisfaction does not appear. If it is located within a factory, collective or state farm, construction site, design bureau, or store, however, it has been specifically assigned the so-called *pravo kontrolya,* the right to check on the substance of managerial decisions.

In this article only those primary Party organizations with the *pravo kontrolya* will be discussed specifically. Yet, while the discussion will be totally irrelevant to the situation within governmental administrative offices (there the role of the Party secretary is quite weak, and Party supervision is exercised instead by the territorial Party organs), the general points to be made apply also to several institutions in which there is no formal *pravo kontrolya;* these include schools, colleges, army units, and perhaps hospitals.

It is quite clear that the *pravo kontrolya* can involve the Party organization deeply in decision-making and in conflicts with the plant director, but the precise meaning of this phrase is not clear at first glance. Part of the difficulty in understanding the *pravo kontrolya* stems from the fact that the word *kontrol* does not really reflect the real nature of the work of the primary Party organization. *Kontrol* has entered the Russian language from the French and has a much more limited meaning than the English word by which it is usually translated. The English verb "control" can often imply the providing of policy direction, but *kontrol* has more the connotations of the word "controller." Consequently, the phrase *pravo kontrolya* conveys the impression of a primary Party organization checking, verifying, inspecting the work of the manager and enforcing his adherence to laws and plans established elsewhere.

However, the role of the primary Party organization and its secretary is stretched far beyond the literal meaning of *pravo kontrolya* by the nature of the instructions and directives that the plant receives from higher Party and state organs. As American authorities have long noted, the Soviet leadership does not provide an enterprise or institution with a precise plan or program to fulfill. Instead, the plant, the farm, the store, is ordered to overfulfill its plan by as much as possible, to do so with optimal efficiency, and to continue to improve the production processes as rapidly as possible. Further complicating the situation is the extreme tautness of the plan in relation to resources. Because of the resulting low levels of inventories, any mistakes in the planning process or any failure of a supplier to meet his schedule can lead to serious difficulties. Consequently, a manager finds it virtually impossible to fulfill his over-all plan without sacrificing some of the regulations that are supposed to govern the work of the enterprise. Schools, colleges, and institutes do not face precisely the same problem, but even they are obligated to achieve an ideal in education or research that can never be reached in the real world.

The effect of this situation on the role of the manager has long been recognized. Because he has no precise set of rules and regulations to follow, he has much more room in which to maneuver than might be expected for an official low in a very centralized hierarchy. Indeed, an American author, David Granick, concluded in 1954 that the plant manager has so much freedom of action that he cannot rightfully be called a bureaucrat in the Weberian sense.

If the nature of the Soviet planning system leaves the manager with some freedom of action in relation to his superiors, it has had a corresponding effect on the nature of the *kontrol* exercised by the primary Party organization. Since there is no precise plan or set of regulations, the *kontrol* cannot be a routine "verification of performance" in the usual sense. The party organization cannot merely check off regulations which have been violated, for, as one higher official expressed it, regulations are constantly being broken "for the sake of production." To be sure, the organization is interested in gross machinations and law violations, but its basic role is much broader. In checking on the over-all performance of the enterprise, it inevitably becomes involved in decision-making, if only for the reason that the mere choice of the indicator or regulation to emphasize constitutes a decision of significance.

Moreover, since the Party organization has the duty of preventing mistakes as well as of reporting and correcting them, it has in effect an opportunity to discuss with the manager any question which it deems important. The official Party handbook is filled with demands that the organization as a whole "raise questions about production," "recommend various measures," "bring up various problems to the administration," and so on. In the realm of personnel action, the Party bureaus do not have the right either to appoint personnel or to confirm appointments, but they do have "not only the right but also the duty to consult with the economic leader and to recommend that this or that official be promoted."

In short, the right of *kontrol* entails both the right to check *after* a decision has been made, and also, more importantly, the right to participate intimately in policy-making *before* the decision is made. It means that the Party committee or bureau of the primary Party organization is the real board of directors of the plant—the place where the top administrative officials, together with the Party secretary, the trade union chairman, and a few workers, discuss the major questions facing the enterprise and make the decisions concerning them.

Although the Party bureau is primarily an "inside" board of directors (that is, composed of men from inside the plant who are subordinate to the manager in their daily work), it does contain at least one man who is always supposed to maintain a position independent of the manager—the secretary of the Party organization. Of course, the crucial question is: What happens when this official and the director do in fact, "argue about questions of principle"? In cases of disagreement, do the Party organization and its secretary have the authority to compel the manager to accept their position?

There are, unfortunately, few other matters on which there are so many contradictory authoritative statements as on the proper relationship between the manager and the plant Party secretary. If at times Soviet officials (for example, Zhdanov in 1939) have criticized "Party organizations [which] take on themselves the improper functions of *executive leadership* [*rukovodstvo*] in economic matters," others have spoken of the "leading [*rukovodyashchaya*] role" of the primary Party organization in the enterprises or of its "providing of political leadership." In one place it is declared that "the decision of the meeting [of the primary Party organization] expresses the opinion and will of the Party collective, [and] it is binding on every Communist" (including, presumably, the director). In another place the statement is made that "the Party organization and its leaders cannot directly give any operational instructions, [nor] can they even require that the director clear his orders and commands with them." It is asserted that a situation should never develop in which "it is not the director who supervises the enterprise but the Party organization which commands the director."

Perhaps the strangest formulation of all appeared in an authoritative attempt to clarify the situation for a confused employee. The director at his plant admitted that the *obkom* and the *sovnarkhoz* could obligate him to take action, but he objected to attempts by the primary Party organization to do so, in addition. The employee wrote for support to the journal of the Central Committee, *Partiinaya zhizn* [*Party Life*]. It answered as follows: "Comrade Razumovsky is mistaken if he thinks that only higher-standing Party and economic organs can obligate him. . . . But it would be incorrect [for the primary Party organization] to abuse its authority by addressing the director in such categorical phraseology as 'obligate,' 'propose,' 'demand.'" Despite the blatant contradictions which seem to exist in these statements about the role of the primary Party organization, Soviet administrative theory is actually not nearly so ambiguous on this point as it appears on the surface.

Part of the explanation for the contradictions has already been suggested in the discussion of the phraseology used to describe *yedinonachaliye*. For example, the assertion that the primary Party organization "cannot *directly* [my italics] give any operational instructions" is surely a reflection of the Soviet insistence that Party officials work through the duly constituted governmental officials in carrying out their decisions. Prohibitions against commanding the director and against forcing him to clear his orders with the Party organizations are likewise expressions of the Soviet belief that managers should be permitted to make minor day-to-day decisions on their own. (The word *komandovat* tends to connote an excessive ordering around of people.)

A second partial expxlanation for the ambiguities in statements about the primary Party organization lies in the diversity of the types of decisions that the primary Party organization may take. Zhdanov's reference to "the improper functions of leadership in *economic matters*" (my italics) reminds us that other decisions of the Party organization deal with various intra-Party matters. Here the authority of the organization and its secretary may be unchallenged.

Even within the economic sphere itself there are many kinds of decisions that may be taken. If the local Party organs issue a *formal* decision about an enterprise, the decision is often directed at the primary Party organization rather than solely at the management. The decision is then echoed by the primary Party organization, its decision obligating all Communists to carry out the different points decreed by higher officials. In such cases there is no questioning the obligatory nature of the "decision of the primary Party organization" for the manager.

There are other decisions of the primary Party organization so general that it would not seem strange if the word "to suggest" were used instead of "to obligate." In 1952, for example, "the Party committee [of the giant plant Elektrosila] obligated Comrade Shevchenko [the director] to be attentive to the workers, to have more contact with them, to take into account criticism which comes from below." A similar obligation was stated in 1965 by the Party conference of the Tbilisi Electric Locomotive Works: "A decision was taken which obligates the Party committee and the Communists: To raise the level of the technical leadership of production. To devote serious attention to the scientific organization of work. More boldly to introduce new techniques and progressive technology into production. . . . To strengthen labor and production discipline, to obtain a rise in labor productivity, to guarantee rhythmic work, to lower costs, and to raise the quality of production."

If it were categorically denied that the Party organization has the right to obligate the manager, then the general decisions quoted above, as well as those on intra-Party matters and those embodying higher Party decisions, could not have been phrased as they are. When the editorial board of *Partiinaya zhizn* states that the director can be obligated by the primary Party organization but that the organization should not abuse its authority by using the word "to obligate," it is possible (or even probable) that it is tacitly differentiating between the type of decision we have been examining and those that deal with specific production questions.

A third step in understanding the role of the primary Party organization and its secretary lies in making a distinction between the organization and the secretary which Soviet theorists are frequently eager to blur. If we closely examine two contradictory statements about the primary Party organization, we often find that one statement refers to the powers and functions of the Party organization as a whole, while the other actually describes the powers and functions of the secretary alone.

Although the primary Party organization has been assigned the right to verify the work of management, we must never forget that the organization also, in fact, contains nearly all of the top members of management itself. From the point of view of Party theory, the organization as a whole (including the managerial team) occupies a special position in relation to the enterprise employees who are not Party members. The organization is part of the vanguard of the proletariat, and its relationship to the proletariat is depicted in the same terms as those used to describe the general role of the Party.

The really sweeping statements about the "leading role" of the primary Party organization almost always refer implicitly to this relationship of the Party organization to the enterprise and to the men in it who are not members of the Communist Party. They do not refer to the relationship of the Party secretary or of a majority of the members to those Communists who occupy the top administrative posts in the enterprise. This is vital to understand if a very frequent type of Soviet press report is not to be misinterpreted. Take, for example, the assertion that "the Party committee [of the Orekhovo-Zuyevo Cotton Combine] skillfully directs the efforts of the Communists, of the 26,000-man collective, in finding and using the internal reserves, in perfecting production, in raising productivity of labor and profitability." This statement does not necessarily imply any limitation on the role of the top managerial officials, for they are among the most important members of that Party committee. It means simply that the major plant decisions are made—or formalized—at a meeting of the plant's "board of directors"; it does not necessarily mean that the Party secretary has had any real impact on the decision.

On the other hand, much Soviet discussion of the primary Party organization is implicitly based on a much narrower conception of the organization—that is, as consisting of the Party secretary at the head of the rank-and-file members. The whole concept of *pravo kontrolya* does, of course, imply a Party organization apart from the top administrators of the unit, and in practice it tends to refer to the role of the Party secretary. Because of the democratic mythology surrounding the primary Party organization, Soviet administrative theorists sometimes find it awkward to discuss the legitimate authority which the leadership really intends to be vested in the Party secretary. However, many of the narrow definitions of the powers of the organization were written with the secretary in mind. When Zhdanov denied that the primary Party organization was to have the role of executive leadership, when *Partiinaya zhizn* stated that it would be improper for the primary Party organization to use the words "obligate" or "demand" in its decisions, they were thinking of the Party secretary and the rank-and-file members he leads.

All Soviet officials interviewed in 1958 and 1962 agreed that both in theory and in practice the powers of the secretary are limited to those of persuasion and of appeal to higher officials, and that the secretary cannot (without the support of higher officials) force the managers to accept his opinion on policy questions. Those interviewed stated that the decision of a meeting of the primary Party organization or its bureau usually does not bind the manager unless he has concurred in the decision. Even a non-Party director of a textile factory insisted that the primary Party organization would take no decision concerning the economic side of the enterprise's life without clearing it with him first.

The interviews indicate that if there is disagreement between the director and Party secretary the secretary's only recourse is appeal to the local Party organs for support. However, one authoritative post-Khrushchev statement about the primary Party organizations suggests that in the realm of personnel selection, at least, it is the director who must take the initiative if he is not to be bound by the opinion of the Party organization. After asserting that the Party committees' "decisions, proposals, and recommendations are obligatory for the [director]," this statement continued, "If the economic leader . . . considers the decision of the Party organization mistaken, he should turn to a higher-standing Party organ and ask it to correct the mistake of the Party organization and to annul its decision."

It is not certain whether the burden of making the appeal has been placed on the director only in the post-Khrushchev period or whether it actually represents a long-standing operating procedure. In fact, the statement does not make clear whether this procedure applies to all decisions of the primary Party organization or just to those involving personnel changes. Another 1965 *Partiinaya zhizn* statement about the primary Party organization defines its role in such a way as to suggest that it still may be compelled to initiate most of the appeals in cases of disagreements with the manager: The Party organizations should, the statement demanded, "work out effective recommendations for the administration and *place important problems* before higher-standing Party organs." The three italicized words were in heavy dark print in the original.

Whoever must make the appeal to the local Party organs, neither the director nor the plant Party secretary can force the other to accept his opinion without the support of higher Party officials. As a result, the essential image of the relationship of the director and the Party secretary emerging from Soviet administrative theory is that of a policy-making team within the enterprise. These two officials, together with the trade union chairman, are to form a three-man directorate—the triangle (*treugolnik*), a term from the 1920's still used today.

Within the policy-making team the director is primarily responsible for day-to-day decisions, but when broader questions arise he must discuss them fully with the secretary, and the two must find a common language, an *obshchy yazyk*. On certain questions dealing with dismissals, housing distribution, and so forth, the agreement of the trade union chairman is also required, but he is closely supervised by the Party secretary and is scarcely an independent power center within the enterprise.

This relationship between administrator and Party secretary in the situation when the Party organization has the *pravo kontrolya* seems also to apply to many other enterprises and institutions in which there is no formal *pravo kontrolya*. To be sure, it has no relevance for the relationship within the central and regional administrative organs, but it is implied even in discussions of such an institution as the army. Marshal M. V. Zakharov, then head of the General Staff of the Soviet Armed Forces, wrote of "the persistent need for businesslike, Party-like cooperation of the commanders and the political workers in the struggle to strengthen the fighting capacity and military discipline of the troops." He criticized "individual political workers who think that they have no obligation to investigate military matters thoroughly," and he condemned any attempt to limit the cooperation of the commanders and the political workers "only to Party-political matters."

Within the policy-making team the two leaders are in a roughly equal position, at least in the sense that neither can compel the other to take a particular action. It is safe to say that the relative influence of the administrator and the secretary varies from enterprise to enterprise, depending upon the personalities and abilities of the two men. No doubt it is also safe to say that most frequently the director is first among equals, both because he has been granted higher prestige and pay and because he is in charge of day-to-day administration. In the army, for example, the head of the political administration (at least at the military district level) seems always to have a lower rank than the commander. In any event, the author has never seen a case in which the political officers had a higher rank. All in all, the relative position of the secretary of a primary Party organization is best expressed in the fact that he may become the chief administrator in his enterprise or unit, but the chief administrator never becomes the Party secretary. Nevertheless, the mere existence of the right of appeal is surely a powerful weapon for the secretary, ensuring a role for him even when the right is not exercised.

The Soviet leaders have realized that a policy-making team within an enterprise can create difficulties, and they have taken a number of steps to avoid them. To prevent one member of the team from becoming dominant, they periodically vary the balance of emphasis between the two roles, and they also follow a policy of replacing Party secretaries after a very short tenure.

The Soviet leaders have also used a number of devices to thwart the development of irresponsibility and indecisiveness in this system. They have held the administrator and the Party secretary strictly responsible for results (basically the same results in each case) and then have given them an extremely difficult plan to fulfill. In this way the two men are given to understand that any poor results ensuing from a failure to work together effectively will bring their prompt removal. Another device has been the insistence upon *yedinonachaliye*—the insistence that orders be carried out along the administrative line and that the administrator have the authority to carry through action which he thinks is needed immediately. Finally, the local Party committee has been given the right and the power to settle any conflict that arises between the administrator and the secretary of the primary Party organization and that cannot be resolved by them.

Above the primary Party organizations in the Party hierarchy we find a series of Party committees, one located within each territorial unit in the Soviet Union—the rural district, the borough, the city, the region [or province] (oblast), and the republic. Like the primary Party organizations, these middle-level committees (termed "the local Party organs") are held strictly responsible for plan fulfillment by the state institutions within their jurisdiction. They too are instructed to intervene to help achieve that plan fulfillment. Yet the relationship of the local Party organs to the state administrators is strikingly different from the relationship of the primary Party organizations to those administrators.

In Soviet administrative theory the key determinant in the relationship of any local Party organ to any state administrator is the territorial level at which the two are located. If the state administrator works at a higher territorial level than the Party organ, the Party organ's position with respect to him is quite weak. In theory the interaction of a Party committee with a higher state official is not that of team decision-making but rather a supplicant-superior relationship. A Party committee can request that a higher administrative official take some action, it can appeal one of his decisions to higher Party officials, but it is not in any real sense an equal. The percentage of success for its requests and appeals is not particularly high; indeed, the well-known difficulties of the local Party organs with the industrial ministries prior to 1957 are a typical reflection of the weakness of the Party organ in this type of relationship and of the unlikelihood of its obtaining consistent support from higher Party organs in its disputes with higher administrators.

If, on the other hand, the state administrator is located at the same territorial level as the local Party organ or a lower territorial level, the Party organ has a very different relationship to him. In fact, in this case the position of the local Party organ is far stronger than that of the primary Party organization within the enterprise. The local Party organ is not called upon simply to exercise *kontrol* over the administrators within its area; instead, it is instructed (in the words of one of the last *Pravda* editorials of the Stalin era) "to realize leadership of the soviet, economic, and public organizations . . . to unite, to direct [*napravlyat*], and to control [*kontrolirovat*] [their] activity."

This difference in the role of the local Party organs and of the primary Party organizations was expressed very well in a 1940 editorial in *Pravda*: "Checking [*kontrol*] by the *plant* Party organization in a given case is combined with correct and capable *leadership* [*rukovodstvo*] of the plant from the side of the Leningrad City Party Committee—daily leadership which is concrete and deep." In the editorial, only the two words *plant* and *rukovodstvo* were printed in boldface type.

The words *napravlenie* (direction) and *rukovodstvo* imply far broader powers than *kontrol*. While *kontrol* implies the absence of the authority to obligate an administrator, *rukovodstvo* denotes its presence. This authority derives formally from the relationship of the local Party organ to the primary Party organization as defined in the Party Rules, specifically from the clause declaring that "the decision of higher [Party] bodies are unconditionally binding upon lower ones." Since the important administrative personnel are for the most part Party members and are enrolled in the primary Party organization at the place where they work, they, too, are subject to the decisions of the local Party organs which supervise their primary Party organization.

That these powers are more than formal and are not limited simply to intra-Party matters is graphically shown in the many references in the Soviet press to local Party organs which "obligate" managerial personnel and which also "promote" or "remove" them. A striking illustration appeared several years ago in a *Pravda* article about the compilation of the plan at the Jelgava Agricultural Machine-building Plant in Latvia. The plant had been ordered by the *sovnarkhoz* to produce air conditioners, and with difficulty its managers succeeded in setting up the necessary rigging. At this stage, however, "officials of the Latvian Party Central Committee suggested that the production of air conditioners be discontinued." The article did not specify which officials were involved, but their "suggestion" was decisive. The plant management vigorously objected to the decision, and they were supported both by the Jelgava City Party Committee and by the *sovnarkhoz*. Indeed, the *sovnarkhoz* twice appealed the decision to the bureau of the Latvian Central Committee, but the production of air conditioners continued to be deleted from the enterprise's plan.

After Khrushchev's removal the Soviet press carried a number of articles indicating that the local Party organs had been calling special operational sessions (*operativki*) and planning sessions (*planerki*) at which they directed the work schedules of state administrators (particularly those associated with construction) in a most immediate way. "At the operational sessions the city committee and borough committee secretaries distribute labor force, urge on the suppliers of materials, establish [daily or weekly] work schedules."

While this article and others like it criticized the Party organs, they accused the Party organs not of exceeding their authority but of using it unwisely. It will be recalled that the plant director who questioned the right of the primary Party organization to obligate him to take action conceded readily the *obkom* [province committee] had this authority, and none of the post-Khrushchev articles suggested that there has been any change in this respect. It was still reported in a matter-of-fact way, for example, that the Kamchatka *obkom* had established a schedule for mail delivery in the oblast and that the Grozny Party officials had required the city's enterprises to send 200 metalworkers to a key construction project temporarily. In short, it was not at all misleading to describe a *gorkom* [city committee] first secretary in a novel as "the highest authority in the city," or to refer to a [borough committee] secretary as "the head (*glava*) of the borough."

As these examples indicate, the local Party organs use their powers to do far more than simply provide general ideological and inspirational leadership for the state administrators. The "leadership" which Soviet administrative theory demands from the local Party organs is that associated with the job of a chief executive. A description of the actual work of the local Party organs is not within the scope of this article, but their duties are as broad—and as difficult to define—as those of any chief executive. They include such functions as selecting important administrative personnel, providing policy direction to the state administrators on "questions of principle," maintaining standards of performance, and, most important of all, coordinating the work of the different administrators and resolving disputes which arise among them.

In carrying out these functions, the local Party organs are to conduct themselves in accordance with the principles implied in *yedinonachaliye*. The Party Rules obligate the Party organs "not to supplant [*podmenyat*] the soviet, trade-union, cooperative, and other public organizations of the toilers, not to permit a mixing of the functions of the Party and other organs or unnecessary parallelism in their work." "The Party organs cannot take on themselves the function of direct administration"; there should be no "detailed interference of the Party committees in the work of the economic organs and their leaders."

These statements are nothing more than the Soviet method of demanding delegation of authority on detailed questions from the Party to the state organs. This is most graphically demonstrated in the fact that Soviet administrative theories use identical language when they discuss delegation of authority from a superior to a subordinate in the state apparatus: "The higher standing administrative bodies in exercising general supervision of the organs subordinate to them do not supplant [*podmenyat*] them."

The essence of the relationship of a local Party organ to a state administrator within its area was best summarized in a 1957 statement by the second secretary of the Sverdlovsk *obkom* about the relationship of the *obkom* and the newly created *sovnarkhoz*. After stating that "the oblast Party committee should not and must not supplant [the *sovnarkhoz*]," the second secretary continued: "The impression might be created that our Party organ takes on the role of a passive inspector. . . . In actuality, this is not so." He then made the crucial distinction: "There is a line where concrete, operational leadership of the enterprise ends and where economic policy begins." Even though the Sverdlovsk *sovnarkhoz* was then headed by a former U.S.S.R. Minister—a man who was a candidate member of the Party Central Committee—the secretary made it clear that questions involving "economic policy" should not be left to the *sovnarkhoz* to to decide. While, of course, the relationship between an *obkom* and a *sovnarkhoz* changed with the raising of the *sovnarkhoz* above the oblast level in 1962, the secretary's distinction has general applicability to the relationship between any local Party organ and a state administrative agency at its territorial level or below.

Since the local Party organs are located at middle levels in a highly contralized hierarchy, naturally there are many questions of "economic policy" which are not left to them to decide either. In general terms the local Party organs are required to operate within the directives and plans established by higher Party and state agencies. (As the state officials at a higher territorial level receive their policy direction from the Party officials at their level, it would be illogical to permit a lower Party committee to thwart a governmental policy which embodies higher Party policy.) In practice, however, the orders which come down the different governmental lines of command are often all-embracing and conflicting, and this increases the scope for action of the local Party organs just as it does that of the lower administrator and the secretary of the primary Party organization.

In our opinion the most important functional responsibility of the local Party organs has actually always been the adjustment of disparities and contradictions in the various plans, directives, and regulations which flow into the area from the various ministries and departments. While all of these plans and directives ultimately derive from the policy of the same Party leadership, they inevitably diverge somewhat as they descend the lines of command and become a bit distorted in meaning and emphasis by different departmental self-interests and perspectives. Moreover, the many regulations which have been issued by the leadership to control undesirable behavior may have untoward results in certain instances and create the need to make exceptions.

A whole series of conflicts and problems result from the contradictions and rigidities in the detailed plans and directives which reach the operational level. A local educational plan for in-factory training may require so much manpower and material from local factories as to threaten the fulfillment of parts of the industrial plan. The completion of the construction of a school by the beginning of the school year may depend upon an extraordinary (outside-the-plan) priority in the delivery of some key item. The harvesting of the local crop may be unsuccessful unless the farmers receive help of "volunteer" labor from city enterprises and institutions. Some local construction emergency may demand the waiving of certain operating regulations if loss is not to be sustained.

In all these cases the administrators involved may take their problem to a local Party organ, and it has the authority to decide the relative priority of two plans or directives, to demand that one institution help another in important marginal cases, or to authorize a state administrator to disregard a particular regulation. And, of course, it also has the power to enforce its decision.

In short, the general authority relationship which Merle Fainsod found existing between the Smolensk *obkom* and the oblast soviet in the 1930's is that which the Soviet leaders intend to prevail generally between a local Party organ and a state administrator within its territory. In this respect there has been very little if any change in three decades.

Indeed, as early as 1923 we find Stalin noting with the greatest approval and encouragement that "the *gubernia**[Party] committees have got into their stride, they have taken up construction work in earnest, they have put the local budgets in order, they have taken control of local economic development, they have really managed to take the lead in the entire economic and political life of their *gubernias*." As the 1940 and 1953 *Pravda* editorials which we have quoted indicate, the mandate of the local Party organs to lead and direct the work of their area's administrators was not abandoned in the last years of the Stalin period.

But to say that the conception of the Party-state relationship at this level has been relatively stable is not to say that the influence of the local Party organs on Soviet decision-making has remained unchanged. When middle-level industrial administrators were moved into the region with the creation of the *sovnarkhozy*, the local Party organs (especially the *obkomy*) were obviously in a position to influence their decisions far more than when they worked in the ministries in Moscow. On the other hand, when the amalgamation of the economic regions raised the *sovnarkhozy* above the oblast level, the principles defining the Party-state relationship dictated a significant reduction in the influence of the *obkom* on *sovnarkhoz* decisions.

Many other factors vary the influence of the local Party organs. When, as in the case of the Smolensk committee in the 1930's, the Party officials in an area were judged primarily on the basis of the performance of one sector of the economy of the region (in the Smolensk case, flax production), the influence of the Party officials might be quite selective as they concentrated their attention upon the particular administrators in charge of that key sector. When, as in the Saratov oblast in 1959, the Party leadershop removes from the first secretaryship an old-line Party official with long experience in agricultural regions and replaces him with a former factory director who has been in industrial management until the age of forty, the supervision over both agriculture and industry takes on a different character (in fact, in the Saratov case that was precisely the result looked for). And, finally, when the secret police became a less feared instrument after the death of Stalin, the local Party organs were clearly able to establish a real superior-subordinate relationship, which had been psychologically difficult to achieve earlier.

Yet, for this discussion, the important point is that (except in the role assigned to the Party committee of the kolkhoz-sovkhoz [collective or state farm] administration) the Party leadership has changed the influence of the local Party organs not by redefining the basic Party-state relationships but by changing the technical qualifications of Party officials, the relative priority of plan fulfillment in different sectors of the economy, the territorial level at which administrators are located; by dividing the

---

* *Gubernia*: Province in pre-Revolutionary and early Soviet Russia.—ED.

Party into industrial and agricultural components to allow Party officials more time for each branch; or, most recently, by reuniting it.

THE RATIONALE OF THE PARTY-STATE RELATIONSHIP

We have seen that officials of the lower Party apparatus have been assigned rather substantial responsibilities in decision-making. Now we turn to an examination of the rationale for this policy of the Soviet leadership.

Unquestionably one of the major reasons has been a desire to strengthen the political control of the leadership. During the early Soviet period the state administration was, in Trotsky's words, "a cell of world counter-revolutionaries, a durable, solid economic nucleus which fights us with weapons in its hands." Even when the administration became increasingly staffed by Party members, the leadership recognized the political dangers of a simple chain of command with only one line of communication open to the center. Under such a " 'simplified' apparatus," Stalin feared, "the ruler, in governing the country, receives the kind of information that can be received from governors and comforts himself with the hope that he is governing honestly and well. Presently, friction arises, friction grows into conflict, and conflicts into revolts."

The desire for political control seems, however, an insufficient explanation for the degree and type of Party participation in decision-making—particularly for the continuation of this scale of participation in recent decades. Given the progressive sovietization of the administrative elite, the development of other lines of communication upward, and the concentration of attention on industrialization, education, science, and public health, the Soviet leadership would certainly long ago have restricted or redefined the supervisory and control functions of the Party apparatus if they had seriously hindered the achievement of the programatic goals. We submit that the Party organs have continued to be assigned these functions (indeed, in practice, to have their involvement deepened and intensified by the increasing appointment of technically qualified personnel to Party posts), because the Party leadership has found that their presence in the decision-making process helps to resolve several important problems inherent in very large organizations.

One such problem is the persistent inability of administrators to obtain all the information they need in order to make intelligent decisions. Few questions are so widely discussed in American administrative theory as that of difficulty faced by administrators in receiving a proper "feedback" of information from lower levels and of the continual necessity for them to make decisions with insufficient information. The Party organs facilitate the flow upward not only of information useful for political control but also of information which will contribute to optimal decisions from a rational-technical point of view.

The primary Party organization is particularly useful in ensuring that more information does flow to those who need it. The higher Party officials receive from the institutions and enterprises independent reports filled with criticism and self-criticism and are also able to participate in the resolution of disputed issues that are likely to provoke major disagreement between the director and the Party secretary. Moreover, the existence of the primary Party organization guarantees that the director (and the secretary) will be provided with a steady stream of information about conditions and trouble spots at lower echelons of the enterprise and will receive alternative suggestions for action.

The local Party organs serve both as a continuation of the line of communication upward and as an important independent source of information. As the local Party organs are the only institutions in the territorial subdivisions responsible for all aspects of life within them, they alone have the proper perspective to point out regional disparities and strains and to speak out for integrated regional development. The very localism that interferes with the performance of the local Party organs as a nationally attuned control instrument is quite functional from the point of view of information flow.

A second problem of large-scale organization which helps to explain the functions assigned to the lower Party apparatus is the amount of discretion which in practice tends to accrue to administrative officials at lower and middle levels of the organization. While the Weberian model implies that decisions within a bureaucracy can always be made correctly and predictably by any technically competent official who applies rules determined by higher policy-makers, Western social scientists have long since realized that this is not necessarily the case, particularly in administrative situations (such as are found in industry) in which many decisions are not routine.

In theory the development of a perfect incentive system might provide a set of "rules" which would ensure that the "independent" decisions of the administrators conformed either to the specific preferences of the leaders or to their generalized desire for efficiency and growth. However, such an incentive system is difficult to achieve within a hierarchical order. The establishment of a measure for success may distort decisions, as the administrators come to focus on the indicator rather than the goal behind it, while the existence of many diverse units in a hierarchy (particularly in the Soviet Union, where all organizations are really part of the same hierarchy) make it quite difficult to ensure that the incentives in the different units do not lead to conflicting actions. Even if these obstacles can conceivably be overcome, it is clear in any case that they have not been in the Soviet Union.

The problem of the discretion to be left to lower officials is complicated by the possibility that the training of these officials may not prepare them well for the exercise of discretion. A number of Western authorities have expressed concern about the type of habits and technique a future executive develops in his first, more detailed jobs and about the isolated environment in which he works (Peter Drukker speaks of the environment in the corporation as being that of a monastery). They fear that this environment tends to produce a parochialism and a mechanical attitude toward men that may seriously limit the executive's effectiveness as he rises to posts in which more and more policy-making is involved.

Soviet authorities on the Party-state relationship show a keen awareness of the problems relating to the discretion exercised below the top policy-making levels. All of the discussions about "democratic centralism," "Leninist principles of administration," and the advantages of "collective" decisions continually express concern about the danger of one-sided, arbitrary decisions by administrators. On the surface, at least, the Soviet leadership worries less about these arbitrary decisions involving too much political independence than about the fact that they will not be well thought out and well rounded. The existence of the secretary of the primary Party organization and of specialized officials within the local Party organs increases the probability that at least two men will be considering questions relating to policy, and this, in the opinion of the Soviet leadership, contributes to decisions which are generally sounder from a rational-technical point of view.

Moreover, the involvement of Party officials also ensures that men with wider responsibilities and often with a less specialized background participate in the solution of many of the most important questions. Even in cases in which the Party officials do not have the general, nonspecialized background to start with, their responsibility for political stability and (in the case of the local Party organs) for many sectors of life gives them a perspective which a man who has always been responsible only for plan fulfillment in one specialized hierarchy might not develop.

Indeed, paradoxically, the existence of the Party organs makes it easier for the administrators themselves to develop the breadth of perspective which is needed. For a number of reasons important administrative personnel are selected for membership in the bureaus of the primary Party organizations and in the committees and bureaus of the local Party organs. While they may be chosen largely because of their technical expertise or because of the desire to give them symbolic recognition, the administrators so selected are compelled to become acquainted with many problems outside their narrow professional field. Those who head the most important enterprises and who are named to the bureau of the local Party organs have an unparalleled opportunity to observe the interplay of all administrative and social forces within the local area.

It cannot be said with any certainty that the involvement of the Party organs in policy-making does contribute to sounder decisions from a rational-technical point of view. It is interesting to note, however, that Arthur M. Schlesinger, Jr., has suggested that the decisions of the Roosevelt Administration were more creative because of the conflicts between men who had been given responsibility for much the same policy realm. It is interesting to read the proposal by Harold W. Dodds that the president of a large college or university should have "a different kind of personal staff officer, one who is fitted by temperament and experience to share his thinking at the highest levels at which he operates . . . one person who will not be troubled, dominated, or compromised by operating responsibilities, [who] may discover trouble brewing of which the president otherwise might not be aware until it explodes, [who] can render an invaluable service by telling the president when he is wrong [and] can serve as a watchdog to see that his chief is not neglecting major matters because of other pressures." It is interesting to note that in American industry the existence of an active chairman of the board in addition to the corporation president is often justified in language very similar to that used by Dodds.

A third major problem of large-scale organization alleviated by the Party organs is the need for regional coordination, particularly the need for the resolution of conflicts among different administrators in the region. While this problem may not be great in a very specialized organization, it becomes much more serious in any organization with a number of divisions, each of which has subordinates interacting in a particular region (the WPA would be a prime American example). The disparities in plans, directives, and regulations which we discussed in the last section demand adjustment, and the only apparent means is through the creation of a regional coordinator, whatever the effect may be on the neatness of the organization chart. This, in fact, has been the solution chosen in such organizations as the WPA.

In the Soviet Union the executive committees of the local soviets are able to serve as a regional coordinator to some extent, but many key officials—including most of those in industry, construction, and transportation, as well as all those in the "public organizations," for example, the trade-union and the Komsomol—are not in any way subordinated to the oblast, city, or *raion* soviets. Consequently, two officials or organizations which come into conflict will often have no common governmental superior below the republic or even the all-Union level to which they can take their problem (in fact, if an official of a "public organization" is involved, there is no common governmental superior at all). Even when there is a common superior at the next hierarchial level, it may be inconvenient to take a problem to him because (as in the case of two factories subordinated to the *sovnarkhoz*) the superior may be miles away and too preoccupied to be concerned with some relatively minor question.

It would be possible to create governmental super-coordinators to fill this gap in the administrative structure (perhaps by widening the responsibilities of the local soviets). In fact, the present practice of subordinating construction to an administrative hierarchy separate from both the soviets and the *sovnarkhoz* requires such detailed and intensive Party coordination of construction activities that some type of reorganization in this realm may be considered.

However, while general regional coordination could be assigned to a governmental body, the local Party organs are in many ways especially well adapted to perform this function. It is interesting to note that the "broker" function is often the responsibility of a political party, and there are a number of reasons why this occurs in the Soviet Union as well. Part of the answer, no doubt, is found in the type of persons who are likely to be attracted to political work. Moreover, while any regional super-coordinator held responsible for the plans of all phases of life in the area would be compelled to develop great sensitivity to the scale of priorities set up by the leadership, the political organ is far better able to take the demands of political stability into consideration in evaluating the relative priority of the factors involved in a particular case.

Another advantage of the local Party organs is their ability to operate with a degree of flexibility that a governmental super-coordinator would find hard to match. It is difficult to imagine precisely how the powers of a governmental super-coordinator would be defined in legal terms. Would the factories, stores, schools, and so on, be subordinated to all of the co-ordinators at the various territorial levels? If so, would not the legal statutes be extremely complicated? If not, could one coordinator solve the problems which arise at the different territorial levels? The rules of subordination found in the Party principle of democratic centralism are sufficiently generalized so that the duties and powers of the local Party organs can be defined flexibly by instructions and by custom.

The powers of a governmental coordinator in relation to the "public organizations" would be especially difficult to define. Whatever their democratic mythology, these organizations are an integral part of the ad-ministrative system and serve a number of useful functions. They interact with the officially recognized governmental administrators, and there must be some effective way of ensuring that this interaction is relatively smooth and that conflicts are resolved along lines corresponding to the leadership's priorities. Yet, if they are to remain "nongovernmental" agencies, it would seem crucial to subordinate them informally to another nongovernmental organization such as the Party rather than directly and explicitly to the government.

A final advantage derived from using the local Party organs as the regional super-coordinator—and probably the most important advantage—is the special mystique which they possess as being part of the ruling party. Just as the position of the President of the United States is enhanced by the fact that he possesses the aura of the chief of state, so the regional coordinator in the Soviet Union has stronger position and may be able to resolve conflicts with greater ease because he can speak as "the Party." This is particularly important because, as James Fesler has pointed out, the area coordinator is inherently likely to be in the weaker position than the functional hierarchies in the type of dual subordination found in the Soviet Union.

In this concluding section we have explained the role of the local Party organizations largely as a response to real problems of very large organiza-tions. While this response may not have been a completely conscious one, we have suggested that the role of the Party organs in decision-making would have been modified had it not been at least partially con-ducive to the smooth operation of the administrative system and the ful-fillment of rational-technical goals.

We have not meant to suggest that there are no costs for the use of the Party organs in decision-making. There is an increase in staff involved and a resulting drain of trained personnel from other work. Moreover, as Stalin admitted, the deviation from a simple line of command "will complicate the work of administration." There are additional conferences, additional conflicts, additional need for clearance.

Yet the costs can be overemphasized. While the lines of authority and influence become rather complex, there is little evidence that the complexity "destroys all sense of responsibility and competence." From the outside the organization chart may appear almost hopelessly confused with its interlocking Party and state hierarchies, but from below (that is, from the point of view of the lower administrator) it is much clearer. When one explores this matter with plant managers, for example, it is obvious that they know the relative standing of the different officials and they have a good idea as to how important a question must be and what type it must be before it is taken to a particular governmental or Party official. Moreover, they insist that basically there is order within the enterprise itself—that the Party secretary is usually consulted regularly and that he and the manager are normally able to find a common language without referring questions upward.

This evidence is scarcely conclusive, but it remains true that, whatever the possibilities of chaos, the administrative system in the Soviet Union does function and has functioned for many years. If we are to judge by such indicators as industrial growth, development of education and science, and progress in public health, the administrative system has functioned reasonably well, and at the least it has produced results in the areas of priority.

It may be that the attempt to supervise all phases of life directly within the framework of a single hierarchical system will ultimately prove impractical as society becomes more complex. Perhaps the system will have to be abandoned in favor of one in which the bureaucracies are more autonomous and are controlled by more indirect ways (such as through the manipulation of the price system). Yet, *once* the leadership has decided to create a unified bureaucratic society, it is difficult to avoid the conclusion that the advantages of Party participation outweigh the costs, for some of the functions the Party organs fulfill seem absolutely required in such a unified system. If for some reason the Soviet leadership decides to restrict the lower Party organs to ideological work, it would seem certain that they will have to create other institutions to carry out at least some of their responsibilities.

* * *

11

KEYNOTE–COMPROMISE

LEONARD SCHAPIRO

The Twenty-fourth Congress of the Communist Party of the Soviet Union, which met from March 30 to April 9, 1971, produced no surprises. Its proceedings were as bland, uneventful, colorless, and smooth as a play being performed on the stage for the third year running. In particular, there were no outward indications of the serious policy disputes which are believed to have been going on within the top Soviet leadership since the Central Committee plenum of December, 1969, whose proceedings were only fragmentarily reported at the time and still remain shrouded in a great deal of mystery.[1]

The subject matter of these disputes necessarily continues to be conjectural, but two broad areas of conflict can safely be identified. One centers on questions of general industrial management policy—in particular, the best ways to increase production. Should greater emphasis be placed on discipline, *dirigisme*, and stern control from the center; or, on the contrary, should greater stress be laid on material incentives, on economic and market price indicators (rather than superplanning), and on decentralization of control over individual enterprises? The second major area of dispute concerns broad economic priorities. Should heavy industry take absolute priority over consumer goods; or should some concessions be made to the long-suffering Soviet consumer even at the expense of heavy industry?

By and large, the views that favor discipline, centralized controls, and absolute priority for heavy industry can be regarded as those of the Party

[1] General Secretary Leonid Brezhnev's speech at the December 15, 1969, session of the plenum was never published, and the official communique issued following the plenum emitted the usual statement that the Central Committee's approval of Politburo policies had been "unanimous." See Sidney L. Ploss, "Politics in the Kremlin," *Problems of Communism* 21, No. 3 (May-June, 1970): 10–11.

Reprinted from *Problems of Communism* 20, No. 4 (July-August, 1971): 2–8.

apparatus, while the views that look toward greater reliance on material incentives, increased application of market principles, decentralization of industrial controls, and higher priority for consumer goods can be identified with the government apparatus, including the planners and managers. Thus, the policy conflicts are inextricably tied in with the whole question of the balance between the Party and the government-administrative apparatus, and this in turn reduces itself, in actual Soviet conditions, to a struggle within the collective leadership between the man who symbolizes the Party, General Secretary Leonid Brezhnev, and the man who stands for the technocratic machine, Premier Aleksei Kosygin. It is not necessarily— indeed, not even primarily—a personal struggle, but in Soviet conditions it tends to become personalized. Viewed in this light, the Twenty-fourth Congress outwardly appeared in many ways, as will be seen later, to mark the personal ascendancy of Brezhnev, but the proceedings shed little light on the implications of this for future policy.

Certainly, no signs of any policy disagreement cropped up during the Congress proceedings. The voting, of course, was unanimous—there would have been something serously wrong with the machinery of Party management had it been otherwise. But not even a hint of any differences of outlook could be gleaned from the speeches of the principal actors. Kosygin, dealing with economic policy some days after it had already been fully expounded by Brezhnev in the Central Committee's report,[2] gave no sign of any concern whatever over the fact that the policy of economic decentralization with which he was closely associated was as dead as the dodo.[3] He endorsed Brezhnev's emphasis on discipline, *dirigisme*, and technical efficiency as the keys to increased production. Yet the debates which had undoubtedly taken place within the leadership on this issue (among others) in advance of the Congress must have been sufficiently furious to necessitate the postponement of the Congress session until March, 1971—even though Brezhnev himself had announced last July that it would be held in 1970,[4] and even though the postponement meant sacrificing the opportunity, so dear to Communist hearts, to associate the occasion with the centenary of Lenin's birth.

Again, if there had been any behind-the-scenes controversy over the issue of "guns versus butter" in the months preceding the Congress, no visible signs of it appeared at the session. Both Brezhnev and Kosygin placed equal stress on concern for the consumer, and the Congress formally endorsed the draft directives on the new Five-Year Plan (published on February 14, 1971), which envisage what would appear to be substantial concessions to consumers.[5] How far these promises by both Party and government leaders will be fulfilled, however, only time will tell. For the moment, it is necessary to bear in mind, first, that the great bulk of capital available for investment is to go into heavy industry and,

[2] *Pravda* (Moscow), March 31, 1971, pp. 2–10.
[3] *Ibid.*, April 7, 1971, pp. 2–7.
[4] *Ibid.*, July 3, 1970, p. 3.
[5] *Ibid.*, April 11, 1971, p. 1.

second, that the promised rise in the standard of living, according to Kosygin, is dependent on a rise in labor productivity as compared with the last (Eighth) Five-Year Plan. "In the Ninth Five-Year Plan period," he told the Congress, "we have to derive 80–85 per cent of the whole increase in material income from increased productivity of labor." This would seem to be an ambitious hope, since increased productivity is in turn to be dependent upon improved discipline, better management and direction, and technological advance.

This cursory glance at the economic background is necessary in order to understand what appears to have been the main political result of the Congress: namely, general acquiescence to increased Party ascendancy within the collective leadership. There were, of course, other equally important factors involved. Outside events may well have made all the leaders more anxious for compromise, peace, and harmony at home. Events in Czechoslovakia in particular, showed how quickly economic reform could lead to demands for political reform and hence to a diminution of the Party's stranglehold over national life—and no doubt every type of Soviet leader, whether a Party boss or a government bureaucrat, has now persuaded himself that to diminish the Party's monopoly of power is to invite counterrevolution. More recently, the events in Poland showed that the working class was prepared even to use force (and risk savage repression) if its standards of living remained too far below its expectations. It is against this background, then, that the changes formalized by the Congress in the leadership and role of the Party must be seen.

Before looking at the new Party leadership, however, it may be useful to summarize the general information on the Party made available at the Congress.[6] The total strength of the Party is now given as 14,455,321, of whom 13,810,089 are full members, and 645,232, probationary members. (According to Brezhnev, the total figure represents 9 per cent of the adult population.) The annual rate of growth of the Party since 1966 has been between 2.6 and 3.9 per cent, according to the latest published statistics. The same statistics show that the rate of growth in the period 1961–65 was substantially higher, ranging between 5 and 6.1 per cent.

It would appear that there has been a continuation of the stress, apparent since the Khrushchev era, on recruiting new members from the working class. Officially, the composition of the Party membership by social status is now given as: workers, 40.1 per cent; peasants, 15.1 per cent; and employees (nonmanual salaried workers), 44.8 per cent. (Of the 3 million admitted to the Party since the last Congress, over half are placed in the workers' category, and the proportion is said to have been higher in the main industrial areas.) The percentage of Party members described as workers had already risen during the period from 1956 to 1967 from 32 to 38.1.[7] (Naturally, however, all these figures have to be treated with caution, since those described as "workers" in past Party

[6] *Ibid.*, March 31, 1971, p. 9.
[7] T. H. Rigby, *Communist Party Membership in the USSR, 1917–67* (Princeton, N.J.: Princeton University Press, 1968), p. 325.

statistics have often turned out to be foremen or other persons in white-collar positions of authority.) According to the data announced at the Congress, there has also been an increase in the number of women Party members, who now number "over 3 million," or between 22 and 24 per cent of total membership [8] as compared with 20.9 per cent in 1967, the last published statistic.

On the all-important matter of the age and seniority of Party members, the information given out at the Congress was confined to the 4,963 Congress delegates.[9] Of these, 4,740 were voting delegates, each representing 2,900 Party members, and the remaining 223 were nonvoting delegates, representing the 645,232 probationary (or candidate) members. These delegates may be described as the aristocracy of the Party rather than a true cross-section of the Party rank and file. Indeed, the presence of only 1,195 "worker" and 879 "peasant" delegates left some 58 per cent of the delegates representing the Party, state, army, and police apparatus and the intellectuals (it should be noted in passing that only very orthodox conformists from the intellectual community were allowed to attend this Congress, marking a shift away from Khrushchev's more tolerant attitude). Of the preponderant group of "white collar" delegates, a very large number—1,698 in all—were secretaries from all levels of the Party apparatus. The age and seniority figures released concerning the delegates provide an interesting comparison with the most recent corresponding date (1967) for the Party as a whole.[10] The figures show that nearly three-fourths of the delegates to the Congress joined the Party after 1946, which closely approximates the corresponding situation in the Party as a whole as of 1967. On the other hand, 88.2 per cent of the delegates were over forty (and 26.6 per cent over fifty)—a substantial deviation from the age composition of the Party as a whole in 1967, when over half of all Party members were under forty. This tends to support evidence available from other sources indicating that the Party apparatus, down to and including the regional (oblast) level, is now in the hands of the over-fifties, and below that, of the over-forties. Certainly there was no sign at the Twenty-fourth Congress that there is any intention to change this age pattern in the near future.

Some other items of interest were disclosed at the Congress. For example, it is useful to know—since the subject has been shrouded in so much mystery—that two-thirds of the Party's budget expenditures are now met out of members' dues.[11] Of still greater interest is the information that in the five years between the Twenty-third and Twenty-fourth Congresses, 200,000 Party secretaries, heads of departments (of Party committees), and editors of Party newspapers at all levels were sent to refresher courses in Party schools.[12] This means that an average of about

[8] *Pravda*, April 3, 1971.
[9] *Ibid.*, p. 4.
[10] Rigby, *Communist Party Membership*, p. 354.
[11] *Pravda*, April 1, 1971.
[12] *Ibid.*

40,000 members of the apparatus were absent from their jobs in each of these years. Obviously, no precise figure for the total size of the Party apparatus can be inferred from these statistics, but they do suggest that an estimate of around 250,000 for the apparatus as a whole may be nearer the mark than the estimates of 180,000, and even 100,000, which some writers have advanced. One in six absent on a refresher course during each year makes sense; one in three, or even one in four, would seem to make no sense at all.

So far the picture is one of stability, conservatism, and an absence of substantial change. But there were some disclosures at the Congress which seemed to indicate new trends. A minor item was Brezhnev's disclosure that the Secretariat, like the Politburo, only meets weekly; under Khrushchev it certainly met much more frequently.[13] A more significant item was the announcement that there is to be a recall and exchange of Party cards.[14] Since the issuance of a new card involves an inquiry into the record of the holder, an exchange of cards usually presages a relatively mild purge of the Party membership. This apparently projected purge, or quasi-purge, would be fully in line with the demand for greater Party discipline and effort which was a key theme of the speeches delivered at the Congress. (Brezhnev revealed incidentally that the last exchange of Party cards took place in 1954.)

The greatest interest of all attaches to the changes in the Party rules adopted at the Congress.[15] All-Union Party congresses are now to meet every five years instead of every four; Union-republic congresses, "at least" once in five years; and lower-level Party conferences, at intervals of two to three years. This change is probably consistent with actual practice and with the growth of the Party; and it also correlates the holding of all-Union congresses with the five-year plan periods. At the same time, there is nothing in the new rules to indicate that Party democracy will be strengthened either by requiring the holding of all-Union Party conferences between all-Union congresses, or even by providing for more frequent Central Committee plenary meetings.

A more important change in the rules illustrates the enhanced role which the Party organizations evidently are now intended to play in directing the whole life of the country. The "control" authority of the primary Party organizations has been considerably extended. Hitherto such "control"—which in Russian (as in French) means "supervision" and in practice signifies responsibility for policy as well as its implementation, with all the powers of interference that this responsibility entails—has been confined to economic organizations. Now the power of control is to be extended to the primary Party organizations of "drafting organizations, design bureaus, institutes engaged in scientific research, educational establishments engaged in cultural and enlightenment work and in medical care."

---

[13] *Ibid.*, March 31, 1971, p. 9.
[14] *Ibid.*, p. 10.
[15] *Ibid.*

This is a formidable list and no doubt reflects a growing concern on the part of the Party leadership over the emergence of dissent, particularly among the all-important scientists. The inclusion of establishments concerned with health could well be a consequence of the fact that both the Academy of Sciences and—in one instance at any rate—the medical profession have displayed opposition to the increasingly frequent official practice of using certification of lunacy as a method of repressing dissenters. No one at the Congress—not even the normally voluble and intemperate Mikhail Sholokhov—had anything to say directly on the subject of dissent, except to imply that certain intellectuals are worthy only of contempt. However, this change in the Party rules seemed to provide a more concrete indication of the future direction of policy on this subject.

"Control" by the primary Party organizations has been strengthened, though in somewhat vague terms, in state bodies as well. Hitherto, the primary Party organizations in government departments, state committees, and the like had no right of "control," but merely the right to complain to higher Party authorities if they disagreed with the policy being pursued. Under the new rules, however, they are to exercise "control" to the extent of ensuring "that directives of the Party and government and observance of the law are carried out"—which, in Soviet practice, is likely to provide quite a large opening for Party interference in state administrative operations. Brezhnev did make it clear that the "control" to be exercised by the primary party organization of a state ministry will not extend to individual enterprises subordinate to the ministry. (Enterprises will, of course, remain subject, as hitherto, to "control" by their own primary Party organizations.)

As was to be expected, this increase in the power of the Party apparatus in relation to a sphere of activity in which the government apparatus had enjoyed relative independence since the fall of Khrushchev in late 1964 is reflected in the new Politburo named by the Twenty-fourth Congress. Headed by Brezhnev as General Secretary, the full members have been increased in number to fifteen. There were no demotions or expulsions. A curious practice which had first been employed at the time of the Twenty-third Congress in 1966 was again followed in announcing the new roster of Politburo members. When the list of those elected was first broadcast over the radio,[16] it was not in alphabetical order but in what must have been some kind of order of ranking, or of importance of function. However, when the proceedings of the Congress were reported in the press the following day (April 10),[17] the names were listed alphabetically. (It was, perhaps, just a happy chance that Brezhnev placed first in both versions, but one might speculate that KGB Chairman Yu. V. Andropov's chances of being elevated from the status of candidate member to full member of the Politburo may possibly have been adversely affected by the fact that alphabetically he would have ranked ahead of Brezhnev if promoted!)

[16] Radio Moscow broadcast, April 9, 1971.
[17] *Pravda*, April 10, 1971, p. 1.

The names of the full Politburo members, in the order of the initial broadcast, were as follows: L. I. Brezhnev, N. V. Podgorny, A. N. Kosygin, M. A. Suslov, A. P. Kirilenko, A. J. Pelse, K. T. Mazurov, D. S. Polyansky, P. Ye. Shelest, G. I. Voronov, A. N. Shelepin, V. V. Grishin, D. A. Kunayev, V. V. Shcherbitsky, F. D. Kulakov. (The last four are the new members who have been added to the previous incumbents, all of whom remain.) The most important changes in ranking from the last congress were Kosygin's demotion from second to third place, below Podgorny, and the relegation of Shelepin—whose rivalry with Brezhnev has been the subject of many rumors (no doubt often inspired) to last place before the new members. Of the new members, Kulakov, the Party secretary responsible for agriculture, was elected to full membership without having previously served as a candidate, while the remaining three had all been candidate members. No new candidate members were elected.

The new makeup of the Politburo illustrates the enhanced position of Brezhnev in several ways. Three of the four new members—Kulakov, Kunayev and Shcherbitsky—are known to be his close supporters, although the position of Grishin is less certain. This reinforcement of Brezhnev's position, moreover, has not been balanced by the elevation of anyone who can be regarded as more likely to support the views and interests of the government side of the hierarchy. There is, for example, no military member of the Politburo. Moreover, D. F. Ustinov, whose position as the Party's "controller" of the armaments industry alone would logically entitle him to full membership, remains only a candidate member, while three of his former fellow candidate members have been promoted over his head. (Ustinov is also believed to head the Administrative Organs Department of the Central Commitee Secretariat, which controls the KGB, the army, the judiciary, and the procuracy.) At the same time, the elevation of Kulakov to full membership strengthens the representation of the Secretariat on the Politburo.

In spite of all this, it still appears quite premature to talk of the end of collective leadership or—notwithstanding Brezhnev's inordinate vanity —of a new "cult of personality." There can be no doubt that Brezhnev has increased his support within the Politburo, but he is still not the undisputed master of that body. Nor is he the single master of the KGB, which remains subordinate to the whole Party leadership. He has increased his influence over the government hierarchy and therefore over the army, since it is administratively subordinate to the Ministry of Defense; and he may well be Chairman of the Supreme Defense Council, although clear information on this is lacking. Nevertheless, both the state machine and the army remain powerful organizations which still retain a good measure of independence and influence. Indeed, insofar as the new Politburo is concerned, all indications are that the action of the congress embodied a compromise—even if it was a compromise in which Brezhnev has come out best.

The new Central Committee also reveals some slight evidence of compromise. The Central Committee has, of course, lost a good deal of status in past years and apparently no longer plays an important part in decision-making. Nevertheless, its membership represents the Party aristocracy, and its composition at least provides an index of the way in which influence is distributed among different segments of the Soviet elite.

The Central Committee elected by the congress consists of 241 full members and 155 candidate members, as compared with 195 and 165, respectively, elected in 1966. (Eighty-one members were also elected to the CPSU Central Auditing Commission.) The stability which characterizes the new Politburo is also evident in the Central Committee, certainly among the full members, 63.9 per cent of whom were re-elected from among the members of the old Committee. In addition, 15.7 and 1.7 per cent of the new full members were elected from among the old candidate members and members of the Auditing Commission, respectively. In both these latter categories, which constitute the next two lower tiers of the Party "aristocracy," the turnover was, as usual, somewhat higher. Thus, of the new candidate members, 45.8 per cent were re-elected from among the old, while 11 per cent were promoted from the old Auditing Commission; and in the new Auditing Commission, 39.5 per cent of the members are re-elected holdovers, while 3.7 per cent are former full Central Committee members who have now been demoted to the Auditing Commission.[18] Interestingly enough, these latter appear to be mostly persons whose careers have associated them with Shelepin—a fact which provides further evidence that he has fallen from grace. At the same time, it illustrates that the consequences of such a fall from grace were relatively mild at this congress by comparison with the past.

There are several other features about the new Central Committee which are worth noting. One is that the total number of military members of the three tiers of the Central Committee remains the same as in 1966—*i.e.*, 36. In percentage, however, their representation has been somewhat reduced (from 8.2 to 7.5 per cent) as a consequence of the increased size of the new Committee. On the other hand, the KGB has very slightly—one might almost say symbolically—increased its representation on the Committee. This increase is not among the full members, where the Chairman alone appears; but three deputy chairmen of the KGB have now reached the lower levels—two as candidate members, and one as a member of the Auditing Commission. There has also been a notable increase in the number of heads of Central Committee Departments—the most senior "civil servants" of the CPSU apparatus—elected to the Central Committee: five of them are now full members, and seven are candidate members, as compared with two and three, respectively, on the preceding Central Committee.

One further development in the new Central Committee merits special attention: namely, the emergence among the full members of twelve regional Party first secretaries of a new and markedly different type. It need hardly be emphasized that the regional (oblast) first secretaries are

[18] *Ibid.*, April 9, 1966, and April 10, 1971.

among the most powerful men in the land. The Politburo may decide and order, but it is the first secretaries of the regions who can make or break policies. The fall of Khrushchev in October, 1964, was, at least in part, due to the fact that he had tried to curb the authority of the regional first secretaries by introducing his short-lived reform dividing the oblast Party committees into two separate committees for industry and agriculture, which had the effect (or would have had the effect, had it been fully implemented) of substantially reducing the first secretaries' powers. The dozen regional first secretaries who have now become full members of the Central Committee were all appointed to their regional posts, which traditionally carry full Central Committee membership, within a few months preceding the congress, replacing men in their early sixties who have apparently been retired. They are all young—in their forties, as against the average of fifty—and what is most important, they have all had long and extensive technical experience rather than just some technical training, while on the other hand their experience in the Party apparatus has been slight or even, in some cases, nonexistent. This development *could* be the beginning of an important change in Party-state relations. If, as is apparently intended, the Party is now to be licensed to interfere more and more in technical matters, it may conceivably sugar the pill if the interference is practiced by men who know the job as well, or almost as well, as the managers and experts whom the Party apparatus proposes to "control." The fact that these regional appointments were made just prior to the Twenty-fourth Congress suggests the possibility that they may have been part of a compromise arrangement between Brezhnev and Kosygin. . . .

* * *

IV

The Economy
and the Bureaucracy

Nothing affects the quality of Soviet life more directly than the system of producing and distributing goods and services. Over the past fifty years this system has been subject to considerable experimentation and modification, and few people today doubt that the methods of organizing production in the Soviet Union will change considerably in the years to come. Lenin himself experimented with two very different approaches: the policies of "war communism," involving extensive nationalization of production and barter exchange, and the "New Economic Policy" (NEP), heralding a partial return to private enterprise and a market economy. Stalin abandoned the NEP in 1928 and through his five-year plans laid the basis of the present system. Indeed, to a large extent, Stalin's programs of industrialization and collectivization consummated the communization of Soviet society begun by the 1917 Revolution. The central characteristics of the system developed under Stalin were, first, the abolition of private ownership of production; second, centralized planning for all sectors of the economy; third, administration by industrial units; and fourth, a complex of incentives that involved compulsory labor discipline mixed with material rewards for meeting required quotas.

The Stalinist system proved to be adequate for transforming an agricultural economy into an industrial one and sustaining a high rate of growth in the early stages of industrialization. It met the essential military needs of World War II and produced for the Soviet populace a higher standard of living than it had ever known. But as the Soviet industrial economy increased in productivity and complexity the system of centralized planning divorced from the market and popular control revealed a number of dysfunctional features. Chief among them was the waste and inefficiency of extensive centralization. Many Soviet planners found themselves drowning in oceans of paper as they attempted to assimilate information about the millions of items that had to be calculated in the plan. A tendency developed for each of the ministries having responsibility for a particular industry—there were thirty-two at Stalin's death—to become self-sufficient and duplicate production and distribution facilities at the local level. Soviet reliance upon quotas as an index of successful completion of state requirements created built-in pressures for deception and falsification of statistics. Enterprises tended to strive for the lowest possible quota and to maximize production of those items that showed the highest gain in quantitative terms. The result was an underutilization of resources and the production of many consumer goods of inferior quality or design. On top of this, labor morale suffered under the compulsion to work, particularly in agriculture, where the rewards have been the least.

Since Stalin's death there have been a number of reforms to overcome these and other problems. During Khrushchev's administration the most important was his scheme for decentralization introduced in 1957. Under this plan, the country was divided into 105 economic regions, each headed by a regional economic council (*sovnarkhoz*). The principle of industrial administration developed under Stalin for planning and management was replaced by the territorial principle. Even with some decentralization of administration, over-all planning authority remained in the hands of central agencies such as the State Planning Committee. Khrushchev hoped by his reorganization scheme to promote greater cooperation of enterprises within each region that previously had gone their separate ways because they were under the jurisdiction of different ministries. It might be added that Khrushchev had a political motive in his reorganization plan: He wanted to strengthen the authority of the Party organization over the economy at the expense of the state bureaucracy.

The decline in Soviet economic growth in the latter years of Khrushchev's rule not only contributed to this overthrow but made inevitable further reform of the economy. In September, 1965, Prime Minister Kosygin introduced a number of reforms designed to improve industrial management and planning and to enhance the effectiveness of economic incentives throughout industry. Administration by industries replaced the territorial principle. Khrushchev's regional economic councils were abandoned altogether. Recentralization, however, was accompanied by reforms giving Soviet managers considerably greater freedom to operate their enterprises. Entirely new incentives were introduced. For those enterprises coming under the reforms, the index of efficiency was determined by profitability (as measured by capital invested) rather than solely by meeting fixed quantitative quotas. It was anticipated that many of the detailed decisions previously left to central planners could be made by the producer according to the dictates of consumer demand. Enterprises that proved efficient and fulfilled their over-all plans were entitled to set aside funds for bonuses as worker incentives.

These attempts to achieve a form of "market socialism" have not been successful. Kosygin himself admitted as much at the Twenty-fourth Party Congress in April, 1971. He was compelled to endorse instead the emphasis of Brezhnev on central control, discipline, and technical efficiency as the keys to economic growth. The prospects are for continued experimentation for the most productive system of economic management.

The article by Hardt, Gallik, and Treml is part of a study proposed in 1966 for the Subcommittee on Foreign Economic Policy of the Joint Economic Committee of the United States Congress. David Granick is Professor of Economics at the University of Wisconsin and author of *Management of the Industrial Firm in the USSR: A Study in Soviet Economic Planning*, among other works. Yevsei Liberman is Professor of Economics at Kharkov University. It was he who first publicly advocated profitability as an industrial yardstick. Though his ideas are not as popular today as they were in the 1960's, they touched off a debate that has not yet been resolved.

*   *   *

12

INSTITUTIONAL STAGNATION AND CHANGING ECONOMIC STRATEGY IN THE SOVIET UNION

JOHN P. HARDT, DIMITRI M. GALLIK, AND VLADIMIR G. TREML

THE SEARCH FOR A NEW PATTERN

The Khrushchevian Approach: The Party's Search for Accommodation. Despite the many administrative changes that have been made in the Soviet economic system since the death of Stalin, the basic elements of the Stalinist model are still in force. A high rate of investment, priority to producer goods industries, collectivized agriculture, and tight central control of the economy are still the cardinal features of the system. In general, the efforts of Stalin's successors, Khrushchev in particular, have been directed toward redressing, in an *ad hoc* and haphazard manner, the grossest imbalances, inequities, and inefficiencies of the system with as little alteration of the basic framework as possible.

Reprinted from *New Directions in the Soviet Economy*, studies prepared for the Subcommittee on Foreign Economic Policy of the Joint Economic Committee, 89th Cong., 2d sess., Part I, Chapters III and IV (Washington, D.C.: GPO, 1966), pp. 44–62. The footnotes have been omitted.

Some of the most significant changes have occurred in the sphere of labor controls. The most abhorrent Stalinist practices—forced labor camps, forced recruitment of labor—have been eliminated or mitigated. Stringent restrictions on the spatial and occupational mobility of labor have been relaxed. The harsh penalties for unauthorized quitting of job, absenteeism, and tardiness have been reduced. Improvements have been made in working conditions, fringe benefits, grievance procedures, and wage rates. In brief, in the area of labor relations, there has been a trend away from coercion and toward positive incentives, away from direct administrative controls toward indirect and more flexible controls. These changes may have been instituted in part to improve labor productivity and efficiency, but they have made it more difficult to enforce strict labor discipline. Much of what the Soviets consider an alarmingly high rate of labor turnover is due to the "spontaneous, unorganized movement of labor." In many cases, this has contributed materially to high labor costs and to regional labor shortages combined with surpluses of labor in other areas.

In other aspects of the economy, Khrushchev's approach to the solution of economic problems was administrative reorganization and a reshuffling of responsibilities. Major reorganizations were followed by the creation of new agencies and the enactment of stopgap measures to fill in the weak spots of the reorganized system as they showed up after it was in operation. Despite avowed intentions of decentralizing and greater local autonomy, the end result was even tighter central control in many respects and greater involvement of Party officials in economic affairs.

In agriculture, Khrushchev made a major institutional change with the abolition of the machine-tractor stations (MTS) in 1958. From the standpoint of relaxation of central control, however, this change was more apparent than real. Although the MTS had originally been established to reinforce the regime's grip on agriculture and to extract for state purposes the greatest possible share of the peasants' product, they had apparently outlived their usefulness in this respect and in addition had become a major source of agricultural inefficiency. Other means of achieving these ends had been established; compulsory deliveries to the state were still exacted, and generally at a high level. Central control of agriculture was even increased through conversion of some collective farms into state farms and through amalgamation of many collective farms. Some improvements were made in the structure of agricultural prices and in the system of income incentives to collective farmers. But on the whole, administrative control of collectivized agriculture remained in full force and may indeed have been even strengthened.

A not insignificant element in Soviet agriculture—individuals' private plots—has generally escaped the tight control exercised over the bulk of agriculture. In respect to this sector, Khrushchev's policy was ambivalent and vacillating, with alternating restrictive and permissive measures. Although compulsory deliveries from the output of the private plots were abolished in 1958, restrictions were later imposed on the size of the plots and on the availability of material inputs.

In an attempt to eliminate some of the bureaucratic fetters imposed on the economy by highly centralized control, in 1957 Khrushchev abolished most of the central ministries dealing with economic affairs and replaced them with a regionally organized system of economic councils. The latter, however, soon developed hindrances of its own; the problems associated with the "departmentalist" tendencies of the ministerial system were supplanted by equally objectionable tendencies toward "localism" under the new setup. To counteract these tendencies, a superstructure of central "state committees" and larger regional and nationwide economic councils was generally superimposed on the system of regional economic councils, and was capped by a "supreme" economic council in 1963. Eventually this system became as cumbersome and rigidified as the one it replaced, and it has undoubtedly contributed materially to the problems of information flow, both upward and downward, and to coordination of planning.

Khrushchev is usually thought of as a champion of "campaignology"—the tactics of instituting change or breaking bottlenecks through an intensive and extensive "campaign" that is often hurried and wasteful and sometimes ill-advised. In agriculture, he is associated with the "campaigns" of plowing up the virgin lands, expansion of acreage under corn, reducing the area in fallow and grasslands; in industry he is given credit for relatively drastic and sudden changes in the sectoral structure, notably the forced expansion of the chemical industry. However, Khrushchev was following a well-established Stalinist tradition that has been used throughout Soviet history, and in fact it is the nature of the system that commands or suggestions from the leaders should be followed up with more than desirable zeal. Although this may have been a useful technique for rapid economic growth during the early period of Soviet industrialization, in a technologically and industrially more mature economy such tactics may cause upheavals and aggravate distortions that become serious obstacles to growth. Some Soviet economists have argued that at least part of the rising capital-output ratio in the economy, and consequently part of the slowdown in the growth rate, is due to the haste with which recent structural changes have been effected.

Planning in Flux: The Economists' Quest for Rationality. Many Western scholars have observed that by the late 1950's the Soviet system had arrived at a crossroads, but all alternatives perceived by the political leadership have certain political and ideological pitfalls and none—at least to Party doctrinaires—represents a failproof guarantee of economic success. The difficulty of choice has been further compounded by the fact that the post-Stalin leadership has been displaying some confusion with respect to the ultimate politico-economic goals of the system. The revolutionary fervor has spent itself, the short-range goals of rapid industrialization and building up of a powerful military machine have been largely achieved, direct support of world Communist revolutions and world dominance has apparently been scaled down on the priority list, as the Chinese ideologists tirelessly keep pointing out. The transformation of the

Soviet socialist society into a Communist world of plenty has ceased to be a heroic, pseudoreligious, distant goal. The vision that has inflamed generations of Communist followers lost some of its appeal when the leaders found it necessary to engage in estimation of per capita shoe production in the future Communist society (Twenty-second Congress Party Program). The normal, for a group in control, goal of preserving one's power leads to a desire for maintaining the *status quo*, but this is precisely what the regime cannot do.

By the late 1950's it was clear that the planning and control system simply could not cope with the new problems. The overcentralized system lacked direction and presented growing evidence of inefficiency. The most painful aspect of this institutional stagnation from the point of view of the leadership has been the gradually declining responsiveness of the system to commands from above, which is eroding the policy-making powers of the Party.

The inadequacy of present over-all economic controls is further illustrated by the unending and so far fruitless discussions on setting up an over-all balance sheet for the national economy that would integrate the balance sheets for individual products, national income flows, consumption and investment, and monetary flows. While the need for such a single equilibrating instrument of planning has been strongly felt since the late 1920's, no serious attempt has been made to design and implement one. Strumilin lamented the absence of such a balance as early as 1954, and other economists and planners have regularly advanced proposals for one. However, as most specialists testify, the problem of a single integrated plan has remained basically unresolved. In the last four or five years, interest has shifted to the construction and operation of *ex-post* and planning input-output tables. Substantial human and financial resources have been allocated to this work, and several rather impressive national and regional input-output tables have been prepared. However, as with other sophisticated tools of economic analysis, input-output techniques remain essentially in an experimental stage and have not been integrated with planning.

The emergence of a new school of economics. Thus the need for change and reform has been clearly recognized. But change in what direction? The difficulty confronting the leadership has been compounded by the very nature of the system which, to say the least, is not conducive to open and thorough examination of meaningful politico-economic alternatives. While many of the oppressive aspects of Stalin's era have gradually disappeared, the debate on economic reforms was and is by no means free, although in looking back over the past two or three years a Western observer is surprised by the candor of the criticism and the unorthodoxy of the alternatives proposed by some of the more recalcitrant economists and planners.

A complete return to Stalinism with or without an omnipotent dictator has never been a feasible choice, and not only for political reasons. Stalin's methods were simply too crude to be applied to a more mature economy, and, furthermore, the inefficiency syndrome has been clearly identified with Stalin's heritage.

A much more appealing choice supported by many professional economists and planners is seen in a highly centralized hierarchic system but with a much more sophisticated control and information mechanism. The supporters of the centralized system have refused to accept any general criticism of the existing state of affairs and see only isolated shortcomings and defects in specific instances—all of which are, in their opinion, correctable. In their defense of the present system, the advocates of the *status quo*, the dogmatists of the economic and planning professions, and the proponents of centralization generally received some unexpected help from a new quarter—the rapidly developing science of data-processing and the emerging school of mathematically oriented economists.

For a long time mathematical economics was condemned in the U.S.S.R. as essentially alien to the Soviet science of political economy. Linear programming, input-output analysis, game theory, the multitude of new techniques offered by econometrics, and other applications of mathematics to economics were developed and applied largely in the West, and this fact in itself made the new methods unpalatable to the Soviet leadership. Under Stalin and well into the 1950's, the responsibility of the emasculated Soviet economic profession was reduced to interpretation and propagation of the tenets of Marxism-Leninism-Stalinism, to favorable elucidation of Soviet economic progress, and to minor, essentially technical, studies of very limited scope. In the somewhat more liberal atmosphere of the post-Stalin years, a slow recovery began but, by and large, nothing of significant theoretical or applied importance has yet appeared, with the exception of one area—that of mathematical economics. Trained almost exclusively by Academicians V. Menchinov and L. Kantorovich and Professor V. Novozhilov—who have long been considered dissenters and heretical—young mathematically oriented economists began to explore Western models and methods. These attempts met with bitter opposition on the part of the older, more dogmatic members of the profession, who accused the new school of employing anti-Marxian methods and of succumbing to "bourgeois vulgar science." The Party, however, contributed somewhat to the progress of the "new economics" by adopting a position of near-neutrality in the dispute. Impressed by the revolutionary progress in computer technology in the West and cognizant of the need for parallel development of "software" such as information systems, theoretical models, and the like, the Party left the new school almost completely free to explore the new methods.

Especially in the early days of debate, the proponents of the new techniques explicitly or implicitly promised a panacea for all the ills of the economy—a streamlined system of reporting and collection of data, invigorated methods of control, rapid estimation of feasible alternatives, and construction of mutually consistent plans. For example, very ambitious plans for "cybernetization and computerization" of planning were

laid out in a paper presented to the April, 1960, Conference on Mathematical Applications in Economics and Planning by an early proponent
of mathematics in planning. All this was apparently to be effected without major changes in the system. The leadership was, needless to say,
enticed by the emerging vision of this paragon of central planning: The
entire country is covered by a network of computers, which receive and
process primary economic data and pass the information on to a few large
computer centers and then to a central master computer complex. This
"giant central brain" would then check and sort out all the information,
correct all inconsistencies, reduce the mass of data to a few macroeconomic indexes, and finally present the political leaders with a set of
feasible alternatives. The first more or less open clash between economists
and planners favoring an extensive computerized system with detailed
microcontrols and members of a new school advocating introduction of
more rigorous mathematical analysis with concomitant decentralization
of decision-making occurred at a March, 1964, "Round Table Discussion
by Economists and Mathematicians." As one participant observed later,
the "round table" proved to have rather sharp edges as economists of
the older generation accused the young radicals of disdain toward Marxism, and the latter retorted that the disdain was directed not toward
Marxism but toward the dogmatic interpretation of it.

It is impossible to say whether all members of the new school were
completely convinced of the feasibility of such a system or whether this
was simply a strategem to lure the Party ideologists into acceptance of
the new techniques. There is strong evidence that the latter was true in
many instances. That the strategem was effective is evidenced by the
position of neutrality taken by the Party in the ideological struggle with
the dogmatic economists and by the substantial resources allocated to
economic experiments.

The hopes for immediate integration of new techniques such as input-
output analysis or linear programing with operational planning soon
proved to have been premature. The more extensive the exploration of
new methods became, the more defects and shortcomings of the existing
system were exposed. Gradual improvement of planning and data-processing through applications of computers and new techniques appeared less
and less promising, and the new school began to demand wide-ranging
radical reforms of the entire system. The grand scheme of a computerized
system with detailed central planning and control also turned out to be
unfounded. Not only the young radicals but also such authorities as
Academician A. Dorodnitsyn dismissed such plans as impossible in practice and advocated "autonomy of individual blocs which would be motivated not by outside controls but by inner economic stimuli." Numerous
other economists of the younger generation, including some of the best-
known names of the U.S.S.R., have joined in rejecting the computerized
paragon of centralization. The same critics have regretfully observed
that so far the introduction of new mathematical techniques and computers has had hardly any effect on planning efficiency and have sug-

gested that piecemeal improvements would not help and that a complete overhaul of the entire system is the only solution. By 1964–65 most members of the new school unequivocally came to support decentralization and the transfer of most controls from the detailed microlevel to the macrolevel. Thus the political leadership came face to face with a new alternative.

It is difficult to find an appropriate term for the incipient system or to describe it accurately, because it is still rather vague. Essentially, the new system calls for a high degree of local autonomy for producers and suppliers. Detailed planning of every important aspect of production would disappear, to be replaced by minimal direct guidance from above. Thus, in contrast to the system which has been used since the early 1930's, the enterprises would have some freedom to choose among alternative production techniques and to decide on levels of utilization of labor and capital equipment, on introduction of new technology, and the like. Tentative steps have been taken toward replacing state-administered distribution of materials among producers with direct commercial relations between suppliers and users. The proper direction of development of the economy would be maintained by introduction of new or reinforcement of existing economic levers and instruments such as a revised price system, profit, credit, taxes, and interest payments. These were essentially the terms of the new reforms announced by the September, 1965, plenary session of the Central Committee. However, while the announced reforms constitute a radical, and probably irreversible, break with the past, the emerging new system appears to be haphazard, with numerous gaps and ambiguities. A thorough analysis of measures already enacted or promised in the near future and statements by leading planners, Party functionaries, and economists leaves the impression of a wide-open field inviting experimentation and further reforms. As of today, a prediction of the emergence of a market economy would appear to be as reasonable as a prediction of the formation of a novel type of system with local autonomy in most production and distribution decisions and powerful over-all controls operating at the macrolevel.

The Soviet economic control engine has developed an inertia of its own, and this may modify some of the proposed reforms. It will be recalled that the abrupt change from the ministerial system to the system of regional economic councils in 1957, which was heralded as a major decentralization reform both in the U.S.S.R. and in the West, rapidly lost its momentum, and trends toward "recentralization" emerged rather soon. The reforms announced in September of 1965 did not spell out in detail either the process of transformation to the new system or the system itself, and elaboration of these details was delegated to the bureaucracies of appropriate state committees and agencies, which had responded faithfully. The character and scope of the resulting new regulations, all of which are termed "temporary," appear to be somewhat more detailed and more stringent than the spirit of the September reforms would warrant. It is also significant that Professor A. Birman, who is emerging as the principal commentator on the 1965 reforms, is critical of some unwarranted restrictions—formulated after the September plenum —on the autonomy of industrial enterprises in the distribution of excess profits.

The key to the future success or failure of the announced reforms, and to the very nature of the new system that will emerge, probably lies with the price system. The discussion on the so-called law of value and price formation under socialism in the U.S.S.R. has a long and tortured history. In a sense, Stalin himself opened the floodgates of the debate in 1952 in his book "Economic Problems of Socialism" by unequivocally stating that values and prices are still relevant in the Soviet system, at least in the sphere of consumer goods. The discussion of what actually constitutes a price under socialism and of a "rational" mode of price formation has continued since that time through endless conferences, congresses, and meetings. No other single topic has taken so much of the attention of economic theorists, statisticians, and planners in the postwar years. While the debate has continued unabated, with all participants stressing the paramount importance of "rational pricing," the functions of value relations and prices have remained rather limited in the actual operation of the system. Unchanged since the early 1930's, the planning mechanism has relied essentially on physical measures for most important planning instrumentalities, such as material balances, gross output targets, and delivery and supply quotas. Prices, in most instances constant prices, fixed by planners' fiat, have been used for control purposes and, in the sphere of consumption, for distribution of consumer goods and extraction of forced savings in the form of a heavy sales tax on consumer goods. Heedless of repeated assertions of the importance of prices, the planning and administrative officials have continued to operate with physical meas- ures and have even tended to expand the scope and importance of nonprice measures.

The theoretical debate has been inconclusive and, if anything, has led to more diversified opinions. Most of the theoretical economists and planners have held tenaciously to the traditional Marxist concept of prices as reflecting the real cost of production and hence not subject to fluctua- tions generated by demand. This group has focused its attention on the mechanics of cost calculations, problems involving the level of profitability of enterprises, the stimulus provided by prices to technological innovation, and problems of the redistribution of national income through sales taxes and profit margins included in prices. A much smaller group, led by Menchinov, Kantorovich, and Novozhilov and consisting mainly of younger, mathematically oriented economists, has gradually adopted the Western concept of flexible prices which serve as indexes of relative scarcity and are essentially bits of "instant information" reflecting con- tinuously changing supply and demand conditions. Defined this way, prices guide decision-makers in their choice of alternatives and generally serve to equilibrate the multitude of interrelated economic processes.

The two positions have remained unreconciled, although the award of the prestigious Lenin Prize in science and technology to Kantorovich, Menchinov (posthumously), and Novozhilov in 1965 greatly strengthened the position of the new school.

However, the apparent isolation of the theoreticians from actual price-setting remains as strong as ever. Various agencies of Gosplan [the State Planning Committee] and other organizations have been working on price reform for years. In July of 1960, the Central Committee of the Party expressed strong dissatisfaction with the haphazard methods of price-setting and ordered a complete revision of all heavy industry wholesale prices to be completed in 1962. Apparently the price specialists encountered difficulties as the introduction of new prices was repeatedly postponed. Finally it was announced that the new prices would be ready for introduction on January 1, 1966. Unfortunately for the specialists who have spent some six years on the project, a few months before the target date the new prices were summarily scrapped by a decision of the September, 1965, plenary session of the Central Committee.

At this plenum Kosygin did call for a complete overhaul of the price system, and a specially established state committee was ordered to prepare the basic outline of a new price reform by January 1, 1966. However, Kosygin's charge to the committee was very general, and no specific guidance was offered on the host of theoretical and practical problems that have been plaguing the formulation of prices in the U.S.S.R. in recent years and that are still being debated by academicians. As could have been expected, the new state committee did not produce the requested outline by January 1 and, judging from articles and papers that have appeared in the press since the September plenum, the profession is as divided on the basic problems of price-setting as ever. Some progress has been evidenced since then, but it is still too early to say what form the new price system will take. Apparently, prices will still be effectively geared to average cost of production with only limited flexibility allowed for effects on the demand side.

The new economics tempered. The procrastination displayed by the political leadership and the state bureaucracy in the case of prices is characteristic of the entire September reform. Most of the changes introduced or projected are not terminal in any sense, and a whole range of problems of macrocontrols remains unresolved. The announced introduction of interest charges on fixed and variable capital and expansion of bank financing for new investment clearly represent a drastic departure from the past. At the same time, it is apparent that the sponsors of the reform have not reached a consensus as to how the interest rates should be differentiated for different users of investment funds. However, most planning functionaries, as opposed to theoretical economists, tend to support differentiated rates.

Lenin's abolition of most direct administrative controls and his retreat to the commanding heights of the economy at the introduction of the new economic policy were reasonable and easily implemented; the commanding heights in that case were key industries, enterprises, and service facilities. While discarding many direct microcontrols, the present Party leadership clearly intends to retain firm control of the economy through the new commanding heights of macrocontrols such as prices, credits, taxes, and interest charges. It may very well be, however, that the Party leaders underestimate the difficulties in effective administration of such a system. The experience of Western Europe and the United States tells us that the art of operating a flexible and efficient monetary and fiscal policy is not mastered in a few years. The advances in theoretical macroeconomics have been quite impressive, and so is the economic stability, employment, and growth record of the postwar West. However, as all government authorities and economists would readily admit, there is still much room for improvement. One may counter this by suggesting that in Soviet conditions the transformation of the system would be comparatively easier. This, of course, is true inasmuch as the political leadership of the U.S.S.R. is still in full control and is relatively unconstrained in its manipulation of prices, taxes, budgets, or the monetary and credit systems. On the other hand, we must be aware of the fact that the Soviet monetary and fiscal systems, which have until now played a very limited role, are rudimentary and completely innocent of intricacies of macrocontrols. One could conjecture, for instance, that the new reforms would possibly lead to inflationary pressures and worsening of the unemployment situation. Adverse developments of this nature would not be easy to handle from the new commanding heights of the economy the Party leadership is so carefully exploring now. . . .

Trends and Prospects

The Agenda of Economic Decisions. The pressure for economic change will continue to place on the Soviet leadership's agenda basic questions as to the organization, concepts, and functioning of their economic system, as well as particular policy questions relating to the allocation of resources among the various claimants. These questions will surface in many ways, including the deliberations of the CPSU Central Committee and Party congresses. The focal point of changes in the pattern of resource allocation and in the system itself is related to reform of the price system and the introduction of indirect fiscal and monetary controls.

Simply put, solutions to the problems will take the form of judgments on the share of resources distributed to the various claimants and on changes in the system that will increase the efficiency of its operation and augment the performance of the Soviet economy in providing the necessary growth of goods and services available to all sectors. This then is the immediate problem for the new planning period of 1966–70.

Decisions on resource allocation must be made within the context of resource availability. It is difficult to abstract from the performance of the Soviet economy and the mechanism within which planning decisions are made and to isolate the problems of the allocation of resources among military and other power augmentation programs, investment for growth, and the consumption needs of the Soviet populace. There are, however, continuing focal points for decisions on resource allocation involving the following:

(a) *Distribution of the national product:* In general terms, every plan sets goals which determine the allocation of resources among military needs, investment, and consumption. The priorities that determine the allocation are generally consistent with the policy context imposed by the political leadership. As noted above, the prescriptions of the leadership are no longer as clear as appeared to be the case under Stalin. Nonetheless, changes in the historical pattern of resource distribution would presumably require some change in the power structure of the Soviet political apparatus and in the external policies of those who exercise the power. The involvement of the Soviet Union in some foreign military activity might thus influence the defense budget upward, or a meaningful detente with the United States in Europe might provide a basis for reduction of the military burden.

At the same time, choices must be made not only between guns and butter but also between guns and the facilities to produce guns or butter. This choice between investment and military outlays was brought home very forcefully to Soviet leaders in the aftermath of the unplanned 1961 shift in priorities from investment to military output. This shift may have been a significant factor in the industrial slowdown that followed, and especially in the problems that emerged subsequently in the energy supply and in development of the chemical industry.

As between consumption/investment/military, there is persistent pressure to increase real wage incentives to workers and peasants as a basis for increasing productivity in factory and farm. Moreover, there may be political pressure to give the more vocal groups in the population a larger share in the fruits of Soviet economic growth. Space spectaculars do not appear to be an adequate substitute for insufficient housing and consumer goods.

Less significant in the aggregate but important in particular areas of industrial bottlenecks or agricultural supply, especially in bad crop years, is foreign economic activity, including Soviet relations with Eastern Europe. The related growth of foreign economic activities may turn on the advantages and costs of expanded trade and aid with the non-Communist nations and the interrelationships between the Soviet and East European economies.

(b) *Structure of the military budget:* Within the military budget the allocation of resources as between the general war/space-missile type of armament and the conventional limited war/ground force type would depend in part on the international climate. Moreover, technological developments in weaponry might open new areas of opportunity in the international contest for power. For example, the development of an effective antiballistic missile system with its implications for the balance of power, might, in the Soviet view, justify a massive production effort and the allocation of substantially more resources than in the past.

On the other hand, military involvement of the Soviet Union along its non–West European borders or elsewhere in noncontiguous areas would presumably require an increase in military capabilities other than long-range missiles and space systems.

(c) *Allocation of investment:* Within the investment budget, decisions must be made on the continuing priority to heavy industry for either expanded defense needs or industrial growth and, on the other hand, higher priority to investment in the infrastructure of the Soviet economy, including transportation, communications, distribution facilities, and housing, as well as investment in agriculture and light industry. The pressure on the Soviet leadership may be more toward increased production in the former low-priority sectors, if in their judgment the over-all efficiency of the economy can be significantly improved only by increasing the effectiveness of these neglected sectors through larger capital outlays for plant and equipment and increased production of consumer goods to provide increases in real income as a basis of incentives for improving labor productivity. Moreover, there may also be a return to the old priority sectors of coal and steel at the expense of petroleum, chemicals, and nonferrous metals for redressing some of the imbalances that have accrued from past planning mistakes.

(d) *Alternate routes for improving living conditions:* In providing resources for consumption, a judgment must be made on both economic and political grounds as to the relative costs and benefits that might accrue from higher priority to various programs for increasing the volume and quality of food, clothing, transportation, housing, and other elements of the living conditions of the Soviet population. If the judgment is that the most effective allocation of resources on all counts would require putting an end to the nagging problem of inadequate grain harvests, then agriculture may receive higher priority in respect to investment for improving state and collective farms; greater flexibility may be introduced into the institution of the collective farm (e.g., by upgrading the private plots or by providing greater incentives through higher prices for agricultural products and a guaranteed annual income for the collective farmers); and progress can be made in ameliorating some of the natural problems faced by Soviet agriculture in raising crop yields, e.g., weather and soil conditions.

Were the quality of food output to be raised—greater production of meat, eggs, butter, etc.—with more investment in distribution and storage facilities and possibly drastic changes in the collective farm system at the same time, the Soviet administration may consider more clothing, more and better housing, or improvement in passenger car transportation as alternative methods for providing the incentives and satisfactions for which there is a felt need among the Soviet citizenry. Passenger car production may indeed be somewhat wasteful in the Soviet view, but the dominant constraint may well be the tremendous cost of providing all the additional investment in roads, repair facilities, service stations, etc., that is implicit in the development of a passenger car society. Soviet citizens may also be given more consideration in terms of the quality and spacious-ness of living space, both in the cities and in the countryside. However, this again may be an extremely expensive program for wide-scale applica-tion throughout the Soviet Union. Some differential programs for reward-ing selected workers may, however, be pursued to provide differential incentives. A particular problem is that of satisfying the requirements of the higher income groups, who can exercise choice in personal demand.

(e) *Growth acceleration as the general palliative:* If the Soviet national income could be made to grow at the rate of 7 per cent per annum that prevailed in the past decade, the decisions on resource allocations noted above would be less agonizing. The hope of the improvisers such as Kosygin or the orthodox "neo-Stalinist" economists such as Ostrovityanov seems to be that somehow the performance of the system will improve. Some growth-stimulating forces are evident: labor shortages may be re-laxed, agricultural weather is likely to improve, the new sectors may profit from the learning process, and problems in such industries as chemicals and petroleum-refining may diminish. Likewise some improvement in the efficiency of planning is possible. It may even be that substantial changes could be made following the logic of Pareto optimality, namely, that some claimants on resources could be better satisfied without hurting other claimants. Still, it appears that in the final analysis the hard choice of attacking the problem of institutional stagnation must be faced. If factors external and internal to Soviet plans do not bring back healthy growth, then the hard choice of changing the system may become an inevitable and central issue.

Political Implications of Economic Change. Changes in the role of the Party and in Soviet society as a whole resulting from economic change may be more significant than the latter itself. If the economic change undertaken goes in the direction implied by the extreme variant in the Soviet search for a new pattern, involving the development of some flexible pricing and market mechanisms in the Soviet economy, then the type of decisions made by the Party leadership and the type of people who make the decisions for the Party may well change substantially. From Lenin's role in the development of the electrification plan of the R.S.F.S.R. (GOELRO) in the 1920's to the convening of the Soviet Party congress in 1966, the top leadership of the Soviet Party has maintained extensive and far-reaching control over the details of economic decisions in the Soviet Union. A transition from physical output planning to fiscal and monetary planning would allow the Soviet leaders to continue developing broad macroeconomic decisions on production levels as well as on final allocation of resources that has been characteristic of the Stalinist ap-proach to economic development. The elite group of decision-makers who influence the pattern and direction of Soviet economic development would thus be likely to be broadened to include more technically oriented, businessman/economist-type leaders. In this context, a Soviet counterpart of our Director of the Bureau of the Budget would be delegated the kind of power previously reserved for the pinnacle of the political power structure in the Communist Party. This delegation of power within the Soviet political structure would be a significant change in the authoritarian state but would not be likely to represent a change which could be described in any meaningful sense as the emergence of a democratic process. The bulk of the population would not be likely to have any strong influence on the production and distribution processes through their demand for goods, nor would the investment program for the expansion of one or another sector of the economy be determined directly by the Soviet consumers' expression of choice in a form of market. The price of investment goods is not likely to be imputed by the scarcity of relevant consumer goods in a market within which consumers are in some meaningful way sovereign. Thus, the Soviet society would still be in a state of political serfdom as described by von Hayek.

One unknown factor which will condition the success of the economic reforms currently being enacted in the U.S.S.R. is the broad attitude toward them. Needless to say, one cannot speak of genuine public opinion as a factor in Party policy, all the recent liberalization notwithstanding. However, there are some encouraging signs, and the support or lack of it on the part of privileged groups—the rank and file of the Party, government functionaries, scholars, the managerial elite, and artists—may well influence the future course of events.

The economic reforms announced by Kosygin at the September (1965) plenum of the Central Committee depart in one respect from all changes previously announced and enacted in the U.S.S.R. This time, practically all points of criticism of the current state of affairs and the remedies proposed by Kosygin were discussed in advance by economists and statisticians in newspaper articles and professional journals prior to enactment of the reforms. Compared with the past, when changes were announced *ex cathedra* by the Central Committee or even the Presidium and then "discussed" or, more correctly, lauded, by the populace, this feature of the current reforms is indeed striking. In his report to the plenum, Kosygin all but quoted the Soviet proponents of change—Nemchinov, Aganbegyan, Belkin, and Birman. This departure from past practice is so radical that it could not have escaped the attention of party controllers. In fact, V. Stepakov, the head of the Department of Propaganda and Agitation of the Central Committee and former chief editor of *Izvestia*, noted with a somewhat defensive air that "one of the present inept tricks of capitalist propaganda is an attempt to describe the current economic reforms as a result of the struggle of a group of economists opposed to the Party line."

It is particularly difficult to analyze fully at this juncture the attitudes of different groups in the U.S.S.R. toward the reforms. We can only say that, on the one hand, the new school of economists, especially the young mathematically oriented ones, are doubtless pleased in general, albeit also probably somewhat disappointed in view of the ambiguities and procrastination in some aspects of the reforms. The bureaucrats of the Party and state apparatus are, on the other hand, probably less than enthusiastic about the proposed changes. It may be recalled that the bulk of the opposition to the original Liberman proposals for greater decentralization came from Party and state functionaries, as well as from the economists of the older school. When Liberman's proposals were tried out in several selected enterprises, some concern was voiced in the press that various government agencies, such as the Ministry of Finance, were not supporting the experiments. In an extremely revealing paper analyzing the announced reform, one of the most outspoken critics of the old system, Professor A. Birman, noted that, during the discussion prior to the reforms, many officials of planning, financial, and other economic agencies spoke against the proposed changes. Now, notes Birman, after the Party and the government have enacted the reforms, the implementation is placed in the hands of these same officials. He, therefore, calls on them to "overcome the attitudes rejected by the reforms" and to assist in introducing the changes. The power of the bureaucracy in the U.S.S.R. should not be underestimated, and lack of support on the part of entrenched officials may well cripple the reforms, especially in view of the reluctance with which the more conservative elements in the Party leadership have supported the reforms. It is also instructive to observe that in the implementation of similar economic reforms in Czechoslovakia and Yugoslavia the strongest opposition has come from Party functionaries and bureaucrats.

Another imponderable in the future of the proposed changes is the specific behavior of the managerial group with their power elite. Even the small measure of independence given them by the reform is not necessarily welcomed by enterprise directors brought up in the Stalinist tradition. While the monetary incentives offered by the new system are attractive, negative sanctions for unsuccessful performances still play a major role in the U.S.S.R. Reluctance to innovate and aversion to risk-taking is typical of the Soviet managerial group, and it is difficult to envisage them as being overly enthusiastic about the new reforms.

The general public can probably be safely dismissed from consideration, as it has very few, if any, outlets for its opinion or political means for affecting the success or failure of proposed changes. The prevalent attitude is probably one of general apathy and indifference. At the same time, the exhortations of a Party propagandist, a former chief editor of *Pravda*, addressed to Soviet youth are very revealing. He regretfully notes that "it is not a secret that many are somewhat tired of reforms and that confidence in innovation has been undermined. Actually they are tired not of reforms *per se* but of the triumphal parade drums that have always accompanied reforms in the past."

If change of a significant nature is undertaken in the Soviet economy involving a substantial expansion of the minority group that controls effective power and a change in the character of that minority from a primarily political orientation to a more technical economist/businessman character, this change might in itself engender other changes within the Soviet society.

What appears to be involved is a revision of the concept of democratic centralism, the guiding principle of decision-making by which the Party develops policy and maintains discipline. As originally conceived by Lenin in 1903, it meant essentially that the members of the Party would freely discuss the issues before a decision was made, but after resolution all were to adhere to the central Party decision without factional dissent. As applied during the Stalinist era, the democratic aspect of this concept was muted at best, as illustrated in Nikita Khrushchev's de-Stalinization speech in 1956. He notes repeatedly the lack of allowable dissent or participation in decisions by even the minority elite that form the Communist Party in the Soviet Union. An outstanding example of this restrictive Stalinist application of democratic centralism in the formulation of economic policy was the discussion of the Fifth Five-Year Plan. This apparently led to the elimination of the head of the State Planning Commission, Nikolai Voznesensky, who "perished physically" as a victim of the Stalinist "cult of personality."

Many changes have taken place since 1953 in the application of democratic centralism and in the formulation of economic policies and other matters. We may now perceive at least four groups within the elite who influence and constrain policy decisions in the Soviet Union and the Party: the military; the economic planners/enterprise managers; the scientific group oriented around the physical sciences in the Academy of Sciences; and the Party bureaucracy. The military have had perhaps the closest approximation to actual decision-making power within their own sphere of professional interest, but even their power in the post-Stalin period has fluctuated. The new group of economists/managers, indicated above, appears to be approaching a position where it may constrain and influence policy on economic matters.

All of these professional elite groups below the top leadership have a common interest in achieving a greater delegation of power from the Party core in this decision-making process. Each group can, presumably, agree that within the guidelines provided by the political leadership, policy can be more efficiently implemented by those trained professionally, formally or by experience, to understand the implications of alternative applications of Party policy guidelines. At the same time, each will likewise tend to compete with the others for priority in policy decisions involving a share of limited resources to attain its particular ends. This is a conflict of interest which doubtless hampers their mutual quest for a broader delegation of power within the Party guidelines of policy. And all of them—those within the elite groups and those at the pinnacle of Party power itself—must be aware that the decision-making power desired may be diluted in the process of implementation in each of these groups. There has been perceived a rising new generation of younger leaders who are in principle allied in the pursuit of a broader delegation of power or a more liberal interpretation of the rule of democratic centralism in Soviet

Party affairs. For the economist/management group, the establishment of indirect controls in the economy would be an implied expression of this kind of delegation of power.

Moreover, the type of revolutionary economic change that appears to be required may endanger the vested interests of many of the present elite groups. To expect the Soviet society to change in an evolutionary way would appear to be un-Marxist and perhaps unrealistic. Truly effective consummation of the apparently necessary changes in the Soviet economy and the political structure within which it operates may take several decades, as it did in the United States in fully adopting a version of the Keynesian approach to fiscal and monetary policy appropriate to our problems in the Great Depression. In his recent Godkin Lectures at Harvard, Walter Heller observed that, insofar as policies proposed and adopted are concerned, the Keynesian revolution was not really completed until thirty years after it was launched in 1936.

In the process, Soviet institutions may go through a gradual evolution, such as step-by-step adoption of effective economic theory, improved data collection, changes in personnel, and modification of institutions. However, it is also possible that the kind of gradual and evolutionary change which has characterized the American accommodation to a change in the nature of the institutional arrangements within which economic problems must be solved is not likely or possible in the Soviet-type society. Therefore, if substantial changes do occur, they may occur rapidly and have far-reaching and immeasurable impacts on the whole fabric of the society. The Soviets used to claim that their system had discovered a law of change, a *zakonomernost*. These claims of orderly controlled change have been singularly muted of late. And if the current quest for a new economic pattern takes concrete forms it is likely to take them well beyond the dimensions anticipated by those who have unleashed the forces of change. The end result may well be a second economic revolution comparable in scope and depth to that launched by Stalin in the 1930's.

*   *   *

13

PLANT MANAGERS AND THEIR OVERSEERS

DAVID GRANICK

The Nature of the Beast

Never have the Russians found a satisfactory solution to the problem of organizational centralization. For as the ministries were splintered, central coordination of decisions was made more difficult. The new splinters were then combined, only to be once more split asunder. Industrial reorganization in Russia, as in large organizations in our country, seems to be an endless process. . . .

The fundamental dilemma of organizational decision-making is that it does not seem possible to make gains in one aspect of efficiency without simultaneously losing ground in other directions. Since the pasture on the far side of the fence always looks greener, the temptation is ever present to reverse direction and regain lost aspects of efficiency.

Centralization of decision-making offers the advantage that relevant information at the disposal of one part of an organization can be brought to bear on the problems of another part. All strings lead to the central decision-maker, and he either has or can get information from all groups. Secondly, the best decision-making and advisory talent in the organization can be mustered at the top; presumably, the resulting decisions will be better than if just "any Joe" had made them.

On the other hand, no central figure at the head of a large organization can hope to keep in touch with nuances of particular, detailed problems. All that he can try to have before him is summary material on which to base a decision. Second, he generally cannot tailor his decisions to individual cases; if he were to attempt to do this, he would soon be com-

From *The Red Executive*, by David Granick (Garden City, N.Y.: An Anchor Book, Doubleday & Co., 1961), pp. 119–40. Copyright © 1960 by David Granick. Reprinted by permission of Doubleday & Company, Inc.

pletely swamped. As a result, he must make decisions of a "rule" nature, indicating to subordinates how entire classes of problems should be handled. Unfortunately, the very act of classifying cases involves riding roughshod over the individual peculiarities of each, and the classification method as a key ingredient of bureaucracy is inherent in central decision-making.

Centralization of the decision process and of planning has an additional major disadvantage, relating to the execution of the plan or decision. For what is a "good" plan? It is one which, once adopted, leads to actions which in turn result in satisfactory outcomes. However, the *process* used in drawing up a given plan may be quite as important in determining action as the resulting plan itself. This is due to the fact that if subordinates are involved in making the decision as to a particular plan, if they accept the plan as their own rather than treating it as a scheme coming from the distant and clouded heights, they are much more likely to work hard to make the plan succeed. Failure of the plan involves a psychological defeat to themselves, rather than bringing sardonic pleasure at the discomfiture of the "all-wise" figure above.

To add to the complications involved in trying to improve the organization of decision-making, it is necessary to recognize that actual patterns of decision-making seldom coincide precisely with those shown by the tables of organization. Generally, it is rather difficult even for the participants to know who made which decision. It is not easy to pin down authority.

Let me give [two] examples. . . .

In 1931, the Central Committee of the Communist Party of the Soviet Union resolved that no new factories should be built in Moscow. The object was to hold down the size of the city. Following this "decision" by the second highest policy-making body in the country, the population of the city proceeded to grow by 50 per cent during the next eight years. In 1939, the highest policy-making body, the Party Congress, reiterated the 1931 decision and demanded its enforcement. As of 1956, the Moscow labor force had grown by an additional third.

Who vetoed the resolutions of the top Party bodies? Stalin? It seems unlikely. Despite the limits on executive power shown in the example above, our knowledge of Stalin's personality does not support the hypothesis that he took this particular means of twice circumventing the Communist Party policy bodies. Stalin's method of asserting authority was more direct. No, the final "authority" was held by officials much lower in the chain of command, men who must have felt that there were good reasons for their own pet projects to be treated as minor exceptions to Party policy. Nor could it be said that they hid their decisions from top Party officials. After all, this great construction was in Moscow itself, the very city in which the policy-makers were living.

Soviet postwar investment decisions raise the same decision-making issue. General policy was to move the base of Soviet industry eastward. Expansion of fuel, electricity, and raw material resources followed this policy and was concentrated in the East.

But new manufacturing firms, built to process the materials and use the fuel, continued to be established in the West and particularly in European Russia. So far did this go, that the National Plan adopted in 1956 had to reverse direction; it called for investment in coal, gas, and electricity in the West in order to service industry which had been constructed there since the war.

How can we account for the fact that this process-manufacturing expansion of 1945–55 occurred primarily in the West? It was due to industrial ministries' following their own narrow departmental interests, attracted by the available labor force of the area, said a professor in a lecture prepared under the auspices of the Central Committee of the Soviet Communist Party.

In this case, as in the previous one, top authorities could not maintain control. It is easy to know who set "policy": the Council of Ministers and the Party Central Committee. But it is much harder for anyone to answer the question of who made the major decisions which violated policy.

The pinning down of authority in the organizational maze is only one complication in the pattern of decision-making. An equally important complication is that people who clearly have no authority control much of the flow of information, and so play a major role in determining when decisions are made.

One need not be in a large organization very long before realizing the tremendous influence exercised by the secretary to the top executive. Control of access to the pinnacle of the organization does in fact often resolve an issue, and may even prevent a question from coming up for explicit decision. . . .

The task of combining communication upward with staff advice to lower echelons is a troublesome one for all staff departments. But the staff department which typically finds particular difficulty in juggling these conflicting functions is the financial accounting and auditing department. In the Soviet Union, for example, factory comptrollers perform a role which embodies all of the traditional dilemmas.

The Soviet factory comptroller is considered a major source of information to higher authorities. In order to preserve his independence and reliability as a communication channel, he is appointed and removed by the higher authorities rather than by the factory directors. But as a result, he has a hard time gaining the confidence of his factory director. Thus, Soviet plant administration suffers from an absence of that pinpointing of problem areas which the comptroller's office is so uniquely capable of providing. All levels of Soviet management recognize the potential value of the comptroller's advice, but the advisory role is hamstrung by enmity and lack of confidence on the part of the plant director. Some directors have even expressed this enmity by such clumsy actions as withdrawing the comptroller's badge, which he needs to enter the plant. How could it be otherwise when the man designated as the plant director's "closest aide" is also the spy who may send upstairs the information which gets the director fired?

BUREAUCRACY AND HOW TO LIVE WITH IT

Soviet theory has always called for decentralization of operational decisions to a local level. But the term "decentralization" has never had the meaning in Soviet parlance which is given to it in American business: that middle managers should have the right of final decision in certain areas. Soviet top administrators have, quite explicitly, reserved to themselves the right to meddle directly in the detailed affairs of even the smallest organizations.

A former lawyer for a Soviet bakery, who is now a Russian refugee, tells the story of the bakery's needing more flour than its normal allotment during the period shortly before the Second World War. A request for additional flour was put through channels, and in time it was approved. The approval bore the signature of V. M. Molotov, Chairman of the Council of People's Commissars. It was as though the President of the United States were to approve the purchase of oil to heat a New York post office substation. Let us grant that this was an extreme case, and that probably some fourth secretary of Molotov's actually did the signing. Even so, the case illustrates the extremes to which Russian centralization of decision-making can go.

Until recently, all of the main administrative bodies of the country were located in Moscow. Since decentralization was primarily along the lines of separate industries, detailed decisions concerning a Tashkent textile mill would be made in a Moscow office. Such decisions applied to annual production plans, to procurement and marketing allotments, even to approval of changes in the mill's management organization. The possibilities for red tape were boundless.

When a huge organization is this highly centralized, two possibilities exist. The organization may founder in its own bureaucracy, or it may ignore its own rules. No one can say that Soviet industry has foundered during the last thirty years. The evidence is conclusive that formal decision-making regulations have been constantly violated. Plant managements have had to make their own decisions if they were to produce the results demanded of them. Top authorities in Moscow have had to wink at violations of rules if they wished industrial production to grind ahead. Both groups have recognized necessity.

It would be difficult to assert categorically that this informal decentralization has been an unsuccessful administrative solution. Soviet industry has expanded at too rapid a rate, over too long a time period, to give grounds for a supercritical attitude. In a broad sense, central authorities have been able to make policy and to get it carried out. Similarly, despite all the uncertainties and major exceptions which exist, plant managements have exercised the authority necessary to maintain operations.

But, as perhaps occurs in any administrative system, the participants have found cause for complaint. Middle management has griped at the red tape in the many cases where they do follow the rules. A good example of what may be involved is illustrated in a story told by a Russian refugee and reported by Joseph Berliner. The refugee had been the chief mechanical engineer of a Soviet mining organization, and his story presumably relates to a prewar period when a law had just been passed, with considerable fanfare, to make the violation of quality standards for final products a criminal offense.

As inspector I once arrived at a plant which was supposed to have delivered mining machines, but did not do it. When I entered the plant premises, I saw that the machines were piled up all over the place, but they were all unfinished. I asked what was going on. The director gave evasive answers. Finally, when the big crowd surrounding us had disappeared, he called me to his office.

"Now we can talk," he said.

"Well," I said, "why don't you ship the machines? We are waiting for them."

"Here is the story," he said. "According to the technical specifications the machines must be painted with red oil-resistant varnish. However, I have only red varnish which is not oil-resistant and green varnish which is oil-resistant. Therefore I cannot complete them. You see, if I send the machines with the wrong kind of varnish I shall not have fulfilled the technical requirements, and for that I shall get eight years in prison. But if I don't ship them this will come under the charge of failure to arrange for transportation. And what will they do with me then? At worst, they will expel me from the Party. Well, the hell with my Party card. So what do you want me to do?"

"But listen," I replied, "the mines cannot work, they are waiting for the machines and you are holding them up because you don't have the right kind of paint."

"But I don't want to get eight years. Give me a written note with your signature and I shall have the machines ready in nothing flat."

Well, I don't want to get eight years either. So what do I do? I cable the ministry and ask permission to use the green varnish. I should have received an answer at once. But it took unusually long. Apparently they did not want to take any chances at the ministry either, and they wanted to cover themselves. Finally I received permission. I put this cablegram from the ministry in my pocket and kept it for the rest of my life, and signed the note allowing the use of green paint, referring to the cablegram. In a short time the machines began to roll from the plant.

Such management concern for legal provisions is doubtless unusual in Soviet conditions, if only because a director of the sort described above would soon lose his job. But certainly the more common type of director, who would have shipped out the mining equipment on his own responsibility, would not have been happy at being forced to engage in such illegal behavior. He would have been well aware that this action might be held against him sometime in the future.

In actual fact, plant directors have possessed great authority. But in theory, they have not; and so they have constantly struggled to legitimatize their power. During the course of this perennial battle, they have often felt sufficiently self-confident to ridicule publicly the laws they were violating. Even at the height of the 1930's there were some plant directors who went out of their way to write signed articles in the national press describing how, in their own work, they had been violating both the law and the instructions from superiors, announcing that they considered these violations to be quite proper, and stating flatly that in the future they had every intention of continuing and even extending the violations.

Central authorities have shown growing concern over their own lack of control in certain key areas of policy. Probably the major area in which central policy has been steadily ignored for thirty years is that of organization autarky, or self-sufficiency of supply. Central authorities in Moscow are quite aware of the cost advantages to be gained through the specialization of individual factories on particular products. Each separate industrial organization, however, is anxious to be as self-sufficient as possible, and thus achieve independence of its neighbors and of an often whimsical national system of allotting necessary supplies.

Since no ministry could be sure of getting the materials, parts, and equipment needed for its operations, the natural tendency was for each to try to expand the coverage of its production so as to supply its own needs. Each ministry was quite willing to pay the price of high-cost production in order to achieve independence. Thirty years of denunciation from Moscow, accompanied by reasoned explanations of the advantages of division of labor, had absolutely no effect.

In 1951, only 47 per cent of the brick production of the Soviet Union was accounted for by the Ministry of the Industry of Construction Materials. High-cost production, often with long railroad hauls, characterized the remainder. In 1955, 390 units of a particular type of excavator were produced. Two-thirds were produced within the appropriate ministry, but the rest were produced elsewhere at a cost 50 to 100 per cent greater. Of the 171 plants in 1957 which specialized in machine-tool production, only 55 were under the appropriate ministry. The other plants were organized within ministries which used their machine tools.

Each ministry, in fact, seemed to act much like an independent nation engaging in foreign trade. Each inevitably dealt with other ministries, but cautiously, jealously safeguarding its independence. Self-sufficiency was treated as the keystone of this independence.

What made this situation even more difficult is that each individual plant copied the example of its ministry, and strove to become an autarkic principality within an autarkic nation. In 1956, the Urals Machine-building Plant, one of the nation's two giant heavy-equipment plants, grossly underutilized its powerful and expensive presses designed for production of forgings 200 tons and over. Of all the forgings produced during January-September, 1956, more than half weighed less than twenty-seven tons apiece. While this was scarcely what one could call small work, it was totally out of line with the capacity of the equipment.

In 1957, no more than half of the nation's standard tooling, nuts and bolts, and electrodes was produced in specialized plants. Yet it was officially recognized that the cost of producing such items in the consuming plants was several times as great as the cost of production in factories where economies of scale could be achieved.

As the thirty-year Soviet experience of factory autarky illustrates, decentralization of decision-making has in fact gone a long way down the organizational ladder. Despite all of the formal centralization, the individual plant director in Russia seems to be much more successful in building his own little empire than is his counterpart in the American giant corporation.

This, however, is in no sense due to the greater belief in decentralization among Soviet top managers. There have been complaints of factory directors who disregarded "on principle" orders from the top management organs of their industry. Plant managements are said to have virtually broken off "diplomatic relations" with these top organs and with other plants, and they have been reproached for considering themselves as feudal lords quite outside Soviet law.

The great strength of the Soviet factory, from an organizational point of view, is that it has been the only stable structure in all of Soviet industry. Ministries and their subdivisions have been split apart, lumped together in new combinations, and then once more splintered. This process continued steadily over a period of three decades, as the Russian leaders have alternately been revolted first by the problems inherent in having only a few large organizations, and then by the large "span of control" required for coordinating a multitude of smaller ones. In all of this shuffling, only the plant organization was left alone.

It is scarcely surprising that this single stable organizational unit should have amassed considerable decision-making power. It is also not surprising that any given plant management should be reluctant to become dependent upon a "sister" plant under the same parent body; for the chances were good that, within a few years, the two plants would be subordinate to different higher bodies.

*   *   *

14

THE SOVIET ECONOMIC REFORM

YEVSEI LIBERMAN

The rapid rate of Soviet economic development, begun in 1921–22, was based upon Lenin's theory that socialism and communism could be built in our country if public ownership of the means of production was established and the economy was centrally planned.

Lenin conceded that the period of so-called military communism (1918–21) had represented an attempt to establish socialism without market relations or trade, but on the basis of direct exchange of commodities between town and countryside and that this attempt had been necessitated by the foreign mlitary intervention rather than having been carefully worked out. Later Lenin pointed out that this had been a mistake, but a mistake that was quite understandable and even helpful. In order to find out the strength of a fortress it was first necessary to try to capture it by direct frontal attack. If this failed, there was no use in persisting in one's mistake; a long siege of the fortress had to be begun. Lenin concluded that the attempt could succeed if enthusiastically supported, but it would have to be based on economic accountability and personal material incentives for the working people.

Thus was laid the cornerstone for the building of socialist society, as a new, planned form of commodity production based on the law of value and commodity-monetary relations. It is important to bear in mind, however, that in the U.S.S.R. the law of value does not operate spontaneously, that is, anarchically, but within the framework of proportions and rates fixed in the over-all economic plan. This is why the operation of the law of value never did and does not lead to economic anarchy, unemployment, or crises and depressions. Just as the means of production could

Reprinted, by special permission, from *Foreign Affairs*, October, 1967, issue (46, No. 1:54–63). Copyright © 1967 by the Council on Foreign Relations, Inc., New York.

not be privately owned for gain, so the operation of the law of value
under socialism has not led and cannot lead to the polarization of
poverty and wealth and the creation of antagonistic class contradictions.

But the law of value leads to the formation of profits. Many persons
in the West cannot understand how profit can be compatible with socialism. Here, too, we may cite history. At one time Lenin demanded that
all Soviet enterprises shift to economic accountability. They should
operate on a "commercial basis," as he put it. Lenin urged that commercial accounting not be ignored and that battle be joined against the
prejudices that hindered it and against adverse recollection of the past.

Lenin's comment about the view advanced in Bukharin's "The
Economy of the Transitional Period" is quite characteristic. Bukharin
had written that production under capitalism was production for the
sake of profit, while production under proletarian rule was production
to meet the needs of the public. He ought, said Lenin, to have made
clear that under proletarian rule the surplus product does not go to
capitalists but to all the working people and to them alone.

Thus, to acknowledge the necessity of commercial operations and
profit-making is to acknowledge the operation of the law of value and
of the commodity-monetary mechanism in the process of building socialist
society.

Actually, these principles have operated throughout the history of the
Soviet state, but we must admit that in particularly critical periods, i.e., in
the years of intensive industrialization and collectivization, in World
War II, and in the postwar reconstruction, the operation and requirements of the law of value were restricted and sometimes even ignored.
These periods demanded the utmost concentration of resources and
centralized rationing of them. Moreover, since the Soviet Union was
not receiving long-term financing and credits from outside, it had to
restrict consumption of the available resources in order to make the
necessary huge investments. This violated the principle of equivalent
exchange between town and countryside, between people and state;
in other words, the requirements of the law of value were not adhered
to in many respects.

Such actions can be historically explained. They were, moreover,
supported by the enthusiasm and heroically selfless efforts of the majority
of the Soviet people. Sacrifice and enthusiasm are an immense force
in the development of society (just as of the individual) at critical
moments of life. But they cannot function for an unjustifiably prolonged
time. Lofty virtues *per se*, they can become faults if reliance is placed
on their effects for too long. They cannot provide the foundation for a
massive daily and continuous improvement in the sphere of production,
distribution, and trade. We must not forget that if restrictions on
consumption are long continued, they undermine the incentive to work,
and this retards the very process of accumulation for the sake of which
consumption has been restricted.

A certain disregard of the requirements of the law of value, observable over a number of years, began to inhibit the growth of efficiency in production in the 1950's and 1960's. Although rates of growth were on the whole quite high in the U.S.S.R., it was evident that we were not making use of all the possibilities and advantages inherent in the socialist system. The substitution of voluntarism and naked administrative fiat for economic stimuli produced distressing disproportions, a lower efficiency in utilizing our fixed assets, deterioration of the quality of goods, and, as a result, insufficient growth of the working people's property. This is why the objective necessity arose to revise the methods of management and bring them into greater conformity with current tasks. This gave rise to the economic discussion of 1962–64, followed by the decision to carry out an economic reform in successive stages over a three-year period.

The essential principle of the reform, now in operation for more than a year, is that what is advantageous for society as a whole should be advantageous for each industrial enterprise. Toward this end a number of measures are being adopted, including: increasing the independence of enterprises; appraising their work by the criterion of profitability; introducing payment for production assets; raising the material incentives for personnel, in ratio to the enterprise's performance, out of profits; increasing the enterprises' direct contracting with one another for the supply of goods; and establishing economically based, as opposed to arbitrarily set, prices.

Last year 704 enterprises, employing more than 2 million persons, or more than 10 per cent of the Soviet industrial labor force, shifted to the new system of operation. For industry as a whole the volume of output rose 8.6 per cent in that year, profit increased 10 per cent, and labor productivity rose 5.2 per cent; but the 704 enterprises which changed over to the new methods of management showed a gain of more than 10 per cent in sales volume, approximately 25 per cent in profit, and 8 per cent in labor productivity. These are average data; at individual enterprises the results were higher. This means that even now, though the economic reform has not reached its full potential, it is already putting vast latent production reserves to work. A total of more than 2,200 enterprises, including almost all the instrument manufacturing plants, many light-industry factories and mills, and ferrous and non-ferrous metallurgical plants, are now operating under the new system of planning and incentives.

From the manager's viewpoint, the reform has thus far brought much that is advantageous but also many cares. The pleasing aspect is that the amount of supervision by superior agencies has been reduced and the possibilities of showing initiative have increased. Practically speaking, the manager now requires supervision only in settling and gaining approval of key goals in his factory's plan; he must also be provided with up-to-date information on technical and economic developments, and, most important, must be helped in solving the practical problems of obtaining supplies for major construction and the introduction of new equipment and machinery. In principle, the manager settles all day-to-day questions independently and directly with his suppliers, clients, and transportation agencies.

As for the manager's cares, they have multiplied, for under the old system, though he had far less freedom of action, his task was essentially simpler, since everything was decreed from above. His responsibility consisted merely in carrying out instructions. Now he has to search, experiment, and take risks; and this is not easy, particularly at the initial stage of the reform, when the enterprises transferred to the new system of management operate in an ocean of others which still are working in the old manner. This simultaneous coexistence of two systems of management creates certain difficulties.

Most questions are now decided at the enterprises themselves and with the broad participation of the workers. It has become much easier to apply proposals for rationalization, since the needed resources are available at the enterprises themselves, out of their own profits. Finally, the wages and bonuses received by the workers have increased substantially.

The data reported indicate that in many instances bonuses issued for the first half of 1966 rose 20 per cent, 30 per cent, 40 per cent, or more over those in the corresponding period of the previous year. It is true that in the opinion of many economists one should judge not merely by the percentage of increase but also by the absolute amount of the bonuses, which still seems insufficient. On the other hand, the rapid rate of growth will naturally lead to an increase in the absolute size of bonuses and in total personal earnings.

The question of profit has been widely discussed in recent times in the U.S.S.R.—not because profit was previously unknown there or was being introduced for the first time, but because prior to the reform profit was not employed as the chief criterion or over-all indicator of the effectiveness of an enterprise. Profit was only one of many required indicators which were set as goals. These indicators established as targets for the enterprise included gross volume of ouput, an excessively detailed list of the items to be produced, cost reduction, number of employees, output per employee, average wage, etc. The number of obligatory targets fettered initiative. Often the enterprises concerned themselves primarily with increasing gross volume of output, since their performance was judged above all by that and not by the amount of output sold, as is now the case. In addition, enterprises gave little heed to the utilization of production assets. Trying to find the easiest way to meet the assigned volume of ouput, they asked and received from the state, free of charge, a great deal of equipment and new structures which they did not always use rationally and fully.

Much of this is explained by the fact that for a long time the Soviet Union was the world's only socialist country. It was faced with the task of creating industry as fast as possible and providing for the country's defense. No thought was given at that time to the quality or attractiveness of goods, not even to production cost or profit. This was entirely justified, for the Soviet Union not only withstood the war of 1941–45 but played a decisive role in ridding the world of fascism. This was worth any price. It was our "profit" and, if you please, the "profit" of the whole civilized world.

But, as Lenin said more than once, our virtues, if carried too far, can turn into faults. This is what happened in our country when the practices of management by administrative fiat were continued into the period after our country had entered the stage of peaceful economic competition with the developed countries of the West.

Success in this competition cannot be gained by the old methods of administrative and excessively centralized management. It was necessary to change so as to give the enterprises themselves a material stake in the better utilization of their assets and in providing the best possible service to their consumers. To do this the enterprises obviously had to be relieved of the excessive number of planned targets and their work had to be judged, first, by how they fulfilled the contracts for deliveries of commodities and, if they did this, secondly by their profit level.

Profit sums up all the aspects of an enterprise's work, including quality of output, since the price for better goods is correspondingly higher than for outmoded or relatively inefficient items. But it is important to note that profit is neither the only nor the chief goal of production. We are interested above all in output of specific commodities to satisfy consumer and producer needs. Profit is used as the chief index of, and incentive to, efficiency of production, as a mechanism for appraising and stimulating the work of an enterprise and also as a source of accumulation and investment.

By means of bonuses drawn from profits we wish to encourage enterprises to draw up their own plans which would be good—that is, advantageous—alike for society and themselves; and not only to draw up such plans, but to carry them out, something which should be encouraged at the expense of the profits. It is a question not of weakening or discarding planning but, on the contrary, of reinforcing and improving it by drawing the enterprises themselves into the planning process, for they always know better than anyone their own real potentialities and should study and know the needs of their clients.

The introduction of contract relations with consumers or clients (for the contractual relationship now exists in a number of light industries) does not at all signify a change to regulation by the anarchy of the market. Effective consumer demand can be predicted more easily in our country than in the West, since we know the wage fund of the urban population and the earnings of the collective farmers. Hence, we can draw up well-based balance sheets of the public's income and expenditure. The total volume of purchasing power is a figure which lends itself easily to planning. But specifically which goods are to constitute this total, what are to be the colors of the clothing, which styles are to be used, and how best to organize their production—this is not the prerogative of centralized planning. It is, rather, a matter for agreement between trade outlets and producers. Thus, our market requirements, the calculation of public demand, and the planning of production not only are integral, they should support and supplement each other.

What is the difference between "capitalist" and "socialist" profit, in my opinion? The difference will be best understood if we consider (1) how the profit is formed, (2) what it indicates, and (3) how it is spent.

From the viewpoint of private enterprise, all profit belongs to the capitalists alone. To justify this, there was long ago devised a theory that three factors—capital, land, and labor—create value. Joseph A. Schumpeter, in his *Theory of Economic Development*, wrote that profit is the excess over production cost. But this "cost" includes "payment" for the entrepreneur's labor, land rent, and interest on capital, as well as a premium for "risk." Over and above this, profit should reward the entrepreneur if, by a fresh combination of production elements, he reduces the production cost below the prevailing average level of expenditures.

The nature of this "combination of elements" can be perceived from the fact that in the private enterprise system most profit is now derived from redistribution of income in the market in the process of exchange. It is common knowledge, for instance, that big profits are most easily obtained by the advantageous purchase of raw materials, by a monopoly-controlled raising of retail prices, by unequal exchanges with under-developed countries, by the export of capital to countries with low wage levels, by a system of preferential duties and tariffs, by the increase in stock market prices through capitalization above profit, and, finally, by military orders.

In our country all these sources of profit are precluded by the very nature of socialism, under which there is neither private ownership of the means of production nor holding of stock (and hence no stock market). The level at which labor is paid depends on the productivity of the labor and is regulated by law. Prices of raw materials and supplies are planned; the market cannot be taken advantage of in purchasing raw materials or hiring labor. Nor is it possible to take advantage of market conditions to raise the prices of finished goods. Exchange with other countries is conducted on a basis of equality and by long-term agreements.

In the Soviet Union, by virtue of the very nature of the mode of production and distribution, profit indicates only the level of production efficiency. Profit is the difference between production cost and the factory sale price. But since in our country the price represents, in principle, the norms of expenditure of socially necessary labor, any increase in profit is an index of relative economy in production. Higher profits in the Soviet Union are based solely on economized hours of working time, economized tons of raw materials and supplies and fuel, and economized kilowatt-hours of electricity. We do not justify profits obtained from chance circumstances, such as excessively high prices, and do not regard such profits as being to the credit of the enterprise. Rather do we consider such profit the consequence of insufficiently flexible price-setting. All profits of this kind go into the state budget; from such profits no bonuses are granted to the enterprises.

Now let us see what is done with profit in the U.S.S.R., that is, what it is spent on. First of all, no private individual and no enterprise as a group of private individuals may acquire profit. Profit may not be invested arbitrarily by any persons or groups for the purpose of deriving personal income.

Profit in our country belongs to those who own the means of production; that is to say, to society, to all the working people as a whole. All profit in our country goes first of all into the planned expansion or improvement of social production, and next into providing free social services to the public, such as education and science, public health services, pensions, and stipends. A part is spent on the administrative apparatus and, unfortunately, quite a large part on defense requirements. We would be happy to dispense with the latter expenditures if a program of universal disarmament were adopted.

Profit used to be given insufficient importance in our country because of a certain disregard of the law of value. Some Soviet economists incorrectly interpreted this economic law as an unpleasant leftover of capitalism; they held that the sooner we got rid of it the better. Disregard of the requirements of the law of value led to the establishment of arbitrarily planned prices—prices which, moreover, remained in force for overly long periods. Prices thus became divorced from the real value of goods; profit varied greatly from enterprise to enterprise, and even from article to article within the same general group of goods. In these circumstances profit did not reflect the actual achievements of the producers. Because of this, many economists and managers began to regard profit as something totally independent of the enterprise and therefore an unreliable barometer of economic management. It is this mistake that many of our economists, including the author, are now trying to eradicate. And our economic reform is aimed at this. We have no intention of reverting to private enterprise; on the contrary, we want to put into operation the economic laws of socialism. Central planning is entirely compatible with the initiative of enterprises in managing the economy profitably. This is as far from "private enterprise" as the latter is from feudalism.

The law of value is not a law of capitalism, but of any form of production for the market, including planned commodity production, which is what socialism is. The difference from capitalism is that ends and means are reversed. Under capitalism, profit is the basic aim, whereas satisfaction of the needs of the public is the means of attaining that aim and is secondary. Under socialism, on the contrary, the aim is to satisfy the needs of the public, and profit is the means toward that end. This is not a verbal distinction but the crux of the matter, since in our conditions profit does not work counter to social needs but helps to satisfy them.

The first stage of the economic reform has confronted us with certain difficulties in realizing its basic principles—difficulties which appear to be inherent in this period of the reform. The transfer of the first 704 enterprises to the new system was not immediately accompanied by substantial changes in their relations with the superior agencies, with other enterprises, with agencies supplying materials and equipment, etc.

Necessary changes have not been fully put into effect in the methods of planning production at the level of the ministries and industry administrations—particularly in the method of setting goals for enterprises. Due to lack of experience, sometimes the same old sharply criticized targets were simply made the new ones. For example, output has been considered as being the same as sales volume; and the assortment of items produced has not always been determined in consultation with the consumer or clients on the basis of direct contract arrangements. Instances of the inevitable deviation of practice from theory could be multiplied, but they all are due to the fact that the reform as yet covers only a limited number of enterprises. It is to be assumed that everything will gradually take proper shape.

The 1966 experience of working by the new method did show that, on the one hand, enterprises are becoming more dynamic and independent in their economic life, but, on the other hand, that the superior agencies frequently have been incapable of freeing themselves fast enough from old habits and from superfluous regimentation of the work of plants and factories. The inertia of thought, views, and ideas which was so characteristic of some executive agencies over a long period has proved more persistent than had been expected.

The reform puts the old established relationships in industry to a severe test. The enlargement of the rights of enterprises is an important condition of the reform. In many cases, however, the superior agencies have proved insufficiently prepared for this development. Sometimes this has taken the form of the old bureaucratic ills—inflexibility, irresponsibility and lack of initiative, reliance upon the formality of issuing orders instead of working out economic as opposed to administrative methods of influencing production.

Perhaps one of the most significant consequences of the economic reform is the growing influence of industrial enterprises on the superior agencies. The reform is destroying and will continue to destroy many established patterns, including the distrust shown by executive agencies for production organizers and economists at the enterprises.

Unquestionably, the reform has strengthened antibureaucratic views and the tendency of enterprises to strive for independence. This, however, does not in the least signify that the principle of democratic centralism in the management of our economy is being abandoned. To strengthen and intensify central planning of production by combining it with the initiative and full economic accountability of enterprises is to realize the principle of democratic centralism.

The reform has not yet sufficiently permeated the administrative interrelationships between enterprises and superior agencies. This is indeed a complicated process of many steps. Complaints and mutual dissatisfactions are inevitable. First of all, the reform requires a sharp improvement in the qualifications of those engaged in the management process. If the economic and organizational level of management is low, the efficiency and profitability of the enterprise are generally low. The point of the reform is to raise production efficiency, increase labor productivity, and open wide the road to rapid technical improvement. As it goes on, the reform inevitably will foster the selection and promotion of the more able, both below and at the top, to executive managerial positions. The reform will not tolerate the retention of anything that is obsolete and that has failed to justify itself in our methods of management.

*　*　*

Part Three

SOCIAL PROCESSES

V

The Political Process

An eminent political scientist has described politics as the process that determines who gets what, when, and how. Stated more formally, the political process is the struggle of individuals and groups to make authoritative decisions for all of society or to influence those decisions. That struggle goes on in the Soviet Union, just as it does in democratic political systems, with the difference that it does not take place openly and involves only a small number of Soviet citizens. Information about the political process in the Soviet Union is elusive. Compared to our knowledge of political behavior in the West, we know relatively little about Soviet politics. This is so partly because the formal description of the machinery and processes of government is so misleading and partly because few social scientists have ever been able to obtain firsthand information about politics in the Soviet Union.

The basic ingredients of political activity are individuals, groups, and classes with conflicting values and interests. Soviet society is stratified much like other industrial societies into broad social-economic classes, including the peasantry, urban industrial workers, and professional, white-collar, and intelligentsia groups. These classes can be further subdivided into numerous small but more cohesive interests, such as artists and writers, scientists, the military, economic administrators, and the legal profession, to name a few. Cutting across these classes and interest groups are large but loose groupings that reflect a common interest or outlook as, for example, advocates of investment in heavy industry or consumer goods, ideological conservatives or liberals, Stalinists or proponents of a reduction in international tensions. Unlike democratic politics, Soviet politics does not permit a free and open interplay of conflicting group interests; nevertheless the competition and conflict are there.

At the national level and every intermediate level down to the cities and districts, the relative scarcity of resources produces an almost continuous bargaining among competitors. Involved in the bargaining process are administrative chiefs, trade unions, customers, suppliers, collective farm chairmen, and Party and government officials. The principal instrumentality through which these interests are aggregated, articulated, and ultimately mediated is the Communist Party. And since the Party operates through a vast bureaucracy, the form and style of Soviet politics tend to be bureaucratic. Policies emanating from central authorities filter down through a complex of administrative bodies, which are structured as hierarchies. Each administrative unit must meet the demands (as modified by negotiation) of its superiors and secure what compliance it can from its inferiors.

Decision-making in Soviet politics is oligarchic. A small group of Party leaders determine the broad line of public policy and resolve those differences that cannot be settled at lower levels. Between them and the masses, who play virtually no part in the decision-making process, are an elite group of Party *apparatchiki*, government officials, industrial managers, professional leaders, and important members of the artistic and scientific intelligentsia, who, while not playing a decisive role, do exercise considerable influence on the laws, regulations, and decrees that make up public policy.

This elite is recruited largely by means of a system of nomination by higher Party committees to all important government, managerial, and professional posts. Advancement in this process requires ability, a talent to cope with the task required by the job. In addition, personal friendships, "pull," knowing the right people are also crucial in promotions and demotions. An important key to success is having the support of the people at they very top or their protégés.

One of the most complex and fascinating aspects of Soviet politics is the process by which the highest leadership emerges. There is no agreed-upon, operative procedure for selecting the head of the Party. Lenin held power because he had molded the Party that led the Revolution in 1917. His leadership was based largely on personal charisma deriving from the force of his intellect and personality. Stalin rose to power partially from his high position in the Secretariat, from which he had placed his supporters in the policy-making organs of the Party; partially by discrediting his competitors through intrigue; and to some extent by espousing policies more acceptable than those of his opponents. Once in control he remained there by means of terror and violence.

Stalin's successors have increasingly relied upon bureaucratic leadership in order to maintain their authority. Like Stalin, Khrushchev manipulated the Party apparatus to his advantage, but he needed in addition to prove his effectiveness in satisfying at least partially the major institutional interests in Soviet society. Violence no longer plays a major role in the struggle for power, nor is terror a central mechanism of control. Khrushchev fell when he lost the confidence of a large number of his colleagues and subordinates in his ability to produce results. It is noteworthy that the Brezhnev-Kosygin team came to power less on the basis of ideological or policy differences with Khrushchev than on their promise of a more rational pursuit of existing policies.

If any one office is associated with political dominance it would be that of General Secretary (First Secretary under Khrushchev) of the Party Central Committee. Stalin, Khrushchev, and Brezhnev have used that office in their quests for power. But Khrushchev's downfall revealed clearly that the office alone cannot guarantee its holder absolute rule. Below the top leader or leaders are ambitious colleagues who are always seeking to maneuver a successful coalition to displace the existing leadership. Factional infighting—even under Stalin—has been a basic feature of Soviet leadership politics. In this struggle issues, interests, and personalities all play a role. The lack of a recognized method for acquiring and transferring political authority is a source of instability and a major weakness of the Soviet system.

The Soviet system is authoritarian in the sense that it lacks an electoral process for mass participation. The public at large has no direct control over its rulers. Elections are common, but their significance is qualified in two vital ways: First, the selection of candidates is limited to individuals approved by the regime, and second, those representatives approved by the public have very little real political power. The Supreme Soviet and lesser legislative bodies in the Soviet Union do not in fact legislate. They approve and confirm decisions made by higher Party authorities. Thus the legislative process is very close to administrative rule-making. Elections, however, are treated as very important affairs by the Soviet leadership. The nominating process, the campaigning, and the election itself constitute an important mechanism by which the government is able to mobilize mass support for its programs and an important prop for the Soviet Union's claim to be a democratic society.

Joel J. Schwartz and William R. Keech are Professors of Political Science at the University of North Carolina. Alfred G. Meyer is Professor of Political Science at the University of Michigan. His books include *Marxism: The Unity of Theory and Practice, Leninism,* and *Communism.* The selection by Max Mote is based upon research carried on at the

University of Leningrad during 1962–63. The circumstances surrounding the accumulation of Khrushchev's reminiscences have not yet been revealed. According to the publisher, the material came "from various sources at various times and in various circumstances." Although this material is widely accepted by Soviet specialists as authentic, there are some experts who contend that it is not.

15

GROUP INFLUENCE AND THE POLICY PROCESS IN THE SOVIET UNION

JOEL J. SCHWARTZ AND WILLIAM R. KEECH

It has become widely recognized that Soviet officials do not formulate public policy in a vacuum, and that, indeed, their deliberations take into account in some fashion the needs and demands of various elements of the society. Further, it has been observed that social groups of various types play a noticeable, if only rudimentary, role in articulating interests to the top of the hierarchy. In fact one author has gone so far as to assert that Communist policy-making results from a "parallelogram of conflicting forces and interests." [1] While such viewpoints are now far more widely accepted than in the early 1950's, relatively little effort has been devoted to illustrating or illuminating how Soviet public policy in

[1] H. Gordon Skilling, "Interest Groups and Communist Politics," *World Politics*, 18 (April, 1966): 449.

Reprinted, with permission of the publisher and authors, from *The American Political Science Review* 62, No. 3 (September, 1968): 840–51. Footnotes citing Russian-language sources other than *Pravda* are omitted.

general or even a given Soviet policy can be importantly affected by group activity.

We propose here to make a contribution. Using the Educational Reform Act of 1958 as an exemplary case, we intend to show how and through what process groups can affect policy outcomes and, by identifying circumstances under which this takes place, to generate some hypotheses about when such influence is most likely to recur. In their excellent analysis of Soviet policy formation, Professors Brzezinski and Huntington identify what they call "policy groups," which come closest of any nongovernmental groups to participating in policy formation. These groups, such as the military, industrial managers, agricultural experts, and state bureaucrats,

> whose scope of activity is directly dependent on the allocation of national resources and which are directly affected by any shift in the institutional distribution of power . . . advocate to the political leadership certain courses of action; they have their own professional or specialized newspapers which, at times and subject to over-all Party control, can become important vehicles for expressing specific points of view.[2]

In this article we will investigate an instance wherein such groups seemed to influence policy with the result of virtually scuttling one of Khrushchev's own major proposals.

We do not mean to challenge the view that ultimate power in the U.S.S.R. resides at the top of the Communist Party hierarchy. Neither do we mean to infer that the top Party leadership was forced by a "policy group" to act against its will. We do not suggest that the instance we cite is modal. Indeed it is the best example we are aware of. We hope that the major payoff in this paper will be in showing why things happened as they did. This is the first step in finding out whether and how often to expect them again.

The first major section of the paper will describe the situation we use as a basis for our speculative analysis about the Soviet decision-making process. The second will attempt to explain why things happened as they did, and the third will report some hypotheses about when such phenomena are likely to recur.

I. Debate over the 1958 Act

A prominent feature of post-Stalin Russia has been the nationwide discussion of certain legislative proposals. This does not constitute a totally new innovation in the Soviet Union. During the preceding period such important laws as the constitution of 1936 received nationwide discussion before enactment. A few differences, however, deserve mention. First, the frequency of these discussions has substantially increased. Second and more important, the impact of these discussions on the

[2] Zbigniew Brzezinski and Samuel P. Huntington, *Political Power: U.S.A./U.S.S.R.* (New York: Viking Press, 1963), p. 196.

proposed legislation has in some instances been far more than peripheral. This especially applies to the debate which surrounded the Educational Reform Act of 1958. A closer look at this debate will afford us an opportunity to consider how the opinion of various "publics" can influence the policy process.

There can be little doubt about whose initiative lay behind the proposed reform. At the Thirteenth Komsomol Congress in April of 1958, Party First Secretary Khrushchev severely criticized the existing school system and demanded fundamental changes. This attack seems to have been motivated by three problems facing Soviet society in the mid-1950's, the cause of which Khrushchev linked to the existing school system.

First, the Soviet press had unceasingly criticized the denigrative attitudes of the younger generation toward physical labor. In the opinion of the First Secretary, the undue emphasis upon classical academic training and the neglect of the polytechnical side of education were largely responsible for this attitude.

Second, competition for admission to higher education had reached an excessive degree, and this likewise had caused great concern among political leaders. The competition itself has largely been a by-product of changes in the economic and educational systems.

Prior to 1950 the rapid growth of the economy and the underdeveloped secondary educational facilities maintained the demand for skilled technical cadres at a higher level than the supply. Throughout this period the number of available places in higher education exceeded the number of secondary school graduates. The postwar years, however, witnessed a remarkable acceleration of secondary school facilities and enrollment. In 1949, out of a total enrollment of 33 million pupils, only about 1 million were in grades eight to ten. Four years later the number of pupils in secondary education had risen to 4.5 million.[3] Now the annual supply of secondary school graduates greatly exceeded the number of vacancies in higher education. Since the Soviet regime, for reasons of its own, was unwilling to widen the availability of higher education, the gates of universities were closed to millions of youth regardless of their educational attainment.

An inevitable consequence has been the intensification of competition for the available number of places.[4] The pressures for admission became abnormally high because of the widespread notion that a college degree represents the key to individual advancement and entrance into the new class of Soviet intelligentsia. Consequently, those high school graduates initially denied admission refused to accept their fate. Instead of

[3] Nicholas DeWitt, *Education and Professional Employment in the USSR* (Washington, 1961), p. 140.

[4] In his speech to the Thirteenth Komsomol Congress, Khrushchev noted that "last year higher educational institutions were able to accept 400,000 new students, half of them for full time study. . . . However, at least 700,000 secondary school graduates failed to gain admission last year to higher or technical schools and between 1953–1956 about 2,200,000 failed to gain admission."

entering the labor force, many of them became perennial college candidates. Very often they applied to schools whose area of specialization was of no genuine interest to them. But in the absence of alternatives they would often enter an agricultural institute just to be able "to study somewhere." Here again Khrushchev charged that the educational system had bred such attitudes. By allowing students to continue their education uninterruptedly and by stressing almost exclusively academic material, the schools naturally generated the expectation that the path to life lay solely through higher education.

The third problem involved the increasing stratification of Soviet society. The notion that higher education was the key to membership in the "new class" had a firm basis in fact. Yet these educational channels for upward social and political mobility were being drastically constricted as a consequence of their pre-emption by the incumbent political and bureaucratic elites. Khrushchev himself admitted that in the competition for admission to college the influence of parents often proved more important than the merit of the candidates. He further stated that only 30 to 40 per cent of the enrolled students in higher education institutions came from worker and peasant backgrounds.[5] The differential access to a prime source of mobility gravely concerned the First Secretary. Both the content and tenor of his statements clearly indicate that Khrushchev sought to eliminate privilege and inequality from the Soviet educational system.

Finally we should mention an additional factor which *may* have influenced the reform movement. At the time of the debate some Western scholars argued that the specifics of Khrushchev's proposals owed much to the serious labor shortage the Soviet economy was about to experience.[6] The argument may be briefly summarized as follows. Because of severe war losses and a declining birth rate in the postwar period, the Soviet Union would have one-third fewer people entering the labor force during the late 1950's and early 1960's than normally would have been the case. Consequently the ambitious economic growth program could be achieved only if the vast majority of young people were channeled into the active labor force instead of higher education. It is important to note, however, that the Soviet press never cited a labor deficit as cause for the reform. Other evidence also casts doubt upon the validity of this thesis.[7]

While there is room for disagreement as to what problems motivated the reform, there is no ambiguity regarding Khrushchev's proposals for dealing with them. In September of 1958, the Party Secretary published his "thesis" on school reorganization.[8] He suggested that continuous academic education be abolished and that all students be required to combine work with study. In effect, this meant phasing out the ten-

[5] *Pravda*, September 21, 1958.

[6] See, for example, DeWitt, *Education and Professional Employment*, p. 15.

[7] For a refutation of the labor deficit thesis see "Facts and Figures," *Bulletin of Radio Free Europe*, September 22, 1958.

[8] See *Pravda*, September 21, 1958.

year school, which at that time constituted a completed secondary education. After finishing a seven- or eight-year primary school, said Khrushchev, every young person should enter the labor force. Those who
wished to prepare themselves for higher education could continue their
studies in evening and correspondence schools. Successful students would
receive two or three days' released time from work to facilitate studying.

The substitution of part-time work and study for full-time education
in secondary day schools had, from Khrushchev's point of view, two advantages. First, it would instill in the younger generation a respectful attitude toward physical labor. Second, it would equalize access to higher
education. The secondary day schools had become the province of children from the urban intelligentsia. Evening and correspondence schools,
on the other hand, recruited most of their students from worker and
peasant families. The difference in the quality of education offered by these
two divisions gave the day school graduate an obvious advantage. By
fusing the two channels into one undifferentiated system, Khrushchev
hoped to eliminate the class bias in Soviet education. The road to a
higher education would be the same for all, irrespective of the positions
or jobs the parents held in society.

Study in higher educational institutions was also to be put on a part-
time basis. The student would acquire the first two or three years of
his college education through evening or correspondence courses. Thereafter he could complete his training on a full-time schedule. Moreover,
no individual was to be granted admission to higher education unless
he had already worked full time after completing secondary school.
Once again we see Khrushchev's determination to de-emphasize the
purely academic side of education and to enhance the importance of
work experience.

If we compare Khrushchev's September Memorandum with the actual
law adopted in December, 1958, we find that the two differ not only in
detail but in basic principle. To begin with, the old secondary day school
was preserved more or less intact both in form and content. Khrushchev's
demand that work be combined with study had received token satisfaction by increasing the number of hours devoted to polytechnical training
within the schools. But the quantity and quality of academic subjects
had in no way been sacrificed. The law established an eleven-year day
school to replace the old ten-year day school system. The addition of
another year permitted greater emphasis upon labor training without
simultaneously diluting the quality of academic education. Indeed, the
number of hours devoted to purely academic subjects proved to be
exactly the same under the new system as it had been under the old.[9]

The maintenance of continuous secondary full-time education must be
seen as a rebuff to Khrushchev's demands. When the new law went into
effect, it became apparent that nearly all the former ten-year schools
would continue to operate as part of the new eleven-year system. Some

[9] For an analysis of this point see an article by Klaus Mehnert in *Die Welt*, July
18, 1959.

figures also suggest that the number of students enrolled in the new system was comparable in size to the two senior grades of the old ten-year school.[10] It is true that Khrushchev recognized in his memorandum the need for *some* full-time day schools. But he envisaged that they would operate only during a transitional period, and he expected their number to be sharply reduced right from the beginning of the reform.

While the eleven-year system might have satisfied the demand that work be combined with study, it could not possibly have achieved Khrushchev's other expressed purpose—the elimination of privilege and inequality. The perpetuation of a bifurcated full-time and part-time school system insured that inequality would persist. Nevertheless the disadvantages faced by the evening and correspondence student might have significantly diminished had the law incorporated Khrushchev's suggestion regarding released time for study. Yet in this area as well important modifications were made. The reorganization decree left this question open, and subsequent legislation resulted in a far less liberal policy.[11] Under these circumstances the vast majority of college students would continue to come from the full-time secondary schools, and an inevitable by-product would be the continuation of class bias in higher education.

The provision for admission to and study in higher educational institutions likewise markedly deviated from Khrushchev's suggestions. Instead of *absolutely* requiring full-time work before admission, the law merely stipulated that *priority* would be granted those with the record of employment or military service. But precedence for people with production experience already existed before the reorganization of the school system. Thus the wording of the law gave only formal recognition to an on-going practice. It cannot be interpreted as a "concession" to the demands made by Khrushchev in his memorandum.

His insistence upon part-time study during the first few college years appears to have been more successfully realized. At least the law accepted it in principle. However, even here some important alterations occurred. The law explicitly exempted from this requirement all students in difficult theoretical disciplines. Similarly, the requirement would be inoperative in both nontechnical higher educational institutions and in arts faculties at universities, since "factory work for students cannot in these cases be connected with their future job."[12]

Generally speaking, the education reform failed to implement the most important goals and purposes that Khrushchev had articulated in

[10] The actual law left this point unclear but later developments indicated that just as many children—about one-third of the total—would attend full-time high schools as had been the case before the reform. See Thomas Bernstein "Soviet Educational Reform" (M.A. thesis, Columbia University, 1962), p. 111, and articles in *The New York Times*, September 2, 1959; *Wall Street Journal*, June 29, 1960.

[11] Instead of the two to three days released time from work as suggested by Khrushchev, students in evening schools receievd only one additional free day for study.

[12] This point was made by the Soviet minister of higher education and was reflected in the final law.

his memorandum. What factors can account for the observable disparity between the September proposal and the December law? To answer that question we must look briefly at the discussion which ensued during this period of time. The content of that debate clearly revealed that different societal groups, or at least some members of them, opposed Khrushchev's reform.

Teachers and administrators identified with the ten-year school obviously wished to preserve and protect their institutional bailiwicks. But a frontal assault on the First Secretary's ideas would not have been good politics. Instead they opposed the reform more deviously. Essentially they argued that to prepare youth for manual labor it was not necessary to send them after the eighth grade to factories or farms. A much better way would be to bring the factories and farms into the schools by setting up first class workshops. Under these conditions it would be possible to teach pupils the same skills they could learn by entering the labor force. To substantiate their case the proponents of this approach assumed the initiative even *before* the appearance of Khrushchev's September memorandum. Prior to the opening of the school year in 1958, Y. I. Afanasenko, Minister of Education for the Russian Republic, announced that the number of schools giving training in industrial and agricultural skills would double. He further announced that the Russian Republic had begun to experiment with extending secondary schools from ten to eleven years. Under the extended program students would spend half of their time at school and the other half at jobs on farms, in factories, or at construction sites. He mentioned that fifty schools with this program had operated the last year and this number would increase to two hundred this year. Here, in embryonic form, was the eleven-year school system that became law in December of 1958. Thus, through word and deed, those occupational groups associated with full-time secondary education sought to protect the organization they had built with effort and care.

Other groups opposed to the reform included higher educational and scientific personnel. Their arguments were perhaps more telling. They warned that it would be impossible under the new system to ensure the supply of highly qualified cadres for economic and societal growth. How can we, they asked, perfect and advance scientific knowledge when new entrants to higher educational schools would have only eight years of regular schooling behind them and, in the following years, would have forgotten the little they had once learned. Several prominent educators and scientists went so far as to assert that a hiatus between incomplete and complete secondary school as well as between complete secondary school and higher education would result in irreparable damage to the state. For creative work in scientific research often manifests itself when the individual has reached his mid-twenties, and the acquisition of theoretical knowledge on a large scale demands uninterrupted study.

The warning of experts reinforced grave doubts raised by many parents. The basic argument of the latter was that a shortened basic school program would adversely affect the physical and intellectual maturation of adolescents. Furthermore, it was said that channeling young people into production at an early age does not give them a chance to adequately choose a skill which best suits them. While both of these points had merit, parental views were somewhat suspect because other motives could be readily discerned. As Khrushchev himself pointed out, many parents were determined that their children receive opportunities for maximum education. They saw his plans as a threat to that opportunity and responded by attacking it. To the extent that pedagogical experts echoed parental concerns, as some did, they served as a linkage between public opinion and political decision-makers. By articulating the interests of an amorphous group in technical terms, the experts transformed their claims into a politically relevant issue.

A few words must also be said about the attitudes of factory managers. Although their opposition did not find explicit expression in the debate, their behavior left few doubts as to where they stood on the issue. Long before the question of reform had arisen, managers had displayed a reluctance to hire and train juvenile workers. Under the new arangements they would become responsible for all sorts of functions for which the factory was ill prepared. Moreover, the large influx of schoolchildren and the necessity to train them would inevitably divert managers from their own duties of production and plan fulfillment. In light of this fact it is not surprising that the reform act failed to implement Khrushchev's suggestions regarding released time from work. That would have greatly complicated the managers' tasks, and we can assume that their views were transmitted to the proper authorities.[13]

At this point, our task is to account for the role of groups in forming educational policy in this instance by interpreting a number of facts. The objective facts we must work from are, in summary, that Khrushchev made a far-reaching proposal to deal with a number of educational problems facing the regime, and that the substance of the proposal was radically modified. The major proponent of the reform was obviously Khrushchev himself. The most important—indeed the only—opponents of the changes we can identify are the social groups cited above.

Here we should note that if one quantifies the number of articles which appeared during the debate, the oppositional point of view is clearly a minority. It is quite possible that a "war of memoranda" may have been raging behind the scenes and that during this exchange the minority position was in fact the majority point of view.[14] Whatever

---

[13] For a scathing criticism of managerial attitudes toward juvenile workers, see the lead editorial in *Pravda*, September 25, 1957.

[14] There is some evidence that the opposition was far greater than one would gather from simply reading the official press. For example, relatively few parental criticisms found their way into print. But during 1963–64, when the first author of this paper was conducting interviews in the Soviet Union, it was learned that a very large number of urban middle-class parents had strongly criticized Khrushchev's proposals at "PTA" meetings held during the reform debate period. Similarly, Professor William Johnson of the University of Pittsburgh told the same author that opposition among educa-

may have been the case, it is undeniable that the oppositional arguments were closer to the form of the finally enacted law.

There are several possible interpretations which would explain the outcome of the educational reform debate. One might argue, for example, that the disparity between the September memorandum and the December law resulted from Khrushchev's changing his mind. Once the technocratic elites had pointed out the potentially dangerous consequences inherent in Khrushchev's proposals, the First Secretary simply revised his original position. There is no way, of course, to verify or falsify this interpretation. Since we have no knowledge of Khrushchev's preference schedule or to whom he would most likely listen, we must allow for the possibility that anyone who had a position and stated it prior to the outcome might have influenced Khrushchev. If we accept this interpretation, however, we must resolve certain questions which detract from its credibility.

When Khrushchev spoke to the Komsomol Congress in April, 1958, he stated that the Party Central Committee had, *for some time*, been discussing the improvement of public education. Presumably, experts had been consulted during the course of such discussions. We might also presume that Khrushchev changed his mind because he heard convincing arguments which had not been made in the far longer period which preceded publication of his memorandum.

It is also important to recall that Khrushchev clearly identified himself personally with the issue of educational reform. He placed his public prestige squarely upon the line. As Richard Neustadt has pointed out, chief executives cannot afford to make indiscriminate public pronouncements. If they are sensitive to the prerequisites of power and influence, they must carefully weigh the consequences which flow from what, when, and how they say things.[15] All the evidence we have on Khrushchev's career suggests that he was highly sensitive to the requisites of power and influence. Thus not only did the First Secretary have ample opportunity to consult expert opinion on the educational question, but he also had a vested political interest in doing so before publicly stating his position.

Our own inclination then is to discount, though not categorically reject, the possibility that Khrushchev simply changed his mind between September and December. An alternative interpretation is that bureaucratic groups prevailed over the First Secretary and forced him to act against his will.[16] To accept this, however, would demand a rewriting of

---

tional officials was far more widespread than the official press revealed. Professor Johnson was in the Soviet Union at the time of the debate and is known to have extensive contacts with Soviet educators.

[15] Richard Neustadt, *Presidential Power* (New York: Mentor Books, New American Library, 1964).

[16] For an analysis of the reform with this type of implication, see David Burg, "Some Thoughts on the Soviet Educational Reform," *Bulletin* 6 (March, 1959): 32–36.

the literature on political power and resources in the Soviet Union that we think is neither necessary nor appropriate. It is quite easy on the other hand to imagine more important actors prevailing over Khrushchev with the social groups associating themselves spuriously, so to speak, with the stronger actors. In suggesting this interpretation we must argue inferentially, because the only direct evidence we have about opposition to the proposal relates to the groups. In the section below we will attempt to account for what happened and to assess the role of the social groups in it.

II. The Role of Social Groups in Shaping the Act

Brzezinski and Huntington express the orthodox interpretation in arguing that the key political resource in the Soviet Union is control of the Party organization, and that such control can be shared only at the top.

> Thus, insofar as there are limits on the power of the top leader in the Soviet Union, they stem from his sharing control of the *apparat* with a small number of colleagues . . . the principal limits on the power of the Soviet leader are inside the Kremlin.[17]

We agree, and we feel that those colleagues were crucially important in defeating Khrushchev's proposal. But the opposition of the groups identified above was not coincidental. We submit that the groups were mobilized after the dispute was left unresolved at the top.

Such an argument forces us to take sides in a dispute among Soviet scholars about whether or not there is conflict within the Soviet leadership at times other than succession crises. It is the position of the "conflict" school that policy issues such as those on agriculture, heavy industry, consumer goods, foreign affairs, Stalinism, economic reorganization, and education are continuous sources of dispute among the top leadership. When one issue is resolved, another is likely to take its place. We think there is strong evidence for this viewpoint, which became more compelling than ever with Khrushchev's political demise in October, 1964.[18]

In this specific case, Khrushchev stated in April, 1958, that the Party Central Committee was presently engaged in preparing a resolution on the improvement of public education. But the September "theses" proved to be simply a note by Khrushchev with the "approval" of the Central Committee, instead of a formal resolution by the august body. This suggests that Khrushchev's educational reform was a highly personal document which lacked support among a substantial element of the top political leadership. Esoteric evidence to support this thesis is pro-

[17] Brzezinski and Huntington, *Political Power*, p. 145.
[18] See for example, Carl A. Linden, *Khrushchev and the Soviet Leadership 1957–1964* (Baltimore: Johns Hopkins University Press, 1966).

vided by the unusual silence of the top political leadership during the educational reform debate. Khrushchev appears to have been the only Presidium member to have played a significant role in the reform discussions and to have clearly and publicly expressed his attitudes. Sidney Ploss has argued that in the context of Soviet politics the silence of leaders on a topical issue must be construed as disagreement with the expressed viewpoint of their colleagues.[19] It is also significant that major amendments to Khrushchev's plan were reflected in the Central Committee resolution on education reform which was finally issued on November 16, 1958.[20]

If, as we have argued, the important conflict was on the top leadership level, and if the persons on that level have the power to determine policy outcomes, what roles did the social groups play? The answer hangs on the nature of conflict among the leaders. It is well known that such conflict involves elements of power struggle and elements of dispute over policy alternatives.[21] Sometimes these elements operate independently of one another; more often they intertwine. Since Khrushchev had decisively defeated his rivals for power in 1957, we can assume that in the case of the education reforms of 1958 the elements of power struggle were less important than at almost any time since Stalin's death, and that the elements of unadulterated policy dispute were correspondingly more important. Indeed, it is unlikely that Khrushchev would have survived such a defeat as this had this policy dispute involved much power struggle.

Insofar as this was really a policy dispute, it involved numerous problem-solving considerations, as we emphasized above. The problems and policy positions associated with them involved a number of questions of judgment about what courses of action would solve the problem, and what the consequences of such action would have for other goals of the regime. It is here that the groups play an important role. Numerous groups have recognized expertise about what problems are in their own area. The ten-year school personnel had an authoritative position for a judgment that students could get work experience without radically changing the school organization and curriculum. The scientific community had good claim to special insight into the needs of training scientists. Parents may be viewed as having some legitimate judgment about the needs of adolescents, although this is less apparently expertise. One student of the reform debate has argued that

> the most important factors responsible for the change in Khrushchev's original proposals probably were the arguments of experts—the function of

[19] See Sidney L. Ploss, *Conflict and Decision-Making in Soviet Russia: A Case Study in Agricultural Policy 1953–1963* (Princeton, N.J.: Princeton University Press, 1965), pp. 17–18.
[20] For an analysis of these amendments see Rudolph Schlesinger, "The Educational Reform," *Soviet Studies* 10 (April, 1959): 432–44.
[21] See Brzezinski and Huntington, *Political Power*, pp. 267, 269–83, 295–300.

expert opinion was to point out to the leadership the possibly harmful consequences to Soviet society of the literal adoption of Khrushchev's original plans.[22]

It is hard to identify any concrete resource other than their own recognized expertise which the groups might have used in the dispute. Neither money, votes, nor popularity were relevant to its resolution. Only the expert judgment was clearly relevant. The only reasonable alternative would seem to be that the regime may have accorded the positions of these groups a certain legitimacy just because they were group preferences, much as an American public official might yield to a constituent's demand simply because he views it as legitimate and because he may view his job as one of servicing such demands when they are legitimate and do not conflict with other goals. We have no reason to believe that Soviet officials view their jobs this way. Communist ideology, unlike democratic ideology, supplies its own policy goals, rather than depending on public expressions of preference to define them. Besides, we have already seen that the goals of these groups conflicted with the goals of none other than the First Secretary of the Communist Party. It does seem apparent that, insofar as groups influenced the outcome of this issue, it was through the communication of their expert judgments to people at the top of the hierarchy who *were* in a position to influence outcomes. The expertise became a resource to be used in making a case that more harm than good would result from the proposed reform.[23] We contend that in the Soviet Union policy issues are often decided on the basis of such debates. If such is the case the arguments of persons who are recognized as being knowledgeable can be an important resource for the proponent or opponent of a policy proposal.[24]

One can see elements of ambiguity in this interpretation of the role of these groups as articulators of expert judgment. It may appear, for example, that the ten-year school personnel are looking out for themselves when they oppose changes in their institution. The position of the parents seems even more transparent. There may even have been some self-interest involved in the position of the scientists. The point is that there is no objective way for either Soviet leaders or American

[22] Bernstein, "Soviet Educational Reform," p. 119. See also Brzezinski and Huntington, *Political Power*, p. 214.

[23] In this instance, many political leaders may have been especially inclined to "believe" these arguments. As primary members of the new class, Communist Party cadres had good reason to support the educational *status quo*. They were among the chief beneficiaries of the existing system. Their children enjoyed advantageous access to full-time secondary and higher education. Their is no question that such cadres hoped to perpetuate the provision of such education for their children. Khrushchev's proposals surely must have caused consternation among Party cadres which other top Party leaders would readily have been conscious of. In this respect the Party itself was probably an important constituent pressure group which reinforced the doubts Khrushchev's colleagues had about the wisdom of his proposals.

[24] For a view of government as problem-solving and adapting to environments in which communications play a crucial role, see Karl W. Deutsch, *The Nerves of Government* (New York: The Free Press, 1963).

scholars to clearly separate the elements of self-interest from those of expert predictions of dire consequences. We would argue that in Western democracies as well there is often an almost indecipherable mixture of preference and prediction in policy debate. For example, social welfare policies in the United States are commonly defended in terms of the prospects of contraction and recession if welfare funds are not fed into the economy. The very ambiguity between preference and prediction may serve to enhance the prospects of group influence through the pressing of interests with the support of expert judgments. The congruence of one's interests with one's predictions is probably less important than the persuasiveness of the predictions and the acknowledged expertness of predictors, no matter whose interests they seem to support.

This almost inevitable mixture of self-interest and expertise provides a channel through which groups in the Soviet Union *may* influence policy when higher powers seek their judgment. We do not know how common this occurrence is, but we are confident that expertise is not used in this way to resolve all policy disputes. We will devote the remainder of this paper to an assessment of conditions leading to such a state, and to hypotheses about when to expect it. Our first set of hypotheses deals with what conditions within the current post-Stalin regime will be associated with such group influence. The second set will attempt to identify what it is about post-Stalinist Russia that makes this possible in contrast with the Stalin era.

III. Some Hypotheses

Leadership conflict has already been cited as an important factor in leading top officials to look to group expertise. It is more than conceivable that monolithic leadership would itself seek expert advice, but we expect that it would do so more surreptitiously than through semi-public debate. More importantly, it could ignore the advice when it chose to rather than in effect being reversed by it. Under conditions of leadership conflict, unresolved disputes may lead some of the participants to broaden the scope of conflict by involving policy groups who might shift the balance. The dynamic involved may be something like the following. There is a split, for example, among the Politburo, wherein the First Secretary is about to prevail. Holders of the minority position may react to their imminent defeat by contacting their sympathizers among the "policy groups" and urging them to state their position on the issue in their specialized publications, in hopes that the balance of power will shift in their favor when more actors are involved. Broadening the scope of conflict may change the outcome.[25]

[25] See Ploss, *Conflict and Decision-Making*, pp. 61, 84, 286, for other examples and a discussion of changes in the scope of conflict in the Soviet Union. See also Elmer E. Schattschneider, *The Semisovereign People* (New York: Holt, Rinehart & Winston, 1960), for a discussion of the impact of other kinds of changes in patterns of conflict in the United States.

We hypothesize that the more and greater the disputes on the top policy-making level, the more likely it is that policy groups will be involved and listened to.

Brzezinski and Huntington point out that policy-makers are "more responsive to the demands or aspirations of groups" during a struggle for power, which would seem to bear out our point.[26] They use Khrushchev's struggle as an example, but they themselves point out elsewhere that victors in power struggles often reverse themselves and adopt the policies advocated by their opponents.[27] This pattern would seem to reduce the long-term impact of group influence in a power struggle. Our own example is of an unreversed policy decided in a period when the heat of the struggle for power had diminished, whether it had completely died or not. Indeed the absence of a threat to his power may well have made Khrushchev more willing to yield. Brzezinski and Huntington say that, while policy is the means to power in succession struggles,

> in stable dictatorial conditions, however, the leader may sometimes exercise power in matters that do not affect the security of his position. Then, as with the education reform of 1958, he can tolerate substantial amendments to his original proposal.[28]

It may be, then, that conditions of tranquility lend themselves more effectively to more or less permanent and far-reaching group influence than do power struggles. Leaders are probably more eager to solicit the support of groups when they are trying to secure power or ward off threats to their position, but group influence may be more permanent and real outside of power struggles. We are not prepared to predict that group influence over policy will be greater under power struggles or more ordinary policy conflicts, but we are prepared to argue that under either of these conditions of leadership conflict group influence will be greater than when leadership is relatively monolithic. Such a hypothesis is at the core of our whole argument.

Bauer, Inkeles, and Kluckhohn observe that the failure of a policy may lead the Politburo to adopt an approach that they recently opposed.[29] Our example does not directly support this observation, although of course it does not conflict with it, but the important point suggested by it is that the nature of the issue may be an important variable. Pursuing the rationale for our argument of group influence in the educational reforms, it is apparent that the problematic character of the issue and the fact that the consequences of a shift were not known with certainty made the judgment of policy groups more important than they

[26] *Political Power*, p. 198.
[27] *Ibid.*, pp. 193, 240–52.
[28] *Ibid.*, p. 270.
[29] Raymond A. Bauer, Alex Inkeles, and Clyde Kluckhohn, *How the Soviet System Works* (Cambridge, Mass.: Harvard University Press, 1956), p. 98.

would have been otherwise. The obvious implication of this is that the more problematic the consequences of a given course of action, the more likely it is that groups would be involved.

A related point that is derived from interest group politics in Western democracies is that groups are likely to be more influential in policy outcomes when the issue is narrow and technical than when the issue is broad and general.[30] In democratic polities, this is partly because other publics are less likely to be paying any attention or to care when the issue is technical. Thus the field is left relatively open for the interested group. A further rationale would be pertinent in the Soviet Union. It is not so much that other actors are or are not concerned; it is rather that technical advice and opinions are at a premium on technical issues.

We hypothesize that the more problematic and technical the issue, the more dependent on expert judgment elites will be. Consequently they will be more likely to consult policy groups, who will thereby be more influential on such issues.

While we hope that the above hypotheses help account for conditions varying *within* the current post-Stalinist regime which we associated with such group influence as we have illustrated, we do not argue that such influence ever occurred in the Stalin era. We know of no such prominent examples. In this final section we will identify several underlying conditions which in part distinguish the two eras and make groups more important in policy formation, or at least potentially so, in the present.

One important change is that the rigid, dictatorial one-man rule of the Stalin period has given way to collective leadership. While there may be one dominant leader, his power is shared among several key figures at the apex of the political structure. Under conditions of a diffused power structure, group influence is far more likely.[31] When power is exercised in an autocratic manner, groups must gain the ear of the all-powerful leader if they are to influence the policy process. During a period of collective leadership the access routes to points of decision-making become more numerous. Indeed, the very nature of collective leadership may make political leaders more responsive to group demands.

Carl Linden has argued that the transition from autocracy to oligarchy bring with it a constant struggle for political primacy at the very top.

[30] See Harry Eckstein, *Pressure Group Politics* (Stanford, Calif.: Stanford University Press, 1960).

[31] Dispersion of decision-making can assume a "personalized" as well as an institutional form. Instead of separation of powers between executive, legislative, and judicial groups one may find a separation of powers between leaders at the top of an outwardly monolithic political structure. See Ploss, *Conflict and Decision-Making*, p. 286. On the relationship between group influence and a diffusion of power, see Harry Eckstein, "Group Theory and the Comparative Study of Pressure Groups," in Harry Eckstein and David Apter, eds., *Comparative Politics* (New York: Free Press, 1963), p. 396.

Since no individual is automatically assured of predominant power, he must secure that position by winning and holding the support of a combination of societal groupings. His actual or potential rivals, on the other hand, can build their own constituency coalitions by identifying with those elements discontented with an incumbent leader's policy. The politics of leadership struggle then intertwines with the politics of group conflict. It is this interdependence which facilitates group influence on the policy process.[32]

We hypothesize that the larger and more collective the top leadership, the greater the prospects for the sort of disputes that can lead to the involvement of social groups in policy formation.

The attitudes of those leaders and their methods of social control will also have an important bearing on the prospects for group influence. Under a system of terror individuals are frightened into silent submissiveness and live in an atomized state. Unaware that others share common attitudes, grievances, and interests, the terrorized citizen accepts his lot and does not attempt to influence the behavior of decision-makers.[33] Only when terror subsides does this condition of "pluralistic ignorance" end and the opportunity for interest articulation emerge. For now communication, both through the formal mass media and through informal personal interaction, assumes a more candid and realistic nature. Under these new conditions the communication process itself facilitates group influence. It serves to generate widespread awareness of commonly shared attitudes which in turn becomes a powerful factor inducing groups to influence policy outcomes in their favor.

The leashing of terror enhances the prospect for group influence in other ways as well. David Easton points out that not all societal claims and demands are converted into policy outputs. Only those which become public issues have this possibility.[34] In any polity this requires the patronage and support of some political authority figure. In a system where terror is no longer all-pervasive, individuals may be far more likely to risk identification with unresolved issues, since the consequences of poor choices are far less serious. At best it may mean that one's power position remains static. At worst it may mean a diminution in political power and perhaps even demotion. But it does not mean internment or execution, as it so often did during the Stalinist period. The individual has lost a political battle but not necessarily the war. He remains on the scene with the possibility of recouping his losses and rising once again to top political positions.

[32] Linden, *Khrushchev and Soviet Leadership*, pp. 20–21.

[33] This condition of "pluralistic ignorance" is discussed in Bauer *et al.*, *How Soviet System Works*, p. 263.

[34] David Easton, "The Analysis of Political Systems," in Roy C. Macridis and Bernard E. Brown, eds., *Comparative Politics: Notes and Readings* (Homewood, Ill.: The Dorsey Press, 1964), pp. 94–95.

We hypothesize that groups will be influential as technocratic spokes-men only when terror subsides and the regime accords them legitimacy of expression of their point of view.

The kind of expert judgment involved in the interest articulation we have described is a function of the nature of the society. Harry Eckstein has noted that modernization increases the significance of groups in the political process.[35] We suggest that the modernization of Russia posi-tively relates to potential group influence in several ways. First, it intro-duces a functional specialization and differentiation into the society, which in turn generates a diffusion of interests competing with one an-other to write the laws of society to their advantage. During the early stages of Soviet rule the Party pre-empts interest articulation not only because it wants to but also, to some degree, because it has to. The society which the Bolsheviks inherited was largely composed of an un-diffentiated mass of peasants who had traditionally played a politically passive role. Thus the task of identifying and articulating interests fell to the Party by default.

This is not to say that at the time of Bolshevik ascendancy there were no functionally specialized groups with political experience in the pro-tection of their interests. They existed but they were far fewer and far less significant than in the present period. Furthermore, those groups tended to be stigmatized by their identification with the old regime. Thus any demands put forth by them lacked an essential ingredient for success—the presumption of legitimacy. The *a priori* belief of the Party that such individuals were disloyal deprived them of any political currency which could be used in the process of trading support for recognition of their demands.

The modernization of Russia has fundamentally altered this situation. Not only has it generated a complex economic and social pluralism but it also has provided new cadres to staff these skilled groups.[36] Those who possess scarce technical capabilities are far more likely to exert influence today than in the past. Such technocrats are products of the new system (the new Soviet man) and their loyalty is not impugned. Consequently, their attempts to influence the political process is per-ceived in legitimized rather than counterrevolutionary terms. The argu-ments of scientific, educational, and managerial experts may have been motivated by selfish concerns. But, as we noted earlier, these arguments were made in the context of what would best serve the interests of the Soviet Union. Given the fact that these experts are the products of the Soviet period, their counsel cannot be ignored on the grounds that the purveyors of such ideas are politically suspect. The handicap which

[35] Harry Eckstein, "Group Theory and the Comparative Study of Pressure Groups," in Eckstein and Apter, eds., *Comparative Politics*, p. 395.

[36] For an interesting, suggestive article on the growth of pluralism in Russian society, see Henry L. Roberts, "The Succession to Khrushchev in Perspective," *Proceedings of the Academy of Political Science* 28 (April, 1965): 2–12.

afflicted old specialists simply does not operate in the contemporary period.

Stalin's transformation of Russia insured the increased importance of groups in the policy process in yet another way, although the full impact of this development had to await the dictator's death. It was during the 1930's and 1940's that the politicization of society reached totalitarian dimensions. As politics came to predominate in all areas of life, individuals realized that the protection of their interests could be achieved only by gaining access to and influencing the political structure. Unlike Western political systems, where many issues are resolved in the private sector of the society, the struggle over who gets what, when, and how in the Soviet Union takes place entirely within the public domain.[37] Thus individuals and groups are perforce compelled to focus their attention and pressure on the decision-making process if they hope to maintain or improve their status.

The fourth contribution of modernization stems from the fact that a complex technological society requires stable occupational group membership. As we have already suggested, the behavior of managers, teachers, educators, and scientists was motivated in part by their desire to protect interests derived from their occupational roles. Such a phenomenon occurs, however, only when individuals have an opportunity to firmly anchor themselves in one occupational role so that it becomes for them an important reference group. This connotes, in turn, an absence of the recurring purge so characteristic of the Stalinist period. Stalin purposefully removed leading strata of important groups lest they become too closely identified with the interests of those groups and more specifically lest they use the economic, social, and political resources inherent in those groups for the purpose of delimiting the decision-making power of the leader.

Now this is a very costly procedure and one that a developed society cannot afford to engage in for very long. Managers, teachers, scientists and other specialists are not created over night, and their summary purge means not only a loss of experienced and skilled personnel but also the forfeiture of scarce economic resources invested in their education and training. As Soviet society has become more complex and sophisticated this type of gross economic waste proved intolerable. We do not imply, of course, that high-ranking Soviet personnel are no longer removed from their positions. The official press is full of accounts concerning the removal of such personnel. We do argue, however, that "the purge" today significantly differs from its Stalinist predecessor. At present

[37] We are identifying here a difference of degree. As Eckstein notes, pressure groups have become very active and significant in the postwar political systems of Britain, France, etc., for similar reasons. "One rather obvious reason for this development is the growth of the social service state—of positive government regulating, planning, directing, or entirely drawing into itself all sorts of social activities. This trend has given social groups a greater stake in politics and therefore mobilized them to a much greater extent while making government increasingly dependent on the collaboration and advice, technical or otherwise, of the groups." Eckstein, "Group Theory," p. 395.

leading occupational strata are not removed in the wholesale manner reminiscent of the 1930's and 1940's. More importantly their removal is seldom if ever accompanied by internment or execution. Most often they seem to be demoted to a less prestigious and influential job but within the same area of expertise, which in turn improve the prospects that groups may influence policy when higher powers seek their judgment.[38]

We have attempted in this article to illustrate that under some circumstances social groups can influence policy formation in the Soviet Union. We have specified those circumstances as clearly as we could, providing hypotheses according to which we expect group influence to vary. If our analysis is sound and valid, we hope that it may provide some guidelines for further research on group influence in the comparative study of Communist political systems.[39] Indeed, we hope that some parts of our analysis may be relevant to the study of the role of groups in policy formation in non-Communist political systems as well.

[38] See S. N. Eisenstadt, *The Political Systems of Empires* (New York: The Free Press, 1963), for a suggestive analysis of the role of skill groups in historical bureaucratic empires.

[39] See Robert C. Tucker, "On the Study of Comparative Communism," *World Politics* 19 (January, 1967): 242–57.

* * *

16

CITIZENSHIP

ALFRED G. MEYER

RIGHTS AND DUTIES

A Soviet citizen has the right to own personal property and to have it, as well as his life and liberty, protected against his fellow-citizens. He has the right to vote, to participate actively in public affairs, and to seek redress of officially wrought inequities through formal and informal complaint channels. His membership in the society entitles him to a certain minimal level of material welfare and security, including not only employment, but also education up to his ability, personal growth, and mobility up the social scale. One might say that each citizen has a share in the nation's economic and cultural resources, that every citizen is a shareholder in U.S.S.R., Inc., the size of the annual dividend depending on the success of the company and on the decisions of the managers. To all this one might possibly add a certain residual right to privacy which is exercised in such matters as the choice of a mate and, to a limited degree, the choice of an occupation.

All these rights are qualified by the proviso that they must not be abused. Participation in public affairs must not disrupt the regime's determined policies. Personal property must not be used for private gain. More generally, the Soviet code of citizens' rights and duties forbids placing individual rights and interests over public ones (as defined by the Party). In a contest between rights or claims, the individual must voluntarily yield to the public authorities. Freedom must not be taken

From *The Soviet Political System: An Interpretation,* by Alfred G. Meyer, pp. 378– 86. Copyright © 1965 by Random House, Inc. Reprinted by permission of the publisher.

absolutely; for absolute freedom disrupts the socialist order.[1] Nor can the regime allow freedom to be "abused" by anyone inimical to communist rule. The constitution and the laws do not protect those Soviet citizens opposing the Soviet system.

Behind this is a conception of citizenship very different from that prevailing in some Western countries, especially the United States. Here, the individualistic ethos prevails, according to which citizenship consists in the right to exercise personal choice and pursue individual interests by participating (or even by not participating) in public political life. Citizenship means contesting with fellow-citizens for advantages. It means being alert, watchful, and critical in guarding one's personal interest, and with deliberation placing the weight of one's vote and influence into the scale of politics. Of course, it also means obeying the law, paying taxes, serving in the armed forces when drafted, and risking one's life against foreign enemies. But these obligations are so basic an attribute of citizenship everywhere that they do not give citizenship in the United States a markedly different character. What does determine its nature in the United States is the emphasis on individual rights and the pursuit of individual interests. In the liberal conception, individual citizens' rights are rights *against* the government, even though, perhaps paradoxically, the political system is designed to guarantee them.

Citizenship in the U.S.S.R. reverses the emphasis. Although certain rights remain with the individual—residually, as it were—the stress is on duty toward the government and toward the community of fellow-citizens, most important among them the duty to do socially useful work, i.e., a job designated as useful. The assertion of individual rights and interests or of the individual personality is regarded as corrosive and destructive by those who have absorbed the ethos of Soviet socialism. Those rights that have been granted are secured, not by struggling against the system, but by relying on it and collaborating with it. "The most substantial guarantee of these fundamental rights of the Soviet citizens is the Soviet regime itself." [2] A life devoted to the pursuit of personally defined goals—be this a career, money, status, power, eternal salvation, sexual satisfaction, or what not—such a life must appear profoundly immoral to the well-socialized member of the Soviet system. If the word "socialism" means anything to them, it means the rejection of the individualistic philosophy.

To be sure, many Soviet citizens obviously have not quite accepted

---

[1] "Socialist democracy differs essentially from the unlimited, uncontrolled 'freedom' of which anarchists love to chatter. Such 'freedom,' incidentally, exists only in their heated imagination, but not in society. As for socialist democracy, it is not directionless democracy, but *directed democracy*, i.e., democracy directed by the Party and the state to further the development of socialism and the building of communism. This is stated by the Communists straightforwardly and openly." *Fundamentals of Marxism-Leninism*, p. 599.

[2] A. Denisov and M. Kirichenko, *Soviet State Law*, p. 321. I [AGM] have translated *sovetskaia vlast* as "Soviet regime."

this idea for themselves and continue to manifest individualistic strivings. Also, the system rewards the individual for his performance, as we
have seen, and thus stimulates his collaborative effort by the promise of
individual advantage. Moreover, on a higher level of abstraction, it is
possible to reconcile the collectivist emphasis on duty, on obligation, on
work for the common good, with an individualistic self-interest: the well-
socialized Soviet citizen may tell himself that work for the community
ultimately means working for himself and his children—hence, that
cooperation coincides with individualism, as obedience does with free-
drom. This collectivist ethos sounds far more convincing to the average
Soviet citizen than to the average American. To the outside, it may seem
as if every Soviet citizen is a civil servant, an employee of the state, a
person in bondage to the community; but many such a servant may feel
that at the same time he is also an integral part of the collective employer and sovereign, and is beneficiary of the joint labors.

PARTICIPATION

Citizenship in the U.S.S.R., ideally, means active participation in
public affairs. In the eyes of the Party leaders, the ideal Soviet citizen,
indeed, is loyal and obedient. But he is not a silent automaton who lets
the authorities do everything with utter passivity. Instead, the ideal
citizen is the *activist* who participates as much as possible. . . . The
scope of this activism is carefully circumscribed. The activist is expected
to participate in executing or fulfilling the commands of the hierarchy,
although in doing this he is to show imagination and initiative. His contributions are to be positive and constructive. He should develop leadership qualities, but use them for the purpose of guiding, leading, in-
spiring his fellow citizens to follow the commands of the authorities.
"What is required from the builders of communism, and still more
from members of communist society, is not mere compliance with
established regulations, but initiative, creative activity, and the ability
not only to work intelligently at one's place of work, but also to take
part in deciding matters of state and public affairs." [3] Obviously, the
ideal society as imagined by the Soviet ruling elite is a bureaucratic
system which combines the hierarchic command principle of *yedinonachaliye* with maximal involvement of all citizens in the administration
of enterprises and organizations, a bureaucracy in which the lower ranks
carry out the commands of the hierarchs cheerfully and expeditiously
because they themselves have "participated" in formulating them. [4] At
the risk of plagiarizing that Madison Avenue genius who coined the
term "people's capitalism" we might give the name "people's bureau-

[3] *Fundamentals of Marxism-Leninism*, pp. 684–85.
[4] This ideal is stated clearly in the decree of the November, 1962, Plenum of the
Party Central Committee. *Spravochnik Partiinogo Rabotnika*, Issue 4 (1962), p. 195.

cratism" to the ideal discussed at such length in current Soviet publications.[5]

For any citizen who wishes to participate in this people's bureaucracy, whether his motives be idealistic or careerist, the Soviet system offers a host of organizations and activities. In his place of work, the citizen can take part in one of the many committees formed by his union. In his community, he can help organize or run parent-teacher associations (called Councils for Assistance to School and Family), neighborhood courts, or perhaps an occasional *ad hoc* committee for some badly needed improvement. Civic duties which demand activists include elections, rallies, and drives, court assessor service, and work with local and provincial soviet standing committees. From civil defense and civilian military training to adult education or organized entertainment, there is a broad range of activities demanding the participation of citizen activists.[6] The many different organizations within which the rank and file of the citizenry can participate in this fashion are called "public organizations" or "mass organizations" in the Soviet Union. The Party has been inclined to lay greater and greater stress on the importance of such organizations; its spokesmen assert that more and more governmental functions will be transferred to such agencies as Soviet society moves closer to the communist ideal of the state's withering away. Whether or not we concede that increased participation in mass organizations conforms to our notion of democracy, we must be aware of the growing importance of these institutions for the Soviet political system.

To this, one might perhaps add one other kind of participation, namely, public opinion. True, the Soviet political system permits no free formation and exchange of opinion on public affairs. Opinion leadership, like leadership in all other matters, is claimed by the Communist Party as its exclusive right, as is the monopoly right over all communications. But the Party has nonetheless shown some interest in the moods of the citizenry. Through the police and, more recently, through polling devices, the Party has sought to gauge these moods.[7] Having one's opinion surveyed might be regarded as some indirect and passive form of participation. But it would be important only if the polling methods were sufficiently refined and if the leaders allowed the results to influence their policy-making. Of this there is no evidence. The regime

[5] See the chapter on "The Role of Public Organizations" in *Fundamentals of Marxism-Leninism*, pp. 528–29.

[6] In addition one could list town or neighborhood committees for the maintenance of housing facilities, production conferences, and *kolkhoz* brigade councils.

[7] One of the most interesting of these experiments so far has been an open questionnaire about the attitudes of Soviet youth administered by the youth newspaper, *Komsomolskaya pravda*, in January, 1961. More recently, there has been extensive polling of industrial workers to investigate job dissatisfaction. See Jay B. Sorenson, "Problems and Prospects," in *Problems of Communism* 13, No. 1 (January-February, 1964): 28–29.

may be interested in receiving feedback on its activities and communications from the population. But it is not in the habit of *consulting* the people. Indeed, there are workshop conferences with foremen and workers; *kolkhoz* meetings, perhaps, with genuine discussion; selection processes in which the Party does eliminate obviously unpopular candidates. In short, the Soviet system involves some consultation with the citizens on a level commensurate with their limited work (or life) experiences, although even this apparently is done rarely and reluctantly. On national issues, however, public opinion is consulted rarely, and then only in ceremonious or perfunctory fashion. The law concerning abortion, in 1936, was submitted to the public for discussion and was then passed, despite evidence of overwhelming popular opposition. Similar public discussions of the 1936 Constitution yielded minor amendments. On such things as foreign policy, missile programs, or the Seven-Year Plan, there can be little genuine consultation.

From all this it is clear that citizens' participation in public life is not supposed to be, and cannot be, free participation. Because it is possible only within the framework of approved associations, groups, and institutions, it is in fact carefully controlled. No association in which activist citizens are expected to participate can legally be formed without clearance from or planning by the Soviet authority having jurisdiction over the sphere of life with which the association plans to deal. No meeting can legally be held without approval of the authorities. In the final analysis, all organizations are creations of the Party. All of them function in prescribed fashion, according to prescribed or patterned plans of organization and by-laws.[8] All organizations function as transmission belts for the Party because their core is always the Party's primary organization or caucus, which often makes decisions before they are submitted to general discussion. Hence if there is discussion, debate, or other grassroots participation, it is rarely more than a prelude to the adoption of policies formulated by the leadership.

Citizens' participation in public affairs therefore does not serve to provide free rein for individual or group interests. Instead, it is designed to mobilize the citizens, that is, to enlist their services for purposes and interests defined by the Party.[9] It is to utilize individual creativity and leadership for this goal; it wishes to tap resources hidden among the population for the Party. Moreover, it serves the purpose of elite recruitment; through participation in committees and associations, suitable activists are discovered who might rise to positions of higher authority. For all participants, whether or not they are made of leadership material, participation serves a socializing function: It introduces them to the

---

[8] For a Soviet discussion of the structure and function of mass organizations, see B. M. Lazarev and A. I. Lukyanov, *Sovetskoye gosudarstvo i obshchestvenniye organizatsii* (Moscow, 1960).

[9] For an excellent discussion of mass organizations as mobilizing agents, see Hartmut Zimmermann, "Der FDGB als Massenorganisation," in Peter Christian Ludz, ed., *Studien und Materialien zur Soziologie der DDR* (Köln: Westdeutscher Verlag, 1964), pp. 115–44.

political system, its values, priorities, forms of organization, and pattern of operations. In addition, the many opportunities for participation which we have discussed undoubtedly provide satisfaction for various personality types which must abound in Soviet society as they do in ours —joiners, operators, careerists, as well as service-minded idealists—and does so in a fashion which furthers the goals of the Party. Finally, it may be of value also as a safety valve through which popular discontent may vent itself without harm to the political system.

SAFETY VALVES

How valuable mass participation is to the regime can be seen in an examination of the institution of *samokritika* (self-criticism). This word connotes public criticism, by individuals, of their own conduct or performance, and also public criticism of an organization by its own members or leadership cadres. *Samokritika*, in other words, includes criticism from below of the activities and failures of some collective body within Soviet society.[10] Self-criticism is usually voiced, in a somewhat formal or ritualized manner, in prearranged public meetings. Such meetings represent, perhaps, an effort on the part of the leadership to include mass participation in decision-making, or to give the appearance of such mass participation. In a *samokritika* session, management itself is facing its subordinates, and it does so without the usual managerial prerogatives. All sorts of complaints and grievances may be aired and must be answered, as the British Government must answer questions in the Parliament.

Although discussions in such meetings may be rather free, there usually is planning even behind the seeming spontaneity of such criticism from below; truly spontaneous self-criticism would doubtless be considered too dangerous by the Party. Instead, *samokritika* doubtless is an effective method of using discontent among the citizens for the purpose of putting lower and middle-range officials under pressure and keeping them in line—even to terrorize them, if that expression is not too strong. *Samokritika* sessions therefore are also safety valves because they allow popular discontent to discharge itself in controlled fashion, so that it does not hit those higher up and does not challenge the political system itself.

There are several other safety valves at the disposal of the regime, i.e., channels through which citizens can voice complaints and give vent to negative feelings without endangering the regime. A person who is very upset about injustices done to him or failings of administrators has a number of agencies to which he can turn with a letter of complaint—his soviet deputy, his Party secretary, his trade union, his public

---

[10] It also includes a form of official humor which in the U.S.S.R. is called satire. This takes the form of cartoons, anecdotes, or jokes designed to lampoon or ridicule persons or institutions that do not live up to the expectations of the regime.

prosecutor, his newspaper.[11] In short, the individual citizen has numerous formal and informal channels providing access to, or communication with, authoritative decision-makers in the Party or the government. The agency set up to receive the complaints coming through various formal and informal channels is the recently created Committee of Party and State Control and its field organizations.[12] All evidence suggests that complaints are treated with some respect and followed up by investigation and, at times, remedial action.[13] At the same time, one must assume that undoubtedly the inspecting authorities acquire a sense for telling which complaints come from the pens of cranks and which deserve attention. Moreover, this form of complaining itself is risky for the individual. It may get him in trouble with the administrator or the agency he is criticizing; indeed, it may get him in trouble with the regime as a whole because it may make the authorities believe that he is disloyal or a grumbler and troublemaker. The use of out-of-channels communications for the purpose of voicing grievances is therefore a safety valve that dissatisfied citizens will probably use only when all the more formal methods have failed. These channels do exist, and they are used; perhaps that is all that should be said.

[11] The press, especially the local and regional press, plays very much the role of the muckraker and often appears to take the initiative in this or to be prodded by complaints from readers, while in general it undoubtedly responds to the cues of the Party. Whoever gives the cues and provides the prodding, however, the newspaper editor easily finds himself in a crossfire and must tread warily lest he offend agencies or administrators to which he is vulnerable, and against whom his appeals to the Party, the courts, or other protectors will not avail him. For the complaint of a local newspaper columnist whose muckraking was rewarded by considerable harassment, see the letter to the editors of *Pravda* (November 16, 1960), p. 6.

[12] *Pravda* (January 18, 1963) printed a Party communiqué on this. The communiqué stresses the need to have representatives from all the mass organizations participate in the committee's field organizations and obliges the committee to render regular accounts to these mass organizations.

[13] Perhaps it would be better to say that complaints of this sort are sometimes treated seriously, but are often neglected. See the Central Committee decree "About Serious Deficiencies in the Review of Letters, Complaints, and Revelations Coming from the Toilers," in *Pravda* (August 26, 1958).

*   *   *

17

CAMPAIGN AND ELECTION

MAX E. MOTE

The final stages of the campaign are, quite naturally, marked by an intensification of publicity. The statute for local elections says that the voters must be informed daily of the date and place of elections during the twenty days prior to the balloting. Thus we find in the local press even before this date . . . frequent biographies of the candidates. Later, such articles appeared daily. Ten days before the election, ballots have to be sent to the polling places by the district commissions. Polling places are prepared for voting and in well managed areas are subjected to public inspection. Then, during the last ten days or so, door-to-door work by the agitators begins; the aim is to visit every single voter and explain the meaning of the election and present biographical information on the candidates. Also during the final stage it is the goal of the Party to have every candidate meet at least once with the voters of his district; these meetings with voters serve two purposes: They give the candidates and organizers an opportunity to present the policy of the government to the people, and the candidates an opportunity to learn and record the wishes or instructions of the voters.

In the week or ten days before the election, attention is turned to the achievements of the Soviet regime vis-à-vis the old Czarist regime as well as Western countries. The superiority of the Soviet system and the glory of its achievements are preached day and night, in meetings, in the papers, and on the radio. It was not just a coincidence that right before elections, immense lines could be seen at some of the Leningrad stores and sidewalk stands: Rare and delectable things were

Reprinted from *Soviet Local and Republic Elections*, by Max E. Mote, pp. 44–83, with the permission of the publishers, Hoover Institution Press. Copyright © 1965 by the Board of Trustees of the Leland Stanford Junior University.

being sold. Eggs were back on the market for the first time since the previous fall (at about ten cents each), and oranges seemed suddenly abundant when compared with the winter months (when they sold for about forty cents each—if the stores had them). The Soviet regime at election time is asking for a vote of confidence in the government and its achievements. So the regime apparently feels the necessity of putting tangible evidence of its achievements into the hands of the electorate. And eggs and oranges appear. At the same time, the evils of the bourgeois world and the antidemocratic machinations of Western politicians, especially Americans, are dwelt on with intensity and ferocity.

The Press Campaign and the Ideal Soviet Deputy

The events described hereafter are taking place simultaneously. We begin with the final stages of the press campaign in which almost entire issues of the local papers are filled with election items. The newspaper campaign for prominent candidates to the Supreme Soviet of the R.S.F.S.R. [Russian Federation] opens about three or four weeks prior to election day. Leningrad papers published series of articles and pictures giving personal biographies of about three-fourths of the city's twenty-three candidates to the soviet of the republic. . . .

Newspapers publish highly stereotyped campaign literature; to give a representative example and impart some of the flavor, the following article is quoted in full:

OUR CANDIDATES FOR DEPUTY:
EVERYDAY EVENTS DESERVING PRAISE

Some biographies seem so simple and ordinary that you don't know what to say about them at first. Tamara Dmitriyevna Mitrakova feels she has done nothing heroic. She has worked underground many years. No startling episodes, no dazzling promotions.

But if you take a close look at every day which she lives through, weigh what she does for people, it becomes clear; these ordinary days, this life deserves praise. Because always and in all things Tamara Mitrakova was with the people—in sorrow and in joy, in the days of wartime tribulation and of peacetime labor.

One autumn day in 1941 she went to the Frunze City-*raion* [Borough] Soviet. There they sent her to a repair-train unit.

The twelve hour shift was coming to a close. The frozen earth creaked, the rails squeaked as they were being piled in a stack. But neither the faces nor the hands of the repair workers felt the deep frost. The cutting wind chafed their skin. Work that day went slower than usual. They advanced cautiously. Two days earlier a repair worker had been blown up by a mine laid by the fascists under a tie.

Tamara brought up the gravel, thinking that she would not go to the warming hut. A long way to go, and she was too tired. She would lie down right there in the snow, like yesterday, and have a good nap.

Searchlights lit up the thick gloom. The low rumble of a motor could be heard. Some military person was driving up in a car. "The Commander of the Front," Tamara heard a loud whisper. The general approached the workers.

"Comrades," he said loudly so all could hear, "much depends on you now. The breakthrough of the Leningrad blockade has begun. But how can we get troops through if there is no rail line?"

"Work through tonight? No—I can't hold out," sounded in her brain. The general continued to speak. The girl saw him through a shroud.

"Let's give our word. Tonight we'll finish the spur," said the brigadier [of the work crew] laconically and solemnly, as if it were a vow.

The fatigue slipped away somewhere, like a weight rolling off their backs, falling from their hands. Like getting your second wind. Tossing the gravel with her shovel, she looked at her comrades. It was hard for them, but they were holding out. She would not give in either.

That night the repair workers kept the word which they had given to the general.

Somewhat later the train on which Mitrakova served was transferred to the Carpathians.

*   *   *

Tamara Dmitriyevna's form-jumbo and the form men work with well-coordinated rhythm. The brigadier gives the signal and the arm of the form-jumbo carefully puts the section of the form into place. The laborers haul off the muck. There is a short breathing spell.

"What's with you, Vasya, you nodding your head? Didn't you get enough sleep last night?" Mitrakova the engineer speaks to the young form man.

"Didn't sleep at all last night. Took my wife to the maternity ward."

"Congratulations. But why didn't you tell anyone?"

"What's there to talk about? Wanted a son and got a daughter."

Tamara Dmitriyevna speaks reproachfully:

"You fool, you, Vasily. Look—I'm a woman. Do I work any worse than you?"

"Wait a minute, Dmitriyevna! You're all right, tops with us. I didn't mean it that way." The young father tries with some embarrassment to set things right.

Other workers come up and congratulate the fellow. He cheers up. The girl's name is Svetlana.

"Thanks, Tamara Dmitriyevna," he says softly, after everyone has gone on about his business.

The subway builders respect engineer Mitrakova. They not only pay attention to her just and pithy words at meetings, they come to get advice from her on family matters. Everyone knows her. Returning sixteen years ago from the Transcarpathian area, she went to work on the construction of the Leningrad subway. There is not a tunnel or a station where Mitrakova has not worked.

When the form-setting machinery and the muck loaders began to appear in the shafts, the subway cadres were the first to make use of the new technology.

"Let's have a look at the assembly," said the mechanic V. T. Kulikov to the tunnel worker Mitrakova, "You're going to work on the machine."

And Tamara Dmitriyevna, after finishing her shift at the shaft, didn't leave the rig. She learned every nut and bolt. Now she can handle any repair job if necessary. Running the form-jumbo, Mitrakova has earned the tile of leading worker. And she has come into her worker's glory: They presented her with the Order of the Banner of Red Labor.

The trees slumber, wrapped in their white hoarfrost. People are coming home from work. At that very moment Mitrakova is descending into shaft number 315. There, deep under the earth, they are outfitting the station for Leo Tolstoy Place. Up above, lights are going on in the windows, children are falling off to sleep in their little beds. But here, tirelessly, the iron hand of the form-jumbo moves, guided by the engineer Mitrakova. They are building the tunnel.

Engineer Mitrakova has been elected deputy twice to the Frunzenskii City-*raion* Soviet. She tries to help people with everything; she can't imagine a life without social activity.

And then the day came when this modest worker was named at a pre-election meeting which nominated candidates to the Supreme Soviet of the Russian Federation.

"Why such an honor for me, why such faith?" Mitrakova asked as she came to the brigade. She looked at the brigadier Vasilii Kalinin, at the shift engineer Aleksei Kuznetsov, at the form man Aleksei Ulitkin.

Ulitkin answered for all: "We believe in you, Tamara Dmitriyevna!"

The above article contains most of the characteristics of a type of literature which is highly, drearily standardized. From it and from many others like it, certain general characteristics of the ideal candidate emerge. The candidate is selected because he or she is a leading, powerful personality; in the case of Mitrakova, there is indeed something extraordinary about the woman's career. The candidate has authority among her peers because she has earned it in difficult circumstances. And this is the point: The deputy is supposed to be a respected leader, but not because this makes him a good legislator—for the Soviet deputy is not supposed to legislate. He is supposed to help secure acceptance of whatever program the regime may be pushing. By their example, deputies are expected to facilitate *execution* of policy, not legislation and formulation of policy. This is why high-caliber candidates are chosen carefully in the advance meetings. This is why deputies are often truly remarkable people. They become symbols of the regime at the local level, and for this reason the regime seeks the best people.

The ideals held up for the candidate are partly those of the society, partly those required by the political system. Following are some of the characteristics of the good candidate and deputy:

In relation to his job or profession:

The candidate gives the impression that work is the key to personal salvation and to social advancement. The regime asks first of all that the person work hard, conscientiously, and well. The best workers are rewarded by being made deputies.

Thus the candidate tends to be a shock worker or an innovator.

He works without mistakes and consistently overfulfills his plan quota.

He is possessed of an inner compulsion to work harder and better.

If the candidate is older, born in Czarist times, then he has come a long way from poverty and oppression, through study and hard work, to a position of respect in the New society.

If the person is a professional or creative worker, he has a compulsion to excellence. He is a thinker.

He is generous with his knowledge and his time; he has a highly developed sense of duty to his job and he knows he must help others develop this attitude. He assists others, the younger workers, in developing not only productivity but also a love for the job. Moving examples of this are cited for the benefit of new candidates. For example, one railway worker, a candidate, spent his days off at the roundhouse, telling young engineers how to run a train on time.

In regard to his personal characteristics:

He is a quiet, modest person whose inner warmth communicates itself (this is the official image; in fact he may be a blatant bore).

He has the respect of his fellows; he leads rather than drives. He is a real person, a *"chelovek."*

The social consciousness of the candidate is highly developed, and he is a leader in various social organizations.

In short, these are the qualities of a natural leader, one who can most easily set an example for his fellows in the execution of given tasks. The newspapers tell us exactly why the "best people" are chosen to be deputies. . . .

Meetings and Instructions

The voter has two possible direct involvements in the pre-election process. One is the candidate's meeting with voters, and the other is a visit from an agitator. Since nominees must be registered within twenty or fifteen days of the election, depending on whether they are candidates for republic or local offices, the meetings with voters begin about this time. . . . Every candidate is supposed to meet at least once with the voters of his district.

These meetings bring the candidates to the voters and bring the complaints and instructions of the voters to the candidates. It is the first opportunity during the campaign for the voters to express themselves. While the meetings with republic candidates tend to preserve a rigidly formal atmosphere, the meetings with the candidates to lower-level soviets of the city and city-*raion* may end in a flood of give-and-take from the floor. It is here that people may rise and tell their representatives what is troubling them. For the first time in the election process one can observe a meeting of real interest, thanks to the rare factor of spontaneity.

The organization of both is the responsibility of the Party organs specializing in mass work; it is largely their job to get the space, provide the entertainment, and get the crowds out to the meetings.

The first type of meeting, the large one for an R.S.F.S.R. candidate, is furnished with a brass band, with speakers, and usually with some form of entertainment afterwards. In many ways it is similar to the nomination meetings except that the candidate is present and delivers a short speech (he is usually not present at his nomination). The meetings are arranged for the evening, as a rule, and last approximately an hour. A large part of the program is devoted to speeches about the policies and plans of the Party and government, and are full of high praise and promise for both. Because of the formal, ceremonial nature of these meetings, probably no one will speak from the floor with instructions for the candidate. And in keeping with the solemn atmosphere on such occasions, the meetings often close with an eloquently worded letter, full of resolve and respect, to the First Secretary and the Central Committee of the Party.

Meetings with candidates to lower-level soviets have a different flavor altogether. These are usually small, less formal, with perhaps one speech by the candidate's sworn supporter and with much discussion from the audience. They are neighborhood meetings, held during the evening in an *agitpunkt*, club, or similar place. Conversation may develop on concrete issues at a lively tempo.

The chairman of the meeting is perhaps a Party organizational worker, or the head of some other social organization such as a house committee. A tally is kept of instructions and of the persons making them; they become part of the record of business of the soviet, and an attempt is made to keep a count on the number of instructions received and the number fulfilled during each two-year session. In Soviet journals and brochures, considerable space is devoted to the subject of voters' instructions, for in theory one of the main tasks of the deputy and his soviet is to hear and respond to the voice of the people as expressed in the instructions. The fulfillment of them is a quantitative gauge for the Soviet degree of democracy.

Following is a sample of a meeting held for candidates to the city and city-*raion* soviets, reconstructed from notes taken while attending several of them. Candidates to the two soviets were meeting some voters at an *agitpunkt*; after they have been introduced and a couple of brief biographical sketches presented, the chairman speaks:

Chairman: Would anyone like to address the candidates?
First Voter: Can you remodel the movie house out here?
Chairman: What is your name and address?
First Voter: (Calls out his name and address; the secretary makes a note.)
Second Voter: I'd like to get the housing office to send a man out

to fix my roof. Pretty soon it's going to be spring and the water will start pouring in.

Third Voter: I think you ought to get the shops next to our apartment to move. They work there three shifts a day, and they make so much noise that we can't sleep. We have to work too.

Candidate: That is a pretty difficult request.

Former Deputy: Do you mind if I interrupt here? During the last session of the soviet we also took up this matter, which was one of the instructions given us by the voters two years ago. We went to our City-*raion* Soviet, to the City Soviet, and finally to the regional Council of the National Economy. Plans have been made to remove the shop to the outskirts of the city during the current Seven-Year Plan. It will be done eventually.

Chairman: Comrade, you have to understand why this situation exists. The shops were built when the city was small. At that time there were no apartment houses around. But you can see that the shops just can't be moved overnight. It is a very expensive undertaking.

Third Voter: Yes, I see that. Well, I just wanted to mention it, because it does bother us.

Fourth Voter: Can't you get the bus route changed so that it doesn't run past the hospital? All the dust it stirs up and the noise of the traffic make things uncomfortable for the sick people.

Chairman: This request is being considered by the Transportation Board of the City Soviet. It is out of our hands.

Fifth Voter: I want to ask you about my pension. I moved here from Kazakhstan and I'm not getting my full allotment.

Chairman: This is a legal question, Comrade, and you had better go to a lawyer for consultation. Now let me remind you other comrades to limit your requests to matters of principle, to questions which have meaning for all the citizens of the area. This is not the place for personal requests

Sixth Voter: We want a place for a club in our apartment house. We need a room to watch television.

Candidate: You really should take this up with your house committee or housing office, but I'll try to help you on the matter. Make sure you get your name and address into the protocol.

Seventh Voter: There are too many people in our apartment, and I've been trying for three years to get some of them moved out. There are more people than the rules allow.

Eighth Voter: Our apartment house is an old one, with a kitchen that was installed where a storeroom used to be. Many families use the one kitchen and children are always playing in the hall next to it. But there is no window in the kitchen itself. What I'm afraid of is that someday the gas will be left on and it will be fatal for the little ones.

Ninth Voter (an older woman): There is something that's been bother-
ing me since two elections ago. That little stand which sells beer
on the corner is an eyesore. A bunch of rowdies and drunks are
always standing around there, and they set a bad example for the
school children in the neighborhood. Besides, there are foreigners
in the area and they should not see this sort of thing.

Voice (not completely sober): You old women just don't like to see
men drink. You don't understand that we need a drink. You don't
know what fun is anyway—all you can do is save up your kopeks.

Ninth Voter: Go ahead and drink if you want. All I want is for them
to move the beer stand around to a back street where people
won't see it.

Chairman: I think we can close the meeting now. We have given
our candidates enough to work on this session.

The meeting is over, but the people go on talking in small groups
which only slowly disperse. It has been an interesting session, the main
feature of which is the immediate, local, rather unimportant nature
of the problems discussed. No vital policy issues are raised. What the
people ask for are minor improvements in conditions close at hand.
Housing matters are frequently touched on, because they are an issue
which receives much official attention and one which can be safely
discussed. We also see that it very often takes a long time, months
or even years, for requests to be acted on.

For a Westerner, the meeting is a curious one. It is not political in
the meaning of a discussion of policies. The meeting deals with minor
inadequacies in the execution, not formation, of plans. The goals and
policies of the government are accepted at the outset; what the people
are asking for is a solution to problems which in the last analysis have
been created by the government. For example, most of the requests
center around questions of housing. But these questions tend to arise
precisely because the government mismanages its monopoly on housing.
And when the public meeting gives people a chance to express themselves on the issue, this is interpreted by the Soviet publicists as an
achievement of Soviet democracy. It is democratic, so their thinking
runs, to let people grumble a bit about the problems which have been
created for them.

THE AGITATOR

Because the Soviet election is mainly a gesture of mass approval of
the government and its plans, the work of the agitator is especially
important. This is the person who makes the face-to-face contact with
each individual voter, enumerates policies and plans, and solicits a
personal commitment to participate in the process by voting. Higher
Party organizers know just as well as any American advertising man that

face-to-face contact is most important, and agitators are sent out in great numbers. . . .

The Party is responsible for organizing the work of the agitators. It does so chiefly by reaching down the chain of command to all kinds of public organizations which are asked to supply the needed agitators from their members. One newspaper stated that some 450,000 persons were enrolled in various social organizations in Leningrad and suggested that all be put to work in the campaign. Another paper gives a more conservative figure, indicating that in the Leningrad oblast there were some 100,000 persons in voluntary organizations. In either event, this is a massive reserve of volunteers who can be called into election work.

Housing offices not only furnish some of the space for election offices and meetings but sometimes organize their own activist groups. One such office put twenty-nine agitators into the field. Aside from this, each office most likely has its own room or corner of a room for political agitation, the "red corner," where political literature is always available. A newspaper account describes a question-and-answer period held in a room maintained by Housing Office No. 16 of the Moskva City-*raion*. At this meeting, the principal figures in attendance were the chairmen of the city-*raion* soviet, the leader of the deputy group (a relatively new type of organization composed of all the deputies from various soviets who live in one area), and some members of the city-*raion* branch of the Society for the Dissemination of Political and Scientific Knowledge. They spoke with the voters, told them about plans for the enormous building program in the city-*raion*, and answered some fifty questions. According to the same newspaper account, "More than 150 requests for such question-and-answer periods were made to the district committee of the Communist Party of the Soviet Union. The *agitpunkty* are supplied with standing groups of speakers by the district Party committee and by the Executive Committee of the city-*raion* soviet. In this group there are more than 120 Party and soviet workers."

The persons in charge of such activities, i.e., of the activist groups, *agitpunkty*, and editors of wall newspapers, are approved by the city-*raion* Party organization. Another newspaper reported that the city Party committee organized agitators and instructed them in the principal themes which they were to carry to the voters; increasing the productivity of labor, achieving new successes in technology, and fulfilling the goals of the Seven-Year Plan. This will strike the Westerner as a strongly progovernment platform, one which ignores the desires of the voter.

Under ideal circumstances, each agitator visits about ten apartments, which brings him in contact with ten to thirty families, depending on how crowded the quarters are. He is supposed to speak to each family or apartment group, and leave with them a printed slip of paper giving the name of the candidates from the given district. If he is slack in his work, he may leave the printed notices in mailboxes without making the personal calls. During the course of the conversation, the agitator not only explains the aims and accomplishments of the government, he not only "sells" the government to the people, he also solicits complaints and divides them on the spot into ills which are being remedied, can be remedied, or cannot be remedied.

The following newspaper account gives a picture of a model visit to an apartment:

A HEART-TO-HEART TALK

There it is, the apartment in the large, bright new house on Gavanskaya Street. On the door—one bell for all. That means the neighbors here get along well, the agitator from the Northern Cable Plant, Ivan Romanovich Gritsai, says to himself as he rings the bell.

It is not the first time Gritsai has been an agitator. Once again in the homes on Gavanskaya, once again at apartment 29. When meeting people for the first time, the agitator wants to find some words from the heart for his conversation. He wants to be a welcome guest.

To do this he thoroughly prepares himself. First of all it is necessary to talk about the way things are going in your own neighborhood.

And these things are gratifying. The decisions of the November Plenum of the Central Committee of the CPSU have inspired the residents of Vasilevsky Island, as they have all Soviet people, to new achievements in labor. At the Elektroapparat Factory they just lately tried out some new 750,000-kilowatt transformers. The shipbuilders of the Baltiisky Factory have taken on the obligation to build, ahead of schedule, some new giant tankers during the fifth year of the Seven-Year Plan. The textile workers from the Vera Slutskaya Factory decided to turn out 10,000 meters more than the plan calls for of dress material.

It will also be interesting for the voters to know how things stand in regard to housing. The agitator Gritsai has the following data ready: Last year on Vasilevsky Island, 50,000 square meters of housing space were begun, and major repairs on about 27,000 square meters. Next year they are going to begin reconstructing old areas. On the sites of little homes, great, bright buildings will rise, some of them twenty stories high. They are beginning to construct a new subway line which will connect Sredni Prospekt with the center of town. The area is being converted to gas.

It is pleasant to mention such facts in a chat. All families have been put on the lists [for new housing] where there is less than four and one-half square meters per person. At the present time, all persons who have been on the lists since 1958 are receiving new apartments.

The agitator rings. An elderly lady in an apron opens the door.

"Hello," says Gritsai, "I am your agitator and I'd like to get acquainted with the voters."

"Lukyanova," the woman introduces herself. "Please come in. We are always happy to have guests. I'll call the other residents right away."

Three families live in apartment 29. This evening almost all of them are home—the lathe operator S. G. Nedorubkov and his wife Vera Ivanovna, a teacher, the electrician German Perov, and Lukyanova. Only the wife of Perov, a worker at the Voskhod Factory, is not there yet. But she should be along soon.

"Well, shall we begin our chat?" Gritsai thinks, meeting the people.

"Oh, what are we standing in the kitchen for," Lukyanova throws up her hands. "Please come into my room," she cheerfully invites the agitator and her neighbors. "I have room for you all."

In a cozy, bright room the lively, soulful conversation gets started by itself.

First of all, the agitator acquaints the residents with the biographies of the candidates to the Supreme Soviet of the R.S.F.S.R. and to the local soviets, for whom they will be voting on March 3.

The name of Anna Arsentyevna Gritskevich, a worker at the Northern Cable Plant whom they have named as their candidate to the Leningrad City Soviet, is well known to them all. The fame of her deeds long since passed far beyond the confines of Vasilevsky Island. That name is famous throughout the country.

"In times past," Gritsai recalls, "Anna Arsentyevna was the first to begin the struggle for a solicitous use of nonferrous metals, and introduced the personal account into the system. And now in our city alone more than 13,000 persons are following the example of this notable worker."

The residents ask him to give some details about the candidate to the Supreme Soviet of the R.S.F.S.R., Yury Zinovyevich Rybakov of the Baltiisky Factory.

"This profound manifestation of confidence [his nomination] was earned by the machinist through his own selfless work. Rybakov holds dearly the honor of his factory and his profession. This remarkable person has time for everything—for education, for social work. The people at the Baltiisky are convinced that he will be a worthy representative of the working class in the Soviet parliament."

Some of the facts which he had stored up on the way to his friends came in handy for Gritsai.

Many things interested the residents—both the building prospects for the district and the growth of service facilities.

It was a heart-to-heart discussion in the apartment, lasting late into the evening.

Then it was time to go. The agitator invited the people to drop around to the *agitpunkt* on Veselnaya Street. "The whole apartment will come," the residents said.

"I'll be back in a few days—if you don't object, of course," says Gritsai, smiling.

"You're welcome," Lukyanova answers for all.

Going out into the frosty air, Ivan Romanovich does not hurry as he goes to the bus stop. He thinks with satisfaction about the way his first meeting turned out to be an exceptional success.

The above article tells many things about the work of the agitator. First of all, he walks a two-way street: He not only promises people things, he quite candidly solicits certain commitments from the electorate —to participate in the election, and to increase their labor efforts. As Party propaganda tells the people, the abundance on which communism will depend can be achieved only if they in return, or in advance, give greater effort to the aims and programs of the Party and government.

The article quoted here resembles much Soviet journalism in that it was not written primarily as a piece of reporting. It was a model for the agitators who in the next few days started canvassing the apartments of Leningrad. Barely below the surface of this heartwarming incident are general instructions for agitators:

The agitator should be well equipped with facts about current policies and programs of the Party and government. He should have data on hand, e.g., about the number of square meters of housing space built already and yet to be built. The promise is important.

The meeting should be a soulful one, with emotions and words coming directly from the heart.

The agitator should be acquainted with the biography of the candidate he is propagandizing.

The work of the agitator provides important spiritual rewards.

Election Day

The polling places, each of which serves two or three districts in a local election, are set up in *agitpunkts*, schools, Palaces of Culture, or other convenient public places. The room for balloting is usually prepared a few days before the Sunday of the election, outfitted with velvet covered tables, red bunting, and a conspicuously locked ballot box. It may also be decorated with flowers, pictures of Central Committee members, Lenin everywhere, and on election day itself there are sometimes refreshments plus a brass band intermittently playing martial music. Liquor is obtainable in stores and bars. Red banners display current slogans in large white letters. Some voting places are decorated more imaginatively, revealing the work of many careful hands.

The polls are open from 6 A.M. until midnight. On duty is the head of the precinct commission, plus several volunteer helpers who pass out and later count the ballots. Machine voting seems to be unheard of. The voter enters the polling place and goes to the section of the long green table which is marked with his letter of the alphabet. There he shows an identification document and receives his ballots (three of them in Leningrad). Care must be taken that he is given the correct set of ballots for his district, but this is the responsibility of the volunteer workers, whose task is made easier by the fact that the ballots come in different sizes and colors according to regulations published by the Central Election Commission of the R.S.F.S.R. . . . His name is checked off the list of voters. There are no control numbers on the ballots.

The voter can then step into a booth to mark the ballot if he wishes, for the statute requires that this be available. However, only a few people utilize this opportunity. The ballot does not even have to be marked; the statute says that a voter only has to "leave on each ballot the name of the candidate he is voting for, crossing out the names of the rest." If the ballot has only one name on it—as did all the ballots in the city of Leningrad, he has merely to drop it in the urn and his voting is done. So the great majority of them pick up their ballots, ceremoniously walk the length of the room, deposit them in the urn without even looking at them, and leave. In some precincts a member of the Pioneer youth organization, dressed up in a white shirt and red neckerchief, salutes them at the urn. That's all there is to voting—no choices, decisions, or questions.

The newspapers appearing on election day provide a convenient summary of the major themes involved. Judging from the treatment it receives in the mass media, election day ranks right after November 7 and May Day in national political significance. It even brings out a poetic flair in journalists when they attach such epithets as "harbinger of spring" to it. Or as one journalist, dwelling on the grandiose achievements of the Soviet regime, had to exclaim, "O brave new world—"

The official attitude toward the elections is capsulized in the headlines, some of which are worth noting: "Everyone to the Polls"; "Day of Unity of the Folk and Party and Government"; "Spring Outside, Spring in Your Hearts"; "For Peace, Happiness, Communism"; "Solicitude for the Soviet People" (referring to Khrushchev's election speech); "The Folk—Master of the Country"; "Russia, My Motherland"; "In the Service of the People"; "A Just Man" (referring to a candidate). In a two-party system, election season is the time for thoroughgoing criticism of the policies of the government. In the Soviet Union, with its single-party system, the opposite is true. Policies may be reviewed and plans presented, but they are all approved (even if it is the policy of disapproving, such as de-Stalinization). One Soviet writer says that voting is a "deed appraising the activities of the Soviet government in the past and defining its program in the future," but the line between appraising and praising is indistinct.

Why should the Soviet citizen be grateful to his government and to the Party? The government press supplies the answer in its review of forty-odd years of history: The Soviet regime smashed the oppressive rule of the Tsars and landlords, held the imperialist armies at bay when the country was weak, and made it possible to found a just government of, by, and for the workers and peasants. In World War II they (almost single-handedly) ended the fascist control of Europe. Now they are modernizing Russia, giving away things like apartments, a larger share of culture, and more free time. And they are ahead of the Americans in launching people into space. The debt from the past is enormous. The one from the future is incalculable—for it will bring communism, the era of plenty. Only the most insensitive cold, the most ungrateful recalcitrant, could fail to be moved by the infinite care bestowed on the people by the government and Party. And this thought too is expressed in an election-day banner, "Citizens, be worthy of the solicitude which the Party surrounds you with." Voting is an expression of gratitude for this omnipresent care.

The 99 Per Cent Vote

Aware that the selection of candidates is managed, and knowing that the ballots carry only one name and that the elections are not a contest in the Western sense, a person is justified in asking whether 99 per cent of the people really go out and vote, and if so, why? Sometimes the voting statistics do seem to be falsified (as one Leningrad volunteer put it, when the ballot-counters turn up with more than 100 per cent of the ballots in the box, then you know that someone has been working too zealously on his election norm). Nevertheless, the overwhelming percentage of eligible voters cast their ballots regularly.

The important question to be answered in regard to a Soviet election is this: Whom does one vote for? Russians vote for the Soviet regime. And if casting a vote on election days is a sign of support of the regime, then not casting a vote is a sign of opposition. So if the Russian is asked, in effect, whether he is voting "for" or "against" the Party and the government, he doesn't have to think. He votes "for." Voting is both a patriotic and a social activity, invested with the diverse pleasures which most people derive from performing a commendable action. It is not an onerous duty. On the contrary, it can be a source of satisfaction.

In addition to these intangibles, an elaborate machinery has been created to increase the total vote. Local Party organs keep a running tabulation of the vote on election day. In Leningrad, for example, the precincts phone in their results to Party headquarters every two hours. The percentage of persons who have already voted is calculated and released to the radio. By mid-afternoon the percentages are already in the nineties.

If a signal comes into Party headquarters that the citizens in a given precinct are not voting in the required numbers, corrective steps can be taken immediately. Party organizers, agitators, the police if necessary may be brought into action. We recall from the description of the voting procedure that as each person comes in and gets his ballot, his name is checked off the list of voters. This list tells who has voted. And it also gives the name and address of everyone in the precinct who has not voted. For those who have not appeared by mid-afternoon, telephones, automobiles, and personnel are ready: Someone will appear at the person's apartment to remind him that it is his duty to get down to the polls. This is usually effective, for if the citizen still refuses to vote after such a visit, his action can be construed as enmity toward the regime, and there are not many in the U.S.S.R. who wish to go on record as entertaining such an attitude. This arrangement brings out many people who would stay home out of sheer indifference.

For those who know they are going to be traveling on election day, elaborate provisions are made. Before leaving his place of residence, the traveler is supposed to present himself at the temporary office where the lists of voters are kept. Here he asks for an absentee voter's certificate. His name is checked off the voting list, and he receives a piece of paper which entitles him to vote at any polling place, even if it is in a neighboring republic. If he is on a train, he can vote in a special car set up for that purpose. In this case he votes for the candidate of the precinct in which he happens to find himself, and not for those representing his own domicile. Whom he votes for is not important. Important only is the fact that he does vote.

To assist the bedridden, election workers are authorized to carry a sealed urn to the invalid's apartment so that he can vote there. Provisions are made for an even more unusual case: Suppose that a person is traveling across the city and falls ill just before election day. He would not have the absentee voter's certificate, since he did not expect to fall ill; and he cannot return to his precinct because the illness has immobilized him. Still he can vote. Official automobiles are assigned to precinct supervisors for a day and can be used to go across town and pick up this ballot for deposit in its own precinct.

In this far-reaching, compulsive effort to get everyone to register approval of the regime, almost all eventualities have been prepared for in advance. And still there must be a few people who do not want to vote—not the sick, the traveling, or the indifferent, but those who simply do not wish to register approval of the regime. Indeed, it would be a strange society which didn't produce such people. Do they exist in the U.S.S.R.? The following conversations suggest that they do, but that most of them also vote.

The following, in question-and-answer form, is an account of some residents of one apartment house, part of which was heard in a conversation at a polling place and part of which came in the form of an anecdote:

Q: Elections in the U.S.S.R. impress Westerners. The overwhelming majority of Russians have come out to vote, and now by mid-afternoon more than 90 per cent have already cast their ballots. But still I wonder: Don't some people ever vote *against* the candidates?

A: Sometimes it does happen that people scratch the name off the ballot. It occurs more often out in the villages.

Q: Does this invalidate the ballot?

A: Yes.

Q: Can persons step into the booth and write in the name of a candidate?

A: Of course a person can do this. But it also invalidates the ballot. You see, a candidate has to be nominated by an organization, approved in advance, and registered according to the statute.

Q: So a write-in would not be valid?

A: It would be meaningless. You can't elect anyone with a write-in vote.

Q: Perhaps this explains why few people make use of the voting booths with the curtains hanging in front of them. It looks like about one person in ten is getting into there.

A: More people go into them now than during the time of the cult of personality [the Stalin era]. In those days, someone was keeping track of the people who went into the booths. We don't do that any more.

Q: Don't some people stay away from the polls altogether? Aren't there any people who just refuse to vote? I can't believe that in any country 100 per cent of the people are totally for the government. That would be an unhealthy sign, don't you think?

A: I heard of a case where some people decided they would not vote. They wanted to make a protest about their housing conditions.

Q: What was the trouble?

A: Several families were living in one of the older apartments. Last fall some workmen from the housing office came to fix the plumbing. Well, they cut a hole in the roof of one of the rooms used by all the residents, but when they finished the job they did not patch up the hole.

Q: It was thirty below last winter.

A: It was cold.

Q: What did they do about it?

A: The residents called the housing office and asked them to come and fix the roof. When this got no results, they called the Executive Committee of their city-*raion* soviet. No help. So they called up their deputy.

Q: Was he able to do anything?

A: No, the matter dragged on for months.

Q: There must have been some way they could have gotten the roof repaired. That isn't much of a job.

A: A minor job, but it became a matter of principle: Of course, they could have given the workmen a bottle or two of vodka and it would have been fixed before they left. But these people wanted to settle the matter honestly. Bribery is not a good thing.

Q: So on election day they decided they would not go to the polls?

A: No, they told the agitator who came to visit them that they were not going to vote unless the roof had been fixed by Saturday, the day before the election. This was an ultimatum.

Q: What could the agitator do?

A: First he had to get over his shock. It was an unusual experience for him. But he called the housing office and told them to get a repairman over there right away.

Q: Did that do the job?

A: No, when Sunday morning came, the hole was still there.
Q: Did they vote?
A: Naturally they voted.
Q: Wasn't the atmosphere a bit tense when they showed up at the polls?
A: It may have been. I heard that the volunteer workers at the precinct gave them special attention when they came in, asking them with perhaps a bit of ambiguity how things were at home. The residents simply put it this way: Is a little hole in the roof any reason to be against the Soviet regime? Of course not.
Q: And so they all voted?
A: They voted, to a man. The roof is still not repaired.
Q: But what if they really had refused to come out to the polls, what would you do in a case like that?
A: I wouldn't *do* anything. But I would begin to think, now why is this person against the government? Yes, I'd want to investigate the matter.

* * *

18

PLOTTING BERIA'S DOWNFALL

FROM KHRUSHCHEV REMEMBERS

Stalin was dead, and at the time, his death seemed like a terrible tragedy; but I feared that the worst was still to come. Each of us took Stalin's death in his own way. I took his death very hard. To be honest, I took it hard not so much because I was attached to Stalin—although I *was* attached to him. He was an old man, and death had been one step

Copyright © 1970 by Little, Brown and Company (Inc.) Reprinted from *Khrushchev Remembers* with an Introduction, Commentary and Notes by Edward Crankshaw, translated and edited by Strobe Talbott, pp. 322–41, by permission of Little, Brown & Co. Reprinted in the British Commonwealth with the permission of Andre Deutsch, Ltd.

behind him for a long time. After all, death is inevitable. Everyone is born and everyone dies. It's a fact of life. More than by his death itself, I was disturbed by the composition of the Presidium which Stalin left behind and particularly by the place Beria was fixing for himself. It all portended serious complications and some unpleasant surprises—I would even say catastrophic consequences.

As soon as Stalin died, Beria was radiant. He was regenerated and rejuvenated. To put it crudely, he had a housewarming over Stalin's corpse before it was even put in its coffin. Beria was sure that the moment he had long been waiting for had finally arrived. There was no power on earth that could hold him back now. Nothing could get in his way. Now he could do whatever he saw fit. You could see these triumphant thoughts in his face as he called for his car and drove off to the city, leaving us at the Nearby Dacha.

I knew that Malenkov had never really had a position or a role of his own and that he was just an errand boy. Stalin used to say very accurately during conversations with his inner circle, "This Malenkov is a good clerk. He can write out a resolution quickly. He's a good person for allocating responsibilities to, but he has no capacity at all for independent thought or initiative." [1] Malenkov had always thought it was profitable to play up to Beria, even though he knew Beria pushed him around and mocked him. And Malenkov was quite right—it was profitable to play up to Beria. It was mainly because he was so close to Beria that Malenkov stayed in favor with Stalin despite Stalin's low opinion of him as a leader. Now that Stalin was dead, Malenkov was sure to "come in handy" for Beria's plans, as Beria himself had once told me he would.

These were the thoughts going through my mind while I stood over Stalin's dead body at the Nearby Dacha.

When Beria had gone, the rest of us decided to call together all the members of the Bureau and the Presidium. While waiting for them to arrive, Malenkov paced up and down nervously. I decided to have a talk with him then and there. I went over and said, "Yegor [Georgi], I want to talk to you."

"What about?" he asked coldly.

"Now that Stalin is dead, we have something to discuss. What do we do now?"

"What's there to talk about? We'll all get together and then we'll talk. That's why we're having a meeting." This seemed like a democratic enough answer, but I took it differently. I took it to mean that Malenkov had already talked things over with Beria and everything had been decided for some time.

"Well, all right," I said, "then we'll talk later."

---

[1] Only five months before, in October, 1952, Stalin had showed his far from low opinion of Malenkov by putting him up to make the General Report to the Nineteenth Party Congress.

Everyone gathered at the Nearby Dacha and saw that Stalin was dead. Then Svetlanka arrived. I went over to meet her. She was very upset and started to cry. I couldn't control myself. I started to weep, too, and I wept sincerely over Stalin's death.

I wasn't just weeping for Stalin. I was terribly worried about the future of the Party and the future of the country. I already sensed that Beria would start bossing everyone around and that this could be the beginning of the end. I'd known for a long time that he was no Communist. I considered him a treacherous opportunist who would stop at nothing to get what he wanted. Ideologically, I didn't recognize his position as a Communist one. He was a butcher and an assassin.

When the meeting was convened, the distribution of our new portfolios began. Beria immediately proposed Malenkov for Chairman of the Council of Ministers. On the spot Malenkov proposed that Beria be appointed his first deputy. He also proposed the merger of the ministries of State Security and of Internal Affairs into a single Ministry of Internal Affairs with Beria as Minister—a seemingly modest post for Beria to settle for.[2] I was silent. I was afraid that Bulganin might object to this improper procedure, but Bulganin was silent, too. I could see what the attitude of the others was. If Bulganin and I had objected to the way Beria and Malenkov were running the meeting, we would have been accused of being quarrelsome and disorderly and of starting a fight in the Party before the corpse was cold. I could see that things were moving in the direction I had feared.

Molotov and Kaganovich were each nominated First Deputy Prime Minister along with Beria. Voroshilov was nominated Chairman of the Presidium of the Supreme Soviet [President of the U.S.S.R.], replacing Shvernik.[3] Beria was most disrespectful in his remarks about Shvernik, saying he was unknown to the nation at large and therefore unsuited to an important position in the leadership. I could see that all these rearrangements of positions fitted squarely into Beria's master plan. For instance, by promoting Voroshilov to the Chairmanship of the Presidium of the Supreme Soviet, Beria was trying to make Voroshilov into someone whom he could rely on when he started his next round of butchery. Then Beria proposed that I be released from my duties as Secretary of the Moscow Committee so that I could concentrate on my work in the Central Committee Secretariat. More nominations and pro-

[2] Not so modest. Earlier Khrushchev said that this was just what he feared. Beria was also chosen to be a First Deputy Chairman of the Council of Ministers (First Deputy Prime Minister).

[3] N. M. Shvernik, one of Stalin's senior old faithfuls, spent most of his career at the head of the Soviet trade unions. The Chairmanship of the Presidium of the Supreme Soviet, or Presidency of the U.S.S.R., was a largely ceremonial function. Bulganin was also appointed a First Deputy Chairman of the Council of Ministers, along with Beria, Kaganovich, and Molotov. Khrushchev held no ministerial appointment. His strength reposed in his position as a member of the Presidium and of the Party Secretariat.

posals were made. Then we decided on the funeral arrangements and how best to announce Stalin's death to the people.[4]

Thus we lost Stalin and started to run the government by ourselves.

During the funeral and right after it, Beria was attentive and respectful to me, which surprised me. He didn't sever his demonstratively friendly connections with Malenkov, but he did begin to establish equally friendly relations with me. Beria and Malenkov started including me in their strolls around the Kremlin grounds. Naturally I didn't resist or object, but my opinion of Beria didn't change. On the contrary, it was confirmed. I understood that his friendly behavior toward me was a trick. It was, as we often put it, Beria's Asiatic cunning coming into play. By this term we meant the quality of a man who thinks one thing but says something else. I knew that Beria was pursuing a hypocritical policy toward me; he was toying with me and trying to put me off my guard, all the while waiting for the opportunity to dispose of me before anyone else.

It was decided that Malenkov and I would work out the agenda for Presidium sessions. Malenkov would preside over the sessions, and I would work with him in setting the agenda.

Beria consolidated his forces with each passing day, and his arrogance grew proportionally. All his shrewdness as a provocateur was called into play.

Then came the first clash between Beria and Malenkov on the one hand and the rest of the Presidium on the other. The Presidium had already changed quite a bit. We had liquidated the large Presidium and small Bureau which Stalin had set up at the first Central Committee plenum after the Nineteenth Party Congress. We had reverted to a narrow circle of about eleven people. At one Presidium session Beria made the following proposal:

"Since many prison and exile terms are coming to an end and all these former convicts and exiles will be returning to their homes, I propose that we pass a resolution not allowing any of them to return without special permission from the Ministry of Internal Affairs. And I propose that we require them to live in regions dictated by the Ministry of Internal Affairs." That meant dictated by Beria himself. This proposal was an alarming sign of what Beria was up to.

I got angry and spoke against him, saying, "I categorically object to the sort of arbitrary rule you're proposing. We've already had this sort of thing in the past. Now that we've started thinking more critically and more correctly about how to evaluate the past, we know we can't impose this sort of illegality disguised as law on the people any more. These convicts and exiles you're talking about were arrested, interrogated, tried, and sentenced by State Security troikas.[5] They were never

[4] The announcement, when it came, included the celebrated plea to the people of the Soviet Union to avoid "panic and disarray."

[5] *Ad hoc* groups of three, who combined the duty of prosecutor and judge and operated with extreme and arbitrary dispatch.

given the benefit of witnesses, prosecutors, or judge—they were just hauled in and imprisoned, or killed. Now you're saying that these people, whose terms of punishment were set by the troikas, should again be deprived of all their rights, treated as criminals, and not allowed to choose where they will live. This is totally unacceptable."

The others supported me. Beria shrewdly withdrew his proposal, and since Malenkov was taking the minutes, the motion was never recorded. Later Beria introduced what seemed to be a liberal motion. He proposed we alter an old ruling which set prison and exile terms at a maximum of twenty years for people arrested and charged by the troikas; he suggested lowering the maximum term from twenty to ten years. This seemed like a liberal enough proposal, but I knew what Beria had in mind.

I said, "I'm categorically opposed to this proposal, too. I'm against it because we should be reviewing the whole system of arrests and investigations, not just modifying the details. Once again, you're trying to promote arbitrary rule. Whether the maximum term is twenty or ten years doesn't really matter because you can always sentence someone to ten years and then another ten years. If necessary you could keep sentencing someone you don't like to one ten-year term after another, right up until he dies. What's required is a radical revision of the inadmissible practice of arresting and sentencing people which prevailed during Stalin's time. What you want to do is legalize arbitrary rule— you want to legalize the *status quo*. Documents are being put together to show how the methods you're proposing have been applied in the past arbitrarily and illegally, and how the Party has been damaged as a result."

Once again Beria withdrew his motion. I had vigorously spoken out against him twice already. I had no doubt that he knew exactly where I stood and that he was planning his next move. Beria could never reconcile himself to the fact that someone was standing in his way.

And what was this scoundrel Beria's next move? Here's what happened. One day we were walking somewhere together—Beria, Malenkov, and I—just taking a stroll, and Beria began to develop the following idea: "All of us are in God's hands, as they used to say. We're not getting any younger. Anything could happen to any one of us, and we would leave our families behind. We should give some thought to our old age and to our families. Therefore I'd like to propose that the Government build dachas which it would then turn over to the leaders of the country for their personal use." The suggestion was typical of Beria. I had come to expect this sort of un-Communist thinking from him. It was completely in keeping with his way of doing things. I was sure that the dacha idea was part of some kind of provocation. But I didn't say anything; I just listened. Then he said, "I propose building these dachas in Sukhumi [on the Black Sea coast] rather than on the outskirts of Moscow and not on the outskirts of Sukhumi, but right in the center. We could clear the center of the city and turn it into a park with peach trees." He started raving about what a marvelous city Sukhumi was and about the peaches and grapes that grew there. He had it all worked out—which personnel would be used and what resources would be needed. He was thinking on a grand and lordly scale. He continued: "The Ministry of Internal Affairs will supervise this project. First of all we'll have to build a dacha for you, Yegor [Malenkov]—then for you, Nikita, and then for Molotov, Voroshilov, and the others."

I heard him out and didn't try to argue with him. All the while he was talking, I just said, "Yes, yes, we'll have to give it some thought" —as though I were agreeing with him.

When we finished talking and returned to our cars, Beria, Malenkov, and I went off to our own dachas in the country. The three of us rode in one car as far as the turnoff on the Rublev road, where Malenkov and I were supposed to turn left and Beria was supposed to keep going straight. Malenkov and I got out of his car and into another one. Once we were alone I said to Malenkov, "Listen, what do you think about this idea of Beria's? It's the most blatant provocation."

"Why do you think so?"

"I can see Beria's a provocateur. He wants to build these dachas as a provocation and nothing else. Let's not object for a while. We'll let him do what he wants, and he'll think no one knows what he's up to."

So Beria began to put his idea into effect. He ordered plans for the dachas to be drawn up. When these were finished, he invited us to come over and showed them to us. He proposed that the constructon start at once. A well-known builder gave a report on the project. This comrade is now in charge of building atomic energy plants. Beria considered him a trusty ally. He worked for Beria and did whatever Beria told him. At the meeting Beria said that the site for Malenkov's dacha had been carefully chosen so that Malenkov would be able to view the Black Sea from his window and keep an eye on the Turks. Beria joked, "Yegor, you'll be able to see Turkey. It's beautiful. You see what a nice house this will be?"

When everyone else had gone, I stayed behind with Malenkov. I said to him, "It's crucial to Beria's plans that your dacha be built in the very center of Sukhumi. The plans call for a great many people to be displaced. The Minister of Housing has said that the dacha project will mean the eviction of a huge number of people. The whole thing will be a calamity for them. They have lived on their property for generations, and now suddenly they're all to be evicted. This is no joke. You still don't see the point of his provocation? Beria wants to start a sort of pogrom, to throw people out of their homes and tear down their houses in order to build you some kind of palace. The dacha and grounds will be walled in. The city will be seething with resentment and indignation. People will ask, "Who are they doing all this building for?" And when it's all finished, you'll arrive and people will see you, the Chairman of the Council of Ministers, get out of your car and disappear into your palace. They'll see that the pogrom and the eviction of people from their homes was all done for you. The hatred against you will spread not only through the whole city of Sukhumi, but everywhere, throughout the land. And this is exactly what Beria wants to happen. He's trying to maneuver you into such a hopeless scandal that you'll be forced to resign. Don't you see? Beria says he's going to have plans drawn up for a dacha of his own, but you'll see, he won't have it built. He'll build one for you and then use it to discredit you."

"How can you say that? Beria talked it all over with me!"

But this conversation started Malenkov thinking.

One day when Beria was showing me the plans for the dachas, he said again, in his thick Georgian accent, "Won't these be lovely houses?"

"Yes, very," I said. "It's a great idea."

"Why don't you take the plans home with you?"

So I took them home, but I didn't know what to do with them. Nina Petrovna [Madame Khrushchev] came across them and asked, "What's this here?" I told her what they were, and she was furious. "That's a disgraceful idea!"

I couldn't explain, so I said, "Let's just put them aside and we'll talk about it later." [6]

Beria tried to push through the construction of the dachas in Sukhumi, but nothing had been done by the time of his arrest. After he was arrested we canceled the whole project. I kept the plans for the dachas at home for a long time afterward.

But in the meantime, things started spinning. Beria was trying to interfere in the workings of the Party, particularly the Cheka. He fabricated some sort of document about the state of affairs in the Ukrainian Party leadership. So he had decided to strike his first blow against the Ukrainian organization! I was ready for this because I figured he would try to implicate me. I was still largely responsible for the Ukraine. Beria started collecting evidence through the regional departments of the Ministry of Internal Affairs in the Ukraine. Strokach was Chief of the MVD [Ministry of Internal Affairs] office in Lvov.[7] He's dead now. He was an honest Communist and a good soldier. Before the war he had been a colonel in command of border troops in the Ukraine. Then, during the war, he had been in charge of the Ukrainian partisan troops' headquarters, so he used to report to me on the situation in occupied territory behind enemy lines. I could see he was an honest, decent person. After the war he was made a representative for the Ministry of Internal Affairs in the Lvov Region. We found out later that when the Minister of Internal Affairs for the Ukraine, who was Beria's henchman, got in touch with Strokach and demanded material from him about local Party workers. Strokach said that he wasn't re-

[6] A fascinating sidelight on the domestic life of Khrushchev and his very remarkable wife.

[7] T. A. Strokach, lieutenant general in the security police. Later (1955–56) he was Chief of the Ukrainian MVD.

sponsible for personnel and that they should get in touch with the local Regional Party Committee. Then Beria himself phoned Strokach and said that if he was going to split hairs, he would be pounded into camp dust. We found out about this incident later, after we detained Beria, but at the time we had no idea that the Party was being undermined and subordinated to the Ministry of Internal Affairs in the Ukraine.

The Presidium began to discuss a memorandum by Beria about the ethnic composition of governing bodies in the Ukraine. Beria's idea was that local [that is, non-Russian] officials should be kept in positions of leadership in their own Republics and shouldn't be promoted to the central organization in Moscow. As a result of his memorandum, it was decided to release Melnikov from his duties as First Secretary of the Ukrainian Central Committee and to put Kirichenko [a Ukrainian] in his place. Beria also proposed putting Korneichuk on the Presidium of the Central Committee of the Ukrainian Party. This was done, and a Ukrainian Central Committee Plenum was held. Korneichuk didn't realize he had been promoted in order to further Beria's anti-Party aims, so he said all sorts of favorable things about Beria and Beria's memorandum during the course of the Plenum. Then a memorandum appeared concerning the Baltic states, followed by another concerning Belorussia. Both stressed the principle of drawing the republic leadership from the local population. We passed a decision that the post of First Secretary in every republic had to be held by a local person and not by a Russian sent from Moscow.[8]

It so happened that Beria's position on this question was correct and that it coincided with the position of the All-Union Central Committee, but he was taking this position in order to further his own anti-Party goals. He was preaching that the predominance of Russians in the leadership of the non-Russian republics had to be reversed. Everyone knew that this was right and that it was consistent with the Party Line, but at first people didn't realize that Beria was pushing this idea in order to aggravate nationalist tensions between Russians and non-Russians, as well as tensions between the central leadership in Moscow and the local leadership in the republics.

At this point I took Malenkov aside and said, "Listen, Comrade Malenkov, don't you see where this is leading? We're heading for disaster. Beria is sharpening his knives."

Malenkov asked, "Well, what can we do? I see what's happening, but what can we do about it?"

"The time has come to resist. Surely you must see that Beria's posi-

---

[8] This refers to the still obscure operation conducted by Beria to encourage local leadership in the component republics. He was arrested and shot before his long-range purpose was clearly manifest, though Khrushchev's explanation is probably correct. A. I. Kirichenko was, in fact, a protégé of Khrushchev, who was to rise to great heights in his master's shadow until his sudden and unexplained downfall in 1960.

tion has an anti-Party character. We must not accept what he is doing. We must reject it."

"You mean you want me to oppose him all by myself? I don't want to do that."

"What makes you think you'll be alone if you oppose him? There's you and me—that's already two of us. I'm sure Bulganin will agree. I've exchanged opinions with him more than once. I'm sure the others will join us if we put forward our argument from a firm Party position. The trouble is that you never give anyone a chance to speak at our Presidium sessions. As soon as Beria introduces a motion, you always jump immediately to support him, saying, 'That's fine, Comrade Beria, a good motion. I'm for it. Anyone opposed?' And you put it right to a vote. Give the rest of us a chance to express ourselves for once and you'll see what happens. Control yourself. Don't be so jumpy. You'll see you're not the only one who thinks the way you do. I'm convinced that many people are on our side against Beria. You and I put the agenda together, so let's include for discussion some matters on which we believe Beria is mistaken. Then we'll oppose him. I'm convinced we can mobilize the other Presidium members behind us and our resolutions will carry. Let's just try it."

Malenkov finally agreed. I was surprised and delighted. We wrote up the agenda for the next Presidium session and included some issues on which the others supported us, and Beria was defeated. This pattern was repeated at a number of sessions, and only then did Malenkov become confident that we could use Party methods against Beria in order to defeat proposals which, in our view, were harmful to the Party and to the country. When Beria realized that the other Presidium members were overriding him, he tried to speed things up. He put on a tremendous show of self-importance, trying to demonstrate his superiority in every way he could. We were going through a very dangerous period. I felt it was time to force the situation to a confrontation. It was time to act.

I told Malenkov that we had to talk with the other members of the Presidium and get them behind us. Obviously it was no good trying to do this during a session with Beria present. We'd have to talk face to face with each individual in order to discover his real attitude toward Beria. At last Malenkov agreed and said, "Yes, we must act."

I already knew Bulganin stood for the Party position and fully understood the danger to the Party which Beria represented. Malenkov and I arranged that, to begin with, I would talk to Comrade Voroshilov. Voroshilov and I served together on some commission or other. I decided this would be my pretext for going to see him. I telephoned him and said I wanted to meet with him about the commission. Comrade Voroshilov said he would rather come see me at the Central Committee building. "No," I said, "please let me come to your office." He insisted that he should come to me, but in the end I had my way. Malenkov and I arranged that I would stop in at his place on my way home so that we could have dinner together and talk over how my meeting with Voroshilov had gone. Malenkov and I lived in the same house and on the same staircase. My apartment was immediately above his.

I went to Comrade Voroshilov's office at the Supreme Soviet, but I didn't accomplish what I'd come for. I was barely inside his office when Voroshilov started singing Beria's praises: "What a remarkable man we have in Lavrenty Pavlovich, Comrade Khrushchev! What a remarkable man!"

I answered, "Maybe not. Maybe you overestimate him." But after Voroshilov had greeted me in this way, I couldn't possibly talk to him frankly about Beria. I thought perhaps Voroshilov had spoken as he did because he thought he was being overheard and that he'd said it for "Beria's ears" [slang for bugging devices]. On the other hand, maybe it was because he considered me Beria's ally. This was conceivable since Beria, Malenkov, and I were often seen together. In any case, my opinion of Beria was completely opposite to Voroshilov's. But if I'd said outright what I wanted to say, I would have put Voroshilov in a very awkward position. He would have been unable to agree with me simply out of pride. He couldn't have come straight over to my position after having just praised Beria as soon as I came through the door. After all, my own position was committed to the need for eliminating Beria.

So Voroshilov and I exchanged a few words on the matter about which I had officially made an appointment with him. It was some trivial question, and I quickly left to have dinner as I'd arranged with Malenkov. I told Malenkov that nothing had come of my visit to Voroshilov and that I hadn't been able to talk openly with him.

Comrade Malenkov and I then agreed that I should talk to Comrade Molotov, who was Minister of Foreign Affairs and who had called me earlier asking if we could meet at the Central Committee office to discuss some matter concerning Foreign Ministry personnel. I used his call as a pretext to set up a meeting and phoned him back, saying, "You wanted to get together with me. I'm ready to see you anytime. If you can, come over here right away. We'll talk about personnel." He arrived shortly and I said, "Let's talk about personnel, but not Foreign Ministry personnel." I gave him my views about Beria's role. I told Molotov what sort of person Beria was and what kind of danger threatened the Party if we didn't thwart his scheming against the Party leadership. I had earlier told him how Beria had already set his plan in motion for aggravating nationalist tensions in the republics.

Apparently Molotov had been thinking a lot about this himself. Of course, he couldn't help but think about it, since he knew about everything that had happened during Stalin's rule. Back when Molotov still enjoyed Stalin's full confidence, I had often heard him speak out strongly against Beria, although never in Stalin's presence. Molotov

had personally been a victim of Beria's hypocrisy and treacherous prov-
ocations during sessions with Stalin, and more than once I heard him
call Beria's activities by their proper names to Beria's face. Therefore,
as soon as I got down to the serious matter at hand with Molotov, I
could see he was in full agreement with me.

"Yes," he said, "I agree with you fully. But I want to ask you one
thing. What is Malenkov's position?"

"I'm discussing this with you on Malenkov's and Bulganin's behalf.
We've already exchanged views on the subject."

Then Molotov said, "It's quite right that you should raise this question. I agree with you fully and you'll have my complete support. But
tell me something else. What do you want to do exactly? Where is all
this leading?"

"First, we have to relieve Beria of his duties as a Presidium member,
Deputy Chairman of the Council of Ministers, and Minister of Internal
Affairs."

Molotov said that wasn't enough: "Beria's very dangerous. Therefore
I think we must, so to say, resort to more extreme measures."

"You think maybe we should detain him for investigation?" I said
"detain" rather than "arrest" because there were still no criminal charges
against Beria. I could easily believe that he had been an agent of the
Mussavatists, as Kaminsky had said, but Kaminsky's charge had never
been verified. There had never been an investigation of Beria's role in
Baku. As far as Beria's provocational behavior was concerned, we had
only our intuition to go on, and you can't arrest a man on intuition.
That's why I said we would have to "detain" him for an investigation.
Molotov and I agreed and parted. Later I told Comrade Malenkov
and Comrade Bulganin what had happened.

We decided that we'd better speed things up because we might be
overheard by "Beria's ears" or someone might let the cat out of the
bag. In short, information about the steps we were taking might reach
Beria, and Beria could easily have us all arrested.

We agreed that I should talk to Saburov, who was then a member of
the Presidium. When I talked to Saburov, he answered very quickly:
"I'm fully in agreement with you." Then he asked, "But what about
Malenkov?" Everyone I talked to asked this same question.

At that time Kaganovich wasn't in Moscow. He was making an
inspection tour of the lumber industry. When he returned, I asked him
to stop in at the Central Committee office. He arrived in the evening,
and we sat and talked for a long time. He told me in great detail about
Siberia and about the sawmills. I didn't try to interrupt him, although
I had other things than sawmills on my mind. I showed proper courtesy
and tact and waited for him to get tired of talking. When he finished
his report, I said, "What you've told me is all very well. Now I want
to tell you about what's going on here." I told him what the circumstances were and what conclusions we had reached.

Kaganovich immediately pricked up his ears and asked, "Who is 'we'?" He put the question like that in order to assess the distribution of power. I said that Malenkov, Bulganin, Molotov, Saburov, and I were of one mind, and I told him that without him we had a majority. Kaganovich declared right away, "I'm with you, too. Of course I'm with you. I was only asking." But I knew what he was thinking, and he knew what I was thinking. Then he asked me, "And what about Voroshilov?" I told him about my awkward meeting with Voroshilov and how Voroshilov had praised Beria. "He really said that?" Kaganovich exclaimed. He was incredulous.

"Yes," I said. "He started to sing Beria's praises the moment I came into his office."

Kaganovich cursed Voroshilov, but not maliciously: "That sly old bastard! He was lying to you. He's told me himself that he can't stand Beria, that Beria's dangerous, and that Beria's likely to be the ruin of us all."

"I thought Voroshilov wasn't being straightforward with me, but that's what he said, all the same."

"What he said doesn't mean a thing."

"Then it seems we'll have to try talking to him one last time. Perhaps Malenkov will talk to him. Since I've already spoken to him, it might be better if I didn't bring up the subject of Beria with him again. I wouldn't want to put him in an awkward position." We agreed on this.

Then Kaganovich said, "And what about Mikoyan?"

"I haven't talked to Mikoyan yet. His case is a bit more complicated." Everyone knew that Mikoyan was on the very best of terms with Beria. They were always together and always following each other around. We'd have to talk to Mikoyan at some point, but it would have to be done later on.

I told Malenkov about my conversation with Kaganovich, and he agreed that it would be better if he talked to Voroshilov himself. That left Pervukhin. Malenkov suddenly said, "I want to talk to Pervukhin myself."

"By all means, if you want to, but Pervukhin is a complex man. I know him."

"I know him, too."

"Very well then, you talk to him."

Malenkov invited Pervukhin to come see him and then got in touch with me later, "You know, I sent for Pervukhin and told him everything. Pervukhin said he'd think it over. That's very dangerous. I think you should get hold of him yourself, and you'd better do it immediately. Who knows what might happen? 'I'll think it over'—that's very dangerous."

I phoned Comrade Pervukhin. He came to see me. I told him everything, very frankly. He said, "If Malenkov had put it to me as clearly as you have done, there wouldn't have been any question in my mind.

I agree with you entirely. There's no alternative." I don't know what Malenkov had told Pervukhin, but now it was settled.

In this way we made the rounds of all the Presidium members except Voroshilov and Mikoyan. We arranged for me to speak to Mikoyan and for Malenkov to speak to Voroshilov. Later, I went by to see Malenkov and asked him about his conversation with Voroshilov. "Well, what happened?" I asked, "Was he still singing Beria's praises?"

"As soon as I told him about our plan," said Malenkov, "Voroshilov embraced me and started crying." I don't know if this really happened, but Comrade Malenkov had no need to lie about it.

Still another question arose. Once we had formally resolved to strip Beria of his posts, who would actually detain him? The Presidium bodyguard was obedient to him. His Chekists would be sitting in the next room during the session, and Beria could easily order them to arrest us all and hold us in isolation. We would have been quite helpless because there was a sizable armed guard in the Kremlin. Therefore we decided to enlist the help of the military. First, we entrusted the detention of Beria to Comrade Moskalenko, the air defense commander, and five generals.[9] This was my idea. Then, on the eve of the session, Malenkov widened our circle to include Marshal Zhukov and some others. That meant eleven marshals and generals in all. In those days all military personnel were required to check their weapons when coming into the Kremlin, so Comrade Bulganin was instructed to see that the marshals and generals were allowed to bring their guns with them. We arranged for Moskalenko's group to wait for a summons in a separate room while the session was taking place. When Malenkov gave a signal, they were to come into the room where we were meeting and take Beria into custody.

We arranged to convene a session of the Presidium of the Council of Ministers but invited all the members of the Presidium of the Central Committee as well. Malenkov opened the meeting as a Central Committee Presidium session rather than a Council of Ministers Presidium session so that we could discuss the situation in the Party. Comrade Voroshilov had to be specially invited, since he was Chairman of the Presidium of the Supreme Soviet and therefore didn't regularly attend sessions of either the Council of Ministers or the Party Presidium.

As soon as Malenkov opened the session he said, "Let us discuss Party questions. There are some matters which we must deal with right away. Everyone agreed. As had been arranged in advance, I requested the floor from Chairman Malenkov and proposed that we discuss the matter of Beria. Beria was sitting on my right. He gave a start, grabbed me by the hand, looked at me with a startled expression on his face, and said, "What's going on, Nikita? What's this you're mumbling about?"

[9] General K. S. Moskalenko, later marshal. At the time of Beria's arrest he was commander of the air defense of Moscow.

I said, "Just pay attention. You'll find out soon enough." And here is what I said. I recalled the Central Committee plenum of February, 1939, at which Comrade Grisha Kaminsky had accused Beria of having worked for the Mussavatist counterintelligence service, and therefore for the English intelligence service, when he was Secretary of the Baku Party organization. I then recalled how immediately after that meeting Grisha Kaminsky had dropped out of sight like a stone in the water: "I've always wondered about Kaminsky's statement and why no one made any attempt to explain what he said." Then I reviewed the moves Beria had made since Stalin's death, his interference in the Party organizations of the Ukraine, Belorussia, and the Baltic states. I described how Beria, like all enemies of the Communist Party, was relying on nationalist antagonisms to undermine Soviet unity. I mentioned his latest proposal concerning policy toward people in exile and in prison camps, stressing that Beria was trying to legalize arbitrary rule. I concluded by saying, "As a result of my observations of Beria's activities, I have formed the impression that he is no Communist. He is a careerist who has wormed his way into the Party for self-seeking reasons. His arrogance is intolerable. No honest Communist would ever behave the way he does in the Party."

After I had spoken, Bulganin asked for the floor and said something very much along the same lines. Then the others spoke in turn. Molotov expressed the proper Party position on the matter. The other comrades stressed the same principles, with the exception of Mikoyan, who spoke last. He repeated what he had told me before the session when we had our talk: namely, that Beria would take our criticisms to heart and reform himself, that he wasn't a hopeless case, and that he could still be useful in the collective leadership.

When everyone had spoken, Malenkov, as Chairman, was supposed to sum things up and to formulate a consensus, but at the last moment he lost his nerve. After the final speech, the session was left hanging. There was a long pause. I saw we were in trouble, so I asked Comrade Malenkov for the floor in order to propose a motion. As we had arranged in advance, I proposed that the Central Committee Presidium should release Beria from his duties as Deputy Chairman of the Council of Ministers and Minister of Internal Affairs and from all the other government positions he held. Malenkov was still in a state of panic. As I recall, he didn't even put my motion to a vote. He pressed a secret button which gave the signal to the generals who were waiting in the next room. Zhukov was the first to appear. Then Moskalenko and the others came in. Malenkov said in a faint voice to Comrade Zhukov, "As Chairman of the Council of Ministers of the U.S.S.R., I request that you take Beria into custody pending investigation of charges made against him."

"Hands up!" Zhukov commanded Beria.

Moskalenko and the others unbuckled their holsters in case Beria tried anything. Beria seemed to reach for his briefcase which was lying behind him on the windowsill. I seized his arm to prevent him from grabbing a weapon from the briefcase. We checked later and found that he had no gun, either in his briefcase or in his pockets. His quick movement had simply been a reflex action.

Beria was immediately put under armed guard in the Council of Ministers building next to Malenkov's office. At this point a new question arose. Now that we had detained Beria, where could we put him? We couldn't hand him over to the Ministry of Internal Affairs because those were all his own men. Beria's deputies were Kruglov [10] and Serov. I hardly knew Kruglov, but I knew Serov well, and I trusted him. I thought, and still think, Serov is an honest man. If there are a few dubious things about him, as there are about all Chekists, then let's just say he was a victim of Stalin's general policy. At first I proposed that Serov should take Beria into custody, but the others were against this. Finally we agreed to entrust him to the air defense commander, Comrade Moskalenko, who had his men transfer Beria to a bunker at his headquarters. I could see that Comrade Moskalenko would do what was necessary for the Party cause.

After it was all over, Malenkov took me aside and said, "Listen to what my chief bodyguard has to say." The man came over to me and said, "I have only just heard that Beria has been arrested. I want to inform you that he raped my stepdaughter, a seventh-grader. A year or so ago her grandmother died and my wife had to go to the hospital, leaving the girl at home alone. One evening she went out to buy some bread near the building where Beria lives. There she came across an old man who watched her intently. She was frightened. Someone came and took her to Beria's home. Beria had her sit down with him for supper. She drank something, fell asleep, and he raped her."

I told this man, "I want you to tell the prosecutor during the investigation everything you've told me." Later, we were given a list of more than a hundred girls and women who had been raped by Beria. He had used the same routine on all of them. He gave them some dinner and offered them wine with a sleeping potion in it.

When Beria was put in solitary confinement, he asked for pencil and paper. We consulted among ourselves. Some of us were doubtful, but we decided to give him what he wanted in case an urge had come over him to tell us candidly what he knew about the things we had charged him with. He started writing notes. The first was to Malenkov: "Yegor, don't you know me? Aren't we friends? Why did you trust Khrush-

[10] S. N. Kruglov, colonel general of the security police, was at one time Deputy Director of Smersh (acronym for "Death to Spies and Diversionists") and responsible for the security of Stalin, Roosevelt, and Churchill at Yalta and Teheran. Even in that gallery he had a reputation for outstanding vengefulness and cruelty. Unlike some of his colleagues, however, he was personally brave. He succeeded Beria as Minister of the Interior, with reduced powers, until his fall in 1957. The head of the MGB at this time was not Serov, but Khrushchev's ally, S. D. Ignatyev.

chev? He's the one who put you up to this, isn't he?" and so on. He also sent me two or three notes swearing he was an honest man and so on and so forth.

We had no confidence in the ability of the State Prosecutor to investigate Beria's case objectively, so we sacked him and replaced him with Comrade Rudenko.[11] When Rudenko started to interrogate Beria, we found ourselves faced with a really awful man, a beast, to whom nothing was sacred. When we opened the archives and brought him to trial, we found out what methods Beria had used to achieve his goals. Not only was there nothing Communist about him—he was without the slightest trace of human decency.

After Beria's arrest the question arose of what to do about Merkulov, who was Minister of State Control.[12] I admit that I held him in high regard and considered him a good Party member. He was unquestionably a cultured person, and in general I liked him. Therefore I said to the comrades, "Just because Merkulov was Beria's assistant in Georgia doesn't mean he was an accomplice to Beria's crimes. Perhaps he wasn't. We can't treat everyone who worked for Beria as his accomplice. Let's call Merkulov in and have a talk with him. He might even help us to clear up some of the remaining questions about Beria." By arrangement with the others, I summoned Merkulov to the Central Committee office and told him what had happened, that we had detained Beria, and that an investigation was under way. "You worked for Beria for many years, Comrade Merkulov," I said, "and therefore we thought you might be able to help the Central Committee with our investigation."

"I will do whatever I can, with pleasure."

"Then write us a report."

A few days passed and Merkulov turned in a lengthy memorandum. It was absolutely worthless. It was more like a piece of fiction. This man Merkulov was something of a writer. He'd written plays and was good at fiction writing. After I sent this material to the prosecutor's office, Rudenko called me and asked for an appointment. When he came to my office he told me that without Merkulov's arrest our investigation into Beria's case would be incomplete. The Central Committee approved Merkulov's arrest. To my regret, since I had trusted him, Merkulov turned out to have been deeply implicated in some of Beria's crimes, so he too was convicted and had to bear the same responsibility. In his last words, after his sentence had been announced by the court, Merkulov cursed the day and the hour when he first met Beria. He said Beria had led him to this end. Thus, in the final analysis, Mer-

---

[11] Roman A. Rudenko, a Ukrainian who was chief U.S.S.R. prosecutor at the Nuremberg trials of the Nazi leaders and became Prosecutor General in 1953.

[12] V. N. Merkulov, an extremely presentable but no less unpleasant secret policeman and a very close associate of Beria's. He was replaced by Abakumov as head of the MGB in 1946, but soon became Minister of State Control. He was tried with Beria and shot.

kulov recognized the criminality of his actions and pronounced his own judgment against the man who had incited him to crime.

One of the people we were able to return to a useful, active life after Beria's downfall was Aleksandr Petrovich Dovzhenko, the brilliant film director who was so unjustly disgraced during the war. Shortly after Beria was arrested, Dovzhenko asked me for an appointment. He came by my office and told me the following story:

One day the director Chiaureli, who made *The Fall of Berlin*, asked Dovzhenko to come and see him. Chiaureli was totally dependent on Stalin's patronage, and it was no accident that his film on the fall of Berlin showed Stalin pondering military strategy in a huge hall surrounded by empty chairs—in solitary grandeur except for General Poskrebyshev, Chief of the Special Section of the Central Committee. In short, Chiaureli was a wretched little toady. After Stalin's death and Beria's arrest we sent him off to the Urals. I don't know what place he holds in the world of film arts today or whether he learned any lessons from the criticism that came his way after his protector Stalin died. Anyway, Chiaureli summoned Dovzhenko and told him, "Comrade Dovzhenko, I'd advise you to go and see Comrade Beria. He's very interested in you and has a proposition to make. It will be to your advantage to go hear what he has to say." Dovzhenko was perplexed: Why was Chiaureli telling him to go and see Beria? What business did he have with the Ministry of Internal Affairs? In the end he decided not to go.

I explained to Dovzhenko: "You see, Aleksandr Petrovich, Chiaureli was trying to recruit you as an agent for Beria. He understood, quite correctly, that you were an influential person and would have been useful to Beria in his plans for the Ukraine. Beria wanted to make you his henchman so that he could count on you when his blood bath began. His plans could only have been bloody because Beria knew no other methods."

I considered Dovzhenko an honest, loyal, upright citizen. He may have sometimes said things which were unpleasant for the leaders to hear, but it's always better to hear such things from an honest man than from an enemy. You can always talk sense to an honest man if he's wrong, and you can learn from him if he's right. After Aleksandr Petrovich's death I urged the Ukrainians to rename the Kiev Film Studio after him, and they did so.

Dovzhenko's story about Beria's attempt to compromise him was only one of the first—and by no means one of the most shocking— in a spate of revelations into Beria's past activities which came to light after his arrest.

*   *   *

VI

The Judicial Process

The judicial process in the Soviet Union has evolved as an accommodation between the demands of Communist theory and the needs of Soviet society. According to Marx and Engels, law, judges, and courts, like other features of the state, were created by the bourgeoisie to protect capitalist property. Justice had no meaning beyond the interests of the class it served. With the elimination of class antagonism in a communist society there is in theory no need for law or the institutions to compel observance of it. In fact, however, the Soviets were from the beginning unable to dispense with a legal system for the administration of justice; and as Soviet society has become socially and economically modernized the corresponding need for a legal system that is stable and reasonably equitable has been met. Today the ordinary problems of civil and criminal offenses in the Soviet Union are administered in a consistent and rational manner, much as they are in other highly developed societies.

Even if the existence of law and a court structure contradicts some elements of Marxist ideology, the judicial system as a whole has been considerably influenced by ideological considerations, particularly the doctrine of Party supremacy. Generally the court structure is characterized by a high degree of centralization and politicization. Law serves the interests of the Party and the state. Soviet justice is designed to protect socialist property, and the courts are treated as one of the many controls to insure implementation of Party and state goals.

The constiutional framework of the judiciary consists of a system of courts and the office of the Procuracy. Both institutions are highly centralized and heirarchically organized to correspond with the structure of the Soviet state. At the apex of the court system is the U.S.S.R. Supreme Court, which has appelate and original jurisdiction over cases of unusual importance. One of its most important functions is to issue general principles and directives aimed at guiding the work of all lower courts. The Supreme Court does not have the right to determine the constitutionality of legislative enactments or executive decrees. Indeed, Soviet rejection of the concept of separation of powers is reflected in the fact that the all-Union and Union-republic courts, as well as all intermediate courts, are elected by the principal legislative organs (the soviets) whose geographic boundaries they share.

At the base of the court structure is the People's Court, which has jurisdiction in cities and local districts. The People's Courts are the principal trial courts for civil and criminal cases. Each court is presided over by a judge and two people's assessors. Judges are elected by secret ballot. People's assessors are laymen elected for a two-year period at public meetings of working people. They are supposed to reflect the wisdom of the common man in the administration of justice. Though limited to a maximum of two weeks of service a year, assessors have the same authority as a judge while on duty. Since decisions are by majority vote, it is possible for the assessors to outvote the judge, though in practice they often defer to the opinion of the judge.

During Khrushchev's administation, an effort was made to expand the role of the public in the administration of justice, to substitute social groups for state organs in the maintenance of law and order. Presumably this was a step in the direction of helping the state to wither away. Two public voluntary groups that have achieved prominance in this effort are the Comrades' Courts and the People's Volunteers. Comrades' Courts are *ad hoc* courts, which may be set up in factories, apartments, collective farms, and other organizations. They are popularly elected by open ballot and are designed to suppress socially undesirable behavior, delinquency, and petty crimes. Cases are tried informally in public. Although a Comrade's Court has the authority to impose minor fines and punishments, its primary utility is supposed to be its educational value and its capacity to shame an offender. People's Volunteer detachments are squads of unpaid, part-time assistants to the uniformed police (militia) who help to maintain order in public areas.

A powerful arm in the defense of public order is the Office of the Procuracy, which resembles the office of Attorney General in the United States. The Procuracy is responsible for overseeing the observance and uniform application of laws throughout the nation. This involves, among other powers, extensive control over judicial proceedings. The Procuracy conducts pretrial investigations, which in the Soviet Union play a major role in determining a person's guilt or innocence. It initiates criminal cases and prosecutes in courts. It may appeal any court decision and determine the legality of sentences, judgments, and decisions of any judicial body.

The Procurator General is appointed by the U.S.S.R. Supreme Soviet and, though legally responsible to it, is in fact supervised only by the leadership of the Communist Party. His office functions in complete independence from all local organs, including local soviets and Party organs. While the Procurator General is responsible for the legality of acts and orders at every level of government, real supervision is limited almost exclusively to that over the lower levels of administration.

Since Stalin's death, the legal rights of Soviet citizens have been substantially increased. Extralegal terror no longer supplements the judicial process. Laws have become more liberal and humanized. Many features of Soviet jurisprudence are considered to be progressive by Western standards. For example, in determining guilt or innocence Soviet courts tend to consider the "whole man," not just the specific facts in the crime; and punishment often is designed to reform, re-educate, and rehabilitate the offender. On the other hand the interests of the state and Party remain paramount in theory and fact over the rights of the individual. Many of the rights considered important in the West—such as habeas corpus and presumption of innocence—are lacking. Though the harshness of the past is unlikely to recur, the political trials of writers like Yuli Daniel and Andrei Sinyavsky and their supporters exposes the continuing capacity of the regime arbitrarily to suppress dissent.

Harold J. Berman is professor of law at Harvard University and a member of the Executive Committee of the Harvard Russian Research Center. His books include *Justice in the U.S.S.R.: An Interpretation of Soviet Law; Soviet Criminal Law and Procedures: The RSFSR Codes;* and (with Miroslav Kerner) *Soviet Military Law and Administration.* George Feifer obtained his information about Soviet trials during a year's observation of the Moscow courts. In 1963 he was a graduate student at Moscow State University. Andreas Bilinsky has been with the Institute for Eastern European Law in Munich since 1957. He is the author of several works on Soviet law published in German and American periodicals.

19

THE EDUCATIONAL ROLE OF THE SOVIET COURT

HAROLD J. BERMAN

The Soviet court plays a double role in the education of popular law-consciousness. On the one hand it is an instrument for teaching law to the public generally. On the other hand it is a means of educating the parties who come before it with their grievances.

The educational role of the Soviet court must be seen in the context of the state's general interest in instilling a knowledge of law and a respect for law, if not a fear of law, among its subjects. Special pains are taken in the Soviet Union to make law a part of the general education of the average citizen. Lawyers are required to give lectures on law at

Reprinted by permission of the publishers from Harold J. Berman, *Justice in the U.S.S.R.: An Interpretation of Soviet Law*, Rev. Ed. (Cambridge, Mass.: Harvard University Press, 1963), pp. 299–311. Copyright 1950, 1963, by the President and Fellows of Harvard College.

meetings of trade unions and other organizations. Law is popularized in pamphlets and tracts written for the general public. The lay assessors who sit with the judges in the three-man People's Courts are given short courses in law prior to their undertaking their duties. The elections of People's Judges, which take place throughout the Soviet Union every five years (formerly every three years), are accompanied by a tremendous propaganda campaign in the press, on the radio, and in street speeches and interviews. In these campaigns Soviet law is praised as a synthesis of personal and collective interests, and various aspects of labor law, housing law, family law, criminal law, ond other fields immediately concerning the general population are discussed.

During the 1949 campaign, for example, one judge reported on seventy cases he had heard having to do with suits against railroads, in sixty-three of which judgment was for the plaintiff, with total recoveries amounting to 146,000 rubles. He went on to describe railroad inefficiency and to urge the creation of a moral atmosphere which would eradicate negligence and theft. The press not only boasted of the achievements of Soviet justice but also criticized deficiencies in judicial administration. *Pravda* reported on the role of the courts in restoring workers to their jobs if they were wrongfully dismissed, citing a case in which a particular People's Court had reinstated a worker who was fired ostensibly because of a general layoff of personnel whereas it appeared on trial that the real reason for his discharge was a critical remark which he had made at a factory meeting.

It may be doubted how effective Soviet legal propaganda is in making drugstore lawyers out of Ivan and Andrei. Much of law is by nature technical, requiring years of special training to understand. However, popular legal literature in the Soviet Union, which formerly was of a low quality, has improved very much in the years since Stalin's death. In any event, it is significant that these efforts are taken to make law comprehensible to the layman, and that the judges themselves are made vehicles of such education, being required to report back to their electors.

With 300,000 agitators active in the judiciary election campaign of 1949, virtually the entire electorate voted. Of the single slate of candidates, 53 per cent were not members of the Communist Party, and 39.2 per cent were women. Apparently at least 30 per cent, and probably more, had no legal education. It may thus be seen that not only did the elections have a "popular" flavor, but the lower courts themselves were "popular" in composition. A serious defect from the point of view of the quality of judicial administration, the lack of legal education of so many People's Judges nevertheless served to bring official law and popular law-consciousness closer together. The People's Judges chosen in 1957 were far better qualified professionally and politically. Nearly all had either higher or intermediate legal education and 93.9 per cent were members of the Communist Party.

In the conduct of trials, also, Soviet judges both on the higher and lower levels are supposed to be continually aware of the effect of their decisions upon the attitudes of the public. In an address on "The educational Significance of the Soviet Court," delivered and printed in 1947, I. T. Golyakov, then Chief Justice of the Supreme Court of the U.S.S.R., stated that "the publicity of our court [procedure] means the attraction of the widest public into the courts." For this purpose, he said, "the court arranges its sessions at such time as is most favorable for the toilers to attend." In addition the court may hold "demonstration trials" of important criminal cases in the enterprises and collective farms where the crimes were committed.

"Trying the case in great detail," Golyakov stated, "strictly observing the law, the court step by step discloses the whole picture of the crime or the civil dispute. It raises the explanations of the parties to a higher level, transforming the whole trial not into a spectacle, as the selfish bourgeois court does, but into a serious instructive school for educating those attending the session to observe and respect law and justice."

In a speech given in 1946, President Kalinin also stressed the role of the judge as a teacher. "As a good artist is able wonderfully to paint a landscape, so a skillful, politically developed judge brings to light during the judicial trial, during a particular, concrete case, all those internal processes that go on in our country." Every decision of the judge must therefore be "as convincing as it is sound," said Kalinin, "so that not only he himself and the people's assessors, but also all the persons attending the session should . . . understand [its] correctness."

From the earliest years of the Revolution, Soviet political leaders as well as Soviet jurists have stressed the educational role of the Soviet court in statements similar to those quoted above. In the years since Stalin's death the number of books, pamphlets, and articles devoted to this theme has, if anything, increased.

A still more important test, however, of the significance of the educational role of the Soviet court is in the actual law of procedure as applied in the trial of cases. Here it is necessary to recognize the points of similarity between Soviet procedure and that of other systems, in order to appreciate the points of difference.

Soviet criminal and civil procedure resembles Western procedure generally in providing for a bilateral hearing, in public, with oral testimony and the right of confrontation of witnesses, and with judgment based on rational as contrasted with purely formal proofs. Appeals may be taken. Parties may be represented by lawyers; in fact Soviet law goes so far as to provide that in criminal cases if the prosecution participates in a case the accused must have a lawyer. If he does not choose one, the court will appoint one.

CRIMINAL PROCEDURE

The most obvious difference between Soviet and Anglo-American criminal procedure lies in the emphasis placed by the Soviets upon pretrial investigation and upon the active participation of the court in the trial itself. Here Soviet law is in the continental European tradition. A preliminary examination is held, in which an examining magistrate (investigator) interrogates the accused and the witnesses and examines evidence prior to preparing the indictment, a document in which the charges and the evidence against the accused are stated in detail.

The 1961 R.S.F.S.R. Code of Criminal Procedure, like that which it replaced, does not provide any punishment for the accused for failing to cooperate at the pretrial examination. The investigator may not use violence, threats, or similar methods—without violating the law. He "does not have the right to refuse the request of the suspect, of the accused and his attorney [or of others involved in the case] to interrogate witnesses, or to have an expert examination, or to have investigations made for the collection of evidence if the facts or circumstances sought to be established may have significance for the case." The accused must be informed of his rights, including the right to state his side of the case during the pretrial investigation and to examine any part of the record, including adverse evidence of which he knows nothing. In the trial proper the prosecutor cannot introduce evidence not previously known to the defendant.

The Soviet system of preliminary investigation has three principal defects in comparison with its West European counterparts. First, appeals from abuses of pretrial procedure may be taken only to the Procuracy, not to the courts. Second, except for minors and persons with physical or mental defects, a suspect under investigation has no right to counsel until the investigation is completed and the indictment is presented to a preliminary session of the court for approval. Third, the time of detention for investigation, though normally limited to one month, may be extended by permission of higher authorities of the Procuracy up to nine months.

On the other hand, the Soviet system, like its counterparts in Western Europe, has the advantage that the indictment must disclose to the accused all the evidence to be used against him at the trial.

Mr. Justice Jackson, in describing his experiences at the Nuremberg trial of German war criminals, writes: "It was something of a shock to me to hear the Russian delegation object to our Anglo-American practice as not fair to the defendant. The point of the observation was this: we indict merely by charging the crime in general terms and then we produce the evidence at the trial. Their method requires that the defendant be given, as part of the indictment, all evidence to be used against him—both documents and the statements of witnesses. [Our] method, it is said, makes a criminal trial something of a game. This criticism is certainly not irrational."

At the trial, the burden of proof of the facts alleged in the indictment is on the prosecutor. However, the judge plays an active part in interrogating the defendant and the witnesses on both sides, and in calling his own impartial experts when necessary. Admissibility of evidence is left to the discretion of the court, though the verdict is supposed to be based on relevant evidence only.

As outlined in the code, Soviet criminal procedure has much in common with general European practice, which places more stress on "inquisitional" features and less on "accusatory" than does Anglo-American law. In a broader perspective, however, both Soviet and American criminal law are a mixture of the so-called inquisitional and accusatory systems. Our judges may and sometimes do interrogate witnesses; they may and sometimes do summon their own impartial experts to testify; they in fact "rule the court" by their decisions about the admission and exclusion of evidence. On·the Soviet side, on the other hand, the adversary features of the trial have been increasingly stressed. Both the prosecutor and the defense counsel question the witnesses and argue their respective cases, and the defendant also may put questions personally, at any time during the trial.

What is most significant about Soviet criminal procedure, however, is not its division into pretrial and trial stages and its emphasis on the leading role of the judge, but rather its educational or parental character, both in its adversary and in its inquisitional aspects. The mere fact that the prosecution and the defense are on an equal basis, each presenting its own side of the case, does not in itself deprive the trial of its educational or parental role. On the contrary, the fact that the parties defend their own rights may itself be a means of teaching them to assume and learn responsibility. On the other hand, the mere fact that the procedure is "inquisitional," with the judge determining the order of witnesses and himself interrogating them, does not in itself guarantee its educational or parental character. The judge may maintain complete formality, and may treat the parties in every way as independent adults.

The clue to the nature of both Soviet criminal and civil procedure lies in Article 3, paragraph 1, of the 1958 Fundamental Principles of Legislation on the Judicial Structure of the U.S.S.R. and the Union and Autonomous Republics:

> By all its activities the court shall educate the citizens of the U.S.S.R. in the spirit of devotion to the Motherland and the cause of communism in the spirit of strict and undeviating observance of Soviet laws, of care for socialist property, of labor discipline, of honesty toward public and social duty, of respect for the rights, honor, and dignity of citizens, for the rules of socialist common-life.

(A corresponding provision of the 1938 Judiciary Act omitted reference to "respect for the rights, honor, and dignity of citizens," and spoke of the "cause of socialism" instead of the "cause of communism," but was otherwise identical.)

In criminal procedure, both the pretrial investigation and the trial proper, and, in the trial, both the adversary and the inquisitional aspects, are designed to fulfill this educational purpose.

From the educational-parental standpoint, the following features of Soviet criminal procedure, though not necessarily uniquely Soviet, are noteworthy illustrations of a shift of emphasis which Soviet law as a whole has carried further than other modern systems.

1. The preliminary investigation is directed toward clarifying the entire situation in the mind of the accused as well as in the records of the investigator.

2. The "entire situation" sought to be clarified includes not merely the circumstances of the case, in the usual sense of that phrase, but also the whole "case history" of the accused, including any past misconduct, his attitude toward the Revolution, his entire motivation and orientation. In addition, the examiner is required to seek the answer to such questions as: Did the commission of the crime take place under coercion, threat, or by reason of economic strain? Was the alleged offender at that moment in a state of hunger or destitution? Was he influenced by extreme personal or family conditions? Was he in a state of strong excitement?

3. Upon indictment, the trial commences with the court's interrogation of the accused directed, again, to his entire biography. Whether or not he is a Party member, whether or not he has been in trouble before, whether or not he has earned rewards for outstanding achievement of any kind, whether or not he took an honorable part in the Great Fatherland War—these and similar questions make it clear that it is not simply the offensive act that is to be punished or exonerated, but the man himself.

4. It is the duty of the court to protect the accused against the consequences of his ignorance, to clarify to him his rights, to call expert witnesses in his behalf when needed whether or not he so requests.

5. On appeal the higher court not only reviews the entire case, both on the law and on the facts, but may also receive evidence not offered in the original trial.

6. The death of a convicted person does not prevent an appeal or a reopening of the case if newly discovered circumstances may lead to the rehabilitation of his reputation.

7. In imposing a sentence, the court has a large range of penalties from which to choose, including public censure, confiscation of all or part of the criminal's property, a money fine in the form of the monthly deduction of a certain percentage of the criminal's pay (so-called corrective labor tasks), prohibition to carry on a particular trade or profession, exile from the city, banishment to remote areas, as well as deprivation of liberty in corrective labor colonies and imprisonment. The punishments prescribed in the Criminal Code often leave to the court a very large leeway between the minimum and maximum. Also worth mentioning in this connection is the provision that punishment may be omitted altogether if the accused is not socially dangerous at the time of the trial. Before December, 1958, the discretionary power

of the court was also enhanced by the doctrine of analogy, despite the limitations imposed on that doctrine since the mid-1930's.

Behind these characteristic features of Soviet criminal procedure lies a new conception of the role of law. In the words of former Chief Justice Golyakov, "The most important function of the Socialist state is the fundamental remaking of the conscience of the people." The chief task of Soviet law, according to another prominent writer, is to educate the people to Communist social-consciousness, "ingrafting upon them high, noble feelings."

In 1947 a Soviet writer criticized the one-judge session established in 1940 for cases of absenteeism on the ground that it lacks "the strictness, officiality, and solemnity" of the regular three-judge court, and that "consequently the educational and deterrent significance of these judicial procedures is undoubtedly diminished."

Soviet criminal procedure deals with the "whole man," but it deals with him in a particular way, as a teacher or parent deals with a child. The court is interested in all aspects of his development, and especially in his mental and psychological orientation, because it is its task to try to "remake" him, or at least to make him behave. The Soviet judge may upbraid or counsel the accused, explaining to him what is right and what is wrong in a socialist society. Even if he is acquitted, the court may deliver an official "admonition," that is, a warning of the dangers involved in conduct which is in itself not criminal but which may lead to criminal activity. If he is convicted, the court imposes punishment as a sign of the state's disapproval or condemnation of both him and his criminal act. Punishment is intended, according to Soviet legal theory, to cause the criminal "a definite suffering." Thereby, it is implied, he will be at least purged and perhaps reformed.

It is not our intention to portray the Soviet criminal court as poles apart from the American criminal court. They have much in common. The difference is a subtle one. The Soviet criminal trial has the atmosphere not so much of our regular criminal courts as of our juvenile courts.

CIVIL PROCEDURE

There is a tendency on the part of Western writers on the Soviet Union to think of the Soviet legal system solely in terms of criminal law. Although criminal law does play a central role in the Soviet system, the importance of claims by one citizen against another (or against a state enterprise) should not be overlooked. Indeed, Soviet legal officials state that 85 per cent of the cases in the courts are civil cases. Most of these concern housing law, labor law, and family law, but many also concern personal injuries, personal property, inheritance, copyright, and other matters of civil law.

The implications of the concept of law as parent and teacher run throughout Soviet civil procedure as well. There is, for example, widespread opportunity for use by public agencies of what in American law is called inter-pleader—an action by a third party to have the conflicting rights of two other parties adjudicated. Thus a Soviet trade union may institute a suit in the name of a member against an employer, without the member's authorization. A local soviet may bring an action on an invalid contract in the name of one of the parties, in order to have determined its (the local soviet's) rights to any unjust enrichment. As we have already seen, the Procuracy may institute a civil suit between two parties if it considers that the "interests of the state or of the toilers" so require, and it may intervene in any case on behalf of either party, and may "protest" any decision to a higher court.

Moreover, once the case is before the court, not merely the issues litigated but any issue arising from the situation may be adjudicated. Also the court is required to certify to the Procuracy evidence of criminal activity revealed in a civil suit. As stated in a Soviet textbook: "In deciding the concrete property disputes of the parties, the court is obliged at the same time to clarify those economic and organizational inadequacies which create the situation out of which disputes arise. On the ground of the defects and inadequacies, established by the court, in the work of state, cooperative, and social organizations, special orders should be handed down (interlocutory orders) and directed to the corresponding organs."

The will of the parties as to the disposition of the case is not decisive, once the court has jurisdiction. Even if they choose to compromise, or if the plaintiff wishes to drop the action, the court may proceed to judgment. It may grant the defendant an unsought remedy against the plaintiff. It may give a remedy beyond the scope of the prayer for relief.

As in criminal procedure, the court in civil cases is concerned not merely with deciding the facts and issues before it, but also with clarifying them to the parties. This is expressed clearly in Article 16 of the Fundamentals of Civil Procedure of the U.S.S.R. and the Union Republics:

> It is the duty of the court, without limiting itself to materials and pleadings submitted, to take all measures provided by law for the detailed, full and objective elucidation of the real circumstances of the case, of the rights and duties of the parties.
>
> The court must explain to the persons taking part in the case their rights and duties, must warn of the consequences of committing or not committing procedural actions, and must render assistance to the persons taking part in the case in realizing their rights.

One is struck by the general informality of the Soviet civil trial. Behind this informality lies the educational and parental role of the court. As the atmosphere of the Soviet criminal trial approximates that of our juvenile courts, so the atmosphere of a Soviet civil suit may perhaps bear an analogy to that of our domestic relations courts.

PROCEDURE IN *Arbitrazh*

Although there is no pretrial investigation in civil suits generally, the procedure of *Arbitrazh* in intercorporate litigation is marked by a preliminary preparation of the case by the judge-arbiter. He studies in advance the materials and documents presented by the parties as well as supplementary materials received from them at his own request. He may summon officials of the disputing enterprises for preliminary explanation of any circumstances. He may join other parties as participants in the case on his own motion. He may investigate questions not raised by the complaint and answer, if such questions appear to him to be relevant.

Though now considered to be bound by the Code of Civil Procedure, *Arbitrazh* nevertheless proceeds even more informally and "parentally" than the regular courts. The hearings generally take place with only six participants—the judge-arbiter and his legal counsel, and a representative of each of the litigating enterprises together with the lawyers for each enterprise.

"The active creative role of the arbiter in the *Arbitrazh* procedure," according to one writer, "does not overshadow, however, the role of the disputing parties, does not diminish their activity in the defense of their interests. On the contrary, the rules of consideration of disputes by *Arbitrazh* give the parties a broad initiative and independence, require from the parties an active defense of their economic interests, in the struggle for the fulfillment of plan."

Here, too, however, as in criminal and civil procedure generally, the judicial contest is waged against the background of a more intimate relationship among the participants, a relationship more akin to that of a family than to that of an impersonal "civil" society.

If we look for an analogy in American law which will throw light on *Arbitrazh* procedure, we may find it in our proceedings in bankruptcy and corporate reorganization, where the judge-referee often makes his own "preliminary investigation" of the case, consulting personally in advance with the various parties involved, though the bankruptcy hearing itself is governed by the regular rules of evidence and procedure. Happily, the analogy bears out our thesis: the Soviet litigant is treated not as an independent and self-sufficient "individual" but rather as someone more helpless, more dependent, more to be protected, guided, and if necessary "reorganized."

*   *   *

20

OBSHCHESTVENNOST

GEORGE FEIFER

In one of the first reckless-driving cases in Dzerzhinsky district the accused driver was represented by two defenders, one a Remnant of the Past, the other a Harbinger of the Future, and this double defense, which I later saw often, is one of the idiosyncrasies of contemporary Soviet law that give it a socialist flavor.

The Past, a plump, middle-aged *Frau*, was counsel for the defense. Engaged by the driver's parents in the normal manner through her College of Advocates, she participated in the trial roughly in the way Russian lawyers have participated in trials for about a century.

The Future, a graying Trevor Howard, spoke too in the driver's cause even though he was not a lawyer at all but a senior driver at the defendant's taxi garage. He had the next shift at noon and came to court in his overalls. He is called an *"obshchestvenny* defender" and personifies one of the few Soviet innovations in trial procedure.

"Obshchestvennost" is one of the first Russian words to learn but one of the most difficult to render into English. Variously, "the community," "society," "the public" or "the opinion-makers" suggest its meaning. In Sovietese it has come to mean principally "public but nongovernmental," or "pertaining directly to the people." Thus the *obshchestvenny* defender in that case of reckless driving was neither a private figure nor a governmental one, and he represented not the defendant but a group of people: the defendant's community, the collective of drivers and mechanics at the taxi garage.

When the collective was informed of the accident and charges against one of its drivers, it scheduled a discussion of them for its next general

From George Feifer, *Justice in Moscow* (New York: Simon & Schuster, 1964), pp. 103–29. Copyright © 1964, by George Feifer. Reprinted by permission of Simon & Schuster, Inc., and the Harold Matson Company, Inc.

meeting. At the meeting the driver's character and working habits were informally reviewed, those who knew him best speaking up in turn from the floor. Most of his peers agreed that he was a steady, reliable worker who consistently fulfilled his work norms, and a good comrade who volunteered for social work around the garage. A mechanic mentioned that he had a fine record in the Soviet Army. Several drivers said that he had a solid family life. The trade union secretary reported that his driving had never before led to any incidents.

In the end, they voted to defend him—to ask the court to reinstate him in his job (he had been demoted to nondriving duties after the accident) and free him from punishment. And they elected the senior driver, who knew him well, to make their will known in court. I emphasize that it was *their* will because this was beyond the desires and control of the defendant. In almost all cases, an accused in Soviet law may refuse the services of a lawyer, but not of an *obshchestvenny* defender, because the latter represents the collective, not the defendant.

The *obshchestvenny* defender (he may be just as easily, it is important to remember, an *obshchestvenny* accuser) rarely knows much about the law, and although on paper he has almost the same procedural rights at the trial—to question, to petition, to comment, et cetera—as the professional lawyer, he rarely talks about it. Usually he talks simply about the accused as a man—his character, his rate of production, his attitude toward his work and his fellows, his family life, his crime in the perspective of his everyday life. It is an institutionalization of the "whole man" approach to the trial. For better or for worse, the defendant's community accompanies him to his day in court—almost always his working community, for Bolsheviks have always felt that a man's nature reveals itself most clearly at work.

Obshchestvennost has a venerable tradition in Soviet law, but it has come to life in the courtroom only in recent years. For—Soviet theorists explain—it is both symbol and agency of a society advancing toward a not-too-distant Communism where government and courts will have withered away, where physical coercion by the state will have become superfluous, where society will discipline itself—simply, without codes, lawyers, or appeals, without the cumbersome formal machinery, like courts, required by the state. It will all be done by *obshchestvennost* itself, by society, the community, the public.

Thus, we are told, the introduction of *obshchestvennost* to the courtroom is a movement forward in the direction of the Great Goal, a bridging of the temperamental distance (even in Soviet society, where state and people are one) between the complexity of state bureaucracy and the simple, natural habits of the collective.

About one trial in ten is attended by an *obshchestvennik*—a representative, in working clothes and with working-class speech, of factory, garage, warehouse, or department store—who takes his commission from the collective seriously. "Ivan Ivanovich is a fine (poor) worker; he has been praised (warned) many times; he is respected (disliked) by his fellow workers; he works hard (does not do his share) to fulfill the plan; he drinks moderately (intemperately); he lives a respectable (shameful) life; this incident is an accident, an excusable loss of control (a natural outcome of his deviant ways); he represents little social danger (his record shows that he is a constant annoyance and a menace); we ask the court to give him the minimum sentence and if possible hand him over to the collective for re-education (we think he deserves strict punishment)."

Judges are not conspicuously attentive when these standardized opinions are offered.

The participation of lay defenders and accusers in trials, and the street patrols of voluntary *druzhiniki* [People's Volunteers] to supplement the police, are but two phases in a massive campaign to draw *obshchestvennost* into the work of law enforcement. In the official declarations, "It is essential that the functions of maintaining social order and safety be discharged by *obshchestvenniye* organizations parallel with such state institutions as the police and the courts," and, "A constituent element in the building of Communism is the active participation of all *obshchestvennost* in the strengthening of socialist legality, the safe-guarding of the Soviet state and social order, the observance of state and labor discipline, and also in the elimination of despicable survivals of the past such as hooliganism, drunkenness, bribery, speculation, and similar vile actions."

Many are the forms—at least on paper—of participation by *obshchest-venniye* organizations. They aid the Procuracy, police, and investigative bodies in a variety of ways. They assume the duties of parole over minor offenders. They supply the lay assessors. They may petition for conditional sentences, or apply measures of social censure in lieu of criminal punishment. "The drawing of *obshchestvennost* into battle with crime," a Soviet jurist wrote recently, "is one of the most important and topical questions in the theory and practice of Soviet criminal procedure, because in the conditions of full-scale building of Communism there is taking place a transformation of socialist *étatism* into Communist *obshchestvennoye* self-administration."

One of the central tasks of *obshchestvennost* is, as one would expect, *prevention* of crime and of noncriminal violations of "communist norms," work discipline, "rules of socialist communal living," and so on. Preventive work, prophylactic work, protective work—these terms appear again and again in Soviet legal literature. And here the work of *obshchestvennost* coincides with another of the literature's central themes: the educative role of the court. For the Soviet court, say its makers, is primarily educative and only secondarily punitive. It teaches rather than punishes, persuades rather than coerces. Its principle task is to re-educate the errant and instruct the waverers; this is established by law.

Moscow courts fulfill their educative functions in a variety of ways. They open their doors to the public, lecture defendants and spectators directly and indirectly from the bench, and hold public evening seminars on crime prevention. But their principal teaching method is more straightforward. They simply take about a fifth of the criminal cases from court to the heart of *obshchestvennost*—to the headquarters of the collective whose members are involved in a crime. This institution is called a "traveling session," and I wanted to find out how it works.

One November day I followed three women, the judge, and two lay assessors, as they traveled—after lunch, on a four-kopek trolley ride— to a red-brick mill ten minutes from the courthouse. It was a printing plant of the Ministry of Communications, where the accused, a printer, and the two men he knifed in a drunken argument were employed. Court was to be held in a large hall that smelled like an old high school auditorium; it was the factory and trade union club, which in one form or another is an essential part of every Soviet organization. It is there that meetings are held, agitation is organized, elections are conducted, lectures are given, dances are held, and entertainment is presented—that the collective life is lived.

The auditorium was full when we arrived: About 700 employees in denim and work shoes (they were ready to start the evening shift at 4 P.M.) jammed the seats and aisles. The court occupied an improvised bench on the stage under the familiar red banner, "FORWARD TO THE VICTORY OF COMMUNISM!"; chairs and tables were arranged for procurator, defense counsel, and defendant in the space directly in front of the stage; and defendant and complainants sat in the first row of benches. It looked as if a school play, rather than a trial, was about to take place.

The crime itself was an "ordinary" one of drink and violence; the most unusual circumstance was the saving of a victim's slashed arm by a new English medical technique. How the trial was going to be conducted under those makeshift, gladiatorial conditions was what interested me most.

It seemed, when it was over, to have been conducted pretty much as it would have been in a regular courtroom, except that the speakers had sometimes to shout over the din of the crowd, and the judge had to rush a bit to free the auditorium by 5 P.M. Sometimes I had the uncomfortable impression that judge and procurator were at least as interested in making points to the audience as in picking the bones of the case, but the facts seemed open-and-shut in any event—no doubt just such cases are chosen for *obshchestvenny* consumption. Naturally, the dignity of the court was considerably compromised in the course of the noisy proceedings. As the afternoon wore on, the audience grew restless. There were sarcastic comments from the rear, then shouts, "*Nu*, enough!"; "Get to the sentence!"; "Finish with it, already!" The judge repeatedly pleaded and warned about the need for quiet. She was ignored. "Oh," a man yelled back at her, "I thought this was a general meeting where we can all talk. I didn't know it was a *court*."

Recollections of mob justice kept running through my thoughts, but this trial never deteriorated to that. And in the end, I felt that the concept of the traveling session was not without some appeal. Obvious unfairness by the court would have been resented by the public and would have defeated the purpose of the session. (The sentence *was* severe, but probably not much more so than it would have been in the courts.) The people around me on the benches knew the accused and his victims—although they knew nothing about the educative role of the court—and felt it a good idea that the trial was held in the factory, because it was a "community affair."

Toward the accused, the sentiment of the audience was mixed. The assemblage groaned when it heard at the outset that he had been convicted before ("He's simply a criminal!"), booed when he testified that he remembered nothing about the stabbings, and roared in approval when the procurator shouted that the man was dangerous and demanded six years' detention. (For five minutes after the procurator's speech, order could not be restored; some of the spectators were shouting, "Six years is too little!") On the other hand, the audience gushed with sympathy when it heard about the hard times of his childhood, applauded lengthily when fellow workers testified that he was a highly regarded toiler, cheered when counsel said that two years' confinement would be enough, and remained respectfully silent when the defendant, in a final statement, said that he knew he must be punished, but begged for indulgence. It was the typical reaction of a Russian theater audience: emotional, naïve, uninhibited, and wildly fluctuating to the action of the moment.

A stunning roar followed the reading of the sentence—five years—but it seemed to be both approving and disapproving: "Yes!"; "No!"; "Ridiculous!"; "Correct!"; "Too little!"; "Too much!" I tried to get closer for a final word with the judge but was carried out the door and to the street by the throng, which started its surge at the word "five." . . .

The great bulk of *obshchestvennost's* work is done on the fringes of the judicial system, not at its innards. An ever growing system of quasi-judicial innovations in method and means is being engineered in order to free Soviet society of all those violations of ethics, morality, and clean living which, although not serious enough to be called crimes, must be eliminated before Communism is reached. In this noble undertaking, the brunt of the job is assigned to *obshchestvennost*, for it is a job to which *obshchestvennost*, with its virtues of flexibility and freedom from the formal and traditional procedures demanded of state agencies, is well suited.

Of all of *obshchestvennost's* quasi-legal, peripheral operations, an invention called the Comradely Court interested me most. This is an authentic Soviet invention; more than anything else judicial it seemed to suggest revolutionary ideology. Its function is to transform bourgeous decadence into socialist virtue. The very name, *Tovarish-*

chesky Sud, suggested Bolshevism. As soon as I unpacked in Moscow I set out to watch a session.

To find a session, however, turned out to be a difficult job, and the fact that I searched for months before finding one and then found three in five days speaks of their nature. For there are hundreds, perhaps thousands, of Comradely Courts in the city but they convene only when a comrade goes astray—which no one can predict. . . .

I ought to mention, meanwhile, something about the judicial characteristics of the Comradely Court. For—as I have been suggesting— it is not a court at all; not, at least, a court in the normal sense. It stands apart from the hierarchy of the regular court system, apart from the criminal and procedural codes of the Russian Republic and all they encompass. In fact, it stands apart from crime itself, dealing instead with "survivals of capitalism," "bourgeois views and morals," "antisocial attitudes," "violations of the socialist order," and "instances of misbehavior." And it stands apart from criminal punishment—applying only "measures of public influence."

A miniature town meeting; a group of neighbors or fellow workers, comrades; *obshchestvennost;* an attempt to set the deviant straight without recourse to the law; one of the Party's myriad methods of mobilizing public opinion, shaping the New Soviet Man, implementing the Moral Code of the Builders of Communism; an attempt to diminish drinking, squabbling, and truancy from work; an organ of *socialist discipline*—the Comradely Court is all these things. "Comradely Courts promote Communist education and upbringing of the masses, strengthen work discipline, increase the productivity of labor—" They operate in factories, institutions, organizations, universities, collective farms, villages, apartment houses, et cetera; members of the court are chosen at general meetings of the collective and serve one year.

Their jurisdiction is limited: violation of labor discipline (truancy and lateness, sloppy work, spoilage); drunkenness and undignified behavior in public places or at work; undignified attitudes toward women or parents, and neglect of children; insults and swearing; damage to trees, greenery, and public property; violation of rules in shared apartments and dormitories; property squabbles involving less than fifty rubles; administrative and petty violations of the law if police, procurator, or court considers transfer of the case to a Comradely Court advisable; other antisocial actions, and so on.

Nothing major, in a word. I suppose for this reason the Comradely Court should be thought of as lower than the People's Court (to which it may turn for advice), although in another sense it is higher than the Supreme Court of the U.S.S.R. For, we are told, it is a prototype of the court of the future: under Communism something like the Comradely Court will settle—simply, in an *obshchestvennoye* way—any minor social disputes that still exist.

Comradely Courts too are an old idea: In the 1920's they were established on collective farms, in housing developments, and especially in factories to deal with minor violations of labor discipline. But the concept was implemented with enthusiasm only in the late 1950's, when Chairman Khrushchev announced the final march on Communism.

At last I saw it. "ON TUESDAY, APRIL 10, 1962, AT 1900, THERE WILL BE A SESSION OF THE COMRADELY COURT OF HOUSING BUREAU NUMBER 5 OF LENINSKY DISTRICT TO HEAR THE CASE OF CITIZENESS KLYUCHKOVA IN THE KRASNY UGOLOK IN THE COURTYARD OF 2b LENINSKY PROSPEKT. ALL COMRADES ARE INVITED." . . .

Sometime after seven o'clock the session began. Court was convened by an elderly woman who sat behind one of the tables. (It turned out that she was a former People's Court judge, retired on pension and filling her time with socially useful work.) To her left was another elderly woman, to her right, an elderly man. Nearby sat an ancient secretary. I was the youngest person there, by perhaps a score of years.

"Will you make it up?" the chairman asked the parties, not yet identified.

"Let's hear the case!" shouted a woman from the rear. "Read the complaint! Get on with it!"

"All right," said the chairman, and she began by reading a tattered letter from one Sobeleva, the complainant.

Sobeleva had written (in her own rules of grammar) roughly this: "Members of our Comradely Court, I ask you to examine the case of Federovna, the woman living with me in our apartment. Last February I was in the hospital recuperating. As soon as I returned, Federovna came to me and demanded money for the electricity and gas bill. [Her share came to twenty-eight kopeks.] When I said, 'No, I was in the hospital that month,' she started insulting me in the filthiest language. It was frightful. This is not the first time she behaved like an animal; you can expect only all sorts of unpleasantness from her mouth. Once she was about to beat me with her fists Her son stopped her just in time. She constantly swears and insults me vilely, as well as all the others in our apartment. To live with her is to live in filth. I ask that the Comradely Court stop her from making my life miserable."

"What else can you add to your complaint, Sobeleva?" asked the chairman when she had finished reading the note.

"Just what I wrote," answered a hurt voice. Sobeleva, a heavy-set housewife, stood up.

"On what day did this last incident take place?"

"I can't remember—sometime in March. I know it was my day of *dezhurstvo* [duty day]." (In shared apartments, as in dormitories and at work, everyone takes a turn cleaning the common bathroom, kitchen and halls.)

At the word *dezhurstvo*, there was an explosion. Federovna, the defendant, who could have been Sobeleva's twin, began shrieking from the other side of the room. "*Dezhurstvo!* Why don't you say anything about your refusing to clean up, you obscenity? How many times did you skip *dezhurstvo?* How many times did I have to clean up for you? You slanderer!" She shot a look of Amazon fury at Sobeleva and advanced a step.

Sobeleva moved back a pace. "I never skipped my *dezhurstvo*. Once, just after I left the hospital. What are you trying to invent, you liar and hussy?"

"*You're* the liar. What about before? What about this winter? You worm, you sneaked out of your turn."

"I washed the floors for three weeks this winter—"

"Shut up. You never washed. Never. We had to do it for you whenever it was your turn."

"I washed in February, I did my—"

"You did not, you refused. And *you* have the gall to complain about *me!*"

After floors, the screams shifted to cleaning rags and cooking smells, while the chairman followed from side to side as if at a tennis match. At last she broke in: "All right comrades, please calm down. *Dezhurstvo* is not the point now; we have gathered to discuss the matter of insults. Federovna, what do you say about that?"

Federovna had a great deal to say. About her son, whom, she screeched, Sobeleva did all in her power to prevent from studying; about her wash, which Sobeleva took from the line while still wet; about the kitchen, which Sobeleva forbade to be used after 11 P.M., although the rules said it should be open until midnight. ("You lie, you lie," Sobeleva now was chanting.) About how that old spinster Sobeleva was impossible to live with because she had no respect for working people and constantly ignored or insulted everyone around her.

The chairman begged her to come to the issue of the gas and electricity bill.

"I simply asked her to pay her share. Twenty-eight kopeks—that's the big deal. She makes a scandal for a kopek, her stinginess is unbelievable. I never said an insulting word to that woman. She insulted *me*. She called me a—excuse the word—prostitute—"

"Tell them what you called *me*, you liar."

"I never called you anything, you shameless slanderer. Why don't you tell them about the filthy language you use? I won't repeat it. You are an impossible egotist—you, an *obshchestvennitsa* [community worker], who is supposed to set an example—"

By this time they were drowned out by the cackling of the spectators, who took sides hotly, defending one, attacking the other. The grandmother-neighbors, almost as aroused as Sobeleva and Federovna themselves (they were all cut from the same homespun cloth), made a deafening din. Later, when something like order had been restored, a few witnesses tried to be heard: Federovna's husband ("Sobeleva is unendurable, she squabbles about everything, every petty little thing") and Mikhailovskaya, a youngish woman who shared the apartment ("I've quarreled with the Federovs too, that's unavoidable, unfortunately,

in one apartment; but Sobeleva fights with *everyone* about *everything*").
The chairman studiously ignored the catcall interruptions from the
floor.

"You forget *my* witness," whined Sobeleva.

"Oh yes, the other witness."

The other witness was the apartment house chairman. He took
Sobeleva's side. "The Federovs are hotheaded, and I heard that Federovna
has been reprimanded at work. Once she swore at me."

One of the pecularities of the Comradely Court is open testimony:
Anyone present is entitled to stand and speak to the issue or around it.
When the chairman opened the floor to the neighbors—"Does anyone
want to express himself?"—the friends of one side and the other used
this rare chance to show their loyalty and pettiness. "Sobeleva keeps
a dirty room." "Federovna pushes her son too hard." "I've lived here
since 1933. Sobeleva is the best neighbor of all." "I worked in a hospital,
I know people. Federovna is an honest person." "Sobeleva swears."
"Federovna spits." While the old women were having their say, the
protagonists continued to shake fists at one another.

Pity the poor chairman—she was nonplused. "It's hard to say who
is lying here and who is not, I don't know *whom* to believe—"

After about an hour she said she thought that the court had better
retire for deliberation. The three went behind a flimsy curtain in a
corner of the room, and soon their perplexed voices could be heard,
since by that time the spectators and partisans had calmed down
somewhat.

Everyone seemed to have lost interest by the time (after 9 P.M.)
the verdict was read. The court concluded that the women were equally
at fault and that their arguments could be easily, amicably resolved.
It encouraged them to face their problems gracefully, in a socialist,
comradely spirit, and warned that further scandals would be punished
strictly. There was no punishment and no censure; the twenty-eight–
kopek debt was divided in half. A cackle of comments followed the
decision—"Correct!" "Very good!" "Sensible!"—and Sobeleva and Federovna looked at each other with shy, tentative smiles.

I felt sadly swindled as I pushed my way out of the airless *krasny
ugolok*. Was *that* a Comradely Court? Were those petty quibblings
typical of an institution about which I had read so many indignant
articles containing so many sinister adjectives in Western journals?
They seemed to be, for later I saw four more Comradely Courts and
none was more exciting, more politically significant, or more ideologically
directed than the Sobeleva-Fedorovna squabble. All involved petty personal
conflicts, the kind that might have been heard in Family Court in
New York and disposed of similarly, if less speedily. . . .

The workings of official *obshchestvennost* still puzzle me in many
ways.

How is it run? On paper, members of Comradely Courts and *obshchestvenniye* accusers and defendants are the people next door; they are

elected at open general meetings of their respective collectives—the apartment-house group or the trade union local. But in practice? I never attended any of their election meetings . . . but from what I learned from firsthand sources they do *not* follow the ordinary Soviet pattern of predetermined "elections." On the lowest level of public affairs in Moscow—trade union and Young Communist committees, local boards, factory and apartment-house meetings—genuinely democratic procedures seem to be followed: More than one candidate is nominated, opinions and proposals are offered, and the voting is free and not unanimous. The Young Communist group of the Juridical Faculty provided a vivid example of this democracy while I was there. At one of its general meetings, the committee—that is, the activist, official leadership—recommended the expulsion of a nonconformist student for poor studies and wild behavior, and in the course of an hour's discussion it furiously assailed him. Yet the rank and file voted almost unanimously not to expel him.

"Do you understand how *obshchestvennost* works?" an old woman, a member of the Comradely Court, asked me. "The people decide. That's democracy. It's the drawing of the people into the administration of public affairs. It's truly people's justice." And indeed, everyone I knew who attended these meetings assured me that at this level the rank and file *does* decide. It is not a rubber stamp.

On the other hand, the one thing most clear from a year's stay in Moscow is the utter absence of "public" or "community" apart from the Party. In Russia, "public opinion" in the professional sense means Party opinion writ into appropriate forms. Nothing can be openly done or expressed against the Party's will. It is the single cohesive element within society. The Party's part in introducing *obshchestvennost* into the law could not have been more prominent; the very concept was a Party invention.

The "opinion-makers," the organizers, the chairmen, the leaders of *obshchestvenniye* organizations are almost always Party members specifically designated by the Party to conduct that kind of work; and even those who are not Party members are responsible to the Party apparatus. One trip to a district Party headquarters is enough to discover that: Party headquarters is the general staff. The Party's direction and coordination is above-board, since in Soviet public life the Party, as the "leading core of all organizations of the working people, both public and state" (according to the Constitution), is *supposed* to coordinate. And so, it would be very easy for the Party to rig the elections, predetermine the decisions of the meetings, and dictate the sentences in the Comradely Courts. The Party's wish to punish or censure a man is a command to the leadership of the local group. Thus, the great campaign to draw *obshchestvennost* into the administration of the law, far from being democratization of public life, may be the very opposite—a gimmick, a cynical and flexible, because so informal, instrument of Party dictatorship.

But I do not believe that that is the practice now in most individual cases. No one ever mentioned to me an instance of direct Party inter-ference, and from what I saw, there was too much confusion and un-certainty behind the desk, too much genuine debate in the auditoriums, and too little preparation on paper to suggest prearrangement. And too little importance in the cases. I saw no *overt* signs of rigging. My free-speaking acquaintances thought it made better sense for the Party to let matters take their own course in these minor affairs—and thus engage the interest of the "broad masses"—than to decide the issues beforehand. And so, the Party actually seems to be encouraging the rudiments of grass-roots democracy in *obshchestvennost*. There may be pressure by higher-ups in some cases to make an example of some poor devil, but on the whole the refreshing experience of a general meeting run by majority rule no doubt stimulates healthy thoughts in the Soviet body politic.

There is, too, a legal question. The cardinal principle of all civilized legal theory—that no one be subjected to criminal penalty except by a duly constituted court after an impartial investigation conducted ac-cording to established procedure—is embodied in the Soviet Fundamentals of Criminal Procedure; but here, in violation of that canon, are the Comradely Courts, imposing fines and publishing censures (no matter that these are called "social measures" rather than "punishment") on the basis of some lesser procedure. No doubt this is potentially dangerous to socialist legality . . . but again, the practice seemed to me much less sinister than the theories about it. A warning, a reprimand, a fine of ten rubles; at most the Comradely Courts refer a serious case to the People's Courts, where regular criminal laws apply. The sanctions at the disposal of the Comradely Courts are simply too insignificant to warrant indignation over their departure from traditional procedure.

Besides, what ought to be done with the women who fight in bath-rooms and kitchens? Should they be sent to the regular courts under criminal charge? To a domestic-relations counselor? Left alone to pull each other's hair and scream away the neighbors' sleep? The Comradely Court does not seem an absurd alternative. Though probably less effective than Soviet legislators had hoped it would be, it is not really an objec-tionable way—except to legal purists—to try to smooth out these petty squabbles and disorders.

*   *   *

21

THE LAWYER AND SOVIET SOCIETY

ANDREAS BILINSKY

The essential characteristic of the indpendent lawyer's profession is that it normally brings him into contact with the state agencies of judicial administration—public prosecutors, investigating magistrates, and the courts—as the advocate, not of his own rights, but of the rights and interests of his client. In a state founded upon the principle that every individual possesses certain inherent rights which can be made to prevail even against the interests of the state itself the lawyer naturally plays a much broader and more effective role than he does in a state which negates the existence of any such inherent rights and recognizes the "rights and legal interests" of the citizen only insofar as they coincide with the interests of the state or society. The latter is the case in a "socialist" state of the Soviet type.

In the absolutist Russia of the first half of the nineteenth century, there was no such institution as an organized bar, and the defense of an accused in criminal proceedings was part of the duties of the state prosecutor. This remained the situation until the Judicial Reform of 1864, which made provision for so-called sworn attorneys-at-law as members of an independent legal profession. They protected the interests of private parties in civil litigations and took charge of the defense in criminal prosecutions. The requirements for eligibility to the bar were an unblemished personal record, legal training through the university level, and five years of preparatory practice in the office of a public prosecutor or an already accredited attorney. For his services, an attorney received fees as fixed either at his own discretion or by agreement with his client. Accredited attorneys as a group were bound together in a self-governing association, whose council numbered among its functions the admission

Reprinted from *Problems of Communism*, March-April, 1965, pp. 62–71. Footnotes citing Russian-language sources are omitted.

of new candidates to the profession. It was from the ranks of these professional lawyers that most of the champions of political and economic
liberalism in pre-Revolutionary Russia sprang.

In addition to the sworn attorney-at-law, there were also so-called private
attorneys. The latter were not university-trained but were permitted to act
as legal representatives in court trials because of the scarcity of fully
qualified lawyers. Close relatives of the parties to trial proceedings also
were allowed to act as their authorized representatives in the courts. In
justice-of-the-peace courts, every private citizen had the right to act as
attorney in three cases per year.[1]

THE POST-REVOLUTIONARY PERIOD

The liberal trend that manifested itself in the development of Russian
legal institutions subsequent to the 1864 reform was interrupted by the
overthrow of the Tsarist regime in 1917. Viewing the judicial organs of the
"bourgeois" state as part of its "bureaucratic apparatus," the Bolsheviks
smashed the Tsarist courts and abolished both the state procuracy (public prosecutors) and the organized bar. The courts were to be replaced
by tribunals chosen by "society," and the problem of prosecution and defense was to be resolved on a social basis.[2]

Initially, a move was made to confer the functions of prosecution and
defense on any private citizens who entered their names on voluntary
lists of "social" prosecutors and defenders. However, after this scheme
failed, the courts were provided in 1918 with locally appointed panels
of "legal representatives," which were to supply both prosecutors and
defense counsels. An accused was to be allowed free choice of a defense
counsel from these panels. This experiment, too, however, proved a failure.
As D. I. Kursky, then People's Commissar of Justice, observed, one of
the reasons was that

> there were few attorneys-at-law and it was impossible to accept into their
> ranks skilled professionals of the bourgeois bar who at that time stood
> without exception on the side of the enemies of the working class. As a
> result, the college of legal representatives turned into a poor copy of the
> former association of sworn attorneys-at-law.

In the search for a "socialist" solution of the problem of legal representation, two opposing viewpoints emerged. One held that defense attorneys (as well as prosecutors and court judges) should be "men of the
people," the other that they should be government officials. The latter
view prevailed in the decree of November 30, 1918, which provided that

---

[1] Lothar Schulz, *Russische Rechtsgeschichte* (History of Law in Russia) (Lahr:
Moritz Schauenburg, 1951), pp. 209 ff.

[2] For a detailed account of the early development of Soviet judicial institutions, see
John N. Hazard, *Settling Disputes in Soviet Society* (New York: Columbia University
Press, 1960).

all district and provincial executive committees should set up "colleges of defense counsels" who would be state functionaries drawing salaries similar to those of people's judges. Conduct of the defense in court trials was made their official duty. However, since criminal trials in the people's courts were conducted without regard for formal rules, it became the dominant view that the institution of defense counsel was altogether superfluous.

The breakdown of "war communism" and the substitution of the so-called new economic policy (NEP), involving a restoration of private enterprise and the free market, brought about a basic reform of the judicial system. The "withering away of law" was postponed indefinitely and a whole series of new legal codes drawn up—criminal and civil codes, codes of criminal and civil procedure, a labor code, a family code, and so on. This meant that judges and state attorneys would require thorough legal training in order to be able to deal with cases according to the new laws. The reform did not go so far as to abolish the popular election of judges lest this detract from the "socialist" character of the courts; however, judges were now to be "elected" from a cadre of nominees designated by the Party apparatus. And so, there was a gradual return to a judiciary organized along West European lines, with a supreme court at the apex.

In May, 1922, the Procuracy was established as a state organ with the following features: (1) It was an instrument of the central power, in contrast to the courts, which were considered "local" agencies; (2) its function was to ensure the uniform interpretation of, and compliance with, standards of revolutionary legality laid down for the entire state; and (3) it was strongly centralized and removed from local and personal influences. Thus, the initial experiments in "socializing" the judicial system ended in total failure, producing as a necessary consequence a change of attitude toward a professional bar.

Simultaneously with the establishment of the Procuracy, a "Law Regarding the Bar" was enacted in May, 1922, providing for a structure and organization reminiscent of the old Czarist bar. The personnel of the new bar consisted mostly of former "sworn attorneys-at-law," who henceforth were regarded as members of a free profession. They belonged to their own autonomous professional organizations—the so-called colleges of defense attorneys—governed by elected presidiums which, as part of their functions, exercised disciplinary authority and passed on the admission of new candidates to the bar.

The colleges were subjected to some degree of supervision by the provincial executive committees, which were empowered to pass on their membership and to act as appellate bodies in case of complaints against decisions of the presidiums. From 1922 to 1924, the colleges remained entirely independent of the courts, but in 1924 the appellate function of the executive committees was transferred to the provincial courts. Members of the colleges carried on what was primarily an "individual" (i.e., private) practice conducted in their own offices with a measure of official support (e.g., in the form of lower taxes and allotments of office space). Their fees were regulated by schedules fixed by the college presidiums and approved by the provincial courts.

Parallel with their private practice, members of the colleges were also required to provide so-called legal consultation services as a public duty. These services were organized by the college presidiums and were performed mostly by young lawyers just beginning their careers. As the services were used mainly in charity cases, however, they did not compete with the lawyers' "individual practice."

As the situation then stood, members of the bar found a fairly broad field for the practice of their profession. They were almost without exception non–Party members, as Party members were forbidden to engage in private law practice. Even so, their earnings as independent lawyers were approximately twice or three times the salaries of judges and state attorneys.

"COLLECTIVIZATION" OF THE BAR

The favorable situation of the professional bar did not last long. After the launching of the First Five-Year Plan, the regime was determined to press ahead with the building of a collectivized economy and to use the full power of the state to ensure fulfillment of the plan and eliminate any hindrances in the path of that objective. This meant the transformation of the organs of justice, particularly the courts and the state procuracy, into political instruments required to function not according to abstract truth and justice, but first of all on the basis of political expediency. What was politically expedient in the existing situation was decided, centrally, by the top leadership of the Party and, locally, by the Party apparatus. Within this apparatus was a special department for administrative organs which saw to it that judicial positions were filled by loyal Party supporters.

This changed concept of the role of judicial administration led to a questioning of the existing form of criminal trial, with its dualism of prosecution and defense. In reality, this questioning was aimed against the independent bar, and as part of the campaign a public discussion was organized in 1928 at the Theater of the Revolution in Moscow to deal with the question, "Is there really any need for a defense?" On this occasion, Soviet justice officials . . . argued for the abolition of the colleges of defense attorneys on the ground that this institution was "inconsistent with the mission of Soviet justice and an impediment to socialist construction."

The opposition, however, was not carried to the point of abolishing the colleges. It may be recalled that at this time there also was a move in favor of abolishing civil contracts on the ground that they were meaningless in relations between state-owned enterprises; but this idea was dropped when it was recognized that contracts and the operation of civil law could provide a valuable means of ensuring the fulfillment of the state's economic plans. Similarly, with respect to criminal trials, it was realized that a defense attorney could play a positive role as long as he carried out his function in court so as to serve the political objectives of the state.

To assure this subordination to state political goals, a reorganization of the professional bar was begun in 1928 and largely completed by 1930. As in agriculture, the regime resorted to the most arbitrary methods in order to impose "collectivization" on the legal profession: independent lawyers were burdened with additional taxes, frequently denied office space, and subjected to other forms of harassment designed to force them to give up private practice. Legal defense activity was centered much more than before in the collectives of defense attorneys: Instead of receiving their power of attorney directly from the client, individual members were ordered by the collective to assume specific defense assignments, and fees were paid to the collective instead of to the individual attorneys. About 50 per cent of the income of the collective was distributed among its members as compensation, the remainder being allocated for other purposes.

The collectivization of the bar did not, however, alter the thinking of professional lawyers or their approach to legal questions. They viewed the actions of the regime as a sort of terror which they could not and dared not resist lest they be completely disbarred from practicing their profession. This attitude of ill-concealed hostility on the part of many members of the defense attorneys' collectives, which included a substantial proportion of "old" (pre-Revolutionary) lawyers, did not escape the attention of the Party authorities, and it is not surprising that between 1930 and 1939 many reputedly "anti-Soviet" lawyers fell victim to systematic purges. At the same time, various concrete measures were taken with a view to developing a new generation of "true Soviet" lawyers.

Many of the U.S.S.R.'s prominent judicial officials joined in the debate concerning the proper position and role of the Soviet lawyer. Among them, the late Andrei Vyshinsky, Procurator General under Stalin, must be regarded as the chief formulator of the professional lawyer's function in the Soviet system of justice. In his *Revolutionary Jurisprudence and the Tasks of Soviet Advocates*, published in 1934, he called upon defense attorneys to bear in mind that what transpires in the courtroom is interlinked with the sociopolitical forces outside and itself develops into a definite political force. Specially noteworthy was Vyshinsky's address to the Moscow Congress of Members of the Lawyer's Collegium in 1936, in which he pointed to the great importance of the defense in court trials and the special character of the defense counsel's function in criminal cases. A court, he said, could not consider a case solely from the viewpoint of the prosecution. The prosecutor's function was to see that the law was obeyed; on the other hand, the defense counsel, though also obligated to uphold the law, had the basic function of assisting the accused—a role that was especially necessary in complex criminal cases. But, Vyshinsky added, the function of the defense counsel was not simply to defend the accused, just as the prosecutor did not appear in court solely in support of the indictment: Both were "parties" to the trial, and their common task was to clarify the facts of the case from all angles.

Thus, Vyshinsky started from the premise that the state was interested solely in convicting the guilty. In his view, it was the task of the court to bring out the substantive truth in a trial. From this standpoint, the function of the defense was no less important than that of the prosecution: The defense attorney was considered, in effect, an "aide" to the court.

In August, 1939, a new "Law Regarding the Bar" redefined the position of the colleges of attorneys. This law remained in force until July 25, 1962, when new regulations were promulgated for the R.S.F.S.R. The new regulations, however, differed from those of 1939 only in details and did not alter the structure or duties of the colleges.

Each oblast has its own college of attorneys. Under the 1962 regulations, the colleges are authorized to provide legal assistance and representation not only to individual citizens but also to state enterprises and organizations. However, their main activity centers in legal assistance to the general public in the form of consultation (advice, information, explanations, etc.); preparation of petitions, complaints and other legal documents requested by citizens; defense of the accused in criminal trials; and representation of the ligitants in civil court actions.

The colleges provide these services through legal consultation centers established at the seats of *raions* and in cities. A citizen in need of legal assistance applies to one of these centers, where he is assigned a lawyer upon payment of a fee fixed by schedule. In some cases, if the head of the center is agreeable, the client may have a particular lawyer assigned to him. The lawyers receive their compensation not from the clients but from the center. Their share is about 70 percent of the fees paid, the remaining 30 percent being retained for the needs of the center. The colleges are regarded as "social organizations" and "voluntary" associations of persons engaged in legal work, and they serve in a sense as the lawyers' professional societies. Their organization, leadership, and activities are controlled by the executive committees of oblast soviets and ultimately by the appropriate organs of the Union republics.[3]

Present Soviet regulations governing the bar stipulate that, in general, a person must have completed formal judicial training on the university level, plus two years of practical work in some branch of the judicial administration, in order to be admitted to practice as an attorney. The colleges of attorneys can, however, accept as candidates persons with the required legal training but without two years of practical experience; such persons must work as apprentices for at least six months before they can be admitted as full members of the college. Also, in exceptional cases, persons without university legal training can be admitted provided they have had at least five years of experience working in state judicial organs;

[3] Ultimate control was formerly exercised by the Ministries of Justice of the Union republics; today it is exercised either by the Councils of Ministers of the Union republics or, as in the R.S.F.S.R., by the Law Commission of the Council of Ministers.

however, their admission must have the concurrence of the oblast executive committee.

Until mid-1964 university training in law lasted five years, but the duration of the course has since been shortened to four and a half years. The curriculum prescribed by the Ministry of Higher Education for university law schools and institutes of law comprises, among others: foundations of Marxism-Leninism; political economy; dialectical and historical materialism; logic; Latin and foreign languages; political and legal theory; history of government and law; history of Soviet government and law; history of political science; foundations of Roman private law; and different branches of Soviet law such as constitutional law, administrative law, fiscal law, criminal law and criminology, etc.

It is through the curriculum described above, supplemented by the required period of practical work experience in state judicial organs or as candidate members of an attorneys' college, that the regime has sought since the 1930's to develop a body of "true Soviet lawyers."

STALINIST PRACTICES

After the failure of the initial experiment in "socialized" justice, the Soviet judicial system was organized within the framework of a state bureaucracy. The bar, it is true, formed a supposedly autonomous branch of the machinery of justice, but its members, in fact, exerted very little influence on the decisions of the courts in the 1930's. In contrast to the lack of qualifications on the part of many state prosecutors, and especially judges, the ranks of professional attorneys contained a high proportion of trained jurists; however, their superior training availed them little in view of the nihilistic Communist ideological conception of the law as a bourgeois institution.

The relegation of professional attorneys to the position of mere supernumeraries in the courts of Stalin's day may be ascribed to a number of factors:

(1) In this period the organs of justice were officially regarded as weapons to be used in waging the struggle against class enemies. As a consequence, a defense attorney could scarcely dare to oppose the specifications of an indictment lest he be suspected of defending a class enemy. Moreover, public prosecutors and judges were, almost without exception, Party members, and even the people's assessors sitting as members of the court dared not oppose them. On the other hand, attorneys generally were not Party members except for those who held executive positions in the attorneys' colleges.

(2) Cases involving political crimes were tried by regional courts or by military tribunals under special provisions (Chapter IV) of the Code of Criminal Procedure, which substantially limited the right of the accused to a defense. Also, only a small number of attorneys were authorized to act as defense counsels in political trials: According to A. Simyonov, only

fifty out of a total of approximately 1,500 attorneys in Moscow had such authorization. When they did appear in political trials, moreover, they were expected to give evidence of their loyalty to the Bolshevik regime, often with the result that, instead of defending the accused, they joined the prosecution in heaping accusations on him.

(3) The public prosecutor's office, which was fully subservient to the organs of state security, enjoyed a complete monopoly of the pretrial in vestigation of cases, neither the defense nor the court being allowed access to the proceedings at this stage. After the pretrial investigation was complete, the case was referred to the court for a so-called preparatory hearing. Until the mid-1920's, there was a conflict of views as to whether the transfer of a case to the court was a function of the court itself or of the prosecutor. The theoreticians of the Stalinist era argued that to assign this power to the court would imply a lack of confidence in the prosecu- tion, and that the court would then be duplicating the function of the prosecution in controlling the work of the investigative agencies. This viewpoint was upheld by a resolution of the All-Russian Central Executive Committee and of the R.S.F.S.R. Council of People's Commissars, dated October 20, 1929. From that time on, for all practical purposes, cases were decided at the preliminary stage, without the participation of the accused or his defense counsel, and the main trial proceedings in court became largely a formal show for the purpose of influencing the masses.

(4) At the "preparatory hearing," it was also up to the court to decide whether to hold the formal trial with or without the participation of prosecution and defense. If it adopted the latter course, the court in effect assumed the role of prosecutor, deciding at the preparatory hearing how the case would be disposed of. In so doing, the court proceeded from the presumption not of the accused's innocence, but of his guilt, because the prosecution—representing the overriding authority of the state—had al- ready found the accused person guilty in its indictment.

(5) Not least important was Vyshinsky's theory which defined "sub- stantive truth" as the highest degree of probability. A mere confession by the accused was enough to convict him and bring about his punishment. This theory was designed to serve the political purposes of the "class struggle," and its practical effect was to make it more difficult for a de- fense attorney to prove the innocence of his client.

FUNCTIONS OF THE DEFENSE ATTORNEY

Even before Stalin's death the position of the attorney in the judicial process became the subject of fresh controversy among Soviet legal schol- ars. As mentioned earlier, the official doctrine, as formulated by Vyshin- sky in the 1930's, held that the attorney for the defense was an "aide" to the court. Professor Mikhail A. Cheltsov, of Moscow University, still upheld this doctrine as late as 1951, arguing that the law recognized the participation of defense counsel in trial proceedings as fundamentally necessary to assist the court in achieving a more complete clarification of the case under trial. On the other hand, a different view was put forward by another leading Soviet jurist, Professor Mikhail S. Strogovich, also of Moscow University. In an article published in 1948, Strogovich sought to base the position of the defense attorney on his relationship, not to the court, but to his client, the accused. He has consistently adhered to this view ever since.

While conceding that a defense attorney does serve as an aide of the court in the sense that, in defending his client, he helps the court to achieve its function of rendering justice, Strogovich contended that this circumstance was not the key to the essential function of the defense counsel, which was to protect the legal rights of the accused. If the defense counsel was an aide of the court, he asked, why should he be paid by his client instead of by the court? He argued further that it was entirely up to the accused, and not to the court, to decide who his defense attorney would be. The accused might even choose to dispense with defense counsel, which would mean that he could deprive the court of its supposed "aide." Strogovich did not, however, construe the legal relationship between a defense counsel and his client as excluding the interests of the state; rather, he emphasized this relationship in order to refute the hitherto accepted interpretation which ignored it.

Basically, the position of the defense counsel in criminal trials is very closely related to the position of the courts in the over-all structure of the state. The position of the courts, in turn, is directly related to the fundamental principles on which the state is founded—that is, to the basic concepts of law, justice, and the relationship between state and citizen. The history of Soviet justice has amply borne this out. During the period when Soviet judicial policy was shaped by Stalin's thesis of an intensification of the class struggle parallel with the approach to socialism, the official attitude toward the bar became more negative to the same extent that the courts themselves became instruments for the liquidation of class enemies.

Following Stalin's death, and especially after the Twentieth Party Congress condemned the thesis of sharpening class struggle, certain modifications of the hitherto prevailing judicial doctrine became necessary. Although Cheltsov still held in 1954 that the function of a defense counsel was to render active assistance to the court in arriving at a correct assessment of the truth concerning an alleged crime and a clarification of the danger presented to society by that crime and its author, members of the Leningrad college of attorneys publicly protested against this formulation in 1955 on the ground that what Cheltsov had defined as the function of the defense attorney was actually that of the prosecutor and the court. The attorney's first and foremost task, they maintained, was to defend the legal rights and interests of the accused citizen; and by so doing he helped the Soviet state and Soviet justice and fortified "socialist legality."

Although these polemics might suggest that a significant change has taken place in the theoretical view of the defense attorney's role, in the author's estimation this would be an exaggeration. Cheltsov continues to maintain that the defense attorney is an organ of the state administration of justice, but that this does not preclude the special character of his function. As already mentioned, Strogovich on the other hand bases the position of the defense counsel on the legal relationship between him and his client; but while placing major emphasis on this relationship, he is nevertheless constrained by the facts of Soviet totalitarianism to recognize that the defense counsel does function as an organ of the judicial administration. Strogovich, indeed, emphasizes that the defense counsel is the champion of the *lawful* interests of the accused—that is, his interests as recognized by Soviet law. Taking into account the special role of law as defined by Soviet political doctrine and jurisprudence, it follows that there is no essential difference between the two interpretations. The two proceduralists both move about within the closed room of Soviet jurisprudence and are unable to introduce any new element.

Nevertheless, the post-Stalin period has seen many important changes in Soviet practice which have affected the position of the legal profession. The most significant are as follows:

(1) The state security service, which in Stalin's time played an important part in judicial administration, has been separated from this function.

(2) The content of "socialist legality" has altered to require that all parties to a trial be held to strict compliance with existing laws. The function of the law as a positive instrument of "socialist construction" has been tremendously enhanced: If a law becames obsolete or fails to meet the requirements of Soviet life, it must nevertheless be obeyed until it is formally repealed. Especially in the field of criminal law and criminal procedure, the relevant norms have become more abstract—i.e., more free from any form of subjectivism.

(3) The courts have emancipated themselves from the influence of the state procuracy. Although the prosecutor still fulfills the dual function of appearing in court as the accuser and exercising supervision over compliance with the law, he no longer has at his disposal any weapon other than lodging a protest against the court's decision.

(4) Whereas the academic preparation of judges in the Stalin era—especially the 1930's—was generally deficient, Soviet judges today have the necessary professional training to enable them to hand down objective decisions. Since prosecutors and defense attorneys also possess the same professional qualifications, court trials take on the character of forensic contests over the law, bearing at least a formal resemblance, insofar as the relations between the trial participants are concerned, to criminal proceedings in Continental European courts.

(5) Trial courts of primary jurisdiction are composed of a professional judge and two people's assessors. The latter are somewhat analogous to jurors in that they participate as representatives of the public. (They are popularly elected to lists of assessors, from which they are successively drawn to serve on the court for a ten-day period each year.) In perform-

ing their temporary judicial function, the assessors are expected to be guided by the law and their socialist consciousness, and not to act as spokesmen of a politically undifferentiated society (which does not exist in the U.S.S.R.). This means that they are influenced directly by the authority of the professional judge, who briefs them on juridical matters, and indirectly also by that of the prosecutor—all of which seriously handicaps the defending attorney.

Since, however, the prevailing doctrine holds that only guilt shall be punished and that it is up to the court to determine the degree of guilt as a measure of the penalty to be imposed, it becomes the duty of the defense counsel to present all facts and circumstances favorable to his client—provided that, in so doing, he does not compromise the allegiance he owes to the ruling ideology and the state. It is not easy to say precisely how far an attorney can go in defending an accused without opening his own political loyalty to question. If he contests the specifications of the indictment, he puts himself in opposition to the prosecutor, who is both a state official and a Party member; if he appeals the conviction of his client, he challenges the correctness of the decision of the court, which is a state agency. These concerns obviously impose restraints upon his freedom of action in conducting the defense of his client.

OFFICIAL VIEWS

There is little question, however, that the post-Stalin period has seen the emergence of a more positive official attitude toward the Soviet bar. The acceptance at long last of professional attorneys as *personae gratae* in Soviet judicial and public life was evidenced in 1957 by the following passage in a speech delivered by I. A. Kairov, an important Party official, before the U.S.S.R. Supreme Soviet:

> Soviet attorneys, by providing legal assistance to the people, fulfill . . . the important task of strengthening socialist legality and the administration of justice. . . . Here and there the alien attitude still persists that attorneys are a disruptive element and do not contribute towards effective judicial administration. Such an attitude towards attorneys is wholly at variance with the real tasks of Soviet justice. We must put an end to it and look upon the attorney as a true, inflexible, and courageous defender of truth and justice.

More important, in response to demands voiced in various professional law journals, Article 22 of the Fundamentals of Criminal Procedure, adopted in 1958, stipulated that the defense attorney should be allowed to participate in a case involving his client by the time the investigative stage came to an end. (This was a compromise solution inasmuch as liberal jurists had wanted defense counsel to be admitted during the entire period of the preliminary investigation, while the procuracy wanted to exclude them altogether.) In addition, the new Criminal Code and

Code of Criminal Procedure did away with certain restrictions on the rights of the accused and rectified Vyshinsky's harmful theories with respect to evidence and "substantive truth."

There are other indications of the increased official confidence placed in the legal profession as an established cog in the machinery of Soviet justice. Books compiled by professional attorneys to serve as guides to the conduct of defense activities in court have been published with official imprimatur. Members of the professional bar have been encouraged to take an active part in campaigns designed to bolster the authority of the law in the eyes of the general public through lectures, educational programs, etc. A resolution adopted by the CPSU Central Committee in 1964 called for the participation of both academic and "practicing" jurists, including professional attorneys, in devising measures "to promote the growth of legal science and improve legal training" throughout the U.S.S.R.

All this does not mean, however, that the Soviet regime is satisfied that it has fully accomplished its objective of building up a cadre of "true Soviet lawyers." In fact, Soviet legal journals and the press continue to publish articles critical of the bar, mainly on the ground that attorneys concentrate too much on vindicating their clients in court and fail to honor their higher responsibility to the state and socialist society. Especially noteworthy was an article published last year by I. Kukarsky, deputy chairman of the Law Commission of the R.S.F.S.R. Council of Ministers (the official organ charged with supervision of the bar in the R.S.F.S.R.). The article contained a good number of criticisms, which may be summarized as follows:

(1) In defending their clients, attorneys sometimes resort to impermissible methods detrimental to the interests of "society" and the state. They contact witnesses for the purpose of influencing them in favor of the accused, and in court they attempt to distort the evidence assembled by the investigative agencies. Also, in some instances, they file unfounded motions motivated exclusively by the interests of their clients. When the pretrial investigation of a case has been concluded, the defense counsel is permitted to study the evidence against the accused and to file a motion for additional investigation if he finds the evidence deficient; however, for tactical reasons, he may delay filing such a motion until the formal trial is already in progress, hoping that if the motion is then allowed by the court, this will discredit the work of the prosecutor and the investigative agencies.

(2) Attorneys are sometimes guilty of accepting illegal "private" stipends paid directly to them by their clients in addition to the compensation they get from the attorneys' college.

(3) Many attorneys shirk their duty to participate in public education activities, either evading giving lectures or giving perfunctory talks of little value.

(4) The attorneys' colleges fail to exercise adequate supervision over

the activities of their members and to cooperate actively enough in combating crime. They often neglect to send an observer to the court when a member attorney is pleading a case and consequently are unable to hold group critiques of the manner in which the attorney conducted the defense. The presidium of each college, composed mostly of Party members, is supposed to exercise broad control over the activities of its members in trial proceedings and to take disciplinary or censorial action in cases of improper conduct.

Kukarsky's article went on to indicate that official steps would be taken to remedy these abuses. In particular, new regulations concerning legal fees would be put into effect with a view to stopping the payment of "private" stipends. Also, the Law Commission of the R.S.F.S.R. Council of Ministers was to tighten its supervision over the attorneys' colleges, which in turn would be obliged to exercise closer control over the activities of their members. All this points to the conclusion that the regime's objective is to assure that the attorney's colleges develop into "socially-oriented" organizations similar in nature to the Soviet labor unions.

THE SOCIAL POSITION OF LAWYERS

The number of students enrolled in university law courses and institutes of law in the Soviet Union is largely fixed by government plan. Up to now there has been little official interest in encouraging the study of law, and for this reason scholarship stipends paid to law students have been lower than those paid to students of the natural sciences.

Since the 1930's, the U.S.S.R. has had a statutory requirement that students who receive higher education at state expense must, upon completing it, accept work assigned to them by the government for a period of three years. Law graduates are subject to this rule, which means in practice that they will be assigned to work for the required three years in either a court, a public prosecutor's office, or the legal department of a state enterprise. Only upon termination of this period can these young lawyers decide whether to continue their work in state judicial agencies or take up a career as professional attorneys. Most of them opt to go on working for the state—as prosecuting attorneys, in the investigative agencies, or in the courts. Those who choose a career as professional attorneys are usually either idealists who consider this to be their natural calling or the untalented who have not been able to make their way in the state judicial administration or with state enterprises.

In the eyes of rank-and-file Soviet citizens, members of the bar occupy a position of great prestige and respect. The reason for this is simply that it is to the professional attorney that the individual citizen accused of violating the law must look for the protection of his rights and interests against the overwhelming power of the state. While official doctrine enjoins attorneys not to place their obligation to a client above their duty to the state and socialist society, this has not deterred them from acting in

accord with the humanitarian dictates of conscience and exerting themselves to the utmost on behalf of those they defend.

The attitude of Soviet attorneys with respect to the observance of professional secrecy illustrates the point. In most democratic countries, lawyers are legally entitled to refuse to disclose any information confidentially
communicated to them by their clients. . . . Soviet law and criminal procedure, on the contrary, do not recognize any right of "confidential communication" between an attorney and his client: Like all other citizens of
the U.S.S.R., attorneys have the formal duty to cooperate with the state
judicial organs in combating criminality. In fact, however, most attorneys
choose to close their eyes to this duty rather than act in such a way as
to undermine the confidential relationship between themselves and their
clients.

This situation has prompted Soviet journals to lecture to members of
the bar on the difference between the Western and Soviet concepts of
professional ethics for attorneys. Whereas the bourgeois lawyer's ethic
sanctions the "right to lie" on behalf of a criminal, one article asserted,
"socialist morality" demands that the attorney exclusively serve the cause
of truth. From time to time, the Soviet press has also carried reports of
alleged "antimoral" conduct on the part of members of the legal profession. The publicity given to such cases is evidently aimed at forcing
attorneys into a more compliant role as tools of socialist justice.

There has been a natural tendency for professional lawyers in the
Soviet Union to gravitate to the principal urban centers of the country,
where the opportunities for earning a livelihood in private legal practice are
greatest. As a result, in the R.S.F.S.R.—which has a total of only 7,000
attorneys to serve a population of 125 millions—there are 103 *raions* without a single attorney, compelling residents of these districts, when in need
of legal assistance, to travel to the nearest—but often very distant—
regional center having an attorneys' college. In the Kuibyshev region,
there are 152 attorneys in all, 100 of them concentrated in the city of
Kuibyshev itself. In the Smolensk region, there are but 34 attorneys divided among the larger cities, with only six more to be found in the
remaining eight cities and *raions* of the region. This suggests that attorneys in the U.S.S.R. are allowed a fairly large degree of freedom in
choosing where to practice their profession. A decisive factor in their
choice, apparently, is whether or not they have good "connections"
among the administrative officials of a particular attorneys' college, as a
good deal of "cliquishness" seems to exist in these bodies.

Until fairly recently, the work of Soviet professional attorneys was
largely confined to criminal cases, employment disputes, and housing litigations, and their opportunities for making money were relatively limited.
However, the last few years have seen a marked increase in the scope of
legal activity, especially in the area of relations between state economic
enterprises and collectives (kolkhozy), with the result that these organizations now find themselves increasingly in need of the services of trained
attorneys. In some cases, attorneys have reportedly performed such services

on an "honorary" basis—i.e., without remuneration—but according to a statement by G. I. Sukharev, deputy chief of the Department for Administrative Organs of the Party Central Committee for the R.S.F.S.R., where attorneys have been pressured into rendering "honorary" legal services to state or collective organizations, they have generally performed them in a careless and perfunctory manner. However, it now seems to have become fairly common practice for enterprises and other organizations to retain attorneys to handle their legal affairs on a contractual basis, paying them handsome retainer fees. One attorney in Kuibyshev was reported to have contracted out his services to four different enterprises, and another, who was retained under contract with an association for the hard-of-hearing, reportedly collected fees for a period of several years without having to handle any legal business whatever.

Thus far, the presidiums of the attorneys' colleges, the executive committees of the local soviets, and even the local Party committees appear to have shown relatively little interest in enforcing more rigorous standards of discipline among members of the professional bar. However, recent articles in leading legal journals suggest that the Party is now giving much thought to this problem. There have even been proposals for the establishment of a fixed income for attorneys with a view to curbing their aspirations to personal prosperity. This will certainly not be an easy task.

*　　*　　*

VII

Political Socialization

Political socialization refers to the process by which individuals learn to become good citizens. It begins with the formation of political ideas in the family, continues with civic training and education in the schools, and includes the political conditioning an individual receives from whatever societal institutions he joins. The end product of socialization in the Soviet Union is a set of attitudes expressing loyalty to the regime and its leaders and hostility to capitalism and bourgeois society, a value system that stresses "communist morality" and a communist attitude toward labor, and an intellectual understanding of the Marxist-Leninist theory of social dynamics, including what the Soviets call a "scientific world outlook." Socialization is a function of every society, but the comprehensiveness of the Soviet effort to transform and control an entire people's political outlook and to reshape the human personality is unique.

The family is the most important socializing institution not directly under the control of either the Party or the state. The Party exhorts the Soviet family to inculate in the young the values of communism and

Soviet patriotism, though with only partial success. While the family has not proved a barrier to ideological indoctrination of Soviet youth, it has impeded the full and enthusiastic acceptance of official orthodoxy within its ranks. Religious influences and, among the non-Russians, national loyalties receive their greatest reinforcement in the home. Also, the efforts of parents to secure for their children the advantages of wealth or status conflict with the ideals of an equalitarian society and reinforce pluralistic tendencies.

The most important socializing institutions in Soviet society are the schools and the youth organizations. From the beginning the regime placed great emphasis on education. Since 1962 compulsory eight-year schooling has been made universal throughout the country. Education involves considerably more than the developing of skills and the transmission of a cultural heritage. It involves molding the "new Soviet man" to live in a communist society. From the time the Soviet child begins school at age seven, he is taught a moral code that emphasizes the importance of the collective, social discipline, respect for labor, love of the socialist fatherland, and other communist virtues. Pedagogic techniques are designed to foster discipline and respect for authority. Formal political indoctrinaton does not generally begin until the latter part of secondary schooling, though all academic subjects at every level are studied from a Marxist point of view. After completion of the eight-year school the typical student continues through grades nine and ten in one of several secondary schools: (1) a general secondary polytechnical school, (2) a technicum and specialized secondary school, (3) a vocational training school, or (4) a school for working and rural youth. Some students complete their secondary education by correspondence.

In 1958 Khrushchev extended the school period by one year and included service in a factory or farm as part of the educational training (see Selection 14, Chapter V, above). This "reform," designed not only to meet manpower needs but also to inculate respect for labor, proved detrimental to the quality of Soviet education and was abandoned in 1964. Like the general ten-year program, higher education in the Soviet Union is vocationally oriented. There are three types of institutions of higher education: the universities, polytechnical institutes, and specialized academies and institutes. Political indoctrination is a part of the curriculum of all institutions of higher learning.

Second only to the schools in importance as instruments of socialization are the youth organization—the Young Communist League (Komsomol)—and its junior affiliates, the Little Octobrists and the Young Pioneers. The Komsomol was established in 1918 as a youth auxiliary to the Communist Party. Membership is limited to the fourteen-to-twenty-six age group. The Komsomol not only provides a source of trained reserves for the Party but is the instrument for mobilizing Soviet youth to build communism and defend the Soviet republic. Primary emphasis is placed upon the acquisition and dissemination of a thorough knowledge of Marxist-Leninist doctrine, Party history, and information about current Soviet policies. Komsomol members are expected to work among the masses combating religious influence, parasitic and antisocial behavior, political apathy, and waste and inefficiency. Their energies are harnessed for a variety of economic tasks, such as organizing socialist competition in factories, cultivating virgin lands, working on conservation and recreation projects, and assisting in all types of socially useful construction.

While approximately one-third of Soviet youth belong to the Komsomol, virtually every youngster at one time or another belongs to the Young Pioneers, for ages ten to fourteen, and the Little Octobrists, for ages seven to nine. Indoctrination among these children is incorporated into the recreational and vocational activities appropriate to these age groups. Athletic and outdoor programs including hiking, camping, swimming, and skiing constitute a major portion of the Pioneer activities. They are supplemented with character-building programs like patriotic drives, organizing Lenin reading corners, and developing skills in a hobby.

To the extent that the regime seeks to reform the human personality along communist lines, Soviet political socialization has not been successful. However, the Party has by means of the instruments of socialization succeeded in creating a general uniformity of outlook and conformity of behavior among the overwhelming majority of its citizens, and that is enough to ensure the regime's continuation.

Jeremy R. Azrael is Associate Professor of Political Science at the University of Chicago. He is the author of *Managerial Power and Soviet Politics*. Ralph T. Fisher, Jr., author of *Pattern for Soviet Youth*, is Professor of History at the University of Illinois. Frederick C. Barghoorn is Professor of Political Science at Yale University. He has written numerous books and articles on Soviet politics, including *Soviet Russian Nationalism, The Soviet Cultural Offensive, Soviet Foreign Propaganda*, and *Politics in the USSR*.

22

EDUCATION AND POLITICAL DEVELOPMENT IN THE SOVIET UNION

JEREMY R. AZRAEL

With a few notable exceptions, students of Soviet politics have largely neglected, or at best treated only indirectly, the process whereby Soviet citizens, and more particularly Soviet youth, acquire their political values, attitudes, perceptions, and sentiments.[1] The task of this chapter

[1] See Samuel W. Harper, *Civic Training in Soviet Russia* (Chicago: University of Chicago Press, 1929), for the first systematic study of this process by a political scientist. See Allen H. Kassof, "The Soviet Youth Program: Socialization in a Totalitarian Society," unpublished dissertation, Harvard University, 1960; Kent Geiger, "Winning Over Youth," in Alex Inkeles and Kent Geiger, eds., *Soviet Society* (Boston: Houghton Mifflin, 1961); Ralph T. Fisher, Jr., *Pattern for Soviet Youth* (New York: Columbia University Press, 1959); and Alex Inkeles and Raymond A. Bauer, *The Soviet Citizen* (Cambridge: Harvard University Press, 1959), for other studies dealing with various aspects of the general socialization process in the U.S.S.R.

Reprinted from *Education and Political Development*, ed. by James S. Coleman (Copyright © 1965 by Princeton University Press), for Social Science Research Council: Jeremy R. Azrael, "Soviet Union," pp. 233–71. Reprinted by permission of Princeton University Press.

is to help fill this gap by discussing one major agency involved in the process of political socialization in the U.S.S.R.—the educational system.[2] . . .

STRUCTURE AND SCOPE

In the period prior to 1958 (and still today) the educational system was part of the monopolistic, centrally controlled communications network of Soviet society. The Department of Schools of the Party Central Committee supervised the functioning of the entire system, and each link of the latter was subject to tight control by local Party organs.[3] Policy-making authority in the sphere of higher education was officially centralized and in the remaining spheres, which were formally under the jurisdiction of the several republics, the Russian Republic Ministry of Education set the basic policy line on all important educational issues. What operative decentralization there was derived from the need to take special local conditions into account in order better to realize centrally determined objectives and tended to be almost exclusively administrative in character.[4] A single basic pattern of school organization prevailed throughout the entire country. The law provided for universal, compulsory, seven-year, or *incomplete* secondary education beginning at age seven, although, in fact, in the years immediately preceding the 1958 reform, only 80 per cent of Soviet children who entered the first grade finished the seventh.[5] Upon completing their compulsory education, the overwhelming majority of students followed one of three paths. One group went more or less directly into the work force. A second group enrolled in technicums, where they received a *complete specialized* secondary education, which qualified them, after three or four years' study, as low- or middle-level technicians. A third group, consisting of those whose parents could meet the moderate, but by no means inconsequential, tuition payments that applied from 1941 on and who received the highest scores on the rigorous qualifying exams, which were instituted in 1944, was allowed to enter the "complete secondary" or ten-year school, where, for three years, they received a *complete general* secondary

[2] See Herbert Hyman, *Political Socialization* (Glencoe, Ill.: Free Press, 1959); Gabriel Almond and James Coleman, eds., *The Politics of the Developing Areas* (Princeton, N.J.: Princeton University Press, 1960), pp. 26–35; and David Easton and Robert D. Hess, "Problems in the Study of Political Socialization," in S. M. Lipset and L. L. Lowenthal, eds., *Culture and Social Character* (New York: Free Press, 1961), for discussions of the process of political socialization.

[3] See George Z. F. Bereday and Jaan Pennar, *The Politics of Soviet Education* (New York: Praeger, 1960), Ch. 3, for a discussion of Party control over schools.

[4] See Bereday *et al.*, eds., *The Changing Soviet School* (Boston: Houghton Mifflin, 1960), Ch. 5, for a discussion of school administration.

[5] Prior to 1943, the starting age for schoolchildren was eight (Bereday, *Changing Soviet School*, p. 82). See N. S. Khrushchev, "On Strengthening the Connection of the School and Life," *School and Society*, February 14, 1959, for the 80 per cent figure.

education.[6] During most of the period under discussion, the first group constituted approximately 60–65 per cent of the total; the second, 15 per cent; and the third, some 20–25 per cent; although, as we shall see, in the years immediately preceding the 1958 reform the relative size of the first group decreased and that of the third grew rapidly.[7] Of those students who entered the work force, the preponderant majority pursued their education no further, although there did exist a skeletal network of "schools of working and rural youth" in which they could continue their studies in their free time.[8] Similarly, graduation from the technicum was ordinarily the final step in the education of students in the second group, although the top 5 per cent of technicum graduates were permitted to apply for immediate admission to higher education, and the remainder could do so after having worked at state-assigned jobs for at least three years.[9] The normal route to higher education was graduation from the ten-year school, and, in fact, prior to 1954 a complete general secondary education was not only a virtual prerequisite for but also a virtual guarantee of admission to higher education.[10] Higher education, which normally lasted five years, was provided in universities or technical institutes and was culminated by enrollment in the lower ranks of the Soviet elite.

CURRICULUM

Just as a single pattern of school organization prevailed throughout the entire U.S.S.R., so a uniform core curriculum was found in all schools of the same basic type. The only significant variations had to do with the language of instruction and, at the upper levels of the educational system, with the particular technical specialty that was stressed.[11] Ideological consideration militated against the development of special programs for "gifted" or "backward" pupils, since the desire for political homogeneity led to an insistence that, within fairly narrow limits, all students were equal or could become equal if they so chose.[12] The same factors led to the politicization of the

[6] See Bereday, *et al.*, eds., *Changing Soviet School*, pp. 74, 83.

[7] See E. Koutaisoff, "Soviet Education and the New Man," *Soviet Studies* 11 (October, 1953): 123, for these estimates, which refer to 1952–53. It is possible that the introduction of fees led to a decrease in the percentage of students going on to the ten-year school, since, according to one source, in 1940–41, 43.3 per cent of all seventh-graders continued their education. K. Hulicka, "Political Education in Soviet Schools," *Soviet Studies* 11 (October, 1953): 147. In the post-1954 period, there was a rapid increase in this percentage, and, by 1958, 70 per cent of those who completed the seventh grade entered the eighth. Nicholas DeWitt, "Upheaval in Education," *Problems of Communism* 8, No. 1 (January-February, 1959): 29.

[8] See Nicholas DeWitt, *Education and Professional Employment in the U.S.S.R.* (Washington: National Science Foundation, 1961), p. 92.

[9] Bereday and Pennar, *Politics of Soviet Education*, p. 12.

[10] See below, note 70.

[11] See below, at notes 61–63.

[12] See Bereday and Pennar, *Politics of Soviet Education*, pp. 64–65.

entire curriculum, although the major indoctrinational burden was carried, as one would anticipate, by the social sciences and humanities.[13] In these fields politicization was particularly intensive and proceeded according to a carefully organized plan designed to synchronize substance and method with the maturation process as understood by Soviet educational psychologists.[14] Broadly speaking, the indoctrinational techniques used corresponded to those which were characteristic of the rest of the Soviet communications network. At the lower levels of the system primary reliance was placed upon *agitation*, with the main effort devoted to inculcating the "spirit" of Bolshevism, conditioning responses to a few relatively simple symbols, acquainting the students with the Party's slogans and principal platform planks, and "explaining" in gross outline the policies of the regime. At the upper levels, and above all in the universities and institutes, increasing reliance was placed upon *propaganda*, with the main effort devoted to "the intensive elucidation of the teachings of Marx, Engels, Lenin, and [prior to 1956] Stalin, and of the history of the Bolshevik Party and its tasks."[15] At all levels, however, the general outlines of the "message" were the same.

In the primary and middle grades an intensive effort was made to establish in the minds of students a full identity among political community (nation), regime (Party), and government (state system and ruling authorities) and to channel commitment from one to another "level" of the political system without discrimination or differentiation.[16] Early initiation into the cult of Lenin and—prior to 1956—into the cult of Stalin was considered an especially useful means of cementing this identification. According to Soviet educators, experience had shown that "children progress most easily to the feeling of love for their motherland, their fatherland, and their state through a feeling of love for the leaders of the Soviet people—Lenin and Stalin," that "they [the children] associate with the concrete images of Lenin and Stalin

---

[13] See Fred M. Hechinger, *The Big Red Schoolhouse* (New York: Doubleday, 1959), p. 167, and G. S. Counts, *The Challenge of Soviet Education* (New York: McGraw-Hill, 1957), p. 93, for examples of the politicization of the natural science curriculum.

[14] See *Soviet Education* 1, No. 2 (December, 1958): 53–91, for an example of such a plan.

[15] Alex Inkeles, *Public Opinion in Soviet Russia* (Cambridge: Harvard University Press, 1958), p. 41, and also pp. 40–43.

[16] See Easton and Hess, "Problems," for "levels" of the political system. The effort to establish an identity among the various "levels" is reflected clearly in the introduction to the official fourth-grade history text where "land of socialism," "Motherland," "Party," and "Soviet state" are used almost interchangeably. (See Counts, *Challenge of Soviet Education*, p. 120, for a translation.) It is noteworthy that the Soviets are pursuing a technique which they recognize as having been characteristic of Czarist education: "In inculcating devotion to the Czar, the Ministry of Public Enlightenment constantly joined the concept 'fatherland' to the concept 'Czar,' striving to consolidate the two concepts." In the case of Czarist education, of course, the consolidation was sought for "reactionary" ends. M. A. Zinoviev, *Soviet Methods of Teaching History* (Ann Arbor: University of Michigan Press, 1952), p. 43.

the Party of Communists, the Party of Bolsheviks created by [the] great leaders," and that "they quickly begin to perceive that under the leadership of the Party of Lenin and Stalin we both build and defend our Soviet state, our fatherland." [17] The desired orientation toward the monolithic political system was summed up in the concept "Soviet patriotism," and the supreme task of the curriculum was to inculcate "Soviet patriotism." [18]

At the lower levels of the education system, "Soviet patriotism" was interpreted primarily in terms of the political community. Thus, history texts—and the primary school song book and readers as well— were designed to convince students that "everywhere, in all spheres of science and art, industry and agriculture, in the works of peace and on the battlefields, the Soviet people march in the forefront of other nations and have created values which are unequaled anywhere in the world." [19] As this suggests, a dichotomous image of the world was an integral part of the inculcation of "Soviet patriotism." While elaborating the glories of the Soviet Union, teachers were instructed to regale their students with vivid "human interest" stories of life in the West—stories of a sort which would insure that students knew "not only with their minds, but with their hearts that capitalism is hunger, unemployment, and eternal fear of tomorrow." It was expected that an emotionally charged juxtaposition of the glories of Soviet life and the horrors of life in the West would "foster a hatred for the exploiters," "teach the students to struggle," and reinforce the students' love of the Soviet system.[20] Out of this syndrome of emotions, in turn, the students would develop a feeling that they stood in debt before their own society and were obliged to repay its beneficence with endless and unstinting service.[21]

The type of service which was expected was made clear to school children by appropriate models. Primary school readers were replete with tales of the careers of political leaders (above all Lenin and Stalin), valiant soldiers, famous scientists, and production heroes.[22] The style of these "biographies" was at once hagiographic and intimate, and they were designed not merely to exemplify right conduct and inspire reverence, but also to facilitate the internalization of desirable

[17] G. S. Counts, *I Want to Be like Stalin* (New York: John Day, 1947), p. 54. (This is a translation of a Soviet pedagogical text.)

[18] See Frederick C. Barghoorn, *Soviet Russian Nationalism* (New York: Oxford University Press, 1956), esp. Chapter One, for a discussion of "Soviet patriotism." See Counts, *Challenge of Soviet Education*, p. 118, for the primary place assigned the cultivation of "Soviet patriotism" in the curriculum.

[19] Zinoviev, *Soviet Methods*, p. 90. See also Merle Fainsod, "The Komsomol: Youth Under Dictatorship," in Inkeles and Geiger, eds., *Soviet Society*, p. 115; and Counts, *I Want*, pp. 53–54.

[20] Zinoviev, *Soviet Methods*, p. 83.

[21] *Ibid.*, p. 90

[22] See Fainsod, "Komsomol," p. 155; Counts, *I Want*, p. 39; Zinoviev, *Soviet Methods*, p. 91.

"ego-ideals." Full identification was encouraged by including many "heroic" children, ranging from the notorious Pavlik Morozov to young partisans killed in the "Great Fatherland War" (World War II). In addition, almost all the "biographies" of adults began with glimpses of the childhood years of their heroes. The fact that the Great Lenin was once *Volodya* Ulyanov and the Great Stalin was once *So-So* Dzhugashvili was stressed, and the idea was constantly driven home that the character traits of the heroic adult were consciously cultivated by the child.[23] As for the character traits themselves, those which were most exalted were love of labor, and, in general, the "protestant" economic virtues so central to industrial development; "personal self-sacrifice with the aim of bringing victory to the fatherland"; and "devotion to revolutionary and scientific ideas."[24] And, once again, as in the case of the picture of the world at large, graphic examples of "negative heroes" were juxtaposed to the portraits of "positive heroes" in order to reinforce commitment to the character traits of the latter. The dichotomous image of the world was complemented by a dichotomous image of human nature, and every effort was made to inculcate a radical intolerance of ambiguity.[25]

At the upper levels of the educational system, the indoctrinational themes were essentially the same. However, the approach became increasingly sophisticated. One change of note was the devotion of progressively more time and energy to the development of proper orientations toward the regime and governmental "levels" of the political system. All complete secondary school students were required (usually in the tenth grade) to take a course on "The Constitution of the U.S.S.R." Here the status of the Soviet state as "the most democratic in the world" was elaborated, the institutional setting of Soviet politics was clarified, and students were instructed in the nature and norms of "socialist legality." History was increasingly Party history, and more and more time was devoted to the contemporary period.[26] While the inculcation of absolute devotion to the nation as such was by no means abandoned, and history texts continued to cultivate not merely chauvinism but xenophobia, the concept of "Soviet patriotism"

[23] See Vasileva, "Study of Episodic Stories from the History of U.S.S.R. in the Fourth Grade," *Soviet Education*, Vol. 3, No. 5, 1960; M. I. Kalinin, *On Communist Education* (Moscow, 1959), pp. 108–9. It is this effort to achieve full identification with appropriate "heroes" which justifies Counts in entitling his translation of sections from a Soviet text *I Want to Be Like Stalin*, although the text itself is entitled simply Pedagogy. See, however, Bertram D. Wolfe, *Communist Totalitarianism* (Boston: Beacon Press, 1956), p. 114.

[24] Zinoviev, *Soviet Methods*, p. 91. See also Counts, *I Want*, pp. 125–26.

[25] The stress on model "heroes"—positive and negative—was not confined to historic personages, nor was it limited to primary education. It was a major theme in the teaching of literature in the secondary schools as well. (See Frederic Ligle, "The Study of Literature in the Soviet School," *Studies in Comparative Education*, December, 1959, p. 34.)

[26] It must be noted, however, that no formal course in party history was offered below the university-institute level.

was more and more infused with manifest political content.[27] Increasing
attention was devoted to cultivating a "class point of view" and to training students to "unmask" and "expose" the "class essence" of ideas.[28]
Prior to 1953, all students from the senior grades on were required to
be intimately familiar with the *History of the Communist Party of the
Soviet Union: Short Course* with its exaltation of Stalin, its cries for
vigilance against any political deviation, and its vigorous assertion of
the vanguard role of the Party. After Stalin's death, texts and guides of
generally similar character, though minus the somewhat hysterical tone
and the "cult of personality," were gradually substituted.[29]

In the middle and senior grades there was no separate study of
Marxism-Leninism, or, as the sequence ran prior to 1953, Marxism-
Leninism-Stalinism. The role of the Party as exclusive custodian of
the ideology was stressed constantly, but no effort was made to cultivate
real ideological sophistication. The fact that the Party had a "scientific"
theory at its disposal was emphasized in order to generate "convictional
certainty." This "convictional certainty" was to rise out of but transcend
the emotional predispositions built up in the earlier grades. To the
students' emotional revulsion against the West was added a "conviction
in the inevitable victory of socialism." [30] However, emphasis was *not*
placed upon the niceties of historical and dialectical materialism. What
was sought was total loyalty to the Party, and there was an implicit
recognition that until such loyalty was secured, familiarity with the
ideology *per se* could lead to "confusion" and provide a standard by
which to judge the Party and resist changes in the Party line.[31] It was
only in the institutions of higher education—after the students had
been exposed to an all-out attempt to socialize them into Party loyalty—
that the formal study of Marxism-Leninism was introduced. At this
level, however, it was a required subject and occupied an important
place in the curriculum.[32] Instruction in ideological theory was
designed to consolidate the world view of that segment of Soviet youth
which was destined to enter the ranks of the Soviet elite. It was designed

[27] See Martin Levit, "Content Analysis of a Soviet History Text for University-
Level Courses," *Studies in Comparative Education*, December, 1959, for a content
analysis of the official university text on Soviet history.

[28] Zinoviev, *Soviet Methods*, pp. 63, 79, 85–90.

[29] See Bereday *et al.*, *Changing Soviet School*, pp. 88–89, for a discussion of some
of the consequences of "de-Stalinization" for the formal school program.

[30] Zinoviev, *Soviet Methods*, pp. 3, 84.

[31] See Hyman, *Political Socialization*, p. 19, for the important role of party loyalty
as opposed (at least partially) to programatic loyalty in preparing the ground for
acceptance of social change.

[32] See *Report of IIE Seminar on Education in the Soviet Union* (New York, 1960),
p. 34. "Marxism-Leninism," together with "The History of the Communist Party of
the Soviet Union" and "Political Economy," which were also required subjects,
occupied over 600 curricular hours over the course of five years' study in institutions of
higher education. In addition, all applicants for graduate degrees were required to pass
an examination in "Marxism-Leninism," irrespective of their proposed field of concentration.

to insure that they would not approach their future assignments from a "narrowly professional" point of view and would make the proper choice—i.e., the choice in conformity with the regime's current schedule of priorities—among the conflicting goals which would confront them as they moved up the ladder of success and were accorded more and more operational autonomy.[33] It was designed to insure that they would become worthy members of an *aktiv* on one or another of the "fronts" of Soviet life. And, finally, it was designed to guarantee that they would be sensitized to the special semantics of Soviet political life and hence able properly to "interpret" the measures of the regime to the masses. It was designed, in other words, to prepare them to serve as agitators in their own right, thus perpetuating the cycle of indoctrination through which they themselves had passed.[34]

ATMOSPHERE AND SPIRIT

Within the educational system, manipulation of the atmosphere and spirit of school life was considered at least as important as manipulation of the formal curriculum in guaranteeing the proper "political upbringing" of youth. Throughout the system, the atmosphere was pervaded by a spirit of discipline and hierarchy. At the lower levels, lessons were marked by the formal recitation of material drawn from the assigned textbooks and by catechetical drill, while at the higher levels standardized lectures propagating the official version of the Truth predominated. Among the very first requirements imposed on entering pupils was that of memorizing and obeying the highly authoritarian "Rules for Schoolchildren" which constituted "a program for the cultivation . . . of habits of disciplined and cultured behavior" both inside and outside the school.[35] It was hoped that behavior, become reflexive, would produce corresponding thought-patterns and that habituation would be the first step in the development of self-discipline. Self-discipline was desired, in turn, because with it *"comformity and obedience [would] become more perfect."* [36] The ultimate goal, in other words, was the internalization of the attitudes toward authority that the "Rules" reflected. Teachers were reminded that they were the principal authority figures with whom schoolchildren had contact and that they had to conduct themselves accordingly, never forgetting, as the late Soviet president Kalinin put it, that "a pedagogue is an engineer of human souls." [37] An authoritative text, after pointing out that "submission to the will

[33] Cf. Jeremy Azrael, "Political Profiles of the Soviet Technical Intelligentsia and Managerial Elite," unpublished dissertation, Harvard University, 1961, Ch. v; David Granick, *Management of the Industrial Firm in the U.S.S.R.* (New York: Columbia University Press, 1954), p. 284.

[34] See Inkeles, *Public Opinion*, pp. 42–43.

[35] Counts, *I Want*, p. 97. See *ibid.*, pp. 149–50, for a translation of the "Rules for Schoolchildren."

[36] *Ibid.*, p. 108 [Azrael's italics]. See also *ibid.*, p. 96.

[37] Kalinin, *On Communist Education*, p. 93.

of a leader is a necessary and essential mark of discipline," directed teachers to "assume from the outset a firm and impressive tone" and warned them not to coax students but rather to demand obedience, for only in this way would students develop the desired moral qualities.[38]

"Conformity and obedience" were secured not only by casting the teacher in an authoritarian role and imposing rigid rules upon the individual pupils, but also by carefully structuring relationships among the pupils. Here the role of the *kollektiv* was crucial. Indeed, *Pravda* proclaimed a strong *kollektiv* to be "the foundation of foundations of the Soviet educational system" and stressed that it was essential that "the organization of a *kollektiv* and the cultivation in each child of a feeling of collectiveness . . . [begin] from the first grade." [39] Teachers were instructed in the ways and means of shaming recalcitrant students into obedience by mobilizing the *kollektivs* against them, thereby at once buttressing their own authority and training students from a very early age to use and respond to such fundamental institutions of Soviet political life as criticism, self-criticism, denunciation, confession, and recantation.[40] However, the *kollektiv's* area of "legitimate" concern was considered to extend well beyond the walls of the classroom, and it was manipulated to break down all attempts on the part of students to develop or maintain a "private" sphere of existence.[41] An attempt was made through the *kollektiv* to exploit the natural vulnerability of youth to peer-group pressure. This was a particularly strategic control technique because, as Kassof has pointed out, the *kollektivs* operated on such a highly personal level and, where they were successful, turned "the abstract question of obeying official norms into issues of friendship and personal emotional security." [42] The first step was to create "citizens . . . able to put social above personal interests," but the long-run goal was "to educate a person . . . who [had] no interests opposed to the collective interests." [43] The hope was that the student

[38] *Ibid.*, and Counts, *I Want*, pp. 122, 140.

[39] Counts, *I Want*, pp. 84, 85.

[40] *Ibid.*, pp. 110, 102, 89, 93. At the lowest levels of the educational system the operative *kollektiv* was the class *kollektiv*. From the third grade to the seventh the class *kollektiv* was in effect a local unit of the All-Union Pioneer organization, which strove to embrace all children between the ages of nine and thirteen (ten to fourteen after 1958). In the 1930's there had been an all-Union organization for younger children, the Octobrist organization, embracing children from seven to nine, but this was abolished before World War II and not re-established until 1957. At the upper levels of the system, the schoolwide or faculty-wide (in institutions of higher education) *kollektiv* became increasingly important. It in effect constituted a local unit of the All-Union Komsomol, which strove to include all or nearly all *students* in the eligible age range (fourteen to twenty-six prior to 1958, fifteen to twenty-seven thereafter). In 1949, over 50 per cent of students from grades seven through ten were members of the Komsomol and in recent years 80 or 90 per cent of all students in institutions of higher education have been members. Kassof, "Soviet Youth Program," p. 204; Bereday and Pennar, *Politics of Soviet Education*, p. 52.

[41] Counts, *I Want*, pp. 84–85.

[42] Kassof, "Soviet Youth Program," p. 204.

[43] Counts, *I Want*, pp. 88, 37.

would ultimately come to make his standing in the *kollektiv* the basis for self-appraisal and would develop such a "pasion for unanimity" that coercion would be superfluous.[44]

The *kollektiv* functioned as an agency of mobilization as well as an agency of control. Here the involvement of the *kollektiv* in "socially useful labor" was considered to be of particular importance.[45] At the lower levels of the educational system, class and school *kollektivs* competed with each other in the collection of scrap metal, ·the planting of trees, the tending of public parks, etc., while at the upper levels Komsomol organizations mustered their members for "Saturdays" and "Sundays" of labor on nearby construction projects and for summer stints on collective or state farms. The objectives which were sought through student participation in "socially useful labor" were chiefly political and ideological, and in only a few instances was student labor of major economic significance. In the first place, participation was designed to inspire respect for physical labor, thereby, at one and the same time, strengthening the appeal of the regime's image as a bulwark of the proletariat and inhibiting the growth of "class-consciousness" within Soviet society. In the second place, it was designed to bring home the reality of socialism. There appeared to be faith in an inverted Lockean logic, whereby, by dint of mixing their labor with the construction projects of the regime, students would develop a sense of the reality of *their* ownership—socialist ownership through membership in the *kollektiv*—of all of the resources of Soviet society.

Finally, the *kollektiv* functioned as an important channel of political recruitmenf. This function was most marked, of course, at the upper levels of the educational system, but even in the primary grades the operations of the *kollektiv* were considered particularly useful in permitting teachers to identify "children of initiative." Once the latter were identified, the task was to discipline them without reducing them to apathy. On the one hand every effort was made to insure that "initiative not be exhibited impulsively." [46] On the other hand something more than "just blind obedience" was desired. The objective was to restrict the exercise.of initiative to a purely instrumental level where it would find expression as "an independent search for the best way to fulfill a

[44] See Margaret Mead, *Soviet Attitudes Toward Authority* (New York: William Morrow, 1955), p. 108. There is obvious tension between the regime's effort to induce students to internalize strong "ego-ideals" on the one hand and its effort to rely on group pressure as a critical technique of social control on the other. Ideally, of course, the two efforts are designed to reinforce each other, but practically considerable tension probably results and the two efforts may tend to contradict each other and lead to tremendous ambivalence on the part of the individual. Further research along these lines might be fruitful, though data would be very difficult to acquire.

[45] "Socially useful labor" can also be viewed as a control technique in so far as it was designed to fill and insure supervision over the use of their leisure time by students. See Jeremy R. Azrael, "Soviet Urban Attitudes Toward Leisure," *Social Problems* 9, No. 1 (Summer, 1961): 75–76, and Kassof, "Soviet Youth Program," pp. 140–41.

[46] Counts, *I Want*, p. 128.

command." [47] To accomplish this delicate task, initiative had to be "directed into organized channels." Here again the *kollektiv* occupied a key position, serving as a forum and a framework for the development of initiative of the desired sort and guaranteeing that "out of children of initiative good organizers . . . [would] come." [48] In the earliest years the position of "class monitors," which entailed assisting the teacher with such things as distributing supplies and maintaining classroom discipline and "cultured" standards of student behavior, served as a training ground for "children of initiative." [49] In addition, from the primary grades on, such children were encouraged to assume special "social obligations" above and beyond their participation in "socially useful labor." "Social obligations" in the lower grades ranged from aiding more backward classmates with their school work to writing articles for local children's newspapers.[50] Later "social obligations" entailed such things as the assumption of leadership (under the guidance of the teacher concerned) of a lower-level class *kollektiv* or Pioneer detachment, participation in the regime's various agitational campaigns, etc.[51] Those students who undertook major "social obligations" and fulfilled them with enthusiasm and skill were singled out, in turn, for further and more intensive initiation into the rites of responsibility. They were apt to be moved into the Komsomol apparatus itself, to be accorded early Party membership, to be enrolled in the special "cadres reserve" maintained by leading Party committees, and thus to be placed on a course which could lead not merely to elite status, but to membership in the "power elite" itself.[52]

The educational system prior to 1958 accomplished many of the tasks set it by the Soviet rulers and, in the process, won admiration and prestige for the regime abroad and support for the regime at home.[53] It transformed an overwhelmingly illiterate population into an almost universally literate one. It fought a largely successful battle against the influence on youth of such traditional institutions as the church. It helped socialize a predominantly tradition-oriented population into the cultural patterns of an industrial society. It trained the technical

[47] Hadley Cantril, *Soviet Leaders and Mastery over Man* (New Brunswick, N.J.: Rutgers University Press, 1960), p. 45, quotes the following definition of initiative by two of the leading educational theorists of the late Stalin era: "Not just blind obedience but an independent search for the best way to fulfill a command." The point, of course, is that there must be a command.

[48] Counts, *I Want*, p. 128.

[49] *Ibid.*, p. 89. In the primary grades "monitors" were directly appointed by the teacher; later they were "elected" by the *kollektiv*, but the influence of the teacher on the outcome was usually decisive.

[50] See Jeremy R. and Gabriella Azrael, "Sasha, Vovo, and Natasha," *The Reporter*, April 27, 1961.

[51] See F. Vigdorova, *Diary of a Russian Schoolteacher* (New York: Grove Press, 1960), for the role of leader of a class-collective.

[52] See Tim Callaghan, "Studying the Students," *Soviet Survey*, No. 33, July-September, 1960, pp. 131, 240.

[53] Inkeles and Bauer, *Soviet Citizen*, pp. 131, 240.

and managerial cadres without whom rapid industrialization and the maintenance of a high tempo of industrial growth would have been impossible. It educated scientists whose researches enabled the regime to pioneer new developments in a wide variety of fields. It played an important role in persuading the bulk of Soviet youth of the merits of socialist principles of production and distribution.[54] It helped generate enough consensus to enable the political system to survive severe shock from within and without. And, finally, it was instrumental in producing enough highly motivated, ideologically committed, and politically active young people that the regime was able to institutionalize tremendously rapid social and economic change and to establish a "permanent purge" of key officials without losing its essential political continuity.

These were no small accomplishments, and the foregoing catalog is by no means exhaustive. However, despite its many "successes," the educational system had not managed to create the sort of all-inclusive, monolithic, and homogeneous political culture that the rulers desired. Its efforts to create such a political culture had been beset by a number of problems which it had been unable to resolve. To be sure, in many cases, the fault lay not with the educational system proper but rather with forces in the broader economic, social, and political environment within which it functioned, but the problems at issue were often rendered more acute by the consequences of its functioning. The most critical of the problems which beset the educational system were those which derived from (1) the multinational character of Soviet society, (2) the tendency of the rigid status hierarchy which the regime had established to turn into a general system of social stratification and take on "class content," and (3) the capacity of the human mind to resist, remain immune to, "misinterpret," or become apathetic in the face of, intensive indoctrination.

THE PROBLEM OF NATIONALITIES

The educational system was still far from having eradicated all of the sources of tension and discord inherent in a multinational polity. It had accomplished a great deal in this direction and had in large measure succeeded in creating a sense of shared destiny among the polyglot nationalities of the U.S.S.R.[55] Even in this respect, however, there were significant exceptions, and, although reliable data are scarce, there is persuasive evidence that educational successes in the area of political socialization were consistently greater among Russian than among non-Russian youth.[56] In part this was a consequence of the fact

[54] *Ibid.*, p. 254.

[55] See *ibid.*, Chap. 15; and Barghoorn, *Soviet Russian Nationalism.*

[56] The fact that the regime felt it necessary to admit that collaboration with the Germans was widespread in several national republics is indicative of the existence of exceptions to the above generalization.

that the launching of the five-year plans had produced a more far-reaching social and cultural upheaval in many of the non-Russian regions than in Russia proper and, quite apart from any strictly political considerations, had engendered widespread hostility against the Bolsheviks as agents of "modernization." Moreover, there was a not altogether unjustifiable tendency to identify the Bolsheviks as Great Russians.[57] This introduction of a nationalistic dimension into an already complex situation made the task of the educational system more difficult. The difficulty was further compounded because the regime had assimilated many—though by no means all or the most important—of the traditional values and attitudes of the Russian people in an effort to win support among the dominant nationality during the "transitional period" to full-fledged totalitarianism.[58] For example, throughout most of the period under discussion, the concept of "Soviet patriotism" was heavily infused with the spirit of Russian nationalism.[59] This unquestionably heightened its appeal to Russian youth, but this was scarcely the case where Ukrainians, Uzbeks, or Tadzhiks were concerned.

One step which the regime had taken to make its indoctrinational "message" more palatable (as well as to insure its wider diffusion) was to propagate "socialist content" in "national form," and most non-Russians were given an opportunity to receive their education, including their higher education, in their native languages.[60] This unquestionably tended to appease nationalist sentiment in some respects, but it also had dysfunctional consequences. For one thing, the perpetuation (or in some cases creation, at least in written form) of native languages served almost automatically to preserve and in many cases to strengthen consciousness of a separate identity. In addition, it reduced the incentive to learn or teach Russian well and contributed to the rise of a situation in which, although the intensive study of Russian was required in all native-language schools, even graduates of native-language secondary schools and institutions of higher education were not really fluent in Russian.[61] This was dangerous for the Soviet system because Russian was the primary language of science, technology, and administration, and was hence a prerequisite for "progress" as the regime conceived it. The existing situation made it difficult for the regime to utilize native cadres and, at the same time, meant that non-Russians educated in native-language schools faced more limited career prospects than Russians

[57] Barghoorn, *Soviet Russian Nationalism*, pp. 68–69.

[58] See *ibid.*, on the assimilation of traditional Russian values. See Dinko Tomasic, *The Impact of Russian Culture on Soviet Communism* (Glencoe, Ill.: Free Press, 1953), for an extreme statement of the degree to which traditional Russian values were easily assimilable to Bolshevik values.

[59] See Barghoorn, *Soviet Russian Nationalism*.

[60] However, see *ibid.*, pp. 44–45, for a reference to the absence of such an opportunity in the former Polish Ukraine.

[61] See Bereday, *Changing Soviet School*, pp. 196–97, and Bereday and Pennar, *Politics of Soviet Education*, pp. 76–77.

with equivalent education.[62] They could normally make their way at the local level, but the odds were disproportionately against them at the national level.[63] The aspirations of the most ambitious were thus apt to be frustrated, while many other educated non-Russians had their tendencies toward "local nationalism" reinforced precisely because their occupational and professional frames of reference were "sensibly" local in character. Opportunities for advancement and access to positions of responsibility were extensive enough that there did not appear on the scene a wholly alienated native intelligentsia similar to that produced by the functioning of so many other "imperial" educational systems. Concessions to national pride were extensive enough so that little real separatist spirit developed. However, "localist" tendencies were prevalent, and forthright nationalist sentiment was by no means eradicated among highly educated non-Russian youth. That this should have been so graphically demonstrated by the violent reaction of Georgian university students to the destruction of the "personality cult" of their co-national Stalin was ironic but, at the same time, both symptomatic and symbolic.

The Problems of Status, Mobility, and Stratification

The Soviet rulers accompanied their turn to a policy of rapid industrialization and total planning with the establishment of a rigid status hierarchy in all walks of life. Extreme wage differentials, clear-cut symbols of rank and office, etc., were introduced in an effort to buttress managerial authority and to create a system of incentives which would draw maximum effort from the labor force and attract the ambitious, but ideologically hostile or indifferent, to the service of the regime.[64] At the same time, however, the rulers were committed to the maintenance of a rapid rate of vertical social mobility. The establishment of a rigid status hierarchy constituted a clear betrayal of those key tenets of Marxist-Leninist ideology which posited social egalitarianism, and the rulers hoped to mask this betrayal by pointing to universal *equality of opportunity* and the complete dependence of status on achievement. More important, the rulers counted upon a rapid rate of vertical social mobility to play a significant part in preventing the transformation of the status hierarchy into a general system of social stratification. Fearing a system in which status would cease to be wholly impersonal, a mere reflection of the regime's evaluation of the benefits

---

[62] Some non-Russians had the option of attending Russian schools in the non-Russian republics, and this option was often exercised by the ambitious. See Makhmatov, "The Outlook for Tartar Schools," *Soviet Education*, Vol. 2, No. 5, 1959–60. However, this option existed only in urban areas, and even in urban areas the number of places in Russian schools was limited.

[63] Distrust of the minorities and Great Russian chauvinism also limited the career opportunities of non-Russians, but here only factors related more or less directly to the functioning of the educational system are at issue.

[64] See Nicholas S. Timasheff, *The Great Retreat* (New York: E. P. Dutton, 1946).

which accrued to it through the exercise of various social and economic functions, the rulers hoped that rapid mobility would inhibit tendencies toward the consolidation of privilege and automatic transmission of privilege independently of the direct sanction of the regime. Rapid mobility was viewed as a desire to help insure against the status gulf's growing into a class gulf and unleashing pressures for social "routinization" and a reduction in the "tempo" of Soviet life. In sum, the commitment of the rulers to the maintenance of a rapid rate of vertical social mobility within the established status hierarchy was part and parcel of their commitment to the consolidation of total power in their own hands and to the creation of a totalitarian political culture.

The rulers always expected the educational system to serve as a major channel of rapid social mobility. In fact, as industrial maturation made problems of management and administration both increasingly critical and increasingly complex, the educational system almost perforce became the primary channel of social mobility. However, although it trained hundreds of thousands of "proletarian specialists," the educational system never managed to create a situation of equal opportunity for all, and in the period after World War II it began to show signs of functioning more and more as an instrument of social stratification.[65] Note has already been taken of the fact that in recent years, despite the seven-year compulsory education law, only 80 per cent of Soviet children who entered the first grade actually completed the seventh. The great bulk of the "delinquents" were concentrated in rural areas. The "delinquency" of rural children was attributable in large measure to the low quality of rural education, the necessity most of them faced of having to transfer to schools in towns and cities in order to continue their education beyond the fourth grade, the inadequacy of transportation and near absence of boarding facilities for transferees, etc.[66] The "underrepresentation" of the peasantry increased as one ascended the educational ladder.[67] This was due to the operative effects of low social status which were not confined to the peasantry although it hit them with particular force.

Among the urban population also differential rates of access to the upper levels of the educational system had become characteristic. Universal seven-year education was a reality in the cities, but the children of the workers were increasingly underrepresented as one moved into the upper reaches of the educational system, access to which had become

[65] See Azrael, "Political Profiles," pp. 252–55; Feldmesser, "Aspects of Social Mobility in the Soviet Union," unpublished dissertation, Harvard University, 1955.

[66] See DeWitt, *Education and Professional Employment*, pp. 142–43. Dropping out was encouraged also by the relative cultural impoverishment of the home and social environment of the bulk of rural children and by the fact that even young children were an economic asset in the countryside, particularly for work on the family's private garden plot. The factors noted in the text were, however, much more critical, and, as their character suggests, they were ultimately rooted in the failure of the regime to provide adequate resources to the educational system.

[67] See Inkeles and Bauer, *Soviet Citizen*, pp. 136–37.

a virtual prerequisite for entrance into the elite. The necessity of
paying tuition fees in the ten-year schools and institutions of higher
education, which applied between 1941 and 1956, militated against the
children of workers continuing their education.[68] An additional factor
was the inability of working-class parents to bring pressure or influence
to bear in order to secure places in institutions of higher education
for their children. This factor acquired great importance in the years
following Stalin's death, for in these years, due partly to widespread
knowledge that the abolition of tuition fees was imminent and partly
to a rise in income which made the payment of fees less burdensome,
more and more working-class children did enter and finish the ten-year
schools.[69] Since the institutions of higher education did not increase
their enrollments, an intensive competition for openings began, and
parental status determined the outcome in many instances.[70] The
combined effect of the fee system and parental influence is suggested
by the fact that, in 1958, 60 to 70 per cent of the students in institutions of higher education were children of "officials" and "members
of the intelligentsia." [71] This represents a marked change from the
situation which prevailed in the early 1930's, when the drive to "prole-
tarianize" education was at its height, and a significant change from the
situation which prevailed in 1938 (after the "proletarianization" drive
had been relaxed), when only 42 per cent of university students were

[68] Tuition fees were also demanded in technicums, but scholarships were rather
widely available for the latter. The question of why tuition fees were introduced in
1941 has never been satisfactorily resolved. Some have suggested that they were
designed to cover the costs of school construction, but the revenue they brought in
was never very substantial. Others have suggested that their purpose was to provide
more manpower for the labor force by limiting educational opportunities. This is
plausible, but the method chosen was bound to bring a derogation of ideological
legitimacy, to cause widespread resentment among the masses, and to increase the
danger that a system of stratification independent of achievement as appraised by the
regime would arise.

[69] The abolition of fees had been foreshadowed in 1952 at the Nineteenth Party
Congress, which decreed a transition to ten-year compulsory education to be completed
in the cities by 1955 and in the countryside by 1960.

[70] Khrushchev, "Educate Active and Conscious Builders of a Communist Society,"
School and Society (February 14, 1959), p. 66; and Khrushchev, "On Strengthening,"
p. 73. The number of openings in institutions of higher education was not expanded
due to the fact that the regime faced an acute adult manpower shortage as a result of
the "generational gap" brought about by World War II. Between 1954 and 1958 the
"surplus" of ten-year school graduates over higher education openings reached
3,000,000.

[71] Khrushchev, "On Strengthening," p. 74. These figures referred to institutions of
higher education in Moscow, and elsewhere the situation was probably more satisfactory. However, Moscow represented a general trend, and a trend that may actually
have been more extreme than Khrushchev's figures revealed, since he suggested that
many of the children of workers and peasants in institutions of higher education were
extension and correspondence students. The quality of correspondence and extension
education was lower than that of resident education, and the former probably brought
fewer opportunities for rapid advancement.

children of professional, administrative, or white-collar parents.[72] This change could not but be highly disturbing to rulers whose ideology posited a movement toward "classlessness," whose political system numbered a widespread opportunity for education among those of its attributes which attracted major support from the population at large, and who were desirous of preventing the transformation of a "service elite" into a "social elite." It was the more disturbing because it was accompanied by a growth of "class-consciousness," which the schools seemed powerless to prevent and often subtly encouraged, e.g., by stressing that the fate of academic failures was to become common workers.[73] The growth of "class-consciousness," in turn, threatened to generate patterns of solidarity and antagonism in society which the regime could not wholly control, and which could undercut its drive to eliminate all dimensions of autonomous social interaction. It also was largely responsible, in the eyes of the regime, for a disturbing tendency on the part of many students to take their privileged status for granted and respond with indifference or hostility to the educational system's attempts to mobilize them.

THE PROBLEMS OF DISAFFECTION AND APATHY

Had the Soviet educational system fulfilled the entirety of the political socialization plan that was assigned it during the period under discussion, the official "de-Stalinization" campaign that began in 1956 would, in one way or another, have resulted in the disintegration of the entire fabric of Soviet life. At a minimum it would have resulted in moral anarchy among the younger generation of Soviet citizens.[74] According to Soviet sources, "de-Stalinization" did cause "a trauma in [some] impressionable young souls" and led a certain number of students to

[72] See Inkeles and Bauer, *Soviet Citizen*, p. 137; Nicholas DeWitt, *Soviet Professional Manpower* (Washington: National Science Foundation, 1955), p. 100; Azrael, "Political Profiles," p. 223, esp. note 63; and Feldmesser, "Aspects of Social Mobility."

[73] According to a major article in *Pravda*, the educational system had contributed to the growth of a situation such that "the editors of youth newspapers frequently had to answer such questions from readers as, for example: 'Can a schoolgirl have a boyfriend who is a worker?' or 'I have a' job and study at night, while a friend of mine is a full-time student. He is condemned for his friendship with me. Is this right?' Etc." (*Pravda*, January 10, 1962, p. 4. See also *Izvestia*, November 24, 1961, p. 6; and Bereday and Pennar, *Politics of Soviet Education*, pp. 80–87.)

[74] Some further sense of the place of the Stalin cult in the school curriculum is provided by the following report which appeared in the official Soviet teachers' newspaper: "From the first day at school our children were brought up in the spirit of genuflection to the personality of J. V. Stalin. The idea was daily inculcated into the schoolchildren that their happy childhood had been created only by him and precisely he had given them the right to education. All the victories gained by the Soviet people both in the struggle against enemies and in creative work were explained only by the genius and wisdom of one man." (*Uchitelskaya gazeta*, August 22, 1956.)

become "skeptics" and "nihilists," believing in nothing and no one.[75] However, despite its disorienting consequences, it would appear that "de-Stalinization" did not profoundly disturb the bulk of Soviet youth, and it is the author's distinct impression that it left the majority of students remarkably untouched.[76] In launching the "de-Stalinization" campaign, Stalin's successors gambled that the educational system had failed in its ultimate task of inculcating an undifferentiated image of community, regime, and government, with faith in Stalin as the unifying cement. They won their gamble, but their very victory could not but disturb them, for it was clear that in part it was due to pervasive political indifference among a sizable segment of Soviet youth, and they were no more willing to tolerate indifference than Stalin had been before them. Moreover, the relaxation of control which accompanied "de-Stalinization" quickly revealed that there was a group of students at the upper levels of the educational system who were politically disaffected and whose disaffection could not be eradicated by the kind of political changes which they, Stalin's heirs, proposed to institute.

Disaffection, derived from a wide variety of sources, took diverse forms and appeared with varying degrees of intensity. Here only a few major variants can be noted.[77] Among some students disaffection took the form of "pandering to Western tastes." Often this amounted to little more than *stilyagism* or "style-chasing," indulged in more or less for its own sake as a protest against the drab, puritanical atmosphere of Soviet life and the depressing uniformity of official Soviet style. Sometimes, however, "pandering to Western tastes" involved genuine cultural "cosmopolitanism" and represented an effort on the part of some of the most cultured members of the younger generation to break free of the stultifying aesthetic canons of the regime and to reestablish contact with the mainstreams of Western art, literature, and music. In a few cases, there was concern with Western political concepts and institutions as well, but most of those who cultivated an interest in the West were not interested in political liberty so much as in liberty from politics. They tended to be apolitical, although in the Soviet context to be apolitical was to be politically defiant.

The major substantive sources of articulate and directly political disaffection were not to be found in the contemporary West, but rather in Marxist-Leninist theory and in the Russian cultural heritage. The students concerned tended to elaborate an "immanent critique" of the political system, contrasting Soviet reality with the theories which were used to legitimize it. The imagery they developed was that of

[75] See Speech of A. N. Shelepin to the Thirteenth Congress of the Komsomol translated in *Current Digest of the Soviet Press* 10, No. 16: 2–9; also, *Current Digest of the Soviet Press* 9, No. 27: 12; *The Soviet Review* 2, No. 11: 14; and S. Dmitriyev in *Molodaya Gvardiya*, April, 1962, pp. 278, 283.

[76] This impression derives from an academic year (1958–59) spent at Moscow State University.

[77] See Callaghan, "Studying the Students," and Burg, "Observations on Soviet University Students," *Daedalus*, Summer, 1960, for further discussion.

"Russia betrayed" or "the Revolution betrayed," and their goal was to recover the pure nucleus which they believed had been present at the inception of the political system, but had been stifled and contaminated by the bureaucratic rigidities and institutionalized brutalities of Stalinism. They were, in a word, idealists—but idealists whose zeal the educational system had failed to harness to Party loyalty and whose enthusiasm it had failed to discipline and direct into "constructive" channels.[78] Although the source of their disaffection was Stalinism, their conception of Stalinism embraced almost the whole of the contemporary Soviet system, and the selective "de-Stalinization" and wary return to Marxism-Leninism that Khrushchev was attempting seemed merely hypocritical.

The disaffected students, while disturbing, were nonetheless a small minority among the student body. A much larger group was politically indifferent and apathetic. As was the case with disaffection, the sources, forms, and degrees of political apathy were highly varied. A sizable group of students, including many of the best students in the pure and applied natural sciences, had developed a deep sense of professionalism and a somewhat technocratic orientation, which made them shun political involvement and become restive at political interference in their own spheres of primary interest, be it interference in the form of demands that they perform political functions or that they pursue their professional callings from a "Marxist-Leninist perspective." Another group was apathetic from sheer overwhelming boredom aroused by the dogmatism and repetitiveness of all political communication sponsored by the regime, whether in the classroom, the Komsomol, or the mass media. And yet a third group—perhaps the largest of all—developed an attitude toward politics that was purely instrumental. Political involvement was for them but a part of the process of acquiring prestige and status. The students in the group were adept at expressing zeal and enthusiasm at appropriate moments and were politically active when occasion demanded, but they were basically self-satisfied and complacent.[79] The artificial quality of the activism of this group was demonstrated with particular force in the years after 1954, when the number of ten-year school graduates began greatly to exceed the number of openings in institutions of higher education. A great many of those ten-year school graduates who were denied admission to the university or institute of their choice refused to enter the labor force and engaged in endless attempts extending over a period of years

[78] Often it was only when these young people left the educational system that they discovered the full extent of the contrast between theory and reality. Only then did they learn the extent to which evasion, suspicion, deception, and dissimulation were built into the prevailing political system. As one young Soviet recently put it: "When we graduated . . . we had no idea what a complex joke life could sometimes be. We walked into it with eyes shut. Many of us got our heads bloodied, and that first painful collision turned into something of a moral crash." *The Soviet Review* 2, No. 12:51.

[79] See Callaghan, "Studying the Students," and Burg, "Observations," for further discussion of the apathetic and "careerist" students.

to gain admittance to *any* department of *any* institution of higher education. They were unwilling to serve the regime in any but a "suitable" station despite the fact that the regime was facing a manpower shortage and could offer such challenging perspectives as labor in the Virgin Lands. As Khrushchev put it, they disdained and had a contemptuous attitude toward labor, and this was not only ideologically disturbing but also boded ill for the quality of their work when and if they achieved "suitable" positions.[80] Soviet executives no less than Soviet laborers were supposed to be "shock workers," and "disdain for labor" was unlikely to be translated into the desired entrepreneurial behavior.

*   *   *

23

THE SOVIET MODEL OF THE IDEAL YOUTH

RALPH T. FISHER, JR.

In this essay, "youth" refers to those between the ages of fifteen and the middle or late twenties—that is, those roughly within the age group of the Communist League of Youth, or Komsomol. The "Soviet model" is that constructed by the top Soviet leaders in their public expressions and actions. This abstraction combines the ideal images appropriate to the countless social roles demanded of Soviet young people. It is a model that

[80] Khrushchev, "On Strengthening," p. 73, and *idem*, "Educating Active and Conscious Builders," pp. 65–66. Khrushchev tended to attribute this complacency to "upper-class" origins, but its prevalence among students who did not gain admittance to institutions of higher education suggests that it was marked among students of worker and peasant origin as well. The educational system tended to inculcate status-consciousness and a variety of "anticipatory" class-consciousness in its own right, irrespective of the social origins of those involved.

Reprinted, by permission of the publishers, from Cyril E. Black, editor, *The Transformation of Russian Society* (Cambridge, Mass.: Harvard University Press, 1960), pp. 625–35. Copyright, 1960, by the President and Fellows of Harvard College. The footnotes have been omitted.

is important because it has been propagated by the immense educational and coercive resources of the Soviet state. This model bears no necessary similarity to those that have actuated the leaders in their own lives. Nor is it the only model that has influenced Soviet youth. Certainly there are widely differing models of youth in operation for many of the sub-cultures within the conglomerate of Soviet society. The coexistence of other models must be kept in mind as we study the most conspicuous ones.

There have obviously been changes, through forty years of the Soviet regime, in what might be called the external appearance and functions of the Soviet model of the ideal youth. Some of these changes reflect shifts in the composition of the Soviet population. For example, the composite model youth of today is better educated and less "proletarian" than his counterpart in the early postrevolutionary years. Other changes reflect the major stages in the development of the Soviet regime. Whereas the model of the Civil War years had a military cast, the model youth of the NEP was waging mainly ideological battles, and each succeeding period left its distinctive imprint. Within each area of Soviet life the detailed functions associated with the model have changed. If in the countryside the ideal youth of 1918–20 was confiscating grain and recruiting soldiers; under the early five-year plans he was collectivizing the farms and wiping out the kulaks. If in the educational realm the ideal youth of the early 1920's sneered at conventional schools and tried to combine education with factory work, the ideal youth of the 1940's was actively reinforcing discipline under the command of the authorities within the regular school system. But a survey of these changes in the multiple roles of youth in each area of Soviet life would involve the whole history of Soviet youth since 1917, and cannot be undertaken here.

Granting these changes in the shell of the model, we must focus our attention on the central core of traits demanded. We want to see what kind of personal character the regime has been trying to produce in its youth and whether the kind of character has changed significantly in the course of the past forty years. To learn this we may first examine the model that characterized the full bloom of postwar Stalinism, after the "abnormal" eras of the Great Purge and World War II, and then proceed to determine how far this model differed from that of the early years of the Soviet regime and that of the post-Stalin era.

The essential features of the ideal youth of postwar Stalinism emerge from the authoritative proceedings of the Komsomol congress of 1949, published at length in the Soviet press for the guidance of those who were training Soviet youth. For example, the letter sent to the Komsomol congress from the Central Committee of the Communist Party declared: "The Komsomol must bring up, among our youth, fighters who are fearless, cheerful, buoyant, confident in their strength, ready to overcome any difficulties—fighters for the freedom and honor of our Homeland, for the cause of the Party of Lenin and Stalin, for the victory of Communism." This passage was often repeated during the congress and was incorporated with little change into the revised regulations of the Komsomol. Another typical characterization appeared in the letter sent by the Komsomol congress to Stalin:

> We vow to you, dear Comrade Stalin, warmly to love our socialist Home-land, mortally to hate her enemies, not to know fear in the struggle, patiently to endure hardships and misfortunes, to display determination and persistence in reaching the goal that has been set. The young generation of our country is ready to carry out all your instructions and all the instructions of the Communist Party and the Soviet Government. We promise you always to be watchful, ready to deliver a crushing rebuff to the imperialist aggressors, ready to give all our strength and, if necessary, our lives in the defense of our socialist Fatherland.
>
> You teach Soviet youth perseveringly to master knowledge, culture, science, and technology.
>
> We vow to you, Comrade Stalin, to carry out with honor these instructions of yours. . . .
>
> Love of you and loyalty to the Fatherland is the life and the spirit of the youth of our country!

From those statements and many others like them, one could draw up a list of traits sought in youth—patriotism, loyalty, courage, vigilance, honesty, persistence, industriousness, optimism, initiative, cheerfulness, idealism, obedience, militancy, ideological purity, and many others.

The central theme that gave the above traits their meaning was that of absolute devotion, respect, and subservience to the leadership represented in the trinity—Stalin, Party, and government. Although the worship of Stalin was then near the peak of its extravagance, even the gaudiest panegyric illustrated that the cult was of Stalin as the leader of the Party and, hence, of the people and their government; when the ideal youth was told to regard Stalin as the incarnation of everything good, the recipient of vows, and the source of inspiration and strength, these demands only reinforced the demand for loyalty, respect, and obedience to the Party leadership. Komsomol orders were an extension of Party orders for the young. The Komsomol regulations declared that "the strictest observance of Komsomol discipline is the first obligation of all members of the Komsomol" and went on to say that each member "must faultlessly carry out the decisions of Party, soviet, and Komsomol bodies." Not only the reference to discipline and to unity and solidarity, but the whole conduct of the congress, including the nature of the discussion and the always miraculously unanimous votes, made it clear that the Party leadership was exercising very tight control and that eager acceptance of this "guidance" was a distinguishing feature of the ideal youth.

It was in that context alone that all the other traits demanded in the ideal youth could be interpreted. Words like patriotism, courage, daring, heroism, self-sacrifice—these were applicable only to those who fought for the Party's cause. "Vigilance" concerned the security of the Party and the Soviet state; "honesty" concerned the observance of principles laid down by the leadership. Persistence, industriousness, all-out effort, the constant striving for perfectionist goals, the refusal to be satisfied with what one has attained—such qualities were of course related to the "building of Communism," that is, the tasks enunciated by the Party leaders. Virtuous conduct in personal life was inseparable from political life. "Initiative" must follow strictly the commands of the Party. The cheerfulness that was part of the ideal did not preclude some satisfaction with the present, but was essentially based upon optimism regarding the promised future. One might conceivably argue that it was that future —the long-range goal, communism—to which the ideal youth was sub-ordinating himself, rather than to the leadership of the Party. When, however, one takes into account the persistent vagueness of all descriptions of that ultimate goal, as well as the leaders' assumption that only they knew how to reach it, then one is bound to conclude that, while references to the goal were used to justify the immediate demands of the leadership, those demands themselves were the essential guideposts for the ideal youth.

The Soviet model of the ideal youth in 1949 was, in short, the "eager robot"—inwardly so complete a tool of Party leadership as to be devoid of a genuine self, yet outwardly seeming to possess such human attributes as will and judgment and enthusiasm.

With this ideal youth of postwar Stalinism in mind, we can now return to the early Soviet period when Stalin had not yet added his impress to the mold. Although there was in those days very little glorification of any leader, including even Lenin, subservience could nevertheless be demanded. How subservient was the ideal youth?

When the Komsomol, which ostensibly embraced the best young people, held its first congress, in October, 1918, the assembled delegates agreed virtually unanimously that while the league was to be "solidary" with the Bolshevik Party it was at the same time to be "independent." It was to safeguard "the principle of the spontaneous activity of youth." In April, 1919, however, a plenary session of the Komsomol's Central Committee "requested" that the Komsomol be brought more closely under the Party's direction, and soon (August, 1919) the two Central Committees jointly declared that the Komsomol must be "directly subordinate" to the Party from top to bottom. While the Komsomol continued to be called "autonomous," the word "independent" dropped out of use and by 1920 was already stigmatized as typical of the dangerous "counter-revolution of the left."

The direct subordination of the league to the Party was evident in deed as well as in word. Some of those whom the first and second congresses elected to the league's Central Committee were unceremoniously removed from their posts by the Party. Already by 1920 the top officials of the league, although ostensibly still elected by the Komsomol congress, were in fact designated by a "Communist faction" operating behind the scenes and subject to Party orders. Pronounced tendencies toward authoritarian rule from the side of the Party were evident in the conditions of deliberation and criticism in the early Komsomol congresses, in the admission and expulsion of members, and in the organizational structure. When some especially zealous Komsomolites launched satellite groups resigned to influence and guide the broad masses of Soviet youth, the Party stopped them, evidently fearing to let Komsomolites gain too much influence over auxiliary youth groups until the Komsomol itself was more firmly under Party domination.

In that early institutional setting the personal quality most insistently demanded in youth was discipline. This discipline was to spring from acknowledgment of the communist goal and was to be conscious, self-willed, and self-enforced, rather than imposed from without in an "authoritarian spirit." Thus it was theoretically not in conflict with the parallel demands for initiative and spontaneity. But it must produce unity and solidarity—in Lenin's words, "a single will" for all the millions of workers and peasants. It must be manifested in strict obedience to higher authority. Said Shatskin at the Komsomol congress of 1920:

> There are some comrades among us who say that there is one discipline in the Party and another in the league. They say that since our organization is an educational one, we can somewhat loosen the reins with which the leading bodies must hold their subordinate Komsomol organizations in check. This opinion must be refuted root and branch. . . . We must finally establish the most unconditional unquestioning subordination of all active workers to the leading bodies of our organization, and the personal responsibility of each responsible official for each member of our league, for that work which these members are performing.

The same congress in closing issued to all members "an appeal for the greatest self-control and discipline." After describing the perils they faced, it proclaimed that

> in such conditions, there stands before the whole proletariat and also before proletarian youth first of all the task of preserving, developing, and strengthening iron discipline in the ranks of their organizations. Only with such discipline, consolidating the proletariat into an impregnable granite rock, can it resist the crowd of enemies and the loose petit-bourgeois element.
> The Third Congress appeals for the preservation of such iron discipline in our ranks. May the ranks of our league be invincible battalions of young proletarians storming the old world.
> Long live our militant front!
> Long live the victorious proletariat!
> Long live revolutionary proletarian discipline!

Other traits much in demand included self-sacrificing bravery for the communist cause, alertness and vigilance against hostile forces, confidence in the victory of communism, a sense of responsibility, and such qualities as toughness, dexterity, precision, and industriousness. Those and other demands—to learn Marxism, to set an example, and to avoid dogmatism and pride—were expressed in harmony with the overriding insistence on conscious discipline and strict obedience. The Soviet ideal youth in 1918–20 was above all a good follower.

Thus the models of 1949 and 1918–20 appear highly similar. Although in the early Soviet ideal there was probably a shade more independence than in the Stalinist version, the characteristics of the eager robot were already predominant.

One might protest, quite logically, that the conditions of the Civil War would have produced the eager-robot ideal, no matter what had been the Communists' original intent. It is therefore pertinent to examine briefly the prerevolutionary Bolshevik model of the ideal youth, as revealed in the writings of the chief prophet of Bolshevism.

Lenin left no finished portrait of his ideal Bolshevik, young or old, even though his program called for remaking man and society. But as a revolutionary leader he demanded and appreciated certain traits in his followers. He especially prized worker and student youth for their turbulence, daring, and revolutionary potentialities and considered young people suited to play the semisacrificial role of a vanguard or skirmishing force which could be sent into battle without committing the main body of the Party. Apart from such notions, however, Lenin's image of the ideal youth was roughly equivalent to his image of the ideal Bolshevik, for he considered his party to be the Party of youth.

Lenin conveniently divorced his model from customary ethical standards by labeling those standards either "feudal" or "bourgeois" and by asserting that the proletariat—whose will he considered himself uniquely fitted to interpret—would establish the moral code of the future. Proletarian ethics admitted all methods. Lenin declared that "Social Democracy does not tie its hands . . . it recognizes all means of struggle so long as they are suited to the available forces of the Party and afford the possibility of gaining the greatest results attainable under the given circumstances."

Lenin insisted that his followers exhibit "Partyness," by which he meant allegiance to his Bolshevik faction of the Russian Social Democratic Workers' Party and observance of Party discipline. In his view a truly nonpartisan approach was impossible. When some of his disciples intimated that Partyness was a negation of freedom within their own group, Lenin retorted that Partyness constituted "freedom from bourgeois-anarchist individualism." The principle of freedom of organization, he declared, gave the Party the right to exclude those who insisted on being individualistic. Lenin was not above declaring support of his own tactics to be a criterion of Partyness. But when he was accused of using Partyness as a mere cloak for his own political demands, he argued that his policy was that of "the majority of class-conscious Marxist workers participating in political life."

He did not always sound completely authoritarian. For example, he could say,

Precisely in order not to become too outspoken and . . . harsh regarding "anarchistic individualism" we must, in our opinion, do everything possible—even to the point of some retreats from the pretty diagrams of centralism and from an unconditional submission to discipline—in order to grant these little groups freedom to express themselves, in order to give the whole Party the possibility of weighing the profundity or insignificance of disagreements, and to determine just where, in what, and *on just whose side* there is *inconsistency*. . . . We must have more faith in the independent judgment of all the masses of Party workers. They, and only they, can soften the excessive vehemence of schismatically inclined groupings; can, with their gradual, imperceptible, but all the more persistent influence, inspire these groups with "good will' toward the observance of Party discipline; can cool the ardor of anarchistic individualism.

But this semitolerance toward "little groups" within the Party was exhibited late in 1903, after the Party had split and Lenin had lost his fight to control the party organ, *Iskra.* In other words, it was at a moment when he had reason to fear that he and his followers might for a time be one of those "little groups"—that is, until they could fight back to a position of power.

Lenin's view of personal relationships fitted into the framework of Partyness and centralism. He condemned clannish or cliquish relations—which included personal loyalties to individuals other than himself—on the ground that they obstructed Party discipline. Comradeliness had for him a special meaning: "We acknowledge the duty of comradeship, the duty of supporting all comrades, the duty of tolerating the opinions of comrades." "But," he went on, *"for us the duty of comradeship stems from the duty to Russian and to international Social Democracy, and not vice versa."* Comrades were comrades, he said, "only because and insofar as they toil in the ranks of Russian (and, consequently, also international) Social Democracy." While Lenin appealed for initiative, this merely complemented his demand for discipline. A reminder on discipline could be used to bring into line comrades who did something wrong, while a request for more initiative could stimulate those who were merely not doing enough of what was right.

Plainly underlying Lenin's concept of the ideal Bolshevik was his preoccupation with fight and struggle. For him there was no possibility of a peaceful compromise. "The question," he said, "can be posed *only this way:* bourgeois or socialist ideology. There is no middle ground." "Therefore," he went on—in a phrase that has since become a Communist slogan—*"any* belittling of socialist ideology, *any deviation* from it means the same thing as a strengthening of bourgeois ideology."

This by no means exhaustive survey of Lenin's prerevolutionary desiderata suggests strongly that the eager-robot ideal of 1949 and 1918–20 was already well developed early in the twentieth century.

The ideal did not die with Stalin. In 1954, at the first Komsomol congress after Stalin's death, the leadership called for a revival of "criticism from below," observance of the collective principle in leadership, and wider democracy within the league. But the congress itself, in its discussion, criticism, and voting, gave no hint of genuine relaxation. Soviet literature was still said to be failing to depict lifelike heroes who could serve as models for the young. Although the Stalin cult was gone, the cult of the Party and its Central Committee provided ample occasion for the same extravagant expressions of devotion. In their letter to the Party's Central Committee, the delegates said:

> The young men and women of the land of the Soviets have boundless love and loyalty for the Communist Party. Their most cherished thoughts and hopes are bound up with the Party; they are obligated to it for all the happiness and joy of their lives. . . . In all its activities the Leninist Komsomol senses the daily, fatherly care of the Communist Party and its Central Committee. . . .
>
> The Communist Party is the wise teacher and mentor of youth. For the Komsomol, the word and deed of the Party come before all else.

And when that letter was read at the final session, all delegates reportedly rose "in a united transport of boundless love for their own Communist Party" and gave a "tumultuous ovation," shouting "Glory to the Communist Party!"

Since 1954 there has been no clear sign of change. The Komsomol Central Committee in February, 1957, while calling for more democracy in the league, insisted also, in the very same sentence, on the need for stronger discipline, and the attitude toward the Party leadership was just as subservient as ever. In July [1957], when Khrushchev's victory over Malenkov, Kaganovich, and Molotov was announced, the accompanying editorial—studded with references to monolithic unity, discipline, and obedience to Party directives—was in the Stalinist tradition.

The Soviet model of the ideal youth—the model expressed by the Party leadership—has had, then, an almost unvarying core. Changes have occurred in the external appearance and functions of the model, but these have not significantly affected the continuity of the eager-robot ideal—the ideal of utter loyalty to the Party chiefs, iron discipline, self-sacrificing bravery, incessant vigilance, burning enthusiasm, unshakable conviction, and uncompromising militancy. While many of those qualities suggest a military figure, the ideal youth, unlike a soldier, is never off duty. There are no areas of human knowledge, appreciation, or action in which he can exercise full freedom and imagination.

The persistence of the eager-robot ideal reflects the continuing importance of doctrine for the Soviet regime, the regime's reliance upon an atmosphere of crisis, and the regime's totalitarian and authoritarian character. The official ideal as treated here could not change significantly without considerable changes in the nature of the regime.

But the answer to the question of continuity and change in the Soviet model of the ideal youth must be termed incomplete. We are driven back to the difficulties suggested earlier, which stem in large part from our lack of free access to Soviet society. We lack the means of penetrating

very far beyond the formal or official or external model, but we can perceive that it does not monopolize the scene. To the extent that it appears
too harsh and uncompromising, to the extent that it fails to *live* for
Soviet citizens, it encourages other models to flourish. The Soviet system,
never completely authoritarian or totalitarian despite its aims and its
dictatorial excesses, can inspire models of careerism, of apathy, of compromise, of opposition. The cynicism of the leaders vitiates the official
model, while beyond the circle of political chiefs there are other model-
makers who play significant but not easily appraisable roles in establishing operating images of the ideal. Thus there is the possibility that while
"the Soviet model" remained the same, other models, without being
formal or official, nevertheless could alter significantly the orientation of
Soviet youth.

*   *   *

24

SOVIET ADULT POLITICAL INDOCTRINATION

FREDERICK C. BARGHOORN

Adult political training is a distinctive feature of the Soviet polity. It supplements and deepens the Marxist-Leninist indoctrination already received in schools and higher educational institutions. The Soviet program
of "political enlightenment" was intensified after the death of Stalin, and
increased efforts were made to expand its coverage to include not merely
members of the Communist Party but also all Soviet citizens. While
greatly expanding its adult citizenship training program the Party simultaneously sought to improve the quality of the much more advanced and
intensive political instruction given to the carefully screened functionaries
chosen for executive responsibilities. A "differentiated" approach to adult

Reprinted from *Ventures, Magazine of the Yale Graduate School*, Volume IV,
Fall, 1964, pp. 23–34.

political socialization was demanded. This approach was not entirely new, but it was apparently implemented with increasing effectiveness after 1956.

There have been three main stages in the development of Soviet adult political instruction or, as it is often called in Soviet sources, "Party propaganda." The first stage included the years of revolutionary struggle before the establishment of Soviet power, the period of Lenin's rule and that portion of Stalin's rule culminating in 1938 with publication of the *History of the All-Union Communist Party (Bolsheviks)*, usually refered to as the *Short Course*. With the exception of a few of Lenin's major works the *Short Course* was probably the most important single publication in the history of the Soviet Union. Presently we shall describe the organization and style of political instruction which prevailed during the fifteen years when the *Short Course* was the bible of Soviet communism. In each of these periods the Party has endeavored to set the pattern of political indoctrination which it considered appropriate at the particular time. Organizational structure, teaching methods, and texts have been standardized. At the same time, a vigorous effort has been made to exclude from the process of political training "incorrect" or "harmful" information and interpretations.

A comprehensive system of political instruction was established in the early 1920's. Because of the generally low educational level of all Soviet citizens prevalent at the time, the Party educational system overlapped considerably with the general Soviet educational network, a situation which was largely corrected in the late 1930's but which to some extent persists even today. However, since both the Party and the general educational structures have been controlled from one center, changes in their practices and curricula have been rather closely coordinated. The political education ladder established in the 1920's set a pattern which, with modifications, has persisted throughout the history of the Soviet regime. In its early form, the structure operated at four levels: schools of "political literacy"; lower-level Soviet and Party schools; higher-level Soviet and Party schools; and communist universities, of which the most famous was the Sverdlov University, founded in 1918. The level of education offered by these Party institutions corresponded roughly to that given in regular Soviet schools of elementary, secondary, and higher education, respectively. However, at all levels these institutions were expected to instill revolutionary fervor and to eradicate "bourgeois" attitudes. The Soviet and Party schools trained lower-level Party functionaries and were particularly oriented to the training of propagandists and agitators. The communist universities specialized in the training of high-level editors, educators, and other workers of the Soviet "cultural apparatus."

Rapid growth of Party membership in the 1930's was accompanied by expansion of the adult political education system. For example, the number of Party schools and study circles grew from 52,000 in 1930 to 210,000 in 1933, and the number of students increased from 1,000,000 during the same period to 4,500,000. Almost half of these students were not Party members at all but fell into the category of "non-Party Bolsheviks," a term used to describe persons who identified with the Party, many of whom eventually became Party members. When, after the rise of Khrushchev, a pattern of mass adult political indoctrination similar to that which prevailed in the early Stalin era was restored, but on a much larger scale, the program was linked to the name of Lenin and its presentation was accompanied by denunciations of Stalin's alleged deviations from Leninism.

In fact, Stalin did alter the political indoctrination program in 1937 and in 1938 in the direction of an elitism designed to strengthen Party control over the new technical, scientific, and administrative cadres which were being rapidly created to staff the fast-growing Soviet industrial and military bureaucracies.

An important 1938 resolution on Party propaganda reflected Stalin's determination to politically integrate the new Soviet intelligentsia into Soviet society. The resolution, entitled "Concerning the Structure of Party Propaganda in Connection with the Publication of the Short Course in the History of the All-Union Communist Party (Bolsheviks)," also reflected the deep suspicions which had given rise to and had been further intensified by the 1936–38 purges, which decimated the Party and especially its upper echelons. Another major effort of tightening up and consolidation was necessitated by World War II. Party indoctrinational efforts had been neglected during the struggle for survival against the Nazis. Also, both rank-and-file Party members and Soviet citizens generally had been led by wartime propaganda of national unity and international cooperation with the Western allies to believe that a more relaxed and less militant world outlook would prevail after the war.

It soon became apparent that these hopes were to be dashed. Particularly in such spheres as the arts, sciences, and education, but also in internal Party indoctrination, Stalin moved in 1945 and 1946 to restore the pattern which had been somewhat shaken by the war and by contacts with the West. On August 2, 1946, the Central Committee adopted a resolution "On the Training and Retraining of Leading Party and Soviet Workers," the preamble to which pointed out that many Party and soviet workers had ceased to systematically work toward the elevation of their intellectual and theoretical level. Once again a straining after quantity at the expense of quality was criticized. The resolution declared that it was necessary in the next three or four years to follow that the "main leading cadres" of the Party and soviet workers should be drawn into Party schools and courses. It set forth highly detailed directives as to how this should be done. It also provided for the reopening of the Higher Party School under the Central Committee, reorganized the system of lower-ranking Party schools, and provided for the establishment of an academy of social sciences to train theoretical workers for the Party under the aegis of the Administration of Propaganda and Agitation of the Central Committee.

Although some significant modifications in the system of political education occurred during the years 1953–56—in 1954 a new textbook on political economy was published and the *Short Course,* at first extolled, gradually ceased to be mentioned—it was not until Khrushchev's report to the Central Committee at the Twentieth Party Congress in 1956 that a new major phase in the Kremlin's approach to all aspects of political indoctrination and communication began. A systematic effort to improve and expand ideological indoctrination has indeed been one of the major preoccupations of the Party leadership since 1955. The demand for a livelier, more "practical," and broader political education program found expression in Khrushchev's main speeches, in a number of Central Committee documents, and in a profusion of handbooks and pamphlets intended for use by Party functionaries and propagandists. The renewed emphasis upon mass indoctrination in Marxism-Leninism was related to the main trends in Soviet policy after the death of Stalin. It was a logical development in view of the Party's proclaimed intention to proceed with the full-scale building of a communist society, one of the requirements of which is the elevation of the consciousness of all citizens to ever higher levels. It may have been motivated also by Kremlin concern regarding political apathy among Soviet young people and among large segments of the industrial working class and the peasantry. Certainly, also, there was concern about certain moods and attitudes among Soviet intellectuals, particularly in an era when the requirements of national policy and of Soviet standing within the international communist movement appeared to necessitate vastly increased contacts between Soviet citizens and representatives of the "bourgeois" world and assurance that the Soviet citizens involved in these contacts be effective in presenting the Soviet policy line and in resisting the blandishments of their capitalist colleagues. It will be useful to examine some representative statements of the post-Stalin program before describing its structure and content.

The gist of Khrushchev's statements on "ideological work" at the Twentieth, Twenty-first, and Twenty-second CPSU congresses was that such work must above all serve as a stimulus to action. It must assist the Party in laying the "material and technical foundations for communism." It must stimulate Soviet workers to increase their productivity. Khrushchev linked up this pragmatic approach to propaganda with quotations from Lenin. He summed up his position well in a sentence in his report to the Central Committee at the Twenty-second Congress, which read as follows: "The ideological work of Party organizations raises the communist consciousness, the labor and political activity of the masses, and serves as a very important constantly active factor in the building of communism." It is important to note that while Khrushchev took the position that propaganda which did not produce tangible results was useless, he did not urge that Communists should be satisfied with production alone. Rather, he reiterated a basic tenet of Marxism-Leninism, namely, the interaction between ideological and practical activity. As he put it in his report to the Twenty-second Congress, the strength of the Party consisted in its ability to "fuse in its revolutionary, transforming activity the theory and practice of scientific communism." The everyday achievements of the Party and the Soviet state were an expression of theory in action, according to Khrushchev. In a word, Khrushchev demanded that the conduct of Soviet citizens be guided by theory and that mastery of theory be demonstrated in action.

The most systematic rationale of Party propaganda policy since the already mentioned 1938 resolution was probably that of January 9, 1960. This resolution began by pointing out that in the period of full-scale building of a communist society ideological work, and, in particular, its "decisive aspect," Party propaganda, took on exceptional significance. The acquisition of a communist world outlook had now become "a vital necessity" for every Soviet citizen. The critical preamble of this resolution demanded that propaganda more effectively than in the past inculcate in Soviet citizens "a spirit of Soviet patriotism and national pride." However, the resolution also demanded that this be done without any tolerance for survivals of "bourgeois nationalism" or other harmful traditions or reactionary customs. The 1960 resolution also criticized previous propaganda work for "the narrowness of its sphere of influence," and also for lack of "massiveness" and weakness of presentation. Local Party organizations, as well as research institutes of the Academy of Sciences of the U.S.S.R., the Institute of Marxism-Leninism, the Higher Party School, and other organizations and institutions were severely criticized because they had, according to the resolution, failed to give sufficient attention to the "bringing up of the workers in a communist spirit." Among the defects of propaganda work criticized were failure to rebuff "manifestations of nationalism, cosmopolitanism, and political indifference," as well as survivals of religious attitudes, violations of labor discipline, and violations of "the principles of communist morality."

The resolution then presented sixteen sets of instructions and demands for the improved conduct of Party propaganda. The general tenor of these instructions was contained in the following paragraph:

> The chief task of Party propaganda consists in a deep and many-sided explanation of the ideas of Marxism-Leninism, the indication as to how they may be successfully applied to life in the course of the struggle of the Party for the victory of socialism and communism in our country, study of their utilization in the practical activity and creative development of the theoretical wealth accumulated by the Party, the raising of the workers in struggle for the realization of the policy of the Party in life, and the training of active and firm fighters for communism.

Perhaps the most significant section of the resolution from an operational point of view was one which instructed Party organizations to achieve an orderly sequence in propaganda work, so that "each Communist from year to year would systematically and purposefully raise his ideological and political level and master Marxism-Leninism as an integrated teaching." The same section of the resolution recommended the following ladder of political education: (1) the political school as the first run of Marxist-Leninist training; (2) circles and theoretical seminars for the study of the history of the CPSU; (3) theoretical seminars and circles for the study of Marxist-Leninist philosophy, political economy, concrete economics, problems of atheism, current politics, the international situation, the international communist movement; (4) economic schools; (5) universities of Marxism-Leninism; independent study according to individual plans, and also in theoretical seminars for the study of particular works of the classics of Marxism-Leninism, or of particular problems of the history of the Communist Party of the Soviet Union, political economy, dialetical and historical materialism, ethics, esthetics, atheism, the world communist, labor, democratic, and national liberation movement, and others.

Another section of the resolution pointed out that the success of Party propaganda depended upon the quality of the cadres of propagandists engaged in it, and it issued instructions to Party organizations on improvement of the recruiting and training of propagandists. This was followed by instructions regarding the establishment of "houses" and "cabinets" for political enlightenment, the purpose of which was to assist propagandists in their training and in their work. Other sections of the resolution were devoted to such methods of propaganda work as lectures, the press, radio, and television. A rather long section stressed the importance of the social sciences in communist indoctrination and in propaganda work, and it called for the preparation of appropriate works on such subjects as the history of the CPSU, philosophy, economics, and history, and also for works on the world communist movement, with proper attention to "the collapse of the colonial system of imperialism and the development of a national-liberation struggle of the peoples of Asia, Africa, and Latin America." This section also requested publication of works "exposing the pseudo-scientific theories of bourgeois, right-wing socialist, and revisionist defenders of capitalism."

The above resolution presented a comprehensive program for the political education of all levels of the Soviet population except for the leaders and cadres of the Party. The data available in Soviet sources indicate that this program, which was already in its early stages of development when the January, 1960, resolution was promulgated, has been carried out with vigor and on a very large scale. Leonid Ilyichev, in a speech reported in *Pravda* for June 19, 1963, stated that "more than 20,000,000 people are engaged in organized study of the history, theory, and policy of the Party in the political enlightenment system." According to another authoritative Soviet source, 22,553,000 persons were enrolled, as of the academic years 1961–62, in the system of political enlightenment. Of these, slightly over 7 million were Party members while the remainder were non-Party persons. What is surprising, perhaps, in these figures is not so much the fact that about 70 per cent of the members of the CPSU were engaged in organized political studies but the very large number of non-Party people so engaged. Yevdokimov stated that in 1958–59 the combined figure for Party and non-Party students in the political instruction network had been 6.7 million, of whom 4.5 million had been members of the Party. It is difficult to know whether or not these figures are inflated, and if so, to what extent. In any case, it is clear that an instructional program of such vastness presents many problems. One problem is that of providing a level of subject matter and of degree of depth of content suited to the varied background of the students. Although the 1960 resolution indicated that the political school was to be the lowest rung of the political education ladder, Yevdokimov stated that the lowest rung was the "elementary economics schools and circles." It appears that the political schools and the economic schools, as well as the more elementary study circles and theoretical seminars, are designed to meet the needs of Party and non-Party students who have not graduated from secondary schools or from higher educational institutions. After obtaining, in these programs, an elementary knowledge of "the laws of social development" and related topics and then studying "the fundamentals of Marxism-Leninism," Soviet citizens can go on to the study of particular aspects of Marxism-Leninism. Finally, the Communist or non-Party activist embarks upon a program of "independent study." However, this independent study is supplemented by group discussions once or twice a month, by lectures and conferences, and by "consultations" for the purpose of clarifying difficulties and correcting mistakes. During the 1961–62 school year about 5.5 million persons were engaged in this form of supervised independent study.

The second major category of political self-improvement is that of persons with secondary schools and higher education. Their political education has already begun in secondary school or in an institute or university. Perhaps the most important institution for the continued political education of relatively well-educated Soviet citizens is the "Evening University of Marxism-Leninism." The evening universities have various faculties and divisions. A person who has completed, for example, the faculty of fundamentals of Marxism-Leninism may then go on to study in one of the special faculties, such as history, philosophy, or political economy. Having completed the courses available in the Evening University of Marxism-Leninism, a highly educated citizen then continues his political training in a theoretical seminar or in a planned individual study program. The principle of sequence is combined with study, at all levels and in all branches of the system, of such basic materials as the Party Program and the most important documents "of the CPSU and the international communist movement, where all the constituent parts and aspects of the Marxist-Leninist teaching are represented in their organic unity." The inclusion of such materials throughout the system insures uniformity of perspective. It also imparts to the total program timeliness and elements of relevance to everyday matters. It may also be noted that this emphasis on the immediate is nothing new. Just as the Stalinist 1938 resolution was critical of the remoteness from reality of much of the teaching in the political education system, so also were the Khrushchevian directives critical, on the same grounds, of the Stalin program. In both periods this criticism of previous practice was both correct and at the same time disingenuous. In both periods, but especially of course during the Stalin era, the propagandists who teach, for example, the history of the CPSU have presumably tended to shy away from touchy topics, and this is probably one reason why, in both periods, one found so much criticism of the practice of permitting students of political courses to remain for years at the same level of content. Similarly, one finds in the documents of both the Stalin and post-Stalin periods criticism of a "mechanical" or an "abstract" approach, which avoids the practical and policy implication of political indoctrination.

The third and highest level of adult political socialization is the one which shapes the outlook and skills of the Party functionaries, who are the driving force, the movers and shapers, of Soviet society. The students of the special schools for Party functionaries and executives are a select group. As is the case with the vastly more numerous students of the programs already described, little is known about the intellectual atmosphere which prevails in the classrooms of the elite political training institutions. However, the inaccessibility of the higher-level institutions to even formal visits by foreign observers is perhaps more significant than the corresponding lack of opportunity for on-the-spot observation in the case of the lower rungs of this political education ladder, for the tiny minority of trusted and seasoned party cadres who attend the higher levels constitute a large proportion of the human material which makes the Soviet system a distinctive one.

It is not difficult to describe the general outlines of the instruction program in the schools for Party functionaries. Like the lower-ranking political education institutions, these schools were affected by the pragmatic post-Stalin emphasis. In his report to the Twentieth Congress, Khrushchev, while expressing satisfaction over the results of the Party cadre training program since 1946, was severely critical of the failure of the Party training schools to give to their students an adequate preparation in the fundamentals of agricultural and industrial administration. He indicated that lack of knowledge of the fundamentals of applied economics adversely affected the performance of Party workers in the direction of the Soviet national economy. In 1956 and 1957 the system of training for Party cadres was reorganized. The main links in the new system, which seems still to be functioning, were four-year inter-oblast party schools in Moscow, Leningrad, Alma-Ata, Tashkent, Baku, Minsk, and some twenty other major cities, and the Higher Party School, which was changed from a three-year to a two-year institution. The June, 1956, resolution which instituted this reorganization also stipulated that in Moscow, Leningrad, Kiev, Minsk, Khabarovsk, Alma-Ata, and Tashkent Party schools should have special programs for the training of journalists. The resolution also provided that the four-year inter-oblast party schools should be included in the category of higher educational institutions together with the Higher Party School. Also, the Higher Party School was authorized to continue to maintain a division for journalistic personnel.

Members of the CPSU, up to the age of thirty-five, with a secondary education, are admitted to the four-year party schools. They must pass entrance examinations on the history of the U.S.S.R., Russian language, geography, and "fundamentals of Marxism-Leninism." Admission to the Higher Party School requires a higher education and "adequate experience" in leadership work. Admission to the Higher Party School is open to persons not more than forty years of age. Among the interesting aspects of the admissions requirements for the Higher Party School is one which makes admission available to "workers, commissioned for study by Communist and workers' parties of foreign countries."

So far as can be determined from available sources, the differences among the levels of adult political education in the U.S.S.R. consist mainly in the quantity, complexity, and intensity of instruction, rather than in content or point of view. To the non-Communist observer, all levels of the program appear to convey a surprisingly uniform, authoritarian, but powerfully systematic and by no means completely inflexible pattern of thought. Thus, the "model study plan for the political schools" provides for about thirty-six sessions, apparently spread over a period of two years. The evening universities of Marxism-Leninism offer a two-year basic course, with from twenty to twenty-four hours per month of instruction for each student, as of 1948–49. Presumably, the study load in the evening universities has been expanded, but no figures appear to be available.

What is the idea content of instruction in these various schools? Generally speaking, the subject matter which they offer may be divided into four main sections: first, the philosophy of "dialectical materialism"; second, the historical-sociological teaching of "historical materialism"; third, political economy; and, finally, political doctrine or political science, taught under the headings "theory and tactics of the international communist movement" and "the doctrine of socialism and communism."

There is now a much wider range of textbooks and other reading material for the political courses than was the case during the Stalin era. Although the basic theme of all of this literature remains the Lenin-Stalin thesis of a struggle between "socialism" and "capitalism," changes have occurred in the official perception of the nature of this struggle and in the style of the language used to describe it. These shifts of emphasis over time may be illustrated by comparing key passages of the *Short Course* with some of the basic post-Stalin political textbooks. The introduction to the *Short Course* asserted that the history of the Party was "the history of the overthrow of tsarism, the overthrow of the power of the landlords and capitalists, a history of the smashing of foreign military intervention during the civil war, the history of the building of the Soviet state and the socialist society in our county." The introduction also asserted that the study of Party history strengthened faith in "the final victory of the great cause of the party of Lenin-Stalin, the victory of communism in the whole world." The *Short Course* was essentially a chronicle—extremely biased and full of calculated distortion—of Lenin's contributions to communism as interpreted by Stalin and particularly of Stalin's policies and Stalin's victories over his enemies. Apart from praise of Lenin and of Stalin, what stands out in the *Short Course* is invective against the "spies," "monsters," and "dregs of humanity"—Trotsky, Bukharin, Kamenev, Zinovyev, *et al.*, presented as the agents of foreign intelligence services, dedicated to the subversion of the Soviet state but destroyed by Stalin, loyal follower of Lenin and loyal servant of the Soviet people.

The elementary textbook, *Foundations of Political Knowledge*, although highly simplistic in its structure of analysis, seems too to be a rather rational, sober, and well-balanced work in comparison with the primitive and hysterical *Short Course*. It is organized more topically than chronologically, beginning with a chapter entitled "What It Is Necessary to Know About the Development of Society," treating of the class struggle, the socialist revolution, and "the problem of power —the chief problem of the revolution." There follow chapters on "socialism—the first phase of communism"; the victory of socialism in the USSR, etc. The third section of the book begins with a chapter entitled "Communism—the Future of Mankind," which is followed by chapters on "the international liberation movement," "peaceful coexistence and the struggle for peace," and, as the final chapter of the book, "The Communist Party—the Leader of the Soviet People." Stalin is ignored in this work, and all credit for the ideas upon which the Soviet state and Party are built is given to Lenin. The book puts heavy emphasis upon the international communist movement and the struggle of the "liberation movement" of Asia, Africa, and Latin America against United States "monopoly capitalism"—this theme is dramatized by numerous derisive cartoons, such as one entitled "Aid à l'Américaine," showing a smoking Uncle Sam, armed with a revolver, holding in his hands a large metal dollar sign with a chain attached. Although the 1963 edition of this text did not criticize the Chinese Communist leadership, it did emphasize the necessity of international communist unity and contained the significant statement that "V. I. Lenin wrote that Bolshevism is suitable as a model of tactics for all." Typical of the sophisticated oversimplification in which this volume abounds is its account of the Cuban crisis of the fall of 1962. This account makes no mention of Soviet rockets or of the measures taken by President Kennedy to assure their removal but asserts that the "ruling circles of the United States of America" were planning an invasion of Cuba using American troops, and that "as a result of the efforts of the Cuban people, and the efforts of the Soviet Union and other countries of socialism, as well as of other democratic, anti-imperialist forces this fully prepared invasion was prevented." The concluding section of the book expresses confidence that if capitalism was mankind's "yesterday," socialism and communism are "the today of many peoples and the future of all of mankind." A considerable part of the text is devoted to attempts to demonstrate that the victory of socialism throughout the world will be assured by the success of the Soviet Union in economic competition with capitalism. At the same time, the work contains numerous warnings that "bourgeois ideology" still possesses a dangerous power "to poison the consciousness" of Soviet people. In general, the tone of this text is less grim than that of the *Short Course*, and more emphasis is given to the benefits attributed to the Party's leadership and less to the dangers threatening from the outside world but the book does contain numerous warnings of the dangers inherent in the international situation. For example, the text asserts that if the "imperialistic maniacs" of the West seek to unleash an aggressive war the rebuff which they will receive will mark "the end of the existence of the antipeople's imperialist system."

Representative of the content of Soviet contemporary political training at intermediate and higher levels was the textbook *Foundations of Marxism-Leninism,* published in 1959 by the State Publishing House for Political Literature. This major work of almost eight hundred pages was prepared by a group headed by the late Otto Kuusinen, at the time an alternate [candidate] member of the Party Presidium. Kuusinen was assisted by leading Soviet scholars and also by "responsible Party and Soviet workers." This work was divided into five sections, headed respectively, "The Philosophical Foundations of the Marxist-Leninist World Outlook"; "The Materialistic Conception of History"; "The Political Economy of Capitalism"; "The Theory and Tactics of the International Communist Movement"; and "The Doctrine of Socialism and Communism." The Russian edition appeared in 600,000 copies and, according to Wolfgang Leonhard, 500,000 copies were published in Soviet-controlled East Germany. More than half of this work was devoted to problems connected with the international communist movement and the transition within the Soviet Union from socialism to a communist society. The work represents a well-organized systematic application of Leninism to contemporary conditions. For example, it reiterates firmly and in detail the Leninist doctrine of the necessity for the "dictatorship of the proletariat" as the first stage of the socialist revolution—a concept also repeated in the 1961 Party Program. In its last chapter this work sets forth an outline of the communist society, which is described as one of "general plenty and abundance" and also one in which true equality and freedom will prevail. The description of the future communist society warns against anarchistic illusions that this will be a society of "individuals who do not recognize any social bonds." In order that production shall function and develop "normally" and so that culture and civilization shall flourish, it indicates, organized direction of society will continue to be necessary. Consequently, the state will be replaced by a system of "public self-administration." This formulation appears to be consistent with the positions taken regarding the organization of society and the relationship between society and the individual at the Twenty-first and Twenty-second CPSU congresses. Regarding international relations, the textbook notes that nations and national cultures and languages will exist, "for a very long time after the victory of communism," but that all conflicts and differences among human groups will gradually disappear. Like other major post-Stalin political analyses, this text saw in the "successes of the building of communism in the Soviet Union" a significant factor which would influence the political development of "that portion of toiling mankind, condemned by capitalism to the most grievous burdens of involuntary labor, poverty, hunger and national humiliation." Also, the text saw as a "mission of salvation" of the "camp of socialism" the possibility of banishing world war from the life of mankind.

Both Stalinist and post-Stalin political indoctrination has been pervaded by the spirit of what one might call political messianism. The systematic teaching of Marxism-Leninism has probably played a significant role in enhancing the cohesiveness of Soviet society. The main appeals of the doctrine consist in its comprehensiveness and apparent consistency —achieved in large part by suppression of information and opinions deemed inappropriate by the Party authorities. Also, the moralistic aspects of the doctrine probably make it attractive to many Soviet citizens, while its emphasis upon the inevitability of the progress of mankind from "feudalism," through "capitalism," up to "socialism," and, finally, "communism"—buttressed by selected data regarding the political history of the world since the emergence of Leninism and especially since the Bolshevik Revolution of 1917, and by an abundance of data on the economic, technological, and scientific progress of the U.S.S.R., can, in the absence of competing points of view, create an impression of irresistible power.

It would, then, be idle to underestimate the effectiveness of a tremendous adult education effort sketched in this chapter. On the other hand, the unwillingness of the Soviet authorities to permit foreign scholars to undertake serious, systematic study within the Soviet Union of the process and effects of the above program raises some doubts regarding the depth and firmness of the convictions which the program engenders. Post-Stalin criticism of Stalinist mistakes in this field also stimulates the outside observer to skeptical reflections—and may well have given rise to a similar response in the minds of some Soviet citizens. However, in the absence of more conclusive evidence of failure than is now available, it would probably be safe to assume that for the foreseeable future the Soviet adult political socialization program will probably continue to function with formidable effectiveness.

*   *   *

VIII

Personal Relations and Daily Life

A half-century of Soviet rule has wrought a number of fundamental changes in the character of Russian life. For the average citizen these changes have brought a higher standard of living and greater opportunity. Among the regime's most notable accomplishments affecting living standards are free education and the elimination of illiteracy, comprehensive welfare measures including free medical care, day nurseries for working mothers, pensions, paid vacations for workers, full employment with a minimum wage for white-collar and manual workers (60 rubles, or $66, a month as of 1968) and the availability of adequate food and consumer goods to meet the necessities of all and provide luxuries for many. By the 1970's affluence had come to large numbers of Soviet citizens.

The benefits of industrialization and socialism have not, however, fallen upon all in equal measure. There are privileged groups—Party chiefs, business managers and executives, artists and scientists—that receive many times the income of manual laborers. Indeed, the pay scales of skilled and unskilled workers are sharply differentiated. Unskilled workers and peasants are at the bottom of the economic ladder. For the average worker the ladder does not go high. According to the state plan for 1968, the average monthly wage throughout the nation was 108.6 rubles ($120). While food is plentiful and relatively inexpensive, the average housewife is compelled to spend a large part of her day waiting in various lines to do her shopping. Staples like potatoes and bread are inexpensive, but meat, fresh fruits, and vegetables are not. Purchasing power has grown beyond the present capacity of the state-run economy to meet consumer demand. Clothes, furniture, many appliances, and even television sets are at times available in large quantities. But refrigerators, washing machines, and dryers are in very short supply, and it is extremely difficult to purchase an automobile or rent an apartment. Probably the greatest general consumer shortage is in adequate housing.

Affluence and social change have transformed urban life much more than life in the countryside. Life in rural Russia is poorer, more of a struggle, and much closer to traditional patterns than in the city. Religious beliefs remain strong in the countryside, and among the many diverse nationalities traditional practices prevail. In the Moslem areas, such as Uzbekistan, many women remain as in the past subordinated to the male in the family. Even arranged marriages persist.

In urban Russia the Revolution has deeply penetrated the roots of social change. Social divisions are considerably less pronounced than under the Tsars. Though class distinctions marked by inequalities of wealth continue to exist, the political and economic elite of Soviet society have not been able to assure transmission of their prerogatives to their children. Class is not fixed by heredity. If communism has not established the equality promised by the doctrine, it has at least provided social mobility and equal opportunity.

Change is particularly evident in the position of women in urban Soviet society. Traditional ideas and practices with regard to courtship, sex, and marriage have given place to new freedoms and opportunities for self-expression. The typical Soviet girl expects to marry for love and to maintain her own identity in the marriage. She wants to plan her family and thus be free to use contraceptives or, if necessary, resort to abortion. Both are supplied by the government. Femininity, clothes, and fashion are important to Soviet women.

Equality of the sexes in the professional and working areas has been achieved to a striking degree, but it has been a mixed blessing for the Soviet woman. On the positive side is the equality of opportunity provided by an educational system based primarily upon ability. There is virtually no profession closed to the Soviet woman. Women account for 75 per cent of the doctors, 70 per cent of the teachers, 40 per cent of the lawyers, and 29 per cent of the certified engineers in the Soviet Union. On the other hand, many women are engaged in strenuous manual labor that is wholly unsuited to their constitution. Excluding the agriculture sector, approximately 50 per cent of the nation's labor force is composed of women—many of them required to work by financial necessity. If agriculture is included, the percentage of women among the unskilled labor force is much higher. Probably the main difficulty of the typical working Soviet woman is the necessity of being a homemaker while she is putting in a full shift in the factory.

The character of Soviet everyday life cannot be easily summarized, because the Soviet Union is not only a large but an immensely diverse nation of many nationalities and cultures. On top of a heterogeneous social system, a monolithic political culture has been superimposed with different results in different regions. In much of the country the modern and the traditional coexist peacefully.

The selection by Bauer, Inkeles, and Kluckhohn is based upon research for the Harvard Project on the Soviet Social System. The data consisted primarily of interviews with hundreds, and questionnaires administered to thousands, of refugees from the Soviet Union in 1950 and 1951. Raymond Bauer is Professor of Psychology at Harvard University and author of *The New Man in Soviet Psychology*. With Alex Inkeles he co-authored *The Soviet Citizen: Daily Life in a Totalitarian Society*. Alex Inkeles is Professor of Sociology at Harvard University. His other books include *Public Opinion in Soviet Russia* and (with H. Kent Geiger) *Soviet Society: A Book of Readings*. Clyde Kluckhohn, who taught at Harvard for a quarter of a century before his death in 1960, was an anthropologist known for his studies of personality and culture. Wright Miller is an English free-lance writer who has lived in and traveled extensively in the Soviet Union. He has published *The Young Traveler in Russia*, a book for children. H. Kent Geiger is professor of sociology at the University of Wisconsin. Besides being coeditor of *Soviet Society: A Book of Readings*, he is the author of numerous articles on the U.S.S.R. Mirra Ginsburg is an editor and translator who has specialized in Soviet literature.

25

SOURCES OF SATISFACTION AND DISSATISFACTION

RAYMOND A. BAUER, ALEX INKELES, AND CLYDE KLUCKHOHN

Day-to-Day Conditions of Life

By the standards of Western society, the day-to-day conditions of life in the Soviet Union are distinctly unrewarding. Yet intergroup differences in rewards, and especially in feelings of satisfaction, are perhaps as striking as is the generally low level of reward and satisfaction. While the Soviet intelligentsia lack much that their opposite numbers in Western society have, the picture of life in the Soviet Union that is given by refugee intelligentsia makes it clear that they would have considered their day-to-day existence satisfactory and enjoyable if they

Reprinted, by permission of the publishers, from Raymond A. Bauer, Alex Inkeles, and Clyde Kluckhohn, *How the Soviet System Works* (Cambridge, Mass.: Harvard University Press, 1956), pp. 118–32. Copyright, 1956, by the President and Fellows of Harvard College.

had been freed from the threat of punitive political action and from excessive politicization of their lives. The manual groups, however, recall their lives as continually dreary and unrewarding.

MATERIAL CONDITIONS

All groups complain about material conditions. Yet there are, of course, substantial intergroup differences. Manual groups uniformly see themselves as worse off than the majority of the population (even though they obviously constituted this majority) and considered their material conditions to be generally highly unsatisfactory. However, in regard to some conditions—food, in particular—a majority of the intelligentsia even reported that they considered their conditions "satisfactory," a considerable concession from a refugee group.

Complaints about material conditions can, for the most part, be supported from official Soviet sources. Refugee respondents, however, reveal an interesting priority of complaints with respect to the three main items in their standard of living. Clothing is the source of greatest complaint, housing follows, and food is last. We base this order of priority on the relative proportion of persons in each social group who regarded each of these items as "satisfactory" in their own life experience.

Even among the intelligentsia a majority of respondents complained that clothing was inadequate. They reported that a professor's new suit would cause a stir in an academic gathering. The quality of clothing was frequently suggested as a good basis for distinguishing a Party member from a non-Party-member. Stories were reported about lower-class children who could not go to school for lack of clothing. Lower-class respondents, particularly peasants, characteristically told of having to wear extremely poor and old clothing which had been repaired many times.

Housing is one of the perennial Soviet problems. Actual shortages of housing facilities are most marked in cities, where there is fantastic overcrowding. The main complaint against urban housing, however, was not so much the actual crowding as the resulting lack of privacy. In the villages, complaints tended to concentrate less on lack of space and more on the state of disrepair of the houses.

The Soviet population has endured several famines, including one in the postwar period. Except for these periods, however, complaints about food are concerned with the extremely high cost and short supply of a large range of items, circumstances which force on the general population an unvaried diet in which bread and potatoes bulk extremely large. Only the privileged escape the necessity of extreme economy in the use of food and the resulting dull and uninteresting diet. Khrushchev admitted in September, 1953, that there were fewer cattle in the U.S.S.R. than in 1941, and far fewer than in 1928. The grain crisis at present appears to be as severe as the cattle crisis and indeed has been partly caused by the means used to "solve" the latter. . . .

The standard of living described here is substantially that which obtains in the mid-1950's.

In our data there are indications, however sparse, that the younger generation may be coming to accept lower material conditions as natural phenomena. The older folk in each social group are about twice as likely to blame their poor standard of living on the absence of consumer goods, while in the younger group about one person in six sees his poor standard of living as a result of not having enough wage-earners in the family—a response that is virtually unheard of in the older generation.

WORK SATISFACTION

The work situation in the Soviet Union ranges from one of frustration and dissatisfaction for the manual groups to one of gratification for the members of the intelligentsia and the white-collar workers. The general problem of standard of living colors work satisfaction. When asked to rate the desirability of jobs on various factors associated with working conditions in the Soviet Union, our respondents revealed that the level of pay was the strongest factor determining the attractiveness of a job. It is interesting as a sidelight on Soviet working conditions that there was, in the opinion of our respondents, an inverse relationship between the over-all desirability of the various jobs we asked them to rate and the degree of political safety they attributed to these jobs. The most desirable jobs were those that paid most and were simultaneously dangerous. An interesting implication of this finding is that, concerned as our respondents professed to be over political safety, this was not a sufficient consideration to offset their over-all evaluation of the attractiveness of various jobs. Until pay rises beyond a critical point, it is the dominant factor in shaping attitudes toward the work situation. When asked what they would want most in their work situation, workers and peasants select good pay as the element they desire, while non-manual workers want interesting work—a luxury that one can consider only after the more basic consideration of income has been taken care of. Fewer than one person in six said he preferred interesting work to good pay in the job situation, whereas the relationship was reversed among the intelligentsia, eight citing interesting work for every one who mentioned pay. This trend illustrates graphically the differences in the life situation of the several social groups in the Soviet Union. The proportion of persons in each social group citing pay as opposed to interesting work is a good index of the point in the system at which preoccupation with standard of living ceases to be an all-consuming consideration. Obviously, it is not only a scale of lesser or greater assurance of basic livelihood that is reflected in these data, but also a shift in the type of work associated with the various class positions and in the values associated with membership in these groups. In every group, those persons with higher pay were more likely to be satisfied with their jobs.

A majority of the nonmanual groups were satisfied with virtually every aspect of their work situation. Compared to persons with other occupations, they considered their pay to be excellent or good and their jobs to be worthy of prestige. Work norms were not considered particularly unreasonable. The work environment was generally pleasant. The nonmanuals were satisfied with their superiors. They felt that they achieved, on the whole, whatever they most sought in the work situation. Most important, however, they enjoyed their work. . . . Members of the intelligentsia, in particular, enjoyed their work. As numerous accounts indicate, many of them found in their work a means of escape from the unpleasantness of other aspects of the Soviet system. They referred to their work as their "internal emigration." Only on one point do they have a distinctive complaint to make: They resented other persons' being advanced beyond them on political grounds.

While members of the intelligentsia and the better-situated employees are not particularly discontented with their income, they have been at various times in the past few decades quite dissatisfied with the unavailability of consumer goods for which they have the money to pay. Under such circumstances, the system of economic incentives seems to bog down for these better-off groups, and the regime is faced with the problem of giving them adequate motives for exerting themselves. . . .

The picture which the ordinary workers and peasants give is an inversion of that given by the employees and the intelligentsia, On every one of the above-mentioned points they regarded themselves as deprived or dissatisfied. Two-thirds of these groups, for example, reported that they did not enjoy their work and did not regard their job as having prestige. Naturally, they said they were underpaid.

The skilled workers fall between the other manual and the nonmanual groups. The profile of their reactions to the several aspects of their work situation is such that we cannot say that they were predominantly either satisfied or dissatisfied.

On one point there was complete agreement by an overwhelming majority of all groups: The attitude of their co-workers was friendly. This quantitative finding is also supported by qualitative descriptions of the work situation and is only one of a number of instances in which refugees indicate that friendly personal relations were one of the rewarding and alleviating features of Soviet life.

The peasants have a pervasive and distinctive complaint: They want more economic autonomy. Complaints about lack of autonomy are not unknown among other groups. The intelligentsia, for example, occasionally complain about restrictions on their activities which kept them from doing the things they wanted to do. But these complaints are minor compared to the peasant's inexorable opposition to the regimentation of his activities by the collective farm. Minimally, he wants more time to work on his private garden plot, but beyond that he wants passionately to return to a system of private farming.

School Experience

School experiences parallel quite closely the work experiences of our respondents. The upper classes get a great deal of direct satisfaction from their school experiences, enjoying their studies and the friendship of their fellow students, and see the schools as training them for a specific life career. They tend to be more satisfied with their opportunities to get as much education as they want. The lower classes do not, by any means, regard their school experience as an unmixed unpleasant experience. There is some tendency among the older peasants and workers, however, to consider it a waste of time which was forced on them and which kept them from working and helping at home. The lower classes are less sanguine than the upper classes about their opportunities for education. To some extent, their optimism on this score seems to be increasing with the expansion of the Soviet educational system. The perceived opportunities of the lower classes, however, do not seem to be advancing at the same rate as those of the upper classes. In other words, all groups see their opportunities as improving, but the upper classes feel their opportunities are increasing at a more rapid rate. Continued expansion of Soviet schools will unquestionably make access to primary and even secondary education routine for all classes in the reasonably near future. It remains to be seen, however, whether apparent trends toward more rigid social stratification will not make it even more difficult for the lower classes to get a higher education.

Family

Family life is an area of strongly mixed experiences for all classes of Soviet society. To some extent it is for everyone the final refuge from the hardships of Soviet life and from Soviet politics, but because Soviet politics and the harsher aspects of life intrude into the very life of the family, the citizen is often frustrated in his attempts to find satisfaction in his family circle. The chief sources of frustration in the enjoyment of family life are: conflict between parents and children over the political beliefs of one or another member of the family; lack of privacy because of inadequate housing; irritability of family members because of poor material conditions and anxiety over situations outside the family; lack of time to spend together because of excessive fatigue or because of the amount of time spent at work and shopping. Thus, the family is, to some extent, a refuge from these external events, but these events in themselves put a strain on family life. This is not as paradoxical as it may seem. When the individual brings his problems home to the family, the other members may be able to help him, but in so doing they must also share his problems. Perhaps the most striking example of this is the need of Soviet citizens to find some area where they can express freely their political feelings. Yet many persons withhold free expression of their opinions in the family circle for various reasons—distrust of some members of the family, concern for the reaction of children in the family, or simply because they do not want to burden the others with the responsibility of sharing these opinions. The evidence available suggests that the family serves as a source of support most effectively in the upper-class groups, both because of stronger cultural values toward mutual support and because the upper groups are better able to avoid physical dispersion.

The relations of family life to the regime can be understood only in the light of Soviet economic history of the past twenty-five years. Since 1929, the U.S.S.R. has been in the process of rapid industrialization, with particular emphasis on the development of heavy industry. This program has resulted in a nationwide shortage of skilled labor. It has also meant that the bulk of the Soviet population was forced to subsist at a low material level. The regime has met this situation by distributing the available stock of consumer goods so as to maximize workers' motivation. Educational and occupational achievement have come to be highly rewarded through the system of markedly differentiated wage and salary rates, referred to above, by which the most highly skilled and responsible occupational positions are best paid. This arrangement has been put into the form of a slogan: "He who does not work shall not eat"; but a more accurate slogan would perhaps be: "He who works best eats best." It appears that the chief result of this policy has not been so much to arouse resentment at the "inequality of reward in a socialist system" as to promote and reinforce popular aspirations for education and occupational mobility. Such aspirations have been still further intensified both by the insistence of Soviet domestic propaganda on "the happy life in the Soviet Union" (a theme which strongly contrasted with the dire economic straits of the bulk of the population) and by the presence of considerable new opportunities for education and occupational advancement.

This set of circumstances—a low average living standard, widespread occupational opportunity, differential reward by quality of performance, and high aspirations and expectations—has strongly affected the value structure and patterns of interpersonal relations in the family. For one thing, educational and occupational achievement seem to have become generally extremely important. Popular valuation of individual occupational achievement and mobility constitutes a point of strength in the system, for it contributes to the effectiveness of the mobilization of the work force and to a higher level of production—one of the main goals of the regime. At the same time, a family value pattern such as this is not without its disadvantageous aspects for the total system. What passes as occupational mobilization could also be seen as occupational "overinvolvement," consuming an inordinate amount of the individual's time and energy and depriving him of the chance to be a political activist, which the regime also desires him to be.

During the past twenty-five years many of the better jobs have involved personal risk, for failure was likely to bring punishment for "antistate activity." Also, a high-level job was likely to require the assumption by the incumbent of some degree of authority in the name of the more or less unpopular Soviet regime. Some persons hesitated to incur such liabilities. But various members of the family were involved in different responsibilities, and, in addition, the regime was not always equally unpopular among all members of the family. Moreover, one or more members of the family may have been unable (as opposed to unwilling) to achieve the occupational or educational goals which the other members of the family valued. Such discrepancies between values and behavior, or conflicts between values in themselves, led to family tensions. Analysis of Project data shows that there was tremendous pressure in most families to improve material living conditions, and that a major source of family tension was caused by the failure of one or more family members to keep up with this expectation. Thus, a correlation is found on all socio-economic levels between economic deprivation and family disruption. Conversely, in the families where material living conditions were felt to be relatively satisfactory, inter-personal relations were more solidary.

INTERPERSONAL RELATIONS

Interpersonal relations are a focal point in the Soviet citizen's quest for pleasure and satisfaction in an otherwise often unrewarding existence. In a variety of situations respondents expressed the satisfaction that they derived from warm, friendly relations with people around them —friends, co-workers, members of the family, fellow students. This must be considered together with the constant complaints which were made about mutual suspicion and protestations that "you couldn't trust anybody." The summary conclusion that we draw is this: Russians —and possibly all of the Slavic nationalities in the Soviet Union—value warm interpersonal relations to an unusually high degree. The need for free, uninhibited social intercourse is both frustrated and accentuated under Soviet conditions. The desire to express pent-up feelings impels the individual to seek out confidants. The fear of talking makes him less likely to talk. The result is not a cessation of confidences, but rather the development of techniques of screening and assessing people in order to decide how much they can be trusted. There seem to be several steps of relation that are established: (1) Relations are carried on at a strictly formal level with suspicion or hostility circumscribing strictly what one will do and say. This probably characterizes most *initial* contacts and persists wherever one has a reason for continuing suspicion or fear. (2) Perhaps the most usual type of relation, one that characterizes contacts with co-workers, colleagues, and most friends, is that of limited friendliness and frankness. Politically delicate subjects are avoided; other topics are treated openly, and there is a warm and frank relation. (3) Intimate, confidential relations in which political confidences are exchanged are rare and are confined to some members of the family and a very few friends. There are unquestionably persons who share such confidences with no one.

The important conclusion is that, despite the barriers which the regime places in the way, warm interpersonal relations remain one of the very real sources of satisfaction in Soviet life.

RECREATION

Again, we find great class differences in patterns of recreation and the degree of satisfaction derived from this source. There were three active sources of interference with opportunity for recreation: lack of time; lack of money; lack of facilities. For the urban intelligentsia, lack of time is most important. For urban workers, money was more important. Lack of facilities (movies, libraries, theaters) was primarily the complaint of rural dwellers.

Attendance at movies, theaters, and concerts and the reading of books and magazines increase regularly as one moves up the social ladder from the peasantry to the urban intelligentsia. There are, however, interesting qualitative changes in the pattern of recreation. Dependence on formal recreation seems to increase up through the employee group. The intelligentsia are characterized by a lesser dependence on such formal sources as the movies and theater, although their absolute use of such means of recreation is very high. In addition to formal recreation, they rely on family activities, vacations taken together, and friends. They tend to rely more on their own resources.

As far as arts and literature are concerned, the regime and the public are in constant conflict. The regime attempts to use these media as strictly political instruments. The public and most artists try to escape politicization.

THE PACE OF LIFE

An aspect of day-to-day conditions in the Soviet Union that appears to be an important source of dissatisfaction is the general pace of existence, referred to by refugees as "the tempo." This derives from the regime's efforts to spur the populace to maximum production with minimum resources. Complaints concerning "the tempo" involved high work norms, overtime (without pay, usually, for white-collar workers), long and difficult hours spent in transit to and from work (also substantiated by the Soviet press), compulsory attendance at meetings outside of regular work hours, precious time spent queuing up for scarce goods, and strict laws of labor discipline which made one liable to strong penalties for being late for work. Urban groups of all classes were depicted as being under extreme pressure because of the laws of labor discipline. Even high officials were said to be anxious over arriving a few minutes late for work. The pressure of the laws of labor discipline was at a maximum in the early 1940's. Enforcement of these laws has been relaxed progressively since then, especially in the post-Stalin era, apparently in response to popular resentment. In the past few years the laws themselves seem to have vanished from the statute books.

Lack of time is one of the important reasons cited for paucity of recreational opportunities. The peasants complain constantly about lack of time to work on their plots. Urban groups, particularly the intelligentsia, said that excessively long work hours interfered with family life.

Violation of Other Allegiances

There are a number of subgroups in the population in whom the regime generates a good deal of hostility and discontent, because it violates the allegiance of these people to other groups. In the past, church members and religious people constituted such a group. This conflict has been somewhat diminished in the last decade. The members of the various national minorities remain perhaps the most significant category of people who experience discontent on this score. . . .

As we have indicated at various points in this chapter, the picture of the sources of satisfaction and dissatisfaction in the life situation of the Soviet citizen is a changing one. Not only are conditions changing, but so are the expectations and aspirations of succeeding generations of Soviet citizens. The youngest people in the Soviet population take for granted many deprivations and more politicization of their lives than do the older people. Furthermore, almost all the conditions we have described have improved or are improving to varying degrees. The worst era of political terror preceded World War II. Even though politics permeated every area of Soviet life during the last years of Stalin's rule, the penalties for failing in one's job or for political incorrectness were less drastic than in the 1930's, and they were imposed less arbitrarily. The post-Stalin regime seems to have gone even further toward relieving this source of tension. The pace of life, the "tempo" referred to by Soviet refugees, seems to have been slackened somewhat by the post-Stalin leaders. The standard of living of the Soviet population has increased markedly since World War II, though not rapidly enough to satisfy the Soviet people. . . . But it should be remembered that these conditions exist not because the Soviet leaders are powerless to rectify them, but primarily because they have in the past been unwilling to cut back their goals of industrial expansion and have preferred to produce guns instead of butter. A relaxation of international tension and an abatement of the armaments race . . . would clearly make it within their power to satisfy many of the desires of their subjects. Not only would it be possible to raise the standard of living, but it would also be possible to relax the pressure on the populace and the use of police terror as a key instrument of social control. Whether or not the leaders will take these steps is, of course, problematical.

Solution of the agricultural crisis and relief of the discontents of the peasantry, however, is another matter. The very institution of the collective farm seems in itself to stand in the way of increased agricultural production and to frustrate the economic aspirations of the peasantry. It is likely that even with the best of intentions for "improving the lot of the people" the Soviet leaders will find it very difficult to do so without abandoning, in some large measure, the present system of collectivized agriculture. And this they do not seem disposed to do.

* * *

26

MANNERS, MORALS, AND TASTE

WRIGHT MILLER

When a foreigner takes his first plunge into Russian life, away from Intourist guides and goodhearted hotel waitresses, his first impression of Russian manners may well be that they are rough or almost non-existent.

Gathering up his Russian words and his fifty kopecks, he is about to speak at the little Metro booking office window when a rough arm thrusts past him and through the window up to the elbow, pushing a crumpled ruble into the hand of the old woman at the ticket-machine. "Two!" grunts the rough arm, obviously in a hurry. Everyone else seems to be in a hurry too, the window is very small, and rough hand after rough hand pushes through until the foreigner realizes that he will never be served with a ticket during the rush hour until he too thrusts in his hand without respect for other hands. He endures the crush in the Metro train—he has heard of that before—and, emerging thankfully into the street, crosses carefully between the pedestrian studs. The Soviet highway code is strict, yet buses, lorries, and cars bear down on him as though the crossing did not exist, and he skips on to the pavement, where he has to look out sharply for other people, for they will not look out much for him. Younger people may stop him, recognizing him as a foreigner, and may speak with a remarkable brusqueness, though no unpleasant intent, asking intelligent questions perhaps and then turning away without a greeting.

The surface impression of Russian city manners is bound to be a poor one, and it contrasts with the gentle warmth and disarming courtesy which Russians nearly always show when they enter into anything which could qualify as even a passing relationship. In crowds they generally appear reserved, offhand, sunk in themselves. They are not one of the nations irresistibly impelled to talk in trains; when they talk they can talk endlessly, but they can also stay monosyllabic and glum. They have a natural tendency to use no more energy, no more faculties, than are required for what they have in hand at the moment. . . .

The old communal ways are still the most powerful element in Soviet manners and morals. They show themselves vigorously, for example, in that most spontaneous and recent Soviet development, the sense of sportsmanship. The state provides grounds and facilities for clubs, but the enthusiasm comes from the people, and it is a very recent enthusiasm. It received an official fillip when the Soviet Government sent the Dinamo team on their victorious tour of Britain; Moscow residents say it was only after this tour that small boys began to make a habit of kicking a ball or a bundle of rags around the backyards.

Organized sport and athletics have made a tremendous outlet for the vitality and "aggression" of Russian players and spectators, but the old feelings of solidarity, of decent relations between man and man, seem to have prevented any development of the dirty play and ugly crowd behavior typical of so many countries where sport is a new thing. Soviet international teams have sometimes made a bad impression through being overzealous about national prestige, but I do not think foreigners have ever had to complain of any lack of sportsmanship on the field. When foreign teams or athletes defeat Russians on Russian ground they never meet with unpleasantness from the crowd unless they have been thought unsporting; the crowds respect the victors and vent their feelings by booing their own side. In domestic matches Soviet crowds are noisily partisan, and Soviet star players sometimes get too big for their boots. The police would step in if crowds showed a tendency to get as rough as the roughest British football crowds, and spoiled star players can be officially penalized in a way which would never happen in Britain, yet the sportsmanship of the Russian crowd and of the average Russian player is too natural to be the result of official discipline.

However, the widespread and healthy survival of old standards is clearly not the only influence in forming Soviet mores. The state has intervened continuously in the field of manners and morals, partly in the attempt to form "Soviet man," but even more because the chaos, confusion, and crime resulting from the Revolution, the Civil War, the industrialization, and the purges made intervention inevitable. There was a brief period when the new State encouraged children to report on their parents' "counterrevolutionary activities," and free love was regarded as "a blow to the bourgeois conception of the family," but in 1928 the First Five-Year Plan put an end to all that.

Since those days the official attitude has been serious, very often solemn, and in general what countries further west would call solid and old-fashioned. It has been expressed not only through regulations but through schools, parents' meetings, and the Komsomol (the Young Communist organization), through discussion in the press, in trade unions and factory units, and through the nonpenal activities of the ordinary police (the "militia"), as well as through films and novels and plays. The public have mostly met official enterprise with earnest interest and they have given the authorities a great deal of cooperation in this field, often taking the initiative themselves. The official attitude, in fact, has largely counted for its support on the Russian care for communal standards; it is an attitude itself partly rooted in that care. The Russian spirit is not offended when private persons take it upon themselves to persuade individuals back into line with accepted behavior, and you have not to be long in Russia before you may see people quietly remonstrating with rude boys, boorish adults, noisy youths, or urchins who have climbed over the fence so as to see a show without paying. Since 1959 volunteers who are willing to deal with breaches of public manners by methods of persuasion have been formed into a *druzhina*, or "company" [volunteer squad] with red armlets.

Most Russians needed little encouragement to return to the idea of a stable family life—if indeed they had ever given it up during the early days of the Revolution. They are not a promiscuous people, and illicit unions are often as stable as the registered ones. During the worst years which came later many spoke of family life as "the only bit of the world you can have to yourself." But campaigns about morals and manners have not only been concerned with such fundamental matters, and it is typical of Soviet Russia that minor points of behavior have been treated with equal seriousness. Town habits had to be inculcated in the mass of city dwellers, whose peasant-born good nature turned to bluntness or apathy in a life where they were herded together, overpoliced, overdisciplined, and for so long almost without leisure. Simple necessary habits of hygiene, tidiness, and self-discipline, restrictions on jaywalking, smoking, or spitting have been treated with the same polite strictness as respect for elders or for women. And attitudes which to a foreigner may appear solemn often miss being priggish in practice, because of the comfortable warmth of the community. This is

particularly so in the training of the young. A collection of lectures on
The Home Training of Children (published in Leningrad in 1959)
deals with the following themes among others:

Before going to school at seven years of age, children should be used to
obeying necessary orders.

Children should always show respect to elders or superiors, greeting them
formally and face to face.

Children should help with the housework. (Instance where the Komsomol
and Pioneer organization of a school persuaded all children to do so, and
received the thanks of several parents.)

At table one should remove the spoon from the cup before drinking.
Bones, etc., should be deposited on the plate, never beside it.

The well-to-do must see that their children enjoy no obviously privileged
position. (Instance of the manager of an important factory who would
never take his son to school in his car.)

Parents should take serious interest in their children's studies but should
not make things too easy for them.

"What will people say?" is a base motive compared with duty to the
community or to one's neighbor.

Modesty and simplicity are marks of the highest culture; children should
not be praised too much nor allowed to show off.

The effects of such precepts as these, it need hardly be said, are far
from being fully realized in Soviet life, but it would be wrong to
imagine that Russians feel them to be priggish, or that the only force
behind them is that which stems from schoolmasters, officials, or police.
The bringing up of children is as common a theme of conversation in
Russia as anywhere else.

The warmth of old-fashioned communal approval is naturally not
always enough to satisfy the more original or more sensitive, especially
among the young. Many have of their own accord taken up some of
the manners of pre-Revolutionary Russia—manners typical of the aristocracy rather than the old bourgeoisie. The stagy or romantic flavor is
often the attraction; some young men sport Pushkinesque sideburns
and affect the manner of a nineteenth-century guardsman, flinging
about such phrases as "devilish good" and twirling their mustaches if
they have them. The dignified contrast of older manners attracts others;
at the opera or in the best holiday hotels it is not uncommon to see
men, by no means elderly, who greet a lady with old-fashioned bows
and kissing of the hand. No doubt some of these manners were originally adopted by way of protest, but the authorities do not now seem
to frown on even the most formal revivals unless someone suggests
that old codes of manners are a necessary guide for Soviet society. This
is inadmissible, but suitable examples from pre-Revolutionary Russia
may be cited for emulation. The Leningrad handbook on the training
of children quoted with approval, under the heading "Training is
Everything," the *mot* of the old actress Sumbatova-Yuzhina, who al-

ways rose to greet her guests in spite of age and infirmity, remarking
when they pressed her to sit down: "It's not me that's standing up—
it's my training."

Revivals of Tsarist manners must seem to the government more
desirable than the aping of "American" ways among the rougher well-
to-do youths of whom so much has been heard abroad. It is only fair
to say that *stilyagi* in Moscow are far less in evidence than teddy boys
are in London, and their loutishness seems to be "American" only in
form. You may be allowed to call it Russian loutishness so long as
you add something about "bourgeois survivals," and at least the youth
committees and similar bodies seem prepared to deal with each *stilyag*
as an individual Russian rather than as part of an "American" problem. . . .

In general the relaxation of political control has released more
spontaneity in public manners. People seem more relaxed, a little more
apart from each other than they used to do; one might say that they
do not seem to need the mass quite as much as formerly. Crowds in
Moscow may not appear very considerate, but they are a good deal
more so than they were earlier, when people wearily sank themselves
into the mass and just pushed.

Meanwhile, the concepts of being moral, considerate, quiet, cultured,
tidy, clean, well-read, respectful, reasonable, and so forth have all
rather fused in the public mind into one general but somewhat fluid
picture—that of the "cultured" (*kulturny*) man or woman. Breaches
of good order, manners, and morals are characterized by the word
which has become well known in the West—*nekulturny* (uncultured)
—though I have the impression that it is somewhat less used, and
more damning when used, than it used to be. The imported word
"hooligan" has almost as wide an application. Small boys who drop
ice cream papers may be "hooligans"; so are noisy, shouting fourteen-
year-olds, and so were the adolescent gangs who used to knife people
in order to steal their clothing.

The scene is full of contrasts in all conscience. One or two hotels maintain American standards of cleanliness, but hotels less visited by foreigners, especially in the provinces, can be nauseating. In city streets there
really is no litter; litterbin-cum-spittoons are set up every twenty yards
or so, and people have been trained to use them. But lavatories are
another thing. Public ones are as discreetly concealed as in New York,
but with this concealment the resemblance abruptly ends. Cubicles,
doors, or partitions are most often nonexistent, even in many hotels, and
elsewhere the foreigner may find it impossible to stomach these places
at all. Back in 1934 one sometimes saw carpenters fitting wooden frames
to prevent anyone from standing on the seat, but the authorities seem
to have given up the unequal struggle on this point since then.

Yet the village bathhouse—something like the Finnish sauna—has been
a flourishing institution for centuries, and through all the years when
soap was scarce one had the impression that Russians were doing their

best to keep clean in circumstances which would have made people from some countries give up entirely. On long train journeys everyone waits in an hour-long queue for the trickling tap, and if water gives out some of the men may dash out at the next stop to sluice themselves under a railway hose. One of the excuses offered for the large single-chamber lavatories is that it is easy to give them a thorough washdown, and that is in fact what they get.

At table one meets with old and new traditions, both pleasant and unpleasant, mingled together. Invitations to share a meal may be very courteous, with polite little Eastern bows, but you may find it hard to suffer the way your host eats his soup. Peasants may apologize engagingly for their clumsy, dirty hands, yet when they share your table they may eat with a diffident delicacy, while next door an intellectual young man with a briefcase shovels up rice disgustingly with his knife. Indulgence in food and drink is comfortably regarded in most Russian circles. It is harder to get hold of drink than it used to be—and rightly so—but both police and public are still remarkably tolerant of drunken men. The average good citizen is represented in cartoons and advertisements as having a figure nearly as well-fed as Mr. Khrushchev's, and if you make friends with Russians, whether men or women, they are certain some time to issue the old challenge: "How many pancakes can you eat at a sitting?"

The break between old and new is clear and definite in another matter—the Soviet conventions about profanity. In "polite society"—say, a good deal more than half of Soviet society in this context—one can resort to nothing worse than "the devil!" and "hell!" and "curse!" to relieve one's feelings. These words preserve some of their nineteenth-century strength in Russia, but to go further is simply taboo. When Eliza Doolittle is asked if she is walking across the park she replies, in the Russian translation, "*Chorta s dva!*," which is approximately equivalent to "Hell, no!" Monstrously unladylike, but not an expression snatched from over the borderline of the unspeakable, as Shaw intended. There is an impassable gulf between polite expletives and peasant or common expletives in Russian. Once you descend below such phrases as "*chorta s dva*" all swearing is based on the ancient ". . . your mother" formula. Not that anyone's real mother need be involved. The peasant uses the expression if it starts to rain or if the sun is too hot, while for more serious occasions he can indulge in obscene and blasphemous elaborations of how he will wrong someone's mother. This is the immemorial kind of profanity; it probably lies at the bottom of the English taboo on the same word. Russian is not sophisticated enough to have developed, as the French have, some *mot de Cambronne* which is delicately balanced on the edge of shockability so that it is taboo enough to have a delicious force when needed, but not so taboo as to be unusable in ordinary circles. So at present it is not possible to render the full flavor of Eliza's word in Russian. Rude stories circulate among Russians, but they have not reached anything like the significance of the exchange of stories among Western men; the dividing line between the shocking and the unshocking is too sharp. The Russians have a tag equivalent to " 'Hell!' said the duchess . . ." but the duchess does not say "Hell!"; she says ". . . your mother!"

The old swearing is being cleaned up; there is a strong teetotal and antismoking movement among the young; there are only occasional and unorganized prostitutes, and only rumors of orgies sometimes in very high society; there is nothing approaching pornography in the theater, the cinema, or in print—there are not even any frivolous magazines nor the sort of paperbacks which Russians call "literature of the boulevard." Isn't "puritan" the obvious label for this society where people appear to restrain so many of their impulses for the sake of the community, and where small children are put into uniform and taught to bow to their elders? Isn't "puritan" the label for the people as well as for their authoritarian government, or the label at least for the leading, energetic, hard-working section of the people, who clean things up, make them run on tramlines, suppress as it would seem a lot of natural instincts, and persuade other people to do the same?

The discipline, the cleaning, and tidying-up are certainly going to continue, and by the most favorable possible interpretation they will continue for so long that it is impossible to foretell what other problems may not arise in the process. Nevertheless, I think it is incorrect to describe the Russians as puritanical, in spite of all their reticences and restraints; they are certainly not puritanical in the sense which the word has historically had in the West.

Russians may be reticent, reserved, shy, or severe for a purpose, but it is quite exceptional for any of them to indulge in austerity for what is called "its own sake." It is quite exceptional for any of them to show the self-lacerating, guilt-ridden asceticism which turns people into gray eminences or Nazi leaders. The teetotal young seem to be enjoying something positive, not repressive, when they try to persuade you not to drink; the reason for not drinking is in order to be able to throw oneself into something else. Young Russians have somewhat more freedom nowadays to try out a variety of personalities and attitudes to life, but few of them apparently choose to turn themselves into smug little section leaders.

When Russians are lazy or idle they seem to feel no guilt. When they have been completely abandoned to a temporary passion they seem to feel little remorse afterwards. Few of them are obsessively clean or tidy in the puritan manner. Few of them will pull in their belts in order to save for a future more than a few months away. Most of them are spendthrift with their money; when the state offered the alternative of interest-bearing loans or lottery loans without interest "everybody," according to my Russian friends, wanted the lottery loan. Russians are permissive in bringing up young children, and when they do discipline them they are not trying to create a sense of guilt; they are simply trying to restore the child to the communal values. In short, they trust and believe in the goodness of human nature more than puritan peoples do.

Russians have their own traditional mistrust of human nature when they think it diverges too much from common standards. But puritanism of the Western kind has had almost no soil in which to grow in Russia. If Russian feudalism had weakened earlier than it did, and if the Old Believers had then become the dominant element in the new middle class of traders, they might perhaps have developed their Old Believer austerity into a conservative puritanism which could have matched the progressive puritanism of the West. But there was no such opportunity. The moral influence remained that of the established Orthodox Church, and "Orthodoxy educates the heart, not the will."

After the chaos and tyranny which they have endured many Russians feel thankful for the existence of strict or formal social standards; they have themselves contributed to these standards, and the standards help to provide a mold for the individual; by voluntarily accepting some of them he gives his new liberties a new point.

It is particularly important, I think, to be clear about the conception of Russian or Soviet "puritanism" when one looks at the relations between the sexes in Soviet Russia. It may seem natural to call this society puritanical where women do not flaunt, where nudity never appears, and delicacy of relations between the sexes seems often to be missing, but I must insist, for the reasons just given, that the word does not fit. The Englishman who said "not puritan but shy" was a great deal nearer the mark.

There have been self-torturing individuals and sects at times—even a castrating sect—in the Russian Church, but the Church in general has never been so much concerned with sin as many other Churches have; purity of heart has been more the theme. Priests are allowed to marry— "to marry one wife" is the canon—and on the whole sexual matters seem to have been left in a sort of elementary simplicity. (We are told, for instance, that it was common for couples to draw a little curtain in front of the ikon when they intended intercourse.)

A kind of innocence, secured by communal good nature, is still the dominant note. Even the crude young men, so blunt in their approaches, seem fundamentally innocent. . . .

Most Russians, especially educated Russians, are by Western standards remarkably embarrassed about sex, nudity, or the private parts, but their embarrassment seems a natural modesty, not a repudiation due to self-discipline. When some of us became blood donors at Kuibyshev the doctor—a middle-aged man—put us through an exhaustive physical examination and asked questions about every ordinary disease; he must have examined at least several hundred donors on these lines, but when he came to ask if we had ever suffered from piles he blushed and stammered like any probationer nurse.

Sex instruction is a subject which both parents and authority seem to shy away from. There is no mention of it in several of the official textbooks for the training of teachers, nor in the Leningrad handbook for parents already quoted. At the Annual Congress of the International Scientific Film Association in Moscow in 1958 a Dutch scientific film on sex education was flatly refused projection. However, the famous educationist Makarenko had something to say about sex education in his lectures to parents. He suggests parents need not fear if their children get sex knowledge from other children and keep it secret: "In this case secrecy is not to be feared!" At a suitable age fathers should talk to sons and mothers to daughters, but explanations which are too "rational" should be avoided. "Sexual love is based on other kinds of natural love— the true follows the true." One may regard all this as elementary, innocent, or even mistaken but I do not think it can be called puritan.

Chasing women is not a national sport with Russians, though men from Soviet Georgia and Armenia have rather a name for it. Russia does not have the highly developed lines of attack and defense which characterize relations between men and women in, say, Italy. Men and women can approach each other freely; "anyone can speak to anyone in the Soviet Union," as one of my friends used to say, and yet there are conventions which regulate the approach. The Russian boy tilts his cap and grins in an obvious, good-natured way when he tries to make a pass at a girl, but unless he is drunk or a very hard case he will accept the girl's hands-off if she doesn't want to encourage him. Convention makes it easy for him to speak to her, but it also makes it easier for her to disengage, and easier for him to avoid feeling embarrassed if she does so.

Apart from a few gold-diggers and sophisticates, Russian girls are usually modest in behavior, attracting by a promised sweetness rather than by flaunting external charms. (The Nazis, among their loathsome statistics, claimed to have examined all the unmarried women when they captured the cities of Rostov and Novorossiisk, and to have established that 85 per cent of them were virgins.) Yet this modesty permits an approach which can sometimes knock a mere foreigner head over heels. Convention allows any of these modest girls to speak to a man first, to make the first approach—roguish or interested or casual—without any implication that she is a bad character. It would be quite improper, of course, for the man to respond by trying to raise the temperature at once; acquaintance proceeds experimentally, allowing either party openings for retreat, just as it does between Russians of the same sex. . . .

Within the freedom which Russian convention allows it is not so necessary for a girl to flaunt, and delicacy between men and women can be a great deal more than one might imagine from a first sight of the rough sex equality so typical of Soviet life. Equality between the sexes is Soviet policy, of course, and in respect of equality before the law, equality in access to jobs, and so on, it is new. But there was a strong tradition of equality also before the Revolution—in the honorable, carefully fostered equality between the men and women of the old intelligentsia, and in the rough functional equality among peasants and industrial workers.

Peasant society was patriarchal, women could be roughly treated by their husbands, they took no part in government by the village *Mir*, and yet there was an equality in the hard life they all shared, in the necessary part played by women as well as men in the fields, and in the simple feeling that all belonged to the one community. One hears strikingly few jokes against women as women in Russia, in spite of the robust Russian sense of humor. There are jokes against the virago, the good-time girl, the lazy wife, the dress maniac, and other individual types, but very few against women in general, whether as a sex or as wives, mothers-in-law, colleagues, or drivers of cars. In principle every kind of job and every rank of job is open to women today, and this not uncommonly means that men find themselves working under a woman; to a foreigner it is remarkable how little this seems to be resented by Russian men, and what straightforward giving of orders and answering back there can be in these cases. Most wives, of course, go out to work as well as their husbands, so that the Western contrast between the mistress of the house and the master at work does not often arise.

In short, Russia is not a country of the sex war. Seventy per cent of Soviet doctors are women, men seem on the whole unjealous of women's position or status, and women behave as equals in conversation, arguing or asserting with a forthrightness which may seem to us unfemale but is merely Russian. All this equality is the background, one should remember, to the inferior status which so many women apparently have to accept in their work. Unskilled work in the Soviet Union seems most often to be done by women—the untrained or the unenterprising, perhaps—and few people seem to think it unfair that women should work at such jobs as spreading asphalt, portering luggage, sweeping the streets, or cleaning engines. Yet there is a kind of equal status in these simple women—they talk to you as people with their own independence and not as inferiors.

The community is the background for all, for women of education and refinement as well as the women who clear away the snow, and it is against this background that Russian women show themselves so often more womanly than English convention allows, though they may be less "feminine" in the Western sense, less concerned about appearance and arts and wiles. One may see this even in some of the smartest and most sophisticated women in the country—the Intourist girls who deal with foreigners in the hotels. Their clothes and shoes are good, even their makeup and hairdressing are sometimes of good Western standard, they know they have a good appearance, they work very hard, and they have plenty of practice at stonewalling difficult foreigners. But when one of these rather frozen-looking young women takes a warmer interest in your request—probably because you have spoken to her in a Russian way—and she breaks into a sympathetic smile, she shows something simpler, more womanly and natural than the equivalent woman in England would show. The Englishwoman could be equally obliging, pleasant, good-hearted, but to exhibit these qualities so frankly, to unveil her essential female goodness to you in a sweetness like that of an Austrian or an Irish maid—that is not the English convention. If an Englishwoman felt she had so much sweetness showing she would probably be embarrassed, but a Russian woman is not embarrassed, because she is simply acting out of the sincerity which Russians show to each other as well as to foreigners. . . .

Now that Russian women are becoming able to dress better and with more individuality I think foreigners will become more aware of something which is fundamental to them, except for the exhibitionist minority. Apart from this minority it has always seemed to me that Russian women—even many Russian women outside the U.S.S.R.—are unable and unwilling to bring themselves to that pitch of self-importance which comes so naturally to a Frenchwoman, for instance, and which the peak of Western fashionableness demands. (The same is true, of course, of Russian men.) Studied charm or dignity in Russian women seems nearly always to be relieved by some comfortable carelessness, some easy slurring over of final elegance, so that it is clear to you that they are presenting themselves not as "appearance" but as something human, as women who for all their smartness are still part of the warm community. Only on certain formal occasions, when she is standing not for herself but for her nation or her group, a Russian woman may appear, by contrast, with a completely formal, rather stiff and cold exterior.

I think this attitude to personal appearance is likely to continue until there is a change in the bases of Russian society, and I also think the well-known reticences and shyness will remain in essence, even though Soviet Russians may be able to lead easier lives and to show relatively more variety of personality, more sophistication and self-possession than in the past. In more relaxed conditions it should be easier, indeed, for foreigners to convince themselves how the reticences and the shyness are neither basically puritan nor enforced from above. . . .

The Russian sense of humor is more catholic than that of many peoples, sharper and finer than the Teutonic, less biting than the French, very close to the English in both its attitudes and its scope. It includes all kinds—irony, ridicule, fantastic exaggerations, "blue" stories, jokes about professions or races or drunks, and of course such political themes as the laziness, corruptibility, or stupidity of officials. Ridicule is sometimes louder than it would be in England, but malice is strikingly absent. The stock comedian in Russia is either a poker-faced clown or a Ukrainian brimming over with Southern gusto and warmth.

In circulation there are classic stories known outside Russia, such as the one about the Chinaman, Russian, Englishman, German, and Jew who found flies in their soup; or native inventions such as the story of the two extremely drunken men who became friends over vodka, were delighted to find that they were both called Ivan Ivanovitch Ivanov, quarreled violently when each of them alleged that he lived at No. 39 Bashkirskaya Street, and finally drank themselves into the realization that they were father and son. The "dumb sniper" was the hero of several wartime stories; he couldn't understand why there was a statue to Pushkin: "He lost the duel, didn't he?" Another wartime theme was the good-time girl—"Of course I'm looking grand. I eat in the American style (*po-amerikanski*); I get shoes in the Italian style (*po-italianski*); I dress in the English style (*po-angliiski*)—and I undress in commercial style (*po-kommercheski.*)"

The broad humor tolerated on the Soviet stage would surprise those who regard Russia as a nation of grim-faced Molotovs and Gromykos. There are sometimes passages which would hardly pass the English censor, in contemporary comedies, or in Mayakovsky's play *The Bug*. In the old favorite *Uncle's Dream* (dramatized from a story by Dostoyevsky) the supposedly rich uncle waddles painfully on to the stage, complaining audibly about the affliction which my Kuibyshev doctor could not mention without a blush. Variety theatres are few, but they often put on an evening devoted entirely to revue-length sketches. In one such performance, among the usual gibes at lazy managers, American politicians, and parents who pull strings for their sons, there were several sketches as "Western" as the following:

The scene is the waiting room of a maternity ward. Among the nervous fathers one Kalmanov is almost in a state of collapse. An astrologer had told his wife before she was married that if her first child was a girl all would be well forever after, but if it was a boy the father would die. His wife had insisted on having her baby just the same, and Kalmanov is consoled by the other fathers and by an orderly who brings vodka. The double doors swing open at last and a beaming nurse announces: "Citizen Kalmanov! It's a boy!" The orderly falls dead. Curtain.

I have made much of certain features of Russian manners and morals, partly because the visitor is more likely to come across these, but also because they help to show how, in a society with the strong communal loyalties of the Russians, people are likely to be addicted to a different pattern of human weaknesses and virtues from those in societies where individualism is more dominant. If some earnest missionary were to examine the Russian people for their proneness to the Seven Deadly Sins I think he would have to award them only very small black marks in respect of Pride, Envy, Avarice, and Lechery; a slightly blacker one for occasional Anger; a fair-sized one for Guttony; and the only really bad one for a still very widespread Accidie—not so much in its old form of hopeless laziness and despair, but as a substratum still showing in all the indifference, the petty adherence to rule, the reluctance to find out the true nature of things, and the tendency to talking instead of doing, which are still characteristic of at least a large minority of Russians.

They are encouraged in these tendencies by the ramifications and multiplication of authorities under the Soviet system, and by the absence of representative institutions except at very low levels. If people want proper attention they have to depend upon correctly interpreting and exploiting the machine—a machine which can often function very badly—and they have to become experts in assessing the status and pliability of the various officials. If they are unjustly treated they can, and do, appeal to their trade union, their local newspaper, or their local representative in the

Supreme Soviet, but the process of appeal can be a very long one. It is often easier to resort to the bribery, corruption, and knavery which are so widespread and which nowadays constitute the chief internal "enemy" of the Soviet state.

Even when one is dealing with Russian officials, however, it is often possible to appeal to their human brotherliness and charity; if you offer passionate sincerity you may be met with understanding. In other kinds of personal relationship Russians retain all that refreshing spontaneity and straightforwardness of which I spoke earlier; since the political relaxation they are able to show it even more than they used to. It has often been asked whether genuine friendship between individuals is possible in Russia, in face of so much state regulation and suspicion and the general sense of all belonging to the same crowd. But any Russian would raise his eyebrows in surprise at the question. What does one ask of friendship—a mirror, a critic, a complementary half, an audience, someone who needs you as you need him? In Russia you can have them all. There is not the same nervousness about the group as there appears to be in America, where the visitor can become depressed at feeling that so much warm but superficial "friendliness" is not personal to him but is due to a deep-seated convention which determines that every stranger must be treated in the same way lest a great American principle be violated. In Russia, in spite of all the group solidarity and egalitarianism, it is not assumed that every individual must be somehow in sympathy with every other. (Nor, if two men find themselves in particular sympathy with each other, are they liable to be suspected of homosexuality.)

There is a pleasant dignity about friendship with a Russian. You have made friends slowly and tentatively, you have not invaded each other's privacy in the possessive way so common for instance among Germans, you have been sincere but not sentimental, frank but not self-humiliating, you have not been exclusive, your Russian friend has introduced you into his group (but you have remained *his* friend)—when you separate you must separate, and after fourteen years you can go back and pick up a friendship almost exactly where you left off.

There can be danger in friendship, of course. One of the first questions asked by the security police is "Who are you friends?" They ask this when they have arrested you, or when they are trying to recruit you, as a patriotic citizen, to do some spying for them. In the past people very often had to be careful about making friends until each knew how far the other was inclined to be "political." This mistrust was not simply because you felt that you might some day express criticism of the regime. If a man was going to betray you he might do so on no evidence at all, since "political offenders" were often charged on evidence so flimsy that they could not possibly have foreseen their arrest.

Yet during the worst periods ties of friendship among Russians were impressive and powerful; I believe most Russians would at any time have put personal loyalties first if they could, and would have tried to protect their friends when it was at all possible. The comparative uselessness of the system in discovering real political offenders seems now to have been recognized, at least for the time being, and such devices as the domestic spy network—three persons unknown to each other in every house block— are thought at the time of writing to have disappeared as a general thing, though they have left an aftermath of apprehension among middle-aged and older persons. . . .

The limitations on experiment in the arts are so depressing in the Soviet Union and so much has been made abroad of the restrictions on Pasternak, Dudintsev, Shostakovitch, and others, and of the moral and political purposes so often assigned to the arts in Soviet education, that it has often been overlooked what enormous work has been done inside the country in fostering interest and spreading opportunities for appreciation and practice of the arts, albeit on restricted lines, among the ordinary population. There never seem to be enough copies of any classical book to meet the demand, so large has the reading public become; an edition of 300,000 copies of a new translation of Shakespeare's sonnets disappears in a very short time, and people queue to put their names on the subscription lists which are opened, in advance of publication, for translations of the collected works of Thomas Mann, Anatole France, Stendhal, or Flaubert. Musical instruments are no longer worth their weight in gold, but the demand for them—largely for use in amateur music clubs—seems insatiable. On a lesser scale painters and sculptors find it easy to sell their works, unoriginal though so many of them are, and shops find it easy to sell classical reproductions to a public which does not easily come by any pictures at all, not even of the lowest merit, in the way that the Western public does through magazines and advertising literature that goes into the dustbin. But the greatest Russian interest—after reading, and after sports and dancing for the young— goes into the theater. The country is covered with amateur dramatic clubs, whose talents seem to arise less from exhibitionism than from what might be called the national passion for human nature. The differentiation between the amateur and professional stage is less marked in Russia than in Britain or many other countries; both amateurs and professionals seem inspired by a similar enthusiasm for all sorts of characters and for perfecting their presentation of them.

The official "line" on the arts has of course relaxed somewhat during the years since Stalin's death. A directive to "discover the best light foreign literature" has resulted in the translation into Russian of *The Quiet American, Our Man in Havana, Lucky Jim, Look Back in Anger,* and *Hurry On Down.* The best of the rich collection of Impressionist paintings are on show again in Moscow, and the explanatory notes on the wall no longer speak of the styles of Matisse and Van Gogh as "reflecting the increasing degeneracy of the bourgeois world," as used to be the case. The Impressionists, in the new version, "followed more and more new paths, often subjective in character," they "turned away from social problems," but their revolt against academic routine is described as "very important." Marquet is praised for his "lyrical rendering of landscape," while the "exceptionally complicated and contradictory" Picasso is praised for the "deep feeling for humanity" in his earlier works, though they were followed by the "formal tendencies" of his cubism.

There is an official reaction also—in the press and in educational works —against the vulgar paper flowers, crude statuettes, "sugary picture post-cards," or "pictures of unnatural swans against a poisonously bright land-scape" which are so often offered to the Soviet consumer. "Why do women not realize," says the magazine *Ogonyok*, "that their most tasteful ensembles are 'killed' by these crudely flowering wallpapers in colors of poached egg and spring onion?" There is a rich soil for the appreciation of the arts, and a fascinating book could be made if some well-equipped foreigner were permitted to spend a couple of years in Russia, traveling everywhere in complete freedom, talking to the public and to teachers as well as to people engaged in the arts, and reporting on people's en-thusiasms, on the abstract sculptures and experimental poetry which are produced in private by a few, and on the occasional preference for clean, simple modern lines in theater décor or shop design, as well as on the academic pictures, the vulgar china vases, the second-rate novels and dance tunes, and so on.

It is impossible to forecast how far the new relaxations may be allowed to develop in the arts, as in every other field. But even in a much freer situation than the present some fundamental tendencies in Russian taste would be likely to persist. . . .

A great deal of Soviet popular music, fiction, and painting, whether "political" or not, has a similar unrefined sentimental quality, and it ap-peals to a large, undiscriminating public. The cultural patterns are still being groped for, since so much of the peasant culture has disappeared and there has not been much time to spare, as yet, for the development towards a self-confident urban or industrial culture with something, say, of the sardonic humor and cheekiness of the Cockney or the Berliner. One of the most popular plays on the Russian stage is a dramatization of *Pickwick Papers*; it is well done with one significant exception—the only character not properly presented is Sam Weller, who is made into a Figaro of a more aristocratic period. The Cockney flavor has not been understood.

There are city jokes, of course, about bus conductresses and football matches, and foremen, there is some city cynicism, and in caricatures and stories one sometimes sees the germ of a conception of the "little man," but it is too soon yet to see what kind of an urban-industrial culture may eventually shape itself out of universal education and the strains and pressures of city life, out of old solidarities and the new acquiring of personal possessions. . . .

The whole of the Russian art and literary world, both producers and public, is at present simmering with discussion, and it is open, sensitively if a little nervously open, to foreign influences as never before since the Revolution. Artists and writers still produce didactic works, but they have no need to feel so self-consciously didactic as they used to, since education has by now given them such a wide, demanding, and discussing public, and the political leadership does not, at least for the present, insist on such direct expression of ideological content. The difference is that plays, novels, films, and paintings are far more concerned with the problems of individual human beings than they used to be. They may still be "ideological," but they mostly express the ideology through the situations of human individuals rather than through organizational symbols and problems. This preoccupation with individual moral situations is partly dictated by the present Party line, but it has naturally opened the doors to a flood of more humane novels, plays, and works of art—good and bad—which it would be extremely difficult for the authorities to check if they ever wanted to. It is not surprising that there is so much uneasiness about the limits which are to be allowed, yet the significant thing even about Dudintsev's *Not by Bread Alone*, it seemed to me, was his concern for the individual rather than the fact that he attacked the bureaucracy and got in trouble for it.

The curiosity about foreign works seems to know no bounds. Abstract artists or tachistes from Poland are usually found laughable, but some Russian artists at least want to see their work in case they might themselves miss some spark which could kindle a response. Ignorance lends a good deal of enchantment, and the name of James Joyce seems to be a sort of talisman for many who can know almost nothing of his work. A few pages of *Ulysses* were translated in one of the literary reviews during the 1930's, and to my knowledge one copy of *Ulysses* in English and one of *Portrait of the Artist* were circulating at the same time, though these are very likely to have been destroyed during the purges. Yet now Kolotozov, director of *The Cranes Are Flying*, alleges that in that film, he was trying "to do something of what Joyce did with words." It is difficult for a foreigner to know what this can mean, especially if he compares Kolotozov's work with that of Cocteau or the early Buñuel for instance. By our standards it is a fairly ordinary, moving film. It does make a poetic use of images from time to time—suggestively in a simple way, instead of directly as in the usual Russian film, and this difference, an obvious one to Russians though small, must be what caused Kolotozov to make his extraordinary comment.

Russians of any culture—and some of almost none—are very conscious of the extent to which they have been out of touch with Western development in the arts since the Revolution. Even those who still indulge in nationalistic boasting are often well aware of this. It is a situation which imposes a delightful but serious responsibility on anyone who comes into contact with Russians, and a responsibility which it may fall to the most innocent tourist to share. Russians are in such an omnivorously receptive state at the moment that it seems extremely important that when we meet them we should bear in mind what an innocent earnestness they bring to the arts. They are bred on Tolstoy, Chekhov, and Turgenev, whom they read in their teens; if they are at all interested in criticism they have the example of more than a century, from the all-powerful Belinsky onwards, in holding as an act of faith that the primary duty of the arts is to reform people and institutions. On the other hand most of them are so little educated in the forms of art that they indiscriminately accept almost any manifestation of the arts in the past. They are not much inclined to put one style against another. They are not put off, for example, by the the Art Nouveau buildings in the old bourgeois quarters, whose carefully preserved stucco still spawns bulbous flowers and submarine macaroni.

So when they come to the arts of the contemporary West they may well want to be shown everything which is going on. They certainly want to see how amusing or lighthearted we can be. But I think it is something of a duty to bring especially to their notice our writers and artists who speak to the heart, who show some compassionate sympathy for human nature and some belief in its capacity for good—Forster, Lawrence, Cary, Arthur Miller, Mauriac, Chamson, perhaps Camus, in literature, and in painting some of the neo-romanticists, for instance, or the leading Australians. Too much acquaintance with our amoral dissections or with our concentration on the subjective in the plastic arts could lead to a serious revulsion from the West. Russians are not well acquainted with what preceded these tendencies, and not many of them would be willing to accept them as temporary and technical explorations.

The Soviet authorities for reasons of their own might take the opportunity of formulating the revulsion and turning it into a prohibition, but it would have a genuine foundation in the taste of the public, much as they might regret the ringing down of another curtain on the West. It is significant that, while "formalistic" experiments of Western artists are nowadays sometimes mentionable in magazines, and in the Hermitage one can see early cubist paintings by Picasso, similar experiments by Russian artists in the free years after the Revolution are not to be seen in public nor reproduced in art magazines. Knowledge of these Russian experiments circulates privately, but if the curtain were to come down again it would thus be foreign and not Russian artists who could be condemned in public.

After such a revulsion the Russian arts might sink into sentimentality again; or if a genius or two appeared we might see a Tolstoy or a Courbet of our day. Even if there is to be no great revulsion, I think, since the Russians have skipped so much in the last forty years, and since they have in that time made so much of their new society, they are unlikely to want to go through the stages they have missed, even if a few Russian artists were to become enthusiasts for Post-Impressionism, Cubism, abstract art, and so forth. I see no likelihood of another Kandinsky or Malevitch arising in Russia, even in private isolation, for much the same reasons that there will not be another Kandinsky or Malevitch in the West. Nor will there be a return to the time when machines, because they were new, were for a brief period the themes of works of art—the cream-separator in one section of The General Line, or a whole factory in Mossolov's Music of the Machines.

The accent will continue to be on the human, for reasons which I have labored often enough. . . . And the human, almost certainly, will be explored more delicately, more intimately, and above all more as a matter of individual personality than in the past. In 1960 more than half the contemporary plays on the Soviet stage had a boy-meets-girl theme or a triangle theme. (Three of them dealt with middle-aged husbands attracted by young girls, each play offering a different solution.)

There has always been a strong preference in Russia, but especially during the Soviet period, for paintings of subjects involving human *situations*—the Zaporozhye Cossacks of Repin, the pyramid of skulls and other antiwar pictures by Verestchagin, and the long-drawn agony of *The Ninth Wave* by Aivazovsky, as well as all the later paintings of gleaming Soviet achievements (though these are now sometimes caricatured in *Krokodil*). But the Impressionists now hang in some of the most prominent places in the galleries of Moscow and Leningrad, and I think their freshness is likely to bring a reaction against the overemphasis on subjects of human situation, just as it brought a reaction, on the first appearance of the Impressionists in Europe, against the prevalence of the pathetic fallacy in salons and academies. For what, in fact, could be more human, more inspired by the delicacy of a human touch than, say, Renoir's rendering of some overlooked hedge corner? Until now the usual Soviet attitude to such a painting was that it was the work of a soul maiming itself in contemplation away from the world of men. But now that Russians can relax a little, now that they do not need the security of the mass quite as much as they used to, now that they can look at each other more as individuals, I think the Impressionist painter is likely to be valued for his rare and precious eye serving as a telescope to hitherto unobserved delights. Pictures of "human situations" will not become entirely out of date, but I think the conception of the human will be enlarged in this way and will inspire Soviet artists, as it has indeed inspired a few in the past. There is a similiar discovery of the poetry and even the uniqueness of individual experience in recent films and novels; it has been there all the time in the work of a very few unfashionables, such as Pasternak. It is a discovery which the Russians, with all their long-established sincerity, are just about ripe to make and to exploit in all the arts. In due course it may bring about another reaction towards the mass and towards art based on "human situations," but the advance which one may hope to see made in the near future is not likely to be entirely lost.

*　　*　　*

27

ELEMENTS AND TYPES IN SOVIET MARRIAGE

H. KENT GEIGER

"There is no love so ardent that it will not be cooled by marriage," says a traditional proverb. Some idea of the distance Soviet men and women have been invited to travel since the Revolution can be obtained by con-trasting the sense of the proverb with the Marxist notion that no marriage is valid *unless* it is bonded by love. As we know, the Soviet regime under Stalin felt obliged to compromise with the Marxist ideal and urged husbands and wives to seek, at least in the transition period, other sources of bondedness in addition to that individual sex love so praised by Engels. Nonetheless, the record suggests that many in the population have found the ideal marriage pattern not only desirable but attainable. These two positions can be regarded as the extremes of the Soviet con-tinuum of marriage types.

THE PEASANT PATTERN

A peasant woman described the proper position of husband and wife in marriage as follows: "In the majority of good families the wife sub-ordinates herself to the husband. Now, with us, when my son comes home my daughter-in-law takes off his boots, cleans them for him, and you see how it is. She is obedient and devoted to her husband. There is no other way." Subordination, obedience, and a slavish devotion comprise the duties of the wife; the husband is the ruler. Anyone who has visited in a traditional Russian peasant household knows the deferential quality of the wife's demeanor. She guards her silence when her husband speaks, serves the food for husband and guest, and remains standing while they

Reprinted, by permission of the publishers, from H. Kent Geiger, *The Family in Soviet Russia* (Cambridge, Mass.: Harvard University Press, 1968), pp. 217–39. Copy-right, 1968, by the President and Fellows of Harvard College. The footnotes have been omitted.

eat. If differences arise between the couple, it is the wife who is expected always to give in. A young collective farm wife says: "If my husband shouted at me because of the children I just remained silent, so there would be no quarrels."

Traditionally, one of the most symbolic of the relative positions of the two sexes has been wife-beating. There are still families to be found in which this male prerogative is practiced. To the women, "Christ is the Head of the Church, the husband of his wife," and often the blows are accepted as in the past, submissively and dumbly, as another aspect of a hard fate.

Love is customarily a muted or entirely missing sentiment. In general, emotional involvement in peasant marriage seems to be minimal, with familiarity constituting the chief source of attraction between husband and wife. The men and women who live in these marriages can rarely describe the details of the relationship; usually the most they can say is that relations are "good" or "bad." The outside observer finds description easier. A fifty-year-old forester is described as religious, patriarchal, and moody. Occasionally he beat his wife. The relation was not a bad one, however, for "in spite of the lack of emotional ties, relations between the spouses were relaxed and always cheerful. He ruled the family with strict, but good-humored patriarchalism." The label "tension-free but superficial" seems apt for the good times, and when the husband is angry, his emotions emerge in spontaneous, full form. The wife then usually forgives him quickly, for it is in the nature of men, she thinks, to be hot-tempered, and her husband is proud of this trait.

Positive feelings between the spouses are held more in check, however. There is a taboo upon overt, certainly upon conspicuous and public, display of affection. Kissing or taking the wife's arm on the street is looked upon as abnormally affectionate and unmasculine.

The relative unimportance of strong positive regard, of love, is seen clearly in mate selection. In the past the custom was for the parents of the prospective couple to take the lead in making the match. In Viryatino the older respondents asserted that there were cases of brides and grooms who had not known each other at all before marriage. A somewhat different aspect, but leading to the same conclusion, is presented by the Viryatino family in which the mother protested against the daughter's intention to marry, "because in the family there were older sisters not yet married."

Even now that the choice is mainly an individual one, the way in which it is made is revealing. A young man, returning to Viryatino after army service, had resolved to marry a village girl with whom he had been friendly before his army days. On his return he found that she had married someone else. He then found another to his liking, a medical student, but she refused, saying she wanted to continue her higher education. He proceeded to quickly decide on another who caught his fancy. He sat down next to her in the club and after about three days asked her to marry. Such dispatch is apparently typical. Another young kolkhoznik says: "We don't look for a great friendship. You like the girl, so you marry her."

It all seems quite casual and matter-of-fact. To the man it seems that "any wife will do" and to the woman that "men are all alike," or at most can be divided into two classes, good men and bad men, those who drink too much vodka and beat them and those who do not. But the formula "any wife will do" is, of course, an exaggeration, and young peasant men prefer wives who are attractive and friendly, good cooks and housekeepers, sensible, and so on. Yet there is some truth in the epigram, and to this extent it fits in with the opposition to divorce. Peasant custom, for instance, does not take kindly to incompatibility as a reason for divorce. One peasant admits that it seems he made a mistake in choosing his wife: "She was a cross one, like a fire. It was hard to get along with her. . . . If I had known it I might not have married her, but if I wanted to divorce, my father would not have permitted it, and I respected my father. [Why would your father not have permitted it?] Because he was religious and did not want people to divorce. 'Marry once,' he always said, 'even if she's an onion and your tears flow.' Thus, he would not permit it." If "any wife will do," then it is obviously inappropriate to divorce.

In the peasant marriage sexuality is seen as a need and prerogative of the man, and sexual relations are usually suffered more than enjoyed by the wife. Marital fidelity on the part of the husband is not considered important—"men are like that"—but both virginity before marriage and fidelity after marriage are expected of the wife. Not only in sexual behavior, but also in other realms of impulse release, the double standard is very strong. Drinking, smoking, fighting, swearing are all prerogatives and symbols of masculinity and are denied to the proper peasant wife. She is expected to obey and to please her husband as best she can, and if he fails to reciprocate with wisdom and kindness, that, too, even though it is resented, is to be expected from men. The chief solace to the wife in an unhappy marriage is the church and her children.

In sexual relations the peasant woman is expected to be innocent, passive, and relatively uninterested. The man takes full initiative, looking upon sexual intimacy as a right which a wife can under no circumstances deny him. To a considerable extent his positive feeling for his wife is linked directly to her sexual desirability; as a consequence, the Soviet peasant husband sees the first period in his marriage as most enjoyable by far—the high point in his relation with his wife. After the initial excitement furnished by novelty, the relations with his wife settle down to a routine form both sexually and in more general terms. A young peasant girl says: "Of course your first year is the best. Your husband treats you better the first year. After that the children—after three or four years."

In the past such a marriage was embedded in a larger, usually patrilocal, extended family, and the tie between the young spouses was only one of the factors to be considered. Central, for instance, was her capacity to adapt to the already established routines of her husband's family of orientation. The submissiveness of the wife was supported by the residence custom, in which she was literally given away by her parents to become a member of another family and thus became economically dependent upon her new family. The real ruler of the family in those days was the old man, the husband's father. The wielding of power was determined primarily by age and sex, the order of precedence being from husband's father to husband's mother to husband. For the newly married husband and wife this worked well in the beginning of their marriage, giving them a chance to get used to each other without the immediate responsibility of exercising power, though by tradition the young wife was "always a stranger in the household of her husband."

These patterns have gradually crumbled, because the economic and legal basis for the aged father's authority has ended. On the kolkhoz, for example, work and payment are assigned and made to the individual, not by the head of household, and the new opportunities and outer status of women make the role of dependent daughter-in-law quite unattractive. Today, when a new wife feels uncomfortable with her parents-in-law she and her husband quickly decide to live by themselves. . . . There are definite advantages to living separately, but the responsibility for maintaining the marriage is thrown directly upon the participants' shoulders. Unfortunately, in the countryside, love—in the sense of that institutionalized expectation of permanent romantic attachment which elsewhere is important as a binding factor—is usually present, if at all, only in the early stages. Thus, it offers little support.

Village custom, religious opposition to divorce, dependency of wife and children on continuation of the marriage, and official divorce policy have all continued to exert some pressure. Sometimes when a peasant wife feels ill-treated and threatens to leave her husband, he uses naked threat of bodily harm, and she stays because she is afraid of what he will do to her. To some degree the traditionally low expectation of what peasant marriage provides helps to maintain it. If "a wife is only dear twice—when brought into the house and when carried out in her coffin," then the peasant husband is not too disappointed about it. Nevertheless, in a time of rapid economic and social changes all these forces have lost some of their sustaining capacity, and Soviet peasant marriage has become more and more unstable with the passing of time.

EQUAL RIGHTS WITH LOVE

This pattern corresponds to the relations deemed proper by modern urban populations around the world. Both spouses share power by conscious agreement and deliberate effort. Sharing does not mean an absence of friction over the question, but when power is abused by one or the other of the sides, usually the husband, it is the wife's right to demand her say. Nor are the spouses required to perform in other respects in any set manner.

In many of the marriages observed the question seems to have been solved without great difficulty. The social unrest and uncertainties in the larger society seem to have combined with the challenging tasks offered by Soviet daily routine to make many Soviet husbands and wives only too glad to share rather than monopolize responsibility and power. The pattern seems often to involve a very rational alternation between two spouses, with an attitude of easy permissiveness for the most qualified to exercise influence, as in a Stalingrad working-class marriage. "In their partnership he predominated at times, and sometimes she did. He then gladly acceded to her guidance."

Often the husband, especially if he is at all "co-opted" by his occupation, is content if the wife takes full charge of running the family household. This is a common factor to the equal-rights pattern. The wife of the busy Moscow factory director, for instance, did not work on the outside, but did take full charge of the furnishing of their luxurious five-room modern apartment near the Kremlin and of planning how to spend the couple's free time. Such spouses often seem quite highly specialized in their marital roles. In the relationship of a research chemist and his wife, also a trained chemist and serving as his assistant at work, the specialization by sex is muted but still noticeable. Their personalities and relationship are described this way: "He was quiet, controlled, serious, and reserved; she was the same. He was very active in his work, but as a person more passive. With her it was somewhat the other way around. While at work she was under him; at home she was really somewhat more the leader. Added together, this led to complete equality of rights between them. All problems were dealt with in common with complete calm." Other equal-rights marriages seem more tense, and apparently much effort has to go into the preservation of the equal status of the spouses. It seems that underlying, less conscious needs press the husband and occasionally the wife in a direction that diverges markedly from their conscious ideal of equality. This situation is especially common in younger families, where idealism is stronger, when husband and wife are still adjusting to each other, and where the limits of each other's desires and capabilities are not clearly understood.

Sometimes, perhaps as frequently as the wife, it is the husband who most seeks this kind of relationship. A young man from Viryatino, a recent version of the "progressive Komsomol youth of the 1920's with its uncompromising view of religion as a class-alien ideology, and with its urge to break with the routine of family life," married a young peasant girl with whom he wanted to establish an equal-rights relation. He became quite a proselytizer, taking his wife to the cinema and Komsomol meetings, reading to her aloud, and "insisting on a baby sitter on evenings when meetings or some other activities were going on in the village club." Another example is a young marriage between a twenty-six-year-old military officer and the daughter of a university professor: "Relations between them were very affectionate, and they did a lot of things together, though she did not share his occupational life. Surprisingly, he was more for equal rights in the marriage than she, who preferred to be somewhat subordinate and made no use of the liberties he was ready to extend to her." The affective bond in this kind of marriage is a deep sense of intimacy and sharing of all aspects of the self. The partners see each other as unique and look upon their relationship as irreplaceable. There is considerable self-control exercised, with the mood swings so typical among the peasantry occurring only rarely. Love is expected and spoken about, the partners are self- and relationship-conscious.

To be sure, mutual understanding and aid are also stressed, as is respect. When referring to the spouse in talk with an outsider (such as an interviewer), a respondent is apt to refer to his spouse as a "friend," or "life comrade" as well as a wife or husband. In general, such spouses seem decidedly more conscious of each other as separate personalities than is the case in the preceding pattern, and also more consciously dependent upon each other. Research into the personalities of Great Russians has repeatedly furnished evidence that dependency and affiliative needs are strong. Marriage is an obvious form for their satis-faction and seems to be the more strengthened by the presence of these needs, provided that they can be integrated with a pattern of distributing power that makes it possible to express them.

As a matter of fact, successful marriages that follow the equal-rights-with-love formula impress one with not only the conscious recognition but the considerable degree of enjoyment afforded by satisfying depend-ency and affiliative needs. A white-collar worker, age sixty-five, says: "It is easier to meet all life's problems when one has a close friend, when one can be of assistance to one another. In that sense I consider my wife as a source of life-giving energy, which enables me to have the strength to meet the struggle for life." In the case of the factory director and his wife, "If he came home from work exhausted, she cheered him up, so that he became visibly transformed—more cheerful and relaxed. . . . The link between them as two human beings was extremely deep." If peasant-style marriage ranges from relatively unfeeling familiarity at best to savage oppression at worst, those at the opposite extreme range in terms of the typical emotional experience from reasonably sympathetic at worst to impressively rich at best. The capacity to enter into a full, intimate relation seems great; perhaps there is an unusual reservoir of stored emotion in the Russian psyche. A Stalingrad couple has an almost idyllic relationship: "They cared for each other not only in the usual sense of marriage, but took an interest in each other's work. Thus she visited him on her free days at his construction site. They also shared the same values and opinions . . . when they had nothing to do, they sat together in front of the door of the house, the wife played the balalaika and the family sang, or the husband and wife played chess."

Attitudes and practice in mate selection and divorce correspond to the elements of the expected nature of the marriage. Love and comradely sympathy are paramount, and the sharing of interests, values, and general philosophy is a secondary criterion for deciding whether and whom to marry. When 800 couples newly married in Leningrad were asked in 1962, "What in your opinion is the chief condition for a stable and happy marriage?" love, it is reported, together with "common views, faith, sincerity, friendship, and such" accounted for 76.2 per cent of the responses. In this kind of marriage divorce is disapproved of in principle but accepted as a necessary evil, for: "If people torment each other, why should they stay together?"

Sexual life is valued by the husband and wife as their personal property, not to be soiled by promiscuity. There is a single standard of fidelity after marriage. Consider the Stalingrad worker, a forty-two-year-old construction trust painter. His wife is forty, a factory worker, and they have two sons, ages eight and nine. Both spouses are of working-class background and live in very modest circumstances in a small wooden house, one and one-half rooms, on the Volga. The husband has a number of the personal traits most valued in the traditional culture: He is lively, fond of singing, courageous, sympathetic, big-hearted, frank, and even outspoken—"whenever necessary, he delivered his opinions point-blank to his work superiors." Also, "he liked the company of women, and liked to joke with them, but never anything serious, for he esteemed his wife too much."

To the observer of such marriages it seems that the two partners are held together mainly by love. Nevertheless, a closer acquaintance often reveals a broader scope in which harmony prevails—in mutual work interests, for example—and in which personal regard looks almost like a by-product. In the case of a scientist and his wife joint occupational achievement was evidently both the goal and symbol of a happy marriage: "Both had studied chemistry in Moscow, and had also met each other, married, and worked together there. Now they were working together in a project which he was directing, on problems of the decomposition of uranium; she served as his personal assistant. . . . Both lived for their professions and for their duty. Everything was subordinated to it. . . . Their life goal seemed to be the Stalin prize." A factory director lives in a different style. Summers are spent in the Caucasus and in the Crimea. Otherwise, in free time the two read, listen to the radio, and like to ice-skate. The observer reports that they love each other. Further: "He was proud of his good-looking wife—she adapted well to managerial circles. She was proud of him because of his achievements. He also impressed her as a man, and there was probably also a certain material factor influencing her. . . . Moreover, they agreed in opinions and values on all matters, and had great trust in each other." All in all, it appears that their love contributes to and is enriched by being in tune with the outer society. Their strong sense of mutuality of fate, and the privileges that go with it, brings them even closer to each other.

THE TREND OF CHANGE

Even in rural areas the old days, when the reins were firmly in the hands of the oldest male, have gone. A saying that until recently the men liked to repeat—"woman has long hair and a short wit"—has ceased to be true or amusing, and the unequal terms of address—by which the patriarchal male was likely to address his wife with the familiar *ty*, while she in speaking to her husband was well advised to use his name, patronym, and the formal *vy*—have been long since replaced by the familiar form. The patriarchal pattern, both as an ideal form for peasant family life as a whole and as an implicit ordering principle for absolute male dominion in marriage, has undergone a gradual and uneven weakening. The process has been under way for some time. Urbanization, education, the emancipation of women— these worldwide trends have had their effect in Russia as elsewhere, and the Revolution has greatly accelerated them.

All sources agree that Soviet marital life is tending toward more equality between husband and wife. The changing pattern of relative age of the two spouses is one particularly significant symptom of the degree to which this is so. Table 26–1 is based on a sampling of 3,000 marriage registration records for the three years 1920, 1940, and 1960, for two urban districts and one rural district in the Leningrad region. If the decline in age disparity indicated by these data is typical for the whole country, the change is a striking one indeed.

Male dominance is still frequent in the peasant marriage, especially in the older generations. Yet even those who still subscribe to the pattern in their own lives express a presentiment of change. A peasant woman says of the new pattern she observes around her: "I am your wife. You say, 'You will not go there. I don't want you to go there.' But I say, 'You have no right. I'll go where I please. The husband does not have the right to tell his wife what to do.' There is a law . . . they call it equality of rights. The wife may want to go into the Komsomol or do something, and she does what she wants, not what her husband wants." In many worker and peasant marriages the confrontation of the old pattern by the new equality brings considerable malaise. As in the above case, there is a tendency for some lower-class women to see the legal equality of woman as extending to family relations as well as economic and political life. Another wife, from a working-class marriage, says, "In the Soviet Union the husband had no say about his wife's working or about his adult children."

Most peasant men have been unwilling to grant such a radical shift in power so quickly, and most of their wives, I believe, have not wanted it either. The transition from the old order has been slow and often painful. Even where the man has remained dominant, however, the

Table 27–1. Relative Age at Marriage of Spouses,
Leningrad Region, 1920, 1940, 1960

Location of Registry Office and Year	Relative Age of Spouses			
	Same or Groom Younger (per cent)	Groom 1–6 Years Older (per cent)	Groom 7 or More Years Older (per cent)	Total (per cent)
Urban				
1920	19.0	49.5	31.5	100.0
1940	32.5	51.0	16.5	100.0
1960	40.0	46.5	13.5	100.0
Rural				
1920	17.5	46.0	36.5	100.0
1940	26.5	50.5	23.0	100.0
1960	41.0	48.0	11.0	100.0

Source: Adapted from Kharchev, *Brak i semya*, p. 190. The rural sample numbered 1,500 and was taken from Mginski district, Leningrad region. The urban sample also consisted of 1,500 cases, taken from Kirov and Kuibyshev districts, Leningrad.

nature of his relationship with his wife has been different. Consultation and mutual agreement about important decisions have become prescriptive. A young collective farm wife is asked who makes the decisions in her family. She says, "My husband, of course. Of course he talks it over with me, asks whether I agree. But he is the husband, he decides mostly. Because he understands more." While the old order involved absolute and irrational hegemony, the new male supremacy is more temperate. Frequently, as in the case above, it is rationalized as "he understands more." Another peasant, who became a tractor driver, presents a different rationalization: "Of course a man should be head of the family. Because I can earn more than my wife. If I get anything my wife has it too."

Actually, in many peasant families today there is a characteristic arrangement, by which the husband is the ruler "in principle," while it is the wife who often makes important decisions and wields considerable influence in other ways. The distinction between public appearance and private reality is more apparent, I suspect, to the wives than to the husbands. An old collective farm woman says: "The husband is the boss, but it's I who tell him, 'Father, we need such and such a thing,' I know the needs of everyone in the family better than he does. I wash their clothing and can see better than he who needs something."

The contradiction between the still lively cultural norm of masculine dominance and the observed behavior of such partners leads to a kind of ritual patriarchalism which can easily be misinterpreted by the casual observer who sees only the outer form and concludes that masculine dominance is more thoroughgoing than is actually the case. A Soviet ethnographer described (perhaps with some exaggeration) the new situation in the families on a Kazakh kolkhoz: "In the overwhelming majority of families in the absence of outsiders the wife has an equal position with the husband, and at times in some families even is the ruler. But in the presence of outsiders, by tradition she must exhibit her supposed submissive position . . . [for example] when visiting she does not sit in the place of honor."

This is probably close to the situation today in the typical Soviet marriage (taking typical to mean modal with respect to the entire population). Masculine dominance, while still present, has become more moderate, and humane, tending gradually toward acceptance of full equality for the wife, though there is still a long way to go among the peasantry. A study of 300 Leningrad working-class families conducted in 1961 offers some good evidence in support. Two types of marital relationships are distinguished, both of which involve masculine predominance—"by tradition the overwhelming majority of women name the husband head of the family." In the first the personal power of the husband is conserved, but it is said to be based not upon constraint but upon "the moral authority of the husband with more or less voluntary submission on the part of the rest of the members of the family to this authority." In the second type the predominance of the husband is merely formal and masks a *de facto* equality of rights in deciding basic intrafamilial questions. Of course, it may be significant, as the researcher claims (but does not support with evidence), that these are all families in which the wife is employed. In any case, the second type, in which the masculine dominance is merely a formal one, is the majority pattern, found in 60 per cent of the sample.

Marital patterns change much more slowly than behavior in public contexts. To the Russian man surrender of power over his wife—a right extended by God, customary law, tradition, and superiority of physical strength—however justifiable in a rational sense and on a conscious level, nonetheless gnaws at his self-esteem. For this reason the outer form so often remains patriarchal even while things are more equal in private and even if feelings of affection and love may have become strongly influential. Thus the typical marriage today combines, in friendly coexistence, male dominance and tender affection, attitudes which do not merge well when they are found in extreme forms. A good example is given by the marriage of a thirty-five-year-old construction foreman from Kiev. His wife is twenty-eight, and they are described as in love: "They met before the war during their student days at a dance, and were married at the time he was drafted. . . . Both expected a mildly patriarchal marriage, and conducted their marriage accordingly. He led the way, but in a gentle and less absolute way than had been the case in the marriage of her parents, his father-in-law. . . . The main influence on both their attitudes was that of their parents' home, mellowed by the advances made by the society which surrounded them."

In addition to ritual patriarchalism with love, there are other signs of what is happening in Soviet marriage. Patterns of the future as well as the past are found in the changing nature of the association between social relations and ceremony. It is usual in Viryatino to go through two wedding ceremonies, one in the Civil Registry, or ZAGS, office and a second, traditional, service in the home of the husband's parents. Significantly, it is reported that sexual relations often are initiated after the first of the two, though the girl continues to live with her own parents until the second ceremony has been completed.

It seems that the link between the girl's continued residence in her parents' home and the traditional wedding ceremony in her husband's parents' home is furnished by the larger circle of persons, mainly kinsmen, who are in some way involved with the young couple. Moving out only after the traditional wedding symbolizes their continuing willingness to see their marriage as contingent upon the larger community, specifically the two parental families, and, perhaps, their desire to express respect for the traditions of their peasant heritage.

The association between the official Soviet agency and their sexual intimacy is also important, the connecting link here being their marriage itself. The initiation of sexual relations before the girl moves out of her parents' home, but only after a trip to the ZAGS office, suggests that the couple sees the Soviet order as supportive of their right to live a separate and independent life as a married couple, and in particular to behave in a fashion independent of and different from that of their parents. However, they assert this right unobtrusively, in terms of the most private aspect of their life together, sexual relations, so as not to offend too greatly against their relatives' or their own sense of respect for tradition.

Such behavior patterns reveal social change in process and the extent to which cultural malintegration is creatively adjusted to by the partners of individual marriages. It is also not without significance that sexual intimacy, perhaps love too, between spouses seems to find its defender in the new Soviet order, whereas the traditional way of life appears to uphold the more repressive, less spontaneous aspect of marriage, namely, the power of the community to influence the young couple's life together.

Of course, this trend toward more individualism in marriage is by no means novel. The shift of solidarity priority from the larger kin group to the marital pair is shown by changes in other patterns of peasant life. In the old days the relationship of man and wife was influenced by the general assumption of male superiority, in connection with which the women were subjected to discrimination and segregation in various guises. The older folks in Viryatino still remember when the mealtime seating order at table in the peasant cottage required the men to sit on one side and the women on the other. But, they report, married couples had begun to sit together before the turn of the twentieth century.

To conclude this portion of the discussion, it is worthwhile to stress several facts about the most typical of Soviet marriages, that which is in transition between the peasant pattern and the pattern of equal-rights-with-love. Transitional forms are compromises, and . . . they do not always work too well. In this marriage not only are power and affection governed by contradictory forces, but often so are other aspects of married life, such as the spouses' religious and political views. Consequently, the continuity from one generation to another is not great, there is a certain fitful unrest to the marriage, as if elemental spontaneity and conscious self-control are vying for supremacy, and very often the spouses work out their uncertainties on their children. In a highly sublimated form of this unrest, husband and wife divert attention from themselves and their own relationship and focus their conscious thoughts and goals upon their children. Such seems to have happened in the case of the happily married Stalingrad couple already referred to: "The children were the purpose of the family. They were to get a better education. He carefully supervised their school work. And when they won prizes for good work he was very proud of them. Their social intercourse was also controlled; the children were not allowed to play with the children of Volga River workers. . . . The family was passively religious, and the children were so reared and they crossed themselves."

Underground Archetypes

1. *The vestigial marriage.* Turning now to a characterization of marriage types that are out of correspondence with any cultural pattern but of frequent enough occurrence to merit attention, I have chosen to label the first "vestigial," since its most typical trait is an absence of content. Other appropriate descriptions would be "casual," "*ad hoc*," or "empty shell." External circumstances rather than love, tradition, or community control predominate as the binding factor. Often forces beyond the control of the individuals concerned bring them together in ways that preclude full commitment to each other, and they live in what they both seem to accept as a union likely to be only temporary. This was so in the case of a forty-five-year-old horse-driver for a Donbas construction trust. As a former prisoner of war he had been sentenced by the Soviet Government to stay in that region, not his original home, and at the time of observation in 1948 had not seen his first wife and three children since 1941. He carried on correspondence with this wife, however, tried to exert some influence over their children in letters, and counted on returning eventually to them. His present *de facto* marriage is described by the observer with eloquent brevity: "He lived in K. with a widow and her son in relations akin to those of marriage. The widow tolerated his connection with his family. With her he did not play the dominant role very much, for he felt more like a guest; moreover, the widow was more independent and active than his own wife." Mobility, both involuntary, in connection with the wars, col-lectivization, resettlement, and so forth, and voluntary, has been very

common. It has brought frequent and long separations between spouses, with temporary *de facto* marriages serving as a substitute.

Moreover, the confusion and disorganization of Soviet history works in a vicious circle, in which deaths, arrests, occupational demotions, divorces, and separations in prior experiences reduce the individual's chances in subsequent marriages. There are many in the population with damaged identity. A construction director, aged sixty-four, is married to a thirty-two-year-old woman with whom his relations are not especially close. He had been a Party member since 1916 and of fairly high rank, but, like the wife, had some liabilities in his past: "After 1945 he was expelled, because he was complaining, wanting to see fulfilled the promises he had had to make to the people in his wartime speeches." Thereafter he lived in S. and followed his original profession of carpenter but as a foreman. His first marriage ended in divorce; his wife had grown too old for him. The second marriage took place in 1946. The wife was thirty-two years younger, parentless, and had been raised in an orphanage. She had been previously married and divorced and brought a child from that marriage into this one. Because of negatively valued personal traits these two partners have little chance to establish a better marriage, they realize it, and they accept the present setup as the best that circumstances can provide.

Deep involvement in one's spouse is lacking in these marriages, and personal convenience seems the main return from marriage. Sexual gratification, regular meals, and a place to live seem central as binding factors, as in this example: "He is interested in his wife only insofar as she cares for the house and the children and affords him a certain comfort. The marriage is for this reason only a physical togetherness; inner feelings are quite absent. From this it is evident why the husband took up with other women and girls from time to time. This is of little importance to his wife who feels, on the contrary: If he has other women sometimes, at least I have some rest from him. . . . Nevertheless the marriage is not bad, nor is the family's integrity endangered." In other cases, the marriage is even more bereft of mutual esteem, and bare sexual satisfaction alone seems salient.

Interestingly, the distribution and exercise of power is not ordinarily problematic, being solved by social distance between the spouses, a grandparent who takes over, or simply indifference. To the casual observer the spouses seem quite equal. An army lieutenant's marriage to a peasant girl in 1945 was described as having the following aims: to help him lead a more orderly life, to gain access to more food products through her kin, who lived on a kolkhoz, and to get sexual satisfaction. The pattern of authority and its background is further described thus: "The two have just about equal rights in the marriage, but he is still somewhat the leader. Basically, however, they lived together without any relationship; each followed his own interests. Just as before [the marriage], he spends much time with his comrades, and she takes care of the small household and chats with the other officers' wives.

The partners were together solely at mealtimes and at night. In addition, there are regular visits to her relatives which, however, serve mainly as an opportunity for them to eat their fill. They do not think about the future nor eventual children, because each of the two partners is happy and satisfied in his situation."

As suggested by the preceding case, the interests of the two partners are essentially individual, or, as the observer put it, "narrow" rather than shared. For the man it is almost like a bachelor's life. Such was explicitly admitted in an interview with a newspaper reporter. He continued his "bachelor-like existence" after his marriage—a pattern aided by work assignments requiring frequent travel. When asked to compare his tie with his wife with that between his own mother and father, who were peasants, he replied, "My wife and I were completely independent of one another, whereas my parents' relations toward one another possessed a patriarchal character." Such a relationship he found pleasing, and, as one can imagine, it was greatly facilitated by the fact that his mother "ran the house."

2. *The mother-wife and the son-husband.* In some marriages the usual roles in wielding power are reversed, and the weaker sex produces the paradoxical phenomenon, in a land of patriarchal tradition, of the strong woman. The most visible characteristic of the wife, as well as of the marriage, is a certain feminine sustaining capacity. The wife is a person of stability and bountifulness. In such marriages the makeup of the wife often tends to take on the shape of the mother role. The observer is inclined to describe the wife's feeling for the husband as one of kindness rather than love. The husband's feeling is harder to characterize, since the relationship, being somewhat illegitimate, and foreign to the conscious masculine self-image, is for him more primitive, ambivalent, and oscillatory.

A description of the interplay of behavior and feeling in this type is taken from a Soviet film. The character traits of the grandmother and her relationship with the grandfather are being described. She has strength, charm, generosity, peace of mind, a calm conscience. Furthermore: "This old woman seems to represent the matter-of-factness of the earth, the self-evident strength of the flesh, and the native stoutness of the heart. [She is] even nursing the wailing grandfather along . . . she lets the senile old man beat her, simply going down on her knees as if he had actually been strong enough to push her down. . . . 'He is my husband,' she says. . . . This woman seems to know no law but that of giving; no principles except the complete trust in her own inner endurance. . . . She accepts the passions of men as she accepts . . . fire: both are external if unavoidable evils. It is as if she had lived long before passions had made men ambitious, greedy, and, in turn, childishly repentant, and as if she expected to outlast it all. . . . The grandmother takes him into her arms, almost her lap. She calms him. . . . He collapses on her in foolish fondness, only to rally suddenly and to knock her down in a rage of jealousy." Although the grandfather is

obviously getting on in years, the senility serves to accentuate the underlying forces that have been there all along.

The pattern itself is in its grosser form quite unmistakable, even
though both partners might subscribe in principle to the traditional
propriety of masculine superiority. A construction worker, in his mid-
forties, of Russian background but living with his wife and two children
in a village in Lithuania, earned about 500 rubles a month and thrice-
yearly bonuses of about 1,000 rubles each time. Relations came to a
focus around the spending of his earnings: "The wife controlled the
money; she took it from him immediately. If he wanted to have a
drink, he had to borrow money. . . . He did not worry about the household—that was her job—but she was somewhat involved in his job.
She sent him off to work punctually, and if he did not come right
home after work, she went to get him, because she was afraid he would
go somewhere to drink." The observer adds that while the wife commanded in the marriage, both were convinced that the man should rule,
and "externally and also in relation to the children . . . he had again
at times to fulfill the patriarchal role." In such a ritual patriarchalism
the ritual is very hollow indeed. In fact, in terms of behavior the
patriarchal roles are turned upside down. The woman is as much a
mother as a wife, while the man is as much a boy, in this case obviously
a bad boy, as a husband.

Seemingly, such marriages have been in existence for quite some time.
Even in a time when tradition, Church, and Tsarist law produced a
picture of a strongly patriarchal way of life in Russia, the outward
appearance of male dominance was often mellowed by an inner permissiveness, the external paraphernalia of the patriarchal way balanced by
the superior personal resources of a woman who had her say behind the
scenes. Vladimir Polunin, for instance, tells how his grandfather, a
wholesale fish merchant in Kursk in the 1840's, "never abused his power
—indeed not infrequently, though unwillingly, he surrendered to grandmother's more forceful character."

An old peasant man whom I interviewed in 1950 tells how it is important to take the intelligence of one's wife into account in arriving
at a proper disposition of authority: "The law of God says 'the wife must
submit to the husband,' but he should also not insult her. Thus, if it is
a wise wife, seek her counsel. But if it is a stupid wife, there is no use
to. [How was it in your family?] If you have a wife, like mine, who
believes in God like I do—thus, I had to share with her. But with a bad
wife, why seek her counsel? She will spend money foolishly and the
husband will suffer." Thus the patriarchal principle, mellowed by the
allowance of this important qualification to masculine predominance,
has for some time been sufficiently flexible, when the need exists, to
permit the wife a considerable increment of power which she exercises
mainly in a motherly way. Apparently in fairly bargained exchange the
husband surrenders power to his wife and receives extraordinary succor,
as if from his mother, in return.

In addition to the sex-typical character structure formed by pre-Soviet tradition, this variety of marriage reflects some of the more unique aspects of recent Soviet social history. A result in later married life of the insecure and aimless life of the homeless child, so common in the early years, is seen in a marriage between a store official and his wife in White Russia [Belorussia]. Although younger than her husband, she is looked up to by him and seems to combine the role of wife and mother quite handily: "The husband, thirty, had been at times a homeless child, and had learned to read, write, and count only as an adult, taught partly by his wife, twenty-five, a nurse. The wife always had the deciding word in the marriage, but he was very attached to her and showed her genuine affection." The turmoil of Soviet history and the shortage of men have brought a considerable number of unequal partners together, especially since many of the men who died prematurely were the more vigorous and courageous specimens. For example, a woman from a Leningrad middle-class background, by profession a medical doctor, was married to a construction-trust official from a lower-class background with considerably less educational experience. She was described as of higher social origin, more intelligent, and less passive. The observer conjectures that the marriage, in 1942, occurred mainly because she wanted to escape the misery of being alone somewhere in the middle of a primitive forest in the Urals. She had been evacuated from Leningrad in midwinter, and "no one but him took any trouble over the crying and abandoned girl." Subsequently, she came to be much more the leader in the marriage than he.

This pattern bears considerable resemblance to the "mother-centered" family, which has come to be associated with the family life of groups under stress, lower-class families generally, and particularly the lower-class Negro family in American society. The Soviet version under discussion differs from that in two ways. The husband is present rather than in-and-out or entirely missing, and he accepts the dominant position of his wife rather easily. In fact, both partners seem quite comfortable about it, much more so than the extent of deviation from the two ideal patterns of Soviet culture would suggest.

3. *The new Soviet woman's marriage.* The two types described to this point seem reasonably successful as marriages. Though deviant from the cultural norms and social modes, they fit the needs of the partners. Two additional types constitute less happy examples. One of them seems extremely common and has probably played a central role in the unfolding of Soviet family policy. . . . The other is another type of marriage in which the wife is the controlling influence. There seem to be two varieties of strong-women marriage in the U.S.S.R. The first is a mother in wifely semblance; the second is a newer product, shaped by Bolshevik, industrial, and cultural revolutions of recent times, newly won economic independence, rising levels of self-regard, and the woman's new determination to exercise her will in marriage.

The key factor in these marriages is the wife's forceful personality.

Often she is a Komsomol activist and Party member. In the marriage of a forty-five-year-old political police lieutenant from a village near Vologda, both spouses are Party members. They differ strikingly in personality traits. The wife, "though short and small-limbed, had a very lively personality, sanguinely vivacious, talkative, and impulsive. She was also dogmatic and very ambitious . . . of above-average intelligence, with her own ideas, and with backbone. Thus she was even able, in resolute fashion, to get her own way with the political police wherever it was necessary. She was sociable and liked to laugh. In relations with others she was self-confident and authoritative. . . . As a personality she was an individual of strong feelings whose impulsiveness was compensated for and controlled by a strong will. In this she was aided by the Party ideals, in which she believed completely, and which were the guiding principle in her behavior. . . . Quite as a matter of course she demanded and received not only equality of rights but also the leadership of the family." The forceful and colorful personality of this woman contrasts remarkably with that of her husband. "He was small, serious, and somewhat shy. Over all, as a person and a personality, he made a colorless impression. He was of barely average intelligence, and in addition quite passive and phlegmatic. . . . His bearing was always unassuming; to his wife he was even somewhat humble."

Most likely this type of Soviet marriage is composed of three elements: a forceful woman; a retiring, passive husband; and some kind of socially recognized superiority—in class background, intelligence, job level, political commitment—which serves as a factor legitimizing her predominance in the eyes of all concerned. In a marriage of similar nature, an energetic young hospital laboratory assistant lived with a man of singularly contrasting personality. He served as an administrative employee of the same hospital: "He was quite passive and lazy, seldom thought things over, and let himself be led. He was superficial in his feelings. He yielded to his wife, and had no rebellious feelings about his inferior position in the marriage." This sounds like an easy and close marriage, yet the observer also notes that the wife, of strong personality, quick and impetuous in temperament, consistent, scrupulous, and duty-oriented, was in addition a Party member, although her husband was not. Moreover, she was "tyrannical and dogmatic by nature . . . always eager to convince others." Not too surprisingly, she sought also "to convince her husband and to drive him out of his [political] indifference. Occasionally they fought about it. All of their conversation had a political tinge to it."

All in all, these marriages usually manifest a serious flaw in the extent to which the positions of the two partners are reversed in terms of sex-role expectations. The wife's leadership is often a result of obvious weakness on the part of the husband, leadership by default rather than preference. Sometimes, of course, the situation is what she needs and enjoys, but more often, probably, she is forced to assume more of the role than she would like. A young construction foreman from Stalingrad is described this way: "Energetic, but somewhat on the fat and chubby side, the husband looked like a big adolescent. And basically, he was one also. He was jolly, affable and good-hearted, not a bad person at all but quite a decent one." However, as a "big adolescent" he was also immature, and in consequence his wife, a "charming and pretty girl, friendly, lively, and jolly, but much more solid and sensible than he," had to take an uncomfortable measure of initiative. "By nature, she was inclined toward subordination to her husband, but since he failed to take this cue, she had to be the leader in the marriage much more than she really wished."

Or, on the other hand, the wife may insist too conscientiously on her equality, to the point where it divests her of her femininity. This seems to have occurred in the life of the secret police lieutenant: "Since at that time these [Party] ideals left little room for femininity, she sought very much to suppress her femininity. She always wore a uniform. When once she was seen in a dress and afterwards received compliments about it, she never put on a dress again, though compliments obviously did not displease her." Bischoff reports the interesting fact that wife-dominated marriages lead to family atmospheres that are more ideological than most. In the older generation such families tend to be very religious; in the younger they tend to be very Bolshevik in outlook. Perhaps this is one of the ways in which the wife struggles with her feelings of doubt and guilt for not following more closely the traditional sex-role pattern.

Quite probably the marriage arrangement of the new Soviet woman is an overly extended form of a general theme in the Soviet feminine character. I suspect that a psychological conflict in which a conscious desire for sex equality struggles with a less conscious drive for a dependent and submissive role is typical for many Soviet women. If so, it must almost inevitably affect the relationship with her husband, who, even though he may be eager, is hard put to give her what she wants. A young daughter of a postal worker seems to fit this pattern. She describes her husband as charming, kind, attentive, unobtrusive, and with a "complacent" temperament. Further, she states that in the relationship between husband and wife "both should have equal authority." Yet, she seems uneasy about her husband's failure to play the traditional role and also feels that "the husband should be the head of the family." Her contradictory yearnings are suggested in her full statement: "The husband should be the head of the family, yet his relation to his wife should be of the closest, as to himself; he should be her friend, her helper, and should consider her opinion."

4. The predominance of the personal factor. Up to this point we have inspected the two extremes of Soviet marriage that correspond with the two ideal patterns, peasant and equal-rights-with-love, have discussed the transitional form that falls between those extremes, and, finally, have inspected some "underground" variations. In social-class terms the most noticeable distinction is between peasant and urban marriages. Most of the former seem to fall into the transitional category, leaning toward the more purely peasant pattern. Probably most urban marriages also are transitional—masculine dominance going together with love—but tending more in the other direction, that of equal rights. Once outside the influence of peasant traditionalism, marriage patterns seem to fan out, presenting a varied assortment to the choice of the individual, but are not correlated in any discernible way with urban social classes. . . .

The breadth of the variation is in itself important, for it contributes, along with the two competing cultural patterns, to what sociologists call anomie, a situation in which important actions have to be taken without a normative standard to provide guidance. From one point of view this generates confusion and uncertainty. From another it suggests greater freedom for the individual couple to attend to its own preferences without too much concern for what others will think.

It is my strong impression that in matters of love and authority in Soviet marriage today there is an extraordinary tolerance and permissiveness among the people, if not in the regime. Not only do individual needs and personality differences play a great role, but many Soviet citizens feel that it is quite proper that they should. For instance, in regard to the proper locus of authority, many would oppose any standardized pattern and would feel, as one respondent suggested to me, that "authority should be enjoyed by the spouse who is better able to organize a family life." Indeed, it is possible to see a parallel between the role of "personal gifts" in determining eligibility for re-election to political posts at the top level in the Soviet Union and the role of the same factor at the bottom level in determining eligibility to wield power in marriage.

An interesting corroboration of the importance of personal character is found in the lack of any discernible statistical correlation between political commitment and the authority pattern found in a given marriage. Although the official line favors equal rights, Party members are no more likely to manifest this relationship with their wives than are nonmembers. A likely explanation is that as a rule only the most able and energetic men join the Party. Such men would tend to assume leadership in marriage because they are usually highly endowed with the trait of dominance, which would nullify in practice their inclination to grant equal rights to their wives on ideological grounds. The solution to the conflict of determining principles involved is exemplified in the words of an army colonel, also a Party member. In our interview the question of reasons for divorce came up. Would, for example, having a politically reactionary wife be a valid reason for a Party member to divorce her? "No. If I would say I want to get a divorce because my wife is apolitical, they would throw the blame on me. 'What kind of a Communist are you, when you can't influence your wife? . . . What? You, an organizer of the masses, can't even convince your wife?' "

*   *   *

28

LETTERS TO AUNTIE

MIRRA GINSBURG

The "Letters to Auntie," with which we have decided to acquaint our readers, are purely personal documents. However, you must not think us guilty of indiscretion in making public a private correspondence; the letters are being published with the knowledge and consent of both the correspondent and the addressee.

It must be said that both of them—the correspondent, a member of the planning department of a certain provincial enterprise, and the addressee, his venerable aunt, retired on pension—were quite astonished to learn that these ingenuous letters had evoked the interest of the editors.

But it is precisely their spontaneity and even naïveté that may, in the editors' view, appeal to the readers of our journal.

A few necessary deletions were made in preparing the letters for publication.

FIRST LETTER

Dear Auntie,

I hasten to inform you that I have arrived safely. The other passengers in my compartment turned out to be the nicest people. One, like myself, was going to Moscow on an assignment from his enterprise; two others were returning from assignments. This gave us all a sense of community, and we spent the whole night playing preference on a suitcase. I won forty-seven kopeks.

The conductor was also a very decent fellow. At three in the morning he knocked at the door of our compartment, thinking there was a fire, but it was only our smoke. Everybody had a good laugh.

Reprinted with permission of the Macmillan Company from *The Fatal Eggs and Other Soviet Satire*, edited and translated by Mirra Ginsburg. © Mirra Ginsburg 1964, 1965.

Incidentally, a waiter comes through the cars at frequent intervals, selling sandwiches, beer, and even cognac. So you need not have worried.

What else can I tell you about my journey? The car was comfortable. True, when we wanted to take a nap (there were still four hours to Moscow), the conductor removed our bed linen, and we had to doze on pillows without pillowcases. I say doze rather than sleep because at dawn the radio on the train wished us good morning and began to play records. One of them, in fact, was repeated several times—the one that says, "You and I are not married." I know the words by heart now.

For the convenience of passengers who may not feel inclined to listen to music at dawn, there is a regulator under the table in each compartment. You can lower the sound or even switch it off altogether. I switched it off. After that, I learned twice again that "you and I are not married"—from the speaker in the corridor. It blared out the information at full volume, but here you could do nothing; no one could switch it off.

I am telling you this, Auntie, so you will understand why I was a trifle shaky when I left the train. But this passed very quickly, and soon I was quite myself again, running from one taxi to another with my suitcase and basket.

Don't imagine that there were no taxis at the station; there were long lines of vacant taxis with their green lights on. But every time, it somehow happened that they would not take me. I noticed that the drivers were collecting groups of three or four people into their cabs and driving off. But I always remained outside any group. Finally, I managed to get into a taxi by myself. The driver turned on the meter and asked me where to go. When I said Cheremushki, he turned off the meter and said that his shift was up. Another driver had no more gasoline when he heard the address. A third made me get out, saying that his tires were worn.

An experienced visitor to Moscow later explained to me that it isn't every taxi driver who will take you where you have to go. Some prefer to go where they have to go. They are a cranky lot and have their favorite routes, from which they will seldom deviate.

Nevertheless, in the end, I too succeeded in finding a taxi.

What can I tell you, Auntie, about Moscow? I have not seen it for several years. Moscow is beautiful! The widest thoroughfares, streams of automobiles, wonderful new houses. As was to be expected, I was especially impressed by the new district—Cheremushki. There is much greenery here, much fresh air, many children, and, unfortunately, many similar street names: Cheremushkinskaya Street, Cheremushkinsky Crossing, Cheremushkinsky Lane, the New Cheremushkinskaya Street, New Cheremushkinsky Crossing, and some other Cheremushkinskoye and New Cheremushkinskoye, so that, by the time I found Semyon Semyonych, my driver and I had become fast friends.

I delivered your parcel. Semyon Semyonych was most grateful, especially for the raspberry jam and the book of Voznesensky's poems. In Moscow, he said, you cannot get it; in the outlying provinces you can.

Semyon Semyonych cordially invited me to stay at his home, but I did not want to impose on anyone and decided to take a room in some hotel nearer the center of town. Especially since, in the course of my wanderings through Cheremushki in the taxicab, I had seen many posters with a pretty girl in a white apron and cap saying: "MAKE USE OF THE SERVICES OF OUR HOTELS."

I must tell you, Auntie, that this appeal is purely abstract in character. Moscow has a great many hotels, but evidently the number of people wishing to use their services is greater. At any rate, such posters are still premature.

In short, by evening I telephoned Semyon Semyonych again and asked for shelter.

As for the taxi driver with whom I had made the rounds of the Moscow hotels, he ended up with a sincere affection for me, having fulfilled his daily mileage norm with me. At the end of the trip, we were calling each other by our first names.

The hospitable Nadezhda Fyodorovna made my bed in the dining room, on a sofa which turns into a bed when you pull out the seat. Now I shall lie down and try to sleep, although I am not sure I can. Too many impressions. The faces of hotel clerks flicker before my eyes, and in my ears there is a constant humming of "but you and I are not married." Good night, Auntie!

I will now continue the story of my visit to the capital, as I promised. I shall not go into the details of my work here; that would bore you. It will be enough to say that everything is going smoothly.

In the morning, when I awakened on the sofa bed, Semyon Semyonych and Nadezhda Fyodorovna were already gone. Only their son Styopa, a fourth-grade student, was home. He attends the afternoon session at school. Like a good host, Styopa served me breakfast and entertained me with conversation. We thoroughly weighed the chances of the various football teams in the coming games, and then Styopa astonished me with his virtuoso skill in twirling a large thin hoop around his waist. This is done by means of rhythmic vibrations of the whole body and, according to Styopa, promotes your general physical development. I recalled that this device is called a hula hoop and that *Krokodil** usually shows Western dandies and idlers of both sexes at this occupation. But Styopa explained that in *Krokodil* it is a hula hoop, but in school, at gym classes, it is a gymnastic hoop and that a hula hoop is bad, but a gymnastic hoop is good. Frankly, I never quite grasped the difference. But I liked the exercise. I think I shall buy a hula-gymnastic hoop, or a gymnastic-hula hoop, for you and me, Auntie. It will help me fight against obesity, and it will help your rheumatic back.

And now I shall tell you how I traveled to my main office in a bus without a conductor. In such a bus the passenger drops his coin into the

* *Krokodil* (*Crocodile*) is the leading Soviet magazine of humor and satire.

box, tears off his own ticket, and rides to his destination. It is an excellent idea, in conformity with the present level of social consciousness among the population. And it is true that when you drop your coin yourself, without the urgings of a conductor, you become imbued with a feeling of profound self-respect. And you begin to regard your fellow travelers in the bus with special friendliness. But this is something I understood only later. At the moment when I was about to drop the coin into the metal box, someone shouted anxiously, "Don't drop it!" I quickly pulled away my hand, thinking that the box was out of order and I might get an electric shock. But the box was in order, and I was stopped because a certain citizen, who had dropped a coin earlier, had to receive forty-five kopeks' change from his fifty-kopek piece and was collecting this sum from other passengers, that is, from those who paid their fares after him.

I gave him my fifteen-kopek piece, and now I had to collect my ten kopeks' change from others. A little old woman in a plush hat gave me six kopeks and demanded one kopeck change. I did not have a kopek, but the man who paid fifty kopeks had two kopeks, so that now the old lady owed him one kopek, and he owed me four. At this point a citizen who looked like a professor intervened and said that I was confusing everything: I, he said, had to collect four kopeks not from the man who paid fifty kopeks—he was still thirty-three kopeks short—but from him. But he did not have four kopeks; he had a twenty-kopek piece, which he was now—what was he doing?—giving to the man who had paid fifty kopeks. Thus, the fifty-kopek man had to collect only thirteen more, but the old lady would have to give her kopeck to him, the professorial citizen, and he would have to collect fourteen kopeks more from others.

I asked a woman sitting across from me to hold my briefcase for a moment, then I took out a notebook and pencil and proved without difficulty that the citizen of professorial appearance was mistaken. But he had a slide rule with him, and according to the slide rule I was mistaken. At this point the whole bus joined in on our calculations, and I did not notice when I passed my stop.

This little incident by no means invalidates the idea of self-service in my eyes. Simply, something still needs to be thought through. Or perhaps it doesn't. Who knows, these mutual computations may even be beneficial—a kind of mental gymnastics, a mathematical hula hoop?

After supper I took a stroll through the Moscow streets, admiring advertisements and store windows, which I think are very beautifully decorated.

However, even here some things made me wonder. Take, for instance, the advertisement that says, "Tea is a tasty and wholesome drink." Is it really necessary to convince anyone of that? And if it is, why not advertise, "Bread is a tasty and wholesome food"? It is inconsistent.

My very best wishes to you, Auntie. Don't forget to water my geranium.

Your Vasya

SECOND LETTER

Dear Auntie,

When I recall what I wrote you in my first letter, I see that my attention is drawn to secondary things, rather than the important ones. Indeed—a man has not been in the capital so many years, then finally he comes, and instead of describing the university building, the Luzhniki Stadium, or the Metro,* he stares at signs, reads advertisements, and investigates the system of computations in a self-service bus.

However, all these things—the university, Luzhniki, the Metro—have been described many times before me, and so much better than I could dream of doing. There is really nothing that I could add. Only, perhaps, that the new stations of the Metro differ from some of the older ones, built in the "Triumph" style, by their good taste and simplicity. And so I hope, dear Auntie, that you will not mind if I continue telling you about all sorts of things, both important and trivial, that I come across in Moscow, just as they strike my attention.

For example, today, after visiting the main office, I strolled through the Moscow streets, looking at the Muscovites and thinking, How well people have begun to dress, such modern and attractive clothing! During the early postwar years the predominant colors were khaki and dull gray. But today the streets are bright with all the colors of the rainbow. Especially, of course, on the women. And I like this very much; it puts you in a better mood, it pleases and delights the eye. And yet our textile plant at home continues to pour out dreary fabrics that make you think of dismal, rainy days. And, again, take the matter of styles. In Moscow, Auntie, you meet any number of young girls wearing slacks and high hairdos, and young men in narrow trousers and brightly colored shirts, worn loosely over the trousers. Our city executive committee chairman would be appalled at the sight! But here nobody bothers. It is permitted. No administrative penalties. No fines. No threats of deportation from the city. And it made me think: Perhaps we are too puritanical in the provinces? After all, there was a time when we gave up caftans and crinolines and, later, overcoats with shoulder capes and ladies' cloaks. Why shouldn't we, in our day, give up wearing wide trousers, long gabardine coats, and jackets nipped in at the waist?

I lunched at a small restaurant, furnished with light, handsome tables and chairs. The service was prompt and polite, and the food tasty. I said to my neighbor at the table that this restaurant was evidently firmly rooted in good traditions. But my neighbor mumbled, spooning down his fish soup, that it was too early to speak of traditions: This restaurant had only been opened two days before. We'll be able to talk of traditions, he said, after five or six months. Then we'll see what sort of traditions they are. Something in his tone suggested that this was a man saddened

* The Moscow subway system.

by wide experience in life. If I am in Moscow again after a year or two, I must try to come back to this restaurant. Just for curiosity's sake.

After lunch I took care of a few more business matters. Then, on a crowded street, I saw a large assemblage of people, and naturally, I hurried to the spot. The people were gathered around a glassed-in billboard, over which there was a sign: "DO NOT PASS BY!" I did not pass by and began to study the cartoons posted on the board. This was much like our own *"Krokodil* in the Street." It pilloried violators of the public order. One would be foolish to assume that there are none among the millions of Muscovites. There are! And here they are exposed to the general view. You showed yourself in a disgraceful state? You caused a row? Up on the board with you, my good man, let everybody know what you are. Ivan Ivanovich Nikiforov, engineer of the SMU Plant No. 39, or Sergei Petrovich Kulebyako, of the regional dramatic theater. . . . This method of public persuasion, it seems to me, should be a strong deterrent both to those who have already found themselves on the board and to future candidates. On the whole, I would say that it is a good method. But when I look more closely at the caricatures and the verses under them, I cannot say I liked them. In Moscow, with its wealth of artistic talent, all this might have been executed on a higher level. You can easily see that the drawings are not by the Kukryniksy.* And the verses are on the order of the following:

> Tipsy Sokolov, Boris,
> Smashed a window with ease.
> Why on earth did he do that?
> You can ask the dirty rat.

Such verses in the home city of a master like Sergei Ostrovoi!

In this verse the offender was called a rat. In others they are called "mugs," "snouts," "swine," and so on. Is this a good thing? Don't think, Auntie, that I am trying to defend rowdies and hooligans. Certainly not. But I think it is wrong to descend to their plane and answer abuse with abuse. In my opinion, this is a wrong educational method. Before you know it, the educator may get so carried away by his educational zeal that he will end up on the board himself—for using foul language.

I stepped into a food store to buy something for supper. It was a self-service store. In the doorway, I had the following conversation with a store employee (I almost said a saleswoman, but she does not sell anything, she only lets the customers in):

SHE: Citizen, take a basket and check your briefcase.

I (*taking a wire basket*): Thank you. The briefcase isn't in my way.

SHE: Naturally, it isn't. Maybe it even helps. Come on, come on, check it, that's the rule. Bags, briefcases, and valises must be checked at the door. You pick them up when you leave.

* A team of three popular Soviet cartoonists.

I: But why?

SHE: So you don't slip something in. All we need is to look away a moment and you'll shove a can of sardines or something else into your bag. And then we have to pay. All sorts of things happen.

I: Such things don't happen with me.

SHE: I wasn't talking about you, but generally.

I: And why don't you sew up the customers' pockets as they come in? You never can tell, some fellow may slip a jar of apricot jam into his pocket—and goodbye!

SHE (*oblivious of the irony*): We have no instructions concerning pockets.

I (*changing my mind about shopping at this store*): Inefficiency! At this rate, you'll go bankrupt before you know it! As for me, I'd rather shop at an ordinary store without self-service. They don't stress their confidence in the customers by allowing them to go to the shelves and counters, but neither do they insult us by demanding that we check our bags and briefcases.

And I proudly walked away.

Don't imagine, Auntie, that this is done in all the self-service stores. I suppose that the director of this particular store had ordered the confiscation of bags and briefcases on his own initiative, which is scarcely to be welcomed.

In the evening, we went to a movie theater, the Russia. It is quite a distance from Cheremushki, But Semyon Semyonych and his wife wanted to show me the new theater and, incidentally, to see it themselves; they had never been there. I have generally noticed that many Muscovites, permanent residents of the capital, let years go by before they find the time to go to the Tretyakov Gallery or the Moscow Art Theatre or any of the places that visitors rush to see as soon as they arrive. The aborigines use the excuse that all these places are always within reach, just around the corner, and they can go whenever they wish. It's a wrong psychological attitude.

Dear Auntie, the Russia is a magnificent movie palace! Modern, spacious, bright. It is so beautiful that it would simply be embarrassing to show poor films there. But we were lucky, we saw a good film. Afterwards, at supper, we got to talking about movies generally, and I learned with astonishment that some of the movies that you and I have, unfortunately, seen at home were not exhibited in Moscow. It turns out that if a movie is not simply inferior but absolutely wretched, it is not released for the Moscow screens. It is, however, sent to us, in the provinces.

And I must say, I consider this unfair! If trash is to be shown at all, let everybody see it. And if it isn't, then no one should see it. And the second alternative, it seems to me, is the preferable one.

And now, dear Auntie, I shall conclude for the day.

Do not water the geranium with cold water—make sure the water is at room temperature.

With fond regards,

Vasya

THIRD LETTER

Hello, dear Auntie,

Your nephew Vasya sends you respectful greetings.

My assignment here is finished. As I had planned, I shall spend two or three days longer in Moscow for my own enjoyment, and then— back home. The other day I was in Luzhniki. I was tremendously impressed by the sports palace. True, what I found there was not a basketball match, but an evening of readings by young poets; however, these readings obviously contained an element of sports as well: Who'll beat whom? The second part of the program was devoted to singers and acrobats, and this combination of sport and poetry was reminiscent of ancient Greece: There, as we know, they also held simultaneous competitions of discus-throwers, poets, and musicians.

I had no difficulty in obtaining a ticket for the Moscow Art Theatre, but some difficulty in getting one for the Contemporary Theatre. I did not get to see a young people's café. I stood in line for two hours on Gorky Street with a number of young men and their girl companions, and suddenly it occurred to me: Here am I, a man considerably past his youth; do I have the right to take up space in this café, where space is at such a premium, when even the young are unable to get in? And so I quietly left the line and went to the Ice Cream Café where I could easily find a table, get my order, and reflect at leisure on why, after all, these young people's cafés are not made more widely available to young people, if they—the young people—have such a strong desire to sit in their own cafés? And what, generally, is the meaning of these "cafés-by-age"?

In the mornings I still converse with Styopa, a fourth-grade pupil, a sober and reasonable young man, but possessed of one noble passion. Styopa is a collector, and he collects matchbox labels and candy wrappers.

Indeed, he owns some unique specimens. What would you think, Auntie, of such a slogan as "Livestock Breeders! Cow-ize Our Pastures"? Or: "Novelists! Novelize Our Magazines"? I believe you would shudder. I also shuddered when I found in Styopa's collection a matchbox label showing a man releasing fry into a lake and urging, "Fishermen! Fish-ize Our Waterways!"

Among the candy wrappers, I found some similarly interesting examples. One wrapper has a picture of a small girl holding a piece of candy high over her head. Near her, a lovable little pup is jumping eagerly —he also wants to taste the candy. But the girl is nobody's fool; she won't share it with him. This brand of candy is called "Try and Take It from Me!" I suppose this series of educational wrappers might be continued indefinitely. My imagination suggests such names for candy as "I Won't Give You Any!" and "Mine!" and even an entire assortment of chocolates called "Get Along, Get Along, God Will Give You!"

I have carried out all your errands, Auntie. I bought the buttons, too, but not at the GUM [State Department Store], for it is not so easy for a stranger to find the needed department in that palace of trade, with all its galleries, rows, and passages. It is true there is a telephone that you are invited to use for inquiries. But the telephone was silent, while a pleasant female voice over the store radio urged you to purchase things, now a camera, now a fishing rod, and now an accordion, and explained how to find your way to the places where they are sold. It said nothing, however, about buttons. One might, of course, wait around until the voice remembered buttons, but I had little time, and so I bought the buttons in a small notions store.

I want to tell you about my visit to still another store, namely, a flower shop. The point is that it was Nadezhda Fyodorovna's birthday, and I decided to bring her some flowers. And as soon as I reached this decision, my mind's eye conjured up an image of a blue-eyed, fragile flower girl, as though freshly off the pages of Balzac (I trust, dear Auntie, that you will appreciate my erudition and style!). With an enchanting smile, condescending and yet encouraging, she helps me to find my way among those gladiolas and cinerarias, and with the taste that only women possess, she selects for me a modest and beautiful bouquet. My mind's eye also envisaged the modest price of the bouquet—say, two rubles or so, but no more, since I had already exceeded my budget.

Well, then, I go into a flower shop. Along the walls, in pickle barrels, there is a row of dim, dusty, wilted shrubs. On the walls hang dreary wreaths made of roofing iron, which is generally in such short supply. And on the counters stand baskets of flowers, some of them real. There is no salesgirl.

As I examine the baskets, I hear a heavy snorting behind me. I look back and see a hulking, unshaven man in a quilted cotton coat.

"We ain't got none," he says in a hoarse voice.

"None of what?"

"No hyacinths."

"And must you have just hyacinths?" I ask.

"Me? What the devil I need them for? They're all asking for hyacinths, so I have none."

"And who are you?"

"I'm the salesman."

There is Balzac for you, Auntie!

"We have wreaths," the salesman says. "Twenty-five rubles and up. Or maybe you don't need one yet?"

"I don't need one yet," I say. "But I want a small basket of flowers. Live. Not artificial. For two rubles or so."

"For how much?"

"Two."

And here, Auntie, he burst into a most insulting fit of laughter. It turns out that there are no such prices here. I ended up by buying one of the baskets for six rubles and thirty-five kopeks, and though it was very heavy, I walked out of the store with a great sense of relief.

Oh, yes! I saw the blue-eyed girl after all! Right there, near the flower shop. She wore a janitor's apron and was sweeping the sidewalk with a huge broom. And I wondered at the inappropriateness of professions that is occasionally observed among us.

Well, Auntie, I guess that is all. Time to wind up.

Goodbye, I'll see you soon. I shall not write any more. If possible, move my geranium further away from the stove.

Your Vasya

1963

* * *

Part Four

SOCIAL TENSIONS

IX

Agriculture and Rural Life

Agriculture has always been and remains today the Achilles' heel of the Soviet economic system. Soviet farms have failed to produce sufficient food to provide an adequate diet for the whole population. There is adequate bread and potatoes but too little meat, butter, sugar, fruit, and milk. And on occasion shortages of grain have compelled the importation of wheat and the rationing of bread. Soviet agriculture has simply failed to match the industrial and the population growth rate. Production is inefficient and costly. When Brezhnev and Kosygin assumed power in 1964, American agriculture produced 60 per cent more than that of the Soviet Union with a labor force one-fifth as large and on an area equal to two-thirds of the Soviet sown acreage. While deficiencies of agriculture affect the entire population, the principal victims are the peasants, who constitute just under half of the population. Their average income is well below that of the industrial worker, let alone the administrative, scientific, and cultural elite of Soviet society, and the quality of rural life lags far behind urban life. Ideologically Russian peasants are aliens in an urban-industrial society.

The problem is rooted in the structure of Soviet agriculture, in the system of collective farming. It is true that farm output can be substantially increased by greater state investment in agriculture—such as higher state prices for farm products, more social benefits to peasants, increased mechanization, irrigation projects, and chemical fertilizers—but this approach alone cannot eliminate the inefficiencies and waste that have made the state farms (sovkhozy) and collective farms (kolkhozy) less productive per unit of land or per man-hour than the agriculture organization in any of the advanced industrialized nations. The regime is caught in a dilemma between the demands of a bureaucratic farming system and the need for local initiative. Among the most chronic problems spawned by collectivization are the following: The peasants lack the incentive to give collective crops and livestock adequate care; detailed instructions from central authorities on what and how to cultivate rob the individual farmer of responsibility and initiative; government authorities and often even kolkhoz chairman and sovkhoz directors are too far removed from the land to make the wisest decisions regarding planting or harvesting; the imposition of high quotas and unrealistic goals encourages the falsification of information by the individual and the theft of communal property; inadequate investment in agriculture has resulted in a tremendous waste of human and material resources.

There is considerable evidence that a self-regulating system of farming based more upon freely operating economic principles and less on planning directives could lead to an increase in agricultural output at a greatly reduced cost per unit of production. In addition, a rationalization of farming would free surplus labor for the expanding industrial and service sectors of the economy, reduce dependence on female labor throughout the economy, halt the drift from the countryside of young people with secondary education, and eliminate a major source of dissatisfaction with the regime. But a substitution of the command principle with a market principle would weaken Party control over the economy and run against the ideological grain of the leadership. In a word, political and ideological constraints stand in the way of economic and social benefits.

In 1964 slightly less than 97 per cent of the total sown area of the Soviet Union was organized into either state or collective farms. A state farm is owned and operated by the state somewhat as a factory is. The director of a state farm is a government appointee, and all the farmhands are paid fixed salaries. A collective farm is a rural cooperative formed by the pooling of land and livestock by those peasants who join. In theory each collective is self-governing, having the power to elect its chairman and board of directors. In practice the Communist Party closely supervises the selection of kolkhoz leadership, and the government maintains heavy control over collective affairs. Unlike the state farmer, whose total income is fixed whether the harvest is good or bad, the collective farmer is to a considerable extent dependent upon the prospects of the farm for his income.

Both state and collective farms are immense compared to farm systems in other countries. In 1967 there were approximately 36,000 collectives and 12,000 state farms, though because the latter are larger in size the total area sown by each type was approximately the same. The average collective had 15,700 acres and 400 families. The average state farm owned more than 50,000 acres and employed about 800 full-time workers. This compares with an average farm size in the United States of about 150 acres tilled by one or two families. Many economists consider Soviet farms too large for efficient managerial decision-making.

An important source of farm produce is the private plot that each household is permitted to use. At the time of Khrushchev's fall, private plots accounted for only 3.1 per cent of the total sown area of the Soviet Union. In size they average about 1.3 acres. Yet in 1966 the private plots produced 64 per cent of the country's potatoes, 42 per cent of the vegetables, 42 per cent of the meat, 40 per cent of the milk, and 66 per cent of the eggs. Unlike the produce of the collectives, whose prices are fixed by the state, privately grown crops are sold in the cities at market prices. The quality of goods at the farmers' markets is noticeably higher than those in state stores, and the prices are usually higher.

Stalin's successors have made agricultural reform a major feature of domestic policy. Nikita Khrushchev, who considered himself a specialist on the subject, attempted to make more workable the system he inherited from Stalin. He increased economic incentives to peasants through higher payments for farm products. He relaxed state controls through the abolition of the Machine Tractor Stations. He sought to expand output by bringing under cultivation vast new virgin lands in Kazakhstan and Western Siberia. His accomplishments were mixed, but on balance Khrushchev failed. During the last years of his rule agriculture was in a state of stagnation.

Khrushchev's successors have inaugurated a series of reforms that in their totality could lead to some fundamental changes. Khrushchev's organizational innovations have been scrapped: The powers of the Ministry of Agriculture have been restored, and the territorial production administrations eliminated, along with the dual Party and Soviet structure of industrial and agricultural organizations at the local level. Brezhnev and Kosygin have abandoned the stringent restrictions their predecessor imposed on the private plots. Probably the most significant reforms are those designed to raise peasant incomes and spur incentives. A new system of collective farm payment has been introduced, providing guaranteed minimum earnings for all farmers. This wage is to be paid monthly and becomes the first charge against collective farm income (not the last, as formerly).

In November, 1969, the Third All-Union Collective Farm Congress met and drafted the first revision since 1935 of the model charter for collective farmers. Many of the post-Stalin reforms, including a plan for a unified social security system for collective farmers, were codified and incorporated into the new model charter, but no radical new directions in agricultural policy emerged from the congress. The generally poor performance of Soviet agriculture in 1969 (production of almost all major farm commodities fell below the 1968 level) suggests that more substantial reforms are inevitable.

Roy D. Laird is Professor of Political Science at the University of Kansas and a member of the staff of the Slavic and Soviet Area Center there. His numerous publications on Soviet agriculture include *Collective Farming in Russia* and (with Betty A. Laird) *Soviet Communism and Agrarian Revolution*. Maurice Hindus, who was born in Russia and died in the United States in 1969, was a prolific writer on Soviet life, particularly on the peasants. Among his numerous volumes are *The Kremlin's Human Dilemma, House Without a Roof, Humanity Uprooted,* and *The Russian Peasant and the Revolution*. Leonid Brezhnev's speech at a March, 1965, plenum of the CPSU Central Committee was a major policy statement on the subject of agriculture in the context of the economic reform that year. Alec Nove is Professor of Economics in the Department of International Economic Studies, Glasgow University. His books include *The Soviet Economy* and *Economic Rationality and Soviet Politics.*

*   *   *

29

THE POLITICS OF SOVIET AGRICULTURE

ROY D. LAIRD

Importance of the Political Factor

Such factors as unfavorable climate, inadequate economic incentives, and shortages (such as of mineral fertilizers) have been major hindrances to the progress of Soviet agriculture. However, such knowledge does not explain the reasons behind the leadership's refusal to make adequate investments in agriculture. Moreover, even on the limited number of farms where relatively generous amounts of equipment, etc., have been available, yields still have been disappointingly poor.

In a series of speeches made during the fall of 1963, when the dimensions of the crop failure were becoming apparent, the Soviet Premier stressed that in addition to the drought, human failure had also caused serious damage. As in previous years, many farms were late in sowing and

Reprinted from Roy D. Laird and Edward J. Crowley, eds., *Soviet Agriculture: The Permanent Crisis* (New York: Praeger Publishers, 1964), pp. 147–58. Footnote references to Russian-language sources other than *Pravda* are omitted.

late in harvesting, and many badly needed machines lay idle due to a serious lag in repairs. In this same series of speeches, Khrushchev noted that even where mineral fertilizer had been made available, much of it was used improperly or not at all. Moreover, according to his own figures, on all the irrigated grain land in the U.S.S.R., yields per hectare averaged only some 11.8 centners of grain and 18.2 centners of corn as contrasted to some 80 centners per hectare on irrigated lands in the United States.[1] Surely, therefore, as Khrushchev himself has implied, the lack of material aids is not the whole cause for such a "disgrace," as he called it. He would hardly agree, however, that the inadequacies of the system, its political faults, must also be at the heart of the matter.

As is the case in agriculture the world over, Soviet farms are not just production entities; they also encompass a way of life for those who work and live in the rural communities. As in every country, this way of life is determined in a very large part by the environmental forces that emanate from the political framework of the society. The American farmer (like his British or German counterpart) is acutely aware of the import to him of political decisions made in the nation's capital. For example, in a democracy, agricultural subsidies constitute a means of providing economic incentives to the farmers, but the decision to give subsidies, the kind and the amount, is a political-economic matter determined by such factors as the balance of forces exerted on the government by both the urban and rural population. Similarly, any listing of the determinants of success and failures in Soviet agricultural production must include not only such factors as climate, the nature and kind of economic incentives, and the level of investment in material aids but also such political elements as the attitudes of workers and managers and the limitations peculiar to the agricultural institutions of communism.

Soviet Agricultural Theory

Politics and economics are never fully separable. Nevertheless, there are politically predominant forces in a society that influence the course of events, particularly governmental decision-making, which cannot be satisfactorily explained solely as a response to economic demands. The actions of individual men and societies alike are not merely responses to the desire to maximize material welfare. Moreover, even when economic forces are obviously the major factor in governmental decision-making (which is probably most of the time) men still must choose among the many paths that might be followed in achieving the desired goal. . . .

Any identification of the political determinants of Soviet agriculture requires an examination of the catalog of the spoken and unspoken assumptions, the theoretical framework that guides the decisions and actions of the Communist Party leadership in regard to kolkhoz and sovkhoz policy. Such a listing would include the following:

[1] *Pravda*, October 2, 1963; *ibid.*, September 18, 1963.

1. Although Marx had little to say about agricultural and peasant affairs, since he derived his theories from an analysis of predominantly industrial nations, the mainstream of his descendants have taken for granted that both industry and agriculture must be organized along communist lines.

2. Lenin's conception of translating Marxism into practice in rural Russia rested largely on the assumption that the application of industrial organization and practice to agriculture would not only result in the communization of rural Russia but also greatly advance production levels.

3. Integral communism requires state ownership, and thus control, of the means of production. Since, at least until recent years, the kolkhozy held some semblance of independence from direct central control—and their means of production are not technically state property—the state-owned and operated sovkhozy have been viewed as closer than the kolkhozy to the ideal communist organizational form.

4. While industrialization of agriculture was the structural key for Lenin, his view of peasant psychology included the belief that they must be indoctrinated into accepting the industrial cooperative farm as superior to their former way of life. Therefore he repeated time and again that collectivized agriculture could succeed only if the peasants voluntarily joined the kolkhozy.

5. From the beginning of Bolshevik rule, traditional Russian gigantomania, arising largely out of a sense of the vastness of the land, was wedded to the Marxist-Leninist conviction that large industrial enterprises are superior organization forms. Therefore it has almost always been assumed that the larger Soviet farms are better.

6. On the strength of Lenin's statement that the peasants should be persuaded to join the kolkhozy voluntarily, the latter have always been advertised as democratic institutions.

The ordinary peasant's alleged participation in farm management (in practice confined largely to voting "yes" at infrequent general meetings of the collective farm membership) is intended to give him a sense of controlling the destiny of his farm. Indeed, the successful translation of Soviet agricultural theory into practice relies very heavily upon the evolution of an attitude whereby the peasant identifies himself with collective land to an even greater degree than the farmer in noncommunist societies feels himself owner of his land. This would be "the new Soviet man" in the countryside.

7. Until the day the "new Soviet man" emerges, the Party must continue to play the role of the "vanguard," and therefore, in agriculture as elsewhere in Soviet society, the word of the Party authorities is final. In practice, as Khrushchev has stated, the leaders must "understand everything." [2] Thus, for example, the first job of an agricultural scientist is to persuade a Khrushchev of the need to incorporate this or that new scientific finding into the corpus of Party-accepted agricultural truth. Similarly, it is the local Party secretaries who take the final decision on

[2] *Pravda*, December 25, 1961.

policy to be adopted in the regional agricultural administrations and on the farms.

8. Stalin and his colleagues concluded that the first priority of Soviet society must be the most rapid possible development of industry, particularly heavy industry, and the only source of the enormous amounts of investment capital for such an achievement was agriculture. Therefore, forcing the peasants into collective and state farms provided a most reliable means of extracting the maximum amount of agricultural produce from them, and in spite of recent changes, agriculture still takes second place to industry.

9. The Communist Revolution in 1917 was very largely a matter of successfully exploiting the much more fundamental peasant revolution against the Tsarist system of land tenure, and the possibility of a new peasant revolution loomed very large in the minds of Russia's new masters. So, in addition to economic reasons, forcing the peasants into collectives provided a means of achieving a maximum degree of Party control and thus served to reduce to a minimum the possibility of future peasant revolts.

10. Centralized planning has been and still is very high on the list of Soviet politicoeconomic dogma. Central planning is seen as the administrative key to expanded material output. Tens of thousands of collectivized farms can be relatively easily incorporated into a centralized planning system, whereas millions of small farms could never be properly planned from the center. A centrally planned economy is seen as demanding some form of large-scale, collectivized agriculture.

11. Although Stalin ignored Lenin's warning that, to be successful, communist collectives must be entered voluntarily, both he and particularly his successors have assumed not only that the passage of time, accompanied by mounting production successes, would wipe out the memory of forced collectivization, but also, and much more important, that the collectives would serve as "schools of communism." Thus, as suggested in paragraph 6 above, the kolkhozy and sovkhozy are not only production entities; they are also educational institutions designed to transform the peasantry into enthusiastic participants in the communist way of life in agriculture.

THE THEORY IN PRACTICE

Such political factors as the above, in conjunction with those of a more strictly economic environmental nature, comprise a very large element in Soviet agriculture. The political element places important limitations upon progress, quite independent of the amount of investment or the degree and kind of economic incentives. . . .

Economic incentives for the worker (many Western economists seem to argue that if only the peasants were offered a high enough wage, the problems of Soviet agriculture would be solved) are not enough to solve a complex socio-economic problem. . . . In the rural U.S.S.R., there are a few so-called advanced collective farms on which peasants earn two or three times the wage of farmers on neighboring collectives. Such farms usually have important economic advantages, but the Soviet leadership is surely largely right in repeatedly stressing that there is no economic factor as such that absolutely prevents the backward farms from catching up with the more advanced. It is highly probable that important administrative and personnel differences also separate the few relatively advanced farms from the backward ones. . . .

Much of Khrushchev's major emphasis in agriculture during the "great decade" has been in the political realm—largely upon the numerous administrative reforms and reorganizations. This emphasis has been in the right sphere of activity but with the exception of three important innovations which have only further compounded Soviet agricultural problems, the changes have, on balance, only affected the surface while leaving the basic political structure untouched.

Originally couched in the promise to create *agrogoroda* (rural cities that would eliminate the differences between town and country), Khrushchev's initiation of the amalgamation campaign in 1950, by joining the existing kolkhozy into even larger collective farms, has been the sources of the three major political innovations in Soviet agriculture in recent years:

1. In 1949, just prior to the amalgamation campaign, there were some 250,000 kolkhozy, each with an average of 557 sown hectares. In 1950 there were some 5,000 sovkhozy, each with an average of more than 3,000 hectares. By 1962, among the remaining 40,000 kolkhozy the average giant kolkhoz was five times larger (2,890 hectares), and of the 8,750 new sovkhozy, the average had 11,500 sown hectares.[3] Part of the growth in the number and size of the sovkhozy has come from the merger of former kolkhozy with sovkhozy, and part stems from the creation of hundreds of new state farms in the virgin lands regions. The 1949 sovkhozy figures (which would be little different from the 1950 figures) cannot be found.

2. Prior to the amalgamations, probably only a minority of the kolkhozy had chairmen who were Party candidate or full members and only 15 per cent supported Party units. Today, virtually every kolkhoz and sovkhoz has a Party member chairman and all have Party units. Thus, the Khrushchev reforms have solidified Party leadership in rural Russia.[4]

3. Largely stemming from the fact that all kolkhozy and sovkhozy are now completely under Party control, the 1940 situation wherein the kolkhozy were somewhat on the periphery of the Soviet bureaucracy has been eliminated. Today, as has long been the case with the factory

[3] Howard Swearer, "Agricultural Administration under Khrushchev," in Roy D. Laird, ed., *Soviet Agricultural and Peasant Affairs* (Lawrence: Kansas University Press, 1963), pp. 9–40; and Roy D. Laird, *Collective Farming in Russia* (Lawrence: Kansas University Press, 1958), pp. 77, 138, 139.
[4] *Ibid.*

worker, the individual peasant is the object of a control apparatus that extends directly from Moscow to his farm.

ADVANTAGES AND DISADVANTAGES OF THE SYSTEM

The Soviet leadership and Western analysts alike now agree that future advances in Soviet agricultural production must depend almost entirely upon increasing grain yields per hectare. Great new quantities of fertilizer are essential if this goal is to be realized, but as Khrushchev has so rightly implied, making all the fertilizer in the world available to Soviet farms would be of little avail unless the human beings responsible for plowing, sowing, cultivating, and harvesting apply the fertilizer in the proper way. In the fall of 1963 Khrushchev asked what the attitude was of Soviet farmers who had received the relatively scant amounts of fertilizer presently available in the U.S.S.R., and answered: "Our leaders treat fertilizer as if it were a burden." [5] What are the political, not economic, determinants of yield and work efficiency in Soviet agriculture? Given the theoretical framework of the kolkhoz-sovkhoz system, is the Soviet agricultural problem rooted in the cooperative form, or in the particular manifestation of that form in the Soviet Union? . . .

Advantages. The previous discussion of Soviet agricultural theory should suggest that any attempt to measure Soviet agricultural successes and failures, or advantages and disadvantages, must account for not only such factors as climatic and soil disparities but also dissimilar historical background and different long-term goals, all involving important forces not present, or not present in the same way, in other societies. Therefore, an examination of pragmatically selected priorities seen as essential to serving the Soviet national interest finds communist Russia placing much less emphasis on the maximization of individual wealth. Thus, the use of economic incentive as a means of social motivation is much less applicable in the Soviet setting than it is in Western economies. There are three reasons for this:

1. The Soviet leadership sees as primary certain national interests that are virtually unknown in Western states. As in all states, security of the regime comes first. But Bolshevism came to power in a hostile world, and from the beginning, the struggle to preserve communism as a system of political organization and rule has been inseparably wedded to the desire to preserve the state. Therefore, political reasons, and particularly reasons of internal security, seemed to dictate the need for controls of a kind and degree that a kolkhoz-sovkhoz, centrally-planned agricultural system can guarantee. Such considerations have placed questions of economic efficiency second in the process of making agricultural policy.

2. The practical demands of centralized planning are inseparable from the theoretical rejection of Western economic concepts. As Khrushchev has stressed, the Soviet planned society rules out much of the value of

[5] *Pravda*, September 18, 1963.

profit as an index of the performance of the economy, saying: "If we take our socialist system of economy as a whole, profit as an economic category does not have the social meaning it has in capitalist society." [6]

3. Although individual economic incentives are stressed today, the future society is seen as being able to do without them, since such incentives are allegedly rooted in a sense of insecurity which will disappear with the advent of communism. Under both Stalin and Khrushchev, the dedication to the future is deeply imbedded in communist psychology, and whole generations are asked to make sacrifices for future goals. The Soviet leadership would naturally like to see an appreciable rise in the standards of living of today's peasants and workers, but the maximization of individual and social welfare is not nearly so important in Soviet communist society as in the West.

Seen from this point of view, several advantages of the Soviet agricultural system become apparent:

1. Stalin's decision to force the peasants onto collective farms did provide a means of extracting much of the capital that has been essential to rapid Soviet industrial growth. Therefore, although the democrat may argue that powers of such magnitude should never be given to heads of government except in wartime, the Soviet dictatorship has the means to act decisively to make agriculture serve what it views as the general welfare in a way that Western governments dare not act.

2. Without a doubt the collectives have very effectively blocked the possibility of a new peasant revolt. Negatively, opposition groups are easily kept from forming, and positively, the kolkhozy and sovkhozy provide captive audiences for propaganda. Among the highly industrialized countries, the Soviet Union is the only one in which the relative political import of agriculture is far below that of industry in relation to the urban-rural population balance. If the American city dweller can justly complain about the cows that seem to count for votes in Western Kansas, the Russian peasant might rightly complain that industrial machines carry much more political weight than farmers.

3. Advances in science and techniques, such as the relatively recent widespread introduction of hybrid seeds in the U.S.S.R., can be put into practice at a speed unknown in noncommunist states, where such decisions are left in the hands of individual, relatively conservative, farmers.

4. Although there is some question as to how successful the Soviets have been in the attempt to use machinery and buildings with maximum efficiency, a kolkhoz-sovkhoz system should at least theoretically be able to achieve a maximum level of benefit from the use of equipment. By contrast, there are few American family farmers who do not bemoan the apparent need to have so much capital tied up in machines and buildings, particularly machines that must lie idle for most of the year.

[6] *Pravda*, November 20, 1962.

This problem is less acute among the larger farms in the noncommunist world.

Disadvantages. A catalog of the disadvantages of the kolkhoz-sovkhoz system must include the following:

1. Apart from the existence elsewhere of successful, but relatively isolated, giant farming enterprises . . . nowhere but in the Soviet Union has there been an attempt to encompass the whole of agricultural production in such huge units. Physically and administratively, virtually all Soviet farms are Leviathans. In addition to such farm residents as children and the elderly, who account for about half of the farm population, the average kolkhoz has some 410 and the average sovkhoz 900 able-bodied workers engaged in full-time farm work. It would appear that the Soviets have gone much too far in the direction of giganto-mania: When compared with the great bulk of highly successful farms in the West, which are tiny by comparison, the Soviets have given no proof that great size carries any decisive production advantage.

2. The claim that the Soviet kolkhozy are cooperatives is false. The successful Egyptian and Iranian schemes are genuine cooperatives with distinct spheres of individual control, and the Israeli collectives allow for much greater opportunity for individual members to influence farm policies. In contrast, very few outside the top Soviet Party hierarchy even pretend that the kolkhozy are genuinely democratic. When general meetings are called only a few times a year, what impact can one peasant among 400 or more have on policy? Soviet press accounts clearly indicate that all important matters to be discussed have to be carefully prepared beforehand by the farm administrators. . . .

3. The prices paid by the state for farm produce and the vagaries of the weather (problems that are similar the world over) plus the skill of the farm administration and the quality of the total effort by hundreds of his fellow collective farm members are among the major determinants of the value of his work over which the Soviet peasant has virtually no influence, whereas the sovkhoz worker receives a guaranteed wage. This is one of the main reasons for the peroccupation with the private plot.

4. Day-to-day agricultural decisions need to be made on the spot, yet in the U.S.S.R. they are often made in distant offices. With the exception of the most menial of hired hands, the non-Soviet farm worker, certainly the family farm operator, participates directly in decision-making, whereas the brigaded kolkhoz and sovkhoz worker tends to be a member of a gang of a score or more of his fellows carrying out an assignment. Not only does the Soviet agricultural system deny the peasant the opportunity to work in his own way, it also ignores the fundamental difference between requirements for industrial and agricultural production. Although the industrial pattern has been im-posed on Soviet agriculture, it does not have the controlled environ-

ment so essential to industry. To ensure this, most of the land would need to be under glass, allowing constant temperature and light control, where all the water desired would be instantly available, and where there would be ample supplies of fertilizers, herbicides, and insecticides (which are still far from perfected aids). . . . In spite of the Soviet system, many of the farmers do go ahead and make the necessary decisions of the moment—otherwise nothing would be accomplished. Nevertheless, the Soviet press continues to report numerous instances of detailed orders being issued from distant Party offices and sometimes by the Soviet Premier himself. For instance, in a series of speeches in 1961, Khrushchev could not refrain from ordering Latvian farmers to plant sugar beet "as widely as possible" and telling those in Lithuania to mix more hay in their livestock feed.[7]

5. The Party leadership's belief that it has a monopoly of truth can cause great harm in many ways. For example, it has not been able to resist turning every major innovation into an excessive campaign which wreaks considerable damage as a result. Thus, the original campaign to establish the Vilyams grass rotation scheme was taken much too far, and the recent anti-Vilyams campaign is probably resulting in the abandonment of the scheme in areas where it is valuable, as well as in those areas where it has proved harmful.

6. Soviet agricultural specialists have far too little influence over production decisions. The Soviet Premier has correctly observed on more than one occasion that everyone tends to fancy himself an expert on agriculture and great harm is done to Soviet agriculture by interference from officials who know little or nothing about farming under a system which insists that the secretaries in the Party hierarchy must take direct responsibility for production successes. Although the drive to have agronomists and zootechnicians who are both specialists and Party members is a move in the right direction, there remain the problems created by having two masters. Furthermore, those Party members–specialists who attain key posts will have done so because their strong point is administrative and not scientific ability. . . . Built into the sovkhoz-kolkhoz system is the inevitable necessity to give Party demands for control priority over production needs.

7. The Soviet planning system tends almost entirely to ignore crucial regional and local differences, not to mention lesser differences between neighboring farms or even neighboring fields. Plan fulfillment and agricultural success do not necessarily coincide. In some of his 1963 speeches, Khrushchev indicated that changes must be made that would put maximum production and work efficiency first and plan fulfillment second. However, the whole rationale of the Soviet system works against the success of any such innovation. Without a free market system, for example, Moscow can be assured of having enough vegetables only if a number of farms are designated to grow such produce (unless other regions are to be robbed of their needs, or plans are made to

[7] *Pravda*, January 12 and 14, 1961.

purchase vegetables from abroad). The Soviet leadership continues to order certain regions and their farms to produce specified foods in stated quantities. By contrast, the successful noncommunist farmer spends much of his energy balancing his output plans with the peculiar climate and soil conditions of his farm, his own talents and preferences, and his judgment of what market conditions will be at harvest time. Therefore, centrally planned production in Soviet agriculture rests on the highly doubtful assumption that on balance central planning offices can arrive at judgments for distant regions and farms that are superior to those made by the farmers themselves.

8. Labor and administrative costs in Soviet agriculture are inordinately high. In all countries where high yields per hectare are the rule, greater numbers of workers are employed per unit of land than is the case in American extensive farming. Undoubtedly, therefore, if Soviet yields are to go up, more manpower is going to be needed in agriculture, or much higher levels of work efficiency must be achieved than has been the rule in the past. Soviet figures imply that output of agricultural produce per Soviet farm worker has been only about one-fourth (perhaps only one-fifth) that of the American farmer. In their article in *Vestnik statistiki* (No. 2, 1961) "Labor Productivity in the U.S.S.R. and the U.S.A.," the Soviet analysts B. I. Bragensky and D. Duminov admit that, according to their calculations, in 1959 Soviet agricultural output per man-hour was some one-third of that of the average American farmer.[8] Much of the reason for this fact stems not only from a lack of economic incentives and investment in material needs but also from such political blocks to worker initiative as those that have been reviewed above. In addition to this, however, there is the undoubtedly high cost of agricultural administration in the U.S.S.R., a cost that is rooted in the political system. Perhaps the administrative costs of collectives and cooperatives elsewhere are also high, but as a Soviet writer has reported, there was one "directing or service worker" for every six kolkhoz—and one for every eight sovkhoz—production workers in 1961. Similarly, 13.8 per cent of all sovkhoz labor payments and 17.4 per cent of all kolkhoz labor payments are said to have gone to administrative and service personnel. Any comparison of the time spent by the American farmer in administrative and service work might well indicate that he spends even more of his total time in such occupations. Nevertheless, a fundamental difference exists between the costs of administration on a Soviet farm and those in individual farming, whatever the country. Not only is the head of a family farm operation his own administrator (making many of his decisions while engaged in production work) but, much more important, the great bulk of his planning, his account work, and his machine repair and construction is done at off-season times when farmers everywhere have relatively little production work to do. By contrast, kolkhozy and sovkhozy demand full-time administrators.

[8] See Harry G. Shaffer, ed., *The Soviet Economy* (New York: Appleton-Century-Crofts, 1963), pp. 176–84.

For example, because of the system of work accounting and remuneration, a number of checkers are required on each farm to do work that is unknown on a privately owned farm (e.g., did the peasant actually weed twenty rows of corn and did he do it properly?). Similarly, full-time accountants are needed to keep both individual peasant work accounts and the general farm accounts as well. Smaller farms in the West, particularly family-owned and operated enterprises, tend to have all hands on full-time production work during peak seasons, and therefore, compared to the Soviet farms, there is very little extra burden of cost for administration and service work.

Since economics deals with the material world, the analyst has the opportunity of transforming his findings into statistical symbols that relatively easily reveal such valuable information as whether one operation is more costly than another. By comparison, political forces are much more elusive. No one can definitely prove that the political costs of the Soviet agricultural system are so high that, without disbanding the present kolkhoz and sovkhoz system, agriculture is destined to continue to be the most serious problem area. Nevertheless, the weight of such evidence as has been presented here does seem strongly to point in this direction. Indeed, such evidence seems to indicate that the Soviet kolkhoz-sovkhoz system is incompatible with intensive agricultural methods.

In the drive to surpass American agricultural achievements, assuming that the Soviets meet their stated goals of mineral fertilizer output, considerably increase the area under irrigation, and sharply increase peasant wages, significant increases in yield per hectare should result. Nevertheless, such achievements do not substitute the political-organizational advantages enjoyed by American farmers, and, in view of the relative political disadvantages in the kolkhoz-sovkhoz system, it is probably impossible to surpass American agricultural output and efficiency. Moreover, future Soviet needs require higher yields than those achieved on American farms, where an extensive system prevails, with low yields compared with those achieved on the intensively farmed regions of Germany, Denmark, or Japan.

For political as well as economic reasons, Soviet Russia seems to be entering a new revolutionary period. Ironically, the problem is not one of a lack of political stability, but the need for the Party leadership to come to grips with a radically new situation in which the present agricultural system does not seem capable of satisfactorily feeding an industrial society with a population that will continue to grow by some 4,000,000 a year, more rapidly than internal food supplies. Just as the United States finds itself in a revolutionary situation, because a society in which the Negro minority is a second-class citizen no longer proves to be viable, so the Soviet leaders now find that the old agricultural system no longer satisfies the changing needs of either society or the Party itself. Unfortunately, as testified by the lopsided emphasis given to the fertilizer campaign (certainly essential in itself), the leadership gives no evidence of facing up to the full implications of this new situation.

The evolution of a parliamentary system allowing the Soviet farmer at least an equal opportunity to express his wishes and his solutions to problems might be a step in the right direction. An attempt to establish a pattern of family-type farms probably would prove to be incompatible with Party social doctrine. Perhaps a turn to much smaller, genuinely cooperative farm enterprises is what is needed. It is certain that the Party leaders cannot afford politically or economically to continue indefinitely to retain the present kolkhoz-sovkhoz system.

The Soviet agricultural system has been successful in serving the social control and industrial priority goals set by the Party, but as satisfactory social institutions, and particularly as efficient production units, the kolkhozy and sovkhozy are proving to be an increasing liability.

*   *   *

30

THE KREMLIN'S HUMAN DILEMMA

MAURICE HINDUS

Trofim Tretyakov, chairman of the Kirov collective, was considered something of an oddity around Krasnodar. He insisted on retaining the old system of paying workers by the *trudoden* (labor day),* which did not mean a day's labor but a prescribed amount of work so that an industrious worker could earn several labor days in one day's work. The reason other collectives in the Kuban had abandoned the old system was because it failed to foster material incentive and entailed

* Referred to in other sources as "workday."—ED.

too much bookkeeping. Yet Tretyakov had made his collective one of the most prosperous in the region. In 1963 it had earned a profit of some $2.5 million, and the following year, though the harvests had been poorer, the collective had shown a profit of over $4 million. In recognition of his continued success, Thetyakov was elected to Moscow's Supreme Soviet, a political reward bestowed on comparatively few chairmen of collectives. . . .

On Sunday morning I drove out to his collective. The two-lane asphalt road was shaded by tall maples and poplars and reminded me that in 1944, shortly after the German retreat and despite the enormous devastation left behind and the acute shortage of labor—made up principally of women and teen-agers—the Soviets, with their passion for trees, had given priority to setting out saplings along the highways. Now I drove on between the green walls of forest that stretched to the far horizon. Nowhere was the natural scene marred by the billboards that desecrate the beauty of American highways; nowhere was there even a printed slogan calling for heroic exertions or with self-congratulatory proclamations of heroic achievement, which one sees on other Soviet highways.

Our Volga [passenger car] sped smoothly between the green walls. Once a Russian driver hits the countryside, he steps hard on the gas—as hard as he can—and woe to the dog that gets in his way. Russian dogs —still inexperienced with automobiles—fall easy prey to Russian drivers' mania for speed. On this trip we scared hawks and crows into flight, but not once did we encounter a dog or a rabbit. This was one of the few bloodless automobile rides I have ever had in the Russian countryside.

Finally we came to the Kirov collective, a huge old Cossack *stanitsa* [village] where, the young driver informed me, lived thirty-eight hundred families. Save for the public buildings and here and there a house of brick, the people lived in neat whitewashed adobe cottages set among vineyards and fruit trees, even as they did in Tsarist times. But the Cossacks' horses were gone from the scene; where they had galloped over unpaved streets, bicycles now sped by on smooth paving. Tretyakov's collective was indeed a shining example of what Russians call "cultural elevation," a triumph over mud and indifference.

There were so many bicycles that I remarked to the driver, a member of the collective, "It looks like everybody here has a bicycle."

Proudly he replied, "Every family has at least two and some young people have motorcycles."

I said I hated the noisy menaces and he laughed, "So does our chairman. He has a saying, 'If you want to do someone an ill turn, give him a motorcycle.'"

Trofim Kirilovich Tretyakov had reached the Soviet retirement age of sixty, but he had not the least desire, he said, "to withdraw into the isolation of a pensioneer." Tall, upright, and handsome, his finely molded head crowned with thick white hair cropped short, he was a man of dignified bearing; and his easy manner, soft voice, and deliberate speech made one think of a schoolmaster rather than a chairman of a kolkhoz. No, he hadn't had much formal education. Under the Tsars he went to the local school, but being the son of an *inogorodnik*—a peasant from outside the Cossack region—he trudged through the mud while sons of Cossacks rode to school on horseback. He had never lived anywhere else and has been chairman for fifteen years. He would continue as chairman as long as the people wanted him.

With him in the cool, thick-brick-walled office were Vasily Kozlov, forty, deputy chairman, and Mikhail Velichko, fifty, the economist, a broad-shouldered man with a long, sharp-featured face and a ready smile. Did I know, he asked, the role the economist was now playing in a Soviet farming enterprise? I replied that I had learned about it from the Production Administration in Krasnodar. Well, he went on, the economist, with his ready figures on profits and losses in any branch of farming, could always point his finger to a farming activity that yielded no profits and should either be abandoned or lifted to a higher productivity so it would show a profit. The economist's mathematical calculations were the compass that kept a farm from straying off the right course, into wastes and losses that should not be tolerated any more. That was what they were doing on the Kirov collective, fighting for an economy of socialist profits that would promote the welfare of the people.

"Libermanism in action," I thought but didn't say it. The Party detests the term Libermanism, named after Liberman, the Kharkov professor-economist who first pronounced the importance of profits in the Soviet economy. My companions were Party members and might have regarded it as an affront to the Party had I identified "the compass" of which the economists had spoken as an innovation not of the Party but of the professor. In conversations with Party members, especially in the countryside, one must be cautious not to say anything that would reflect on the prestige of the Party or to question any of its directives and prerogatives. The conversation might suddenly become stiff and unrewarding. Yet as the economist kept on talking of the importance of economic science in the administration of Soviet farms, it was clear that Libermanism had penetrated deep into his mind.

A woman brought in big bowls of freshly picked cherries and strawberries, but no vodka or wine, a relief to a poor drinker like myself. Tretyakov, it turned out, was a total abstainer, the only one I ever knew among chairmen.

The giant collective spread over 48,000 acres, of which 45,000 were in cultivation, principally in grains—wheat, barley, sunflower, corn, and rye, which was sown not for grain but for green fodder in the spring. The work force consisted of 4,500 men and women, so each worker averaged ten acres of cultivated land, a small area, very small, by American standards. If one allows for a one-third reduction of the work force during the winter months, the collective still suffered from an enormous waste of labor.

The kolkhoz also grew sugar beets and specialized in grapes and other fruit and in vegetables—lettuce, cucumbers, radishes, onions, and others—though chiefly for seed, which was highly profitable. No, they didn't eat lettuce. People said, "Why eat lettuce for vitamins when you get them from young onions and from cherries?" They didn't eat corn *kasha* (mush), either, though in the old days Cossacks loved corn *kasha* boiled with pumpkin and eaten with hot or cold milk. But people were developing a taste for sweet corn, and planting more and more of it in kitchen gardens. In the community bread bakery, which worked round the clock in three shifts, they used 28 per cent corn flour and 72 per cent wheat flour. But they didn't sell bread, they exchanged it for the wheat, which workers received in part payment for their labor days. The cost of baking a kilogram (2.2 pounds) of bread was 2½ kopeks, and the kolkhoz met the expense.

The farm was divided into six self-sufficient brigades (units) each equipped with its own machinery, its own livestock, its own labor force, though the over-all plan of production was drawn by the executive committee made up of nine specialists, including the chairman. Tretyakov and his associates assured me that there was no interference either from the re-established district Party secretary, the production administration, or the soviet in the planning or in the rotation of crops. But they too had plowed up much of their alfalfa land—3,500 acres. Now they were bringing it back as fast as they could, having already seeded about 3,000 acres. In the absence of alfalfa or hay, in spring they fed cattle green winter rye and green winter wheat, the most expensive fodder to grow—how expensive can be judged from the fact that, according to Tretyakov, each ruble invested in wheat gave a return under the new prices of three and a half rubles. But Tretyakov, aware of his Party membership, would not commit himself on the financial loss the collective had suffered from the Party's violent drive against alfalfa during Khrushchev's last two years in power. Had they not plowed up their alfalfa, they would have had it for spring feeding and would not have needed to cut precious green winter wheat. They could have allowed the wheat to ripen, harvested it and sold it at the high price the state was now paying.

Still, the kolkhoz dairy was profitable, because the average annual yield of milk per cow was 5,250 pounds, some 2,000 pounds more than the average in the Soviet Union, though some 2,000 pounds short of the average in the U.S.A. No, they didn't have enough milking machines for all their milkmaids, though some 80 per cent of the cows were milked by machines, each maid averaging twenty-eight cows. No, there was no scramble here among milkmaids to outdo one another in the number of cows they could milk with machines, as there was on other collectives. Here they treated cows gently. Never, never, Tretyakov emphasized, would his veterinarian allow milkmaids to yank machines on and off cows, as under the spur of socialist competition the maids had done on the giant Don Cossack collective I had told him about.

Socialist competition? No, they didn't allow any chase for mere quantity output. They insisted on quality performance. And if the operator of a tractor or any other machine broke it through haste or recklessness, he was twice penalized. He had to pay for the repairs and he was docked while his machine was out of use. Nor did he alone suffer. His brigade ran the risk of forfeiting the 20 per cent premium for quality achievement. It was therefore to the interest of the whole brigade, Tretyakov explained, to pressure mechanizers into conscientious care of their machines.

We argued back and forth, I insisting that socialist competition necessitated quantity output, which entailed haste and recklessness; Tretyakov and his associates arguing that with the threat of penalties on mechanizers and their brigade they eliminated these dangers. "Our farm," observed Tretyakov, "is called a 'collective of communist labor,' and we never would have earned the title had we been slovenly or reckless in performance. We don't use the expression 'socialist competition' in the sense in which you do."

Sorevnovaniye is the Russian for competition, and in reply I said, "To my mind, on your farm you have substituted *stremleniye* (aspiration) toward good work for *sorevnovaniye*."

I was not quibbling over the meaning of words. One has only to travel in the Soviet countryside to become aware of the appalling breakage of tractors and combines. One sees piles of them in open fields, and the press complains endlessly over the reckless use of machinery. As long as the Kremlin calls for drives in socialist competition, breakage is unavoidable, though as far-sighted a man as Tretyakov can take stern measures to minimize or prevent it.

Like Tretyakov the Soviet press and Soviet officialdom keep demanding quality work, but fulfillment of the demand is seriously frustrated by the endless campaigns for socialist competition. To my mind, it is a self-defeating, indeed a nefarious speed-up method of production, and not only in agriculture, which, however justified in the early years of planning, has long ago outlived its usefulness. But "socialist competition" has through the years acquired the power of a mystique which Soviet leaders appear unwilling or unable to relinquish.

I asked Tretyakov whether his kolkhoz too was investing heavily in boarding schools. "No, we don't," he replied. "We have built only one, a small one for children who live too far away from schools." The mania for boarding schools at the expense of urgent community improvements, which under Khrushchev the Party had assiduously fostered, had obviously left Tretyakov unmoved, as it had other practical-minded chairmen. Only those with a zeal to fulfill the Party's ideological precepts succumbed to the mania. . . .

Tretyakov's system of payment to workers is a complicated affair, and involves three forms of calculation: the output of each worker, the output of his brigade, the total output of the kolkhoz. The individual worker gets advance cash payment of one ruble per labor day, the cash increments which are paid at the end of the year come from individual performance, from the profits of the brigade and the profits of the entire kolkhoz. Tretyakov is convinced that his mode of payment rouses the worker's interest not only in his individual performance but in the performance of his brigade and of the entire collective. It promotes, he insists, the cooperative spirit that socialism demands of workers.

The Kirov collective is regarded as one of the richest in the Kuban, with more money to distribute among workers than other rich collectives. I was assured that, because of the money they earned and the other material advantages they enjoyed, young people were glad to remain in the kolkhoz.

In addition to cash earnings, workers had their private plots from three-fifths to more than one acre, depending on the size of the family. They all had pigs, chickens, geese, and ducks. Only about one-half of them had their own cows, but they could buy all the milk they needed from the kolkhoz at 18 cents a liter in summer and 22 cents in winter. They also had small vineyards and small orchards.

"You must remember," the economist put in, "that our people have their homes here and bring up their children here, which of itself is an incentive to work well on our farm."

"And we do all we can to help them," Tretyakov added. "We maintain seven kindergartens free to all members. We have a hospital with seventy-five beds and twelve physicians—one of them a surgeon. In May we opened our modern mechanized bakery, and now our women have fresh bread every day without having to sweat over a tub of dough or tend a hot oven. We are building a nine-hundred-seat theater. We have thirteen letter-carriers, and we need that many because every family here subscribes to at least two publications, and the load is heavy. Though at present our people have to raise their own supply of winter vegetables on private plots, we are arranging for the kolkhoz to supply them with vegetables at low prices all year round, which means that they will be able to use their land for more fruit trees or another vineyard. So you see, the more efficiently we plan, the richer we grow and the higher our living standards rise, both materially and culturally."

We drove through fields whose rich stands of barley, wheat, corn, and sunflower stretched to the horizon. Grain fields in the Kuban are always beautiful to look at, even the fields of the less-thriving collectives, but the lush beauty of these fields, which Tretyakov ascribed to work well done and on schedule and to the use of large amounts of fertilizer, promised an unusually abundant harvest.

Then we drove around the sprawling village, whose wide streets were lined with neatly whitewashed adobe cottages surrounded by greenery. They called to mind the old Cossack sense of order and cleanliness, and though their design was simple to the point of primitiveness, I thought they had far more architectural distinction than the clumsy modern structures in the cities. Some new brick houses—the kolkhoz had its own brickyard—struck an incongruous note among the old country-style dwellings. Cool in summer, warm in winter, with greenery all around them, they give one a sense of home that apartment houses never can offer. And the *kazachki* [Cossack women] are magnificent housekeepers, with an eye not only for comfort but for beauty. They adorn the walls with framed family portraits, homemade embroideries inherited from the past, and now and then ikons, which lend a luster of their own to a home.

Trofim Tretyakov was sensitive to the special needs of women in the community. They did not want boarding schools and he did not build them. After childbirth they could stay at home as long as they wished —six months or a whole year. It was for them to decide when they were ready to go to work again. The more they mechanized the farm, the less need there would be for women to work, and even now heavy work was performed by men. Women were wives and mothers, said Tretyakov, and their health must never be jeopardized; nor must their love of children and the care they personally wished to bestow on them ever be interfered with. . . .

We drove out to a parking lot for combines, all repaired and ready for harvesting. The gigantic machines were lined up in a row in the shade of trees and presented an impressive sight. Tretyakov had his own skilled mechanics who did all the repairing, and who when necessary could manufacture their own spare parts. "Harvest time is almost here," he said, "and we are ready. Nothing is missing, not a bolt, not a screw, and we do everything with our own hands. Nothing like having cadres of your own to prepare machines for the harvest so that no time is wasted and every stalk of grain can be gathered on time."

So while the press was sizzling with indignation at the lagging manufacture of spare parts and at farm managers who were neglecting to repair harvesting machines, Tretyakov was free of all worries: His barley and wheat would be gathered on time.

We sat down to dinner in a grove of white acacias. The food was abundant, but again no alcoholic drinks were served. Again the economist was eloquent in holding forth on the benefits the science of economics was destined to bring to socialized farming. It would eliminate wastes in everything—in labor, in machinery, in fertilizer. Profit and loss would no longer depend on general estimates or on guesswork; there was no substitute for scientific mathematical calculation to boost production and profits. And the more I heard Tretyakov himself, the more impressed I was with his deep solicitude for the welfare of his people, an attitude rooted not in democracy but in the paternalism inherent in the Soviet system. Here paternalism was at its best and most humane.

* * *

31

PEASANTS AND OFFICIALS

ALEC NOVE

The object of this contribution is to discuss the relationship between the local officials and the peasants. It includes the chairmen of the kolkhozy, though they sometimes behave like officials, sometimes like peasant headmen. The emphasis is on the local situation. Needless to say, the behavior of the officials is to a considerable extent conditioned by national policy, by what the leaders want, or by the general priorities of the regime. In these instances, the local secretaries are merely levers, connecting rods. However, it is becoming clear that the methods used by the Party secretaries, though no doubt developed as a consequence of policies insisted on by their superiors, now have a life and logic of their own. It could well be that it represents a major obstacle to the implementation of reforms which the top leadership appears to be considering. Their behavior may have distorted some of Khrushchev's measures, so that they had an impact other than he wished. Finally, the influence of the rural Party officials in the Party itself may affect the kind of proposals which are made. It is never realistic, under the guise of "totalitarianism," to assume that the men on the spot are mere cogs in a machine. Their character, interests, habits can help to determine how the machine works.

Let us look at some of the characteristics of official attitudes, and then proceed to explain why they arose.

ATTITUDES TO THE KOLKHOZY

The Party secretary has regarded it as his primary responsibility to ensure the fulfillment and overfulfillment of the procurement plan.

From *Soviet and East European Agriculture*, edited by Jerzy F. Karcz (Berkeley: University of California Press), 1967, pp. 57–72. Reprinted by permission of the Regents of the University of California. The footnotes have been omitted.

As Ovechkin's * fictional but realistic character, Borzov, put it: "The state needs bread grains." Ovechkin's protest, "it is not merely for simplifying procurements that we created kolkhozes," is in itself significant enough. He describes the Borzov type of secretary as a "procurement agent." Since local procurement plans were seldom fulfilled, and since, even if they were, a deficiency in other regions was probable, farms were constantly under pressure to deliver *all* their surpluses, and more, to the detriment of farms and peasants.

This has led, as is well known, to the repeated dishonoring of pledges about the size of the delivery quota, or promises to return "borrowed grain," or the removal even of seed grain (although there was more than one decree forbidding this), and impossibility of planning even the feeding of the kolkhoz livestock. ("Our concentrates were taken away as over-plan deliveries.")

This reflects a deeply rooted feeling that kolkhozy and peasants exist to be exploited, to be prevented from using for their own purposes produce which officials are obliged to secure for the state. There is no equivalent of this in other sectors of the economy.

It is also the practice of the officials in agriculture to issue orders about sown areas, output, livestock holdings, dates of sowing and harvesting, methods of sowing and harvesting, and so on, and this regardless of any legislation . . . which instructs them not to do this. Results, as is known, were often deplorable. This is not the place to set out the ample evidence, given by men as varied as Khrushchev and a whole list of contributors to literary journals. To cite one of the latter, Ivanov, who expressed his indignation at orders to increase sowings of corn and sugar beet where there was no means—through lack of labor and machinery—to cultivate them: "What basis was there for the doubling of sowings of corn and sugar beet? Was this not intended for the report, soullessly, without thinking of the consequences, without any economic analysis?"

One sees here, of course, the consequence of pressure from above. This was the meaning of the statement, cited by Abramov, that a chairman was reprimanded for "political underestimation of silage." But it is more than this. Some secretaries take the initiative. One sees "a desire to shine" . . . in much the same way as a company commander wants to show off when an inspecting general comes. This is the way to promotion, or to avoid demotion, and the longer-term effect is ignored; its source may ultimately be unidentifiable, or the official may have been transferred. Some secretaries, with the same motives but less bold, show a tendency merely to obey others blindly, to be "levers." . . . Sometimes this type of behavior takes the form of simulation. The latter fits into the absurd behavior of the secretary in the Grodno Province, criticized by *Pravda*, who fulfills the plan by ordering the delivery of

---

* Valentin Ovechkov, Yefim Dorosh, Fyodor Abramov, Vladimir Tendryakov, and Leonid Ivanov, whom Nove cites throughout, are writers of essays and fiction on rural subjects.—Ed.

all grain, part of which is then transferred back to the kolkhozy in scarce trucks by overworked peasants at the height of the harvest. Asked why, the secretary replied that for him the plan was an order to be obeyed. Other forms of cheating are familiar to students of the subject.

The Party exercises tight control over appointments and also plays an active role in directly controlling agriculture. Local agricultural officials, indeed rural state officials in general, have always been weak. Khrushchev himself described them as the Party secretary's office boys. . . .

The priority of "ruling" may help to explain the predilection of many local Party secretaries to amalgamate kolkhozy and sovkhozy too, a process which, as Brezhnev admitted, has gone beyond all reason. As Dorosh has pointed out, not only does it facilitate the exercise of control to have fewer to control, "but the illusion is created that there are no backward kolkhozy in the region." Another form of simulation!

A further familiar feature of Party rule is distrust of kolkhoz officials, table-thumping abuse, cursing, and reprimands. All writers on rural themes—Ovechkin, Dorosh, Abramov, Ivanov, and Tendryakov—comment on this and deplore it. It constitutes one reason for the reluctance of self-respecting men to become kolkhoz chairmen.

An additional consequence of distrust is the repeated dispatch of "plenipotentiaries," charged with ensuring obedience to current orders about current priority campaigns. Their crudity, ignorance, and effect on the responsibility of kolkhoz officials are well known.

This brings me to campaigns in general, and the role of the Party in forcing them on the kolkhozy, regardless of their interests. This, too, is a familiar phenomenon. It is worth emphasizing that not only have the kolkhozy been victims of sharp practice, but in general their needs have been systematically ignored, and particularly so in comparison with . . . sovkhozy. This helps to explain the increased difficulties which arose with spares and supplies, and even in the production of farm machinery, after the transfer to kolkhozy of the machines in 1958. Similarly, the financial terms of the transfer, the insistence by local officials that the machinery be paid for in a year, despite the more liberal provisions of the law, constitutes one reason among others for the financial difficulties of many kolkhozy.

ATTITUDES TO THE KOLKHOZNIKI

A characteristic, amply documented, of such attitudes is the ignoring of the material interests of peasants. In insisting on deliveries of produce, in financial policy, in ordering the expansion of unremunerative productive activities, the officials seem to have no concern with the peasants, who, they must presumably assume, can devise their own means of keeping alive. Dorosh described such an official in vivid terms. He boasted that "mice would break their heads in the kolkhoz barn searching for just one grain" when he had finished "procuring," and a dismayed chairman is cited as saying: "The hand of such a man would not tremble when he leaves the children without milk—he would not leave a drop."

This leads to ignoring the need to ensure an adequate collective income, in cash and in kind. Gradually this is being corrected, but the correction seem to come from above, not from the regional Party level. Thus the Party secretary of the Estonian Republic is evidently pleased to be able to report that all "kolkhozy in Estonia pay peasants a regular guaranteed minimum." Others remain prone to ordering loss-making activities, ranging from lavish capital expenditure to the purchase of butter (at retail prices) for redelivery to the state "as milk." The cost of simulation often falls on the peasants.

The same neglect extends to the provision of amenities in villages, despite talk about "eliminating differences between town and country." Admittedly the story about an official who was accused of being "an enemy of the people" because he looked after them too well belongs to the 1930's. Yet many have noted that little attention is paid to elementary comforts and that officials who have abundantly proved their inefficiency are apt to be appointed to manage rural cooperatives.

Officials are particularly apt to regard the private plot with suspicion. True, they have been encouraged to restrict it on occasion, but they do not seem to need much encouragement, and the fact that there have been local variations in policies shows that there is no clear and enforceable guidance from the center. The way in which these restrictions are imposed must be a source of endless bad blood between officials and peasants. Instances can be quoted almost *ad infinitum* from Soviet literature. When willing labor is scarce, the obvious way out—to encourage effort by giving a share of it to the peasants—is regarded as almost anti-Soviet, even if the alternative is all-round loss. . . . Recent evidence, published in *Voprosy ekonomiki* [*Questions of Economics*, monthly of the U.S.S.R. Academy of Sciences' Economics Institute] showed that restrictions on the private plot are counterproductive, since all additional difficulties in getting fodder compel the peasants to devote *more* time to a smaller number of private livestock. The same, no doubt, applies to the effect of lack of facilities to get to market.

All this must have had a profound effect on the peasants' view of officials. They are usually strangers. . . .

At the same time, many officials seem to have regarded the peasants as untrustworthy, tricky backsliders, always willing to act against state interests, backward technically. This, at any rate, is an integral part of the frequently repeated criticism of the "old methods of work" which are to be (or are being) replaced by a new approach.

THE CHAIRMEN

What about the situation of the chairmen of kolkhozy situated uncomfortably between officials and peasants? And what of directors of sovkhozy? The latter were at one time quite different types of men, though now, with the great increase in numbers of sovkhozy and of the size of kolkhozy, and a tendency to merge the control system, the differences might be less than before. Traditionally, sovkhoz directors received orders from trusts or regional bodies in their own hierarchy, while kolkhozy were ordered about by the *raikom* [district Party committee] secretaries. For lack of information, rather than a desire to neglect sovkhozy, I will concentrate on the chairmen of kolkhozy.

Here evidence of great variety is abundant. The sheer size of a kolkhoz makes close human contact impossible. Kuznetsov's vivid story showed that the chairman appeared in outlying hamlets only when something went seriously wrong, which is scarcely surprising with existing road conditions. He often remains unknown to many of the members; the more so as it has become physically impossible to call a kolkhoz meeting. It follows that his relationship with the peasants, and with his superiors, has greatly changed since the average size of kolkhozy has quintupled, when compared with the period before 1950. . . .

Some chairmen, as Dorosh puts it, "tend to introduce all sorts of novelties," others "are quite indifferent." There is a sad account of the first kind, involving, again, ducks. A chairman, described as basically hostile to peasants and anxious to get rid of them and substitute machines, acquires vast quantities of mandarin ducks, which were subsequently killed by pike. The resultant heavy losses were borne by the peasants. The author comments that the large landowners also had their brain waves, but at least they paid for the failures out of their own pockets. He also noted the tendency, common also among officials, to pick schemes which give publicity to themselves. ("Who will be surprised with potatoes or garlic? But a mandarin duck, that's different! They will write in the papers about the ducks.") A similar point was made about a sovkhoz director who, to the horror of his agronomist, ploughed under trees on a hillside and caused many to fall, all to exceed 100 per cent of the ploughing plan. "100 per cent, that's just average. With just average indicators one will just work on indefinitely, no one will notice."

Then there is another kind of chairman, the skilled maneuverer. One is described by Tendryakov. He once got into endless trouble by growing cabbages to order when other officials had "forgotten" to organize their storage, transport, and distribution. He learned his lesson. His two slogans were: "A reprimand, unlike turberculosis, can be carried about," and "A wise man does not climb a mountain, he goes around it." He seems to be in league with some, at least, of his peasants in an endless struggle with the bosses above him. Thus "he met the terrible corn as a wise general," made speeches about the "queen of the fields," and then announced that it had all been killed by frosts and that his fields had to be resown with oats and barley. However, he kept a couple of hectares to show the *raion* officials that, by great efforts, he had managed to save some. He lied shamelessly to the officials, "but in the autumn they had bread grains and were able to pay the peasants." Similarly he dealt with the "Ryazan miracle," the great meat campaign. "In all the country they followed [the Ryazan example], fulfilled and overfulfilled meat sales, slaughtered not only calves and milk cows, but pregnant cows and breeding bulls." This chairman made speeches, and carefully disposed only of his inferior breed of pigs. The point of Tendryakov's story is that the chairman "infected" the heroine with his sly methods, so that she too cheated. But Tendryakov is clear that this chairman, as many others, was himself reacting to campaigns, pressures, reprimands. Others may well be in collusion with Party officials at local level, jointly to mislead those above them. Still others do their best to be honest, although, as is often remarked, circumstances make it difficult not to be in breach of some regulation. . . .

CAUSES

These types of behavior have deep roots in history and in institutional arrangements. A two-faced attitude to the peasants is inherent in Bolshevism. H. G. Wells, reporting Lenin's remarks about the socialized agriculture of the future, commented: "At the mention of the peasants, Lenin's manner became confidential . . . as if, after all, the peasants might overhear." Lenin sought to secure peasant support for the Revolution and then to change matters somewhat after it.

The problem of procurements was already a vital one in the NEP period. The "Ural-Siberian method" of forced collections was devised by Stalin personally early in 1928. Despite Ovechkin's pained remark, collectivization *was* carried out largely to facilitate procurement. Thus generations of rural Party secretaries were judged by their success in running the procurement campaign. This deeply affected their behavior.

Collectivization itself was a major surgical operation, which affected patients and surgeons deeply. Collectivization was not merely based on large-scale coercion, carried out by local officials, but also on a series of lies, or at best half-truths, concerning what was happening and why it was happening. Officials would not, at least in their official capacity, admit to each other what all knew to be the truth. This habit persisted. . . . Party officials in rural areas had a tough and unpopular job, and were themselves at the receiving end of reprimands and threats. The efforts they made to show their superiors that they were carrying out orders caused, and still causes, numerous distortions in agricultural planning and in human relations with those below them. All this has been technically related to overambitious plans, a tendency for the men at the top to ask for the impossible. This has frequently meant that the honest official who aims for the sound and the realistic has been held up to ridicule, while deranged individuals like Larionov of Ryazan, the man who promised to treble meat deliveries, were praised by the First Secretary [Khrushchev]. It is a puzzling matter that the evident harm done by encouraging absurd plans has not been obvious long ago to the top leadership.

The low priority of agriculture was, of course, inherent in the nature of Stalinist industrialization, and in the purpose for which kolkhozy were set up. Therefore the relative neglect of the needs of farming and especially of the peasants was no accidental deficiency of local Party secretaries. Times changed, needs changed, but the habits of officials at all levels lagged behind and must have contributed to the otherwise inexplicable "reaction" in agricultural incomes, inputs, and investment which occurred after 1957.

Similarly, it was logical to have substitute orders (and threats of punishment) for incentives when there were no incentives and when prices were confiscatory. When there is no profit in farm activity, then both chairmen and peasants must be ordered to carry out even such elementary tasks as sowing and harvesting, and the production pattern must be the subject of instructions too. . . .

The lack of economic incentives explains campaigns, which, in part at least, are the *modus operandi* of the Party and provide success indicators for Party officials. . . .

Substitution of commands for incentives also explains the tendency of some officials to resort to various forms of statistical manipulation since their careers depend on claiming success in the fulfillment of basically unrealistic plans.

Moreover, distrust of private plots has deep roots, since the plots are symbolic of private enterprise, uncontrolled initiative, and other undersirable phenomena. They also visibly take the peasants' attention away from the collective sector, from which, since January, 1958, practically all state procurements have been drawn.

In the historical and institutional circumstances, it seems clear that officials have some basis for thinking that the peasants, their brigade leaders, even at times their "elected" chairmen, have interests other than those of maximizing state procurements; that, left to themselves, they will do the wrong things. Therefore they must be kept on the right track by plenipotentiaries, inspectors, and threats. Some officials presumably also believe that peasants are traditionalist, unenterprising, lacking in initiative. Khrushchev once put it colorfully to an American journalist. Russian peasants, he said, had not been through the capitalist school. (He did not add that those who had were deported as kulaks in 1930.) Therefore it seemed natural that peasants had to be ordered to be modern, to change the old patterns, and the officials who did this may well have reminded themselves of Catherine's insistence on the planting of potatoes in the eighteenth century. The peasants resisted, but they were wrong and Catherine's officials were right about the peasants' own interest. Such reasoning provides cover for a multitude of sins.

Yet there is also an ingrained distrust of peasant initiative which the officials feel may involve actions contrary to the interests of the regime.

The mental makeup of rural officialdom was shaped in the Stalin era. It takes time to make any radical change in their ideas and their methods. They are the local bosses, with special responsibility for agriculture. It is not enough to urge them—as Khrushchev often did— "to work in a new way." How? By persuasion? But if they cannot persuade, they *must* order. . . .

Khrushchev's policies concerning local officials were inconsistent and contradictory. He condemned the old crudities and spoke of the need for a better deal for peasants, more facilities for their private activities, reduced taxes, higher priority for farms, and more autonomy for management. Yet his campaign and his speeches at the plenum made nonsense of his own recommendations. The unrealistic targets made excesses by local officials unavoidable. It is true that in themselves these excesses were sometimes not desired. Thus Khrushchev was doubtless horrified by the story of a field of growing clover, ploughed in for no better reasons than to show a reduced acreage of grassland. He specically warned against administrative pressure to sell private cows. Yet he so acted as to cause these local excesses to happen. He added to confusion and irresponsibility by repeated reorganizations of the Party, and by in effect eliminating the powers of the Ministry of Agricultue, especially after 1959. His price reform of 1958 was insufficiently logical, in the sense that price relativities conflicted with the plan; thus a large increase in meat output was desired, though meat production involved heavy loss. This conflict compelled officials to intervene and this, in the campaign atmosphere, led to excesses. . . .

Let me illustrate, by two quotations, the pressure to which head officials were subjected. One comes from an excellent article by Yu. Chernichenko. He describes an actual meeting in Slavgorod (Kulunda steppe), attended by an unnamed "plenipotentiary from the capital," evidently Khrushchev's right-hand man (Shevchenko?). A *raikom* secretary was speaking, "when the plenipotentiary from the capital interrupted him."

"Why do you fail to keep up the delivery schedule?"

The secretary referred to the weather. Then the mighty visitor, winding himself up, started questioning: Have any Communists remained in the *raion* center? Why so? What right have they to stay there when the fate of the grain harvest was being decided? The Slavgorod secretary shrugged his shoulders: These are officials of the *raion* finance office, the posts, railways. What should they be doing in the fields?

It was there that the plenipotentiary blew up. He jumped from the table, he shouted: "Such a capitulator still sits on the *raikom*? Remove him, remove him! What are you afraid of? We removed countless officials in Tula until we found the right man! People like him should be thrown out! Who gave you the right to be so soft?" . . .

It was not only his rudeness that was so insulting. We were oppressed by the pettiness of the plenipotentary's requirements. We would understand if he were angry because the land was in poor state, because of the wild oats, the roadlessness, lack of grain storage space—because good grain was mixed with rubbish, or because cultivation methods had not changed since the first year of the virgin lands campaign. Sharpness or even rudeness would be explained by the worry of a true husbandman. But the plenipotentiary required only one thing: that this very day, the day of his arrival, grain should be delivered to the elevators and local storage dumps. No matter what kind, dry or in damp lumps, that intended for deliveries or seed grain (later we discovered: He left the Novosibirsk oblast without seed that autumn).

One after another the *raikom* secretaries went up to speak and were met with the same shouting: "When will there be a plenipotentiary with each combine harvester? Take Communists from wherever they might be, send them to the *machines!* Make them stay there all the time! Let them be personally responsible for the threshing! A thousand combine harvesters? Then—a thousand plenipotentiaries. If two thousand are needed, we'll send them."

A young chairman could not refrain from shouting from his seat: "But all our combiners are Communists. Are they also [to have plenipotentiaries attached to them]?"

"What is his name? Consider this at once in the bureau! At once in the bureau," cried the plenipotentiary, gasping with fury.

The effect on grain quality, and on the morale of officials, hardly needs stressing. The author himself comments: "Crude shouting and directives engendered a reluctance to think. Reluctance to think engendered stereotyped methods. Stereotyped methods make the harvest the helpless victim of weather conditions, weeds, and pests. The official who deprives himself of the right to act according to circumstances deprives himself of the right to make demands upon others. There arises a vicious circle of irresponsibility. This is the family tree of the standardized scheme."

The same picture emerges from many speeches made at the Central Committee plenum of March, 1965. Here, for example, are the words of I. Gustov, Secretary of the Pskov Province Party Committee: "Much harm was done by the imposition [from above] of sown-area structures. . . . All of us *obkom* secretaries recall how we were called annually to the Agricultural Department of the Central Committee of CPSU for the R.S.F.S.R., where the sown-area structure was imposed, we were compelled to put our signatures to this structure, and afterwards it was all presented as proposals from below."

Obviously, this could not but affect the behavior of *obkom* officials.

It must be added in fairness that many speakers at this plenum drew attention in strong language to the necessity of improving pay and amenities in rural areas, pointing to the dangerous loss of labor, especially by kolkhozy. It may well be that they had made these representations in earlier years too, but they were given less publicity.

How far did the policy errors of the period after 1958 also originate with local officials? *They* seem to have pressed for amalgamations of farms, *they* favored lower prices at the winter plenum in 1958–59, *they* said they were worried about "excessive" peasant incomes in the better-off farms, and *they* took the initiative against private plots in a number of instances. It is easy to blame Khrushchev alone. But was he not, in these instances, reflecting the instincts of local Party officials?

WHAT NOW?

The post-Khrushchev era has opened the way for important reforms in agriculture. Among these is to be a change in the *modus operandi* of officials which will affect their relations with peasants and with farm management. At the same time, the leadership principle is maintained, the key role of the Party secretary emphasized. The following quotation gives a fair representation of what appears to be the present policy: "These differences [will be] big! In the place of pressure and arbitrariness has come persuasion, explanation, education, control not over people but through people, relying on people. It is perfectly possible to do without orders, without definitive instructions." (There follows an example of how an argument about whether calves should suckle the cows would have been dealt with by orders binding on everyone, whereas now there was consultation and experiment.) "The way to success lies in the increased role of rural Party organization, the direct influence of Communists on the economics of kolkhozy and sovkhozy. And as for the purely productive side of the work—*and the* raikom *cannot leave it aside, it is still responsible for everything*—this is now decided in far better conditions and by different methods of control." The same point is repeated in other articles. The work is to be done not by campaign methods, but thought out in detail, with the long term in mind, with the *raikom* consulting the experts.

This suggests that the Party will still be very much in charge, but they are to take wise decisions, taking into account local conditions and the ideas of experts, management, agronomists, even peasants. . . . The local Party and state officials are to have a key role in deciding the delivery obligations of farms, and thereby their specialization, if any. They are enjoined not to vary arbitrarily the delivery obligations of farms, to let over-quota sales be genuinely voluntary, to let the farm management have much greater freedom to choose the farming methods, and (within limits) the crop pattern and livestock holdings which they prefer. Private interests of peasants are to be given greater attention, the restrictions on the private plot were relaxed.

Yet these are apparently the same *obkom* and *raikom* officials. There is no sign of any major new broom. On the contrary, the top leadership has been weakened and seems more dependent than ever on the good will of the intermediate grades of the *apparat*. The latter can therefore largely determine the way in which reforms are implemented. It may well be that they will continue to interfere with farm management and exercise the same pressure as before to overfulfill procurement targets. They are hardly the kind of people to study patiently the demands of specialization, and they might well throw out proposals from below (as has happened often enough in the past) and substitute what they think

Moscow wants to hear. Thus skepticism would be in order. The same applies to their reaction to a variety of new proposals and experiments, which are being discussed and (here and there) tried out. The Party secretaries may be, in this respect too, an obstructionist and conservative force.

However, this view may be proved wrong, if Moscow's pressure on local officials is relaxed. One of the causes of "campaigning" pressures by officials, of their neglect of the long-term health of agriculture, and of peasant interest in favor of immediate results, is that they were forced by their superiors to behave in this way. If Brezhnev keeps his promise to have modest delivery quotas for each region, and does not publicly announce excessively ambitious production plans, local officials may after all be able to take expert advice and avoid the stupidities of the past. Many of them may well sincerely desire to do the right thing. If price relativities are improved, then, with the considerably higher general level of purchase prices, incentives could be more closely linked with the pattern of production actually needed, and so the objective need for issuing orders on farming operations could be reduced considerably. Thus, changes toward a less strained relationship between officials and those below them, which seems to be consciously sought by the leardership, might perhaps come about. In this connection the bad weather of 1965 is most unfortunate, since shortage is likely to inhibit relaxation of controls.

But another obstacle to progress must be briefly mentioned in conclusion. The peasants, conditioned to skepticism by many past promises, may not believe Brezhnev, however sincere he may be. The peasant's own status is still that of a second-class citizen, passportless, without assurance of freedom of movements or even of study Of course, the desire of skilled or ambitious villagers to go to town is a universal phenomenon, and not peculiar to Russia. However, the willing participation of the peasants, the willingness of men to operate and repair farm machinery—these are obviously essential if the new policies are to succeed. Involved in all this is a new spirit between the rulers and the farmers. Evidence of good intention exists. Evidence of the ability and willingness of officials to change long ingrained habits and methods of work is still lacking. We can just wait and see.

*   *   *

32

URGENT MEASURES FOR THE
FURTHER DEVELOPMENT OF AGRICULTURE
IN THE U.S.S.R.

REPORT BY L. I. BREZHNEV

I. Basic Results of the Development of Agriculture in Recent Years

Comrades! Our agriculture is based on the most advanced social system, which has withstood the test of time and through the entire course of historical development has proved itself an irresistible, vital force. Relying on the socialist system, the Communist Party has done substantial work to develop agriculture. . . .

Unfortunately, however, these positive results were not further consolidated and developed. We were faced with the fact that in the past few years agriculture had slowed in its development, and our plans for an upsurge in agricultural production remained unfulfilled.

According to the control figures, the gross output of agriculture during the seven-year plan (1959–65) should have risen by 70 per cent; in fact, during the first six years the increase came to only 10 per cent. Whereas the gross output of agriculture grew by an average of 7.6 per cent a year during the period 1955–59, in the past five years its average annual rise has been only 1.9 per cent. The growth in the yields of basic crops has slowed down. Thus the average yield of grain crops increased by 1.7 centners in 1955–59 as compared with the preceding five-year period, while in the period 1960–64 it rose by only .8 centner.

A similar phenomenon is to be observed in animal husbandry. The increase in the number of cattle over the past five years was only half as great as in the preceding five years. As for the number of pigs, sheep,

Pravda, March 27, 1965. Translation copyright 1965, by *The Current Digest of the Soviet Press*, published weekly at The Ohio State University by the American Association for the Advancement of Slavic Studies; reprinted by permission of *The Digest*. Brezhnev "Report" reprinted from Vol. XVIII, No. 12, pp. 3–11.

and poultry, it has actually declined substantially during this time. The average milk yield per cow on the collective and state farms has decreased by more than 370 kg.

The data that have been cited make it possible to draw a conclusion: Whereas there was a notable upsurge in agriculture up to 1959, in the period since then it has to all intents and purposes begun to mark time.

What are the basic reasons for this situation?

First, a weak spot in the guidance of agriculture is the fact that the demands of the economic laws of development of a socialist economy were not fully taken into acount and were frequently even ignored. I have in mind first of all such laws as those of planned and proportional development and of expanded socialist reproduction, as well as the principles of the combination of public and personal interests, material incentives, and others. But, as we know, life sternly punishes those who do not take these laws into account, who scorn them and are guilty of subjectivism.

Actions of a purely willful nature, especially in the fields of planning, price formation, financing, and the extension of credits, increasingly came to the fore in the practice of agriculture guidance in the past few years. It cannot be considered normal, for example, that the purchase prices of a number of agricultural products do not even cover the cost of their production. As a result the collective and state farms suffer large losses.

The numerous and sometimes ill-conceived reorganizations gave rise to an atmosphere of nervousness and confusion, deprived managers of a long-range view, and undermined their faith in their abilities. Instead of painstaking, thoughtful work and profound analysis of the state of affairs, the practice of administration by fiat, of issuing commands to the collective and state farms, was often permitted.

Second, agriculture was faced with very great tasks, but they were inadequately backed up by the necessary economic measures, particularly the correct determination of the level of prices for agricultural products and goods needs for production, the allocation of the appropriate capital investments, and the improvement of material and technical supply. Thus in the five years 1954–58 state investments in agriculture amounted to 11.3 per cent of all investments in the national economy, while in the control figures of the seven-year plan (1959–65) they were set at only 7.5 per cent.

In contrast to other branches of the national economy, construction on the state farms and particularly on the collective farms was not fully provided with materials and integrated equipment. Large amounts were frequently channeled into projects whose construction was not demanded by the urgent interests of production. As a result these expenditures did not yield an economic effect, and the national economy thereby suffered losses.

Third, practically nothing was done to raise farming standards or increase fertility. Many collective and state farms violated the crop rotation and failed to observe the elementary rules of agrotechnology. The central agencies issued various kinds of stereotyped instructions on tilling the soil, on determining the structure of sown areas and replacing one farming system by another, and on caring for and feeding livestock, without taking into account natural-economic and production conditions or local experience. All this prevented the planned management of the farms, reduced the role of the land agencies, and did not contribute to the productive utilization of the land.

Finally, in speaking about the reasons for the lag in agriculture, we must also acknowledge that there have been serious shortcomings in the work of Party, soviet, and land agencies. Of course, the work of our cadres was made more complicated by the atmosphere of frequent reorganizations and changes. Nevertheless, we have not utilized all the possibilities at our disposal. We have done insufficient work with people, we have been lax in basing ourselves on specialists and on agricultural science, we have been unable to organize properly the generalization and dissemination of advanced experience. . . .

We understand that an upsurge in agriculture is something that is vitally necessary to us for the successful construction of communism. In order to resolve this nationwide task, we must put a firm economic foundation under agriculture. V. I. Lenin regarded this question as one of the most important questions of the Party's economic policy, since it touches upon the very foundation of the Soviet state—the relationship of the working class and the peasantry.

We must correct the mistakes that have been made in agriculture more quickly and put an end to subjectivism. We must utilize on a broad economic basis material and moral incentives for the development of production. Great efforts and a decisive change in methods of work is demanded of Party, Soviet, and economic agencies, of all of us.

II. Improve the System of Procurements of Agricultural Products

Comrades! The Presidium of the Central Committee attaches serious importance to improving the system of procurements and purchases of agricultural products. It now suffers from many shortcomings and needs to be perfected.

The chief shortcoming consists in the fact that the present procurement system introduces uncertainty into the work of the collective and state farms and does not allow them to plan their production correctly. Plans for procurement of agricultural products are assigned to the collective and state farms for one year only, and often quite belatedly. Furthermore, these plans are repeatedly changed during the course of the procurements, and the collective and state farms receive additional assignments that often exceed those of the plan.

There have been instances when collective and state farms have had to call on the state for seeds after the completion of the grain procurements. In 1962 the state sold the collective and state farms 1,373,000 tons of grain for seed purposes. This year they have again requested about 2,000,000 tons of seeds from the state.

In a number of zones the purchase prices for grain do not cover production expenses. Such a practice harms the state, undermines the economy of the farms, and gives the farmers no material interest in the results of their labor.

We all know from our experience the difficulties that surround grain procurements. The fact that in the past ten years the grain procurement plans have been fulfilled only three times—in 1956, 1958, and 1964—testifies to how unrealistic and imperfect they have been.

Life insistently demands the improvement and perfection of our entire procurement system. First of all, it is necessary to shift to firm plans for procurements of agricultural products covering a number of years. The interests of the state as a whole and of the individual farms must be harmoniously combined in them.

The Presidium of the CPSU Central Committee submits the following proposals for the consideration of the plenary session of the Central Committee:

First, that the approved plan for grain purchases for this year be reduced from 4,000,000,000 to 3,400,000,000 poods;

Second, that this plan for the purchase of 3,400,000,000 poods be established as fixed and unalterable for all the years of the coming five-year period, including 1970.

It is proposed that a fixed, unalterable plan for grain purchases over the six years be established for the republics, provinces, territories, districts, and collective and state farms. . . .

As you see, comrades, the Presidium of the Central Committee is proposing a practice of planning grain procurements that is new in principle. Such a procedure is an urgent necessity that meets the interests of the progressive development of the productive forces of agriculture. We are confident that it will receive the approval and support of the Party and the people.

Simultaneously, beginning with this year's harvest, it is proposed that we raise the basic purchase prices for wheat, rye, and certain other grain crops, and also for sunflower seed bought from state farms. The so-called sliding prices will be abolished. . . .

Comrades! The Presidium of the Central Committee considers it necessary to report to the CPSU Central Committee's plenary session that the proposed volume of grain purchases will not fully satisfy the growing needs of the country and the creation of state reserves. Therefore, in addition to the planned procurements, we should organize above-plan purchases of the basic food crops from farms that have an excess of marketable grain.

The state will sponsor free purchases of farm products and stimulate them with stable prices, furthering the all-round development of commodity relations. In order to encourage the sale of products above the fixed plan by the collective and state farms, it is proposed to establish an added payment of 50 per cent of the basic purchase price for wheat and rye. . . .

Comrades! It is generally known that animal husbandry depends directly on the development of field farming, and first of all on grain growing. In striving for an increase in the production of grain we will at the same time be creating a firm base for the development of animal husbandry. Together with this, the Presidium of the CPSU Central Committe intends to implement a number of economic measures that will contribute to an upsurge in this important branch of the economy.

Animal husbandry is now unprofitable on many collective and state farms.

An obviously abnormal situation has taken shape: The more meat a farm produces, the bigger the losses it suffers. Is it really possible to run a farm in this way for very long? . . .

Taking into account the proposals of the Central Committees of the Communist parties and the Councils of Ministers of the Union republics, and in order to maintain the livestock herd for a further increase in the output of animal husbandry products, it has been decided to establish a 1965 state plan for the procurements of livestock and poultry in the amount of 8,500,000 tons, rather than the previously established 9,000,000 tons. It is also necessary to lower slightly the plans for the purchase of other livestock products. . . .

In order to accelerate the growth of the output of livestock products, it is necessary to undertake certain additional measures of state assistance to the collective and state farms. The drafts that will be handed out to you propose the establishment, with due regard for specific zonal features, of increments to the existing purchase and procurement prices on the collective and state farms: for cattle, from 20 to 55 per cent; for pigs, from 30 to 70 per cent; and for sheep, from 10 to 70 per cent, and up to 100 per cent in the high-mountain districts.

It must be stressed that the increase in purchase prices will be carried out without raising the existing retail prices of grain, groats, meat, and meat products.

As you see, the state is investing large additional sums in animal husbandry as well. We are doing this in order to help the collective and state farms make this branch a profitable one. Party, soviet, and land agencies and the leaders of collective and state farms should use this help to ensure a radical improvement in the development of animal husbandry in the next two or three years. . . .

Comrades! The establishment of firm plans, the raising of the basic prices for a number of agricultural crops and livestock products, and the system of above-plan purchases at higher prices will create new conditions for each farm, each leader, and each Party organization; will open good prospects for their fruitful activity; and will create assurance in work.

Now, taking local features into account, it is possible to determine in advance the structure of sown areas, to restore the violated crop rotations, and to work out and introduce progressive agrotechnology, based on the achievements of science and advanced experience, and a system of measures for increasing the livestock herd and raising its productivity.

A stable six-year plan for purchases and stimulation of the growth of commodity output will be an important means for a further upsurge in agricultural production. They will unleash the initiative of farm specialists and leaders, offering them an opportunity to exercise their creative abilities, to develop economic enterprise, and to eliminate stereotypes in field farming and animal husbandry.

The central committees of the Union-republic Communist parties, province, territory and district Party committees, and soviet and land agencies are faced with a complicated and responsible task: to assign to each collective and state farm, with due regard for its soil, climatic, and economic features, firm plans for the purchase of agricultural products over the next six years. Mistakes cannot be permitted here, comrades!

The success of the cause will largely depend on the correct planning of purchases: Either all the farms will begin to grow quickly in the new conditions or, if mistakes are made and the plans are not assigned objectively, some farms will rise in their economic development while others will be unable to do so. Therefore thoroughgoing economic and agrozootechnical work must now be instituted on the compilation and assigning of stable plans for each collective and state farm.

We must firmly agree that no one has the right to change these plans. A permanent plan does not weaken but on the contrary raises the responsibility of Party and soviet agencies for increasing the output of farm products and for the fulfillment of the state's assignments.

If we say that the plan has the force of law, then it should be mandatory for everyone: It cannot be changed, and it cannot go unfulfilled!

All the state's regulatory levers must contribute to placing the country's collective and state farms, which have different possibilities, in approximately equal economic conditions for development. The success of this or that farm will depend in decisive measure on its leaders and specialists, on the enthusiasm and industry of the agricultural workers, and on the fruitful activity of Party and soviet organizations and land agencies.

III. On Strengthening the Material and Technical Base of Agriculture

Comrades! The material and technical base of the collective and state farms has grown somewhat during the years of the current seven-year plan, and the number of tractors, trucks, and farm machines has increased. The supply of power for farm labor has also risen. Our industry and its workers and engineering and technical personnel have done much to provide agriculture with modern equipment.

However, the technical supply of the collective and state farms is still inadequate. We do not have enough tractors, trucks, combines, and other complex agricultural machines, as well as cultivators, harrows, and seed drills. This leads to prolongation of the time needed to carry out field work and to a reduction in yields.

It can hardly be considered normal when autumn plowing often stretches out over two months, instead of taking only eighteen to twenty days, and ends only with the coming of frost, since every peasant knows that a good harvest can be obtained only from early autumn plowing. Because of the shortage of combines and other equipment, the harvesting of grain crops frequently extends over thirty to forty days, which causes enormous losses in the harvest.

The interests of an upsurge in agriculture demand the resolute intensification of the material and technical supply of collective and state farm production, a sharp increase in the output of farm equipment, and a rise in its quality, reliability, and durability.

In developing the production of tractors and other machines, it is necessary to ensure the standardization of parts, assemblies, and mechanisms. We must no longer tolerate a situation when with the appearance of each new machine there arises the problem of spare parts for it, when the assortment of spare parts increases year after year.

Workers, engineers, technicians, and the Party organizations of industrial enterprises must do everything necessary to ensure the prompt delivery of equipment to agriculture and to raise its quality sharply. In turn, the agricultural agencies must put an end to the practice of repeated changes in orders for agricultural equipment that have been placed with industry.

The question of the production utilization of available equipment and its careful maintenance is also a very acute one. It is necessary to raise the responsibility for the correct use of equipment, to strengthen the material interest of agriculture's engineering and technical workers and equipment operators, and to improve the supply of spare parts and materials to the collective and state farms.

Above all, we must strengthen the repair base of agriculture. This is a very important question, and we cannot postpone its solution. Large amounts of new equipment can be given to the collective and state farms, but if a firm repair base is not created we shall not obtain the proper results. The present repair base makes it possible to implement only 60 per cent of the necessary repairs in good time and with high quality. Almost 13,000 farms lack workshops capable of carrying out even routine repairs. . . .

Gigantic power plants have been built in our country in recent years. Yet 12 per cent of the collective farms do not yet have electricity even for illumination. Agriculture consumes only 4 per cent of the power generated in the country, including only 2 per cent for production purposes.

The question of the electrification of agriculture must be fundamentally solved. The State Planning Committee, the State Committee for Power and Electrification, the Ministry of Agriculture, and scientists must be charged with drafting a plan for solving this highly important task in the next few years.

In speaking about measures for an upsurge in agricultural production, one cannot fail to emphasize the important role in this matter that belongs to the chemical industry. We must be clearly aware that the effectiveness of all the planned measures will increase substantially given the broad chemicalization of agriculture. The chemical industry must improve its work and must step up the rates of production and delivery of high-quality mineral fertilizers, chemical poisons, herbicides, and defoliants. . . .

IV. Put Science and Advanced Practice at the Service of a Comprehensive Upsurge in Agricultural Production

Comrades! Agricultural science has been given an important role in the measures the Party Central Committee is taking to correct shortcomings and ensure a further upsurge in agriculture. The mighty strength of science lies in the unity of theory and practice. Service to the people is an excellent feature of our Soviet science.

In addition to their profound scientific researches that have enriched world science, outstanding Russian scientists have directly engaged in important practical questions. We must comprehensively develop the traditions of our brilliant scientist compatriots. . . .

At the same time the achievements of our agricultural and biological science and its practical assistance to production would have been even more successful if the erroneous theories and dogmas that arose without adequate scientific foundation and that were supported by administrative methods had been eliminated in time.

Science does not tolerate subjectivism or over-hasty conclusions that have not been verified in practice. At its basis there must be only objective data, confirmed by precise experiments, production experience, and life itself.

Genuine science accepts nothing on faith; it cannot be the monopoly of individual scientists, least of all of administrators, no matter what authority they enjoy. Unfortunately, in recent times there have been instances when scientifically incompetent people have sometimes assumed the role of arbitrator in disputes between scientists and have thus fettered their initiative and prevented the free, creative discussion of scientific problems. . . .

Comrades! Our agriculture has at its disposal an enormous army of highly qualified specialists. Unfortunately, an incorrect attitude toward specialists has formed in recent years; their knowledge and experience have often been ignored, and in a number of cases they have actually been prevented from fulfilling their lofty duty.

V. I. Lenin taught us to be attentive, sensitive, and responsive to specialists and to value them. He said: "To correct the work of hundreds of the best specialists in an offhand way, to brush them off with vulgar little jokes, to brag about one's right 'not to approve'—is this not shameful?

"We must learn to value science, to repudiate the 'communist' swaggering of dilettantes and bureaucrats, we must learn to work systematically, using our own experience, our own practice!" Excellent words!

We must resolutely change the attitude toward agricultural specialists and scientists, give them constant assistance and support, encourage their initiative, and surround them with concern and attention. We must turn them in fact into organizers of production, the champions of agrotechnical and zootechnical knowledge, of everything new and progressive.

Agronomists and zootechnicians are the technologists of agricultural production; their role is just as great as the role of engineers in industry. In the specialists the Party sees its reliable, skilled mainstay in the struggle for an upsurge in agriculture. We trust our specialists, who have been reared by the Communist Party. Given the active support of farm managers and Party and soviet organizations, the rural specialists will be able to develop their creative abilities and to ensure the steady growth of the yield of the fields and the productivity of animal husbandry.

V. Certain Questions of the Further Organizational and Economic Strengthening of the Collective and State Farms

Comrades! A highly important condition for an upsurge in the productive forces of agriculture is the correct development of social and economic relations in the countryside. As you know, two types of communal economy have evolved historically in our country's farming, the state farms and the collective farms, which are based on two forms of socialist ownership—state and collective-cooperative.

Experience has shown that the skillful combination of the development of these two types of farms has enabled us to reconstruct agriculture on a socialist basis. It must be assumed that these two types of communal farming will continue to exist and develop for a long time to come. *At the present stage, our obligation consists not in accelerating the transformation of one form into the other, but in promoting in every way the development and prosperity of both types of communal farming.*

The economic measures outlined by the CPSU Central Committee will create the conditions for the successful development and strengthening of both the collective and state farms. However, in order to take better advantage of the new possibilities for a rapid upsurge in agriculture production, it is necessary to eliminate a number of serious shortcomings in the management of the state farms and, in particular, the collective farms.

Very many impulsive and, to put it plainly, ill-conceived decisions that sometimes contradict the essence of the collective farm system and the real conditions of life have been introduced here. In recent years, for example, the amalgamation of farms has been carried out on a broad scale in many provinces of the country. Certain collective farms became so large that they proved unmanageable. The necessary economic grounds did not always exist when state farms were set up on the basis of collective farms, as a result of which many of them proved to be cumbersome and barely manageable, and some of them are still unprofitable.

All this indicates that fundamental questions of socio-economic relations in the countryside cannot be resolved by campaigns or administrative methods. It must be borne in mind that they concern the vital interests of millions of Soviet people, and consequently are questions of policy, which must be resolved circumspectly, without haste, as economic conditions grow ripe. At the same time, it would be no less rash to deal with the question of breaking up the large farms with the same haste.

We cannot ignore the fact that the democratic foundations of the collective farm system have in many instances been crudely violated. On a number of collective farms, the majority of farm members find themselves left out of the discussion and resolution of vital questions of the artel's economy. Furthermore, in recent times certain farms have not even been guided by the statutory requirements, though after all the Collective Farm Statutes are the *cornerstone* of the management and social life of the artel.

The collective farm is a communal, cooperative organization; it cannot live and develop normally if its democratic foundations are violated. It is therefore necessary to ensure the strict observance of democratic principles in the management of the artel's affairs on every collective farm.

It must be admitted that much in the Collective Farm Statutes has become obsolete. Life insistently demands the improvement of the Statutes. The time has come to begin drafting new Collective Farm Statutes that take into account everything positive that has been accumulated in the practice of collective farm development in recent years. Preparations for a Third All-Union Congress of Collective Farmers should be initiated at the same time, so that such a congress might be called as early as next year. This congress should be preceded by district, territory, province, and republic congresses of collective farmers.

Many other questions concerning the organizational and economic strengthening of the collective and state farms have accumulated. It is known that a farm can be run correctly only on the basis of a well-organized economic work and precise cost-accounting. The level of profitability must be placed at the foundation of an objective evaluation of the economic activity of the collective and state farms. But, unfortunately, cost-accounting principles are at present being poorly applied to our farms.

Take the state farms, for example. The state gives them capital investments, establishes plans for the delivery of products and their prices, determines the wage fund and even the size of the staff, the category of workers, and administrative and service personnel. Losses incurred by the state farms are compensated by the state. Cost-accounting is violated in the very economic relations between the state and the state farms, as well as the collective farms.

We must abandon excessive regimentation in the distribution of capital investments and subsidies to the state farms and shift the state farms to full cost-accounting as soon as possible. The state farms will retain for their own uses the profits they receive, which should be employed for expanding operations, for capital construction, for encouraging good workers, and for improving the cultural and everyday conditions of the workers and employees.

In order that the state farms may actually utilize the profits received as a result of their skillful economic activity for expanding production, the planning agencies are obliged to authorize the hiring of manpower for these purposes, and also to allocate the necessary funded supplies of building and other materials and of mechanisms and equipment.

The Ministry of Agriculture, together with the Union republics and other authorities and with the help of economic scientists, should prepare concrete proposals for shifting the state farms to full cost-accounting.

No small importance attaches to the financing and extension of credit to the collective farms. We are also faced with the task of analyzing and putting in order this important sector. The Ministries of Agriculture and Finance and the State Bank must be charged with drafting and submitting to the CPSU Central Committee proposals for improving the system of financing and crediting the collective farms.

Many collective farms are now deeply in debt to the state, which makes their economic activity difficult. In order to ease the situation of the collective farms, primarily the economically weak ones, and to give them an opportunity to work normally, the Presidium of the CPSU Central Committee deems it possible to write off their indebtedness.

It is also necessary to change the existing procedure in the levying of the income tax on the collective farms. The collective farms are now taxed on part of the expenses of production, that is, on the expenditures on labor payments to the collective farmers, and also on the value of the goods still in production. This cannot be considered correct. A draft resolution on changing the decree on the collective farm income tax has been prepared with respect to this question, establishing a new procedure whereby the tax will be applied not to the gross but to the net income of the collective farms.

We must call attention to and adopt appropriate measures on the further strengthening and preservation of the socialist public property of the collective and state farms. It is necessary first to put in order the matter of land utilization, and instances of squandering land and a predatory attitude toward it must be done away with.

We need thrift now as never before. We must be economical in everything. This is not a matter of campaign, but of daily thrift in everything —equipment, fuel, expenditures on the operation of vehicular transport; we must not tolerate the loss and squandering of materials, products, and funds. This concerns everyone—from the collective farmer and the worker to the leader. We must wage a resolute struggle to strengthen labor and state discipline on the collective and state farms.

One of the important conditions for an upsurge in agricultural production is the question of material and moral incentives for agricultural workers. We have many unresolved questions here. The system of remunerating labor on the collective and state farms is still far from perfect.

The U.S.S.R. Ministry of Agriculture, together with the Union republics, must be charged with enlisting scientists, specialists, and the collective farm *aktiv* in generalizing the experience that has been amassed and preparing proposals for improving the remuneration of labor on the collective farms, and also in considering the question of creating monetary and in-kind funds for the guaranteed payment of the collective farmers' labor.

We must also study questions of material incentives for the collective farmers and state farm workers who are directly engaged in growing agricultural crops and in animal husbandry and who have achieved the highest results.

The system of remunerating the officials and specialists of state farms and trusts that was introduced in the past has not justified itself. We must abandon it and establish remuneration for state farm managers and specialists according to their posts, depending on the volume of work and taking into account their education and period of service, and must pay these wages in full every month.

I want to dwell on yet another question. Letters from workers in the countryside have proposed the extension to rural localities of the prices for manufactured goods and foodstuffs that are in effect in the cities. The Presidium of the CPSU Central Committee considers it possible to do this with respect to most goods beginning in May, 1965, and for certain goods beginning in January, 1966. Former collective farm members whose lands have gone to state farms and other state enterprises and organizations have raised the question of the extension to them of the law on pension insurance for collective farmers. This question is also being resolved favorably.

The economic measures for an upsurge in agriculture that are being submitted for the consideration of the Central Committee plenary session will undoubtedly make it possible to strengthen the collective and state farms organizationally and economically, to raise the material interest of the toilers of the countryside, and to increase the output of agricultural products.

VI. Raise the Level of Party Work in the Countryside

Comrades! The great tasks of economic and cultural construction in our country immeasurably increase the guiding role of the Communist Party and its cadres in the life of society. The construction of communism relies on the mighty creative forces of the people. This places special obligations on the Party——to improve constantly its organizational, political and economic, and ideological work.

The situation itself places high demands on Party cadres. The cultural level of our country's people has grown, and their political horizon has expanded. If our Party and soviet cadres are to execute the role of leader successfully, to solve the tasks of communist construction successfully, they must tirelessly master Lenin's skill in guiding the masses.

The proposed economic measures for the further development of agriculture insistently demand that the organizational guidance of the Party be raised to a new level. Life has shown that the higher the level of organizational guidance, the more fruitful are the economic successes.

It should be recognized, however, that certain Party organizations still exert only a weak influence on the economic activity of the collective and state farms, ignore major shortcomings, and carry out work with people, with the masses, on a low level. There is no militancy or purposefulness in the practical work of a number of Party organizations.

The Central Committees of the Union-republic Communist Parites, the territory and province Party committees, all of us must take definite steps to readjust ourselves, must resolutely get rid of everything superficial and harmful in Party work. We must put an end to the practice of command and administration by fiat, to petty tutelage, to the usurping of the functions of the leaders and specialists of the collective and state farms, must eradicate any manifestations of ostentation and ballyhoo.

The task consists in arousing people for the fulfillment of the measures of the CPSU Central Committee and ensuring their firm and constant implementation. This depends most of all on the efforts, energy, and persistence of the Party organizations and their leaders, on their ability to organize the masses.

Special attention must be paid to strengthening and raising the role of the primary Party organizations of the collective and state farms. They are in the forefront of the struggle and are directly translating the policy and directives of the Party into life. There are now 50,000 primary Party organizations, numbering more than 2 million Communists, in the countryside. This is an enormous force, comrades, one that is capable of solving in a militant way the tasks advanced by the Party.

Serious assistance and support must be given to the secretaries of the primary Party organizations of the collective and state farms, especially since many of them have been elected to these posts for the first time or are overburdened with their basic work. Possibly we should somewhat increase the number of full-time secretaries of Party organizations on the collective and state farms. . . .

At the same time, the Party organizations must constantly concern themselves with satisfying the cultural and everyday needs of the toilers of agriculture in order to improve housing conditions year by year and to see to it that there are good clubs, libraries, schools, and stores in the countryside. It is a well-known truth of life that in the development of any social system the decisive role belongs to production. But it would be wrong to forget questions of the culture and everyday life of the rural workers. The creation of good cultural and everyday conditions is a mighty lever for advancing collective farm and state farm production.

Our work will be successful only if we are able to employ such powerful forces as the soviets, trade unions, and the Young Communist League. Whenever the Party has taken this or that major step on the path of communist construction, it has intensified in every way the activity of these mass political organizations of the working people.

The CPSU Central Committee hopes that the soviets and the trade union and YCL organizations will occupy a proper place in the nation-wide struggle for a further upsurge in agriculture.

We must make far better use of so powerful a lever for the organization of the masses as the Soviet press. We publish several hundred central, republic, territory, and province newspapers. The Central Committee recently adopted a decision on resuming the publication of district newspapers.

The task consist in orienting our press toward the businesslike and thorough illumination of questions of the development of agriculture. The newspapers must promptly note and propagandize everything new, must raise vital questions of collective farm and state farm production and teach the masses through progressive examples.

A vast army of agitators and propagandists is taking part in the practical implementation of mass-political work in the countryside. At meetings and in personal talks with collective farmers and state farm workers, these toilers on the political front always endeavor to explain the policy of our party and the most important events taking place in the country and abroad and to mobilize the people for excellent feats of labor. They must do much work on explaining the decisions of the present plenary session of the CPSU Central Committee.

The Party organizations must give the agitators comprehensive assistance in their great and important work. The leaders of Party committees should meet with them more often, generalize their experience, and improve agitation and propaganda work. It is necessary to help them rouse the people to feats of labor in an effective and revolutionary way.

In the face of the complex and great tasks in the sphere of agriculture, we must emphasize with renewed force that ideological tempering, inflexible conviction in the correctness of Party policy, is the force that helps all of us to overcome any difficulties, to resolve practical tasks skillfully.

The experience of the Communist Party convincingly shows that the higher the ideological level and theoretical training of Party, soviet, and economic cadres and the more skillful their guidance of the masses, the more fruitful will be their entire practical activity. Our cadres must continue to master the theory of Marxism-Leninism, profoundly study the laws of socialist economics, and improve the forms and methods of political work among the masses.

The measures the Presidium of the CPSU Central Committee has worked out for an upsurge in agriculture create favorable conditions for work in the countryside by the Party organizations. The task now lies in putting these enormous material and organizational forces into operation, in making maximum use of them for an upsurge in the labor activeness of the masses and for the achievement of high labor productivity, which in the final analysis is the chief thing in the further development of agriculture. "To build a new labor discipline," V. I.

Lenin said, "to build new forms of social ties between people, to build new forms and methods of attracting people to labor—this is the most gratifying and noble work."

Comrades! The proposals for an upsurge in agriculture that have been submitted for your consideration and the major state investments linked with them have been dictated by life itself, by an urgent, nationwide need. We are deeply convinced that they will help to put the collective and state farms on a firm material base and to create objective conditions that will make it possible to manage agriculture confidently and according to plan in the future.

The chief thing now consists in resolutely putting an end to subjectivism in the practice of managing socialist agriculture and in making broad use of economic and moral incentives in all sectors of the production activity of the collective and state farms. We must grant them more economic independence and raise the role and responsibility of Party, soviet, and agricultural agencies and of leaders and specialists for the state of affairs in agriculture.

All our measures and all our efforts must be concentrated on the successful solution of the central problem of agriculture—raising the standards of farming, obtaining high yields, raising the productivity of animal husbandry, and ensuring the profitability of all branches of agricultural production.

Concern for the steady growth of the material and cultural level of the entire Soviet people, for strengthening the alliance of the working class and the peasantry—such is the political meaning of the measures of the Presidium of the CPSU Central Committee.

*   *   *

X

The World of the Intellectual

The intellectual in the Soviet Union is in an anomalous position: He is relatively well paid for his talents, but he may be severely punished for challenging the wisdom, let alone the authority, of the state. Writers and artists exist to articulate ideas and emotions, but Party guidelines, not their own instincts, determine the scope of such expression. There has been a constant tug-of-war between the intellectual and the state because of the dilemma that freedom of expression poses for the latter. In a developed society some individuals will inevitably express ideas that conflict with those of the ruling elite and pose a challenge to its authority. The regime can therefore suppress some of its creative artists and writers or tolerate dissenting ideas that might in time nourish political opposition. Compounding the dilemma for the Soviet Union is the fact that many of Russia's most esteemed writers—Mayakovsky, Akhmatova, Pasternak, and Solzhenitsyn, to name a few—have had the greatest difficulty adhering to the strictures of the Party line.

The term used by the Russians to classify the intellectual in the

Soviet social structure is "intelligentsia," though the "new Soviet intelligentsia" encompasses a wider range of occupations than just scientist, writer, and artist. According to the 1959 census the Soviet intelligentsia constituted approximately 8 per cent of the population. By occupation it could be subdivided into three groups: the "creative intelligentsia," those professionals in the arts and sciences who are usually thought of when the term intellectual is used in the West (0.5 per cent); the "technical intelligentsia," administrators and technical personnel in industry and agriculture (3.5 per cent); and professional service personnel in education, architecture, medicine, law, entertainment, and mass media (4.0 per cent).

Traditionally the Russian intelligentsia was defined not by occupational status or even education, but by its attraction to the culture of Western Europe and its demands for reform of Russia's social, economic, and civic life. As a social critic Lenin himself carried on the tradition of Russia's intelligentsia. However, once in power he demanded of Russia's intellectuals the same subordination to Party policy that was required of all other groups; and under Lenin's administration the techniques of censorship and control—the hallmarks of Soviet policy toward the intellectual—were initiated. Shortly before Lenin's death Glavlit (Chief Administration of Literary and Publishing Affairs) was established as the primary government censorship agency. Notwithstanding the increasing demands for political conformity, the 1920's witnessed a wide range of experimentation in nearly all of the arts.

Stalin destroyed the last vestiges of intellectual freedom and in the process completely modified the social structure of the intelligentsia. A new group of scientific, technical, and administrative specialists—the "working intelligentsia"—replaced the large number of artists and writers who perished in the 1930's. Their function was to assist in the construction of the economic and industrial infrastructure of communism. Those who became designated as "the creative intelligentsia" were required to use their talents to build popular support for the Party and its policies and, later, for Stalin personally. During the 1930's the Communist Party achieved complete bureaucratic control over culture through the formation of such organizations as the Union of Soviet Artists and the Union of Soviet Writers.

Under Stalin Soviet art and art education were dominated by the canons of socialist realism. This standard, which remains the aesthetic doctrine of the Soviet state, is designed to bring culture to the masses while it glorifies communism and the Party. Art must be intelligible to the common man, meaning that music should be tuneful, not cacophonous; painting must depict recognizable themes, not abstractions; literature must flatter the state, romanticize the common life of the people, and uphold civic virtue. Socialist realist art is meant to inspire optimism; conflict shown to be resolved on the side of good, which invariably is the side taken by the Party and the state. This populist doctrine has resulted in the stifling of experimentation and the encouragement of only the most conservative, if not banal, in contemporary art.

Since Stalin's death, government policy has alternated between periods of relaxation and tightening of ideological controls. As in other areas of public life, Khrushchev liberalized many of the restrictions imposed upon writers. He personally authorized the publication of Aleksandr Solzhenitsyn's *One Day in the Life of Ivan Denisovich*, an exposé of life in a forced-labor camp and a landmark in Soviet literature. A new genre of writing appeared, treating honestly and critically some of the unpleasant characteristics of Soviet life. Novels like V. Dudinstev's *Not by Bread Alone* for the first time portrayed Party bureaucrats in an unsympathetic light. Many writers who had been shot or disgraced under Stalin were officially "rehabilitated." Khrushchev's liberalization—indeed, his entire de-Stalinization campaign—was rooted in his struggle for political control. When the volume of writings critical of life in Stalin's time threatened to raise the larger questions not only of Stalin's authority but of the legitimacy of Party rule, Khrushchev reacted with a campaign to reimpose ideological controls on dissident intellectuals.

Khrushchev's successors have pursued an even harder line. The repression began in earnest in September, 1965, when two Russian writers, Yuli Daniel and Andrei Sinyavsky, whose satirical attacks on the Soviet establishment and "socialist realism" had been published abroad under pseudonyms, were arrested for anti-Soviet slander. Their trial led to protests by other intellectuals, further arrests, more demonstrations, and a number of trials of intellectuals on such charges as "anti Soviet propaganda" and "agitation." These proceedings, reminiscent of Stalinist terror, were often semisecret. They subjected the defendants to lengthy pretrial detention, intimidation by the secret police, vicious attacks by the press and resulted in unusually harsh sentences (Daniel and Sinyavsky received five and seven years at hard labor, respectively).

But repression has failed to silence completely the nonconformist and the critic. Aleksandr Solzhenitsyn, though expelled from the Writers' Union and no longer published in the Soviet Union, continues to protest government censorship publicly. An underground world of forbidden literature and avant-garde art thrives in the major cities. Manuscripts that cannot be published legally are reproduced by hand and circulated from person to person—a form of publication known as *samizdat*. Many Russians are writing, as they put it, "for the drawer," to be filed away until a change in circumstances might permit publication.

The Soviet regime is based upon a theory of history, not an aesthetic theory. There is no reason inherent in the Soviet system why any one form of esthetic expression—be it Cubism or neo-Dada in art, stream of consciousness in literature, serialism or electronics in music—should be suppressed or preferred. Even a dictatorship can permit a display of artistic taste that differs from the personal preferences of the ruling elite. There are, however, limits to free expression in any authoritarian system. Any subject matter directly concerned with political issues, and here literature would be particularly vulnerable, must be supportive of the group or person in power. Soviet intellectuals cannot demand an abstract right to act independently—even on questions remote from politics—simply because such an assertion might constitute an example for other social groups. Quite likely one of the concerns of the Brezhnev-Kosygin leadership in bringing the intelligentsia to heel was simply the need to restore respect for authority.

Merle Fainsod, formerly Director of the Russian Research Center at Harvard University, and Director of the Harvard University Library until his death in 1972, was the author of widely acclaimed studies of Soviet society, including *How Russia Is Ruled* and *Smolensk Under Soviet Rule*. Nikita Khrushchev was deposed as First Secretary of the Soviet Communist Party and Prime Minister in October, 1964. He lived comfortably in retirement until his death in 1971. Anatoly Kuznetsov is a young Soviet writer who defected to Great Britain in July, 1969. One of his major works is the novel *Babi Yar*. Andrei Sakharov, considered the "father of the Soviet hydrogen bomb" is one of the leading Soviet physicists. He is a cofounder of the unofficial Soviet Committee on Human Rights and a vigorous spokesman for civil liberties in the Soviet Union.

33

THE ROLE OF INTELLECTUALS
IN THE SOVIET UNION

MERLE FAINSOD

We begin with a problem of definition: What do we mean when we speak of intellectuals in communist countries? In contemporary Soviet usage, the term "intelligentsia" is officially defined as "a social stratum consisting of people who are occupied professionally with mental labor." It excludes workers, peasants, and low-level clerical personnel, but among the occupations included are all managerial personnel in industry, trade, and agriculture; the Party apparatus; technical personnel in industry and agriculture, including engineers, architects, technicians, foremen, agronomists, and veterinarians; scientific workers, physicians and intermediate medical personnel, including midwives, nurses, laboratory workers, and pharmacists; teachers, librarians, journalists, writers, and artists; economists, accountants, and planners; lawyers, army officers, and students in the universities and technical institutes.

Reprinted from *The Texas Quarterly* 13, No. 4 (Winter, 1965): 88–103. Reprinted with permission of the author and publisher.

Obviously, the current Soviet conception of the intelligentsia includes many categories not commonly thought of in noncommunist countries as entitling their members to credentials as intellectuals. At the same time, Soviet definitions go part way toward accommodating themselves to Western usage by distinguishing between the technical intelligentsia, which has grown so rapidly in numbers and importance with industrialization, and the *tvorcheskaya intelligentsia,* or creative intelligentsia, of writers, artists, scholars, and other representatives of the world of culture whose concerns more closely approximate those of the Western intellectual.

The role of the creative intelligentsia, and, more particularly, the literary intelligentsia, claims attention here. First, it is important to understand the milieu in which Soviet writers operate. Their assigned task, in the words of the Party program, "lies in strengthening ties with the life of the people, and in the truthful and highly artistic depiction of the richness and diversity of Socialist reality, in inspired and vivid portrayal of all that is new and genuinely communist, and exposure of all that hinders the progress of society." Khrushchev, before his downfall, was more explicit. He pronounced, "The press and radio, literature, painting, music, the cinema and the theater are a sharp ideological weapon of our Party. The Party is concerned that its weapon be always in battle readiness and that it hit the enemy accurately. The Party will allow no one to blunt its edge, to weaken its effect. In questions of creative art the Party Central Committee will seek to obtain from all—from the most honored and best known writer or artist and from the young, fledgling creative worker—unswering execution of the Party line." His successors have somewhat modified these strictures. While still insisting that Soviet intellectuals must conform to the Marxist-Leninist philosophy of dialectical materialism and the principles of socialist realism, they have promised that Party controls will be exercised in a less heavy-handed way. Quoting from a 1925 Central Committee resolution on literature, A. H. Rumyantsev, editor of *Pravda,* declared, "Communist criticism must rid itself of the tone of literary command. The Party must in every way eradicate attempts at homebred and incompetent administrative interference in literary affairs."

Rumyantsev's words of encouragement to writers and artists who seek more elbow room to experiment should not be taken to mean that the Party is prepared to abdicate its role as ideological spokesman and guide in literary matters; nor will it tolerate any form of literary or artistic activity that places its own principles in peril. In the words of L. F. Ilyichev, the former chairman of the Central Committee's Ideological Commission, "The question of creative freedom must be fully clarified. . . . We have full freedom to fight for communism. We have not and cannot have freedom to fight against communism."

The Party possesses a formidable armory of weapons to enforce its views. It can tempt writers to meet its demands by rewarding conformists with large editions, swollen royalty accounts, and the amenities and perquisites these can command. It can punish the deviant and the recalcitrant by subjecting them to public criticism, censoring their output, denying them publication, and, in the most extreme cases, consigning them to prison or exile under the criminal or antiparasite laws.

But there are also certain things that the Party cannot do. It cannot force a writer to write if he is prepared to shoulder the consequences of not writing. It cannot make talented writers out of hacks, and it has learned more than once that to rely on hacks to transmit its message is to deaden and kill its appeal. It seeks to enlist the creatively gifted in its service but frequently finds itself impaled on the horns of a dilemma where the needs of creativity and conformity clash. . . .

Since Stalin's death, the Soviet Union has provided a fascinating laboratory to study the potentialities and limits of intellectual freedom under Communism. The repudiation of the Stalinist legacy of mass terror encouraged the more venturesome among the creative intelligentsia to explore the boundaries of their new freedom and even to function, in the nineteenth-century tradition of their intelligentsia forebears, as critics of the established order. The regime, on the other hand, sought to engage the support of the intelligentsia, while setting limits to its more dangerous critical proclivities. This policy, perhaps best summed up in the ambiguous formula of controlled relaxation, has consisted thus far of alternating phases in which a loosening of bonds has been followed by tighter restrictions which, in turn, have given way to easings of pressure.

To understand post-Stalinist developments, one needs to view them in the perspective of what went before. The early years after the Revolution were still a period of relative freedom. Party controls were not as rigid as they were later to become. The period of the tightening of controls began with the consolidation of Stalin's power in the late 1920's. Literature during those years received its Five-Year Plan, along with industry and agriculture. The writers were now christened "engineers of the human soul," and they had their set themes and their set goals. With the organization of the Union of Soviet Writers in 1934, controls became even more sweeping. Writers were expected to serve the Party cause and glorify Stalin. This was the perdominant line down to the war and the Nazi attack on the Soviet Union in June, 1941.

The war period opened up new possibilities for the writers. There was less stress on the Party and more on patriotic-national themes that would have an inclusive appeal. The necessities of the Alliance bred more tolerance of cosmopolitan interests, and the sufferings of the war were also permitted an outlet in the form of deeply personal poetry that had little or nothing to do with glorification of the Party or of Stalin. . . .

As the war drew to a close and victory was within grasp, a mood of demobilization set in. After the grim hardships, people longed to relax, to taste the joys of victory and peace, and to lead an easier life. . . . But it was not to be. Stalin was not interested in demobilization. The

end of the war was marked by a tightening of Party controls; there was
no room for poems expressing longing for the beloved, for relaxation,
pleasure, and joy.

The Party entered the fray with the Central Committee resolution
of May 14, 1946, on the journals *Zvezda* and *Leningrad*. The speeches
of Zhdanov, the new cultural Tsar, which accompanied the decree,
marked a vigorous reassertion of the Party's role in literature. Said
Zhdanov:

> Any preaching of ideological neutrality, of political neutrality, of Art for
> Art's sake, is alien to Soviet literature and harmful to the interests of the
> Soviet people and to the Soviet state. Such preaching has no place in our
> journals. . . . The task of Soviet literature is to aid the state to educate the
> youth correctly and to meet their demands, to rear a new generation strong
> and vigorous, believing in their cause, fearing no obstacles and ready to
> overcome all obstacles.

Soviet literature, said Zhdanov, must concern itself with current themes,
inculcate loyalty to Party and state, attack bourgeois culture, show
Soviet man as positive and optimistic, and educate the youth to be
cheerful, confident in its own strength, and unafraid of any difficulties.
The Zhdanov pronouncements threw the literary world into a turmoil.
They were marked by ugly attacks on many writers, including such
talented figures as Anna Akhmatova and Mikhail Zoshchenko. Some
stopped writing, while others adjusted and conformed by writing made-
to-order novels, plays, and poems without any literary merit. The
Zhdanovschina, as it was called, cast a dark blight on Soviet literature,
which lasted, with some slight moderation after 1949, until Stalin's
death.

After this occurrence came the Thaw, with its promises of a better
life to come, of an end to mass terror, and of more attention to man
and his well-being. The writers began to revive their courage and explore
new themes. Some were courageous indeed. . . .

Two . . . works, L. Zorin's play *The Guests* and Ilya Ehrenburg's
novelette *The Thaw*, may serve to illustrate the new notes that were
being struck in the immediate post-Stalinist years. Zorin's play is
essentially a study in generations: the grandfather, a hero of the Revolution who lives austerely and retains his ideals; the son, a high-ranking
bureaucrat, remote from the people, poisoned by power, and leading
a "gluttonous" life as a member of the new Soviet state bourgeoisie;
the grandson, sharing the values of his father and accepting all the
amenities which he has inherited as his due. One sees the outlines
of a new privileged class emerging. This is apparent, too, in Ehrenburg's
The Thaw, in which the principal negative character, Zhuravlev, a factory
director, is portrayed as narrow and self-seeking, neglecting the welfare
of his workers and using whatever means are at his disposal to advance
his own career. Running through Ehrenburg's story is a recurring note
of discontent with Soviet society and the cultural values which pervade

it. In the words of one of his characters: "We have taken a lot of trouble over one half of the human being, but the other half is neglected. The result is that one half of the house is a slum. I remember that article of Gorky's I read long ago, while I was still at school; he said we needed our own Soviet humanism. The word has been forgotten, the task is still to be done. In those days it was only a presentiment, now it's time we tackled it." Speaking through the mouth of another of his characters, Volodya, a disillusioned and cynical hack painter, Ehrenburg has this to say: "Raphael wouldn't be admitted to the Artists' Union. . . . Everybody's shouting about art and nobody cares a fig for it really; that's the sign of our time." Volodya is equally critical of the content of Soviet literature. A writer, he points out, is not expected to have ideas. "What you're meant to look for in a book is ideology. If it's there, what more do you want? It's lunatics that have ideas."

All this was too much. Zorin's attack on the new privileged class and Ehrenburg's pessimistic picture of the cultural values of Soviet society touched tender spots; by mid-1954, chill winds began to blow again. The writers seemed to be getting out of hand, and it was necessary to discipline them. The Second All-Union Writers' Congress, which opened on December 15, 1954, was designed to bring the writers back into line. It was not altogether successful. The congress's proceedings were marked by sharp attacks on the bureaucrats who ran the writers' organization; on the whole, the organizers of the congress were on the defensive. There was a noticeable absence of forceful guidance; indeed, the Party spokesmen at the congress, while denouncing Zorin and his ilk, tried to occupy middle ground. In effect, their message was this: We don't want to go back to the worst excesses and rigid doctrinarism of the Zhdanov era, but at the same time the writers must behave. They must realize that their literary output must serve the interests of the Party. During the next year (1955), the Party controllers of literature tried to enforce this uneasy compromise. They enjoyed only moderate success. It was clear that beneath the surface there was a great deal of resentment among some of the better writers against this new effort to tighten the bonds.

Then came the Twentieth Party Congress in 1956 and Khrushchev's dramatic attack on Stalin. A number of writers interpreted this as the signal for a new era of liberalism, and bold new themes began to be aired. Real criticism of some of the more unsavory aspects of Soviet reality began to find its way into literature; some of the most sacrosanct features of the regime were openly challenged and condemned.

What were these themes? First, there was a continuation of the attack on the privileges of the New Class of Party and state bureaucrats. Second, there was an attempt to escape the compulsions of the political by retreating into a world of private and personal concerns. Third, there was a revolt against what the Russians call *lakirovka*, against varnishing and prettifying Soviet reality, which expressed itself in a passion for truth and for the tearing away of masks. And finally, there was a new stress on humanitarian values, on the need to respect people and to treat them decently, on a call for courageous people who will speak up and fight for their rights, on the need for compassion and the airing of a deep sorrow for the harshnesses and injustices of Soviet life.

Let me illustrate these themes as they found expression in Soviet literature after the Twentieth Party Congress. Vladimir Dudintsev's novel *Not by Bread Alone* may serve as an example of the attack on the New Class. What gave the novel its sense of urgency was not its rather shopworn plot of the inventor who struggles for recognition against bureaucratic opposition but rather the sharpness of its criticism of the bureaucracy as a home of narrow-minded, unprincipled self-seekers concerned primarily with their comforts and their careers. These qualities were summed up in the character called Drozdov, who was portrayed as a typical member of the class.

The novel quickly became a subject of controversy, and the discussion it inspired touched on some of the most sensitive areas of Soviet life. At a public meeting in the Moscow Writers' Club in October, 1956, Konstantin Paustovsky, one of the most respected of the older generation of Soviet writers, rose to Dudintsev's defense and was rebuked for his pains. The cautious summary of his remarks in *Literaturnaya Gazeta* (Literary Gazette) read: "K. Paustovsky went on to tell of his trip to Europe on the liner *Pobeda*, on which he chanced to meet with certain 'responsible' workers who, in his opinion, are akin to Drozdov. From these observations K. Paustovsky drew a series of incorrect conclusions and generalizations to the effect that Drozdovs are a mass phenomenon." The full text of Paustovsky's speech, not published in the Soviet Union, was transcribed at the meeting and subsequently appeared in *L'Express*, in France. It was an amazingly frank denunciation of bureaucratic philistinism. Charging that there were "thousands of Drozdovs" still around, he illustrated their vulgarity and arrogance with descriptions of their behavior on the European tour. Paustovsky continued: "This is not merely a matter of describing a few careerists. It's not simply a matter of careerists. It's all much more complex and more important than that. The problem is that in our country a completely new social stratum exists with impunity and even flourishes up to a certain point—a new petty bourgeois caste. It is a new population of rapacious and propertied persons who have nothing in common with the Revolution, with our regime, or with socialism." He then went on to charge them with having served as Stalin's hatchetmen. "If it weren't for the Drozdovs, such people as Meyerhold, Babel, Artyon Vesyoly, and many others would still be living among us. They were destroyed by the Drozdovs. And they were destroyed in the name of the stinking comfort of these Drozdovs."

Dudintsev and Paustovsky were not alone in directing their fires at the New Class. One of the most moving documents of this period was

Nikolai Zhdanov's story "A Visit Home," which appeared in *Literaturnaya Moskva* early in 1957.* It attacks the great gulf which exists between kolkhoz peasants and Party officials. The story describes how a busy official, now a big shot, returns to his native village to attend his mother's funeral. It is many years since he has been there, and he finds the villagers living in great poverty. The visitor is deeply depressed, most of all when one of the women of the kolkhoz, a soldier's wife, half-apologetically describes how things are to him, a former villager but now a Man from the Center, who presumably can do something about the situation.

"I wanted to ask you," she says, "have they done right by us here? This year we sowed seventy-four acres with hemp. It was just ready when the summer wheat also got ripe for cutting. We should have gathered the hemp, but they ordered us to thresh the grain deliveries and take the grain to the collection center. You know, if you don't do the hemp in time, you lose it, but they wouldn't listen to us; they wanted their grain deliveries and that was that. . . . And so we lost the hemp. And now we've no bread again. Now tell me, is that good or not?"

"She thinks it all depends on me," says the official to himself. And out loud, he answers importantly, "That is a political question. The State must always come first. Everything depends on the level of consciousness of the masses." He's not at all satisfied with his explanation, but the peasant woman looks pleased, and he thinks, "She is happy because the conversation has reached a high level." But the official's conscience gnaws at him; he can't face the misery of the people. He longs to escape back to his comfortable office in Moscow, and at the end of the story we see him on the train going back to Moscow, half-dozing in his compartment, unable to fall asleep, still thinking about the village. He begins to dream uneasily. He sees his village again. He sees his mother as he saw her being buried, her face small and dark as she bends toward him, expectant and hopeful, and she asks, as the soldier's wife had asked, "Have they done right by us here?"

Here is still another story—really more a sketch than a story—Yury Nagibin's "The Light in the Window." In a convalescent home, a suite of rooms has for years been kept in readiness for a Very Important Person, who never comes. Day after day, the rooms are thoroughly cleaned by a woman especially hired for the job; even when the home is jammed full these rooms are not used. One fine day the cleaning woman breaks the regulations. She and the porter and his children all sit down in the luxurious room and they turn on its new television set, to the speechless horror of the director, who sees them through the window. In a single act of indiscipline, the cleaning woman sweeps aside the barrier erected between "them"—the New Class—and the people.

* An English translation of this story appears in Edmund Stillman, ed., *Bitter Harvest: The Intellectual Revolt Behind the Iron Curtain* (New York: Praeger Publishers, 1959).

This is literature teaching a new kind of moral; the political symbolism of the story is daring, almost a call to revolt. Not surprisingly, the writer soon found himself under sharp attack.

Side by side with these strictures directed against the state bourgeoisie there also emerged an apolitical literary trend, a turn away from politics to personal concerns, love, family, marriage, and its problems. A popular play by Aleshin called *Odna* (*Alone*) may serve as an example. The plot of the play is simple. A middle-aged engineer, married for sixteen years to an attractive schoolteacher and with a teen-age daughter, becomes hopelessly infatuated with the beautiful wife of a younger colleague. She also falls madly in love with him. They try to fight their love for each other, but in the end they surrender to it. The beautiful young wife leaves her husband; the engineer abandons his wife and child. There is no happy ending. At the conclusion of the play, the abandoned wife simply proclaims her faith that, despite all that has happened, one must try to go on living, one must live decently, and try to fulfill one's capacities.

To understand the excitement and controversy which this play aroused, one must appreciate how far removed it was from the usual political morality play served up to the Russian theatergoer in Moscow. There was no typology, nor were there clearly demarcated positive and negative heroes. All the parties concerned were portrayed as decent people betrayed by their emotions; all acted as human beings, with all their frailties. Western audiences would hardly regard the play as shocking. For Soviet audiences it was new, and they found themselves caught up in what seemed a daring and frank confrontation of an eternal human problem rather than a Party message.

Still other recurrent themes were the protest against prettifying Soviet reality and the call for a new humanism. These received particularly forceful expression in the works of the younger poets. . . .

These were the themes of 1956—love people; seek the truth; let us have a personal life again; we're fed up with the privileges of the bureaucracy. As can be imagined they were not very palatable to the Party leadership. Genuinely shocked and outraged by the unintended consequences of de-Stalinization—the Hungarian revolt, the Polish October, and the intellectual ferment in the Soviet Union—the regime replied in a not unfamiliar pattern: with force in Hungary, with suspicion and reluctant acquiescence in Poland, and with a renewed war on "unhealthy" ideological manifestations in the Soviet Union. After Hungary, the swing of the cultural pendulum moved for a time in a neo-Stalinist direction. The more restive spirits among the Soviet literary intelligentsia were subjected to sharp criticism, called upon to recant, and summoned to meetings to confess their sins.

But some of them were stubborn. They refused to confess their errors and when called upon to speak they said nothing. This led the Party bureaucrats to charge that the writers had joined in what they called a conspiracy of silence. L. Sobolev, one of the most orthodox of the non-Party writers, expressed the regime's concern. Addressing those who had remained silent, he said:

> Your silence is dangerous. It causes disorientation among the readers. What does it mean? What does it conceal? An arrogant contempt for the opinion of others? A contemptuous belief in one's own infallibility? An insulting "How could you possibly understand us?" The pathos of readiness for sacrifice? What does this silence signify? We do not understand it. Neither do the people. Do you know what became known to me yesterday and what shocked me, so that I felt compelled to mount the platform and excite myself beyond the measures permitted by my physician? That in the Western press hypocritically friendly sentiments are being voiced concerning you, you who should speak today but do not. That a "friendly" [Western] hand is being extended towards you. That they are ready to embrace you, that a rope is ready for you that would draw you even further from your own people? Do you know that you are being enjoined to commit "the heroic act of being silent"? The heroics of silence? What strange and poisonous word!

And Sobolev concluded his speech with the fervent hope that the writers would not follow this diabolic advice from the West.

Then came pressure and discipline (though not arrests), and finally the heavy artillery of Khrushchev himself was mobilized to lay down the line. Essentially, Khrushchev's message was this: You must not slander Soviet reality; you must write about the favorable aspects of Soviet life. One may expose the shortcomings and mistakes of individuals, but one cannot attack or challenge the Soviet order itself. All literature must adhere to Party positions, celebrate the nobility of labor, and arouse the people to struggle for new victories in the building of communism.

Some writers obliged. There was a new rash of official, made-to-order novels, such as Kochetov's *The Brothers Yershov*. But the drive toward orthodoxy also met with resistance. Despite the favor shown by the regime to such untalented official hacks as Kochetov, despite Khrushchev's warnings at a series of receptions for writers that they must follow Party directives, and despite the campaign launched against Pasternak for defying the ban on the publication of *Dr. Zhivago*, a number of writers continued to maintain courageous independent positions. . . .

At the Third Writers' Congress, in 1959, Khrushchev called on the writers to settle their own quarrels. Despite this summons, the breach widened between the old-line conformists and the writers pressing for greater creative freedom. It received open expression at the Twenty-second Party Congress in 1961, when Kochetov spoke for the Old Guard and Tvardovsky for the liberals. In the aftermath of the Twenty-second Party Congress, with the renewal of the assault on Stalinism, it appeared for a time that the liberals were carrying the day. There was a new upsurge of hope, a new outburst of critical realism. . . . Writers hastened to exploit the theme of the conflict of the generations. Perhaps the most talented work in this genre was Vasili Aksenov's novel *Ticket to the Stars*, which was published in 1961 and provided a remarkably outspoken airing of the desire on the part of at least some young people to be free to find their own way in life without constant tutelage and official direction.

Perhaps the most powerful work of this period was Aleksandr Solzhenitsyn's description of life in a concentration camp, *One Day in the Life of Ivan Denisovich*, which was published with Khrushchev's personal blessing, but which in turn unleashed a flood of concentration-camp literature that Khrushchev undertook to check by warning that the theme was a delicate one. In the same critical vein as Solzhenitsyn's novel, though less talented, was Fyodor Abramov's *Round and About* [*The New Life*], a frank exposure of the lack of interest of collective farmers in kolkhoz work and a plea for dealing with the problem of improving incentives. An equally unorthodox note was struck by the novelist Viktor Nekrasov, whose objective account in *Novy Mir* of his travels in Italy and America laid him open to the charge of having failed to display the necessary ideological militancy in dealing with bourgeois phenomena. The literary ferment which both preceded and followed the Twenty-second Congress enlisted some of the most creative voices in the younger and middle generations—such poets as Yevtushenko, Voznesensky, and Akhmadullina, and such talented writers of fiction as Aksenov, Kazakov, Nagibin, Nekrasov, and Solzhenitsyn. They numbered among their supporters such respected elder literary figures as Tvardovsky, Ehrenburg, and Paustovsky.

But this time, too, high hopes met frustration. The crackdown began when Khrushchev visited the Manege exhibition in Moscow on December 1, 1962, and singled out the abstract art on exhibition for his now famous dictum, "Such pictures were not painted by the hand of man but by the tail of a donkey!" From painting and sculpture the attack spread to music and literature. Artists, composers, and writers were accused of producing "formalist monstrosities" alien to the people. Nor were the criticisms limited to style and form. Members of the "liberal" group were also accused of besmirching Soviet reality, of failing to defend correct Party positions, of setting themselves up as representatives of the youth against the Party, and even of giving comfort to the enemy. During the next months, the forces of orthodox conformity gave every appearance of being in the saddle, and they joined in a chorus of full-throated denunciation of their liberal rivals.

But appearances turned out to be deceptive. By May, 1963, there were already signs that the conservative campaign had spent its force. Tvardovsky, one of the leaders of the liberal forces, not only retained his editorship of *Novy Mir* but, in a noteworthy interview with Henry Schapiro, the United Press-International correspondent in Moscow, which was published in *Pravda* on May 12, 1963, was able to indicate in an authoritative manner that his cause was far from lost. The Central Committee plenum on ideology which followed in June, while providing a forum for severe criticism of such recalcitrant writers as Nekrasov, stopped short of a heresy hunt. The turning of the tide became more evident in August, when Khrushchev invited Tvardovsky to read his new poem, "Vasili Tyorkin in the Other World," at a reception for foreign writers. The poem itself, as outspoken an attack on the cant and humbug of the Stalinist era as has yet appeared in the Soviet press, was a clear indication that the conservatives would no longer have a clear field to themselves. The rehabilitation of such writers as Voznesensky and Yevtushenko was quick to follow, and though their first works to see the light of day after their disgrace revealed that they had been chastened by their experience, they at least had a public platform again. In the wake of Khrushchev's removal, there were further signs of liberalization. The publication of Ilya Ehrenburg's memoirs, which had been suspended in 1963, was resumed. New poems and short prose pieces by Boris Pasternak were printed in *Novy Mir*. The same magazine, still under Tvardovsky's editorship, provided a home for such controversial writers as Nekrasov, Yefim Dorosh, and Yevtushenko. The swing of the pendulum pointed, at least temporarily, toward some easing of literary controls.

As one looks back on the cultural history of the Soviet Union since the death of Stalin, with its alternating phases of restriction and relaxation, what is most striking is the continued pressure of the more talented writers for greater creative opportunities. One can almost feel them rediscovering their heritage, edging their way toward greater freedom, and becoming, in the grand tradition of the Russian intelligentsia, the voice of conscience against the rulers of society.

Yet it would be profoundly misleading to conclude that the bulk of the so-called liberal wing of the creative intelligentsia is in open rebellion against the Soviet system. There are, of course, isolated heretics who are completely alienated and disillusioned, who write for the drawer, and whose works are not, and cannot be, published. But the goals of the great majority of the so-called "liberals" are more modest. Running through most of the literature which articulates their spirit of protest is a desire for more independence, a search for fresh forms, a distaste for embellishment, a passion for truth, and a concern with the personal life of man. But those who express these values also consider themselves good Soviet patriots, loyal to the communist cause as they understand it. If there is a political program concealed in the interstices of their collective works, it is essentially a plea for a more libertarian form of communism. They do not undertake to present a direct challenge to the system itself.

In this respect the case of Yevtushenko is instructive. A handsome poet of modest talent, he has played a tremendous role as a symbol of youth's discontent. His outlook on the world and his almost messianic attraction for many Soviet young people provide a fascinating mirror of the complexity of their beliefs and aspirations. On the one hand, he shares with them many attitudes which are politically unexceptionable. His patriotic poems, his poems of praise for Castro's Cuba (which he sees as a symbol of the pure uncorrupted revolution), his denunciation

of fascism, his anti-Stalinism and neo-Leninism not only win official
approval but give every appearance of reflecting his own sincere beliefs
as well as those of his youthful auditors. On the other hand, much
of his appeal to the more restive spirits among the youth derives from
the fact that he bursts the bonds of the prescribed orthodoxies. His
highly subjective and even erotic poems, his defense of so-called nihilists
and beatniks, his openly expressed admiration for abstract art, his calls
for the right to travel ("I'm irked by national borders"), his courageous
denunciation of Soviet anti-Semitism in the poem "Babi Yar," and
his insistence on the right of youth to make mistakes all find support
in a generation seeking more elbow room to express its own individuality. But beyond these relatively mild heterodoxies, there are other
dimensions of Yevtushenko's outlook which border on open defiance
of the regime's values. They include declarations in the course of his
travels abroad that he did not believe that capitalism was "going
downhill" and that both East and West had "their failings and unhealthy phenomena," and, finally, the very un-class-conscious pronounce-
ment in his autobiography that "I loathe nationalism. For me the entire
world is composed of two nations only: that of good men and that of
bad men." Such heresies explain the massive effort to discredit him
which was launched in early 1963. . . .

Yevtushenko provides an index of the kind of problem which the
more rebellious young intellectuals present for the regime. Despite
pampering and special privileges, trips abroad, and large editions, he
still overstepped the bounds of approved conduct and invited forms
of repressive control which the Party leaders would probably have
preferred to avoid if they could have achieved their objectives by other
means. In the conservative Kochetov's most recent novel, *Secretary of
the Obkom,* the obkom secretary Denisov, described in the novel as a
"leader of the new type," observes that the younger generation has
"higher demands in everything" than its elders and that "one must
work with it more cleverly . . . without didacticism and shouting; it must
be attracted, led, but not shoved around."

It is a prescription which is not easy to enforce. With every relaxation
of discipline, new heterodoxies are opened. The very fact that so many
of the most talented of the younger (as well as some of the older)
literary figures have rallied to the so-called liberal banner immensely
complicates the task of control. Desirous of using their talent, the
regime still cannot give them their head. It alternates between phases of
liberalization and of tightened controls because no more effective way
of harnessing their energies lies ready at hand. Meanwhile, there is
always the danger that this form of manipulation will alienate the
so-called liberals and turn loyal oppositionists into enemies of the regime.

The creative intellectual in any society is a special breed that cannot be
easily haltered. He seeks outlets for his creativity, and if outlets are
closed, he ceases to function. A very talented writer, E. I. Zamyatin,
who fled Russia in the 1920's, once said, "The best way to kill art

is to canonize one form and one philosophy." And on another occasion he wrote, "The main thing is that there can be a real literature only where it is produced by madmen, hermits, heretics, dreamers, rebels, and skeptics, and not by painstaking and well-meaning officials." In the Soviet Union today, the officials are still in the saddle, but it remains to be seen whether the voices of the heretics, dreamers, rebels, and skeptics can be permanently stilled. It was Jean Cocteau who said, "It is the dictators of art who make possible the disobedience without which art dies." What has been happening on the Soviet literary scene since Stalin's death may serve as a reminder that both disobedience and literature are still alive.

* * *

34

KHRUSHCHEV ON MODERN ART

The first extended pause is in front of one of Falk's paintings.

N. S. Khrushchev: "I would say that this is just a mess. It's hard to understand what this still-life is supposed to represent. I will probably be told that I have not reached the point where I can understand such works—the usual argument of our opponents in culture. Dimitry Stepanovich Polyansky told me a couple of days ago that when his daughter got married, she was given a picture of what was supposed to be a lemon. It consisted of some messy yellow lines which looked, if you will excuse me, as though some child had done his business on the canvas when his mother was away and then spread it around with his hands."

Then, further along: "I don't like jazz. When I hear jazz, it's as if I had gas on the stomach. I used to think it was static when I heard it on the radio. I like music a lot and often listen to it on the radio.

Reprinted, with permission, from *Encounter* (London), April, 1963.

I even went so far as to carry a little Japanese radio around in my pocket. They make them very well there. . . .

"Even Shostakovich surprised us once in this connection. At the final concert of the plenary meeting of the Composers' Union we were regaled with a trio which wasn't entirely pleasurable listening. . . .

"Or take these new dances which are so fashionable now. Some of them are completely improper. You wiggle a certain section of the anatomy, if you'll pardon the expression. It's indecent. As Kogan once said to me when she was looking at a fox-trot, 'I've been married twenty years and never knew that this kind of activity is called the foxtrot!' . . .

"Jazz comes from the Negroes. They've had it for a long time, and here it's treated as a novelty. I understand our own Russian dances a lot better—Georgian and Armenian ones too. They are wonderful dances. . . .

"People tell me that I am behind the times and don't realize it, that our contemporary artists will be appreciated in 100 years. Well, I don't know what will happen in 100 years, but now we have to adopt a definite policy in art, emphasizing it in the press and encouraging it materially. We won't spare a kopek of government money for any artistic daubing. . . .

"As long as I am Chairman of the Council of Ministers, we are going to support a genuine art. We aren't going to give a kopek for pictures painted by jackasses. History can be our judge. For the time being, history has put us at the head of this state, and we have to answer for everything that goes on in it. Therefore we are going to maintain a strict policy in art. I could mention that when I was in England I reached an understanding with Eden. He showed me a picture by a contemporary abstractionist and asked me how I liked it. I said I didn't understand it. He said he didn't understand it either, and asked me what I thought of Picasso. I said I didn't understand Picasso, and Eden said he couldn't understand Picasso either."

When passing by the satirical drawings of Reshetnikov and the Kukriniksy, N. S. Khrushchev indicated his approval, laughing in particular at Reshetnikov's satire on abstractionist painters.

In front of paintings by Andronov, Mikhail and Pavel Nikonov, Basnetsov, and Yegorshina—

V. A. Serov (pointing to these paintings, and especially to "The Raftsmen" by Andronov and "The Geologist" by Nikonov): "Some connoisseurs claim that these pictures are programmatic. We dispute that."

N. S. Khrushchev: "You are entirely correct." Then, in front of "The Geologists": "He can paint and sell these if he wants, but we don't need them. We are going to take these blotches with us into communism, are we? If government funds have been paid for this picture, the person who authorized it will have the sum deducted from his salary. Write out a certificate that this picture has not been acquired by the government. . . .

"But who ordered it? And why? This painting shouldn't have been hung in the exhibition. Pictures should arouse us to perform great deeds. They should inspire a person. But what kind of picture is this? One jackass is riding on another. . . .

"No, we don't need pictures like these. As long as the people support us and have confidence in us we will carry out our own policy in art. And if pictures like these appear, it means that we are not doing our work properly. This includes the Ministry of Culture and the Central Committee's Commission on Ideology."

S. A. Gerasimov (or V. A. Serov): "People say, by the way, that pictures like these are supported in the press. For instance, Konenkov's article in *Izvestia* praises the sculptor Neizvestny and some of the other formalists."

In passing by paintings of Korzhevsky and Zhevadronova, N. S. Khrushchev says: "These are good pictures, especially that one over there. You can feel the essense of youth in it. But why these bad pictures— a spoonful of pitch in a barrel of honey."

A propos a painting by Kugach: "It looks like a real winter scene!"

After a quick look at the upper halls, where the formalist paintings are hung, N. S. Khrushchev says: "What is this anyway? You think we old fellows don't understand you. And we think we are just wasting money on you. Are you pederasts or normal people? I'll be perfectly straightforward with you; we won't spend a kopek on your art. Just give me a list of those of you who want to go abroad, to the so-called 'free world.' We'll give you foreign passports tomorrow, and you can get out. Your prospects here are nil. What is hung here is simply anti-Soviet. It's amoral. Art should ennoble the individual and arouse him to action. And what have you set out here? Who painted this picture? I want to talk to him. What's the good of a picture like this? To cover animals with?"

The painter, Zheltovsky, comes forward.

N. S. Khrushchev: "You're a nice-looking lad, but how could you paint something like this? We should take down your pants and set you down in a clump of nettles until you understand your mistakes. You should be ashamed. Are you a pederast or a normal man? Do you want to go abroad? Go on, then; we'll take you free as far as the border. Live out there in the 'free world.' Study in the school of capitalism, and then you'll know what's what. But we aren't going to spend a kopek on this dog shit. We have the right to send you out to cut trees until you've paid back the money the state has spent on you. The people and government have taken a lot of trouble with you, and you pay them back with this shit. They say you like to associate with foreigners. A lot of them are our enemies, don't forget."

Then, in front of a painting by Gribkov: "What's this?"

Gribkov: "It's the year 1917."

N. S. Kh: "Phooey. How much the state has spent on you, and this is how you repay it. My opinion is that you can all go to hell abroad. This is an art for donkeys. . . .

"Comrade Ilyichev, I am even more upset by the way your section is doing its work. And how about the Ministry of Culture? Do you accept this? Are you afraid to criticize? . . .

"They say that some of our writers praise these pictures and buy them. That's because our honoraria are high. Our writers are too prosperous and have money to throw away."

Belyutin, one of the ideologists of the formalists, comes up.

N. S. Kh: "Who are you? Who are your parents?"

Belyutin answers.

N. S. Kh: "Do you want to go abroad? Who supports you?"

Belyutin: "I am a teacher."

N. S. Kh: "How can such a person teach? People like him should be cleared out of the teaching profession. They shouldn't be allowed to teach in the universities. Go abroad if you want; and if you don't want to, we'll send you anyway. I can't even talk about this without getting angry. I'm a patriot."

In front of a painting by Shorts: "Why aren't you ashamed of this mess? Who are your parents?"

Shorts gives information about his parents, mentioning that his mother is dead.

N. S. Kh: "It's a pity, of course, that your mother is dead, but maybe it's lucky for her that she can't see how her son is spending his time. What master are you serving anyway? Our paths are different. You've either got to get out or paint differently. As you are, there's no future for you on our soil."

One of the bystanders says, "These are graphic artists. They do these pictures in their spare time to improve their skill" (general laughter).

N. S. Kh: "I remember the Ukrainian satirist, Ostap Vishnay. In one article he gives the following conversation: 'Do you believe in God?' and the answer, 'At work I don't, and at home I do.' That's what these scratchings of yours are like. . . .

"I used to be on friendly terms with the sculptor, Merkuryev. He was a great man, a real man. Once, in the Dresden Gallery, he pointed to some paintings of the Dutch masters and told me that our artists maintain that to appreciate a painting you have to stand back from it. The Dutch masters painted differently. You can look at their pictures through a magnifying glass and still admire them. But your paintings just give a person constipation, if you'll excuse the expression. They don't arouse any other feelings at all."

Turning to Zhutovsky's self-portrait: "Externally there is no resemblance. The picture is unnatural. But there is certainly a spiritual resemblance between the portrait and the original. You are stealing from society. You are a parasite. We have to organize our society so that it will be clear who is useful and who is useless. What right do you have to live in an apartment built by genuine people, one made of real materials?"

Zhutovsky: "But these are just experiments. They help us develop."

N. S. Kh: "Judging by these experiments, I am entitled to think that you are pederasts, and for that you can get ten years. You've gone out of your minds, and now you want to deflect us from the proper course. No, you won't get away with it. . . .

"Gentlemen, we are declaring war on you."

*   *   *

35

RUSSIAN WRITERS AND THE SECRET POLICE

ANATOLY KUZNETSOV

It is a frightful story that I have to tell. Sometimes it seems to me as though it never happened, that it was just a nightmare. If only that were true.

The Soviet system remains firmly in power in Russia only thanks to an exceptionally powerful apparatus of oppression and primarily thanks to what has been called at various times the Cheka, the GPU, the NKVD, the MGB, and the KGB. In other words, the secret police, or the Soviet Gestapo.

Everybody knows that the number of people murdered by the secret police runs into many millions. But when we come to reckon the number of people who are terrorized and deformed by them, then we have to include the whole population of the Soviet Union. The KGB's tentacles reach, like cancerous growths, into every branch of life in Russia. And in particular into the world of Soviet literature.

I do not know a single writer in Russia who has not had some connection with the KGB. This connection can be one of three different kinds.

The first kind: You collaborate enthusiastically with the KGB. In that case you have every chance of propspering.

The second kind: You acknowledge your duty toward the KGB, but you refuse to collaborate directly. In that case you are deprived of a great deal, and in particular of the prospect of traveling abroad.

The third kind: You brush aside all advances made by the KGB and enter into conflict with them. In that case your works are not published and you may even find yourself in a concentration camp.

How all this works out in practice I shall explain by reference to my own experience. As a matter of fact a similar story could be told by any Russian writer who is even slightly known. But they are there, and they want to live, and so they keep quiet.

In August, 1951, I was preparing for the first time in my life to travel abroad, to France. I had been included in a delegation of writers. It was a most impressive experience, because in the Soviet Union the only people who are allowed to travel abroad are those with "clean" records, who have been thoroughly "vetted," who had not been in any trouble at their work or in their political activities, who have never in their lives consulted a psychiatrist, who have never been before the courts, and so on and so forth.

What is more, the whole process of getting one's papers in order lasts many months and requires a mass of references, questionnaires, secret signatures, and confidential advice on how to behave. By the time a person has gone through this procedure he is so intimidated and tensed up that the trip begins to seem like some religious ritual.

I had already gone through this intimidating procedure and was packing my case when someone telephoned to say that people from the secret police were going to visit me. A couple of men appeared and showed me their identity cards. They made a few jokes, chatted about literature, then got down to business:

"You realize, of course, why we've come. One of our comrades will be traveling, as usual, with your delegation. But it will be difficult for him to cope on his own. So you will help him. You just keep an eye out to see that nobody slips away and stays abroad, to see who talks to whom, and to see how people behave."

"No, I don't want to," I said.

"You must."

"Let somebody else do it."

"Others will be doing it."

"I don't want to."

"Well, then, we shall have to reconsider. In that case, what's the point of your going."

I remained silent, quite overcome. And the two men started to explain to me that this was the most usual and most natural thing: No group of tourists and no delegation could do without its "comrade" and the voluntary assistants attached to him. The Western world was devilishly cunning, and we had to be incredibly vigilant. Either I would undertake to maintain contact with the "comrade" or else my trip would be canceled and I would never be allowed to travel anywhere abroad. The "comrade" would be a very pleasant person, and he would approach me himself, saying: "Greetings from Mikhail Mikhailovich."

Our delegation consisted of some fifteen writers and editors of Moscow magazines, and we all gathered at the harbor in Leningrad to embark on the liner *Latvia*. I looked at each of the delegates and wondered: Which one of them is it? The person in charge of the delegation was a woman from Intourist who kept counting everybody as if we were chickens. Maybe she was the "comrade"?

But when we were aboard the ship it was one of the editors who came up to me and, with a crooked grin, said "Greetings from Mikhail Mikhailovich."

He was a boorish fool, who spied openly and cynically on everybody, who also kept counting up the delegation, and who listened greedily to every conversation. But I noticed that some of the writers were also keeping their eyes about them, especially a certain Sytin, who now holds one of the key jobs in the Soviet film world. Of the fifteen members of the delegation, one was from Intourist, one was the "comrade" and at least five were "voluntary assistants." Later I came to understand that this was the usual arrangement.

If five people are traveling abroad, at least two of them are informers. If two are traveling, at least one must be an informer. And if there's only one person, then he is an informer on himself.

Perhaps some other Russian writer will also, like me, be reduced to blind horror and will wrench himself out of the control of the KGB and reveal what they did to him. Perhaps Yevtushenko will one day tell of the conditions on which he was allowed to travel round the world and the reports he had to write.

Because we are all obliged to write reports after a trip abroad.

I was ordered to write such a report after my trip to Paris. I went through agonies trying to guess what our "comrade" would write, so that I would agree with him. On one occasion someone had turned up late for the bus, and the "comrade" had been green from fright. I described that incident in detail and others like it. I devoted about half the report to reporting on myself, because that is essential—where I had gone, whom I had met, and what had been said.

But my report wasn't to the liking of someone high up. Eight years passed before I was again allowed to travel abroad, this time to Britain. You will now learn the price I had to pay for that.

I lived the whole of those eight years in Tula, and throughout that time the "comrades" kept coming to see me. When I came to inquire

of other writers it appeared that this was the most ordinary occurrence—
they went to see everybody, everybody. And it depended on the extent
of the writer's decency which of the three categories of collaboration he
would choose.

They would ask me gently and politely about my life, about what I
was working on, what my friends Yevtushenko, Aksenov, Gladilin, and
others were doing, what they were saying, and what sort of people they
were. At first I said only favorable things and spoke highly of them. But
they objected. Yevtushenko was committing mistakes, I was not watching
carefully enough, I must provoke him to argument and report what was
really going on inside him. They started to talk to me more sharply and
to use threats.

At this I could take no more. I shouted at them that it was not proper
behavior and I asked them to keep away from me. I said I didn't see
anything bad around me, no conspiracies and nothing anti-Soviet. If I
did see anything, then I would ring them up. And with that they vanished.

I couldn't believe my luck. So that, it seemed, was the way to talk to
them. After all, what could they do to me? I was already a well-known
writer, my books were being published in forty different countries, and
I could permit myself the luxury of having nothing to do with such
characters.

How very wrong I was! I was simply transferred to the second category.

My home in Tula was open to everybody. One day there appeared a
very pleasant young man, a student at the Polytechnic Institute, who
unburdened himself to me at great length. He told me that he and his
fellow students were being taught how to make missiles and were made
to sign terrifying documents about the preservation of state secrets. He
said he had dreamt of being an inventor, but instead of that he was
obliged to work out, according to special "man-kill" formulas, how many
missiles were needed per thousand human lives.

The Soviet Union was, in his opinion, a fascist country. The students,
he said, were publishing a handwritten magazine and were being arrested.
Finally he burst into tears. I tried to calm him. Through his tears he
screamed that he would produce the magazine himself. I said that was
stupid and that he would prove nothing like that.

Not long afterward somebody phoned me and asked me to meet him
on the square outside. It was one of the "comrades" I knew, who invited
me to sit on the bench and said: "Why didn't you ring us up? Somebody
reveals state secrets to you and tells you various formulas, gives you information about underground papers, and you simply object that that
is not the right way. What is the right way, then, in your opinion?"

I tremble when I write now about that conversation on the bench in
the square. For me it was like a red-hot frying pan. I was forgiven and
allowed to go, but I was warned.

From that time in 1963 I was regularly followed. Not, of course, that
I was an anti-Soviet element or that I was intending to organize some
plot. On the contrary, I was a member of the Communist Party, a recog-

nized Soviet writer, and I wanted only one thing: to go on writing. But I had automatically to be followed, because I came in the second category.

Then I took a room in Yasnaya Polyana where I wrote a novel. I became friendly with the scholars working in the Tolstoy Museum, and they were very kind to me, especially the intelligent and attractive Luiza Senina.

One day she came to my room and told me she had been appointed to follow every step I made and report every word I said. But, she said, I was good and trusting and she couldn't do it any more; she was having nightmares.

One of the "scholars" at Yasnaya Polyana was an officer of the KGB, and everybody, from the director down to the guides, had to report to him. Every foreigner who visited Yasnaya Polyana was kept under specially strict surveillance. The fact that I had taken a room there was especially suspicious, and they were trying to get something out of her about me. What was she to do? She would be sacked!

I was particularly shaken by the fact that this was taking place on the revered territory of Tolstoy's estate. "Well," I said, "let's try and save you; let's make something up together."

I did not succeed in saving her. On the contrary, out of inexperience, I wrecked her life. One day in the café a KGB officer in civilian clothes sat down opposite me and started joking and asking odd questions. I looked him straight in the face and said: "Listen, by dint of pure logic, I have realized that you are from the security and that you're interested in me. So let's talk like man to man. What do you want to know? You ask the questions and I'll give you straight answers. It'll be easier for you and for me."

He was terribly embarrassed and started muttering that he was not interested in me personally, that I was above any suspicion, that I had well-known friends in Moscow, that they sometimes behaved rather strangely, and that in general my circle of acquaintances. . . .

Later, in his own time, he reached his own conclusions. Luiza Senina was dismissed after a frightful row, was given a hopeless reference, was a long time without work until she was given a job as a librarian in some trade school, where she still is today.

I hurried away from Yasnaya Polyana as if a curse had been laid on it.

But wherever you live you still have contact with people. Young writers kept coming to see me, bringing their works with them. There was one very sweet girl, a student at the teacher's institute, Tanya Subbotina, who came along in this way and then one day asked me to go outside on the street with her.

Once she was sure we were alone she said she had been forced to come to me and told to try and become my mistress and report on everything I did. Otherwise, they threatened, she would be turned out of the institute. She was not doing very well there, and they could well have done it.

Heavens above! I have recounted only two incidents, because they are no longer secret and everything is already very well known to the KGB in Tula. Poor Tanya got completely confused and told everything to her "comrades."

But I was struck with the way people would immediately tell me everything, warn me and give me advice. I cannot say any more, so as not to harm them. After all, they are there, they are not to blame, they are the victims.

There are others whom even I do not know. A stranger phoned me from a call box at a tram stop and told me what was in my letters to my mother and which foreign magazine I had at home:

"What on earth are you doing? Don't you realize that all your mail is opened? That your neighbors on both sides and above you are watching you? That your phone conversations are recorded?"

He gave no name and hung up. Thanks. But I just couldn't understand: What was the point of this horror? I was writing literary works and had no intention of engaging in political activity. I was a writer. What do you want from me? That I should stop to think before every word I said on the telephone?

In fact, on one occasion the telephone at home started tinkling in an odd way. I took off the receiver but heard no ringing tone, so I started banging on the cradle. Suddenly a tired voice at the other end of the line said: "Please don't keep banging; have patience. We're switching you over to another recording machine. It's a complicated system—you understand."

Later an electrician appeared and changed the electricity meter, fitting a new one, freshly sealed, with a microphone, no doubt.

In 1967 I locked up my flat and went off on a long trip. Two days after I left, in the middle of the night there was a fire in my study and everything in it was destroyed. The firemen who came to the scene prevented the whole flat from being destroyed but never discovered what caused the fire. But my papers and manuscripts escaped by a real miracle: Literally on the day of my departure I had moved the cupboard with the manuscripts into another room, intending to move my study there on my return.

After that I kept my manuscripts buried in the ground. Another reason was that, whenever I left my flat for any length of time afterward, I recognized by various signs that someone had been in the flat in my absence.

I frequently asked various top people about my having a trip abroad but without much hope. I wanted to see the world. They were always ready to promise me, but that was the end of it. Others went traveling, but not me.

Then, unexpectedly, the Paris publishers, Les Editeurs Français Réunis, invited me to spend a month in Paris as part of the payment for my *Babi Yar*. I thought that the authorities must understand at last that I was no enemy, so I made my application and started to go through the procedural marathon. I got right on to the end of it only to be told that the Union of Writers had no money for my trip. Then they told me in a whisper that it was simply that the authorities in Tula had formally sanctioned my departure, but that Safronov, the Propaganda Secretary, had said by telephone that I should not be allowed to go.

I said in my statement how my writings were maltreated. But they also deformed my whole life. I couldn't speak on the telephone; I practically stopped writing letters; and I saw an informer in every one of my acquaintances. I began to ponder: What sense is there in such a life at all?

Here is an extract from my diary in October, 1967. "I have not been able to sleep for several days now. I am just a great lump of nostalgia. I turn over in my mind what I have written and compare it with what I would like to write and what I could write. I see before me years and years of life in which I could have got to know and study and understand and create so much and which have been wasted. On what, it is frightful to think about. . . . When I quote what I wrote in *Babi Yar* I feel like an ant, cemented up in the foundations of a house. All around there is nothing but stones, walls, and darkness. To live to the end of my life with this feeling of being stifled, in this state of being buried alive."

That was just after the trial of Sinyavsky and Daniel. Solzhenitsyn's writings were no longer being published. The process of rehabilitating Stalin had begun.

I had my own troubles. There was an unpublicized row over *Babi Yar*. They suddenly decided that it ought not to have been published. At *Yunost* they told me that it was practically an accident that it had ever appeared at all and that a month later its publication would have been out of the question. In any case they forbade the reprinting of it.

Before the Writers' Congress, to which I was to be a delegate from Tula, Solzhenitsyn sent me a copy of his famous letter [in which he denounced censorship]. I spent several nights thinking it over. At home they wondered what was the matter with me. I said: "Solzhenitsyn is inviting me to commit suicide with him."

Yes, I could not find in myself the courage, and I probably fully deserved Solzhenitsyn's contempt. I simply did not attend the congress. I signed no protests, either then or later. I saved my own skin and kept out of things. Others were expelled from the Party and from the union and were no longer published. But they continued to publish me, and the "comrades" resumed their kindly and friendly attention.

How movingly they explained to me that the situation among the intelligentsia was very complicated. That people as high-strung as the writers, however clever they were, were in revolt and they did not want to resort to tough measures. . . . I had done very well, they said, not to sign any protests; that was not the business of an artist. But I ought to try and influence my misguided friends and make them understand that if they did not stop causing trouble, then—well, you understand.

I went from town to town trying to keep out of the way of these "comrades," from Moscow to Leningrad, to Kiev. Many people there probably remember my asking: What are you going to do? What is the way out? What is there to hope for? Nobody knew anything. Intelligent people in Russia feel only horror. There is nothing but darkness ahead.

On the night of August 20, 1968, Russian tanks entered Czechoslovakia. I spent several days listening to the radio. Many people in Russia wept during those days. It marked, they said, the turn to fascism.

It came over me somehow of itself. I realized that I could not remain there any longer, that every day, every month, and every year would see only a piling up of horror and cowardice inside me. . . .

But Russia is as well-defended as a prison. Just read Anatoly Marchenko's remarkable *My Testimony*. He wanted only one thing: to get out. They caught him forty yards from the frontier and threw him into the same camp as Daniel. Marchenko's description of that present-day concentration camp is enough to make your hair stand on end.

Then I received another invitation, this time from America, from the Dial Press, which had allotted $5,000 for my trip. I began to attend all the meetings in Tula; I presented Safronov with signed copies of my books; and I always turned up on time for talks with the "comrades" and spent six months fixing my papers for America.

Then I was turned down again, with the explanation that the Dial Press had published Solzhenitsyn as well as me and they were therefore enemies. It was clear from certain details that once again it was the KGB who would not let me out. This coincided with some fierce criticism of my latest writing in the press.

Now I began to feel myself run down and hemmed in like a wolf. I went down to Batumi to study the lie of the land. The whole of the holiday coast of the Black Sea is under the strongest guard. When darkness falls patrols drive everybody away from the water. Seachlights play over the beach and the sea. Radar installations detect even a child's ball floating on the surface of the sea.

But I had made up my mind to swim under water to Turkey with the help of an aqualung, entering the water before the patrols appeared and pushing in front of myself an underwater raft with spare oxygen containers. I would swim by compass just one night, otherwise I would be detected in the morning by helicopters that were about like flies. I had trained myself to swim without stopping for fifteen hours. I started on the building of my raft.

It was frightening all the same. I imagined myself being cut in two in the darkness by a submarine at full speed. They are about the place like sharks. Or I would drown.

So I decided to make one last desperate effort to obtain permission for a trip abroad. I no longer thought of anything but getting out, at any price.

Night and day I had going round in my mind only that: to get away, away, away from that monstrous country, from those scoundrels, from that KGB. Let me get out, even to the Antarctic, even to the Sahara, so long as they are not there. I just could not go on.

It was stronger than me; it was the animal instinct for self-preservation probably—I was at least a living being. I wrote in *Babi Yar* that by the time I was fourteen I should have been shot twenty times. That I was still alive was practically by a miracle, a sort of misunderstanding. So there we are: According to the rules of the KGB I should now be shot for the twenty-first time. If only because I went straight at them and got out. If only because I am writing this. And I shall go on writing, as long as there's life in me.

Now listen to what the Russian writer, Anatoly Kuznetsov, did. He said to himself: "You have to imagine that they are the Gestapo and think what they like most of all. Informers are what they like. Fine. So they'll get a real piece of informing." I hinted to the "comrades" that it seemed as though an anti-Soviet plot was being hatched among the writers. They were really impressed and believed me. They demanded some facts, and of those I had a headful.

My report revealed that the writers were preparing to publish a dangerous underground magazine called *The Polar Star* or *The Spark*, but they were still arguing about the name. I said that the people who are going to publish it included Yevtushenko, Tabakov, Arkady Raikin, etc., etc. I said they were collecting money and manuscripts. The first number would start with Academician Sakharov's memorandum. I very much wanted to add that they also intended to blow up the Kremlin, but that would have been too obvious an exaggeration. I was transferred to the first category.

That's how I came to be in Britain. I brought a copy of my report with me, photographed on film, because it is the most remarkable work I have ever written. The rest was easy. Only six months' filling in forms, a promise to write a novel about Lenin, just one personal agent—Andzhaparidze—and I didn't have to go swimming in the Black Sea. (Who knows? Maybe they have got radar that operates even under water.) On July 24 I got out of Russia on the same plane as Gerald Brooke, and I don't know which of us was the more moved, as he looked out at the blue sky.

I managed to get out and I'm still alive. You can try me if you wish. I have still not come round; I still feel as if I lay on the edge of a sea, groaning, exhausted, and bleeding. But it is the sea. I have got away from them.

I now believe that the main reason why many highly intelligent and able people do not escape from there is that the Soviet regime has forced them to commit such cowardly acts that no amount of repentence can absolve them. There is no way out.

But really, what would you say if you learned that Leo Tolstoy had been a secret police agent and had written reports on all the foreigners visiting his Yasnaya Polyana? Or, that Dostoyevsky informed on his best friends? Would it be possible after that to have any respect for their works, however, brilliant they were? I personally have no answer to that question. The only thing I can say is that Dostoyevsky and Tolstoy did not live in Soviet Russia.

If you are a citizen of Soviet Russia, you automatically cannot be a 100 per cent decent person. Cowardly silence or half-truths—are those not lies? I have told you only about myself. But, believe me, there are very many others who could tell a similar story. Let me leave it at that.

*　　　*　　　*

36

THE THREAT TO INTELLECTUAL FREEDOM

ANDREI D. SAKHAROV

This is a threat to the independence and worth of the human personality, a threat to the meaning of human life.

Nothing threatens freedom of the personality and the meaning of life like war, poverty, terror. But there are also indirect and only slightly more remote dangers.

One of these is the stupefaction of man (the "gray mass," to use the cynical term of bourgeois prognosticators) by mass culture, with its intentional or commercially motivated lowering of intellectual level and content, with its stress on entertainment or utilitarianism, and with its carefully protective censorship.

Another example is related to the question of education. A system of education under government control, separation of school and church, universal free education—all these are great achievements of social progress. But everything has a reverse side. In this case it is excessive standardization, extending to the teaching process itself, to the curriculum, especially in literature, history, civics, geography, and to the system of examinations.

One cannot but see a danger in excessive reference to authority and in the limitation of discussion and intellectual boldness at an age when personal convictions are beginning to be formed. In the old China, the systems of examinations for official positions led to mental stagnation and to the canonizing of the reactionary aspects of Confucianism. It is highly undersirable to have anything like that in a modern society.

Modern technology and mass psychology constantly suggest new possibilities of managing the norms of behavior, the strivings and convictions of masses of people. This involves not only management through information based on the theory of advertising and mass psychology, but also more technical methods that are widely discussed in the press abroad. Examples are biochemical control of the birthrate, biochemical control of psychic processes, and electronic control of such processes.

It seems to me that we cannot completely ignore these new methods or prohibit the progress of science and technology, but we must be clearly aware of the awesome danger to basic human values and to the meaning of life that may be concealed in the misuse of technical and biochemical methods and the methods of mass psychology.

Man must not be turned into a chicken or a rat as in the well-known experiments in which elation is induced electrically through electrodes inserted into the brain. Related to this is the question of the ever increasing use of tranquilizers and antidepressants, legal and illegal narcotics, and so forth.

We also must not forget the very real danger mentioned by Norbert Wiener in his book *Cybernetics*, namely the absence in cybernetic machines of stable human norms of behavior. The tempting, unprecedented power that mankind, or, even worse, a particular group in a divided mankind, may derive from the wise counsels of its future intellectual aides, the artificial "thinking" automata, may become, as Wiener warned, a fatal trap; the counsels may turn out to be incredibly insidious and, instead of pursuing human objectives, may pursue completely abstract problems that had been transformed in an unforeseen manner in the artificial brain.

Such a danger will become quite real in a few decades if human values, particularly freedom of thought, will not be strengthened, if alienation will not be eliminated.

Let us now return to the dangers of today, to the need for intellectual freedom, which will enable the public at large and the intelligentsia to control and assess all acts, designs, and decisions of the ruling group.

Marx once wrote that the illusion that the "bosses know everything best" and "only the higher circles familiar with the official nature of things can pass judgment" was held by officials who equate the public weal with governmental authority.

Both Marx and Lenin always stressed the viciousness of a bureaucratic system as the opposite of a democratic system. Lenin used to say that every cook should learn how to govern. Now the diversity and complexity of social phenomena and the dangers facing mankind have become immeasurably greater; and it is therefore all the more important that mankind be protected against the danger of dogmatic and voluntaristic errors, which are inevitable when decisions are reached in a closed circle of secret advisers or shadow cabinets.

It is no wonder that the problem of censorship (in the broadest sense of the word) has been one of the central issues in the ideological struggle of the last few years. Here is what a progressive American sociologist, Lewis A. Coser, has to say on this point:

"It would be absurd to attribute the alienation of many avant-garde authors solely to the battle with the censors; yet one may well maintain that those battles contributed in no mean measure to such alienation. To these authors, the censor came to be the very symbol of the Philistinism, hyprocrisy, and meanness of bourgeois society.

"Many an author who was initially apolitical was drawn to the political left in the United States because the left was in the forefront of the battle against censorship. The close alliance of avant-garde art with avant-garde political and social radicalism can be accounted for, at least in part, by the fact that they came to be merged in the mind of many as a single battle for freedom against all repression." (I quote from an article by Igor Kon, published in *Novy Mir* in January, 1968.)

We are all familiar with the passionate and closely argued appeal against censorship by the outstanding Soviet writer A. Solzhenitsyn. He as well as G. Vladimov, G. Svirsky, and other writers who have spoken out on the subject have clearly shown how incompetent censorship destroys the living soul of Soviet literature; but the same applies, of course, to all other manifestations of social thought, causing stagnation and dullness and preventing fresh and deep ideas.

Such ideas, after all, can arise only in discussion, in the face of objections, only if there is a potential possibility of expressing not only true, but also dubious ideas. This was clear to the philosophers of ancient Greece, and hardly anyone nowadays would have any doubts on that score. But after fifty years of complete domination over the minds of an entire nation, our leaders seem to fear even allusions to such a discussion.

At this point we must touch on some disgraceful tendencies that have become evident in the last few years. We will cite only a few isolated examples without trying to create a whole picture. The crippling censorship of Soviet artistic and political literature has again been intensified. Dozens of brilliant writings cannot see the light of day. They include some of the best of Solzhenitsyn's works, executed with great artistic and moral force and containing profound artistic and philosophical generalizations. Is this not a disgrace?

Wide indignation has been aroused by the recent decree adopted by the Supreme Soviet of the Russian Republic, amending the Criminal Code in direct contravention of the civil rights proclaimed by our Constitution. [The decree included literary protests among acts punishable under Article 190, which deals with failure to report crimes.]

The Daniel-Sinyavsky trial, which has been condemned by the progressive public in the Soviet Union and abroad (from Louis Aragon to Graham Greene) and has compromised the communist system, has still not been reviewed. The two writers languish in a camp with a strict regime and are being subjected (especially Daniel) to harsh humiliations and ordeals.

Most political prisoners are now kept in a group of camps in the Mordvinian Republic, where the total number of prisoners, including criminals, is about 50,000. According to available information, the regime has become increasingly severe in these camps, with personnel left over from Stalinist times playing an increasing role. It should be said, in all fairness, that a certain improvement has been noted very recently; it is to be hoped that this turn of events will continue.

The restoration of Leninist principles of public control over places of imprisonment would undoubtedly be a healthy development. Equally important would be a complete amnesty of political prisoners, and not just the recent limited amnesty, which was proclaimed on the fiftieth anniversary of the October Revolution as a result of a temporary victory of rightest tendencies in our leadership. There should also be a review of all political trials that are still raising doubts among the progressive public.

Was it not disgraceful to allow the arrest, twelve-month detention without trial, and then the conviction and sentencing to terms of five to seven years of Ginzburg, Galanskov, and others for activities that actually amounted to a defense of civil liberties and (partly, as an example) of Daniel and Sinyavsky personally. The author of these lines sent an appeal to the Party's Central Committee on February 11, 1967, asking that the Ginzburg-Galanskov case be closed. He received no reply and no explanations on the substance of the case. It was only later that he heard there had been an attempt (apparently inspired by Semichastny, the former chairman of the KGB) to slander the present writer and several other persons on the basis of inspired false testimony by one of the accused in the Ginzburg-Galanskov case. Subsequently the testimony of that person—Dobrovolsky—was used at the trial as evidence to show that Ginzburg and Galanskov had ties with a foreign anti-Soviet organization, which one cannot help but doubt.

Was it not disgraceful to permit the conviction and sentencing (to three years in camps) of Khaustov and Bukovsky for participation in a meeting in defense of their comrades? Was it not disgraceful to allow persecution, in the best witch-hunt tradition, of dozens of members of the Soviet intelligentsia who spoke out against the arbitrariness of judicial and psychiatric agencies, to attempt to force honorable people to sign false, hypocritical "retractions," to dismiss and blacklist people, to deprive young writers, editors, and other members of the intelligentsia of all means of existence?

Here is a typical example of this kind of activity.

Comrade B., a woman editor of books on motion pictures, was summoned to the Party's district committee. The first question was, "Who gave you the letter in defense of Ginzburg to sign?" "Allow me not to reply to that question," she answered.

"All right, you can go, we want to talk this over," she was told.

The decision was to expel the woman from the Party and to recommend that she be dismissed from her job and barred from working anywhere else in the field of culture.

With such methods of persuasion and indoctrination the Party can hardly expect to claim the role of spiritual leader of mankind.

Was it not disgraceful to have the speech at the Moscow Party conference by the president of the Academy of Sciences [Mstislav V. Keldysh], who is evidently either too intimidated or too dogmatic in his views? Is it not disgraceful to allow another backsliding into anti-Semitism in our appointments policy (incidentally, in the highest bureaucratic elite of our government, the spirit of anti-Semitism was never fully dispelled after the 1930's).

Was it not disgraceful to continue to restrict the civil rights of the Crimean Tatars, who lost about 46 per cent of their numbers (mainly children and old people) in the Stalinist repressions? Nationality problems will continue to be a reason for unrest and dissatisfaction unless all departures from Leninist principles are acknowledged and analyzed and firm steps are taken to correct mistakes.

Is it not highly disgraceful and dangerous to make increasingly frequent attempts, either directly or indirectly (through silence), to publicly rehabilitate Stalin, his associates, and his policy, his pseudosocialism of terroristic bureaucracy, a socialism of hypocrisy and ostentatious growth that was at best a quantitative and one-sided growth involving the loss of many qualitative features? (This is a reference to the basic tendencies and consequences of Stalin's policy, or Stalinism, rather than a comprehensive assessment of the entire diversified situation in a huge country with 200 million people.)

Although all these disgraceful phenomena are still far from the monstrous scale of the crimes of Stalinism and rather resemble in scope the sadly famous McCarthyism of the cold war era, the Soviet public cannot but be highly disturbed and indignant and display vigilance even in the face of insignificant manifestations of neo-Stalinism in our country.

We are convinced that the world's Communists will also view negatively any attempts to revive Stalinism in our country, which would, after all, be an awful blow to the attractive force of Communist ideas throughout the world.

Today the key to a progressive restructuring of the system of government in the interests of mankind lies in intellectual freedom. This has been understood, in particular, by the Czechoslovaks, and there can be no doubt that we should support their bold initiative, which is so valuable for the future of socialism and all mankind. That support should be political and, in the early stages, include increased economic aid.

The situation involving censorship (Glavlit) in our country is such that it can hardly be corrected for any length of time simply by "liberalized" directives. Major organizational and legislative measures are required, for example, adoption of a special law on press and information that would clearly and convincingly define what can and what cannot be printed and would place the responsibility on competent people who would be under public control. It is essential that the exchange of information on an international scale (press, tourism, and so forth) be expanded in every way, that we get to know ourselves better, that we not try to save on sociological, political, and economic research and surveys, which should be conducted not only according to government-controlled program (otherwise we might be tempted to avoid "unpleasant" subjects and questions).

*   *   *

XI

The National Minorities

The lack of a national identity in its name reflects the multinational character of the Soviet state. No nation in the world has such an ethnically variegated population. There are 177 distinct nationalities, tribes, and linguistic groups in the Soviet Union, of which some 20 number more than a million people. By far the dominant nationality is the Great Russian, comprising slightly more than half of the entire population.

A society composed of so many diverse and often antagonistic races and nationalities could be expected to have difficulty achieving a general consensus on social and political goals. The problems are magnified in a centralized, highly authoritarian regime. From the Tsarist legacy, the Bolsheviks inherited a tradition of Russia as a "prison of nations." Lenin and the Communist Party made the 1917 Revolution in the name of national self-determination in order to enlist the support of the national minorities; the Soviet regime, while not conceding genuine self-determination, has done much to encourage the cultural self-expression of the non-Russian peoples. But the Tsarist legacy remains. The dilemma of how to maintain a politically centralized regime and at the same time permit each nationality to possess cultural and administrative autonomy has yet to be solved. Nowhere is the dilemma more evident than in the field of education, where many minority groups want instruction in the local language while the central authorities in Moscow press to make Russian the lingua franca of the country. Also, because the Russians have dominated the Soviet state, there exist among several of the minorities deep undercurrents of anti-Russian feeling.

The nationality problem has led to the constitutional device of a federal system of government. Fifteen of the largest nationalities have a special status as Union republics with the legal right to secede from the Union. Other nationalities are administratively organized into autonomous republics, autonomous regions, and national areas. While size is one criterion for status as a Union republic, it clearly is not the only one. Several nationalities—the Jews, Crimean Tarters, the Volga Germans, the Chuvash, and the Finnish Mordvinians for example—are more numerous than several of those organized into Union republics yet have a lesser political status. Each of the four national administrative subdivisions is permitted to use the native language for all official purposes, and the native culture is supposed to be encouraged. In addition, the nationalities are represented individually in the Council of Nationalities, one of the two houses of the Supreme Soviet.

Soviet federalism, however, is a constitutional fiction that fails to conform to the realities of politics. The power of national leaders at every administrative level is sharply curtailed by authority centered in Moscow. It would be unthinkable, for example, for one of the republics to consider seriously seceding from the Union. In reality, the Soviet political system comes much closer to being unitary than federal. This is the result of Communist Party domination of the organs of the state coupled with the highly centralized character of the Party. The fate of the nationalities lies not in their own hands but in those of the Party leadership.

Soviet nationalities policy since the Revolution has alternated between restraining Great Russian chauvinism and curbing local nationalism. The long-term goal is to forge a new multinational nation with a common culture. This objective is similar to the pre-Soviet policies of Russification, because the Russian language is to become the unifying medium of communication, and inevitably this will hasten the "Russification" of the Soviet peoples. An important step toward this end was the education reforms of 1958–59, which permit the parents of every non-Russian child to determine whether their children will be instructed in Russian or the native language of the Republic. Since virtually all higher educational instruction is carried out in Russian, this law is expected to intensify the trend toward Russifying the educational systems of the minorities.

At the same time Soviet policy eschews any effort to impose forcibly the Russian language or culture on a minority or to suppress any national culture. So long as the non-Russian peoples do not threaten the political and social objectives of the regime nor the external security and territorial integrity of the Soviet Union, they are free to practice their traditional ways. One notable exception is the Jews. Though classified as a separate nationality, they are denied the rights of one. They are not permitted to maintain educational, cultural, or religious institutions. There is no Jewish theater and virtually no publication in Yiddish. To some extent Soviet policy reflects the traditional anti-Semitism of the Slavic peoples (principally the Russians and Ukrainians), and partially it is a reaction to the enthusiasm of Russian Jewry for the State of Israel, which conflicts with the regime's demand for unquestioned and total loyalty to the Soviet state, as well as with its foreign policy.

It is impossible to measure the resistance to Russification, but its existence is unquestioned. There is considerable native resentment in areas such as the Baltic states, Kazakhistan, and Kirgzia, where Russian migration and settlement has been extensive. Many Ukrainians have openly opposed the educational reforms, which permit schools in the Ukrainian Republic to substitute Russian for Ukrainian language instruction. So forceful were the protests of a number of Ukrainian educators and intellectuals that more than a dozen were tried secretly in the winter of 1965 and 1966 and imprisoned. There is widespread resentment against the preferential treatment accorded to Russians for all the higher positions in Soviet society—in the Party, the military, and the industrial hierarchy. It is very possible that national frustrations and animosities may be the single most important source of dissatisfaction with the regime.

Richard Pipes is Professor of History at Harvard University. Among his works are *The Formation of the Soviet Union* and *The St. Petersburg Labor Movement, 1885–1897*. Yaroslav Bilinsky is Professor of Political Science at the University of Delaware and the author of *The Second Soviet Republic: The Ukraine after World War II*. Vyacheslav Chornovil is a young Ukrainian jouralist whose reporting of the 1965–66 secret trials of Ukrainian intellectuals resulted in his arrest and imprisonment for "slandering the Soviet system." One of the documents in his book is an account of the arrest and imprisonment of the Ukrainian poet and linguist, Svyatoslav Karavansky.

37

"SOLVING" THE NATIONALITY PROBLEM

RICHARD PIPES

Nationalism is a natural ally and concomitant of democracy. This connection is often lost sight of in the West where nationalism, once it matured, shed its democratic affiliations and became increasingly identified with conservative and reactionary causes. But this had not been the case in Europe originally, and it is still not the case in those areas of the world which have only recently experienced the first stirrings of national sentiment. Here, nationalism and democracy are closely linked.

There are good reasons for this close affinity between the two. Democracy, by the mere fact of asserting the principle of popular sovereignty, raises the question: Who are the "people"? How many and what kind of "people" rule the given state? These questions are most readily answered by reference to nationality. The "people" are the "nation"—that is, those who share a common language and secular culture. Indeed, in most European constitutions of the late eighteenth and early nineteenth cen-

Reprinted from *Problems of Communism*, Vol. XVI, No. 5, September-October, 1967, pp. 125–31.

turies, the terms "people" and "nation" are used interchangeably. Now, in multinational empires where one nation rules many, this identification of democracy with nationalism is inherently an explosive force. Here the "sovereignty of the people" means not only the introduction of democratic institutions but the overthrow of foreign rule. This is the reason why, under the impact of democracy, imperial structures previously considered viable, like the Austrian and British, came under severe internal stress in the past century.

Until the end of the nineteenth century, the Russian Empire was generally regarded as a viable political organism—except by the Poles, who had been acquired late and refused to assimilate. One can dismiss accusations that Russian imperialism was more brutal than its Western counterparts, exactly as one can disregard the claims of Stalinist and post-Stalinist Soviet historians that it was somehow more "progressive." The Russian Empire was an empire like the others, perhaps less efficiently administered, especially in the remote provinces, where lack of supervision by the center permitted serious abuses. Its political inefficiency, however, did have its good side, for it also allowed a great deal of diversity. Until the 1860's, vast areas of Russia were allowed to escape the authority of the central bureaucratic apparatus and to rule themselves (e.g., Livonia, Finland, and the Kazakh steppe).

A complicating feature of the history of Russian imperialism is the fact that the Great Russians developed a sense of national consciousness more or less concurrently with their subject peoples (the Poles again excepted). In other words, at the very time when they acquired an awareness of their own national identity, they were forced to contend with nationalist movements directed against themselves. I believe that this coincidence had much bearing on the whole development of Russian nationalism and, in particular, on Russian imperial practices. The French in North Africa, the Germans in the Cameroons, or the Japanese in Korea had no doubt about their own identity. They crossed bodies of water, put down local resistance by force, and incorporated the conquered areas. But the Russians were never fully conscious of being strangers in their vast and amorphous land. The absence of any sharp land or water frontiers between Russia proper—the upper Volga and Oka region—and the Pacific, the Himalayas, or the Black Sea, permitted Russian colonists to move steadily outward, engulfing or bypassing other ethnic groups, often without realizing that they were engaged in an imperial venture. The historical fusion of nationalism and imperialism, as well as the geographic contiguity of national state and empire, helps explain why the Russians never developed either an imperial mentality or an imperial constitution. They created and ruled an empire as if they were creating and ruling a national state.

The first stirrings of national sentiment among the subjugated peoples toward the end of the nineteenth century produced a distinct shock in Russian public opinion, well reflected in the programs of political parties.

The parties of the right, of course, rejected out of hand any idea of autonomy for the various ethnic groups, being committed to uphold the supremacy of the Great Russian nationality and its Orthodox religion. But even those of the center and the left—parties which would have no truck with racial or religious discrimination—were strangely embarrassed whenever the "national problem" reared its head. They were all for abolishing disabilities imposed by the Imperial Government on minorities, such as the Jews; they were even prepared to concede independence to Poland. But beyond this they hesitated to go. Russian liberals and socialists, in their desperate fight against Tsarism, feared nationalism as a divisive force and preferred to ignore it.

Though by the time World War I broke out most political parties had formulated programatic solutions of the nationality problem, they did so in an unmistakably halfhearted manner. Deep inside, the liberals believed that the national problem would solve itself with the introduction of political democracy, while the socialists were equally certain it would vanish with the expropriation of private property. That the desires of the minorities not only stemmed from political or economic dissatisfaction but also expressed positive aspirations of a democratic nature was not seriously entertained by any prominent opposition group in Russia, despite ample evidence to that effect from neighboring Austro-Hungary.

Lenin and the National Question

Fundamentally, Lenin had a similar attitude toward the national question, notwithstanding the boldness of his nationality program. Like his socialist colleagues, he viewed nationalism as a byproduct of the capitalist mode of production, doomed to disappear with the introduction of socialism. More than any socialist leader, however, he took seriously the possibility of exploiting the frustrations of the national minorities for revolutionary purposes. Lenin always looked for allies, no matter how distasteful they or their ideals may have been to him. It was while living in Austria on the eve of World War I that he became aware of the explosive force of nationalism and formulated a radical programatic "solution." This solution was political self-determination, defined to mean that every national minority had the right to separate and form an independent state; if it did not wish to avail itself of this right, it had to acquiesce to assimilation. Lenin rejected any middle way, such as federalism or cultural autonomy, because he felt they institutionalized and therefore perpetuated national distinctions. His thesis on national self-determination was criticized at the time of its formulation (1913) by fellow Bolsheviks on the ground that it would split Russia into many small states and thereby hamper the development of capitalism and socialism. Lenin, however, had no such fears. He felt certain that capitalism would inexorably fuse the national minorities with the Russians and create out of the empire an indissoluble whole, so that in practice no minority peoples would or could take advantage of the right to independent statehood. His solution, therefore, was also essentially declarative. It was so bold because he did not expect it to be exercised.

Within a few years, however, events made a mockery of Lenin's calculations.

Once the Revolution got under way, the nationalist movement among the non-Russian peoples matured with great rapidity. The phenomenon had no single cause. In some areas, separatism was due to a desire of local groups to escape the bloodshed of the civil war. In others, it was the result of intervention by Germans, Austrians, and Turks. In others yet, it came into being because of pent-up hatred between the native population and Russian settlers. Whatever the reason, however, once launched, separatism gained great impetus. The local governments which came into being in the years 1918–20 may have been as ephemeral as the money or postage stamps they issued, but the independence which they proclaimed and in some way embodied struck root in popular consciousness. The native intelligentsias in particular developed a strong appetite for authority during those years. The history of the formation of the Soviet Union offers many striking examples of individuals who as late as 1916 had pledged loyalty to Russia, yet fought for separation from it two or three years later.

The unexpected disintegration of the Russian Empire confronted Lenin with a dilemma: either to acquiesce in it and reduce the domain of the Bolshevik regime to the size of Muscovy in the reign of Basil II; or to seize the separatist areas by force of arms and thereby abandon the entire Bolshevik nationality program. As we know, Lenin chose the second alternative. Wherever possible, he ordered the separated borderlands to be reconquered and reincorporated into the Russian state. At the same time, as a sop to their nationalist feelings, he granted the so-called Soviet republics pseudo-federal status and a considerable measure of cultural autonomy—the very devices which he had condemned before the Revolution as nationalistic and reactionary.

The foundations of Soviet nationality policy thus were laid not in Lenin's pre-1917 writings but in the practical directives issued in the midst of the civil war. At the time the Communists did not think about the long-term effects of any policy, for they were fighting for survival. They needed Ukrainian wheat, coal, and iron; Caucasian oil; and Turkestani cotton. They had to prevent the borderlands from turning into White outposts. It must also be kept in mind that in 1918–19 the Communists believed in the imminence of world revolution. In subjugating the breakaway republics, they were motivated not so much by a desire to re-establish the frontiers of the old Russian Empire as by a wish to "liberate" as many countries as possible from the "capitalist-imperialist yoke." Their attack on the government of the Ukrainian Directory in early 1919 basically had much the same purpose as the support which they extended that year to Bela Kun's government in Hungary, a country which had never formed part of Russia. The fact that Soviet nationality policy was devised as an emergency measure in the civil war, that it was not thought out but improvised as a makeshift arrangement to tide the new regime over until the outbreak of world revolution, is essential to an understanding of both its philosophy and its operation.

By 1920 it became clear that the world revolution would not come, at least in the foreseeable future. It was necessary, therefore, to bring order to the helterskelter arrangement which had come into being in the preceding three years. The Constitution of the Soviet Union, promulgated in 1923–24, froze the system of administration evolved in the course of the civil war. It is testimony to the fundamental conservatism of all Russian politics, whether imperial or Soviet, that this system has remained virtually intact to this day. This fact permits us to review the successes and failures of Soviet nationality policy over the past fifty years as a whole. Let us carry out the survey under the rubrics of political, economic, and cultural policies.

Politics

The Soviet Union has been from the beginning a strictly centralized state, ruled both horizontally and vertically by the Communist Party. The Party does not recognize national divisions. Its structure is homogeneous, cutting across ethnic lines. This much can hardly be disputed.

Despite its own centralization, the Party recognizes constitutionally the existence of national republics, some of which—the so-called Union republics—are in theory able to separate and form independent, sovereign states. In reality unitary, the Soviet Union is in form federal. The fiction of federalism is a legacy of the civil war, when it was found expedient, for both domestic and foreign reasons, to leave the conquered borderlands a semblance of sovereignty. In 1922, when the new constitution was being drafted, Stalin urged that this fiction be abandoned and the national republics incorporated into the Russian Soviet Republic. But Lenin refused because he foresaw the necessity of formally dissociating the new Soviet state from the name "Russia" in order to permit the absorption into it of future communized countries. (Lenin originally even proposed to call the new state "Union of Soviet Socialist Republics of Europe and Asia"). Lenin also attached importance to the federal fiction as a psychological asset in overcoming the suspicion of the national minorities toward the Russians. For these reasons the pseudo-federal system remained on the books.

Now it is needless to elaborate that the republics do not—and, given the Communist Party's view of itself, cannot—enjoy anything resembling genuine authority, and that their "right to separation" is meaningless. Historically viewed, the functions of the so-called republican governments resemble not those of bona fide federal states but those assigned before the Revolution to the provincial *zemstva*. Nevertheless, the Soviet national republics with their token governments must not be written off. The *zemstva*, too, lacked legislative authority, yet they became with time important foci of political resistance. The same may well happen with the administrations of the Soviet republics.

In the first place, national governments, even when impotent, are known from historical experience to arouse strong feelings of loyalty among both their officials and subjects. Napoleon had this disagreeable experience with the satellite governments he had set up over Europe. Even some of his own brothers identified themselves so closely with their domains that they resisted him and had to be removed. The puppet Napoleonic Kingdom of Italy and the Confederation of the Rhine became the nuclei, respectively, of the united Italian and German states. We can observe the same phenomenon in twentieth-century Africa. The African states which came into existence after World War II follow the frontiers carved out in the nineteenth century by their imperial masters. They are legacies of conquests accomplished by Western armies and legalized by Western diplomats without regard either to the wishes of the native population or to its ethnic composition. Yet the "imperialist" origin of their states has not inhibited the Ghanaians or the Congolese from developing a genuine sense of patriotism. Undoubtedly this is also true of the Soviet national minorities. The fact that the Uzbek Republic is a Soviet creation, and that its government enjoys no meaningful authority, probably does not make it any less real for the Uzbeks, and especially for the Uzbek intelligentsia.

In the second place, the bureaucratization of Soviet life and the spread of education have markedly increased the number of intellectuals with administrative experience. In 1917–20, the nationalist movement in the borderlands of Russia had been led by a handful of lawyers, teachers, and journalists, few of whom had had any practice in statecraft. By contrast, there are today in every minority republic thousands of persons employed in the Party and state apparatus who could, if permitted, assume full responsibility for local administration. The hunger for power among the intelligentsia in so-called underdeveloped countries is well known. They tend to consider a secondary school diploma a ticket to political office, and they chafe when positions to which they feel entitled are occupied by civil officials from another region or of another nationality. There is little doubt that the native intelligentsia in the Soviet borderlands have similar ambitions and experience similar frustrations. To enjoy the appearance of power without its substance is not something which they like or will acquiesce in forever.

These two considerations—the psychological reality of statehood and the discontent of the native intelligentsia, especially those serving in the bureaucracy—endow Soviet federalism with a significance which it lacks when viewed purely from the point of view of power distribution. Devised to mollify nationalism, it in effect intensifies it and provides it with institutional outlets.

Economics

The economic benefits of imperialism are familiar. Imperialist rule brings with it capital and technical skills, opens up markets for local produce, and thereby contributes to "economic development." Thanks to these benefits, areas which once were colonial possessions are today at a higher economic level than those which were not. On the debit side, however, imperialism entails regional specialization, which results in unbalanced economies overdependent on one or two basic commodities.

Broadly speaking, Soviet imperialism has brought with it the same advantages and disadvantages as did so-called capitalist imperialism.[1] Russian investments have stimulated and continue to stimulate economic activities which would have been beyond the capacity of the borderlands were they independent. The construction of railroad lines alone (many of them, to be sure, laid before the Revolution) has linked the borderlands with markets that would not have been otherwise available to them, thereby substantially enhancing the value of their produce. At the same time, however, the borderlands have not been permitted to develop rounded economies. Soviet planning offices treat the entire Soviet Union as an economic entity, placing industries and assigning crops where they are most profitable or strategically useful, without regard to local desires. . . . This policy of regional specialization and dependence on the all-Union economy arouses considerable resentment in the national republics.

Setting aside the question of how well the borderlands would have fared economically had they not been subjected to communist economic regulation, it seems fairly certain that by being part of a large economic entity they do enjoy distinct benefits.[2] Statistical computations purporting to show that Russia withdraws more wealth from the national republics than it puts into them are not convincing, because they usually do not take into account the costs of administration and defense which these republics would have to bear if they were independent. They are indeed no more realistic than Marxist statistics adduced to show imperialistic exploitation of colonies by the "capitalist" countries. Nevertheless, many intellectuals in the borderlands passionately believe that they *are* being exploited by Russia, and this belief is politically significant.

Confined for half a century within a closed economy and unable to reach foreign markets directly, the national republics have become, for better or worse, welded economically to the other regions of the Soviet Union. It would be dangerous, however, to draw from this economic fact conclusions about their political future. We know, for example, how closely Algeria was formerly integrated into the French economy, and

[1] This statement is meant to apply only to areas within the U.S.S.R. and not to the so-called satellite states of Eastern Europe.

[2] There is little doubt in the author's mind that Russia and its empire would have been very much better off economically had the Revolution not occurred, but this is irrelevant to the present discussion.

how much its own economy has declined since independence. Yet this predictable fact did not prevent Algerian nationalists from waging a determined struggle for independence. Nor would they now trade their independence for the economic advantages of reunification. If economic considerations were the determining factor in such matters, nationalism would not exist, because it is inherently an economic absurdity. The integration of the various regions of the U.S.S.R. into an economic whole, therefore, is not likely of itself to retard the development of national sentiments or movements. The mere fact that many intellectuals in the national republics believe they would be better off without Russian tutelage may have more bearing on their political actions than the objective realities of the situation.

There is another aspect to this matter. Even if separation from the imperial metropolis usually brings with it an economic decline of the ex-colony taken as a whole, it does improve the economic status of some of the native social groups. How many clerks in French Algerian enterprises have become executives since Algeria gained independence! How many sergeants have been promoted to colonels, how many teachers have become school inspectors, how many reporters have secured editorial desks! The general deterioration of the Algerian economy has not adversely affected *their* climb up the social and economic ladder. And after all, it is just these groups—resentful intellectuals and white-collar workers—who everywhere furnish the leading cadres of nationalist movements. It would be difficult to dissuade them from engaging in separatist activities by the force of general economic arguments. No matter what would happen to their particular country as a whole, their personal position would be likely to improve under independent statehood.

The Algerian example provides a further corollary for Russia. After the protracted and vicious war waged between the French and Algerians, one might have expected that relations between them would remain permanently poisoned. Yet as soon as France had granted Algeria independence, the two countries re-established normal economic ties. The point is that Algeria and France, having become economically interdependent over a long period of common statehood, need each other. France requires Algerian labor (and, more recently, oil); Algeria requires French markets. It is likely that future relations between the national republics and Russia will develop along similar lines. Even if some day the Ukraine, the Caucasus, and Central Asia should secure independence, they would probably want to continue close economic relations with Russia proper, to which they are linked by transport and a long tradition of trade. Russia thus seems likely to remain the hub of a large economic community, regardless of political vicissitudes.

CULTURE

In the borderlands which they reconquered during the civil war, the Communists at first granted the minorities a considerable measure of linguistic and cultural autonomy in addition to pseudo-federal institutions. In particular, they permitted the native intellectuals great latitude in matters of historical and political thought. This policy was abandoned in the early 1930's, when Stalin, for reasons of political expediency, found it necessary to appeal to Great Russian nationalism; however, it left lasting traces. For many of the nationalities, the 1920's were a decade of unprecedented cultural activity, in the course of which they laid the foundations of a national ideology. Indeed, some of the smaller, more primitive ethnic groups became aware only then of their national identity. If for the Russians the Revolution marked the beginning of a tragic cultural decline, for some of the minorities it meant the very opposite: the birth of a national culture.

Much of the "instant culture" that sprang up in non-Russian republics during the 1920's is comical, but it is nevertheless taken very seriously by the population concerned. For example, I recall once being told by an Azerbaijani refugee that the Russians must have no culture of their own, otherwise they would not translate into Russian so many works by non-Russian authors of the Soviet Union. Even so civilized and ancient a nation as the Armenians can get carried away and . . . make claim to having invented cybernetics a thousand years ago.

No single aspect of the nationality question evokes more passion than the matter of assimilation. And rightly so, for this issue is indeed critical. If in fact the minorities are gradually losing their ethnic identity and fusing with the dominant Great Russian population, then the Bolsheviks may be said to have successfully "solved" the nationality problem. To answer this question with any degree of assurance, we would have to have access to a great deal of statistical and ethnographic information—such, for example, as data on intermarriage or domestic habits. We do not, however, possess such information, and all we can go by is the census figures on linguistic habits—data which are at best of limited significance, and at worst of dubious reliability. Without going into the detailed results of the linguistic censuses, suffice it to say that while they indicate rapid linguistic assimilation of smaller and territorially scattered ethnic groups, they also reveal a remarkable persistence of linguistic loyalty among the larger, more compact minorities with their own republics. There has been no significant Russification of the Ukrainians, Georgians, Uzbeks, or other major borderland peoples. The fact that in these republics much of the administration and education is in the hands of native intellectuals makes it possible to resist efforts at Russification emanating from the center and from the local Russian population.

The prevalence of bilingualism among intellectuals in the borderlands need not, of itself, be taken as a symptom of denationalization. The phenomenon has parallels in other colonial areas. The most rabid Indian nationalists, for example, spoke English as their second language, and even today English continues to serve as the official language in the parliament of independent India. Similarly, in Algeria, the war for independence was led by French-educated Arab nationalists, to whom French was a second language. English was for the Indians, and French for the Algerians, not a substitute for their local, native languages but a link with the Western world. Russian performs the same function for Azerbaidjani or Tadjik intellectuals.

The linguistic data are thus not enough to permit any firm opinion on the question of ethnic assimilation. It can be said, however, that neither the scanty information coming from the U.S.S.R. nor the lessons taught by the experience of other empires would suggest that such assimilation is taking place. The onus of proof in this matter rests with those who argue the opposite hypothesis. The intense debate carried on in Soviet journals . . . on the subject of the "merging" of nationalities in the communist state of the future is indicative of the concern this question causes the Soviet authorities and shows they are far from convinced that the issue of assimilation has been solved in a positive sense.

In addition to politics, economics, and culture, there is one more aspect of Soviet nationality policy that should be mentioned, one that cuts across all three: the relationship between ethnic groups. Official Soviet propaganda sidestepped this question for a long time on the ground that there can be no national antagonism in the Soviet Union, either because it has been constitutionally outlawed, or because the Russians are immune to it by virtue of their peculiar "all-human" ethos. It is perfectly clear, however, that the Soviet Constitution, of itself, can no more eliminate national or racial tensions in the U.S.S.R. than the U.S. Bill of Rights can assure the civil equality of American Negroes. More is needed than laws. The belief that the Soviet constitution has "solved" the relations between ethnic groups is a widespread Russian self-delusion. Much the same holds true of Russian "pan-humanity." It may have carried the day for Dostoyevsky in his Pushkin Speech of 1880, but as a serious contention it will not hold water. The Russians are as susceptible to anti-Semitism, anti-Negroism, and every form of xenophobia as are members of other nations.

It is difficult to speak with any assurance on ethnic relations in the Soviet Union, because the material is even scantier than on the question of assimilation. There is much evidence that friction exists not only between the Russians and the other nationalities, but also among the different national minorities themselves. . . . Many of the minority intellectuals blame the Russians for the poverty and lack of freedom in their regions; others, not without justice, accuse them of discrimination in higher schooling and career advancement. In areas where the Russians have penetrated and settled *en masse* in this century (e.g., the Baltic areas and Kazakhstan) there is deep resentment against the newcomers and acute racial tension. . . . (The Muslim regions of the U.S.S.R. have been more heavily colonized by non-Muslims than any other Muslim area in the world.) But there does not seem to be widespread hatred of Russians, even among ethnic groups which have suffered most from communism. For although the Russians rule, they are not a "Herrenvolk" as were the Germans in their shortlived empire. A Russian *qua* Russian does enjoy certain advantages, but he does not automatically have a privileged status. Indeed, some Russian settlers in the non-Russian republics believe that they are worse off than the native citizens, and they grumble about having to toil for the indolent Caucasians or Turkestanis. There are also local tensions among different national groups. The Armenians and Azeri Turks, for example, seem to have developed a healthy dislike for the neighboring Georgians, whom they accuse of having lorded it in the days of Stalin and Beria. In the Ukraine, the traditional anti-Semitism has not subsided.

All these antagonisms are undoubtedly exacerbated by that intense Russian nationalism which has since the 1930's penetrated the whole Soviet apparatus, but they cannot be entirely ascribed to it. In recent times we have seen similar ethnic conflicts arising in democratic states (e.g., Canada and Belgium) where the minorities are given very wide latitude. As pointed out at the beginning of this essay, nationalism is an intrinsic aspect of the democratization of modern life which goes on relentlessly everywhere, even in countries with a political system that is the very antithesis of democracy.

To summarize: The national problem in the Soviet Union surely has not been "solved." On the contrary, if by a "solution" we mean the disappearance of national frustrations and animosities, the problem is in many ways more acute than it was when the Communists seized power fifty years ago. True, the Soviet regime is in theory an international government, the bastion of "world socialism," and it cannot afford to tolerate, let alone excite, national animosities as the Imperial Government was wont to do in its final decades. For this reason, although anti-Semitism, for example, seems to have greatly intensified in the past fifty years, it is not allowed to take violent outlets. On the other hand, all the evidence available both from within the Soviet Union itself and from historic parallels with other countries indicates that the nationalism of the minority peoples of the U.S.S.R. (like that of the Russians themlseves) has grown and intensified since 1917. There is a great deal of nationalist frustration in the Soviet Union. Unless the Soviet rulers face up to it and begin the process of decentralization voluntarily, it is likely someday to explode in a most destructive manner.

*   *   *

38

SVYATOSLAV KARAVANS'KY

VYACHESLAV CHORNOVIL

Svyatoslav Yosypovych Karavans'ky was born on December 24, 1920, in Odessa, into the family of an engineer. In 1938 he graduated from Odessa secondary school No. 119 and enrolled in the Industrial Institute (and at the beginning of 1939, he also enrolled in the correspondence course of the Institute of Foreign Languages). Even during his school days he wrote poetry and short stories, some of which were published in youth magazines. He also tried his hand at translating while in the institute. Dissatisfied with his chosen profession, he voluntarily left the Institute in 1940 and joined the army, intending after completing his service to enroll in the faculty of literature at the university. In July of 1941, the detachment in which Karavansky served was surrounded by the Germans in Western Belorussia. Avoiding capture, Karavans'ky managed to get to Odessa at the beginning of 1942. There he enrolled in the faculty of literature at the university, where he joined an illegal group of Ukrainian youth connected with the OUN. He organized a bookshop and transferred the profit from the sales of books to student groups and to the Ukrainian theatre. Karavans'ky was persecuted by the Rumanian political police.[1]

He left for Rumania in 1944, and later in the same year he returned illegally to the liberated Odessa. However, on the third day of his return, while attempting to establish contact with his former associates, he was arrested. He did not commit any actions (neither armed nor through propaganda) directed against the Soviet Government during his stay on the liberated territory. During interrogations, Karavans'ky was promised freedom if he agreed to inform the police about attitudes among the

[1] Odessa, as well as other southwestern regions of Ukraine, was occupied for a time by Rumania during World War II (translator's note).

From *The Chornovil Papers* by Vyscheslav Chornovil, McGraw-Hill, Toronto, Canada, 1968, pp. 166–80. Reprinted by permission of the publishers.

students. He rejected this offer. On February 7, 1945, the Military Tribunal of the Odessa Region sentenced Karavans'ky to twenty-five years of imprisonment. He served his sentence in many hard-labor camps of the North and the East. He worked on the construction of a railway in Pechora, felled trees in Magadan, mined gold in Kolyma, worked on the construction of the highway between the Taishet and the Lena, and sewed overalls in Mordvinia.

When the conditions in hard-labor camps improved slightly after Stalin's death, he resumed his literary work. He wrote poems, tales in verse, plays, and made translations. Some of his works, sent from the camps, were even published in republic publications (for instance, in *Literaturna Hazeta* [*Literary Gazette*]). In 1954 he began a major project —the preparation of a dictionary of rhymes in the Ukrainian language.

After sixteen years and five months of imprisonment, he was released on December 19, 1960, on the basis of the decision of the Dubravny ITL (Corrective Labor Camp) which was based on the Decree of September 17, 1955, Art. 2, dealing with amnesty. His sentence was reduced by half—to twelve years and five months.

After returning to Odessa, Karavans'ky completed a course for mechanics, specializing in the repair of calculating machines. He worked as a mechanic in the provincial automobile workshop; as a senior mechanic at a factory which manufactured adding machines; as a mechanic in the servicing section for calculating machines; as a book-hawker; as a translator in the editorial office of the regional newspaper, *Chornomors'ka Komuna*; as a part-time correspondent of the magazine *Ukraina*; as a subscription salesman for Soyuzdruk (a publishing house); and then left for several months for Intu (Komi Autonomous Republic) to increase his earnings. The frequent changes of work were caused by the fact that at times he was able to find only temporary work or because he was dismissed from work after his past in the camps became known.

The intensity of Karavans'ky's literary work after his release from imprisonment was amazing. He completed the work started in the camp on the dictionary of rhymes in the Ukranian language (1,000 printed pages). He translated many English poets, prepared a book, *The Biographies of Words*, frequently wrote articles to newspapers and magazines on linguistic problems, had a column in the magazines *Ukraina* and *Znannva ta pratsya* [*Knowledge and Work*], and newspapers *Sil's'ki Visti* [*Village News*] and *Ukrains'ke Zhyttya* [*Ukrainian Life*] and others, prepared a collection of humorous short stories and feuilletons for the publishing house Mayak, and published short interludes. In agreement with the publishing house Dnipro, he was translating Charlotte Bronte's novel, *Jane Eyre*.

S. I. Karavans'ky actively participated in Ukrainian community life. He organized subscriptions for Ukrainian publications in workingmen's hostels in Odessa, collected Ukrainian books for libraries in the Kuban, addressed extensive proposals to public and government organizations concerning such matters as the nationwide observance of the jubilee of

M. Lysenko,[2] the introduction of the dubbing of all films in the Ukrainian language, the creation of special councils of spectators at film studios, the improvement of sales of Ukrainian books, etc. In 1965, disturbed by the growing Russification of Ukrainian schools and universities, he wrote two articles (an accusation of the Minister Dadenkov and *About One Political Error*), which he sent to official institutions.

Karavans'ky was married in 1961. In 1962 he enrolled in the correspondence department of the Philological Faculty of the Odessa University, where he made good progress in his studies.

On September 4, 1965, when arrests were made in Ukraine, Karavans'ky's home was searched but nothing illegal was found. The next day Karavans'ky sent a categorical protest against the unjustified search to official organizations and to the press. Somewhat later he handed letters to the Consuls of Poland and Czechoslovakia in Kiev, explaining the violations of Lenin's principles of nationality policy in the Ukraine and describing the arrests of Ukrainian intellectuals in August–September of 1965.

For all this Karavans'ky was arrested on a street in Odessa on November 13, 1965. Since there was no formal cause for a trial, on the recommendation of the KGB, the General Prosecutor of the U.S.S.R., Rudenko, revoked Karavans'ky's 1960 release. Upon his decision Karavans'ky was sentenced, without an investigation or a trial, to eight years and seven months in severe hard-labor camps (the term which remained from the original sentence of twenty-five years). As a protest Karavans'ky went on a hunger strike. At the end of November of 1965, he was deported to the Mordvinian camps (camp No. 11, Yavas).

In the camp Karavans'ky wrote a number of petitions to official organizations and to representatives of the public, for which he was twice sentenced to punitive isolation for ten days. On October 8, 1966, he was sent to a camp jail, BUR, for a term of six months. He was formally charged with failing to fulfill the required work quotas (which the majority of prisoners fail to accomplish). In the solitary confinement cell and three times in the prison jail, Karavans'ky went on hunger strikes, demanding a meeting with the public prosecutor. In all, since his arrest, Karavans'ky went on five hunger strikes, which were usually broken on the ninth or tenth day by forced feeding.

During those brief periods when he was not sitting in the prison jail or in solitary confinement, Karavans'ky managed to finish the translation of Bronte's novel, *Jane Eyre*, and also wrote several chapters of his book, *The Biographies of Words*.

On January 3, 1967, a search was made in the house of Karavans'ky's wife in Odessa. Among the confiscated documents there were drafts of statements written by Karavans'ky's wife concerning the illegal arrest of her husband, as well as the manuscript of Karavans'ky's poem written in camp under the title, *To the Heirs of Beria*. In 1967 the camp administra-

[2] The outstanding Ukrainian composer (translator's note).

tion deprived S. Karavans'ky of the right (guaranteed by law) to have a meeting with his wife.

To the Prosecutor of the Ukr. SSR
PETITION
*by citizen Svyatoslav Yosypovych Karavans'ky, residing in the
city of Odessa, Chornomors'ky shlyakh, 56, Apt. 47.*

I beg you to indict the minister of higher and secondary education of the Ukr. SSR, Yury Mykolayovych Dadenkov, according to the articles of the CC Ukr. SSR [Criminal Code of the Ukrainian Soviet Socialist Republic] which provide penalties for:

1. Violation of national and racial equality (Art. 66, CC Ukr. SSR).
2. Opposition to the restoration of Leninist principles of opportunity for higher education in the Ukr. SSR (Articles 66, 167, CC Ukr. SSR).
3. Failure to implement the resolutions of the Twentieth Congress of the CPSU concerning the liquidation of all traces of the personality cult, and obstructing the restoration of normal conditions for the development of the Ukrainian socialist nation (Article 66, CC Ukr. SSR).
4. The training of unqualified teaching cadres and the disorganization of the educational process in the system of secondary and incomplete secondary education (Article 167, CC Ukr. SSR).

I base my petition on the following facts:

1. During his tenure as minister of higher and secondary education in the Ukr. SSR, Yu M. Dadenkov committed serious mistakes; as a result people of Ukrainian nationality, whose native tongue is Ukrainian, do not enjoy the same rights in entering the *vuzy* [institutions of higher learning] as do those whose native tongue is Russian. Russian language and literature are a compulsory part of the *vuz* entrance examinations and so the graduates from Russian schools are more successful in passing this examination with higher marks than the graduates from Ukrainian schools. Furthermore, entrance examinations for special disciplines are also conducted in Russian, and this, too, makes it difficult for graduates from Ukrainian schools to pass special subjects. And so Ukrainian-speaking applicants get lower marks in competitive examinations. Because those with higher marks in the competitive examinations are accepted by the institutions, the majority of students entering the *vuzy* in Ukraine are graduates from Russian secondary and incomplete sceondary schools. Most of the institutes on the territory of the Ukr. SSR demand from their entrants an examination in the Russian language and literature. To this petition are added two clippings with the announcement of admissions to the Dokuchayev agricultural institute in Kharkov and the credit-economic institute in Odessa.

As a result of such a faulty anti-Leninist approach to applicants to the *vuzy*, Ukrainians comprise a considerably lower percentage in comparison with the percentage of Ukrainians in the production of material amenities on the territory of the Ukr. SSR. Among those who entered the Odessa Polytechnical Institute in the 1964–65 school year, Ukrainians amounted to 43 per cent. Of 1,126 Ukrainians who applied for admission, 453 were accepted, i.e., 40 per cent. But of 1,042 Russians who forwarded documents to the institute, 477 were accepted, i.e., 46 per cent. This is the result of the system of admission, which makes it difficult for Ukrainians to enter institutions of learning. This established practice of admission to the republic's higher and secondary institutions of learning is anti-Leninist and constitutes an indirect restriction of the rights of citizens because of their nationality. Actions of this kind must be punished according to Article 66 of the CC Ukr. SSR.

"*Article 66. Violation of national and racial equality.*

Propaganda or agitation for the purpose of arousing racial or national hostility, or dissension, or the direct or indirect restriction of rights, or the establishment of direct or indirect privileges for citizens depending on the race or nationality to which they belong, shall be punished by the deprivation of freedom for a term of six months to three years or by exile for a term of two to five years."

2. In the resolution of the CC RCP (b) [Central Committee of the Russian Communist Party (Bolsheviks)] of November 29, 1919, concerning the Soviet regime in Ukraine, Lenin himself wrote the following:

"In view of the fact that Ukrainian culture (language, school, etc.) has been suppressed for centuries by tsarism and the exploiting classes of Russia, the CC of the RCP enjoins all members of the Party by all means to remove all hindrances to a free development of the Ukrainian language and culture. In view of the centuries-long oppression, one can observe nationalist tendencies within the backward part of the Ukrainian masses; in treating these tendencies members of the RCP must show greatest patience and caution and counter them by explaining in a friendly way that the interests of the toiling masses of Ukraine and Russia are identical. The members of the RCP on the territory of Ukraine must implement the right of the toiling masses to learn and to use their native tongue in all Soviet institutions, and always counteract attempts to relegate the Ukrainian language to an inferior position. On the contrary, they should aspire to transform the Ukrainian language into an instrument of the communist education of the toiling masses. Measures should be taken at once so that all Ukrainian institutions will have a sufficient number of employees with a command of the Ukrainian language and that in future all the employees will be able to speak the Ukrainian language." (Lenin, *Works*, Vol. 39, pp. 334–37.)

As a result of Lenin's instructions, higher and secondary specialized education in Ukraine was Ukrainized during the twenties and thirties. Teaching in the institutions of higher learning was conducted in Ukrainian. This paved the way to an education for the majority of the Ukrainian working masses and created conditions for a normal development of the Ukrainian socialist nation.

During the period of the Stalin personality cult, this Leninist principle of higher education in Ukraine was forgotten. Later the Party passed resolutions to enable the ministry of higher and secondary specialized education in the Ukr. SSR, headed by Yu. M. Dadenkov, to liquidate the remains of the personality cult. But in most higher and secondary specialized institutions of learning in Kiev, Kharkov, Odessa, Dnepropetrovsk, and other cities, the instruction is still not in the Ukrainian tongue. The ministry allowed the Ukrainian language to be "relegated to an inferior position," against which Lenin had forewarned. And it continues to tolerate the elimination of Leninist norms in the organization of higher education in the Ukr. SSR.

3. A normal prerequisite for the development of any socialist nation is the training of cadres of the national intelligentsia. During the time that Dadenkov has held his post, the training of such cadres has not been restored in the Ukr. SSR. The Ukrainian intelligentsia is being trained in isolation from its people, its culture, its language. The cadres of lecturers at the *vuzy* of the Ukr. SSR "do not understand" the Ukrainian language. In the Ushyns'ky Pedagogical Institute in Odessa, which trains cadres for the secondary schools, instruction is not offered in Ukrainian because the lecturers "do not know" the language. At the Mechnikov State University in Odessa, in the Ukrainian section of the Department of Philology, which trains Ukrainian philologists, most of the disciplines (the history of the CPSU, foreign languages, logic, psychology, foreign literature, Marxist philosophy) are not taught in Ukrainian. This is a direct result of the minister's negligent attitude towards his duties: (a) The textbooks required in the Ukrainian language for the *vuzy* are not being published— manuals for foreign languages, textbooks on logic, on foreign literature, anthologies of foreign literature, etc. (b) There are no cadres of national teaching intelligentsia being trained. There is no doubt that such a state of higher education in Ukraine ruins the normal conditions for the development of the Ukrainian socialist nation.

4. As a result of the "relegation" of the Ukrainian language to a secondary position in the system of higher education, graduates of universities and pedagogical institutes have no command of the Ukrainian tongue. Such instructors working in Ukrainian schools do not teach their subjects in Ukrainian. Fifty per cent of the graduates from the Odessa University and the Odessa Pedagogical Institute decline to teach in Ukrainian schools because they do not know the Ukrainian language. Such a situation interferes with the normal pedagogical process in Ukraine.

Thus Minister Dadenkov's negligent attitude toward his duties affects the training of cadres and interferes with the normal work of the institutions of popular education.

All the facts I have presented attest to the abnormal work of the ministry of higher and secondary specialized education of the Ukr. SSR, headed by Yu. M. Dadenkov.

I beg you to take these facts into account in ascertaining the degree of guilt of Yury Mykolayevych Dadenkov.

February 24, 1965
(S. Y. Karavans'ky)

About One Political Error

According to Article 9 of the "Law on the ties between school and life" adopted in 1959, in the Russian-language secondary schools of the Union republics, study of the national language is not obligatory and is carried out only at the request of the parents.

Lenin expected to bring the Ukrainian language into all aspects of the republic's social and political life. In that case there is no doubt that a knowledge of the Ukrainian language should be obligatory for those who acquire education in the territory of the Ukr. SSR.

From a juridical point of view, Article 9 of the "Law on the ties between school life" is anticonstitutional, for it contradicts both the Constitution of the USSR and the constitutions of the Union republics. The Constitution of the Ukr. SSR states: "The equality of rights of the citizens of the Ukr. SSR, regardless of their nationality and race, in all fields of economic, governmental, cultural, and social-political life, is an inviolable law. Either direct or indirect limitations of rights or the establishment of direct or indirect privileges for citizens depending on their race and nationality and also any propaganda of racial or national exclusiveness or of hatred and contempt is punishable by law" (Article 103).

The language of a nationality is a clear expression of its national image. But where are equal rights if one language must be taught in school, but another (in this case the language of the basic part of the population of the republic!) is taught only at the request of the parents?

This article of the law is discriminatory, for it places the language of the republic in an inferior position and degrades the dignity of the citizens of the republic who use the native tongue. It is also wrong from the viewpoint of the international communist upbringing of the children. When parents are reluctant to teach their children the language of the republic whose bread they eat, the child is imbued from its infancy with chauvinistic views, unworthy of Soviet people, of the exclusiveness of its own nationality—a direct departure from the standards of international communist education.

Article 9 of the law is absolutely wrong from the pedagogical point of view. In the practice of Soviet education, there was never a precedent when the teaching of subjects was left to the discretion of the parents. Leaving the question of whether the children should study this or that subject to the parents is a profoundly unpedagogical measure. The parents often do not understand what advantage or harm they cause a child by the decision they make. It can be said that one of the very responsible aspects of international upbringing is being transferred to the discretion of the parents. Such "democratic solution" of this very question could be justified if the question of the language of instruction in the *vuzy* were solved in our country in a similar democratic way. But it is in this sphere of popular education that, for decades (during the personality cult of Stalin and Khrushchev), the instruction has been given in Russian and a knowledge of the Russian language has been required at the entrance examination. After decades of discriminatory measures against the Ukrainian language, to place the question of teaching it at the discretion of the parents is, to a great extent, strange and unpolitic. This action could be justified if the question of wages for the various categories of workers and employees were submitted to the judgment of the citizens. For the public is not any less interested in the just distribution of material amenities in the country, all the more so since this distribution is one of the basic principles of communism.

As a result of the adoption of Article 9, the number of Ukrainian schools on Ukrainian territory has decreased. In Odessa and the Odessa region in the 1962–63 school year, there were 821 Ukrainian schools; in 1963–64 the number was reduced to 693, and in 1964–65 to 603. Of that number in Odessa, respectively, there were 10, 8, and 6 schools instructing in the Ukrainian language. (The total number of schools in Odessa is 104.) The few Ukrainian schools that survived are under the threat of being closed. All this is the result of the anti-Leninist, discriminatory Article 9.

How are the Ukrainian schools being closed? Even before the Ukrainian language was removed from the *vuzy* in Odessa, the parents only reluctantly sent the children to Ukrainian schools because of the impossibility of continuing their education after graduating from a Ukrainian school. . . . Indeed, the graduates from Ukrainian schools are only a small percentage of the total number of graduates from the Odessa *vuzy*. The system of admission that existed till recently, and still exists in some places, gave preference to graduates from Russian schools. So the parents, who earlier reluctantly sent the children to Ukrainian schools, now (after the appearance of the discriminatory article) began to demand that Ukrainian schools adopt the Russian language of instruction. At first a few Russian classes appear in a Ukrainian school, then their number gradually increases, until finally the school becomes entirely Russian. Ukrainian parents, who speak Ukrainian, come to the schools and beg that their children be transferred to "Russian" classes. Such a request is dictated not by an indifference towards the native tongue, but by those discriminatory obstacles which for decades have barred the road of graduates from Ukrainian schools to the attainment of education, and which still exist in some places.

Characteristic of the parents' attitude is the request of Citizeness Balok, a resident of the village of Kryva Balka, to transfer her child to a Russian school. Citizeness Balok, in a conversation with me, stated that she wishes to have her child attend a Russian school, because she herself at one time had completed seven grades in a Ukrainian school and had gone to Odessa to continue her schooling. And here, because she spoke Ukrainian, her classmates laughed at her. Citizeness Balok had to terminate her education, and she wishes to have her daughter taught in such a way that no one will jeer at her.

One cannot listen calmly to such confessions. How could such discriminatory acts penetrate into the environment of the Soviet people—who are militant internationalists—discriminatory acts that compelled the child of honest workers to quit school and to ask that her child be enrolled in a Russian school, so that in future the child would not become a victim of national discrimination? This same thought prompted many other Ukrainian parents to insist that their children be taught in Russian schools. After all, it is no secret that in Odessa (and in other places in Ukraine, including Kiev) among a certain chauvinistically inclined part of the populace, derision of the Ukrainian tongue and of the Ukrainian nationality became a very popular pastime. Such acts were observed in buses, in offices, libraries, institutions of learning. Madame Mel'nyk, a lecturer in history at the Party school in Odessa, declared in the presence of students that she did not like the Ukrainian language and did not wish to make use of it. Such a declaration from a pedagogue, an educator of the Ukrainian masses, is in this case more than characteristic.

All this shows that, during the time of the Stalin personality cult, discriminatory tendencies towards the Ukrainian language and the Ukrainian nationality developed in Ukraine. These tendencies were bolstered in recent times by the so-called "Law on the ties between school and life," as a result of which the number of the Ukrainian schools in Odessa, in the Odessa region, and indeed all over Ukraine decreased catastrophically. The number of Moldavian schools in the Odessa region has also become smaller. Furthermore, in the Russian schools the vast majority of pupils refuse to learn the Ukrainian tongue. It is not taught at all in the schools of the Volgrad district of the Odessa region, in the town of Izmail, and in the Izmail district.

Thus Article 9 of the "Law on the ties between school and life" is directed against teaching the national tongue in the schools. What true internationalist could be worried by the fact that a child learns the language of a brother-nation? Only chauvinists can lock their children in narrow national frameworks, hiding behind theories of the exclusiveness of their nationality. Article 9 of the law placed the cards in the hands of these chauvinistic elements, kindled and fanned chauvinistic sentiments among parents and pedagogues. The director of the Odessa Ukrainian School No. 125, O. I. Kryuchkov, for example, incites the teachers and parents to introduce the Russian language in the school as the medium of instruction. Not having received permission from anyone to do this, he twice arranged meetings of the parents, who voted to adopt the Russian language of instruction in the school. Rather than trying to improve teaching techniques, to master the Ukrainian language himself, which incidentally he cannot speak, and to acquire, at least by a correspondence course, the pedagogical training which he also lacks, this "educator" does everything to install the Russian language as the means of instruction in the school.

This law also develops undesirable tendencies among the pupils. Pupils being instructed in the Russian language are divided into two categories: those who study the Ukrainian language and those who do not. Thus, instead of leveling the national differences among the pupils, the school fosters and emphasizes them. The division of the children into two categories also engenders discrimination. The appearance of improper nicknames, such as *khokhol*,[1] *katsap*,[2] etc., has been observed among Soviet children in Odessa schools.

The children whose parents refused to teach them the Ukrainian language develop a contemptuous attitude toward the Ukrainian language and nationality. Among the children who do study it there arises a feeling that their nationality is inferior; the study of their national language is not obligatory, is of secondary importance, and can be derided openly by chauvinistically inclined elements.

No less painful is the effect of this law upon the pedagogical process and upon the teachers who offer the Ukrainian language. For the instructor is constantly aware that the pupil may refuse to learn the Ukrainian language; therefore, God forbid, one must not give him a low mark. After all, the study is not obligatory. If the pupil is given a low mark, he simply asks his parents that he be completely relieved of the study of the language. Such cases are very common. Thus the law places an entire category of Soviet teachers in an impossible situation; the normal process of teaching this subject is violated.

All these facts show that the adoption of one discriminatory law during the time of the Khrushchev personality cult created impossible conditions for the normal functioning of the Ukrainian school system. This law belittles the national dignity of citizens of Ukrainian nationality, strikes a blow at international communist education, and prepares the ground for the kindling of national animosity. It contradicts the last will of Lenin and, being basically discriminatory, encroaches upon the friendship of peoples of the U.S.S.R.

It is essential that the general public speak out against this situation. It is dreadful to commit a political error, but it is much more dreadful to be afraid to rectify it. The desire to rectify the error compelled me to write this article.

On my part I suggest the following measures;

1. To revise at once Article 9 of the "Law on the ties between school and life."

2. To transfer the teaching in the higher and secondary specialized institutions of learning in the Ukr. SSR to the Ukrainian language in

[1] Derogatory term for Ukrainians (translator's note).
[2] Derogatory term for Russians (translator's note).

order to facilitate the education of the broad masses of the Ukrainian people.

3. To set up a coordination committee between the Ministry of Education of the Ukr. SSR and the Ministry of Higher and Secondary Specialized Education of the Ukr. SSR to establish normal conditions for the training of graduates from Ukrainian secondary schools in the institutions of higher learning and the technical schools of the republic.

4. To remove chauvinistically inclined instructors from among cadres of popular education.

5. To apply decisive measures to stop discriminatory acts against the Ukrainian language and Ukrainian nationality.

6. To select for the teaching staffs of Ukrainian schools people who can instill love for the native tongue and culture.

7. To stop the pedagogically erroneous practice of setting up Russian classes in national schools, which leads to the Russification of national schools.

8. For a truly international training of national minorities, the system of popular education should include schools offering Yiddish, Armenian, and other languages of instruction.

9. In the institutions of higher learning which train teachers, special attention must be given to the training of national teaching cadres, to establish groups and courses which would graduate qualified cadres for national schools.

10. To inform the general public of all the measures taken. Only the implementation of these points will make it possible to remove in practice, in the Leninist manner, all the hindrances to a normal development of Ukrainian education.

S. KARAVANS'KY

*   *   *

39

EDUCATION OF THE NON-RUSSIAN PEOPLES IN THE U.S.S.R., 1917–67

YAROSLAV BILINSKY

In any multinational state the language and content of elementary and secondary education are liable to become controversial political issues. The dedicated nationalist will be concerned about safeguarding the purity of his people's heritage. On the other hand, many parents want their children to achieve responsible positions that call for higher education. Equal access to universities and technical institutes by students of all nationalities then becomes the touchstone of equitable educational policy. This essay seeks to evaluate briefly Soviet educational policy toward the non-Russian peoples that together make up nearly one-half of the total population of the U.S.S.R. (45.4 per cent in 1959). . . .

After briefly surveying the Soviet educational facilities open to non-Russian peoples, I shall concentrate on two specific problems: I shall try to show to what extent Soviet children have been taught in their native languages, and then shall try to present and interpret statistics on college admissions of different nationalities. This study will largely be limited to the fourteen non-Russian peoples that have Union republics, because evidence on the ninety-four others is very difficult to obtain in this country. An effort, however, has been made to account for the developments among two others: the Jews and the Tatars, the most numerous and important Soviet nations without a Union-republic status. I hope to be able to show that in this area, as in many other fields, the Soviet record is an uneven one: Achievements of which the most progressive countries would have been proud are tarnished by relapses into barely disguised reaction.

From Yaroslav Bilinsky, "Education of the Non-Russian Peoples in the USSR, 1917–1967: An Essay," *Slavic Review*, Vol. XXVII, No. 3 (September, 1968), pp. 411–37. Reprinted with permission of the publisher and author.

It is the paper's premise that elementary and secondary education—not necessarily higher education—should be given in the native language of the pupils. Opening a new world to a seven-year-old is difficult enough without forcing the child to think, speak, and write in a foreign language.[1] . . . It may be argued, on the other hand, that children of very small nationalities should be immediately exposed to the lingua franca of the state, lest their education be cut short; but even in such cases teaching in the native language in the first grades will smooth the later transition to the predominant language of the state. Larger peoples, in contrast, can afford to maintain even higher education in their languages—not to mention elementary and secondary education—provided, of course, that scientific and engineering subjects do not suffer from being taught in a language incomprehensible to most Soviet citizens. Exaggerated stress on the perfect command of the lingua franca in higher education may result in discrimination in favor of Russians.

Education had been a relatively neglected area in the Russian Empire. Before 1917 there were only 285 nursery schools in the entire state, with a maximum enrollment of 5,000 children.[2] Moreover, according to the 1897 census, only 24 per cent of the population over nine years old could read and write in any language.[3] There were simply not enough schools. Even thirteen years later, in 1910–11, the number of children attending school was exceedingly low. In the United States the pupils of elementary and secondary schools then numbered more than 19 per cent of the total population, in England and Germany around 17 per cent, in Spain almost 12 per cent, in relatively backward Portugal 4.4 per cent, and in the Russian Empire as low as 3.85 per cent.[4] In the school year 1914–15, only 20 per cent of the children between eight and seventeen attended schools in the Tsarist empire, and 51 per cent of the children of elementary school age (eight to eleven).[5] As for higher education, in 1913 there were ninety-five institutions throughout the empire, including nine universities. In 1914 their total enrollment was 127,000 students.[6] The only academy of sciences was the one located in St. Petersburg. . . .

Whatever criticisms we may have of the Soviet approach, by 1959 the regime appears to have liquidated illiteracy at least among the major

[1] Unesco, *The Use of Vernacular Languages in Education* (Paris, 1953), pp. 47–48, as cited by John Kolasky, *Education in the Soviet Ukraine* (Toronto, 1968), pp. 168–69.

[2] E. N. Medynsky, *Prosveshchenie v SSSR* (Moscow, 1955), p. 47.

[3] Tsentral'noe upravlenie narodnokhoziaistvennogo ucheta Gosplana SSSR, *Kul'turnoe stroitel'stvo SSSR: Statisticheskii sbornik* (Moscow and Leningrad, 1940), p. 7. Figures refer to the territory of the USSR as of January 17, 1939.

[4] See Tadeusz Pasierbiński, "Problem narodowościowy w szkolnictwie," in J. Bohdan et al., eds., *Oświata w Związku Radzieckim* (Warsaw, 1962), p. 200.

[5] *Pedagogicheskii slovar'*, II (Moscow, 1960), 392.

[6] Nicholas De Witt, *Education and Professional Employment in the U.S.S.R.* (Washington, D.C., 1961), pp. 216b and 634.

nationalities and to have equally extended primary education to all of them.[7] To have expanded the total school enrollment in Tadzhikistan, for example, from 400 in 1914–15 to 361,000 in 1955–56 is a considerable achievement by any standard, the more so if we consider that in 1955–56 14,400 persons attended college (none did before 1917).[8]

Essentially, the present Soviet educational system starts with voluntary crèches for infants up to two years old and voluntary nursery schools for children between three and six, proceeds through the increasingly selective ten-year primary-secondary schools, and culminates in the even more selective institutions of higher education. A few outstanding researchers, teachers, and graduate students are drawn into the system of the academies of sciences. (I omit here all kinds of vocational schools, including technical schools and schools for a special clientele, such as working youths and gifted children.) Preschool education is heavily subsidized by the state;[9] all other education is free, with scholarships widely available at the college and graduate level.

In theory, all preschool, primary, and secondary educational establishments, most of the institutions of higher education, and all republic academies of sciences are directly subordinated to certain republic ministries. In practice, their curricula, admission standards, and research programs have been centrally established since the 1930's, through either the Party or certain administrative arrangements or both, subject to whatever modifications the republic authorities could obtain through political influence. Since 1966 formal administrative centralization has been stressed again. . . .

At the pinnacle of the Soviet research institutions is the system of the academies of sciences—the Academy of Sciences of the U.S.S.R. in Moscow and the fourteen republic academies of sciences. For simplicity's sake, we omit some other academies: those grouping together scholars in one discipline only, such as the Academy of Medical Sciences. The majority of these specialized academies are found only in Moscow. To be sure, most of the research—applied research in particular—is undertaken in institutions subordinated to various central and republic ministries.[10] It is in the academies, however, that the really crucial basic research is carried out. Moreover, the academies are not purely research institutes; they also teach a few carefully selected graduate

[7] See Tsentral'noe statisticheskoe upravlenie pri Sovete ministrov SSSR, *Itogi vsesoiuznoi perepisi naseleniia 1959 goda: USSR* (Moscow, 1962), Table 26, p. 89. It excludes people of fifty years and older and does not correlate literacy with nationality, only with the populations of the Union republics.

[8] Tsentr. stat. upravl. pri Sov. min. SSSR, *Kul'turnoe stroitel'stvo* (Moscow, 1956), pp. 32–33.

[9] See De Witt, *Education*, p. 23.

[10] According to Alexander Korol, *Soviet Research and Development: Its Organization, Personnel and Funds* (Cambridge, Mass., 1965), p. 45, in 1961–63 the ministerial sector included about 75 percent of the "R & D" institutions and well over 500,000 professional employees (80 per cent of all R & D personnel with higher education). The *general* academies of sciences, on the other hand, in 1963 employed only 44,503 scientific workers (p. 24).

students. In theory, the republic academies, whose full and associate members and professional staff taken together exceed those of the U.S.S.R. Academy of Sciences,[11] are subordinate to the republic councils of ministers. In fact, they are subordinated to the U.S.S.R. Academy of Sciences through the mechanism of so-called joint consultations between the Presidium of the U.S.S.R. Academy and that of the republic academy.[12] This had not always been so. In the 1920's a public and initially successful struggle was waged by the proponents of the autonomy of the republic academies, the Ukrainian Academy in particular, vis-à-vis the supporters of immediate centralization.[13] And even under Khrushchev the subordination of the republic academies to the U.S.S.R. Academy was not absolute; in 1961, for example, the republic academies did not follow the action of the U.S.S.R. Academy in casting off industrially oriented research institutes.[14]

Having surveyed the Soviet educational system in general, let us now take up two specific problems, starting with the availability of teaching in the mother tongue at the primary and secondary levels.

Not only has the Soviet regime extended elementary and secondary education to the non-Russian peoples on a more equal basis, but it has also introduced large-scale education in the native languages. This is particularly true for the 1920's and early 1930's, the period of the so-called *korenizatsiya*, when the central regime sought to "take root" among the non-Russian peoples. Statistics from the 1920's show for the first—and last—time how many pupils from the various nationalities were actually taught in their native language. In December, 1927, to take only the major nationalities, 93.9 per cent of Ukrainian pupils in the Ukraine received elementary education in Ukrainian, 90.2 per cent of Belorussian school children went to Belorussian-language schools in the Belorussian S.S.R.; the respective figures for pupils being taught in their native languages in their own republics range from a low of 74.1 per cent (Tadzhiks) to a high of 98.1 per cent (Georgians). Moreover, in the Ukraine 49.6 per cent of the Jewish schoolchildren were taught in Yiddish, in Belorussia as many as 55.5 per cent. Education in the native language was even extended to those living outside their own republics: For example, 56.7 per cent of the Armenian school

[11] On Jan. 1, 1963 the total of scientific workers in all republican academies was 24,474; in the U.S.S.R. Academy, 20,029. See Korol, *Soviet Research*, Table 3, p. 24.
[12] G. I. Fed'kin, *Pravovye voprosy organizatsii nauchnoi raboty v SSSR* (Moscow, 1958), p. 112; Korol, *Soviet Research*, pp. 23–25.
[13] See Loren R. Graham, *The Soviet Academy of Sciences and the Communist Party, 1927–32* (Princeton, N.J., 1967), pp. 75 ff. Also N. Polons'ka-Vasylenko, *Ukraïns'ka Akademiia Nauk: Narys istoriï*, Vol. I (Munich, 1955). The Ukrainian Academy of Sciences was established in November 1918, when the Ukraine was under Hetman Skoropads'kyi, *not* in 1919, as alleged by the Bolsheviks and erroneously repeated by Korol, *Soviet Research*, p. 24. The Belorussian academy was established on Jan. 1, 1929 (Korol gives the year 1928). The academies of the other republics were established between 1943 (Uzbek) and 1961 (Moldavian).
[14] Korol, *Soviet Research*, p. 38.

children living in the Russian republic were taught in Armenian elementary schools, and 5.5 per cent of Ukrainian pupils in Russia went to Ukrainian-language schools. On the *secondary* level (grades 6–9) the percentage spread between pupils of different nationalities *living in their own republics* and being taught in their native language was much more pronounced: It ranged from a low of 0 (in 1927 all four of the Turkmen and all thirty-one Kirgiz were taught in Russian), through 49.21 (Kazakhs), 53.99 (Tadzhiks), 76.12 (Belorussians), and 77.39 (Tatars), to 83.67 (Ukrainians), 93.85 (Azeris), 94.57 (Uzbeks), with the prize being shared by the Armenians (98.51), and the Georgians (98.91).[15] In other words, except for most of the Central Asian nationalities, all were able to send their children to national-language secondary schools.

In the 1930's the situation changed in disfavor of the non-Russian nationalities. At the Seventeenth Party Congress in early 1934, Stalin declared that non-Russian nationalism now constituted a greater danger than "Great-Russian chauvinism." [16] By 1937 the last Ukrainian-language schools in the Russian Republic were closed down despite the existence of a compact Ukrainian minority, and since 1938 the study of Russian has been strongly emphasized in all republics. The Russification drive was further increased after World War II and Stalin's toast to the Great Russian people. Under Khrushchev, after a brief liberal interlude following the Party Congress in February, 1956, Russification efforts were resumed in mid-1958 and entrenched in the Party Program of 1961.[17] Moreover, by the mid-1930's the regime also stopped releasing data on the number of pupils of a given nationality who were taught in their native languages; henceforth only the number of schools and the number of students using a certain language of instruction were given. Even these incomplete data were withheld between 1940 and 1956. Since 1956 statistical information even more abbreviated has been issued, only to be stopped again around 1958, except for a few republics. Nevertheless, a graphic picture of Soviet educational policy can be obtained by tracing the development of schools in the non-Russian republics for which more data are available. We shall look at the distribution of students being taught in different languages, which is more significant than the number of schools.

The Belorussians and Ukrainians belong to the same East Slavic family of nations as the Russians and hence are potentially more assimilable in language and culture than a Muslim people, such as the Tatars. In the school year of 1926–27, only 38.5 per cent of all school-

[15] *Nats. pol. VKP(b)*, pp. 278–79, 294.

[16] See *History of the Communist Party of the Soviet Union (Bolsheviks): Short Course* (New York, 1939), pp. 321–22.

[17] See Y. Bilinsky, *The Second Soviet Republic: The Ukraine after World War II* (New Brunswick, N.J., 1964), pp. 11–26; Oleh S. Fedyshyn, "Khrushchev's 'Leap Forward: National Assimilation in the USSR after Stalin," *Southwestern Social Science Quarterly* (June 1967), pp. 34–43.

children in the Belorussian S.S.R. attended schools with Belorussian
as the language of instruction, 11.7 per cent of the pupils attended
Russian-language schools, and 4.9 per cent Yiddish-speaking schools.
(According to the census of 1926, Belorussians numbered 81 per cent
of the republic's total population, Russians and Jews 8 per cent each.)[18]
But the statistics are incomplete: Only 180,348 pupils out of a total
of 326,897 are accounted for by language of instruction. (The largest
omission is among elementary school pupils.) We notice, however, that
among students of so-called nine-year and second-division schools
(schools including grades 6–9) as many as 37.5 per cent of the students
were taught in Russian, and only 19 per cent in Belorussian (4.6 per
cent in Yiddish). Six of the eight nine-year schools were located in
cities, and so were five of the eleven second-division schools.[19] Incomplete as these statistics may be, and given the not unreasonable
assumption that schools that have failed to report on the language of
instruction are not exclusively Belorussian-language schools, the figures
tend to suggest the ascendancy of Russian in the more comprehensive
nine-year and second-division schools, that is, on a more advanced level,
in the school year of 1926–27.

By the school year 1938–39 the total number of schoolchildren in
Belorussia had almost tripled to 1 million, of whom 93.3 per cent were
taught in Belorussian and 6.6 per cent in Russian (no Yiddish schools
were listed). In the upper grades (8–10), however, the number of
students being instructed in Belorussian declined to 87.8 per cent and
the number of students attending Russian-language schools increased
to 12.1 per cent.[20] Unfortunately, no figures are available on the number of Russians in the total republic population in 1939. In 1955–56,
after Stalin's wave of Russification, the number of pupils being taught
in Belorussian declined to 78.5 per cent, while 21.5 per cent attended
Russian-language schools. No breakdowns according to grades were
released.[21] The number of Russians in the total population in 1959
was 8.2 per cent, the number of Belorussians 81.1 per cent. The next
two most numerous minorities in Belorussia were the Poles (6.7 per
cent) and the Jews (1.9 per cent),[22] but they were not served by any
schools teaching in their own languages. No statistical evidence on

[18] Frank Lorimer, *The Population of the Soviet Union: History and Prospects*
(Geneva, 1946), Table 25, pp. 63–64, gives data on the percentage of the titular
nationality and that of the Russian in each republic in 1926. Percentage of Jews from
Bol'shaia sovetskaia entsiklopediia (1st ed.), XXIV, 86.

[19] See [Tsentr. stat. upravl. SSSR], *Narodnoe prosveshchenie v SSSR, 1926/27
uchebnyi god* (Moscow, 1929), Pt. V, Tables 2–4, pp. 134–43. The totals and percentages were calculated by the present author.

[20] *Kult. str.*, 1940, p. 73.

[21] *Kult. str.*, 1956, pp. 186–87. More precise figures in Stat. upravleine BSSR,
Narodnoe khoziaistvo Belorusskoi SSR (Moscow, 1957), p. 285.

[22] These and the following nationality percentages in 1959 were taken from *Itogi
perepisi SSSR*, Table 54, pp. 202–8.

subsequent developments under Khrushchev has been released, but there was a noteworthy complaint in the Belorussian press in 1965 that all urban secondary schools and a part of the rural schools in the republic had been transformed into Russian-language schools. In protest, in 1964 students at the Lenin pedogogical institute in Minsk had set up a "Club of the Living Belorussian Language," whose object was the defense and the spreading of the native language and culture.[23]

Azerbaidjan (Azerbaidjanis 62 per cent and Russians 10 per cent in 1926; 67.5 per cent and 13.6 per cent, respectively, in 1959) has published the most comprehensive statistics, which allow us to determine precisely the technique used for Russification. In 1938–39 Russian-language schools in Azerbaidjan numbered 173.[24] By 1940–41 they had increased to 178, but then actually declined to 174 in 1953–54, and 152 in 1958–59. Under Khrushchev's Russification drive their number increased to 166 in 1963–64. . . . But the number of Azerbaijani-Russian schools, of which there were 158 in 1940–41 . . . almost doubled to 295 in 1963–64. Moreover, their rate of increase was accelerated under Khrushchev: In 1953–54 there were but 183 such schools, by 1958–59 their number had grown to 231, and in 1963–64 there were 295.[25] This technique of commingling students of different nationalities under the same roof, with one group being taught in Russian and another in their native language, has also been employed in Latvia and in Central Asia.[26] Explicitly this is designed to strengthen the friendship of peoples, but it can also be used as an intermediary stage in the transformation of the entire school to an all-Russian one. (Such transformations have been reported from the Tatar A.S.S.R. and the Ukraine, but not from Azerbaidjan.) [27]

The result of the government's policy in Azerbaidjan has been on the whole an increase in the number of students taught in Russian: In 1940–41, 18.8 per cent attended Russian-language schools; in 1953–54, 21.4 per cent; in 1955–56, 23 per cent; in 1958–59, as many as 24.6 per cent; but by 1963–64, despite Khrushchev's Russification drive, their number leveled off to 23.4 per cent (it should be recalled that ethnic Russians constitute only 13.6 per cent of the total population). At the

[23] *Literatura i mastatstva* (Minsk), Sept. 28, 1965; as cited by P. K. Urban, "Vozrozhdenie 'natsionalisma' v istoriografii BSSR," in Institut po izucheniiu SSSR (Munich), *Soobshcheniia*, No. 12 (1967), p. 50. Partly confirmed by Kolasky, *Education*, p. 72.

[24] *Kult. str.*, 1940, p. 73.

[25] Tsentr. stat. upravl. pri Sov. min. Azerbaidzhanskoi SSR, *Azerbaidzhan v tsifrakh: Kratkii statisticheskii sbornik* (Baku, 1964), pp. 192–93.

[26] See V. Stanley Vardys, "Soviet Nationality Policy Since the XXII Party Congress," *Russian Review*, XXIV (Oct. 1965), 334; Kolasky, *Education*, p. 206.

[27] "Voprosy postavlennye zhizn'iu," *Uchitel'skaia gazeta*, Aug. 2, 1958; S. I. Karavans'kyi, "Pro odnu politychnu pomylku," in Viacheslav Chornovil, ed., *Lykho z rozumu: Portrety 20 zlochyntsiv* (Paris, 1967), p. 119 (collection of underground materials, apparently authentic); Kolasky, *Education*, p. 75.

same time the number of students taught in Azerbaidjani increased from
68.9 per cent in 1940–41 to 69.4 per cent in 1953–54, dropping back to
68.5 per cent in 1958–59, and rising to 71 per cent in 1963–64 [28] (Azerbaidjanis number 67.5 per cent of the total population). Especially noteworthy are the decrease in the number of students being taught in
Russian and the increase in the number of students being taught in
Azerbaidjani between 1958–59 and 1963–64. Possibly the Russians are
becoming the victims of a *vengeance des berceaux*: a higher population
increase among the non-Russians, particularly among the Muslim peoples.[29] But another and probably better explanation is to be found in the
sharp resistance of the republic authorities to Khrushchev's 1958 Russification policy. Azerbaidjan, together with Latvia and Estonia, produced
the strongest opposition.[30] There is one complicating factor, however.
Next to the Russians there is also a substantial minority of Armenians
(12 per cent in 1959). How many ethnic Azerbaidjanis actually are
taught in Russian? In a recent Soviet book it has been claimed that,
whereas in 1940–41, 12 per cent of the Azerbaidjani schoolchildren attended Russian-language schools or groups in bilingual schools, by 1960–
61 their percentage had increased to 25.1, and "this percentage keeps
growing at the present time." [31] I find this last figure inordinately high:
15.1 per cent would have agreed more with the other available statistics
—possibly a printing error is involved. It would appear, in any event,
that some of the increase in Azerbaidjani-language instruction might be
due not to the winning back of Azeri students from Russian-language
schools, but to restrictions on the instruction in other minority languages.
This hypothesis is borne out by the statistics on students taught in
Armenian: 12 per cent in 1940–41, 5.4 per cent in 1963–64.[32] The Russians thus seek to keep Russifying the Azerbaidjanis, and the Azerbaidjanis retaliate by Azerifying their Armenians.

Even Georgia does not seem to have escaped a small amount of
Russification.[33] Most interesting, however, is the case of the Turkmen,
one of the least developed peoples at the time of the October Revolution of 1917. According to the census of 1897 only 0.8 per cent of the
Turkmen were literate in any language, and in 1926 2.3 per cent were

[28] *Azerbaidzhan v tsifrakh* (1964), pp. 192–93; *Kult. stir.*, 1956, pp. 186–87.

[29] Rein Taagepera, "*Vengeance des berceaux* Soviet Style," forthcoming in *Soviet
Studies.*

[30] Y. Bilinsky, "The Soviet Education Laws of 1958–9 and Soviet Nationality
Policy," *Soviet Studies*, XIV (Oct. 1962), 138–57 and *passim.*

[31] F. G. Allakhiarov, *Sblizhenie kul'tur sotsialisticheskikh natsii v period stroitel'stva
kommunizma* (Baku, 1966), p. 124.

[32] *Azerbaidzhan v tsifrakh* (1964), pp. 192–93.

[33] *Nar. prosv.*, 26/27, Pt. V, Tables 2–4, pp. 134–43; *Kult. str.*, 1940, p. 73; *Kult.
str.*, 1956, pp. 186–87; Tsentr. stat. upravl. pri Sov. min. Gruzinskoi SSR, *Narodnoe
khoziaistvo Gruzinskoi SSR v 1961 g.: Stat. ezhegodnik* (Tiflis, 1963), p. 466, and
Nar. khoz. Gruz. SSR v 1964 g. (Tiflis, 1965), p. 343.

literate, compared with a Union average of 39.6 per cent.[34] Books were published in the Turkmen language only after 1917. . . . In 1926, Turkmen numbered 72 per cent of the republic's population and Russians totaled 8 per cent; in 1959 Turkmen constituted 60.9 per cent of the total population and Russians 17.3 per cent. By 1938–39 great improvements had been made. The number of students increased to about fifteen times their total in 1926; 61.5 per cent of them attended Turkmen-language schools, 13.2 per cent Russian-language schools, and 12.1 per cent bilingual schools with Turkmen groups.

Pupils in the three top grades of secondary schools were mostly taught in Russian: They comprised 78.8 per cent of all students in their age group, compared with 9.7 per cent attending pure Turkmen schools and 11.7 per cent going to bilingual schools with Turkmen groups.[35] In 1955–56 already 21 per cent of all students attended Russian-language schools. In 1956–57 22 per cent attended Russian-language schools, compared with 71.5 per cent going to Turkmen schools. In 1958–59 the number of students enrolled in Russian-language schools was not given directly; it was only stated that 69.7 per cent of the pupils attended Turkmen-language schools.[36] On the surface, it appears to be a great achievement for the Turkmen, who numbered 60.9 per cent of the population. But how many of those were drawn from Asian minorities (in 1959 Uzbeks were 8.3 per cent of the total population, Kazakhs 4.6 per cent, Tatars 2 per cent)? There are two indications that a substantial number of Turkmen did attend Russian-language schools: a statement to that effect by a Soviet author in 1964 ("many" Turkmen children do so) [37] and the curious fact that in the Turkmenian capital, Ashkhabad, twenty-one out of its twenty-four schools were Russian, with the result that only 13.7 per cent of the pupils attended Turkmen schools (though Turkmen constituted about 29.7 per cent of the capital's population at that time and 96.7 per cent of them considered Turkmen their native language).[38]

The Tatar case is significant, too, because the Volga Tatars had made the greatest socio-economic progress of all Muslim nationalities in the Russian Empire. In 1926 the Tatars formed 45 per cent of the total population of the Tatar A.S.S.R., with Russians constituting 43 per cent; in 1959 the percentage was virtually unchanged: Tatars 47.2 per cent

[34] Lorimer, *Population*, pp. 55 and 59 for 1926 figures. For 1897, *Pedagogicheskii slovar'*, Vol. II, under "Natsional'nye shkoly."

[35] *Kult. str.*, 1940, p. 74.

[36] *Kult. str.*, 1956, pp. 186–87; *Narodnoe obrazovanie Turkmenskoi SSR za 40 let* (Ashkhabad, 1957), p. 21; Tsentr. stat. upravl. SSSR–Stat. upravl. Turkmenskoi SSR, *Kul'turnoe stroitel'stvo Turkmenskoi SSR: Stat. sbornik* (Ashkhabad, 1960), pp. 76–77.

[37] Sh. Annaklychev, "Rol' promyshlennykh tsentrov v protsesse sblizheniia natsional'-nostei (na primere Turkmenskoi SSR)," *Sovetskaia etnografiia*, No. 6, 1964 (Nov.–Dec.), p. 33.

[38] Cf. *Kult. str. Turkmenskoi SSR*, pp. 76–77; and *Itogi perepisi: Turkmenskaia SSR* (Moscow, 1963), p. 132.

and Russians 43.9 per cent. The Russians were not new settlers but had been living there for centuries. For 1926–27 there are no school figures available that single out the Tatar A.S.S.R., but for 1938–39 it is recorded that 46.8 per cent of the schoolchildren went to Tatar schools, and 44 per cent to Russian-language schools (in the three top grades 35.6 per cent learned in Tatar and 53.3 per cent in Russian).[39] By 1956–57 the number of students attending Tatar schools had diminished to 34 per cent,[40] dropping still further in 1959–60 to 31.6 per cent,[41] despite vigorous protests of Tatar Party officials in 1958.[42] It seems probable that the Volga Tatars are subject to even stronger Russification pressures than other peoples because, instead of having a Union-republic status and the small amount of political autonomy that goes with it, they are merely an autonomous part of the Russian republic.

Soviet Jews are in an even worse position as a national group despite the strong representation of individual Jews in Soviet arts, sciences, and education. Being dispersed throughout the state and lacking any real territorial political base (for the Jewish autonomous province of Birobidzhan is both ridiculously small and remote), the Soviet Jews find it difficult to resist a central denationalization policy. As is well known, no Yiddish schools whatsoever have been allowed anywhere in the Soviet Union since 1948. This is not to say that a stronger territorial Jewish political organization would have prevented Stalin's and Khrushchev's anti-Semitic drives, but it might have tempered them somewhat and might even have retained a few Yiddish schools.

Finally, a few remarks on the progress of Russification in the Baltic States. In Lithuania, for which very detailed data are available from 1953–54 through 1965–66, we see a slight diminution in the number of students attending Lithuanian-language schools, from 83.4 per cent in 1953–54 to 82.6 per cent in 1965–66. During the same period, we find a relatively larger increase in the number of pupils being taught in Russian, from 10.1 per cent to 12.6 per cent, and a considerable decrease in the number of students studying in Polish, from 6.5 to 4.8 per cent.[43] As Lithuanians constituted 79.3 per cent of the total population in 1959, Russians 8.5 per cent, and Poles 8.5 per cent, Russification does not seem to be a problem in the school system of the Lithuanian S.S.R.; indeed, discrimination against Poles would be a more likely consideration.

Nor does *scholastic* Russification seem to constitute a great danger in

---

[39] *Kult. str.*, 1940, p. 77.

[40] *Kult. str.* RSFSR (Moscow, 1958), p. 207.

[41] Tsentr. stat. upravl. Tatarskoi ASSR, *Tatarskaia ASSR za 40 let: Stat. sbornik* (Kazan, 1960), p. 30. In 1962/63 only 6 percent of Tatar pupils living in the fifteen cities of the republic attended Tatar-language schools. Kolasky, *Education*, p. 34.

[42] "Voprosy postavlennye zhizn'iu" (see n. 27).

[43] Tsentr. stat. upravl, pri Sov. min. Litovskoi SSR, *Prosveshchenie i kul'tura Litovskoi SSR: Stat. sbornik* (Vilna, 1964), pp. 44–45; *Narodnoe khoziaistvo Litovskoi SSR v 1965 g.: Stat. sbornik* (Vilna, 1966), pp. 240–41.

Latvia and Estonia.[44] Vardys points out that, after repeated representations by Lithuanian, Latvian, and Estonian leaders, in August, 1965,
the regime allowed all Baltic schools to maintain their traditional eleven-
year curriculum, while all the other schools in the Soviet Union, *includ-*
ing the Russian-language schools in the Baltic States, were being
switched back to ten-year programs.[45] Thus, at least so long as this
anomaly will last, the Lithuanian, Latvian, and Estonian schools will be
able to offer to their pupils an extra school year and thereby a better
preparation for admission to college.

From this survey we can see that by 1938–39 (the end of *korenizatsiya*)
virtually all peoples, with the possible exception of the Turkmen, received public education in their native languages in the first through
tenth grades. Since then there has been a tendency to increase the
number of students in Russian-language schools beyond the number
warranted by the influx of Russians into the non-Russian republics. But
this has been an uneven development: Some republics—such as Lithuania, Estonia, Latvia, Georgia, and Turkmenistan—seem to have resisted
those pressures rather well, whereas the Belorussians and Tatars have
yielded perceptibly in their republics. In some republics, such as Azerbaidjan, a modest trend toward assimilation is beclouded by a parallel
process that denies some of the non-Russian minorities, such as the
Armenians, their freedom in choosing the language of instruction.

Several prickly questions are raised by this analysis, quite apart from the
most obvious—and unanswerable—one: Why do some republics continue
to publish data on this subject, while others regard it as a state secret?
(1) Does the over-all language of instruction really matter, considering
that in the senior grades of non-Russian schools Russian language and
literature are given more hours than native language and literature? [46]
I think it does. A non-Russian will find it harder to master the Russian
language when the other subjects are taught in his native language. (2)
Do not the girls in the Muslim areas, when they reach the traditional
marriage age, drop out of school before graduation and thereby decrease
the number of students attending native-language schools? True, Edward
Allworth notes that out of 5,151 Kirgiz girls entering the first grade in
Osh oblast in 1950–51, all but 421 dropped out of school by the tenth
grade in 1959–60.[47] According to Elizabeth E. Bacon, an American

[44] *Kult. str.*, 1956, pp. 186–87; Eesti RSV Rahva majandus, etc., *Narodnoe khoziaistvo Estonskoi SSR* (Tallinn, 1957), p. 228; Bilinsky, "Soviet Education Laws," *passim;* V. Stanley Vardys, "The Baltic Peoples," *Problems of Communism*, XVI, No. 5 (Sept.–Oct. 1967), 60.

[45] Vardys, "Baltic Peoples," p. 61.

[46] For evidence, see Nicholas De Witt, *Education*, p. 113 (Uzbek SSR, 1960); V. Stanley Vardys, "Soviet Colonialism in the Baltic States, 1940–65," *Baltic Review*, No. 29 (June 1965), pp. 23–24; Kolasky, *Education*, pp. 64–65 (Ukraine, 1956 and 1964). Russian-language instruction in non-Russian schools starts with grade 2 or grade 1, depending on the republic.

[47] E. Allworth, "The Changing Intellectual and Literary Community," in E. Allworth, ed., *Central Asia: A Century of Russian Rule* (New York, 1967), p. 393.

anthropologist, this is not a uniform phenomenon: The problems seem to be more serious in the Turkmen S.S.R. and Tadzhik S.S.R. than in Kirgizia and Kazakhstan.[48] (3) Is it not true that a number of parents may send their children to Russian-language schools voluntarily? Must we assume, for example, that all of the ethnic Kazakh pupils who attend Russian-language schools have been forced by the government to do so?[49] Certainly not. Some parents want their children simply to pass for Russians, and some send them to Russian-language schools in order to prepare them for college, whose admission requirements in turn are manipulated by the government.

In summary, this article and a parallel study[50] show that, with the exception of the Tatars and the Jews, there has been no precipitous decline in the number of primary and secondary school pupils learning in their native languages. The main reason for this seems to lie in the resistance to Russification offered by the non-Russian peoples and the republic authorities. . . .

Higher education is the gateway to any responsible position in the Soviet Union: Even professional politicians often have university degrees. An equitable distribution of college admissions becomes the acid test of Soviet nationality policy, a policy that has so often proclaimed the goal of leveling economic standards between the republics and peoples. To an outside observer the record appears mixed. A tremendous amount was done in the 1920's and 1930's to allow the less well developed nationalities to catch up on higher education. But in the 1950's and 1960's the drive seems to have been run aground. Indeed, here and there we can observe instances of national discrimination in college admissions in favor of Russians and a few other nationalities; admissions of Jews, on the other hand, are being deliberately restricted. The concept that is being stressed now is the planned interrepublic ex-

[48] Elizabeth E. Bacon, *Central Asians Under Russian Rule: A Study in Culture Change* (Ithaca, N.Y., 1966), pp. 146, 171. Soviet data indicate that the problem has been solved in Kazakhstan. In 1958/59 even in the rural schools girls numbered 47 percent of the enrollment in grades 8–10. Admittedly, no breakdown is provided according to nationality of pupils. See Statisticheskoe upravlenie Kazakhskoi SSR, *Kul'turnoe stroitel'stvo Kazakhskoi SSR: Stat. sbornik* (Alma-Ata, 1960), pp. 60–61. For more precise and recent data see K. A. Aimanov (Kazakh SSR Minister of Education), "Razvitie narodnogo obrazovaniia v Kazakhstane," *Sovetskaia pedagogika*, XXXI, No. 5 (May 1967), 29.

[49] See V. Stanley Vardys, "Soviet Nationality Policy," p. 334. The original source is N. Dzhandil'din, "Voprosy internatsional'nogo vospitaniia trudiashchikhsia v sovremennykh usloviiakh," *Voprosy filosofii*, XV, No. 6 (June 1961), 8. They number 27 percent of all ethnic Kazakh students.

[50] Harry Lipset has attempted to reconstruct the number of pupils studying in their native languages from the number of school textbooks in various languages printed for 1964/65. His results, while occasionally less precise than mine, encompass all Union republics. In general, his and my data are very close. See his article, "The Status of National Minority Languages in Soviet Education," *Soviet Studies*, XIX (Oct. 1967), 181–89.

change of "cadres" of different nationalities.[51] If consistently implemented, this program is bound to result in relative neglect of the socio-economically weaker peoples (i.e., those who have to rely on outside personnel) and relative favoritism toward the stronger nations (the "exporters of cadres").[52] Insofar as many of the imported professionals are Russians, the new policy also amounts to a thinly disguised socio-economic and demographic Russification. In any case, it constitutes the reversal of the *korenizatsiya* policy of the 1920's, which made a good start toward establishing greater equality among the peoples of the U.S.S.R. . . .

[A detailed illustration of Soviet educational policy in the late 1950's comes from] the Tatar Autonomous Republic, a part of the Russian S.F.S.R. In 1960 the Tatar A.S.S.R. celebrated its fortieth anniversary, and it is to an unusually solid jubilee article that we owe some fascinating figures on Tatar college graduates.

Kazan University, which had been founded early in the nineteenth century, graduated only six Tatars before the Revolution, though it was located amidst the Volga Tatars.[53] The Soviets did better: From 1928 to 1940 institutions of higher learning in the Tatar A.S.S.R. graduated approximately 18,000 professionals in the following fields: more than 5,000 medical doctors, of whom 649 were Tatars; 4,124 teachers (1,300 Tatars); 2,383 veterinary doctors (236 Tatars); 1,580 agronomists and foresters (512 Tatars); 1,333 chemists (243 Tatars); and 1,029 construction engineers (197 Tatars).[54] As one can see, the share of Tatar graduates was far from being comparable to the Tatar share in the total population; but perhaps this inequity can be partly attributed to the difficulty of overcoming centuries of educational backwardness.

Even more fascinating are cumulative figures on graduates from individual institutions. During the Soviet period Kazan University has graduated more than 15,000 professionals, of whom 2,420 were Tatars; in 1960 the University had 1,840 Tatars among its 5,440 students, and 91 Tatars on its faculty of 326. The Kirov chemical engineering institute in Kazan had graduated 6,563 engineers (1,104 Tatars); the aviation institute (in 1960) counted 1,315 Tatars among its 7,742 students, but the number of Tatar graduates was not given.[55] The medical school had graduated 2,233 Tatars out of a total of 11,156 (1960 Tatar enrollment was 890 out of 2,769 students); the Kazan institute for veterinary medicine had graduated a total of 4,767 doctors, of whom 724 were Tatars. Similar figures (with the numbers of Tatar graduates in parentheses) are as follows: Gorky School of Agriculture in Kazan, 3,582 (1,120); Kazan Institute for Construction Engineering, 2,050 (374); Kuibyshev Institute

---

[51] See the editorial "Leninskaia druzhba narodov," *Pravda*, Sept. 5, 1965, p. 1.

[52] For some documentation see my "The Rulers and the Ruled," *Problems of Communism*, XVI, No. 5 (Sept.–Oct. 1967), 17–19.

[53] M. Makhmutov, "Za novye uspekhy narodnogo obrazovaniia v Tatarii," *Sovetskoi Tatarii 40 let* (Kazan, 1960), p. 170.

[54] Sh. Mukhamed'iarov *et al.*, "Vysshee obrazovanie i nauka v Tatarii za 40 let," in *ibid.*, p. 138.

[55] *Ibid.*, p. 142.

for Finance and Economics in Kazan, 5,030 (816); Kazan Pedagogical Institute, 17,652 (6,980).[56] Not only is the number of Tatar graduates disproportionately low in general, but the fields in which more Tatars are admitted (agronomy, teaching, general medicine) are among the less well remunerated in the Soviet Union. Only a relatively small number of Tatars have been admitted to well-paying engineering jobs. The authors of the article do try to reassure us that at the time it was written (in the 1959–60 academic year) there were 10,600 Tatars among a total of 33,800 students and that the 1,340 Tatar freshmen admitted that year constituted 34.1 per cent of their class.[57] This was still considerably below the Tatar share in the total population (47.2 per cent), but even that small figure was an improvement: In 1958 only 939 Tatar freshmen were admitted (27.7 per cent), and in 1956 there were only 919 Tatar freshmen (25.4 per cent). After forty years of Soviet rule the argument cannot be fairly made that the Tatars, who had been the most advanced of the Muslim peoples in the Russian Empire, are incapable of following college courses as easily as their Russian fellow citizens. More plausible is the hypothesis that national minorities without a Union-republic status are discriminated against more than those who are enjoying such a status.

Most Soviet institutions of higher learning teach in Russian,[58] a practice that easily lends itself to national discrimination. Only fragmentary information is available to substantiate this. I am not convinced that an analysis of the publications of individual universities would yield their language of instruction, even if such an analysis were possible. Nor is it feasible to try to ascertain the examination requirements for languages of the schools of higher education without access to the local press. In one republic prospective candidates for admission are given all possible information about the institution of their choice except the language in which they will be instructed.[59] It does appear, however, that in 1965–66 all twenty-eight schools in Belorussia taught in Russian,[60] that in the Ukraine in 1966–67 thirty-one teachers' colleges taught in Ukrainian, and that history was taught in Ukrainian at Lvov University (the total number of Ukrainian institutions was 133).[61] In Armenia, the university in Yerevan was reported in 1946 to have been teaching all

---

[56] *Ibid.*, pp. 143–44.

[57] *Ibid.*, pp. 141, 144.

[58] De Witt, *Education*, p. 357a.

[59] I have examined the *Dovidnyk dlia vstupnykiv do vyshchykh uchbovykh zakladiv Ukraïns'koi RSR na 1965 rik* (Kiev, 1965), and its successor volume for 1966 (Kiev, 1966).

[60] See *Literatura i mastatstva* (Minsk), Sept. 29, 1965; as cited by Urban, pp. 48–49 (see note 23).

[61] Education Minister Udovychenko's declaration to the Canadian Communist Party delegation, "Report of Delegation to Ukraine," p. 3; E. Babenko-Pivtoradni and L. Zuyeva, "After the Anxieties of Competition," *Radians'ka Ukraina*, Sept. 27, 1967, p. 4, as translated in *Digest of the Soviet Ukrainian Press*, Nov. 1967, p. 23 (referring to 1967/68). See also Kolasky, *Education*, p. 137.

classes in Armenian;[62] chances are that it still does. In some technical areas (e.g., nuclear physics) use of the lingua franca may be fully justified in the interests of better communication; and a uniform language of instruction does facilitate transfers between universities. But at the same time it should be borne in mind that lecturing in Russian may present genuine difficulties to many non-Russian students, especially in Central Asia, at a time when a disproportionate number of positions in the republic are still filled by nonindigenous personnel (at the end of 1960, for example, Uzbeks filled only 37 per cent of the professional positions in their republic).[63]

During the liberal period of 1956–57 several interesting complaints were published in the Soviet press. In 1957, for example, Kazakh secondary school graduates complained that they had difficulty in getting admitted to institutions of higher learning in Kazakhstan because they were required to pass an entrance examination in Russian language and literature. The official reply was that they were mistaken: They could have taken an examination in Kazakh instead if they had wanted to, and, anyway, Kazakhs accounted for 43.8 per cent of the newly admitted freshman class in 1956–57—an unusually high proportion.[64] There have been complaints of the poor quality or even lack of non-Russian university textbooks in Uzbekistan [65] and Estonia,[66] as well as a complaint of poor teaching of Tatar in Tatar teachers' colleges.[67] Earlier, in June, 1953, Ukrainian First Party Secretary Leonid G. Melnikov, a Russian by nationality, had been fired for, among other things, Russifying Ukrainian colleges in the western Ukraine.[68] But the most telling example from the late 1950's has been found by De Witt: in the Kirgiz S.S.R. during the three-year period 1955–57, about one thousand students of local nationality were forced to drop out of college, mostly because of a "lack of knowledge of the Russian language." [69] From another source we know that the total enrollment of Kirgiz students in 1955–56 was 4,085, which would be a dropout of 333 students, amounting to about 8 per cent.[70]

In more recent years the most amazing evidence of discrimination is that which has come from the Ukraine. On February 24, 1965, the

[62] Mary A. K. Matossian, *The Impact of Soviet Policies in Armenia* (Leiden, 1962), p. 190.

[63] *Vysshee obrazovanie v SSSR* (Moscow, 1961), p. 70.

[64] "Za dal'neishii rastsvet kul'tury kazakhskogo naroda," editorial in *Kazakhstanskaia pravda*, Jan. 31, 1957, p. 4.

[65] Dotsent M. Rakhmanov, Director of the Bukhara Pedagogical Institute, in *Pravda Vostoka*, Feb. 11, 1958, p. 2.

[66] De Witt, *Education*, p. 357a, citing *Sovetskaia Estonia*, Jan. 31, 1957.

[67] "Voprosy postavlennye zhizniu," *Uchitel'skaia gazeta*, Aug. 2, 1958, p. 2. This state of affairs had been criticized at the Tatar Party obkom meeting.

[68] See *Pravda*, June 13, 1953; *Radians'ka Ukraina*, June 28, 1953 (editorial); or Bilinsky, *Second Soviet Republic*, pp. 166, 233 ff., esp. 239.

[69] De Witt, *Education*, p. 357a. The quote is from *Sovetskaia Kirgiziia*, No. 4, 1957.

[70] Tsentr. stat. upravl. pri Sov. min. Kirgizskoi SSR, *Narodnoe khoziaistvo Kirgizskoi SSR v 1960 godu: Stat. ezhegodnik* (Frunze, 1961), p. 230.

Ukrainian journalist, poet, and translator Svyatoslav I. Karavans'ky addressed a formal complaint to the Procurator of the Ukrainian S.S.R. demanding that Ukrainian S.S.R. Minister of Higher and Specialized Secondary Education Yu. M. Dadenkov be held criminally liable for national discrimination and for the violation of Leninist principles in higher education in the republic. (For this and similar complaints Karavans'ky was remanded, without a trial, to serve out the rest of a twenty-five-year sentence imposed upon him originally in 1944, of which he had already served some fifteen years. He was sent back to a labor camp for eight years and seven months.) [71] In his closely argued and partially documented complaint, which despite its conveyance through underground channels appears to be authentic, Karavans'ky stated that in the Ukrainian S.S.R., Ukrainian applicants to higher schools were being discriminated against in two ways: through the requirement of passing an examination in Russian language and literature, the results of which were counted in the admission competition, and through the device of holding examinations in special disciplines (e.g., physics) in Russian. These practices resulted in more examination points being obtained by ethnic Russians and graduates of Russian-language schools in the Ukraine and discriminated against ethnic Ukrainians, especially those who graduated from Ukrainian-language schools. For instance, in 1964–65 the total student body of the Odessa Polytechnical Institute was only 43 per cent Ukrainian; in the freshman class, Ukrainians constituted 40 per cent and Russians 46 per cent. He further charged that in the preponderant majority of schools of higher education in Kiev, Kharkov, Odessa, Dnepropetrovsk, and other cities, instruction was being given in Russian, with the result that a considerably lower percentage of Ukrainians were being admitted to these institutions than there were Ukrainians working the economy of the republic.[72] . . .

There have also been complaints of discrimination in graduate study,[73] which has an impact on the supply of non-Russian scientists. The interpretation of statistics on the national composition of graduate students in 1960 shows that in the case of Ukrainians, Belorussians, Kazakhs, and Moldavians there was a smaller number of graduate students than would have been warranted on the basis of the total populations.[74] The following three facts substantiate the complaints still further. First, the Central Committee of the Communist Party of the Soviet Union and the U.S.S.R. Council of Ministers decide which institutions in the U.S.S.R. are em-

[71] See Chornovil, ed., *Lykho z rozumu*, p. 129 (see no. 27). See also Chornovil's letter to the procurator of the Ukrainian SSR *et al.*, printed in *Novy Shliakh* (Winnipeg), Nov. 11, 1967, p. 14.

[72] "Petition to the Procurator of the UkrSSR by Citizen Svyatoslav Karavans'ky, resident in Odessa, at . . . ," reprinted in Chornovil, ed., *Lykho z rozumu*, pp. 110–15. It has been translated in John Kolasky, *Education in the Soviet Ukraine: A Study in Discrimination and Russification* (Toronto, 1968), pp. 222–24.

[73] Kolasky, *Education*, pp. 125–29, 139, 155–56

[74] See Table XXIV and Appendix I, *ibid.*, pp. 133 and 213.

powered to grant graduate degrees (the "candidate" and "doctor of sciences" degrees).[75] Second, the Higher Certification Commission in Moscow, an elaborate body, which is itself appointed by the U.S.S.R. minister of higher education, in turn confirms the personnel of the academic councils in all institutions authorized to recommend graduate degrees (those councils supervise all the work toward degrees).[76] Third, for good measure, the Higher Certification Commission must approve all candidates' and doctors' dissertations.[77]

The emphasis in this study has been on the availability of primary and secondary education in the native languages of the Soviet peoples and on the opportunities for these nationalities to obtain higher education. . . .

I have . . . omitted an extensive analysis of the latest educational reforms of 1966 because it is too early to assess their full impact. Briefly, in August, 1966, the Union-Republic Ministry of Education was set up in Moscow. Previously, in theory at least, primary and secondary education had been within the exclusive jurisdiction of republic ministries of education. Now those ministries have been formally converted to *de facto* branch offices of the ministry in Moscow.[78] In September, 1966, the Party Central Committee and the U.S.S.R. Council of Ministers issued a decree, which, among other things, subordinated a number of institutions of higher education in the republics directly to the Union-Republic Ministry of Higher and Specialized Secondary Education in Moscow.[79] In practice it means that, for example, the Ukrainian S.S.R. Ministry of Higher and Specialized Secondary Education, starting with the academic year 1967–68, no longer has any control over such well-known schools as the Dnepropetrovsk State University and the Kharkov Institute of Aviation.[80] In November, 1966, the Party Central Committee and the U.S.S.R. Council of Ministers passed another decree, which, among other things, standardized the curricula of elementary

[75] See the lists of institutions approved by those bodies on Aug. 20, 1956, in A. V. Topchiev, ed., *Nauchnye kadry v SSSR: Sbornik dokumentov i spravochnikh materialov* (Moscow, 1959), pp. 171–92, and a statistical summary of those lists in Kolasky, *Education*, Table XX, p. 126.

[76] See "Polozhenie o Vysshei Attestatsionnoi Korissii po prisuzhdeniu uchenykh stepenei i zvanii pri Ministerstve Vysshego Obrazovaniia SSSR," of Aug. 20, 1956, Arts. 1 (i) and 2, in Topchiev, ed., p. 168. Korol, *Soviet Research*, p. 94, describes the Commission in 1959 as consisting of 67 expert subcommissions meeting twice a month, with 68 academicians, 93 corresponding members of the Academy of Sciences, 365 professors (and doctors of science), 188 candidates of science (and docents), and 62 industrial specialists.

[77] See "Polozhenie . . . ," Art. 1 (b) and (v) in Topchiev, ed., p. 167; and Kolasky, *Education*, pp. 139, 154–56.

[78] *Pravda*, Aug. 4, 1966.

[79] "O merakh po uluchsheniiu podgotovki spetsialistov i sovershenstvovaniiu rukovodstva vysshim i srednim spetsial'nym obrazovaniem v strane," *Vestnik vysshei shkoly*, XXIV, No. 9 (Sept. 1966), 4; also *Pravda*, Sept. 9, 1966, p. 1.

[80] Kolasky, *Education*, p. 207.

and secondary schools throughout the Soviet Union. It would appear that in the non-Russian-language schools the native language has to be taken on top of the full class load of Russian-language schools—a measure not designed to make the former schools more attractive.[81] Insofar as formally separate ministries in the republics served as nuclei of opposition against Russification,[82] the 1966 reforms seem designed not only to centralize administration but to advance Russification from above, almost by administrative fiat.

In conclusion, judging by the proportion of ethnic Russians living in the non-Russian republics and by the increasing number of pupils being taught in Russian since 1938–39, Russification of primary and secondary education is gaining, though not at an equal pace. The Lithuanians, Latvians, Estonians, and Georgians seem to have resisted the trend rather well. The Russification has not gone unchallenged even in Belorussia, where linguistic Russification seems to have proceeded very far. On the other hand, though at the price of frequently being compelled "voluntarily" to attend Russian-language schools, all peoples of the Soviet Union are guaranteed at least eight years of primary and secondary education. National discrimination, however, does prevail in entrance to institutions of higher education, both through national admission quotas and through the use of Russian as the language of entrance examinations and lectures. Thus, in essence, in comparison with the tsarist rule, national discrimination has been shifted from primary and secondary school to higher education, an area of great importance in the second half of the twentieth century. The progress is undeniable, but limited.

Finally, this study opens up two broad questions, which can be discussed only briefly: (a) What is the effect of education in the mother tongue on ethnic identification? (b) How does education itself affect ethnic allegiance? Addressing myself to the first question, I would agree with the conclusion of Richard Pipes, who has analyzed the results of the 1959 census. In his apt words:

> Language, of course, is only one of several criteria of national viability, and it would not be sound to base one's whole evaluation on the pattern of linguistic development. But it is a most important criterion. The transition from one language to another is, perhaps, the single most dramatic manifestation of a shift in national allegiance. The fact that it is not occurring among the major peripheral nationalities gives some ground for arguing that the burden of proof in discussing the fate of Soviet nationalities lies on those who foresee their imminent dissolution in a single Soviet nationality.[83]

[81] ["On Measures for Further Improving the Work of the General-Education Secondary School"], *Pravda*, Nov. 19, 1966, pp. 1–2, or *Current Digest of the Soviet Press*, XVIII, No. 46 (December 11, 1966): 6–8. Comments in Kolasky, *Education*, p. 66.

[82] The Ukrainian S.S.R. Ministry of Education allegedly resisted hints from Moscow that in the interests of overworked students Ukrainian should not be taught in Russian-language schools in the Ukraine. See Kolasky, *Education*, p. 74.

[83] Richard Pipes, "The Forces of Nationalism," *Problems of Communism*, XIII, No. 1 (January–February 1964), p. 6.

Soviet policy has certainly increased the availability of education in non-Russian languages as compared with 1914. Despite the reaction since the 1930's the major languages (with the exception of Yiddish) still serve as an important medium of instruction. On balance, the Soviet educational system helps to keep the major languages alive and thus contributes to ethnic identification.

In discussing the second question (the effect of education on ethnic allegiance), we should observe the following limitations on statistical hypotheses. We could correlate educational levels and nationality identification, as disclosed by the population censuses of 1926, 1939, and 1959. But the official definition of nationality has been changed between 1926 and 1939. More important, national identification in the census could mean many things: In a few cases it could mean a reluctant admission of ethnic origin (the assimilation of certain non-Russians is not being encouraged); in other instances it might signify a quasi-reflexive response, or a proud affirmation of one's ethnic origin, or a claim to assimilated status. The so-called native language, which is only slightly less precise, has not been correlated with education in the 1959 census publications. We are, therefore, forced to rely on our own interpretations of events. From my knowledge of the events in the Ukraine and some acquaintance with those in the Baltic countries in the past ten years, I conclude that it is not ordinary peasants and workers who have been in the forefront of political nationalist resistance, but educated men. E. K. Berklavs, who was purged in mid-1959, was a deputy prime minister of the Latvian S.S.R. Viacheslav Chornovil, the thirty-year-old author of *The Crime of Thought*, who was twice arrested and jailed in 1966 and 1967, is a Ukrainian journalist and radio and television reporter. He is also a candidate for a Ph.D. degree in Marxist-Leninist philosophy! His position should perhaps not be generalized, but he does not stand alone. In these cases, at the very least, education has not extinguished national allegiance, but quite the contrary—it has affirmed it.

＊　　＊　　＊

Part Five

THE FUTURE

XII

The Future of Soviet Society

The previous chapters have demonstrated that Soviet society is anything but static. We can be certain that the Soviet system in the future will undergo change even though we may not know the limits of that change. It is doubtful that the Soviets themselves know the limits of social change in their country. It would be futile to attempt to predict specific changes: For the short run that would be useless and for the long run very hazardous. But the same concern to comprehend the present compels us to speculate at least on the broad profile of what Soviet society will look like two or three decades from now.

In many ways Soviet society is unique. Will it continue to retain its present character? Can we say that the Russian social structure has found its permanent shape? Or will the demands of an increasingly advanced industrial state produce a radical restructuring comparable to the changes made under Stalin's rule? How stable is Russia's government? Can the regime indefinitely manipulate and balance the many social forces pressing for attention in Soviet society? Might a new tyrant come to power? Is an evolution toward some form of constitutional democracy within the capability of the Soviet system? These are the kinds of question that prompt speculation about where Soviet society is moving.

To a considerable extent the answers depend upon assumptions one makes as to the causes of social change either generally or specifically within the Soviet system. One can approach the subject of change from one of several frameworks. We might, for example, simply extrapolate present trends into the future. This approach would stress quantitative change and would basically show the future as an expanded version of the present. The economy would be larger, the standard of living would be higher, the ratio of service output to production will have increased, Russification of the Soviet culture will have advanced, more of the population will live in cities, and so on. While perhaps the safest and easiest approach, projection alone fails to illuminate qualitative changes in the system.

Another approach might be to apply the analytic concepts of systems theory to the Soviet Union and ask what changes are likely to be necessary to guarantee the survival and growth of the system. System theorists stress functional needs that must be performed, such as interest articulation and aggregaton, political socialization, and recruitment, to name a few. How effective is the Communist Party, the systems theorist might ask, in adjusting the demands of administrators, peasants, industrial workers, intellectuals, and other interest groupings and reconciling them in broad policies satisfactory to all? Which policies are dysfunctional to system maintenance and must be modified? Systems theory might be useful to focus on problems that the Soviet Union has in common with other polities. However, by itself systems theory cannot point out developments likely to take place because of conditions unique to the Soviet Union. There are too many different ways by which the requirements of any one of the several requisites of functional analysis can be met.

A third approach, and a very popular one, is to look at the Soviet Union as illustrative of some particular type of a model, and on the basis of the parameters established by the model to deduce future developments. By far the most common model developed to explain the Soviet Union is the totalitarian model. Stressing as it does the autocratic character of Party rule, the subordination of society to the state, mobilization of the masses through propaganda and coercion, and the ideological fervor of the rulers to reconstruct both man and society, the totalitarian model adequately described Stalinist Russia. It suffers, however, as a conceptual model for explaining fundamental social change. As post-Stalinist Russia changed not only from above through concessions by the rulers but from below with the development of new relationships between social groups and public policy, criticism of the totalitarian model increased. The totalitarian model, for example, fails to explain the sharp decrease in the use of terror since Stalin's death.

Other models have described the essential characteristics of the Soviet Union in terms of industrial growth and change. The nation's commitment to economic growth and the creation of an affluent welfare state is viewed as the overriding factor of contemporary Soviet Russia by some. The "industrial" or "modernizing" model emphasizes those requirements—technical competence, national integration, education, and so on—which the Soviet Union has in common with all highly industrial powers. A "bureaucratic" model looks at the Soviet Union as a large complex bureaucratic organization and stresses the importance of rational management, much as in the administration of corporate affairs. These and other models are by no means incompatible with the totalitarian model; indeed almost all observers do integrate their newer concepts with some features of the older model. But where Soviet society was seen as an almost uniquely totalitarian model (shared as a prototype only by the Nazi regime in Germany), the newer models focus upon dynamic factors shared by many other countries as well.

The articles in this chapter, which offer a forecast of Soviet society in the years and decades to come, do not rely on any single one of the several approaches just mentioned. They are eclectic in the sense that they incorporate in varying degrees elements of several of them.

Marshall Shulman is Professor of Government at Columbia University and Director of its Russian Institute. Formerly he was a research associate of Harvard's Russian Research Center. He has written *Beyond the Cold War* and *Stalin's Foreign Policy Reappraised*. Allen Kassof is Associate Professor of Sociology at Princeton University. He is the author of *The Soviet Youth Program: Regimentation and Rebellion*. Andrei Amalrik, a young Soviet historian, has been a critic of Soviet controls over its intellectuals. In 1970 he was sentenced to three years' confinement in a labor camp for "defaming the Soviet state."

40

TRANSFORMATIONS IN THE SOVIET SYSTEM

MARSHALL D. SHULMAN

In dealing with a distant society, we sometimes permit ourselves to reduce things to manageable simplifications which we would hesitate to accept in dealing with the jumble of detail closer at home. This phenomenon has been particularly apparent among the ventures of some foreign observers into quite sweeping generalizations about trends in Soviet society.

We need, of course, to try to form some notions, however tentative, about what is happening to the Soviet system, for both intellectual and practical reasons. The evolution of the Soviet social structure, under conditions that illustrate the interaction of modern totalitarianism and advancing industrialization, represents an intriguing contribution to the

From *Beyond the Cold War* by Marshall D. Shulman (New Haven: Yale University Press, 1966), pp. 33–49. Copyright © 1966 by Marshall D. Shulman. Reprinted with permission of the publisher.

comparative study of contemporary political and social development. On the practical side, there is the obvious linkage between Soviet internal developments and the dynamism of Soviet foreign policy.

The range of Western speculative responses to these questions has been broad and far from unanimous. Some writers have seen recent developments as part of a process of liberalization; others emphasize the continuing dominance of the Communist Party. Some stress the rapidity of social change; others say such changes are but superficial and that fundamental transformations are proceeding at a glacial pace. Many observers are attracted by the notion of the rise of a "managerial class" in the Soviet Union and, with it, the replacement of revolutionary ideology by pragmatic problem-solving. A companion of this view—mildly Marxist in perspective—is what has come to be called the "fat-man thesis," that Soviet society is becoming and must necessarily become more conservative as it reaches a higher level of economic development. Others, to balance the picture, see economic development as leading to a depersonalized technocratic dictatorship, no less dynamic in its foreign policies.

For our present purpose, which is to consider the relationship between transformations in the Soviet system and the evolution of the Cold War, we begin by reminding ourselves how intricate is the society we are trying to analyze, and how much our speculative hypotheses are dependent upon selected fragmentary impressions and the culling of printed materials which refract more than they reflect even limited aspects of Soviet life. We direct our attention, therefore, not so much to broad general theories, nor to the propensities of the present Soviet individual leaders—about which we have little certain knoweldge—but rather toward some of the underlying forces that seem to be at work, influencing the longer-term evolution of the Soviet system. From this perspective, our concern is not only with the conscious changes by the Soviet leadership, but even more so with those that may be partly or wholly unintended—the kind of transformations that come about over a period of time as the consequence of actions taken to meet immediate felt needs, but going far beyond the intentions and perhaps even the awareness of the actors themselves.

In response to a number of factors in international politics . . . the Soviet leadership has been brought to the view that greater emphasis upon the further development of its economy is a fundamental key to the enlargement of its power and influence in the world. It is obvious that an arsenal of modern weapons systems and activities in outer space require a highly developed technology supported by a strong economy. Further, the inhibitions against general war and the blunted promise of direct revolutionary action, in Europe at least, have combined to encourage reliance upon other instrumentalities for a long-term advance, including foreign aid, trade, and the example of a successful system, all of which add urgency to the repair of shortcomings in the domestic economy. Historically, the Soviet regime under Stalin had concentrated its resources upon rapid industrilization at all costs, with the result that spectacular advances in certain fields were purchased at the expense of others, chiefly agriculture and consumer goods, as well as an increasingly inadequate system for administering the industrial complex that emerged. The effect of this unbalanced development could not be held off indefinitely. Declining growth rates and serious shortages in critcial areas were but symptoms of profound, cumulative disorders which demanded attention. The Party was faced with the necessity of repairing the imbalances and adapting itself and its methods of governing to the requirements of administering an increasingly complex industrial society. Here we have, I believe, a fundamental factor in the transformation that has been taking place.

We are somewhat aware from our own experience how advancing industrialization continues to transform our own societies—shifting our populations, changing social patterns, complicating the functions of government and business organizations, creating an increasingly complex, delicate, and interdependent mechanism. How much more so is this the case for the Soviet Union, where the functions of control over all aspects of life are gathered in the hands of a small group of men. The contrast between the functions of the Communist Party in the early days and now can be compared to the difference between running a Roman trireme, where coercion and exhortation were sufficient to keep the galley slaves pulling at their oars—and, on the other hand, operating a modern ocean vessel, where regularity of authority and highly developed leadership skills are required to encourage and coordinate the exercise of a variety of specialized functions. Responding to the requirements of industrialization, the Party leadership has been trying to find ways to modernize its system of administration and control, without—if possible—fundamental alterations in its political system.

Indeed, this last reservation is the question of questions for the Soviet system. Can so centralized a political control system efficiently administer an advanced industrial economy? If not, must it accept a metamorphosis in its fundamental political character? Can it do so, gradually, experimentally, without cataclysm?

These are the questions that loom over the process of de-Stalinization, which represented a major effort to chip away at the encrustations of bureaucratic inertia, of safe routines, cautious evasion of responsibility, and the paralysis of initiative, habits deeply imbedded in the middle generation of Soviet bureaucrats as part of the Stalinist heritage. Along with this have come other experimental efforts to modernize the system and make it more efficient: the reduction in the overt use of mass terror, to give a greater sense of personal security and to encourage initiative; more use of material incentives to raise productivity; an experimentation with market forces in place of overcentralized economic planning; somewhat wider latitudes in artistic and intellectual realms and in cultural and technical contacts with the West.

But, such is the nature of the Soviet system, these practical measures had to be given ideological rationalization and sanction, and this is the point at which friction bursts into flame between orthodoxy and the impulse to adapt and modernize. In the new Party Program adopted in 1961, and elsewhere, the Party has sought to get away from its characterization as a dictatorship. In place of the previous self-description as a "dictatorship of the proletariat," it now seeks to identify the system as "a state of the whole people"—which is intended to carry the implication of a wider sense of voluntary participation by a classless population in the administration of the economy and the service functions of government. Along with this, the Party Program identifies the present period as one in which the main task is "building communism," which implies, but does not define, the promise of abundance widely shared.

Necessarily, these practical and ideological measures for the easement of internal tensions have been accompanied by a commitment to international peace as a positive motivation for popular support, in place of the earlier habit of mobilizing political support through the pressure of external tensions and hostilities. This has been registered on the ideological plane by the extended commitment to "peaceful coexistence" as a long-term strategy leading to ultimate victory, while the ups and downs of international tension have been accompanied by a broadened concept of struggle under conditions of "peaceful coexistence."

How far, then, does the model of totalitarianism still apply to the Soviet system under these conditions? A Soviet citizen, asked this question, would be likely to reply that the most important thing from his point of view is that the cruel and despotic use of mass terror has been mercifully eased. But from the point of view of an outside observer, the most significant characteristic of the regime is that control over all aspects of public life continues to be exercised by the governing group at the top of the Party, with the assistance of a still formidable police apparatus. Clearly, it would be misleading either to continue to apply the Stalinist model of totalitarian dictatorship, or to speak of liberalization in a Western sense. A more differential conceptual tool of analysis is required.

If a distinction is made between a traditional autocratic regime, which involves a high degree of concentration of political power and authority, and a totalitarian regime in which the control of all public aspects of life remains in the hands of one man or a small group and the society is not distinguished from the state, then what we know of the Soviet development obliges us to regard the Soviet system as passing into some mature form of totalitarianism. We have learned a great deal in recent years about the structure and functioning of totalitarian systems, but we still know very little about the laws that govern their evolution under conditions of modern industrialization. Whether a mature form of totalitarianism can remain a more or less stable condition, or whether it is necessarily but a way-station on the path to pluralism and the diffusion of political controls, is of course the crucial and still unanswered question. Those writers who incline to the latter view tend to give much weight to the technocratic quality of the Party leadership, to the pressure of managers and functional interest groups, to the emergence of a "bourgeois middle class," and to the voices of protest of liberal intellectuals, artists, lawyers, or scientists.

It must be said, however, that so far at least these developments have not altered the essential structure of totalitarian control. There can be no doubt of the primacy of the small, co-opting group at the top of the Party hierarchy exercising control through a large professional Party apparatus and a large political police apparatus, whose operations are more subtle and sophisticated than before, but no less pervasive into all aspects of life and especially those involved in contacts with foreigners. Even casual and unsystematic investigation can identify significant groups in Soviet society with varying degrees of influence and a sense of group identity and group loyalty, but the Party has so far succeeded in preventing such groups from becoming political entities, with independent sources of political power. This would include economic administrators, managers, technocratic specialists, government bureaucrats, scientists, police, military, intellectuals, artists, peasants, and the youth, as well as local regional interest groups. These are of course very broad categories, and further significant distinctions can be made within each of these groups. For example, conflicting interest groups within the military establishment have pressed their claims in public exchanges. Among the intellectuals there are some who function as spokesmen for the Establishment and some bolder and more independent spirits who press for modifications in Party control over the arts, with the great majority somewhere ambiguously in between.

We are, quite naturally, drawn to those among the intellectuals and artists who voice aspirations for freer expression, and who keep pressing, within the limits of their situation, for less interference by Party functionaries and for the expression of humane values in art. We are right to recognize the universal moral significance of their courage, but we are not right, and we do them a great disservice, when we claim them as Westernized heroes. For the most part, the liberal intellectuals as a group, including the younger generation of intellectuals, if one may generalize from limited experience, appear to be patriotic—in the sense that they are deeply committed to Russian national traditions— and it must not be assumed that their pressure on the regime for less Party interference or their private criticism of particular officials is equated with a rejection of the system as a whole. Those few within this group who have an ideological commitment—and there are some, particularly among the young—idealize the Revolution in a pure sense, detached from the realities and the compromises that the Party has made. Most, however, are thoroughly and by deep habit apolitical: Politics for them is the business of a disembodied, gray anonymous "they" who run things. As a group, they are not politically effective. Being an articulate segment of the population, and because of the functions they perform in the society, they do exert some pressure against one sector or another of the limits established by the governing group, but the prospects for their exercise of a dominant influence over the evolution of the system as a whole do not appear to be bright—the more so because "the system" in which they live is bulwarked by a large Party and police apparatus, which bureaucracy has a dynamic of its own. . . .

The relationship of the ruling Party group to each of the functional groups and subgroups we have identified is a subtle process of interaction. Upward pressures do get registered and sometimes accommodated, the more so as the efficient functioning of the group is necessary to the system, but the accommodations are within well-defined limits of acceptance of the Party's ultimate control. This point is particularly important to appreciate in weighing the expectation that the technocrats are taking over the system. It is certainly true that the present Party leadership is better trained in technical and management experience than its predecessors have been; it is also true that it is obliged to give weight to the imperatives reflected through the managers and the technical specialists. But the fundamental point is that the ultimate decision-making is still a political act, and it is securely in the hands of men whose vocation and experience are *primarily* those of political overseers, moving from one sector to another as needed.

We may be led into error if we analogize too directly from our own experience with "interest groups" and pressure lobbies, as some analysts tend to do. Undoubtedly functional interests have developed in the Soviet Union as part of the process of industrialization, and it seems to be the case that the process of decision-making increasingly provides for regularized consultation among the diverse interests affected, particularly in the post-Khrushchev period, but the Party's control of personnel in each of the other hierarchies and the shifting of Party personnel from one function to another tend to limit the independent pressure that any interest group can exert upon Party decision-making.

There is a question whether there is a Soviet equivalent to what in this country has come to be called "the military-industrial complex"—that is, some identification of groups that may have an interest in higher tension and in emphasizing the conflict aspect of foreign relations. It might appear from the available literature that certain of the military interests, certain of the heavy industrial interests, the Party professional ideologists, and the middle generation of the Party professional apparatus may be among the groups reflecting a commitment in this direction. But our group analysis is still largely an *a priori* affair, and we need to press our search for knowledge in this direction, in order that we may better identify the dominant political groups within the leadership and have some insight into their perceptions of the world, their values and their goals, as a differentiated matter, rather than generalizing about *the* Soviet leadership group as a whole. Group politics, within and outside the Party, obviously affect policy and personnel changes within the limits of a largely unified hierarchical system, but we cannot speak categorically about this, for the process is one of subtle personal interactions, permeated by informal private arrangements. It would, however, be stretching the evidence to suggest that the process yet resembles the interplay of independent pressure groups familiar to us. . . .

It has been evident, even in this brief synthesis, that at each turn we are dealing with processes of change that are subtle, ambiguous, and in motion. There is little empirical evidence available, and it is extremely difficult to say with certainty how far along the path any of these processes have advanced or even to be sure in what direction they are moving. The main point that emerges, relevant to our concerns in these pages, is that it would be premature to base present policy judgments upon an estimate that these domestic factors have already deflected the main direction of Soviet foreign policy, although we may want to encourage such possibilities over the long run.

Certain more limited conclusions, however, do have a bearing upon present policy formulation. It seems clearly evident that domestic problems, particularly the repair of economic deficiencies and the political consequences of these reorganizations, occupy a position of high priority in the attention of the Soviet leadership. It also appears to be the case that the system has moved toward less reliance upon external tension for domestic consolidation than formerly. Corresponding to the reduction in internal tension, which is found useful in the operation of an advancing industrial society, the leadership seems to find the generation of external tension less useful in cementing popular support and evoking productive energies than the peace symbol, given the weary reaction of the population to the tragic effects of the last war, unless external events appear to require a further mobilization of the economy. It may also be the case that a broadening of the decision-making process among a larger number of technical interests, also required by the complexity of the economy, serves to impose some restraint upon the political leadership, reducing the possibility of sudden changes, of dramatic surprise, and of caprice. . . .

Probably the determining factor is likely to center around the future of the Party—whether the Party can maintain its primacy and its essential character. The ideological authority of the Party has been weakened by the de-Stalinization process and by the present emphasis upon economic progress rather than revolution. At the same time, the structural authority of the Party has been strengthened relative to other institutions. Whether the erosion of ideological justifications for the Party's command role will undermine its authority may depend primarily upon its success or failure in the management of the economy. Perhaps it is something of a Marxist conception to argue that if the Party is successful in achieving a thriving economy this will produce its own kind of ideological justification, quite distant from its revolutionary origins. But if so, what would the ascendancy of technical specialists (and the passage of several generations) do to the values and goals of the Party? We are predisposed to hope that it will encourage liberal values, but might it not equally well tend toward an organization of society with greater efficiency, greater depersonalization, in which power is an end in itself, unrestrained by humane values? Some of these possibilities, of course, are but a magnification of those that concern us in examining the values of the Organization Man in our own society.

And can the economy be efficiently run? Can a system so highly centralized in its power structure adapt itself to the multiplicity of interdependent functions required by advanced industrialization? When one contemplates the present bureaucratic encumbrances that have barnacled Soviet planning, production, and distribution, the prospect does not seem favorable. Still, it would probably be a mistake to extrapolate from present economic troubles in the Soviet Union. We have had a tendency in the past to project too readily from Soviet successes at one time, or from its backwardness at another, and have been led into error as a consequence. Sometimes this is because both successes and backwardness are difficult to see in proportion, and also because it is difficult to estimate the flexibility of the Party leadership in dealing with the reallocation of resources.

Moreover, beyond the uncertainty whether the Party will be able to repair present deficiencies and learn to administer so complex an economy, there is a further uncertainty whether the concentration of effort and resources provided by the Soviet system will turn out to have been upon the decisive levers of economic power. The criteria of success or failure may depend in part upon external factors. Whether a balanced development such as is now prized in the West, or a planned concentration upon certain sectors of the economy judged by the Soviet leaders to be decisive, will produce the more effective system may depend upon whether the world environment will favor peace and stability or continued mobilization, and, therefore, which forms of economic power will be the more influential.

In short, to return to our central question, while we may judge that the process of adaptation to advancing industrialization is a determining force, tending toward the ascendancy of technically trained executives and administrators, we cannot predict whether this will have the effect of diluting the Party's monopoly of power, or be internalized within the Party; nor can we be confident that it will tend toward a pluralism of independent forces within the society, from whose interplay will emerge a form of democracy defined and shaped by Russian historical and cultural experience. We may hope that this will be so, and we may, within the limits of our influence, try to encourage a development along these lines, but we should not assume that this is a determined outcome or that it has already begun to appear. . . .

*   *   *

41

THE ADMINISTERED SOCIETY:
TOTALITARIANISM WITHOUT TERROR

ALLEN KASSOF

As an orchestra conductor sees to it that all the instruments sound harmonious and in proportion, so in social and political life does the Party direct the efforts of all people toward the achievement of a single goal.

Each person must, like a bee in the hive, make his own contribution to increasing the material and spiritual wealth of society. People may be found who say that they do not agree with this, that it is coercion of the individual, a return to the past. To this my answer is: We are living in an organized socialist society where the interests of the individual conform to the interests of society and are not at variance with them.—Nikita Khrushchev, March 8, 1963.[1]

More than a decade after Stalin's death, the time is ripe for a fresh view of Soviet society. Many of the conventional patterns of analysis, developed largely during the period of Stalinist absolutism, seem to be no longer adequate for this purpose. This article proposes that a new concept, the "administered society," may be useful in summarizing and evaluating recent changes in the Soviet system and in identifying current trends.

Like other ideal-typical concepts, that of the administered society by no means pretends to account for all of the concrete detail of a social order. Instead, it draws attention (through emphasis, and hence a certain exaggeration) to very general features which constitute a society's ethos or prevailing themes—in the Soviet case, centering

---

[1] Reported in *Pravda* and *Izvestia*, March 10, 1963; translation from *Current Digest of the Soviet Press*, XV, No. 11 (April 23, 1963).

Reprinted with permission of the publisher from *World Politics*, Vol. XVI, No. 4 (July, 1964), pp. 558-75.

around the drive of the regime to establish a highly organized and totally coordinated society, and the consequences of that drive.

The administered society can be defined as one in which an entrenched and extraordinarily powerful ruling group lays claim to ultimate and exclusive scientific knowledge of social and historical laws and is impelled by a belief not only in the practical desirability, but the moral necessity, of planning, direction, and coordination from above in the name of human welfare and progress.

Convinced that there should be complete order and predictability in human affairs, the elite is concerned not merely with the "commanding heights," but also to an overwhelming degree with the detailed regulation of the entire range of social life, including those institutions which, in the West, typically have been regarded as lying beyond the legitimate scope of public authority and political intervention. The rulers of the administered society refuse to grant the possibility of unguided coordination and integration; they believe, on the contrary, that not only the masses but responsible subgroups (for example, the professions) are incapable of maintaining a viable social order on their own, without the precise and detailed supervision of an omniscient political directorate. The elite believes, and through a far-reaching program of education and propaganda tries to teach its subjects, that the only possible good society is one that is *administered.*

The administered society is thus a variant of modern totalitarianism, with the important difference that it operates by and large without resort to those elements of gross irrationality (in particular, the large scale and often self-defeating use of psychological terror and physical coercion as basic means of social control) that we have come to associate with totalitarian systems in recent decades.

The administered society, however, should be distinguished from the conventional welfare state in that it is not involved simply or principally in creating minimal conditions of social welfare within an otherwise pluralistic political framework, but instead treats welfare as an incidental—and instrumental—element in the larger scheme of social planning and reform. While an administered society may display more or fewer welfare features of a material or service nature, they are neither final goals nor the most important determinants of over-all policy. To put it another way, the elite regards the promotion of total coordination as itself the ultimate form of welfare under modern conditions.

Plainly enough, the administered society is not the authentic good society of faithful Marxists, for it is characterized by the growing size and importance of an elite party and state bureaucracy, in contrast to the withering away of governmental apparatus which Marxism predicts and upon which it insists.

Nor, finally, should the administered society be confused with a rational technocracy, even though here there are some superficial parallels. The leadership of the administered society, to be sure, is forced to rely on scientific and technical cadres as sources of essential information and in the execution of highly complex economic and social planning. But the political elite is not bound solely or principally by considerations of technical rationality; the technicians and experts operate only under license of the political elite and in terms of the latter's self-proclaimed ultimate knowledge about the proper uses of science and technology in the larger sociohistorical setting. The experts, in short, are servants rather than masters or even independent practitioners. They lack the power of veto on grounds of technical rationality over political decisions (though in the end the limits of technology itself, if not the will of the technocrats, of course impose certain restraints). And their potential for independent influence in the society is decisively cut short by the elite's consistent practice of defining *all* decision-making as political and therefore beyond the competence of any group other than itself. Similar considerations are applied—if anything, with more vigor—to the producers of the more "esoteric" goods and services—the artists and writers, professors and critics and journalists. Like technicians in the more literal sense, they are construed by the elite as turning out "commodities" whose creation, distribution, and consumption demand coordination from above in the pursuit of order and planned progress.

Let us see how this preliminary definition of the administered society can be applied to an understanding of Soviet developments, and with what advantages.

TOTALITARIANISM WITHOUT TERROR

By now it must be clear even to the most reluctant analyst that the cumulative change in Soviet society since Stalin's death is too great to dismiss as merely superficial. The transformation of Soviet society during this period, though by no means a wholesale departure from earlier patterns, nevertheless has been extensive. The conventional label for this change has been "liberalization." The reference point is to the state of Soviet totalitarianism under Stalin and to the degree of departure from that condition.

To be sure, the totalitarian model could only approximate the underlying reality. Even at the zenith of Stalinism, we know, there were major and numerous exceptions to the effective realization of absolute despotism. Piecemeal information such as the testimony of refugee informants showed that many individuals were able to preserve for themselves or to create tiny islands of privacy and to maintain attitudes of doubt and skepticism about the system in the face of the relentless propaganda that penetrated every corner of the society. We know, too, that in the midst of what was surely the most thoroughgoing system of political and social controls ever devised, there were widespread and patterned evasions of official demands in places high and low. The factory manager engaged in self-defensive falsification of production statistics; the peasant stealing time from the collectivized sector to work on his private plot; clandestine listeners to forbidden foreign radio broadcasts—these and other types are amply familiar to students of Stalinist Russia. For those who were caught (as well as for many of the totally innocent) the costs were horrendous, often final. But even at its most extreme the system of surveillance and punishments did not stamp out pockets of resentment, awareness, inner resistance.

Nevertheless, if Soviet totalitarianism under Stalin was not exactly an Orwellian 1984 and if, in important respects, it departed from the analysts' model of the totalitarian society, it came very close indeed (perhaps as close as is possible in a modern complex society) to approximating that model. Extraordinary was the near-completeness, if not actual totality, of the invasion of society by Party and state. The efforts to regulate in minute detail cultural activity, patterns of material consumption and taste, attitudes towards love and friendship, professional routine and aspiration, scholarly research, moral virtue, recreation and leisure, informal social relationships, sex and childbearing and childrearing—these efforts, though far from always successful, had the most profound effects in creating a condition of unfreedom. If one also recalls the elaborate development of control mechanisms designed to promote the institutionalization of anxiety (that state of affairs in which even the most innocent act is likely to be arbitrarily greeted with harsh and capricious punishment), then it is clear that the Soviet system under Stalin, by any practical definition, was totalitarian.

It is also clear that substantial liberalization has taken place since the dictator's death. But this measure, useful in many ways, creates very serious problems in analysis and evaluation. For although liberalization tells something about where the Soviet system has come from, it does not say very much about where it is *going.* To say that the system is being liberalized is like walking away backwards from a receding reference point, a procedure that gives too little information about what lies on the road ahead. After all, if the society has become less totalitarian, then what is it? To conclude, in effect, that it is still more of the same but somehow less so than it used to be may be essentially correct, but it is not a very satisfactory answer. And the understandable fascination with the political drama of on-and-off-again de-Stalinization has led to a partial neglect of its *social* consequences— in some quarters, too, to an imprecise assumption that political liberalization (the moderation of one-man despotism and the probably genuine efforts to avoid extreme abuses of absolute power) also spells some kind of broad social liberalization (even leading, perhaps, to a form of society more familiar—and less antagonistic?—to the Western experience).

Indeed, it may be that the use of liberalization as the key criterion for measuring changes in Soviet society is responsible for some of the confusion and disagreement among analysts of various persuasions. Thus, those of a conservative or pessimistic disposition have been inclined to deny that the changes are so significant (or that some of them have really taken place) because of the implication that liberalization also means *liberation,* a prospect they reject as too unlikely; while their more optimistic colleagues (especially those who see in Khrushchevism the harbinger of a welfare state) have attached far more significance to the same developments.

The core of the difficulty lies in the fact that, under Stalin, there was an amalgamation of totalism with terror and coercion, and that we may have overlearned a lesson about the necessary association between the two on the basis of that highly convincing record. The concept of the administered society is proposed as a way of saying that there can be totalism *without* terror; it recognizes that the changes in the Soviet Union have been real and vast (after all, totalism without terror is something new); but it insists that, far from developing alternatives to totalism, Soviet society is being subjected to new and more subtle forms of it, and that the Stalinist past is being streamlined rather than rejected.

The implications of this assumption will have to be explored, but first a few illustrations are in order to give a necessarily rather abstract discussion some concrete grounding.

Some Examples

The case for the administered society is not subject to proof of an absolute kind, for not only is such a concept more or less useful rather than right or wrong, but its application to the affairs of a live society cannot possibly cover all contingencies. It does, however, provide a general framework for depicting the Soviet system under Khrushchev (and probably his successors as well), sensitizing us to interpretations that otherwise might go unnoticed and enabling us to see patterns in apparently unconnected trends. The following examples (at this early stage it would be too much to call them evidence) are chosen from a number of important areas of the Soviet system: social stratification, educational policy, administrative shifts in industry and agriculture, the youth program, Khrushchev's position on art and literature, and the recent activity of Soviet sociologists.

Social Stratification. Under Stalin, the differences in income, life-style, and perquisites of the various occupational strata came to be very wide indeed, certainly so in contrast with the Marxist vision of the classless order, also in absolute terms. By and large this development could be accounted for by the functional importance of differential rewards in maximizing output and performance, particularly among the technical and managerial cadres, among symbol-makers and bureaucrats, and in assuring the loyalties of these strategic groups during the critical periods of economic expansion and political consolidation.

Under Khrushchev, however, this trend toward increasingly sharp social stratification has come into question and concrete measures have been adopted to slow its progress, if not to reverse it. And so in recent years we have seen reductions in income and privileges of some of the highest groups, along with serious efforts to improve the lot of the most deprived peasants and workers. Certainly these steps have not been sufficient to overturn the established order of priorities, a revolutionary change that would involve long-range costs and penalties too great for a system still bent on rapid expansion and dependent on a proven, if quite un-Marxist, system of motivations. But the official talk has revealed an apparently deep concern over the excesses of the stratification system given impetus under Stalin.

The Soviet explanation for these changes is that they represent a renewal of Marxist intention now that the requisite material base for establishing full communism, and with it full equality, has been achieved. A somewhat more likely explanation is that the regime under Khrushchev is making strenuous efforts to enhance its popularity by easing and improving living conditions, and probably this is true as far as it goes. But neither explanation accounts for the simultaneous attack against the privileged groups: In purely practical terms, the redistribution of part of their share of the national income could hardly have much of an impact on millions of new recipients and would also threaten to undermine the good will of the strategic strata towards the post-Stalin regime.

Then what does lie behind this new policy? The most convincing answer has been given by Robert Feldmesser, an American student of Soviet affairs who has for some years carried on painstaking studies of social-class policies. Feldmesser's examination of the evidence leads him to the conclusion that class policy under Khrushchev represents an effort to prevent the formation of vested interest groups, in the form of durable social strata, that might interfere with the Party's freedom to plan and manage the affairs of society in its own way. According to Feldmesser, the growing privileges of the upper strata

> threatened to contravene the cardinal dogma of the Soviet system, which has come to be known as Stalinism though it could as well be called Leninism or Khrushchevism: that ultimate power belongs exclusively to the party—or more accurately, to the head of the party. Whenever any group jeopardizes that principle, it must be struck down, and that is what Khrushchev is doing. Stalin, in other words, forgot his Stalinism; and Khrushchev is not repudiating Stalinism, he is, if anything, reinstating it.[2]

The significance of this development, then, is very great. The growth of pluralism, or at least of the capacity of a population to erode the monolithism of a social system, seems to depend to a considerable degree upon the opportunities available to various social groupings (especially, perhaps, in the upper ranges of the stratification system) to develop over the generations, without undue manipulation and interference from the outside and with reasonable probabilities of

[2] Robert A. Feldmesser, "Equality and Inequality under Khrushchev," *Problems of Communism* 9 (March-April, 1960): 38.

continuity, their own traditions, expectations, and behavior patterns—in short, upon opportunities to develop into subcommunities of interest. This is why sociologists and others have sometimes looked to the possibilities of an incipient "bourgcoisification" of Soviet society as an important clue to the easing of totalitarianism, on the grounds that an increasing concern among a growing professional and middle class with preserving advantages once gained might lead to restraints on the freedom of the Soviet regime to pursue harsh programs at home or to engage in risky overseas adventures. But the Soviet record shows us how important it is not to confuse a bourgeoisification of taste and style (which undoubtedly is taking place) with a realignment of power and influence stemming from the interests of this stratum. Public displays of affluence and refinement, which in other times and places have been associated with the political ascendancy of a middle class, do not have this meaning in the contemporary Soviet Union.

It is precisely the prospect of such an ascendancy that is so intolerable to the leadership; it would make it more difficult to administer the society from above. The regime depends upon the privileged groups —else they would not be privileged—but refuses to allow them the kind of long-run security of position that might dilute power. And so the Khrushchev policy can be seen as part of the drive to administer from above.

Educational Policy. A parallel development has taken place in educational policy. Although the reforms of recent years, beginning in the late 1950's, reflect in part the influence of practical problems of manpower allocation (one intended consequence of the reforms is to reduce the pressure on university admissions by shunting more aspirants into the labor force instead), they are also designed to enhance administration from above. That the educational system continues to be construed as a preparatory instrument for quite specific and narrow adult occupational roles rather than as an agency of general enlightenment is highly revealing. Moreover, the new provisions requiring most applicants for admission to higher education to have spent some years either at work or in the military forces are quite consistent with the ethos of a system in which the official emphasis is on treating people as aggregate resources and elements of planning rather than as individuals whose voluntaristic impulses will be sufficient to keep the system running.

In the same connection, the efforts currently under way to establish the new boarding schools on a more extensive basis are, by Soviet assertion, designed to prepare children from the earliest possible age for the institutional atmosphere of the highly organized society. And it is no accident that the main theme of recent Soviet pedagogical and youth literature centers now about the task of raising the new generation in a spirit of "group and collective life" that will surpass in scope and intensity the experiences of the earlier generations. Such bold intentions, of course, may not be effectively realized (and this is a question that will have to be taken up later) but the intentions are unmistakable.

Controls in Industry and Agriculture. An especially convincing example is to be found in the record of industrial and agricultural organization. Early reaction to the widely publicized administrative reorganizations that gained momentum in the latter half of the 1950's saw in them a kind of decentralization that might lead to the development of an incipient grassroots autonomy on the local level. The announced desire to improve productive efficiency by granting more discretionary powers to plant and farm managers, it was speculated, also held forth the possibility of autonomies that would go beyond the intended area of purely economic or managerial decision-making; that is, might lead by tiny but cumulative steps to local patriotisms whose long-run effect would be to encourage a modicum of genuine political independence.

The proposition is reasonable enough, for there is a connection between one kind of autonomy and another, even though the actual political consequences of such a situation are necessarily difficult to forecast. However that may be, we now know that the new independence of industrial and agricultural managers has turned out to be largely illusory. As early as 1960, Arcadius Kahan could conclude in a study of agricultural reorganization that the practical consequence of administrative shifts had been to *tighten* Party control by reducing the overweight bureaucratic machine between Moscow and the farm, thereby enhancing the Party's effective presence in local operations. He writes:

> The new collective amalgamations, the influx of agricultural specialists and former MTS personnel (often party members) into the farm organizations, along with a drive for new party recruits in rural areas, have made it possible to organize party cells on most collective and state farms. The consequent opportunity to exercise control from within, and to present the party to the mass of peasants as a local rather than an alien force, has undoubtedly increased the party's influence over the behavior of the farm population.[3]

On the industrial side, Herbert Ritvo has made a similar point even more emphatically:

> The economic bureaucracy has undergone a series of sweeping reorganizations designed to improve its efficiency and to strengthen direct controls. There can be little doubt that not only the power of leading representatives of this group, but also many of their personal privileges, have diminished as a result of Khrushchev's administrative changes and reforms. As one reads the familiar complaints of industrial managers, it becomes only too apparent how little the "rights of managers" have been expanded since the decree of August 9, 1955. In addition, this sector, more than any other, has felt the greater severity of the new penal laws of 1961–1962; thus, the reorganization of management has revealed that the opinions of this part of the bureaucracy could be silenced and ignored in a matter affecting its vital interests; the harshness of the revised penalties for economic crimes has demonstrated that, despite the importance of the technical elite in an

[3] Arcadius Kahan, "The Peasant, the Party and the System," *Problems of Communism* 9 (July-August, 1960): 34.

industrial society, their prerogatives are limited—not least by an educational system which can now provide a sufficiency of replacements.[4]

These are not only the conclusions of Western analysts; the fight against the dangers of local autonomy is a matter of high-level policy in the U.S.S.R.

> From the very beginning Comrade N. S. Khrushchev, to whom belongs the initiative for the reorganization, directed the attention of our economic cadres to the impermissibility of localism in any form and cautioned them against understanding an integrated economy as self-contained and autarchical. Was such a warning necessary? Undoubtedly it was. The relatively small size of many of the economic administrative regions was an objective basis for attempts to develop a self-sufficient economy within the framework of the economic councils.[5]

Both in industry and agriculture, then, the Khrushchev reforms have been liberalizing insofar as they attempt seriously to amend the rigid and inefficient Stalinist pattern of multiple, overlapping, and cross-checking hierarchies between the center and the localities. But at the same time they have given the Party a freer (because more direct and efficient) hand in administering its own interests within the production units.

The Youth Organizations. An additional illustration comes from the Soviet youth organizations. Far from loosening their grip on the new generation in comparison with their practice in Stalin's time, the Komsomol and Pioneers have been involved in intensive efforts to extend their network of influence, both in membership coverage and in the range of youth activities that they originate or supervise. It is true that some steps have been taken to reduce some of the most extreme consequences of excessive bureaucratization and neglect of local interests and, at the most recent Komsomol Congress in 1962, there was some guarded talk about democratizing the internal structure.[6] But a close examination of the recent Komsomol record suggests that the impulse for such changes comes not so much from a serious intention to democratize the youth program as to alter its widespread reputation as boring, repressive, and offensive in order to make it more appealing to youth. At the same time there has been no sign at all of a withdrawal from interference in personal life; if anything, the reforms are meant to make that interference more effective by replacing swivel-chair

---

[4] Herbert Ritvo, "The Dynamics of Destalinization," *Survey*, No. 47 (April, 1963), pp. 27–36.

[5] V. Pavlenko, "Ekonomicheskoe raionirovanie v novykh usloviiakh [Economic Regionalism under the New Conditions]," *Ekonomicheskaia gazeta*, October 19, 1963, pp. 12–13; translation from *Current Digest of the Soviet Press*, Vol. 15, No. 42 (November 13, 1963).

[6] *Komsomol'skaia pravda*, April 18, 1962, 2. A detailed discussion of the youth organizations since Stalin is given in Allen Kassof, *The Soviet Youth Program: Regimentation and Rebellion* (Cambridge, Mass.: Harvard University Press, 1965).

organizers with energetic enthusiasts who will not be afraid to grapple directly with problems of youthful nonconformity.

Certainly it is true, as in other areas of Soviet life, that the resort to coercion and threat has become less important than under Stalin. But their replacement with more reasoned tactics of persuasion should not be taken as a surrender of the principle of total involvement and control. On the contrary, the youth program is now regarded as more essential than under Stalin, for it has become increasingly important to remind the new generation—which does not share the caution born of experience in the old days—not to confuse the relatively more benign outward character of Khrushchevism with a grant of autonomy. A genuine test of change in the youth sector would be a surrender (more realistically, a partial surrender) of the organizations' claim to a monopoly over formal and informal youth activities. Concretely, such a step might take the form of allowing youngsters (especially in higher educational institutions) not to join if they have no desire to do so. But there has been no change in the Komsomol's policy of covering an ever larger proportion of those of eligible age, including 100 per cent of the university students and large majorities of key categories of young professionals. And the Pioneer organization, as before, continues to maintain total coverage in its group. Finally, the content of the youth program (as revealed in recent policy literature) centers around renewed efforts to exercise total control over the young on the grounds that the reforms now make the organizations such benign and authoritative agencies of society that no one could possibly object to their paternalistic concern.

Literature and Art. In art, literature, and intellectual affairs generally, recent events in the Soviet Union have attracted such intensive scholarly and journalistic coverage in the West that it is hardly necessary to review them here. Most analyses have stressed the alternating thaws and freezes in the intellectual world since Stalin's death, seeking to discern in them an over-all trend or to attribute cyclical changes to shifting alignments in the Party leadership or to general characteristics of the political climate.

Granting that the end of this complex story is yet to be told, Khrushchev's now famous speech of March, 1963,[7] in which he upbraided errant artists and writers, must stand as a landmark in the publicly proclaimed policy of the administered society. The essence of his message is that the Party's willingness to allow at least some frank discussion of the Stalin period and the decision to loosen somewhat the straitjacket of rigid conformity must not be understood as permission to stray from Party control; that what the more optimistic members of the artistic and intellectual communities have taken for liberalization, or liberation, is only a readjustment in the form and content of Party supervision.

[7] *Pravda* and *Izvestia*, March 10, 1963; translation from *Current Digest of the Soviet Press*, Vol. 15, No. 11 (April 23, 1963).

In effect, said Khrushchev, either the writers, artists, and others must work out a satisfactory system of self-censorship conforming to the needs of the Party, or the Party will do the censoring itself.

Khrushchev made it clear, then, that artistic and intellectual output is a commodity to be mobilized as the regime sees fit in furthering its domestic and international programs, and that the leeway granted in the process of de-Stalinization has been a measure to improve the quality of the product for these purposes—not a signal that the instrumental approach has been modified or abandoned. The thaws and freezes, that is, have been generated by uncertainty as to how the product could be improved without violating unchanged political requirements. So long as this uncertainty remains, the ups and downs of the artistic and intellectual communities may be expected to continue as the limits of experimentation are redefined in practice. But the basic principle has been reiterated, and unmistakably so.

Khrushchev's statements on that occasion are in fact more interesting for what they reveal about his idea of social order than merely as strictures against disobedient poets. He could not have expressed more precisely the ethos of the administered society when he said that the denunciation of the Stalin cult does not signify that "a time of drift has set in, that the reins of control have been slackened, that the ship of society is drifting at the will of the waves, and that each person can follow his own whim and behave in whatever way he sees fit. No. The Party has pursued and will consistently pursue the Leninist course it has mapped out, irreconcilably opposing any ideological waverings and attempts to violate the norms of life in our society." And, he said in the same speech,

> among certain people one can hear talk about some kind of absolute freedom of the individual. I do not know what they have in mind, but I believe that there will never be absolute freedom of the individual, even under full communism. . . . And under communism the will of one man must be subordinated to the will of the entire collective. Unless this is so, anarchic self-will will sow dissension and disorganize the life of the society. Without the organizing, directing principle, neither socialist society nor any other society, even the smallest collective of people, can exist.

To give him proper credit, Khrushchev is probably quite right in an elementary sociological or philosophical sense when he denies the possibility of absolute individual freedom. But there is an enormous difference between saying this as an abstract assertion about the limits of human experience and the active promotion of an all-encompassing social policy dedicated to the proposition of individual subordination to a superorganized society. And Khrushchev is not speaking as a sociologist or philosopher, but as a man of action.

Sociology. A final illustration concerns the current work of Soviet sociologists. Sociological writing and research were taboo in the Soviet

Union until recent years, and even the word "sociology" was regarded as a synonym for "bourgeois apologetics." But beginning in the late 1950's, a number of academics began to identify themselves as sociologists and to write under the heading of sociology. Much of what they have produced up to now consists of little more than political slogans of old dignified with a new professional vocabulary; this aspect of their work need not concern us here. More revealing are their research and their conception of the proper uses of sociology.

It is only a slight oversimplification to conclude that, so far, the principal assignments of the sociologists have been to prove the "superiority" of the Soviet Union over "bourgeois" societies and to provide policy-makers with how-to-do-it information of a rather limited scope. Conspicuously absent are even the most timid efforts at criticism, evaluation, or basic questioning about social structure. That is, there is no sign of an uninhibited, nonpolitical search for answers that are not already predetermined by general dogma. There is also an intriguing (and probably not altogether accidental) parallel with the kind of industrial and personnel research that is popular in some American corporations, where the micro-techniques of the social sciences are applied to the purposes of administration and manipulation. (So far, it must be said, the Soviet sociologists have barely begun to develop the kind of technical sophistication displayed by their Western counterparts, but they have declared their intention to do so.) In particular, there is a strong resemblance between the organizational ethos that is becoming increasingly evident in Khrushchev's Russia and the internal behavior of some American corporations depicted by observers such as William Whyte.[8] The concrete, human consequences of "being administered" may be more or less benign for the individuals involved—but that it takes place at all is the critical fact. On the one hand in a large corporation, on the other in an entire society, the insistence on the superiority of superorganization emphasizes the relevance of the whole life for the task-oriented area and results in efforts to bring together into a coherent pattern—under influence and guidance from above—such a wide variety of roles that social character and individual aspiration become increasingly a public affair. Probably it is no accident that, at a recent international sociological conference, a Soviet participant is reported to have said that David Riesman's "other-directed man" (that modern type whose behavior is motivated by what others think of him more than by a stable core of inner values)[9] comes very close to the ideal of responsible social behavior so ardently fostered by the Soviet educational and propaganda systems.[10]

[8] William H. Whyte, *The Organization Man* (New York, 1956).

[9] David Riesman, Nathan Glazer, and Reuel Denny, *The Lonely Crowd* (New Haven, 1950).

[10] Recent developments in Soviet sociology are reviewed in Leopold Labedz, "Sociology as a Vocation," *Survey*, No. 48 (July, 1963), pp. 57–65.

Some Implications

These illustrations go only a small way toward showing the potential applications of the concept of the administered society to an understanding of contemporary currents in Soviet life. Others, no doubt, would be equally appropriate—for example, the growing emphasis on "public" participation in social control through voluntary assistance to the militia; the Komsomol street patrols' enforcing of dress, decorum, and taste; the quasi-judicial comrades' courts, and so forth.

There are also *a priori* reasons to expect the Soviet leadership to stress this approach. The organizational problems of the Soviet economy, for example, become more rather than less complex with technological advance; if economic successes under Stalin solved a number of relatively primitive problems of accumulation and investment, they in turn have created new problems of organization and coordination that are less easily solved. When Khrushchev rejects the notion that the ship of society can sail wherever the waves carry it, he refers not only to the narrow problem of political unity and ideological correctness but to the larger, underlying issue of how to manage a modern industrial order. In one sense the Soviet case is a qualitatively extreme example of the problem of coordination faced in all modern industrial societies, aggravated by the peculiar ferocity with which the issue of backwardness was handled under Stalin.

The passion for organization, for perfect coordination and integration of social life—a kind of compulsive's dream of beehive order projected upon an entire society—has partly replaced the original impetus of Bolshevik ideology. The denial that there can be any real conflict in the good society, the belief that all legitimate human needs can be satisfied simultaneously, that interest groups are subversive, that only uninformed selfishness or disregard of organizational principles stands between the present and the utopia of the future—these are some of the ingredients of the new ideology. If it lacks some of the romantic appeal of barricade-storming, it is perhaps no less revolutionary in its consequences, for its purveyors insist that they will not rest until all societies have undergone the transformation to superorganization. Its potential impact on an audience, say, of hard-pressed political leaders and court philosophers of developing nations may be considerable, for the idea of total coordination must tempt many of them as the answer to problems and frustrations of economic backwardness and the awkward necessities of coping with competing political interests. And for mentalities especially sensitive to the real and apparent disarray of human affairs or philosophically intolerant of ambiguity in social structure, there is, after all, a great utopian charm in such an image: Much like the classical Marxist formula of salvation, it seems to promise a final answer to the centuries-old dislocations generated by modernism and science and a return to a latter-day version of a medieval world where everything—and everyone—apparently had a proper place in the universe.

Assuming this assessment of the basic aspirations of the Soviet regime to be correct, there is the quite different question of how far they are likely to be realized in practice. Naturally it would be unrealistic to expect complete and literal fulfillment of the dream, any more than one could have expected perfect totalitarianism to exist under Stalin. The issue, then, is how closely it will or can be approximated. Without going into the kind of detailed discussion that is far beyond the scope of these early notes, the best that can be done is to suggest some of the factors in a balance sheet of probabilities.

In the background is the ancient dilemma of how to combine personal with public interest in such ways as to put an end to politics. If the record of other complex societies (not to mention the history of the Soviet Union itself) is a guide, we may be excused for having serious doubts about such a grandiose conception. To deny that there is social conflict, as the Soviet leadership essentially does, is not to be rid of it. Even the most superficial reading of the Soviet press daily provides an endless catalog of the stresses and strains arising from the pursuit of private or group interests against the demands for conformity emanating from the center. Some of the examples are petty, more of them are serious, all of them reflect the underlying tensions of an imperfectly coordinated society; they usually fall short of posing immediate threats to the political directorate but often have cumulative consequences of an unplanned and unintended nature. Moreover, broad areas of deviant behavior and subversive attitudes which once were suppressed by the application of prophylactic terror now have to be handled by more patient and indirect means. It is too early to say whether the new machinery of social control will be as adequate to the task as was pure Stalinism.

Then there is the paradoxical discovery, finally dawning on the regime, that the gradual alleviation of extreme material want that has been behind so many traditional problems may produce new and more subtle issues of control over a long-deprived population experiencing relative affluence for the first time. Failures to satisfy these wants are the obvious danger; success breeds more subtle risks, however, for a rising standard of living (as we have seen in the case of other industrial nations) often results in new forms of emotional investment that are to a great extent antithetical to he high level of public commitment obviously essential in realizing the administered society. We already have some evidence of this in the form of a troublesome youth problem in the Soviet Union: One of the greatest headaches of the post-Stalin regime has been how to prevent the drive for individual advancement and the intoxication with consumption from becoming the basis for a privatism that could easily wreck long-term intentions. So far the problem has been most visible among youth, but there is reason to believe that it is widespread.

To these and equally powerful impediments in the road to the administered society—for example, the articulate and sometimes effective objections of at least parts of the scientific, artistic, and intellectual communities to being as totally mobilized as they were under Stalin— must be added the even more vexing "technical" problem of *how* to administer and coordinate an entire enormous society effectively even in the absence of any special opposition. Yet when all this is said, what stands out is the remarkable success of the Soviet regime, during and since Stalin's day, in making a very impressive start.

Most important is the fact that, during almost half a century of Communist rule, the possibilities for alternative institutional forms have been largely wiped out. Even were the will to democratic or pluralistic institutions substantially present—and it is not—it is highly doubtful that the resources currently available by way of formal structures, source philosophies, or practical experience would go very far. The Bolshe-vization of a society, if it goes on long enough, is an irreversible process, because it is so intense and so total that it indelibly alters not only earlier institutional forms but the entire pattern of a population's expectations of reasonable and workable alternative possibilities for social order. This is not to say that the Soviet leaders have mastered history, for even a process that is irreversible can move forward in unintended and undesired directions. But the prospects of developing viable substitutes for a social system that has so long been based upon extreme and centralized organization are very poor. Ironically, the regime is probably correct—at least in the case of Soviet society—when it insists that any form of pluralism is impossible. The best that can be expected is a more or less benign totalism within the limits of the administered society, with a very slow erosion of the Bolshevik heritage; the worst, a surrender of good intentions to manage the society without terror and a return in some form to the excesses and cruelties of classical Stalinism.

How one evaluates this situation depends on his general political outlook and his preferences about the good society. Surely no one will deny that the Soviet citizen is, in the most elementary sense, better off today than he was under Stalin. And certainly no one will claim that the Soviet citizen prefers to be brutalized as he was then. Still, the thoroughgoing bureaucratization, the superorganization, of social life contains a special nightmare quality of its own even when shorn (as probably it must be if it is to operate efficiently) of raw psychic brutality and terror. And the easing of the terror, while an obviously welcome development, also has the consequence of diminishing the awareness of living in an essentially closed society and of reducing the capacity to act from moral indignation toward a freer life.

Perhaps the concept of the administered society, in this preliminary form, errs on the side of pessimism by making too much of the dream and not enough of the sheer confusion of reality. Daily life in the Soviet Union is far richer, far more problematical to its rulers, far less certain than an abstraction can depict; no doubt the framework of this modest idea will have to be considerably filled in before it can be of much use in practical analysis. But it does call attention to the inadequacy of the liberalization formula in understanding contemporary Soviet developments and the new ideology driving the regime. And if this is the dream of the post-Stalin leadership, then the Soviet system under Khrushchev may be moving not toward its Western counterparts but even farther away from them. If Khrushchev and his heirs succeed, the developments of the last decade in the Soviet Union will have been only a tactical regrouping on the march from a relatively primitive to a far more advanced variety of twentieth-century totalitarianism.

* * *

42

WILL THE SOVIET UNION SURVIVE UNTIL 1984?

ANDREI AMALRIK

We are aware that the regime underwent very dynamic internal changes in the five years before the war.[1] However, the subsequent regeneration of the bureaucratic elite was carried out by the retention of those who were most obedient and unquestioning. This bureaucratic method of "unnatural selection" of the most obedient members of the old bureaucracy, together with the elimination from the ruling caste of the boldest and most independent-minded, created over the years an increasingly weaker and more indecisive generation of elite. Accustomed to obey unconditionally and without thought in order to attain power, bureaucrats, once they have attained that power, are very good at holding onto it but have no idea how to use it. Not only are they incapable of conceiving

[1] A reference to Stalin's purges of the entire Soviet hierarchy.

new ideas; they regard any novel thought as an assault on their own prerogatives.

Evidently we have reached the sad point where the idea of power is no longer connected with either a doctrine, the personality of a leader, or a tradition, but only with power itself. Every governmental institution and position is sustained by no other force than the realization that it is an essential part of the existing system.

Naturally, self-preservation is bound to be the only aim of such a regime, at least in its domestic policy. This has come to mean the self-preservation of the bureaucratic elite. In order to remain in power, the regime must change and evolve, but in order to preserve itself, everything must remain unchanged. The contradiction can be noted particularly in the case of the "economic reform," which is being carried out so slowly and yet is so vital to the regime.[2]

Self-preservation is clearly the dominant drive. The regime wants neither to "restore Stalinism" nor to "persecute the intelligentsia" nor to "render fraternal assistance" to those who have not asked for it, like Czechoslovakia. The only thing it wants is for everything to go on as before: authorities to be recognized, the intelligentsia to keep quiet, no rocking of the system by dangerous and unfamiliar reforms.

The regime is not on the attack but on the defense. Its motto is: "Don't touch us and we won't touch you." Its aim: Let everything be as it was. This is probably the most humane objective the regime has set for itself in the last half-century, but it is also the least appealing.

Thus we have a passive bureaucratic elite opposed to a passive "middle class." Moreover, however passive the elite is, it really does not need to make any changes, and in theory it could remain in power for a very long time, getting away with only the slightest concessions and minor measures of repression.

It is clear that a regime in such a quasi-stable condition requires a definite legal framework, based either on a tacit understanding by all members of society of what is required of them or on written law. In the days of Stalin and even of Khrushchev, there was a sense of direction emanating from above and felt by all, which guided every official unerringly to an awareness of what was currently required of him (reinforced, however, by special instructions) and enabled everyone else to sense what was expected of him. At the same time there existed a "décor" of laws from which the authorities chose whatever they needed at any given moment. But gradually, both "from above" and "from below," a desire became noticeable for more stable "written" norms rather than this "tacit understanding." This desire created a rather uncertain situation.

The necessity of a modicum of the rule of law had made itself felt "at the top" earlier, during the period when the role of the state security organs was being curbed and mass rehabilitations were taking place. In

---

[2] The "economic reform" of 1965, involving some decentralization of decision-making.

the decade beginning in 1954, gradual, though very slow, progress was achieved in the fields both of formal legislation and of the practical implementation of the laws. This took the form of the signing of a number of international conventions and of an attempt to bring Soviet law into some kind of harmony with international legal norms. Furthermore, personnel changes were carried out among investigative and judicial authorities.

This very slow movement toward the rule of law was further retarded by the following factors: First, the authorities, for various reasons of current policy, issued decrees and regulations which directly contradicted the international conventions they had just signed as well as the approved principles of Soviet law. For example, the decree ordering five years of exile and forced labor for persons with no fixed employment, which was approved in 1961, was not made part of the Criminal Code. Then there was the decree which increased the penalty for illegal currency dealing to include death and which was given *de facto* retroactive force.

Second, the personnel changes were carried out on a very limited scale and with little consistency. They were hampered by a shortage of administrative officials who understood the concept of the rule of law.

Third, the professional egotism of the administrative officials led them to oppose anything that might lessen their influence or abolish their privileged position in society.

Fourth, the very idea of the rule of law had virtually no roots in Soviet society and was in blatant conflict with the officially proclaimed doctrines about the "class" approach to all phenomena.[3]

While the movement toward the rule of law, which had begun "from the top," thus gradually bogged down in a bureaucratic swamp, suddenly voices demanding the observance of the laws were heard "from below." And, indeed, the "middle class"—the only class in Soviet society to understand and to feel the need for the rule of law—had begun, albeit very timidly, to demand that it be treated not in accordance with the current requirements of the regime but on a "legal basis."

It now became evident that in Soviet law there exists, if I may use the term, a broad "gray belt"—activities that the law does not formally forbid but which are, in fact, forbidden in practice—for instance: contacts between Soviet citizens and foreigners; a concern over non-Marxist philosophies or art inconsistent with the notions of socialist realism; attempts to put out typewritten literary collections; spoken or written criticism not of the system as a whole, which is forbidden under Articles 70 and 190/1 of the Criminal Code, but of particular institutions within the system.

Thus two trends are evident today: the efforts of the regime to "blacken" the gray belt—by means of amendments to the Criminal Code, trials designed to serve as examples to others, and instructions to ad-

[3] This approach involves always putting the interests of "the working class"—in reality, of the regime—above all others.

ministrative officials on how to enforce existing regulations—and an effort by the "middle class" to "whiten" the belt, simply by doing things that had earlier been considered impossible and constantly referring to their lawfulness.

All this places the regime in a rather awkward situation, particularly if one bears in mind that the idea of the rule of law will begin to take hold in other strata of society. On the one hand the regime, in the interests of stability, is constantly forced to observe its own laws, while on the other it is constantly forced to violate them so as to counteract the tendency toward democratization.

This has given rise to two interesting phenomena: mass persecution outside the judicial system and selective judicial persecution. Nonjudicial persecution is exemplified primarily by dismissals from work and expulsions from the Party. In the course of one month, for instance, over 15 per cent of all those who had signed petitions demanding observance of the law in connection with the trial of Galanskov and Ginzburg were dismissed from their jobs, and almost all those who were Party members were expelled from the Party.

Selective judicial persecution has the aim of frightening those who might be liable for trial on the same charges. Thus it may happen that persons who have committed a more serious crime—from the regime's point of view—may be allowed to go free, while persons who have committed a lesser infraction may be thrown into prison if this requires less expenditure of bureaucratic effort or the circumstances of the moment make it more desirable.

A typical example was the trial of the Moscow engineer, Irina Belgorodskaya, in January, 1969. She was accused of "attempting to circulate" what the court held to be an "anti-Soviet" appeal in defense of the political prisoner Anatoly Marchenko and was sentenced to one year's imprisonment. At the same time, the authors of the appeal, who publicly acknowledged that they had written and circulated it, were not even called as witnesses.

Another contemptible repressive measure is becoming increasingly widespread—forcible commitment to psychiatric hospitals. This is done in the case both of persons who are completely sane and of those with slight mental disorders who do not need hospitalization or compulsory treatment.

As we can now see, the existence of a "Stalinism without violence," while calming the fears of the people which date from the previous era of violence, inevitably produces a new kind of violence: first, "selective persecution" of malcontents, then "lenient" mass persecution. And what next?

Still, looking back over the last fifteen years, we observe that the process of regularizing the legal system has advanced, slowly but rather steadily, and has gone so far that it will be difficult to reverse it by the customary bureaucratic methods. It is a moot point whether this process represents part of the liberalization of the regime, which is—or at least was until recently—supposed to be taking place in our country. After all, it is well known that the evolution of our state and society has gone forward not only in the field of law but also in the economy, in culture, and in other areas.

In fact, not only does every Soviet citizen feel that he is living in greater security and enjoying more personal freedom than he did fifteen years ago, but the director of an industrial enterprise now has the right to decide for himself matters that previously were not his to decide, while the writer or theater director works within much wider limits than he did before. The same can be said about almost every area of life in our country. This has given rise to yet another ideology in our society, possibly the most widespread one; it can be called the "ideology of reformism."

It is based on the view that a certain "humanization of socialism" will take place and that the inert and oppressive system will be replaced by a dynamic and liberal one. This will be achieved through gradual changes and piecemeal reforms, as well as by replacing the old bureaucratic elite with a more intelligent and more reasonable group. In other words, this theory is based on the belief that "Reason will prevail" and that "Everything will be all right."

This is why it is so popular in academic circles and, in general, among those who are not badly off even now and who therefore hope that others will also come to accept the view that it is better to be well fed and free than to be hungry and enslaved. I think that all the American hopes about the Soviet Union are derived from this naïve point of view. We know, however, that history, and Russian history in particular, has by no means been a continuous victory for reason and that the whole history of mankind has not followed an unbroken line of progress. . . .

In addition to this faith in reason, Americans apparently also believe that the gradual improvement in the standard of living, as well as the spread of Western culture and ways of life, will gradually transform Soviet society—that foreign tourists, jazz records and miniskirts will help to create a "humane socialism." It is possible that we will indeed have a "socialism" with bare knees someday, but not likely one with a human face.[4]

In my view, the growth of material conveniences of everyday life and economic well-being does not in itself prevent or eliminate oppression. As an example, one may cite such a developed country as Nazi Germany. Oppression is always oppression, but in each country it has its own specific traits, and we can correctly understand the causes that brought it about and that can lead to its elimination only in the historical context of that country.

In my opinion, the trouble lies not so much in the fact that the degree of freedom available to us is minimal as compared with that needed for a developed society, and that the process of liberalization, instead of

[4] A reference to the slogan used by Czechoslovak reformist leaders in setting forth their aims.

being steadily accelerated, is at times palpably slowed down, perverted or turned back, as in the fact that the very nature of the process gives us grounds to doubt its ultimate success.

It would seem that liberalization presupposes some kind of purposeful plan, put into effect gradually "from above" through reforms and other measures, to adapt our system to contemporary conditions and lead it to a radical regeneration. As we know, there has been, and still is, no such plan, and no radical reforms have been, or are being, carried out. There are only isolated and uncoordinated attempts at emergency repairs by tinkering in various ways with the bureaucratic machine.

The so-called "economic reform," of which I have already spoken, is in essence a half-measure and is in practice being sabotaged by the Party machine, because if such a reform were carried to its logical end, it would threaten the power of the machine.

Liberalization could, however, take a "spontaneous" form. It could come as the result of constant concessions on the part of the regime to the demands of a society that had its own plan for liberalization, and of constant efforts by the regime to adapt itself to the storm of changing conditions all over the world. In other words, the system would be self-regulating: Difficulties in foreign and domestic policy, economic troubles, etc., would constantly forewarn the ruling elite of changing conditions.

We find, however, that even this is not the case. The regime considers itself the acme of perfection and therefore has no wish to change its ways either of its own free will or, still less, by making concessions to anyone or anything.

The current process of "widening the area of freedom" could be more aptly described as the growing decrepitude of the regime. The regime is simply growing old and can no longer suppress everyone and everything with the same strength and vigor as before; the composition of the elite is changing, as we have mentioned; the contemporary world, in which the regime is already finding it very hard to keep its bearings, is becoming more complex; and the structure of society is changing.

We can visualize all this in the following allegory: A man is standing in a tense posture, his hands raised above his head. Another, in an equally strained pose, holds a Tommy gun to the first man's stomach. Naturally, they cannot stand like this for very long. The second man will get tired and loosen his grip on the gun, and the first will take advantage of this to lower his hands and relax a bit. In just this way, we are now witnessing a growing yearning for a quiet life and for comfort— even a kind of "comfort cult"—on all levels of our society, particularly at the top and in the middle.

If, however, one views the present "liberalization" as the growing decrepitude of the regime rather than its regeneration, then the logical result will be its death, which will be followed by anarchy. . . .

One may, of course, hope—and this will probably come true—that the emerging movement will succeed, despite persecution, in becoming influential, will work out a sufficiently concrete program, will find the structure necessary to its goals and attract many followers. But at the same time, I think that its base in society—the "middle class," or, more exactly, a part of the "middle class"—is too weak and too beset by internal contradictions to allow the movement to engage in a real face-to-face struggle with the regime or, in the event of the regime's self-destruction or its collapse as a result of mass disorders, to become a force capable of reorganizing society in a new way. But will the Democratic Movement perhaps be able to find a broader base of support among the masses?

It is very hard to answer this question, if only because no one, not even the bureaucratic elite, knows exactly what attitudes prevail among the wider sections of the population. The KGB, of course, supplies the bureaucratic elite with information, gathered by its special methods, about popular feelings in the country. This information obviously differs from the picture drawn daily in the newspapers. However, one can only guess how true to reality the KGB's information is. It is, incidentally, paradoxical that the regime should devote enormous effort to keep everyone from talking and then waste further effort to learn what people are talking about and what they want.

As I see it, popular views can best be described by the words "passive discontent." The discontent is directed not against the regime as such—the majority do not think about it, or they feel that there is no alternative—but rather against particular aspects of the regime, aspects which are, nevertheless, essential to its existence.

The workers, for example, are bitter over having no rights vis-à-vis the factory management. The collective farmers are resentful about their total dependence on the kolkhoz chairman, who, in turn, depends entirely on the district administration. Everybody is angered by the great inequalities in wealth, the low wages, the austere housing conditions, the lack of essential consumer goods, compulsory registration at their places of residence and work and so forth.

This discontent is now becoming louder, and some people are beginning to wonder who is actually to blame. The gradual though slow improvement in the standard of living, due largely to intensive housing construction, does not diminish the anger though it does somewhat neutralize it. It is clear, however, that a sharp slowdown, a halt or even a reversal in the improvement of the standard of living would arouse such explosions of anger, mixed with violence, as were never before thought possible.*

Inasmuch as the regime, because of its ossification, will find it increasingly more difficult to raise industrial output, it is obvious that the

---

* For this reason, I believe, the regime did not carry out early in 1969 its intention of raising prices sharply on many goods, preferring instead a kind of creeping inflation. The possible consequences of sharp price increases were brought home to the regime by the "hunger riot" in Novocherkassk [June, 1962] after Khrushchev raised the prices of meat and dairy products.

standard of living in many sectors of our society may be threatened. What forms will the people's discontent take then? Legitimate democratic resistance or an extreme form of individual or mass acts of violence?

As I see it, no idea can ever be put into practice if it is not understood by a majority of the people. Whether because of its historical traditions or for some other reason, the idea of self-government, of equality before the law and of personal freedom—and the responsibility that goes with these—are almost completely incomprehensible to the Russian people. Even in the idea of pragmatic freedom, a Russian tends to see not so much the possibility of securing a good life for himself as the danger that some clever fellow will make good at his expense.

To the majority of the people the very word "freedom" is synonymous with "disorder" or the opportunity to indulge with impunity in some kind of antisocial or dangerous activity. As for respecting the rights of an individual as such, the idea simply arouses bewilderment. One can respect strength, authority, even intellect or education, but it is preposterous to the popular mind that the human personality should represent any kind of value.

As a people, we have not benefited from Europe's humanist tradition. In Russian history man has always been a means and never in any sense an end. It is paradoxical that the term "period of the cult of the personality"—by which the Stalin era is euphemistically designated—came to mean for us a period of such humiliation and repression of the human personality as even our people had never previously experienced.

Moreover, official propaganda constantly makes the utmost effort to set the notion of the "communal" against the notion of the "personal," clearly underlining the insignificance of the latter and the grandeur of the former. Hence, any interest in the "personal," an interest that is natural and inevitable, has come to be regarded as unnatural and egotistical.

Does this mean that the masses have no positive ideas whatever, except the idea of "strong government"—a government that is right because it is strong and that therefore must on no account weaken? The Russian people, as can be seen from both their past and present history, have at any rate one idea that appears positive: the idea of *justice*. The government that thinks and acts in everything for us must be not only strong but also just. All must live justly and act justly.

It is worth being burnt at the stake for that idea, but not for the right to "do as you wish." For despite the apparent attractiveness of the idea of justice, if one examines it closely, one realizes that it represents the most destructive aspect of Russian psychology. In practice, "justice" involves the desire that "nobody should live better than I do" (but not a desire for the much-vaunted notion of equalizing wages, since the fact that many people live worse is willingly accepted).

This idea of justice is motivated by hatred of everything that is outstanding, which we make no effort to imitate but, on the contrary, try to bring down to our level, by hatred of any sense of initiative, of any higher or more dynamic way of life than the life we live ourselves. This psychology is, of course, most typical of the peasantry and least typical of the "middle class." However, peasants and those of peasant origin constitute the overwhelming majority in our country.

As I have observed myself, many peasants find someone else's success more painful than their own failure. In general, when the average Russian sees that he is living less well than his neighbor, he will concentrate not on trying to do better for himself but rather on trying to bring his neighbor down to his own level. My reasoning may seem naïve to some people, but I have been able to observe scores of examples in both village and town, and I see in this one of the typical traits of the Russian psyche.

Thus two ideas that the masses understand and accept—the idea of force and the idea of justice—are equally inimical to democratic ideas, which are based on individualism. To these must be added three more negative and interrelated factors: first, the continued low cultural level of the greater part of our people, especially in respect to everyday culture; second, the dominance of the many myths assiduously propagated by the mass information media; and, third, the extreme social disorientation of the bulk of our people.

The "proletarianization" of the countryside has created an "alien class"—neither peasant nor working class. They have the dual psychology of the owners of tiny homesteads and of farm hands working on gigantic and anonymous farms. How this class views itself, and what it wants, is known, I think, to nobody. Furthermore, the mass exodus of peasants to the city has created a new type of city dweller: a person who has broken with his old environment, way of life, and culture and who is finding it very difficult to discover his place in his new environment and feels ill at ease in it. He is both frightened and aggressive. He no longer has any idea to what level of society he belongs.

While the old social structure in both town and village has been completely destroyed, a new one is only just beginning to form. The "ideological foundations" on which it is being built are extremely primitive: the desire for material well-being (relatively modest from a Western viewpoint) and the instinct for self-preservation. Thus the concept "profitable" is confronted with the concept "risky."

It is hard to tell whether, aside from those purely material criteria, the bulk of our people possess any kind of moral criteria—such as "honorable" and "dishonorable," "good" and "bad," "right" and "wrong," the supposedly eternal principles which function as inhibiting and guiding factors when the mechanism of social constraint begins to fall apart and man is left to his own devices.

I have formed the impression, which may be wrong, that our people do not have any such moral criteria—or hardly any. The Christian ethic, with its concepts of right and wrong, has been shaken loose and driven out of the popular consciousness. An attempt was made to replace it with "class" morality, which can be summarized as follows: Good is what at any given moment is required by authority. Naturally, such a morality, together with the propagation and stimulation of class and national animosities, has totally demoralized society and deprived it of any nonopportunistic moral criteria.

As an example, I might cite the unusual increase in casual thievery (as compared with a decrease in professional theft). Here is a typical case: Two young workers are on their way to visit friends. Walking along the street, they see an open ground-floor window. They slip in and grab some trifle or other. Had the window been shut, they would simply have passed on without more ado. One constantly sees people enter a house without a greeting, eat without removing their hats or swear coarsely in the presence of their small children. All this is normal behavior and not in the least exceptional.

Thus the Christian ethic, which in Russia had a semipagan as well as official character, died out without being replaced by a Marxist ethic. (There is not space here to discuss it at length, but it is worth mentioning that Russia received her Christianity from Byzantium, which was rigid and moribund, and not from the developing and dynamic young Western civilization. This could not but deeply influence subsequent Russian history.) "Marxist doctrine" was revised and reversed to suit current needs too often for it to become a viable ideology. And now as the regime becomes ever more bureaucratic, it becomes ever less ideological.

The need for an ideological underpinning forces the regime to look toward a new ideology, namely, Great Russian nationalism, with its characteristic cult of strength and expansionist ambitions. Something similar took place at the beginning of the century, when the traditional monarchist ideology was replaced by a narrow nationalism. The Tsarist regime even introduced into everyday speech the expression "genuinely Russian people" in distinction to the simpler term "Russian," and inspired the creation of the Union of the Russian People.[5]

A regime grounded in such an ideology needs external and internal enemies who are not so much "class" enemies (for instance, "American imperialists" and "anti-Soviet elements") as national enemies (for instance, Chinese and Jews). Such a nationalistic ideology, although it may prove temporarily useful to the regime, is very dangerous for a country in which those of Russian nationality constitute less than half the total population.

The need for a viable nationalist ideology is not only acutely felt by the regime, but nationalist feelings also appear to be taking hold in Soviet society, primarily in official literary and artistic circles (where they have evidently developed as a reaction to the considerable role of Jews in official Soviet art). Beyond these circles, these feelings have a center of sorts in the "Rodina" (Fatherland) Club.[6] This ideology can perhaps

[5] A patriotic and chauvinistic Russian society formed at the beginning of this century. It organized pogroms against the Jews, often with official encouragement.

[6] A club whose members glorify Russian culture and its history.

be called "neo-Slavophile," although it should not be confused with the "Christian ideology"—partially tinged with Slavophilism—which we discussed earlier. Its central features are an interest in Russianness, a belief in the messianic role of Russia and an extreme scorn and hostility toward everything non-Russian. . . .

What, then, are the beliefs and guiding ideas of this people with no religion or morality? They believe in their own national strength, which they demand that other peoples fear, and they are guided by a recognition of the strength of their own regime, of which they themselves are afraid. (It goes without saying that most Russians approved, or regarded with indifference, the Soviet military invasion of Czechoslovakia. On the other hand, they resented deeply that the Chinese went unpunished for the March, 1969, clashes on the Ussuri River border between China and the Soviet Union.)

Under this assessment it is not difficult to imagine what forms and directions popular discontent will take if the regime loses its hold. The horrors of the Russian revolutions of 1905–7 and 1917–20 would then look like idylls in comparison.

There is, of course, a counterbalancing factor to these destructive tendencies. Contemporary Soviet society can be compared with a triple-decker sandwich—the top layer is the ruling bureaucracy; the middle layer consists of the "middle class" or the "class of specialists"; and the bottom layer, the most numerous, consists of the workers, peasants, petty clerks, and so on. Whether Soviet society will manage to reorganize itself in a peaceful and painless way and survive the forthcoming cataclysm with a minimum of casualties will depend on how rapidly the middle layer of the sandwich expands at the expense of the other two and on how rapidly the "middle class" and its organization grow, whether faster or slower than the disintegration of the system.

It should be noted, however, that there is another powerful factor which works against the chance of any kind of peaceful reconstruction and which is equally negative for all levels of society: This is the extreme isolation in which the regime has placed both society and itself. This isolation has not only separated the regime from society, and all sectors of society from each other, but also put the country in extreme isolation from the rest of the world. This isolation has created for all—from the bureaucratic elite to the lowest social levels—an almost surrealistic picture of the world and of their place in it. Yet the longer this state of affairs helps to perpetuate the *status quo*, the more rapid and decisive will be its collapse when confrontation with reality becomes inevitable.

Summing up, it can be said that as the regime becomes progressively weaker and more self-destructive it is bound to clash—and there are already clear indications that this is happening—with two forces which are already undermining it: the constructive movement of the "middle class" (rather weak) and the destructive movement of the "lower classes," which will take the form of extremely damaging, violent and irresponsible action once its members realize their relative immunity from punishment. How long, though, will it be before the regime faces such an upheaval, and how long will it be able to bear the strain?

This question can be considered in two ways, depending on whether the regime itself takes decisive and forthright measures to rejuvenate itself or whether it merely continues to make the minimal necessary changes so as to stay in power, as it is doing now. To me, the second alternative appears more likely because it requires less effort, because it appears to be the less dangerous course and because it corresponds to the sweet illusions of today's "Kremlin visionaries." [7]

However, some mutations within the regime are also theoretically possible: for instance, a militarization of the regime and a transition to an openly nationalistic policy (this could be accomplished by a military *coup d'état* or by the gradual transfer of power into the hands of the military).

Such a policy would no longer disguise the regime's actions beneath the cloak of "protecting the interests of the international Communist movement" in order to make some sort of gesture toward the independent and semi-independent Communist parties in the outside world. (As for the role of the army, it is constantly growing. This can be seen by anyone, for example, who compares today's ratio of military officers to civilians on the reviewing stand on top of Lenin's Mausoleum during parades with what it was ten or fifteen years ago.)

Another possible and very different mutation of the regime could occur through economic reforms and the relative liberalization of the system that would follow such reforms. (This could be achieved by increasing the role in the political leadership of pragmatic economists who understood the need for change.)

Neither of these possibilities appears unlikely on the face of it. However, the Party machine, against which either coup would in effect be directed, is so closely intertwined with the military and economic establishments that both groups, if they pursued the aim of change, would very soon bog down in the same old quagmire. Any fundamental change would require such a drastic shake-up in personnel from top to bottom that, understandably, those who personify the regime would never embark on it. To save the regime at the cost of firing themselves would seem to them too exorbitant and unfair a price to pay.

On the question of how long the regime can survive, several interesting historical parallels may be cited. At present, at least some of the conditions that led to the first and second Russian revolutions probably exist again: a caste-ridden and immobile society, a rigid governmental system which openly clashes with the need for economic development, general bureaucratization and the existence of a privileged bureaucratic class, and national animosities within a multinational state in which certain nations enjoy privileged status.

[7] A phrase used often in the past to describe admiringly Lenin and the early Bolshevik leaders.

Under these same conditions, the Tsarist regime would probably have survived quite a while longer and would possibly have undergone some kind of peaceful modernization had the governing class not fantastically misjudged the general situation and its own strength, and pursued a policy of foreign expansion that overtaxed its powers. In fact, had the government of Nicholas II not gone to war against Japan, there would have been no Revolution of 1905–7, and had it not gone to war against Germany, there would have been no revolution in 1917. (Strictly speaking, it did not start either of these wars itself, but it did its utmost to see that they were started.)

Why regimes that have become internally stagnant tend to develop a militantly ambitious foreign policy I find hard to say. Perhaps they seek a way out of their domestic problems through their foreign policies. Perhaps, on the other hand, the ease with which they can suppress internal opposition creates in their minds an illusion of omnipotence. Or perhaps it is because the need to have an external enemy, deriving from internal policy aims, builds up such momentum that it becomes impossible to halt the growth of hostility. This view is supported by the fact that every totalitarian regime decays without itself noticing it.

SELECTED BIBLIOGRAPHY

CHAPTER I. INTRODUCTION

HULICKA, KAREL and IRENE. *Soviet Institutions, the Individual and Society.* Boston: The Christopher Publishing House, 1967.

JUVILER, PETER H. and HENRY W. MORTON, eds. *Soviet Policy-Making, Studies of Communism in Transition.* New York: Praeger Publishers, 1967.

KULSKI, W. W. *The Soviet Regime, Communism in Practice.* Syracuse: Syracuse University Press, 1954.

McCLOSKY, HERBERT and JOHN E. TURNER. *The Soviet Dictatorship.* New York: McGraw-Hill, 1960.

MEYER, ALFRED G. *The Soviet Political System, an Interpretation.* New York: Random House, 1965.

RAYMOND, ELLSWORTH. *The Soviet State.* New York: The Macmillan Co., 1968.

RESHETAR, JOHN S., JR. *The Soviet Polity, Government and Politics in the U.S.S.R.* New York: Dodd, Mead and Co., 1971.

SCHAPIRO, LEONARD. *The Government and Politics of the Soviet Union.* New York: Random House, 1965.

SKILLING, H. GORDON and FRANKLYN GRIFFITHS, eds. *Interest Groups in Soviet Politics.* Princeton: Princeton University Press, 1971.

TATU, MICHEL. *Power in the Kremlin from Khrushchev to Kosygin.* New York: Viking Press, 1969.

CHAPTER II. THE IDEOLOGICAL HERITAGE

DENNO, THEODORE. *The Communist Millennium: The Soviet View.* The Hague: Martinus Nijhoff, 1964.

GOODMAN, ELLIOT R. *The Soviet Design for a World State.* New York: Columbia University Press, 1960.

KUUSINEN, O. V., ed. *Fundamentals of Marxism-Leninism.* 2d ed. Moscow: Foreign Languages Publishing House, 1961.

LENIN, V. I. *Selected Works.* 2 vols. Moscow: Foreign Languages Publishing House, 1952.

LICHTHEIM, GEORGE. *Marxism: An Historical and Critical Study.* New York: Praeger Publishers, 1961.

MARX, KARL, and FRIEDRICH ENGELS. *Selected Works.* 2 vols. Moscow: Foreign Languages Publishing House, 1951.

MEYER, ALFRED G. *Leninism.* Cambridge, Mass.: Harvard University Press, 1957.

TUCKER, ROBERT. *Philosophy and Myth in Karl Marx.* Cambridge: Cambridge University Press, 1961.

ULAM, ADAM. *The Unfinished Revolution: An Essay on the Sources of Influence of Marxism and Communism.* New York: Random House, 1960.

WOLFE, BERTRAM D. *Marxism: 100 Years in the Life of a Doctrine.* New York: The Dial Press, 1965.

CHAPTER III. THE COMMUNIST PARTY

ARMSTRONG, JOHN A. *The Politics of Totalitarianism: The Communist Party of the Soviet Union from 1934 to the Present.* New York: Random House, 1961.

DJILAS, MILOVAN. *The New Class: An Analysis of the Communist System.* New York: Praeger Publishers, 1957.

FAINSOD, MERLE. *Smolensk Under Soviet Rule.* Cambridge, Mass.: Harvard University Press, 1958.

GEHLEN, MICHAEL P. *The Communist Party of the Soviet Union: A Functional Analysis.* Bloomington: Indiana University Press, 1969.

History of the Communist Party of the Soviet Union. Moscow: Foreign Languages Publishing House, 1960.

LENIN, V. I. *What Is To Be Done?* Moscow: Foreign Languages Publishing House, 1952.

MEISSNER, BORIS, and JOHN S. RESHETAR. *The Communist Party of the Soviet Union: The Party Leadership, Organization, and Ideology.* New York: Praeger Publishers, 1956.

RESHETAR, JOHN S. *A Concise History of the Communist Party of the Soviet Union.* New York: Praeger Publishers, 1960.

RIGBY, T. H. *Communist Party Membership in the U.S.S.R. 1917–1967.* Princeton, N.J.: Princeton University Press, 1968.

SCHAPIRO, LEONARD. *The Communist Party of the Soviet Union.* New York: Random House, 1960.

CHAPTER IV. THE ECONOMY AND THE BUREAUCRACY

AZRAEL, JEREMY R. *Managerial Power and Soviet Politics.* Cambridge, Mass.: Harvard University Press, 1966.

BERGSON, ABRAM. *The Economics of Soviet Planning.* New Haven, Conn.: Yale University Press, 1964.

BERLINER, JOSEPH. *Factory and Manager in the USSR*. Cambridge, Mass.: Harvard University Press, 1957.

BRODERSEN, ARVID. *The Soviet Worker: Labor and Government in Soviet Society*. New York: Random House, 1966.

BROWN, EMILY CLARK. *Soviet Trade Unions and Labor Relations*. Cambridge, Mass.: Harvard University Press, 1966.

CAMPBELL, ROBERT W. *Soviet Economic Power: Its Organization, Growth and Challenge*. Boston: Houghton Mifflin, 1966.

EVENKO, I. A. *Planning in the USSR*. Moscow: Foreign Languages Publishing House, 1961.

GRANICK, DAVID. *The Red Executive: A Study of the Organization Man in Russian Industry*. Garden City, N.Y.: Doubleday & Co., 1961.

NOVE, ALEX. *The Soviet Economy*. New York: Praeger Publishers, 1961.

SCHWARTZ, HARRY. *The Soviet Economy Since Stalin*. Philadelphia: J. B. Lippincott, 1965.

CHAPTER V. THE POLITICAL PROCESS

BARGHOORN, FREDERICK C. *Politics in the USSR*. Boston: Little, Brown & Co., 1966.

CONQUEST, ROBERT. *Russia After Khrushchev*. New York: Praeger Publishers, 1965.

DALLIN, ALEXANDER, and ALAN F. WESTIN, eds. *Politics in the Soviet Union: 7 Cases*. New York: Harcourt, Brace, Jovanovich, 1966.

FAINSOD, MERLE. *How Russia Is Ruled*. Cambridge, Mass.: Harvard University Press, 1963.

FARRELL, R. BARRY, ed. *Political Leadership in Eastern Europe and the Soviet Union*. Chicago: Aldine Publishing Co., 1970.

GRIPP, RICHARD C. *Patterns of Soviet Politics*. Homewood, Ill.: The Dorsey Press, 1963.

KHRUSHCHEV, NIKITA. *Khrushchev Remembers*. With an Introduction, Commentary, and Notes by EDWARD CRANKSHAW. Translated and edited by STROBE TALBOTT. Boston: Little, Brown & Co., 1970.

LINDEN, CARL A. *Khrushchev and the Soviet Leadership, 1957–1964*. Baltimore: The John Hopkins Press, 1966.

PETHYBRIDGE, ROGER. *A Key to Soviet Politics: The Crisis of the Anti-Party Group*. New York: Praeger Publishers, 1962.

RUSH, MYRON. *Political Succession in the USSR*. New York: Columbia University Press, 1965.

CHAPTER VI. THE JUDICIAL PROCESS

BERMAN, HAROLD J. *Justice in the U.S.S.R.: An Interpretation of Soviet Law*. New York: Random House, Vintage Books, 1963.

DENISOV, A., and M. KIRICHENKO. *Soviet State Law*. Moscow: Foreign Languages Publishing House, 1960.

FEIFER, GEORGE. *Justice in Moscow*. New York: Dell Publishing House, a Delta Book, 1965.

GRZYBOWSKI, KAZIMIERZ. *Soviet Legal Institutions: Doctrines and Social Functions*. Ann Arbor: University of Michigan Press, 1962.

Gsovski, Vladimir, and Kazimierz Grzybowski. *Government, Law and Courts in the Soviet Union and Eastern Europe.* 2 vols. New York: Praeger Publishers, 1959.

Guins, George. *Soviet Law and Soviet Society.* The Hague: Nijhoff, 1954.

Hazard, John N. *Law and Social Change in the U.S.S.R.* London: Stevens & Sons, Ltd., 1953.

————. *Settling Disputes in Soviet Society: The Formative Years of Legal Institutions.* New York: Columbia University Press, 1960.

Kelsen, Hans. *The Communist Theory of Law.* London: Stevens & Sons, Ltd., 1955.

LaFave, Wayne R, ed. *Law in the Soviet Society.* Urbana: University of Illinois Press, 1965.

Chapter VII. Political Socialization

Barghoorn, Frederick C. *Soviet Russian Nationalism.* New York: Oxford University Press, 1956.

Bereday, George Z. F.; William W. Brickman; and Gerald H. Read, eds. *The Changing Soviet School.* Boston: Houghton Mifflin, 1960.

Bereday, George Z. F., and Jaan Pennar. *The Politics of Soviet Education.* New York: Praeger Publishers, 1960.

Fisher, Ralph T., Jr. *Pattern for Soviet Youth.* New York: Columbia University Press, 1959.

Grant, N. *Soviet Education.* London: Penguin, 1964.

Harper, Samuel W. *Civic Training in Soviet Russia.* Chicago: University of Chicago Press, 1929.

Kassof, Allen. *The Soviet Youth Program.* Cambridge, Mass.: Harvard University Press, 1965.

Kline, George L., ed. *Soviet Education.* New York: Columbia University Press, 1957.

Meyer, Frank S. *The Moulding of Communists: The Training of the Communist Cadre.* New York: Harcourt, Brace, Jovanovich, a Harvest Book, 1961.

Mickiewicz, Ellen Propper. *Soviet Political Schools: The Communist Party Adult Instruction System.* New Haven, Conn.: Yale University Press, 1967.

Chapter VIII. Personal Relations and Daily Life

Bauer, Raymond A; Alex Inkeles; and Clyde Kluckhohn. *How the Soviet System Works.* New York: Vintage Books, 1960.

Geiger, H. Kent. *The Family in Soviet Russia.* Cambridge, Mass.: Harvard University Press, 1968.

Hindus, Maurice. *House Without a Roof: Russia After 43 Years of Revolution.* New York: Doubleday & Co., 1961.

————. *The Kremlin's Human Dilemma: Russia After a Half Century of Revolution.* New York: Doubleday & Co., 1967.

Inkeles, Alex, and Raymond A. Bauer. *The Soviet Citizen: Daily Life in a Totalitarian Society.* Cambridge, Mass.: Harvard University Press, 1959.

Mace, Vera, and David Mace. *The Soviet Family: Love, Marriage, Parenthood and Family Life Under Communism.* Garden City, N.Y.: Doubleday & Co., 1963.

Makarenko, A. S. *The Collective Family: A Handbook for Russian Parents.* Garden City, N.Y.: Doubleday & Co., 1967.

Mehnert, Klaus. *Soviet Man and His World.* New York: Praeger Publishers, 1962.

Miller, Wright. *Russians as People.* New York: E. P. Dutton & Co., 1961.

Vladimirov, Leonid. *The Russians.* New York: Praeger Publishers, 1968.

Chapter IX. Agriculture and Rural Life

Belov, Feder. *The History of a Collective Farm.* New York: Praeger Publishers, 1955.

Bienstock, Gregory, Solomon M. Schwarz, and Aaron Yugow. *Management in Russian Industry and Agriculture.* London: Oxford University Press, 1944.

Dinnerstein, Herbert S. and Leon Gouré. *Communism and the Russian Peasant: Moscow in Crisis.* Glencoe, Ill.: The Free Press, 1955.

Goldman, Marshall I. *Soviet Marketing: Distribution in a Controlled Society.* New York: The Free Press, 1963.

Jasny, Naum. *The Socialized Agriculture of the USSR.* Stanford, Calif.: Stanford University Press, 1949.

Karcz, Jerzy F., ed. *Soviet and East European Agriculture.* Berkeley and Los Angeles: University of California Press, 1967.

Laird, Roy D., and E. L. Crowley, eds. *Soviet Agriculture: The Permanent Crisis.* New York: Praeger Publishers, 1965.

Laird, Roy D., and Betty A. Laird. *Soviet Communism and Agrarian Revolution.* Harmondsworth, Middlesex, England: Penguin Books, 1970.

Maynard, Sir John. *Russia in Flux.* New York: The Macmillan Company, 1948.

Ploss, Sidney I. *Conflict and Decision-Making in Soviet Russia: A Case Study of Agricultural Policy, 1953–63.* Princeton, N.J.: Princeton University Press, 1965.

Chapter X. The World of the Intellectual

Billington, James H. *The Icon and the Axe: An Interpretive History of Russian Culture.* New York: Alfred A. Knopf, 1966.

Blake, Patricia, ed. *Dissonant Voices in Soviet Literature.* New York: Pantheon Books, 1962.

Hayward, Max. *On Trial: The Soviet State Versus "Abram Tertz" and "Nikolai Arzhak."* New York: Harper & Row, 1966.

Johnson, Priscilla. *Khrushchev and the Arts: The Politics of Soviet Culture, 1962–1964.* Cambridge, Mass.: The MIT Press, 1965.

Observer. *Message from Moscow.* New York: Alfred A. Knopf, 1969.

Pipes, Richard, ed. *The Russian Intelligentsia.* New York: Columbia University Press, 1961.

Sakharov, Andrei D. *Progress, Coexistence and Intellectual Freedom.* New York: W. W. Norton & Co., 1968.

Shub, Anatole. *The New Russian Tragedy.* New York: W. W. Norton, 1969.

Simmons, Ernest J., ed. *Through the Glass of Soviet Literature: Views of Russian Society.* New York: Columbia University Press, 1961.

Swayze, Harold. *Political Control of Literature in the USSR, 1946–1959.* Cambridge, Mass.: Harvard University Press, 1962.

Chapter XI. The National Minorities

Bilinsky, Yaroslav. *The Second Soviet Republic: The Ukraine After World War II.* New Brunswick, N.J.: Rutgers University Press, 1964.

Conquest, Robert. *The Soviet Deportation of Nationalities.* London: Macmillan & Co., 1960.

Goldhagen, Erich, ed. *Ethnic Minorities in the Soviet Union.* New York: Praeger Publishers, 1968.

Kolarz, Walter. *Russia and Her Colonies.* New York: Praeger Publishers, 1955.

Pipes, Richard. *The Formation of the Soviet Union: Communism and Nationalism, 1917–1923.* Cambridge, Mass.: Harvard University Press, 1964.

Schlesinger, R. *The Nationalities Problem and Soviet Administration.* London: Routledge & Kegan Paul, 1956.

Sullivant, Robert S. *Soviet Politics and the Ukraine, 1917–1957.* New York: Columbia University Press, 1962.

Tsamerian, I. P., and S. L. Ronin. *Equality of Rights Between Races and Nationalities in the USSR.* Paris: UNESCO, 1963.

Vardys, V. Stanley, ed. *Lithuania Under the Soviets: Portrait of a Nation.* New York: Praeger Publishers, 1965.

Wheeler, Geoffrey. *The Peoples of Soviet Central Asia.* London: Bodley Head, 1966.

Chapter XII. The Future of Soviet Society

Amalrik, Andrei. *Will the Soviet Union Survive until 1984?* New York: Harper & Row, 1970.

Braverman, Harry. *The Future of Russia.* New York: Grosset & Dunlap, 1966.

Fischer, George. *The Soviet System and Modern Society.* New York: Atherton Press, 1968.

Fleron, Frederic J., ed. *Communist Studies and the Social Sciences.* Chicago: Rand McNally & Co., 1969.

Hendel, Samuel, and Randolph L. Braham, eds. *The U.S.S.R. After 50 Years: Promise and Reality.* New York: Alfred A. Knopf, 1967.

Inkeles, Alex. *Social Change in Soviet Russia.* Cambridge, Mass.: Harvard University Press, 1968.

Kassof, Allen, ed. *The Prospects for Soviet Society.* New York: Praeger Publishers, 1968.

Laqueur, Walter, and Leopold Labedz, eds. *The Future of Communist Society.* New York: Praeger Publishers, 1962.

Moore, Barrington, Jr. *Terror and Progress: Some Sources of Change and Stability in the Soviet Dictatorship.* Cambridge, Mass.: Harvard University Press, 1954.

Shulman, Marshall. *Beyond the Cold War.* New Haven, Conn.: Yale University Press, 1966.

INDEX

Joyce, James, 383
Judicial Reform (1864), 299, 300
Judiciary Act (1938), 283
Juviler, Peter H., 5n

Kaganovich, Lazar, 7n, 140, 261, 269, 270, 343
Kahan, Arcadius, 565
Kairov, I. A., 309
Kalinin, M. I., 281, 322n, 324n
Kamenev, L., 353
Kaminsky, Grisha, 269, 272
Kantorovich, L., 181, 184, 185
Kapitonov, I. V., 137
Karachai, 136
Karavans'ky, Svyatoslav, 514–24
Karol, K. S., 131
Kassof, Allen, 317n, 325, 326n, 549n
Kautsky, Karl, 23, 41
Kazakhstan, Kazakhs, 103, 395, 419, 502, 504, 512, 529, 533, 536, 539, 540
Kazan University, 537, 538
Keech, William R., 215
Keldysh, Mstislav Y., 498
Kennedy, John F., 353
Kerner, Miroslav, 278
Khabarovsk, 351
Kharkov, 519, 540
Khrushchev, Nikita, 7, 8, 10, 12, 13, 15, 16, 23, 71, 73, 121, 126, 130, 134, 137–39, 146, 155, 168–70, 173, 175, 177–79, 192, 215, 230, 255, 277, 294, 318n, 332n, 335, 336, 339, 340, 343, 347, 348, 360, 436, 468, 528, 531, 532, 534, 558, 562, 563, 565, 566, 570, 579n; and agriculture, 419, 421–23, 425–27, 429, 435, 439, 441, 444–46, 448; and educational reforms, 218, 230, 315, 564; and intellectuals, 467, 470, 473, 477–79, 481–85, 567, 568; and youth, 336–40, 342, 343; reminiscences of, 259–75
Khrushcheva, Nina Petrovna, 265
Kiev, 120, 519, 522, 540; Academy of Sciences in, 135; University of, 135; Party schools in, 351
Kirgizia, 502, 529, 536, 539
Kirichenko, M., 237n, 266
Kirilenko, Andrei, 135, 138, 171
Kitchko, Z. T., 138
Kluckhohn, Clyde, 230, 258
Kolasky, John, 526n, 531n, 534n, 535n, 538n, 541n, 542n
Komsomol (Young Communist League), 55, 63, 81–83, 89, 95, 102, 107, 109, 120, 131, 137, 162, 219, 225, 297,

315, 316, 325n, 326, 327, 335, 370, 371, 390, 462, 463, 566–68, 570
Kon, Igor, 496
Korneichuk, A. E., 266
Korol, Alexander, 527n, 528n, 541n
Kosygin, Aleksei, 7, 11, 134, 136, 137, 166, 167, 171, 173, 175, 176, 185, 189, 190, 215, 419, 468
Koutaisoff, E., 319n
Krokodil, 407, 410
Kruglov, S. N., 273
Kuibyshev, 312, 313
Kukarsky, I., 310, 311
Kulakov, F. D., 171
Kunayev, D. A., 171
Kursky, D. I., 300
Kuusinen, Otto V., 23, 354
Kuznetsov, Anatoly, 468; and secret police, 485–94

Labedz, Leopold, 569n
Laird, Betty, 420
Laird, Roy D., 420, 425n
Larson, Thomas B., 5n
Lasselle, Ferdinand, 23, 24
Lasswell, Harold D., 128n
Latvia, 155, 429, 531, 532, 542, 543
Law regarding the bar (1922), 301; (1939), 304
Lazarev, B. M., 240n
Lenin, Vladimir I., 5, 7, 8, 22, 23, 45, 46, 54, 58, 62, 71, 76, 83–86, 90–92, 138, 139, 145, 146, 166, 174, 185, 189, 192, 201, 202, 205, 214, 320–22, 340–42, 353, 444, 452, 457, 463, 464, 466, 495, 584n; and national question, 505–7, 518–20, 523; on state and revolution, 39–44
Leningrad, 120, 126, 136, 154, 243, 244, 251, 254–56, 351, 371, 385, 392–95, 401
Leonhard, Wolfgang, 354
Levit, Martin, 323n
Liberman, Yevsei, 176
Liberman reforms, 15, 176, 183–85, 190, 191, 201–9, 434
Ligle, Frederic, 322n
Linden, Carl A., 226n, 231, 232n
Lipset, Harry, 536n
Lipset, Seymour M., 318n
Lithuania, 136, 429, 534, 535, 542
Little Octobrists, 315, 316, 325n
Lorimer, Frank, 530n, 533n
Lowenthal, L. L., 318n
Lowenthal, Richard, 5n
Ludz, Christian, 240